The World and Its People

A WORLD VIEW

CLYDE P. PATTON
Professor of Geography
University of Oregon, Eugene, Oregon

ARLENE C. RENGERT
Professor of Geography
West Chester University, West Chester, Pennsylvania

ROBERT N. SAVELAND
Professor of Social Science Education
University of Georgia, Athens, Georgia

KENNETH S. COOPER
Professor of History, Emeritus
George Peabody College for Teachers
Vanderbilt University, Nashville, Tennessee

PATRICIA T. CARO
Assistant Professor of Geography
University of Oregon, Eugene, Oregon

ANNOTATED TEACHER'S EDITION

SILVER BURDETT COMPANY

MORRISTOWN, NJ
Atlanta, GA • Cincinnati, OH • Dallas, TX •
Northfield, IL • San Carlos, CA • Agincourt, Ontario

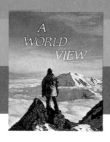

TABLE OF CONTENTS

THE WORLD AND ITS PEOPLE

Built on a solid factual foundation

The Silver Burdett social studies program THE WORLD AND ITS PEOPLE was developed to help pupils understand themselves and the world around them and to instill in them the knowledge and skills necessary for responsible citizenship. Built on a solid factual foundation, the program examines the pupils' world in an ever-widening circle. THE WORLD AND ITS PEOPLE begins with a study of self and family, expands to a study of neighborhood, community, state, region, nation, world, and ends with a study of the history of the United States.

Instills knowledge and skills

Each book in the series reflects the following belief: *Pupils need to know, to appreciate, and to do.* A grasp of basic facts is essential in gaining an understanding of social studies. To that end, a wealth of material is provided. Lesson checkups, chapter and unit reviews, and chapter tests ensure the pupils' understanding of the text material. Opportunities for development of language, reading, and social studies skills are provided throughout the series through vocabulary study, skills development exercises, and other skills-related activities.

Encourages active learning

THE WORLD AND ITS PEOPLE involves *doing.* Pupils work with maps, charts, graphs, tables, and time lines as a vital part of the learning process. Pupils build models, conduct interviews, hold debates, and take part in a variety of other activities. In short, pupils are *active participants.*

Fosters responsible citizenship

THE WORLD AND ITS PEOPLE enables pupils to appreciate themselves, the world around them, and their role as citizens of the United States. Pupils learn to understand some of the important links between them and their families, communities, states, regions, nation, and world. In doing so, they develop an appreciation of historic and geographic factors and economic and political relationships that have shaped their world. Moreover, pupils are given specific suggestions for assuming a responsible role — in capacities commensurate with age and ability — in their community, state, region, nation, and world. THE WORLD AND ITS PEOPLE not only prepares pupils for the future but also helps them function meaningfully in the present.

An Expanding Horizons Approach That Teachers Like to Use

THE WORLD AND ITS PEOPLE is a social studies series that begins with the pupil's familiar world of self and family, broadens into a study of neighborhoods, communities, states, regions, the United States, other countries around the world, and ends with an in-depth study of the history of the United States.

PROGRAM COMPONENTS

- PUPIL'S TEXT
- ANNOTATED TEACHER'S EDITION
- TEACHER'S PLANNING GUIDE
- WORKBOOK
- TEACHER RESOURCE PACKAGE

The World and Its People
MY WORLD AND ME

EUROPE, AFRICA, ASIA, AND AUSTRALIA
CANADA AND LATIN AMERICA
THE UNITED STATES AND ITS NEIGHBORS
STATES AND REGIONS
COMMUNITIES AND RESOURCES
NEIGHBORHOODS AND COMMUNITIES
FAMILIES AND NEIGHBORHOODS

A WORLD VIEW

ONE FLAG, ONE LAND

A World View
Is Organized to Excite Student Interest

 Care is taken to integrate regional and topical geography throughout the text. The historical dimensions of each country studied are consistently given.

 The study of people and how they live is part of each unit.

Page 316

Page 317

Page 319

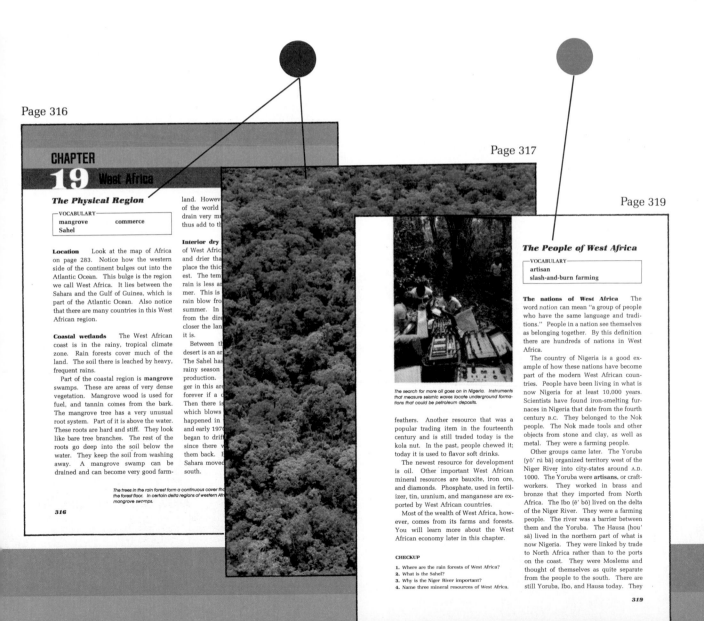

CHAPTER
19 West Africa

The Physical Region

┌─VOCABULARY─
mangrove   commerce
Sahel
└─

Location   Look at the map of Africa on page 283. Notice how the western side of the continent bulges out into the Atlantic Ocean. This bulge is the region we call West Africa. It lies between the Sahara and the Gulf of Guinea, which is part of the Atlantic Ocean. Also notice that there are many countries in this West African region.

Coastal wetlands   The West African coast is in the rainy, tropical climate zone. Rain forests cover much of the land. The soil there is leached by heavy, frequent rains.

Part of the coastal region is **mangrove** swamps. These are areas of very dense vegetation. Mangrove wood is used for fuel, and tannin comes from the bark. The mangrove tree has a very unusual root system. Part of it is above the water. These roots are hard and stiff. They look like bare tree branches. The rest of the roots go deep into the soil below the water. They keep the soil from washing away. A mangrove swamp can be drained and can become very good farm-

*The trees in the rain forest form a continuous cover that
the forest floor. In certain delta regions of western Afr
mangrove swamps.*

316

land. Howev
of the world
drain very mu
thus add to th

Interior dry
of West Afric
and drier tha
place the thic
est. The tem
rain is less an
mer. This is
rain blow fro
summer. In
from the dire
closer the lan
it is.

Between th
desert is an ar
The Sahel has
rainy season
production.
ger in this are
forever if a d
Then there is
which blows
happened in
and early 197
began to drif
since there w
them back. B
Sahara move
south.

feathers. Another resource that was a popular trading item in the fourteenth century and is still traded today is the kola nut. In the past, people chewed it; today it is used to flavor soft drinks.

The newest resource for development is oil. Other important West African mineral resources are bauxite, iron ore, and diamonds. Phosphate, used in fertilizer, tin, uranium, and manganese are exported by West African countries.

Most of the wealth of West Africa, however, comes from its farms and forests. You will learn more about the West African economy later in this chapter.

*The search for more oil goes on in Nigeria. Instruments
that measure seismic waves locate underground formations that could be petroleum deposits.*

CHECKUP

1. Where are the rain forests of West Africa?
2. What is the Sahel?
3. Why is the Niger River important?
4. Name three mineral resources of West Africa.

The People of West Africa

┌─VOCABULARY─
artisan
slash-and-burn farming
└─

The nations of West Africa   The word *nation* can mean "a group of people who have the same language and traditions." People in a nation see themselves as belonging together. By this definition there are hundreds of nations in West Africa.

The country of Nigeria is a good example of how these nations have become part of the modern West African countries. People have been living in what is now Nigeria for at least 10,000 years. Scientists have found iron-smelting furnaces in Nigeria that date from the fourth century B.C. They belonged to the Nok people. The Nok made tools and other objects from stone and clay, as well as metal. They were a farming people.

Other groups came later. The Yoruba (yō´ rū bä) organized territory west of the Niger River into city-states around A.D. 1000. The Yoruba were **artisans**, or craft-workers. They worked in brass and bronze that they imported from North Africa. The Ibo (ē´ bō) lived on the delta of the Niger River. They were a farming people. The river was a barrier between them and the Yoruba. The Hausa (hou´ sä) lived in the northern part of what is now Nigeria. They were linked by trade to North Africa rather than to the ports on the coast. They were Moslems and thought of themselves as quite separate from the people to the south. There are still Yoruba, Ibo, and Hausa today. They

319

Unit Introductions Provide Capsule Previews of the Units

Each unit opens with an introduction to the region to be studied, giving broad information pertaining to the region as a whole.

Maps highlight the countries that students will study in the unit.

A convenient table of information about the countries in the unit allows students to find facts quickly.

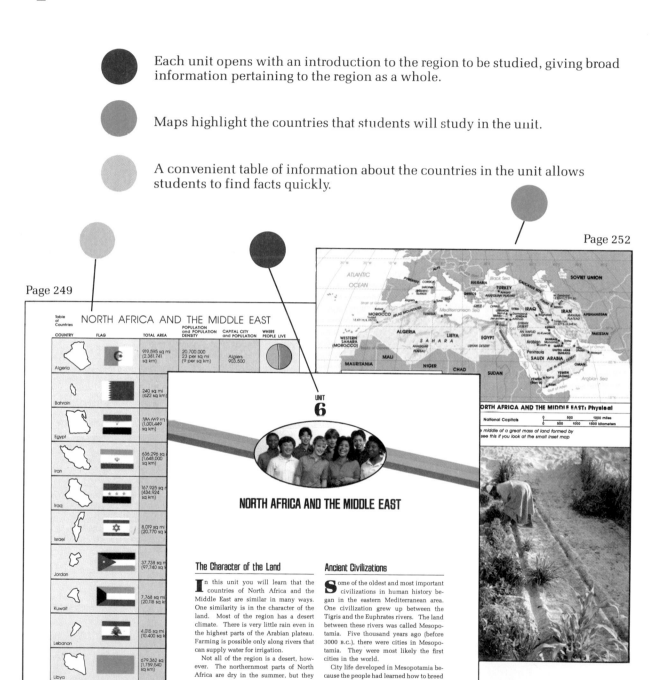

Page 252

Page 249

Page 248

Table of Countries
NORTH AFRICA AND THE MIDDLE EAST

COUNTRY	FLAG	TOTAL AREA	POPULATION and POPULATION DENSITY	CAPITAL CITY and POPULATION	WHERE PEOPLE LIVE
Algeria		919,595 sq mi (2,381,741 sq km)	20,700,000 23 per sq mi (9 per sq km)	Algiers 903,500	
Bahrain		240 sq mi (622 sq km)			
Egypt		386,662 sq mi (1,001,449 sq km)			
Iran		636,296 sq mi (1,648,000 sq km)			
Iraq		167,925 sq mi (434,924 sq km)			
Israel		8,019 sq mi (20,770 sq km)			
Jordan		37,738 sq mi (97,740 sq km)			
Kuwait		7,768 sq mi (20,118 sq km)			
Lebanon		4,015 sq mi (10,400 sq km)			
Libya		679,362 sq mi (1,759,540 sq km)			

252

UNIT 6

NORTH AFRICA AND THE MIDDLE EAST

The Character of the Land

In this unit you will learn that the countries of North Africa and the Middle East are similar in many ways. One similarity is in the character of the land. Most of the region has a desert climate. There is very little rain even in the highest parts of the Arabian plateau. Farming is possible only along rivers that can supply water for irrigation.

Not all of the region is a desert, however. The northernmost parts of North Africa are dry in the summer, but they get quite a bit of rain from the winter storms that cross the Mediterranean Sea from west to east. The same thing is true in the mountainous lands of Turkey and Iran.

Ancient Civilizations

Some of the oldest and most important civilizations in human history began in the eastern Mediterranean area. One civilization grew up between the Tigris and the Euphrates rivers. The land between these rivers was called Mesopotamia. Five thousand years ago (before 3000 B.C.), there were cities in Mesopotamia. They were most likely the first cities in the world.

City life developed in Mesopotamia because the people had learned how to breed animals and plant crops. The domestication (də mes ti kā′ shən) of plants and animals meant that people could live in settled villages and raise enough food. A dependable food supply freed some peo-

In this photograph an Algerian farmer tends his vegetable garden in the Sahara. An underground spring provides the water necessary to raise these few crops.

248 INTRODUCTION

NORTH AFRICA AND THE MIDDLE EAST: Physical

National Capitals

0 500 1000 miles
0 500 1000 1500 kilometers

...n middle of a great mass of land formed by ...see this if you look at the small inset map

A Focus on People Enlivens and Motivates

 Stimulating **Biographical Features** offer vivid descriptions of the lives of individuals who have made outstanding contributions throughout history.

 Thought-provoking **Slice-of-Life** features give students an insight into the everyday lives of people in countries throughout the world.

Page 445

Rachel Carson: Biologist and Author

*I*N THE SUMMER OF 1919 a 12-year-old girl named Rachel Carson excitedly read a story entitled "A Famous Sea Fight." It excited her because she was its author. Years later Rachel Carson wrote many magazine articles and several books, but she doubted if their publication had ever excited her as much as seeing her first words in print.

Rachel Carson was interested in the outdoors as well as writing. She liked to learn about all sorts of living things. When Carson went to college, she studied biology — the science of living things. Later she took a job as a biologist for the U.S. Fish and Wildlife Service. She never lost her love of the outdoors.

While working as a government biologist, Rachel Carson became concerned with the widespread use of DDT and other powerful new pesticides. She became convinced that spraying pesticides to kill mosquitoes, elm beetles, and fire ants also destroyed many beneficial insects and fish, birds, and other wildlife. In 1962, Rachel Carson published a book, *Silent Spring,* in which she summed up what she had learned about the widespread use of pesticides. She described how the careless use of poisons had produced "silent springs" by killing off so many songbirds. But *Silent Spring* was more than a book about pesticides and birds. It was a plea for a more thoughtful relationship between people and nature.

Page 61

A SLICE OF LIFE

Joel: Growing Up a Farm Man

Joel Holland wants to be a farmer when he grows up. He lives on a corn and live-stock farm in northwestern Illinois. He is the youngest of six children. Only he and his 16-year-old brother, Martin, still live at home with their parents. The house Joel was born in was built by his great-grandfather James, an Irish immigrant. The 245-acre (99-ha) farm has been in the family since 1860.

Joel's mom and dad usually shout into his room to awaken him about 7:30 A.M. He's really not a morning person and has a hard time getting going. In the spring he has to feed the calves before going to school.

The school bus stops on the highway to pick up Joel and the other farm boys and girls who go to school in the town of Scales Mound. The school is a brick building that houses both grade school and high school. There are 235 students, and Joel knows practically everyone in school. Few people leave or move into the community every year, so Joel usually has the same classmates. He is a good student and especially likes the experiments in science.

The first thing Joel does when he gets off the school bus in the afternoon is to take off his sneakers and put on boots. He is no longer a typical teenager. He has farm work, called chores, to do. He has to clean out the farrowing house after a litter of pigs is born. He runs the mixer mill to grind corn for the cattle and hogs.

There is different work at different times of the year. Depending on the season, the corn must be planted, harvested, or stored.

Joel keeps the hogs as a business of his own. Two days after the pigs are born, he squirts serum containing liquid iron into their mouths. Then he cuts their needlelike baby teeth. After that he cuts off their tails and notches their ears to identify them. If the pigs' teeth and tails were not cut, the pigs would chew on each other's tails.

Joel is learning a lot about farming. He would rather live on a farm than in a city. He feels that people don't work together as a family as much in the city as on a farm. He also likes the freedom and the responsibilities on the farm.

But life is not all work on the farm. Joel always has energy left over for sports. He shoots baskets on a backboard nailed to a tree. He plays softball in the spring, goes water-skiing and fishing in the summer, hunts deer in the fall, and rides a snowmobile in the winter.

His mother says the best words to describe Joel are *energetic* and *enthusiastic*. On one summer day he jumped 15 fences, drove farm machinery 25 miles, fed 320 animals, opened and closed 8 gates, walked and ran about 8 miles, jumped on and off the tractor 26 times, lifted 900 pounds of grain and shoveled 4,000 pounds, and ate about 2,600 calories!

Joel's story is told in a good book by Patricia Demuth. The photographs were taken by her husband, Jack. Ask your librarian if you can get a copy of *Joel: Growing Up a Farm Man* (New York: Dodd, Mead & Company, 1982). It tells many more interesting things about Joel, such as how he helped when cows gave birth, and how he built a Fly Zapper that killed bushels of flies.

61

A Practical Three-Part Lesson Format Structured to Save Time for Teachers

- Each lesson opens with a list of key social studies vocabulary words that are defined in the Glossary. The words are in boldface where they first appear in the lesson, and difficult words are followed by phonetic respellings.

- Every lesson is divided into parts identified by descriptive headings, which facilitate student comprehension.

- Checkup questions at the end of every lesson provide students with immediate review of key points.

Page 44

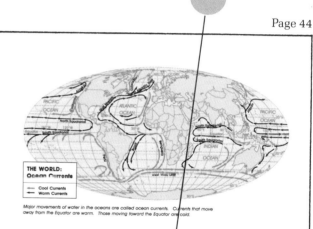

THE WORLD: Ocean Currents

— Cool Currents
→ Warm Currents

Major movements of water in the oceans are called ocean currents. Currents that move away from the Equator are warm. Those moving toward the Equator are cold.

Oceans influence temperatures

Oceans and seas moderate, or make less severe, the temperatures on nearby land. This is because water warms more slowly and cools more slowly than land. In the summer the ocean waters often have a lower temperature than the continents, so they cool the nearby lands. In the winter the nearby lands are warmed by the oceans. Places near a large body of water tend to have warmer winters and cooler summers than places that are inland.

The different rates of heating and cooling of land and water produce land and sea breezes. During the day the land heats up more quickly than the water. As a result the air over the land is warmer than the air over the water. Warm air rises and creates a low-pressure center. Cold air sinks and creates a high-pressure center. Air moves from centers of high pressure to centers of low pressure. So the cooler air over the water moves toward the warmer air over the land. During the day the breeze in coastal areas is often from the water to the land. At night the land cools more quickly than the water. The process is then reversed. This daily reversing of the wind happens quite regularly along the coasts.

CHECKUP

1. In what ways does the earth move in space?
2. What is the difference between a solstice and an equinox?
3. Describe the three temperature zones into which the earth can be divided.
4. How does the earth's rotation from west to east affect time in the United States?
5. What is the International Date Line?
6. Describe the general movement of the major ocean currents. Name the four major oceans of the world.

44

Page 38

CHAPTER 3 / World Patterns

The Earth in Motion

— VOCABULARY —

petroglyph	Antarctic Circle
revolution	equinox
axis	temperate
Tropic of Cancer	rotation
	contiguous
Arctic Circle	International
solstice	Date Line
Tropic of Capricorn	ocean current

An ancient stone formation In Chaco Canyon in northwestern New Mexico, scientists have been studying a formation of stones. Three large stone slabs are stacked against the side of a cliff. The slabs are 6 feet (1.8 m) to 9 feet (2.7 m) tall and weigh about 2 tons each. Scientists believe that the stones were carefully arranged against the cliff hundreds of years ago. Until recently, however, scientists did not know why the stones had been placed in this exact position.

The answer was discovered by an artist named Ann Sofaer. In June 1977 she was climbing near the stone slabs, looking for carvings on the rocks. The carvings, called **petroglyphs** (pet' rə glifs), had been made by the Indians who once lived in the canyon. While Ann Sofaer was looking at two petroglyphs on the cliff wall beside the stone slabs, she saw a dagger of sunlight appear on the larger petroglyph. It took about 12 minutes for the sun dagger to move down through the center of the petroglyph and disappear.

Further studies showed that the sun would shine through the slabs and make a dagger of light on the petroglyphs at particular times of the year. Today, scientists believe that the Indians used the pattern of sunlight on the rock carvings as a calendar. The sun daggers marked the four seasons of the year. In the smaller photograph on the facing page, the sun dagger is marking June 21 on the petroglyph. June 21 is the beginning of summer in the Northern Hemisphere.

The changing seasons The sun daggers mark the seasons of the year because of the earth's movement around the sun. As you saw in the diagram on page 37, the earth revolves around the sun in an oval path called an orbit. It takes 365¼ days for the earth to make one **revolution** around the sun. The revolution of the earth around the sun and the tilt of the earth's **axis** cause the change of seasons. The earth's axis is an imaginary line that goes through the earth from the North Pole to the South Pole. This tilt never changes as the earth revolves around the sun.

The inset photograph shows a sun dagger on a petroglyph. The petroglyph is on the cliff wall beside the stone slabs shown in the large photograph. This ancient stone formation is found in Chaco Canyon, New Mexico. (36°N/108°W; map, p. 53)

38

A Complete Map and Globe Skills Program Encourages Student Achievement

The many maps included in A WORLD VIEW reinforce the map and globe skills learned in previous grades. The first chapter of this text is devoted entirely to the development of map and globe skills. A world time zone map is introduced. The Atlas in the back of the book includes a variety of political and physical maps. THE WORLD AND ITS PEOPLE series includes more than 450 colorful maps.

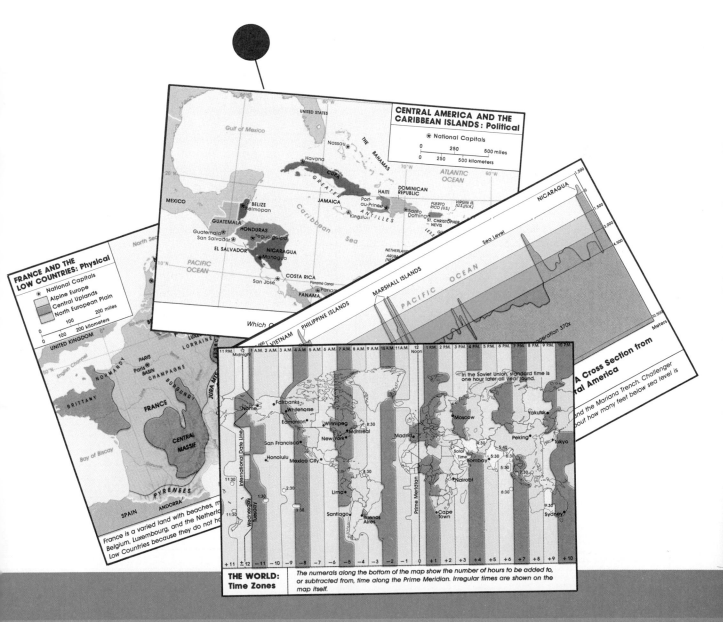

A Gazetteer Helps Students Develop Skill in Using Reference Tools

 THE WORLD AND ITS PEOPLE is the first social studies series to include a Gazetteer, or geographer's dictionary. This tool, which is found in Books 3–7, helps students successfully complete place geography exercises.

 The Gazetteer lists most of the places discussed in the text. For each place, the Gazetteer provides (1) the pronunciation, (2) a brief statement about the place, (3) the latitude and longitude when appropriate, and (4) the page number of a map on which the place is shown.

Adelaide (35°S/139°E). **Capital of the Australian state of South Australia. Located near a gulf of the Indian Ocean. p. 419.**

Page 48 9

Page 419

The coming of the settlers The reports of Cook and Banks encouraged the British to send settlers to New South Wales. The government decided that the faraway land would be a good place to send some convicts from the prisons. The convicts could be made to work the land, and it seemed unlikely that many would find their way home from halfway around the world. The first group of convicts, 570 men and 160 women, arrived in New South Wales in 1788. They were accompanied by 250 free persons. The convicts at first worked on government land. However, as they completed their terms, they could take up farms of their own. The British government sent about 160,000 convicts to Australia before stopping the practice in 1868.

Many free people also went to Australia. They went for the same reason that other Europeans went to America. They wanted land of their own. The settlers brought seeds and animals previously unknown in Australia. They changed the look of the land by clearing forest and bushland and planting fields of wheat, barley, and oats. They pastured sheep and cattle on grassy plains where only kangaroos had once fed.

As the number of settlers increased, the British established other colonies along the coast and on the island of Tasmania. Each of the colonies was separate, much like the 13 colonies the British established in North America. Each colony had its own government. In time the settlers gained control of these governments. In 1901 the colonies united to form the Commonwealth of Australia. A federal government somewhat like that

AUSTRALIA: Political
⊛ National Capital
★ State Capitals
• Other Cities
0   500 miles
0   500 kilometers

Australia is the only continent on which all people are under the same government.

of the United States was set up. Each of the former colonies became a state. There are six Australian states: New South Wales, Victoria, South Australia, Queensland, Western Australia, and Tasmania. Northern Territory is not yet a state, but it has limited self-government.

The Commonwealth of Australia has kept certain ties with Great Britain. It is a member of that other commonwealth, the Commonwealth of Nations. The queen of the United Kingdom is also queen of Australia. The Australian flag carries the Union Jack in the upper left corner. The Union Jack is the British flag. The five smaller stars on the Australian flag stand for the Southern Cross, a reminder that this country lies in the Southern Hemisphere.

CHECKUP

1. How did the Aborigines live 200 years ago?
2. Who were some early explorers of Australia?
3. Why did Europeans go to Australia?
4. What kind of government does Australia have?

419

GAZETTEER The Gazetteer is a geographical dictionary. It shows latitude and longitude for cities and certain other places. Latitude and longitude are shown in this form: 9°N/39°E. This means "9 degrees north latitude and 39 degrees east longitude." The page reference tells where each entry may be found on a map.

Key to Pronunciation

a	hat, cap	i	it, pin	ou	house, out	zh	measure, seizure
ā	age, face	ī	ice, five	sh	she, rush	ə	represents:
ä	care, air	ng	long, bring	th	thin, both		a in about
ä	father, far	o	hot, rock	ᵺ	then, smooth		e in taken
ch	child, much	ō	open, go	u	cup, butter		i in pencil
e	let, best	ô	order, all	u̇	full, put		o in lemon
ē	equal, see	oi	oil, voice	ü	rule, move		u in circus
ėr	term, learn						

This Key to Pronunciation is from Scott, Foresman Intermediate Dictionary, by E. L. Thorndike and Clarence L. Barnhart. Copyright © 1983, by Scott, Foresman and Company. Reprinted by permission.

Accra (ä′ krä). Capital of and most populated city in Ghana. Port city located on Atlantic Ocean. (6°N/0° long.) p. 287.

Addis Ababa (ad′ə sab′ə bä). Capital of and most populated city in Ethiopia. Located at an elevation of 7,900 ft (2,408 m). (9°N/39°E) p. 287.

Adelaide (ad′ əl ād). Capital of the Australian state of South Australia. Located near a gulf of the Indian Ocean. (35°S/139°E) p. 419.

Aden (äd′ ən). Capital of Yemen (Aden). Located on the Gulf of Aden. (13°N/45°E) p. 251.

Adriatic Sea (ä drē at′ ik sē). An arm of the Mediterranean Sea located between Italy and the Balkan Peninsula. p. 145.

Aegean Sea (i jē′ an sē). Part of the Mediterranean Sea located between the eastern coast of Greece and the western coast of Turkey. Bounded on the north by Greek mainland and on the south by Crete. p. 145.

Alexandria (al ig zan′ drē ə). Second most populated city in Egypt. Located in the Nile Delta. (31°N/30°E) p. 251.

Algiers (al jirz′). Capital of Algeria. Located on the Mediterranean Sea. (37°N/3°E) p. 251.

Alps (alps). Mountain system extending in an arc from the Mediterranean coast between Italy and France through Switzerland and Austria and into the northwest coast of Yugoslavia. The highest peak is Mont Blanc, with an elevation of 15,771 ft (4,807 m). p. 143.

Amazon River (am′ ə zän riv′ ər). Second longest river in the world. Tributaries rise in the Andes Mountains and Guiana Highlands. Flows into the Atlantic Ocean near Belém, Brazil. p. 89.

Amman (ä män′). Capital of Jordan. (32°N/36°E) p. 251.

Amsterdam (am′ star dam). Capital of the Netherlands. Connected to the North Sea by canal. (52°N/5°E) p. 145.

Anatolia (an ə tō′ lē ə). Peninsula on which Asian Turkey is located. This peninsula lies between the Black and Mediterranean seas. p. 482.

Andes Mountains (an′ dēz mount′ ənz). High mountains that stretch north to south along the western side of South America. Highest peak, with an elevation of 22,840 ft (6,690 m), is Mt. Aconcagua. p. 89.

Ankara (ang′ kə rə). Capital of Turkey. (41°N/33°E) p. 211.

Antwerp (ant′ warp). Chief port of Belgium. Located on the Schelde River about 50 miles (80 km) from the North Sea. (51°N/4°E) p. 170.

Apennines (ap′ ə ninz). Mountains in Italy. They extend from northwest Italy near Genoa to the southern tip of the Italian Peninsula. Its highest peak is Monte Corno, with an elevation of 9,560 ft (2,914 m). p. 143.

Appalachian Mountains (ap ə lä′ chən mount′ ənz). Chain of mountains stretching from Canada to Alabama. The highest peak is Mt. Mitchell at 6,684 ft (2,037 m). p. 53.

Arabian Peninsula (ə rā′ bē ən pə nin′ sə lə). Large peninsula located east of the Red Sea. p. 249.

Arabian Sea (ə rā′ bē ən sē). Part of the Indian Ocean located between India and the Arabian Peninsula. p. 251.

489

Meaningful Social Studies Activities Support the Teaching of Reading Skills

 Many of the Skills Development pages, which follow each Chapter Review, consist of questions and activities that develop reading and language arts skills through social studies content.

 A WORLD VIEW can function as an extension of the teaching of reading skills. Reading for understanding, outlining, identifying main ideas, using the library, stating a point of view, using context clues, paraphrasing, using primary source material, and similar skills arc developed.

Page 246

14/SKILLS DEVELOPMENT

IDENTIFYING MAIN IDEAS

WHAT IS A TOPIC SENTENCE?

As the name suggests, a topic sentence states the topic, or main idea, of a paragraph. Usually the first sentence in a paragraph is the topic sentence. In some cases, however, the first sentence of a paragraph does not state the main idea, and the second or third sentence may be the topic sentence. The other sentences in a paragraph supply details that support the main idea. They are called supporting sentences.

Some topic sentences try to cover more than can be developed in one paragraph. They try to tell everything in one sentence. A good topic sentence states a subject or idea that can be properly developed in one paragraph.

SKILLS PRACTICE

In the passage below, the paragraphs have been run together purposely. Read the passage and decide where you would divide it to make three paragraphs.

The Volga

The Volga River rises in the Valdai Hills, to the northwest of Moscow, and after a course of 2,300 miles (3,701 km), it enters the land-locked Caspian Sea. It is a wide, slow-flowing river, and from the earliest times it has been used for navigation. A thousand years ago it carried the trade between the peoples around the Baltic Sea and China and India. Small boats were carried downstream by wind and current, and on the return voyage they were rowed. Today things have greatly changed. A series of dams have been built, and the great river has been transformed into a succession of lakes that drop like gigantic steps from the Valdai Hills to the Caspian. No longer does one hear the melancholy song of the rowers; it is the shrill whistle of a ship's siren and the beat of stern paddle and screw. The Volga is busier than ever before. It carries much of the internal trade of the Soviet Union: coal and oil, lumber, and cement and building materials. It is also joined by canal with other rivers. But some of the problems that confront the modern riverboats and their tows are the same as those faced on the Volga in the past. During the long Russian winter, the river is frozen, and shipping comes to a halt. In the spring the snows melt, and the current is swift. In the fall the water level is low, and navigation is difficult except on the lakes. Still the Volga continues its long tradition of serving as an important trade route.

Write the title of the passage on a sheet of paper. Then write the topic sentence of each paragraph. Does each of the sentences you chose state the main idea of the paragraph? For each topic sentence write a short explanation telling why you think the sentence does or does not state the main idea. Copy the entire passage as three separate paragraphs on your paper. After you have copied the passage in paragraphs, answer the following questions.

1. What are some of the details given in the supporting sentences of the first paragraph? Write two words from the first paragraph that describe the Volga River.
2. What does the second paragraph describe?
3. How many supporting sentences are there in the third paragraph? What kinds of details do they give?

246

Page 12 3

7/SKILLS DEVELOPMENT

UNDERSTANDING SEQUENCE

COFFEE FROM BERRY TO POT

Read the following material carefully. Notice especially the sequence, or order, in which coffee is produced.

Coffee grows as berries on fairly low-growing trees. There are machines that can harvest the berries, but most coffee berries are still picked by hand. Then the berries are dried. Sometimes they are spread out in the sun, but they can also be dried by machine.

During the next step a machine removes the two beans that are inside each coffee berry. It sorts them according to size, shape, and color. Then the beans are graded. A person called a "cupper" tastes coffee made from each type of bean and decides how good it is. After the sorting and testing, the coffee beans are bagged. Most of the coffee is exported.

Manufacturing is usually done in the country where the coffee will be sold. The coffee is roasted in large ovens at high heat. The various beans are blended and then ground. The coffee is packed into vacuum tins or bags and is shipped to markets.

SKILLS PRACTICE

Place the following statements in the sequence in which they happen.

The berries are dried and cured.
The beans are roasted at high heat.
Coffee beans are picked by hand.
The beans are graded and tested.
Machines remove the beans from the berries and sort them.
The coffee is ground and packed in tins.
These pictures show parts of the coffee-making process. On your paper write the letter of each picture next to the statement that it illustrates.

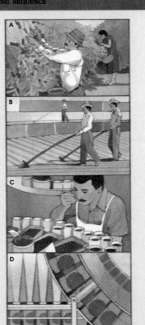

123

Chapter and Unit Reviews
Measure Growth and Reinforce Ideas

Chapter Reviews present the chapters' main ideas, test vocabulary knowledge, ask recall and thinking questions, and suggest activities that require a minimum of teacher direction.

Unit Reviews consistently include the following categories of skill-building activities:

- Reading the Text
- Reading a Map
- Reading a Picture
- Reading a Diagram, Table, Chart, or Graph

Page 358

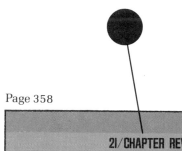

21/CHAPTER REVIEW

KEY FACTS
1. Japan is a very mountainous island country; only one sixth of its land is arable.
2. Japan is in a zone of volcanic eruptions and earthquakes.
3. From the time of the Tokugawa shogunate until 1868, Japan was isolated from foreign countries.
4. Under the Meiji Restoration, Japan began a new push for industrial development.
5. Japan was seriously weakened by World War II.
6. Only the United States and the Soviet Union have a gross national product larger than Japan's.
7. Most Japanese live in cities.

VOCABULARY QUIZ
On a sheet of paper write the letter of the word or phrase that correctly completes each statement.

1. The average length of time people live is (a) gross national product, (b) life insurance, (c) life expectancy.
2. A violent, hurricanelike storm is (a) an atomic bomb, (b) a shogun, (c) a typhoon.
3. A group of islands is (a) an archipelago, (b) a fish farm, (c) a continent.
4. A school that helps students prepare for examinations is called a (a) middle school, (b) test school, (c) juku.
5. Another word for an inactive volcano is (a) dormant, (b) marine, (c) vacant.
6. Not knowing how to read or write is (a) hearsay, (b) illegal, (c) illiteracy.
7. An example of a social reform is (a) compulsory education, (b) a dance class, (c) a shogun.

8. The total value of all the goods and services a country produces is its (a) life expectancy, (b) gross national product, (c) bank account.
9. A military ruler of early Japan was (a) a president, (b) a prime minister, (c) a shogun.
10. A leader without power is a (a) typhoon, (b) figurehead, (c) shogun.

REVIEW QUESTIONS
1. What are the names of the four largest Japanese islands?
2. How is Japan's climate affected by its island location?
3. What effect did each of the following have on Japan: (a) China, (b) Tokugawa shogunate, (c) Meiji Restoration.
4. How do we know Japan is a wealthy country?
5. Name three important Japanese industries.

ACTIVITIES
1. Find three advertisements for products made in Japan in a magazine or a newspaper.
2. Politeness and courtesy have a high value in Japanese culture. Children usually address their parents and teachers with terms of respect, such as "Ma'am" and "Sir." For one day use nothing but politeness toward your parents and teachers, and address each of them at least once as "Ma'am" or "Sir." Write an essay describing this experience, including how easy or difficult it was for you and people's reaction to your behavior.
3. Ask someone who remembers World War II what she or he can remember hearing of Japan's attack on Pearl Harbor. People who were adults then often remember where they were and what they were doing.

358

Page 389

8/UNIT REVIEW

READING THE TEXT
Turn to page 340 and read the section "A nation develops." On a sheet of paper, write the answers to these questions.
1. What event that affected Chinese history happened in 221 B.C.?
2. During which dynasty did China's population reach 100 million?
3. Which Chinese religion was based on the idea that people should live in harmony with nature?
4. In which religion was respect for the past important?
5. Which of these religions influenced the government of China?

READING A MAP
Turn to the map on page 357, which shows population density in Japan. On a sheet of paper, write the answers to these questions.
1. How many cities in Japan have a population of 1 million or more?
2. What is the population density per square mile in and around Tokyo?
3. Which major Japanese island has a population density of under 100 people per square kilometer?
4. Look at the city index below the map. Are most of the cities listed in the index on the east or the west coast of Japan?
5. What are the grid coordinates on this map for the capital city of Japan?

READING PICTURES
Pictures give information just as written words do. Below is a list of page numbers. On each page is a picture that falls into one of the following information categories: Industry (I), Agriculture (A), Religion (R), and History/Culture (H/C). Study each picture. On a sheet of paper, write the letter of the category that identifies the subject of the picture.

1. p. 360	6. p. 335	11. p. 341
2. p. 380	7. p. 355	12. p. 369
3. p. 379	8. p. 365	13. p. 338
4. p. 388	9. p. 352	14. p. 343
5. p. 366	10. p. 384	15. p. 370

READING A TABLE
Turn to the tables on pages 332–333. Use the tables about the countries of Asia to find out whether the statements below are true or false. On a sheet of paper, write **T** if the statement is true and **F** if it is false.

1. The population density is greater in Bangladesh than it is in China.
2. Japan is bigger in area than Indonesia.
3. The country with the largest population also has the largest area.
4. The greater part of India's population lives in nonurban areas.
5. Singapore is the smallest country in area in South and East Asia.

389

Varied Workbook Activities
Strengthen Student Skills

Concise directions to the student are clearly marked with a blue triangle (▶), allowing students to work with a minimum of teacher direction.

Workbook activities are based on information provided in pictures, drawings, maps, graphs, illustrations, word puzzles, and symbols as well as reading selections.

The lesson in the textbook on which the workbook exercise is based is clearly indicated. Sample pages shown are from the annotated Teacher's Edition of the workbook for A WORLD VIEW.

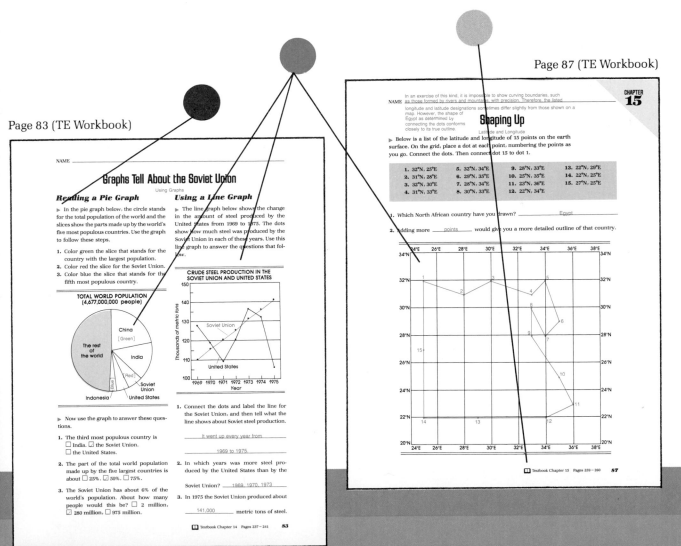

Page 87 (TE Workbook)

Page 83 (TE Workbook)

An Annotated Teacher's Edition
Saves Teachers Time and Work

The high quality and diversity of annotations in the Teacher's Edition make A WORLD VIEW easy to use. The annotations include questions, suggested activities, interesting facts, and supplementary information, all of which enrich the subject matter.

Answers to all questions for every Checkup section, Chapter Review, Unit Review, and Skills Development page are provided in a special Answer Key in the back of the book.

Refer your pupils to the Graph Appendix in the back of this text to determine the five leading countries in the production of each resource described in the section below.

Page 198

Note that cork has been used for various items since 44 B.C. The ancient Romans wore sandals made of cork.

climate variations. Northwestern Spain has very rainy winters and cool summers. The southern half of Portugal is a little less rainy and warmer in the summer. The Meseta is the driest part of Europe. The Meseta is also colder in the winter than the rest of the Iberian Peninsula. In southern Spain, summers are very hot.

The mineral resources of the Iberian Peninsula are varied. Spain has some coal and iron ore and is the world's leading source of mercury. Mercury is used in thermometers and in making paint and paper. There are other less important resources, such as **tungsten** in Portugal. Tungsten is a hard, heavy metal that is used to make steel hard and strong. It is also used to make the filaments in

electric light bulbs. Some hydroelectric power is produced in the rainy northwest of the peninsula. Although many trees have been cut down, there are still large forests of cork oak in Spain and Portugal. Cork comes from the bark of the cork oak tree. Many products you use are made from cork. Floats for fishing nets, bottle stoppers, insulation, floor and wall coverings, engine gaskets, bulletin boards, hotdish pads, and shoe soles are some of the many items made from cork.

Romans, Goths, and Moors The Iberian Peninsula was a part of the Roman Empire. Except for Italy itself, the Iberian Peninsula was the most Romanized part of the Mediterranean. Even now, Roman

Olives are grown throughout the Mediterranean region. It takes 15 years for olive trees to mature and produce fruit. The tree and the fruit provide many useful products.

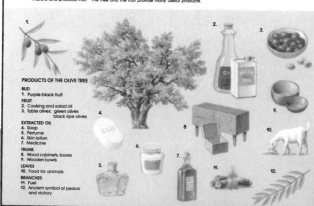

PRODUCTS OF THE OLIVE TREE
BUD
1. Purple-black fruit
FRUIT
2. Cooking and salad oil
3. Table olives: green olives
   black ripe olives
EXTRACTED OIL
4. Soap
5. Perfume
6. Skin lotion
7. Medicine
TRUNK
8. Wood cabinets, boxes
9. Wooden bowls
LEAVES
10. Food for animals
BRANCHES
11. Fuel
12. Ancient symbol of peace
    and victory

Page 238

Refer your pupils to the Graph Appendix in the back of this text to determine the five leading countries in the production of each resource described in the section below.

Resources A country as large as the Soviet Union has a big share of the world's natural resources. In addition to fertile soils and huge forests, the Soviet Union has large deposits of petroleum, coal, iron ore, and other minerals. Unfortunately, the forests and many other resources are in Siberia. Severe climate and great distance make it difficult to use some of the country's natural wealth.

The Soviet Union is the world's leading producer of oil. Large petroleum fields are in the Caucasus Mountains. The Baku (bä kü') field is the oldest of these. Today, however, the major oil-producing region is in the Ural Mountains. Coal deposits found in the Ukraine and Siberia make the Soviet Union the

world's second largest coal-producing country. More than one third of all the coal mined in the Soviet Union comes from the Donets Basin, in the Ukraine. Iron ore also is mined in the Ukraine, Siberia, and the Ural Mountains. The Soviet Union leads the world in the mining of iron ore. Locate these natural resources on the map on page 239.

The Soviet Union is also rich in natural gas, chromium, aluminum, nickel, lead, zinc, gold, silver, and tungsten. The Soviet Union leads the world in the production of manganese, a metal needed to make steel. The Soviet Union's great supplies of almost every resource needed for industry mean that the country does not have to import many natural resources.

Automobile factories benefit from the country's vast supply of iron ore, used to make steel.

A Distinctive Teacher's Planning Guide Offers an Abundance of Teaching Suggestions and Activities

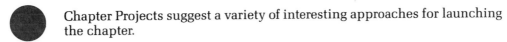 Chapter Projects suggest a variety of interesting approaches for launching the chapter.

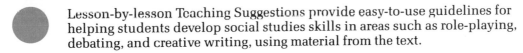 Lesson-by-lesson Teaching Suggestions provide easy-to-use guidelines for helping students develop social studies skills in areas such as role-playing, debating, and creative writing, using material from the text.

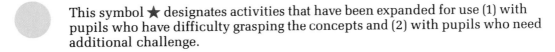 This symbol ★ designates activities that have been expanded for use (1) with pupils who have difficulty grasping the concepts and (2) with pupils who need additional challenge.

 Frequent Supplementary Information sections offer helpful sidelights on topics related to the text.

Page 2

Page 3

CHAPTER 1 PAGES 4–25

THEME

Globes and various kinds of maps provide a wealth of information. Tools such as these help people to study and better understand the earth on which we live.

CHAPTER PROJECTS

1. An interesting source of information that pupils should learn to use is a world almanac, such as *The World Almanac*. Ask pupils to use an almanac to find the following: the latitude and longitude of your state capital, the population density of your state, and the climatic features of your state.

2. Have pupils write to various places in the United States to request a variety of maps. They might write to city, county, and state government offices; state and national parks; amusement parks; museums; state departments of transportation; and local banks or real estate firms. Review letter-writing skills with pupils and be sure they explain why they are requesting maps. Make a class collection of maps that pupils receive in the mail. As different types of maps are discussed throughout the chapter, refer to the collection.

3. Have pupils search magazines and newspapers for various types of maps. Ask them to bring these maps to class to add to the classroom map collection.

4. Maps are made by several organizations. The United States Geological Survey (USGS) is especially important. It surveys the land, prepares maps, and then prints and publishes them. Many of its maps are very beautiful. They are on many different scales, and they use different methods of showing relief and certain features. Select a pupil to obtain a USGS map by writing to U.S. Geological Survey, 582 National Center, Reston, VA 22092. An index map of your state should be requested. The index will tell what maps are available and how to order them directly from the USGS.

LESSON 1 PAGES 4–10

GOALS **1.** To identify specific physical features in pictures and in the local area. **2.** To define *canyon, continent, delta, fjord, gulf, harbor, island, isthmus, lake, mountain, ocean, peninsula, plain, river, strait,* and *valley.*

TEACHING SUGGESTIONS

1. **Discussion/Research Report.** At times the *Double Eagle II* pictured on p. 5 traveled at heights low enough so that the balloonists could see the different shapes of land and water below. Perhaps some pupils know a balloonist, have seen a sport balloon, or have even been to a balloon race. Ask pupils to share with other class members any experiences or knowledge they may have of balloons. You may wish to have pupils do research and report back to the class on the different kinds of balloons and how they operate.

★ 2. **Making a Notebook.** You may wish to have pupils begin a geography notebook to be used throughout the term. Suggest that they keep a list of the vocabulary words and definitions in the notebook. To start, have them list and define each of the boldfaced terms on pp. 6–9. Have partners quiz each other on their understanding of the terms and their definitions.

The organization of the notebook should reflect the lesson topics. Various assignments, answers to Checkup Questions, answers to Chapter Review exercises, and reports may be kept in the notebook. Emphasize to pupils that the notebook should be neatly kept and carefully written.

REMEDIATION Ask pupils who have difficulty grasping the meaning of the vocabulary terms to find pictures of the physical features on post cards, in magazines and brochures, and in other printed material. Have them identify each picture as the kind of physical feature it represents and then add these pictures to the appropriate section of their notebook.

ENRICHMENT Pupils who need a challenge can write definitions of the vocabulary terms by paraphrasing the definitions given in the Glossary. Have them add this list of definitions to their notebook.

---

3. **Learning Definitions.** Make a set of 3″ × 5″ index cards for pupils to use as a study aid. Half the cards should show a vocabulary word that names a physical feature from pp. 6–9. The other cards should give a definition of a vocabulary word. Have pupils match the vocabulary cards with the appropriate definition cards.

4. **Vocabulary Building.** Have pupils make a list of the words given in the vocabulary box on p. 4. Have pupils write their own definitions for each of the words. As they write, walk around the classroom and tell pupils which of their definitions are correct. After they have attempted their own definitions, have them turn to pp. 6–9 in the text to find the meaning of the words they did not know.

5. **Identifying Local Landforms.** After pupils have read pp. 6–9, assist the class in identifying any physical features discussed on these pages that may be found in your local area. Ask:

a. Is our community near a sea or an ocean?

b. Is our community on a plain?

c. Are there mountains and rivers in or near our community?

d. Are there lakes near our community?

e. Is our community on an island or a peninsula? If it is not, name the nearest island and peninsula.

f. What other physical features shown on pp. 6–9 are in or near our community?

Make use of a local or state map to further examine the area in which your community is located.

SUPPLEMENTARY INFORMATION

1. **The Earth Wobbles.** Scientists have established that the earth wobbles as it spins on its axis. The shift is as great as 72 feet (22 m) over a period of 14 months. The north-south axis zigs and zags in a generally circular motion, much like a spinning top when it loses its speed. Several theories have been suggested by scientists to try to explain this phenomenon. It may be the result of melting polar ice caps; it may be due to the movement of the seas; or it may be due to the uneven distribution of the earth's landmasses.

2. **Constant State of Change.** Though we may not realize it, the surface of the earth is in a constant state of change. Physical features disappear, and water and land form new configurations.

Islands sink beneath the sea, and ocean bottom becomes land. The reason we do not realize that these changes are occurring is that they take place over a long period of time. The earth's surface is very different today from centuries ago.

There are many different forces that carry out this slow but steady process of change. Pressures generated deep within the earth exert tremendous force on the surface, pushing it upward. Today the fossils of sea creatures can be found in the rock layers of mountain ranges. In other places, what was once dry land is now many feet below the surface of the ocean. Other forces that destroy physical features and create new ones include wind, water, and ice. Soil is moved by these forces. This process of constant change has always gone on and probably always will.

LESSON 2 PAGES 10–19

GOALS **1.** To appreciate the functions and importance of maps. **2.** To use a map scale to determine distance between two points. **3.** To draw a map to scale. **4.** To know that map symbols stand for real places and things. **5.** To use a map key to determine the meaning of map symbols. **6.** To define *compass rose, latitude, longitude, hemisphere, parallel,* and *meridian.* **7.** To locate places on a map, using latitude and longitude. **8.** To locate places on a map, using grid boxes. **9.** To interpolate the location of a place if the parallel or meridian of that place is not shown on a map.

TEACHING SUGGESTIONS

1. **Understanding Scale.** Bring, or ask pupils to bring, various models to class, such as a model car, airplane, or a piece of dollhouse furniture. Use the models to help pupils realize that not only are models smaller than the things they represent, but that all the parts of a model are built to the same scale. Ask: *Why is it necessary for these models to be smaller than the real things?* (It would not be practical for models to be as large as the things they represent.) *Why must a consistent scale be used on all parts of a model?* (All parts of a model must be accurately proportioned to the parts of the real thing that the model represents.)

Point out to pupils that maps are drawn smaller than the areas they represent. On the chalkboard,

2

3

PROGRAM CONTENT OUTLINE

MY WORLD AND ME

FAMILIES AND NEIGHBORHOODS

NEIGHBORHOODS AND COMMUNITIES

The World and Its People

COMMUNITIES AND RESOURCES

STATES AND REGIONS

PROGRAM CONTENT OUTLINE

THE UNITED STATES AND ITS NEIGHBORS

CANADA AND LATIN AMERICA

The World and Its People

EUROPE, AFRICA, ASIA, AND AUSTRALIA

PROGRAM CONTENT OUTLINE

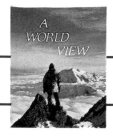

A WORLD VIEW

The World and Its People

ONE FLAG, ONE LAND

MAP AND GLOBE SKILLS
SCOPE AND SEQUENCE

SKILLS

SKILLS	MY WORLD AND ME	FAMILIES AND NEIGHBORHOODS	NEIGHBORHOODS AND COMMUNITIES	COMMUNITIES AND RESOURCES	STATES AND REGIONS	THE UNITED STATES AND ITS NEIGHBORS	CANADA AND LATIN AMERICA	EUROPE, AFRICA, ASIA, AND AUSTRALIA	A WORLD VIEW	ONE FLAG, ONE LAND
Globe	●	●	●	●	●	●	●			●
Continents and Oceans	●	●	●	●	●	●	●			●
Landform Identification	●	●		●	●	●	●			●
Shape Identification	●	●	●	●	●	●	●			●
Cardinal Directions		●	●	●	●	●	●			
Legend (Key)		●	●	●	●	●	●			●
Symbols		●	●	●	●	●	●	●		●
Color		●	●	●	●	●	●			●
Political Boundaries		●	●	●	●	●	●			●
Pictorial		●	●	●	●	●	●			●
Abstract		●	●	●	●	●	●			●
Transition from Photo to Map		●	●	●	●	●	●			●
Comparative Size		●	●	●	●	●	●			●
Labels		●	●	●	●	●	●			●
Location	●	●		●	●	●	●			●
Inset Maps			●	●	●	●	●			●
Picture Maps		●	●	●						
Directional Arrows		●	●	●						
North Pole				●	●	●	●			
South Pole				●	●	●	●			●
Floor Plan			●	●	●	●	●			●
Thematic Maps				●	●	●	●			
Atlas				●	●	●	●			●
Intermediate Directions				●	●	●	●			●
Compass Rose				●	●	●	●			
Latitude				●	●	●	●			●
Equator				●	●	●	●			●
Arctic Circle										●
Antarctic Circle										●

SKILLS

Latitude (continued)	MY WORLD AND ME	FAMILIES AND NEIGHBORHOODS	NEIGHBORHOODS AND COMMUNITIES	COMMUNITIES AND RESOURCES	STATES AND REGIONS	THE UNITED STATES AND ITS NEIGHBORS	CANADA AND LATIN AMERICA	EUROPE, AFRICA, ASIA, AND AUSTRALIA	A WORLD VIEW	ONE FLAG, ONE LAND
Tropic of Cancer				●	●	●	●	●	●	
Tropic of Capricorn				●	●	●	●	●	●	
Longitude				●	●	●	●	●	●	
Prime Meridian				●	●	●	●	●	●	
Using a Coordinate System				●	●	●	●	●	●	
Hemispheres				●	●	●	●	●	●	
Shaded Relief				●	●	●	●	●	●	
Scale				●	●	●	●	●	●	
Elevation Tints						●	●	●	●	
Mileage Chart				●	●	●	●	●	●	
Subway Map				●					●	
Railroad Map						●	●	●	●	
Physical-Political Map					●	●	●	●	●	
Road Map					●	●	●	●		
Isolines (e.g., contour lines)					●	●	●	●	●	
Profile Maps					●	●	●	●	●	
Travel Routes						●	●	●	●	
Historical Maps						●	●	●	●	
Weather Map							●	●	●	
Time Zones						●	●	●	●	
Projections								●	●	
Diagrams				●	●	●	●	●	●	
Graphs	●		●	●	●	●	●	●	●	
Pictograph	●		●	●	●	●	●	●	●	
Pie Graph			●	●	●	●	●	●	●	
Bar Graph	●	●	●	●	●	●	●	●	●	
Line Graph										
Climograph						●	●	●	●	

READING SKILLS
SCOPE AND SEQUENCE

SKILLS	MY WORLD AND ME	FAMILIES AND NEIGHBORHOODS	NEIGHBORHOODS AND COMMUNITIES	COMMUNITIES AND RESOURCES	STATES AND REGIONS	THE UNITED STATES AND ITS NEIGHBORS	CANADA AND LATIN AMERICA	EUROPE, AFRICA, ASIA, AND AUSTRALIA	A WORLD VIEW	ONE FLAG, ONE LAND
VOCABULARY BUILDING										
Understanding and defining words by:										
Using objects	●	●	●	●	●	●	●	●	●	●
Using illustrations	●	●	●	●	●	●	●	●	▪	●
Using a glossary			●	●	●	●	●	●	▪	▪
Using a dictionary				●	●	●	●	●	●	▪
Using context clues					●	●	●	●	●	
Alphabetical Order		●	●	●	●	●	●	●	▪	●
Synonyms/Antonyms	●	●	●	●	●	●	●	●	●	●
Prefix/Suffix				●	●	●	●	●	●	▪
Acronyms/Abbreviations				●	●	●	●	●	●	▪
Word Origins				●	●	●	●	●	▪	●
DEVELOPING READING COMPREHENSION										
Understanding and identifying the main idea		●	●	●	●	●	●	●		●
Following directions	●	●	●	●	●	●	●	●	▪	●
Understanding relationships	●	●	●	●	●	●	●	●	▪	●
Understanding sequence	●	●	●	●	●	●	●	●	▪	●
Understanding cause and effect	●	●	●	●	●	●	●	●	▪	●
Recalling information	●	●	●	●	●	●	●	●	●	●
Recognizing attitudes and emotions	●	●	●	●	●	●	●	●	●	●
Understanding different literary forms		●	●	●	●	●	●	●	●	●
Understanding that facts support main idea			●	●	●	●	●	●	●	●

SKILLS

Skill	MY WORLD AND ME	FAMILIES AND NEIGHBORHOODS	NEIGHBORHOODS AND COMMUNITIES	COMMUNITIES AND RESOURCES	STATES AND REGIONS	THE UNITED STATES AND ITS NEIGHBORS	CANADA AND LATIN AMERICA	EUROPE, AFRICA, ASIA, AND AUSTRALIA	A WORLD VIEW	ONE FLAG, ONE LAND
DEVELOPING READING COMPREHENSION (continued)										
Identifying purpose for reading			•	•	•	•	•	•	•	
Reading schedules and calendars			•	•	•	•	•	•	•	
Identifying topic sentence				•	•	•	•	•	•	
Distinguishing between the main idea and details				•	•	•	•	•	•	
Skimming				•	•	•	•	•	•	
Distinguishing between fact and opinion				•	•	•	•	•	•	
Summarizing				•	•	•	•	•	•	
Reading mileage charts				•	•	•	•	•	•	
Reading time lines				•	•	•	•		•	
Reading and interpreting facts from tables				•	•	•	•	•	•	
Using details to support main idea					•	•	•	•	•	
Distinguishing between relevant and irrelevant data						•	•	•	•	
Paraphrasing						•	•		•	
Recognizing and identifying author's or speaker's purpose						•	•	•	•	
Understanding primary and secondary sources						•	•		•	
Recognizing propaganda						•	•	•	•	

LANGUAGE ARTS SKILLS
SCOPE AND SEQUENCE

SKILLS	MY WORLD AND ME	FAMILIES AND NEIGHBORHOODS	NEIGHBORHOODS AND COMMUNITIES	COMMUNITIES AND RESOURCES	STATES AND REGIONS	THE UNITED STATES AND ITS NEIGHBORS	CANADA AND LATIN AMERICA	EUROPE, AFRICA, ASIA, AND AUSTRALIA	A WORLD VIEW	ONE FLAG, ONE LAND
WRITING SKILLS										
Letter Writing (personal)		●	●	●	●	●	●			
Descriptive Writing	●	●	●	●	●	●	●			●
Narrative Writing	●	●	●	●	●	●	●			●
Report Writing	●	●	●	●	●	●	●			●
Letter Writing (business)	●	●	●	●	●	●	●			●
Book Reports				●	●	●	●			●
Writing a Diary				●	●	●	●			●
Outlining				●	●	●	●			●
Persuasive Writing					●	●	●			●
SPEAKING SKILLS										
Expressing a Point of View	●	●	●	●	●	●	●			●
Oral Reports		●	●	●	●	●				●
Debate						●	●			●
LIBRARY SKILLS										
Choosing References				●	●	●	●			●
Card Catalog				●	●	●	●			●
Encyclopedia				●	●	●	●			●
Newspapers and Magazines				●	●	●	●			●
Vertical File					●	●	●			●
Readers' Guide to Periodical Literature						●	●			●
Almanac						●	●			●

REASONING SKILLS
SCOPE AND SEQUENCE

SKILLS	MY WORLD AND ME	FAMILIES AND NEIGHBORHOODS	NEIGHBORHOODS AND COMMUNITIES	COMMUNITIES AND RESOURCES	STATES AND REGIONS	THE UNITED STATES AND ITS NEIGHBORS	CANADA AND LATIN AMERICA	EUROPE, AFRICA, ASIA, AND AUSTRALIA	A WORLD VIEW	ONE FLAG, ONE LAND
Identifying and expressing preferences and opinions	●	●	●	●	●	●	●	●	●	●
Generalizing		●	●	●	●	●	●	●	●	●
Making inferences	●	●	●	●	●	●	●	●	●	
Drawing conclusions	●	●	●	●	●	●	●	●	●	
Comparing and contrasting	●	●	●	●	●	●	●	●		
Classifying	●	●	●	●	●	●	●	●		
Interpreting cause and effect				●	●	●	●	●		
Gathering information	●	●	●	●	●	●	●	●	●	
Observing	●	●	●	●	●	●	●	●	●	
Interviewing			●	●	●	●	●	●	●	
Using primary sources				●	●	●	●	●	●	
Using secondary sources				●	●	●	●	●	●	
Polling						●	●	●	●	
Identifying a problem					●	●	●	●	●	
Identifying alternatives					●	●	●	●	●	
Recognizing and identifying points of view					●	●	●	●	●	
Defending a point of view						●	●	●	●	
Predicting						●	●	●	●	
Developing objectivity						●	●	●	●	
Making or withholding judgment					●	●	●	●		
Evaluating relevance of information						●	●	●	●	

SOCIETAL SKILLS
SCOPE AND SEQUENCE

SKILLS	MY WORLD AND ME	FAMILIES AND NEIGHBORHOODS	NEIGHBORHOODS AND COMMUNITIES	COMMUNITIES AND RESOURCES	STATES AND REGIONS	THE UNITED STATES AND ITS NEIGHBORS	CANADA AND LATIN AMERICA	EUROPE, AFRICA, ASIA, AND AUSTRALIA	A WORLD VIEW	ONE FLAG, ONE LAND
LIFE SKILLS										
Telling time		●	●							
Reading a calendar		●	●							
Practicing pedestrian and bicycle safety	●	●	●							
Reading traffic signs	●	●	●	●	●	●	●			●
Recognizing warning signs and symbols	●	●	●	●	●	●	●	●		
Knowing full name and address	●	●	●	●	●	●	●	●		
Understanding the importance of good nutrition	●	●	●	●	●	●	●	●		●
Knowing fire drill procedure	●	●	●	●	●	●	●	●		
Knowing when and how to call fire or police help	●	●	●	●	●	●	●	●		
Practicing basic safety techniques in home and school	●	●	●	●	●	●	●	●		
Knowing emergency telephone numbers		●	●	●	●	●	●	●		
Using a telephone		●	●	●	●	●	●	●		●
Becoming aware of job opportunities		●	●	●	●	●	●			
Budgeting and banking		●	●	●	●	●	●			
Addressing an envelope			●	●	●	●	●			
Using a telephone directory				●	●	●	●			
Reading a schedule				●	●	●	●			
Filling out forms and applications					●	●	●	●		
Reading newspaper ads						●	●			●
HUMAN RELATIONS										
Developing personal friendships	●	●	●							
Developing respect for self	●	●	●	●	●	●	●			
Developing respect for others	●	●	●	●	●	●	●	●		●
Working in groups	●	●	●	●	●	●	●	●		●
Recognizing interdependence among people	●	●	●	●	●	●	●	●		

SKILLS

HUMAN RELATIONS (continued)

Skill	MY WORLD AND ME	FAMILIES AND NEIGHBORHOODS	NEIGHBORHOODS AND COMMUNITIES	COMMUNITIES AND RESOURCES	STATES AND REGIONS	THE UNITED STATES AND ITS NEIGHBORS	CANADA AND LATIN AMERICA	EUROPE, AFRICA, ASIA, AND AUSTRALIA	A WORLD VIEW	ONE FLAG, ONE LAND
Understanding the importance of courtesy	•	•	•	•	•	•				
Recognizing other points of view				•	•	•	•	•	•	

CITIZENSHIP AND VALUES

Skill	MY WORLD AND ME	FAMILIES AND NEIGHBORHOODS	NEIGHBORHOODS AND COMMUNITIES	COMMUNITIES AND RESOURCES	STATES AND REGIONS	THE UNITED STATES AND ITS NEIGHBORS	CANADA AND LATIN AMERICA	EUROPE, AFRICA, ASIA, AND AUSTRALIA	A WORLD VIEW	ONE FLAG, ONE LAND
Respecting our American heritage and beliefs		•	•	•	•	•	•	•	•	
Understanding the democratic process		•	•	•	•	•	•	•	•	
Understanding the role of the citizen in a democracy		•	•	•	•	•	•	•	•	•
Understanding and accepting the need for laws		•	•	•	•	•	•	•	•	•
Developing a respect for rules and laws	•	•	•	•	•	•	•	•	•	•
Appreciating ethnic heritage		•	•	•	•	•	•	•	•	
Appreciating basic American values		•	•	•	•	•	•	•	•	•
Appreciating the dignity in all occupations	•	•	•	•	•	•	•	•	•	
Developing pride in one's own work	•	•	•	•	•	•	•	•	•	
Developing good work and job habits	•	•	•	•	•	•	•	•	•	
Understanding the importance of responsibility	•	•	•	•	•	•	•	•	•	•
Participating in decision making	•	•	•	•	•	•	•	•	•	•
Understanding the importance of leisure time						•	•			
Respecting the rights of others while exercising one's own						•	•	•	•	
Recognizing that responsibility and freedom are related						•	•	•	•	
Recognizing and avoiding negative stereotypes						•	•	•	•	

BOOKS, FILMS, RECORDS

Some of the books mentioned may be out of print. However, they may be available in your school or local library.

UNIT 1

BOOKS FOR STUDENTS

Earth in Motion: The Concept of Plate Tectonics. R.V. Fodor. New York: William Morrow & Co., Inc. (1)

Map Making. Lloyd A. Brown. Boston: Little, Brown & Co. (1)

Our Violent Earth. Washington, D.C.: National Geographic Society. (2)

Sky Watchers of Ages Past. Malcolm E. Weiss. Boston: Houghton Mifflin Co. (3)

This Book Is About Time. Marilyn Burns. Boston: Little, Brown & Co. (3)

BOOKS FOR TEACHERS

The Atmosphere, Third Edition. Edward J. Tarbuck and Frederick K. Lutgens. Columbus, Ohio: Charles E. Merrill Publishing Co. (3)

Children's Spatial Development. John Eliot and Neil J. Salkind. New York: Charles Thomas. (1)

Climate, History and the Modern World. H.H. Lamb. New York: Methuen Inc. (3)

Geography Teaching with a Little Latitude. L.J. Jay. Boston: Allen & Unwin, Inc. (1)

Image and Environment. R.M. Downs and David Stea. Chicago: Aldine Publishing Co. (2)

Killer Weather: Stories of Great Disasters. Howard Everett Smith. New York: Dodd Mead & Co. (3)

Media Planning and Production. Michael R. Simonson and Roger P. Volker. Columbus, Ohio: Charles E. Merrill Publishing Co. (2)

FILMS

Maps for a Changing World. Chicago: Encyclopaedia Britannica Educational Corp. 14 min, color. (1)

UNIT 2

BOOKS FOR STUDENTS

Canada Coast to Coast. Photography by Paul von Barch and others. New York: Oxford University Press, Inc. (5)

Children's Choices of Canadian Books, Volume 2. Margaret Caughey, ed. Ottawa, Ont.: Citizens' Committee on Children. (5)

Facts on Canada. Ottawa, Ont.: Secretary of State for External Affairs. (5)

Safeguarding the Land. Women at Work in Parks, Forests, and Rangeland. Gloria Skurzynski. New York: Harcourt, Brace, Jovanovich, Inc. (4)

Shale Oil and Tar Sands: the Promises and Pitfalls. Richard B. Lyttle. New York: Franklin Watts, Inc. (4)

BOOKS FOR TEACHERS

The American Weather Book. David McWilliams Ludlum. Boston: Houghton Mifflin Co. (4)

Anglo-American Realm, 2nd ed. Otis P. Starkey and others. New York: McGraw-Hill, Inc. (4, 5)

Centennial. James Michener. New York: Fawcett Book Group. (4)

Chesapeake. James Michener. New York: Fawcett Book Group. (4)

FILMS

Here Is Canada. National Film Board of Canada (Obtain from Canadian Embassy, 1746 Massachusetts Ave. N.W., Washington, D.C.) 28 min, color. (5)

The Story of the St. Lawrence Seaway. National Film Board of Canada (Obtain from Canadian Embassy, 1746 Massachusetts Ave. N.W. Washington, D.C.) 13 min, color. (5)

RECORDS

"The Chivalrous Shark." *Silver Burdett Music 7* 1985 ed., Record 2. (5)

"Every Night When the Sun Goes In." *Silver Burdett Music 7,* 1985 ed., Record 7. (17)

"New River Train." *Silver Burdett Music 7,* 1985 ed., Record 3. (5)

"I'se the B'y." *Silver Burdett Music 6,* 1985 ed., Record 1. (1)

UNIT 3

BOOKS FOR STUDENTS

Coming to North America from Mexico, Cuba, and Puerto Rico. Susan Garver and Paula McGuire. New York: Delacorte Press. (6, 7)

Feathered Serpent: The Rise and Fall of the Aztecs. Ruth Karen. New York: School Book Service. (6)

First Book of the Ancient Maya. Barbara Beck. New York: Franklin Watts, Inc. (7)

First Book of Central America and Panama. Patricia Maloney Markun. New York: Franklin Watts, Inc. (7)

Latin America. Lawrence J. Pauline. New York: Globe Book Co., Inc. (6, 7, 8)

Looking at Brazil. Sarita Kendall. New York: Harper & Row, Publishers, Inc. (8)

Lost City in the Clouds: The Discovery of Machu Picchu. Elizabeth Gemmings. New York: Coward, McCann & Geoghegan. (8)

Mexico. Larry Cuban and E.H. McCleary. Glenview, Ill.: Scott Foresman & Co. (6)

People of the Dawn. Richard B. Lyttle. New York: Atheneum Publishers. (6, 7, 8)

Puerto Rico: Island Between Two Worlds. Lila Perl. New York: William Morrow & Co., Inc. (7)

The Tropical Forest: Ants, Animals, and Plants. New York: Harper & Row, Publishers, Inc. (8)

BOOKS FOR TEACHERS

Environment, Society, and Rural Change in Latin America. David A. Preston, ed. New York: John Wiley & Sons, Inc. (6, 7, 8)

Latin America: Geographical Perspectives. Harold Blakemore and Clifford T. Smith. London: Methuen & Co., Ltd. (6, 7, 8)

Middle America: Its Lands and Peoples. Robert C. West and John P. Augelli. Englewood Cliffs, N.J.: Prentice-Hall, Inc. (6, 7)

Sex and Class in Latin America. June Nash and A.J. Safa, eds. New York: Praeger Publishers. (6, 7, 8)

Sons of the Shaking Earth (The People of Mexico and Guatemala — Their Land, History, and Culture). Eric Wolf. Chicago: The University of Chicago Press. (6, 7)

FILMS

Amazon. Irvington, N.J.: Journal Films, Inc., 23 min, color. (8)

Bolivia, Peru, and Ecuador. New York: Sterling Educational Films, 19 min, color. (8)

A Brazilian Family. New York: International Film Foundation, 20 min, color. (8)

Central America: A Human Geography. Chicago: Coronet Films, 16 min, color. (7)

Latin American Overview. New York: McGraw-Hill Films, 25 min, color. (6, 7, 8)

South America Today. New York: International Film Foundation, 26 min, color. (8)

RECORDS

"Carmela." *Silver Burdett Music 7,* 1985 ed., Record 9. (22)

"El Capotín." *Silver Burdett Music 8,* 1985 ed., Record 2. (3)

Ginastera: *Estancia Ballet Suite,* "Wheat Dance." *Silver Burdett Music 8,* 1985 ed., Record 3. (4)

UNIT 4

BOOKS FOR STUDENTS

e Alps. Washington, D.C.: National Georaphic Society. (11)
e Black Death, 1347–1351. Daniel Cohen. New York: Franklin Watts, Inc. (9, 10, 11, 12)
ts from the Greeks: Alpha to Omega. Sophia ... Boyer. Skokie, Ill.: Rand McNally & Co. (12)
ler's War Against the Jews. David A. Althuler. New York: Behrman House, Inc. (11)
ince: the Invisible Revolution. Sabra Holbrook. Chicago: Nelson-Hall Publishers. (10)
ion in the Sun. Edward F. Dolan. New York: Parents Magazine Press. (9)
king Expansion Westward. Magnus Mansson. New York: H.Z. Walck. (9)

BOOKS FOR TEACHERS

The European Culture Area. Terry G. Jordan. New York: Harper & Row, Publishers, Inc. (9, 10, 11, 12)
A Historical Geography of Europe. 5th ed. W. Gordon East. New York: E.P. Dutton, Inc. (9, 10, 11, 12)
Reading the Landscape. May Theilgaard Watts. New York: Macmillan Publishing Co. (9, 10, 11, 12)
A Social Geography of Europe. J.M. Houston. London: Duckworth. (9, 10, 11, 12)

FILMS

France. New York: Goldberg-Werrenrath Productions; Journal Films. 19 min. (10)
Germany. New York: Screenscope. 25–27 min. (11)
Mediterranean Prospects. New York: Time-Life Films. 60 min. (12)
Spain. New York: Goldberg-Werrenrath Productions; Journal Films. 20 min. (12)

RECORDS

"Barb'ra Allen." Silver Burdett Music 7, 1985 ed., Record 1. (3)
Debussy: Prelude to the Afternoon of a Fawn. Silver Burdett Music 7, 1985 ed., Record 6. (13)
"Parting Song." Silver Burdett Music 7, 1985 ed., Record 7. (16)
Falla: El Amor Brujo, "Ritual Fire Dance." Silver Burdett Music 7, 1985 ed., Record 1. (1)

UNIT 5

BOOKS FOR STUDENTS

rlin: City Split in Two. Nancy Gardner. New York: G.P. Putnam's Sons. (13)
e Cold War. Morris Herlitzer. New York: Franklin Watts, Inc. (14)
urney Across Russia: the Soviet Union Today. Bart McDowell. Washington, D.C.: National Geographic Society. (14)
e Kremlin: Citadel of History. Mina C. Klein. New York: Macmillan Publishing Co. (14)
land in Pictures. Robert Obojski. Sterling Publishing Co., Inc. (13)
Poland: The Threat to National Renewal. Richard Worth. New York: Franklin Watts, Inc. (13)

BOOKS FOR TEACHERS

Eastern Europe. Roy E.H. Mellor. New York: Columbia University Press. (13)
Geography of the USSR. Paul E. Lydolph. New York: John Wiley & Sons, Inc. (14)
Poland Between East and West. Norman J.G. Pounds. Searchlight Book No. 22. Princeton, N.J.: Van Nostrand Co., Inc. (13)
The Soviet Union: The Fifty Years. Harrison E. Salisbury, ed. New York: Harcourt, Brace & World. (14)

FILMS

Poland: The Will to Be. New York: Emlen House Productions; Pyramid. 58 min. (13)
Sadja's Yugoslavia. New York: Ramsgate Films. 11 min. (13)
Soviet Agriculture. Lincoln, Neb.: Great Plains ITV Library. 25 min. (14)

RECORDS

Prokofiev: Classical Symphony. "Gavotte." Silver Burdett Music 8, 1985 ed., Record 1. (2)

UNIT 6

BOOKS FOR STUDENTS

e Euphrates. John Batchelor. Morristown, N.J.: Silver Burdett Co. (16)
ael: Land of the Jews. Mina C. Klein. Indianapolis, Ind. Bobbs-Merrill Co., Inc. (16)
wait and the Rim of Arabia. Gilda Berger. New York: Franklin Watts, Inc. (16)
banon. Gerald Newman. New York: Franklin Watts, Inc. (16)
gacy of the Desert: Understanding the Arabs. Boston: Little, Brown & Co. (15, 16)

The Oil Countries of the Middle East. Emil Lengyel. New York: Franklin Watts, Inc. (16)
The Pyramids of Egypt. I.E.S. Edwards. New York: The Viking Press. (15)

BOOKS FOR TEACHERS

The First Cities. Dora Jane Hamblin. Alexandria, Va.: Time-Life Books Inc. (16)
The First 3000 Years. C.B. Falls. New York: The Viking Press. (15, 16)
Makers of Arab History. Philip K. Hitti. New York: Harper & Row, Publishers, Inc. (15, 16)
The Middle East: A Physical, Social, and Regional Geography. W.B. Fisher. London: Methuen Inc. (16)

The Source. James A. Michener. New York: Fawcett Book Group. (16)

FILMS

Israel: The Story of the Jewish People. Chicago, Ill.: International Film Foundation. 28 min. (16)
Mosaic of Peoples (An Overview). Chicago: Coronet. 27½ min. (15)

RECORDS

"Dayenu." Silver Burdett Music 7, 1985 ed., Record 7. (16)
"Shalom, Chaverim." Silver Burdett Music 7, 1985 ed., Record 12. (25)

UNIT 7

BOOKS FOR STUDENTS

rica. Milton Jay Belasco and Harold E. Hammond. New York: Globe Book Co. (17, 18, 19)
hiopia: Land of the Lion. Lila Perl. New York: William Morrow & Co., Inc. (17)
nya. Edward J. Soja. Glenview, Ill.: Scott, Foresman & Co. (17)
uth Africa: Coming of Age Under Apartheid. Jason Laure and Ettagale Laure. New York: Farrar, Straus & Giroux, Inc. (18)
e Story of Africa from the Earliest Times. A.J.
Willis. New York: Africana Publishing Co. (17, 18, 19)
Through African Eyes. Leon E. Clark, ed. New York: Holt, Rinehart & Winston. (17, 18, 19)

BOOKS FOR TEACHERS

Africa and the World. Lewis H. Gann and Peter Duignan. San Francisco: Chandler Publishing Co. (17, 18, 19)
African Women in Towns: An Aspect of Africa's Social Revolution. London: Cambridge University Press. (17, 18, 19)
Population, Migration, and Urbanization in Africa. William A. Hance. New York: Columbia University Press. (17, 18, 19)

The Strong Brown God: The Story of the Niger River. Sanche de Gramont. Boston: Houghton Mifflin Co. (19)

FILMS

Africa: An Introduction. Santa Monica, Calif.: BFA Educational Media. 22 min, color. (17, 18, 19)
Tanzania: of People and a Vision. Albany, N.Y.: Carousel Films, Inc., 19 min, color. (17)

RECORDS

"African Noel." Silver Burdett Music 7, 1985 ed., Record 11. (24)
"Mangwani Mpulele." Silver Burdett Music 7, 1985 ed., Record 9. (22)

BOOKS, FILMS, RECORDS

UNIT 8

BOOKS FOR STUDENTS

Children of Vietnam. Betty Jean Lifton and Thomas C. Fox. New York: Athenum Publishers. (23)

The Chinese, How They Live and Work. T.R. Tregear. New York: Praeger Publishers. (20)

Gandhi: Fighter Without a Sword. Jeanette Eaton. New York: William Morrow & Co., Inc. (22)

India. Sandra Hineley and Ralph Mitchall. Glenview, Ill.: Scott, Foresman & Co. (22)

India, Pakistan, Bangladesh. Milton J. Belasko and Harold E. Hammond. New York: Globe Book Co., Inc. (22)

Japan, Korea, Taiwan. Rudolph Schwartz, Harold Hammond, and Adriane Ruggiero. New York: Globe Book Co., Inc. (21, 23)

The Land and People of the Philippines. John Nance. Philadelphia: J.B. Lippincott Co. (23)

The People of New China. Margaret Rau. New York: Julian Messner. (20)

Through Chinese Eyes, Volume 1: Revolution, A Nation Stands Up. Peter J. Seybolt. New York: Praeger Publishers. (20, 21, 22, 23)

Through Chinese Eyes, Volume 2: Transformation, Building a New Society. Peter J. Seybolt. New York: Praeger Publishers. (20)

BOOKS FOR TEACHERS

Modern Japan. Irwin Scheiner. New York: Macmillan Publishing Co. (21)

The Southeast Asian City. T.G. McGee. London: G. Bell & Sons, Ltd. (23)

Women in China. Marilyn B. Young, ed. Ann Arbor, Mich.: Center for Chinese Studies. (

FILMS

Asia: An Introduction. BFA Educational Me 22 min, color. (20, 21, 22, 23)

China: A Class by Itself. Part I and Part II, Fil Inc., each 26 min, color. (20)

India, An Introduction. International F Foundation, 30 min, color. (22)

Japan, Interdependent Nation. Internatio Film Foundation, 24 min, color. (21)

RECORDS

"Crescent Moon." *Silver Burdett Music 6,* 1 ed., Record 13. (26)

"Ahrirang." *Silver Burdett Music 6,* 1985 Record 5. (10)

UNIT 9

BOOKS FOR STUDENTS

Australia. Elizabeth Cornelia. Chicago: Macdonald Educational, Ltd. (25)

The Australian Outback. Ian Moffitt. Alexandria, Va.: Time-Life Books Inc. (25)

Captain Cook and the Pacific. David W. Sylvester. New York: Longman, Inc. (24, 25)

Hawaii. Robert Wallace. Alexandria, Va.: Time-Life Books Inc. (24)

Kon-Tiki. Special edition for young people. Chicago: Rand McNally & Co. (24)

The Land and People of New Zealand. Edna Mason Kaula. New York: Harper & Row, Publishers, Inc. (25)

Vikings of the Sunrise. Peter Buck. Chicago: University of Chicago Press. (24, 25)

BOOKS FOR TEACHERS

Aku-Aku: The Secret of Easter Island. Thor Heyerdahl. Chicago: Rand McNally & Co. (24)

Coming of Age in Samoa. Margaret Mead. New York: William Morrow & Co., Inc. (24)

The Exploration of the Pacific. J.C. Beaglehole. Stanford, Calif.: Stanford University Press. (24, 25)

The Fatal Impact: An Account of the Invasion of the South Pacific. Alan Moorehead. New York: Harper & Row, Publishers, Inc. (24, 25)

The Maoris of New Zealand. Joan Metge. Boston: Routledge & Kegan Paul of America, Ltd. (25)

New Lives for Old: Cultural Transformation — Manus, 1928 – 1953. Margaret Mead. Westport, Conn.: Greenwood Press. (24)

Southwest Pacific. Kenneth B. Cumberland. New York: Praeger Publishers. (24)

Tales Told to Kabbarli: Aboriginal Legends Col-

lected by Daisy Bates. Retold by Barb Wilson. New York: Crown Publishers. (25

FILMS

Australia: Down Under and Outback. Wa ington, D.C.: National Geographic Soci 25 min. (25)

Captain James Cook. New York: Time-L Films. 52 min. (25)

New Zealand. Toronto, Ont.: Film Arts. 15 m (25)

Polynesian Adventure. Washington, D.C.: tional Geographic Society. 52 min. (24)

The South Pacific. End of Eden? Santa Mon Calif.: Pyramid Films. 16 min. (24)

RECORDS

"Tongo." *Silver Burdett Music 6,* 1985 ed., R ord 8. (18)

UNIT 10

BOOKS FOR STUDENTS

Alternate Energy Sources. Jane Werner Watson. New York: Franklin Watts, Inc. (26)

As We Live and Breathe: The Challenge of Our Environment. Washington, D.C.: National Geographic Society. (26)

Careers to Preserve Our Shrinking World. Robert V. Doyle. New York: Julian Messner. (26)

Earth, Water, Wind and Sun: The Energy Alternatives. D.S. Halacy. New York: Harper & Row, Publishers, Inc. (26)

Geothermal Energy: A Hot Prospect. Augusta Goldin. New York: Harcourt Brace Jovanovich, Inc. (26)

Oil in Troubled Waters. Madelyn Klein Anderson. New York: Vanguard Press, Inc. (26)

The Sea Around Us. Rachel Carson. New York: Oxford University Press. (26, 27)

The Sea Miners. John T. Foster. New York: Hastings House. (26, 27)

Silent Spring. Rachel Carson. Boston: Houghton Mifflin Co. (26)

Water: A Scarce Resource. Henry Gilfond. New York: Franklin Watts, Inc. (26)

Water: Too Much, Too Little, Too Polluted? Augusta Goldin. New York: Harcourt Brace Jovanovich, Inc. (26)

BOOKS FOR TEACHERS

Basic Facts About the United Nations. New York: United Nations Publications. (27)

Towards a Politics of the Planet Earth. Harold Sprout and Margaret Sprout. New York: Van Nostrand Reinhold Co., Inc. (26)

The United Nations and the Control of International Violence. John F. Murphy. Totowa, N.J.: Allanheld, Osumun & Co. (27)

FILMS

Energy for the Future. Chicago: Encyclopaedia

Britannica Educational Corp., 17 min. (26

Energy from the Sun. Chicago: Encyclopae Britannica Educational Corp., 18 min. (26

Energy: The Fuels and Man. Washington, D National Geographic Society. 23 min. (26

Energy Where You Least Expect It. Cambri Mass. Third Eye Films, 28 min. (26)

Erosion. Chicago: Encyclopaedia Britann Educational Corp., 14 min. (26)

Water: A Precious Resource. Washington, D National Geographic Society. 23 min. (26

RECORDS

"Roll On, Columbia." *Silver Burdett Music* 1985 ed., Record 12. (25)

"This Land Is Your Land." *Silver Burdett Mu* 7, 1985 ed., Record 12. (25)

"If I Had a Hammer." *Silver Burdett Music* 1985 ed., Record 3. (6)

"A World of Musical Experience." *Silver B dett Music 7,* 1985 ed., Record 7. (16)

The World and Its People
A WORLD VIEW

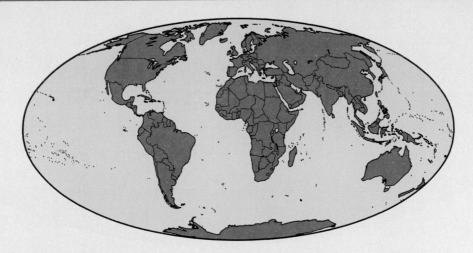

INTRODUCING THE TEXTBOOK

Help your pupils to become familiar with their textbook by reviewing the different parts of the book. Turn first to page 1 and have pupils read silently or aloud "A Letter to You from the Authors." Then have pupils turn to each part of their book, from the title page to the Index. Discuss the purpose and use of the Contents; the lists of Maps, Graphs, Diagrams, Table of Countries, Other Tables and Time Lines, Biographies, A Slice of Life; the Chapter Review pages; the Skills Development pages; the Unit Review pages; the Atlas; the Gazetteer; the Glossary; the Graph Appendix; the Index; and the Picture Index.

Chapters 1 and 2 provide pupils with the basic skills and knowledge of tools useful for studying the world and its people. Chapter 1 teaches pupils how to read and use maps and globes. Chapter 2 teaches them how to read and use photographs, tables, graphs, and time lines. These basic skills are presented in a series of lessons for ease in teaching and learning. The material in Chapters 1 and 2 is designed so that you may use it to introduce, review, or reinforce skills. Although the chapters were written to be taught as a unit of knowledge, you should feel free to adapt the material to meet the specific needs of your class and local and state curricula.

SERIES AUTHORS

Val E. Arnsdorf, Professor,
  College of Education, University of Delaware,
  Newark, Delaware
Herbert J. Bass, Professor of History,
  Temple University, Philadelphia, Pennsylvania
Carolyn S. Brown, Late Principal,
  Robertson Academy School, Nashville, Tennessee
Richard C. Brown, Former Professor of History,
  State University of New York College at Buffalo
Patricia T. Caro, Assistant Professor of Geography,
  University of Oregon, Eugene, Oregon
Kenneth S. Cooper, Professor of History, Emeritus,
  George Peabody College for Teachers, Vanderbilt
  University, Nashville, Tennessee
Gary S. Elbow, Professor of Geography,
  Texas Tech University, Lubbock, Texas
Alvis T. Harthern, Former Professor of Education,
  University of Montevallo, Montevallo, Alabama
Timothy M. Helmus, Social Studies Instructor,
  City Middle and High School, Grand Rapids,
  Michigan
Bobbie P. Hyder, Elementary Education Coordinator,
  Madison County School System,
  Huntsville, Alabama
Theodore Kaltsounis, Professor and Associate Dean,
  College of Education, University of Washington,
  Seattle, Washington
Richard H. Loftin, Director of Curriculum and Staff
  Development,
  Aldine Independent School District, Houston, Texas
Clyde P. Patton, Professor of Geography,
  University of Oregon, Eugene, Oregon

Norman J. G. Pounds, Former University Professor
  of Geography,
  Indiana University, Bloomington, Indiana
Arlene C. Rengert, Associate Professor of Geography,
  West Chester University, West Chester,
  Pennsylvania
Robert N. Saveland, Professor of Social Science
  Education,
  University of Georgia, Athens, Georgia
Edgar A. Toppin, Professor of History and Dean of
  the Graduate School,
  Virginia State University, Petersburg, Virginia

GRADE-LEVEL CONTRIBUTORS

Phyllis Connell, Teacher,
  Martin Spalding High School, Severn, Maryland
Sarah B. Duvall, Teacher and Chairman of Social
  Studies, Norman C. Toole Middle School,
  Charleston, South Carolina
Frances Flannery, Teacher,
  South Plainfield Middle School,
  South Plainfield, New Jersey
Robert M. Foster, Coordinator of Social Studies,
  Allentown School District, Allentown,
  Pennsylvania
Dale L. Knapp, Social Science Instructor,
  Meredith Junior High School,
  Des Moines, Iowa

The World and Its People

A
WORLD
VIEW

CLYDE P. PATTON
Professor of Geography,
University of Oregon, Eugene, Oregon

ARLENE C. RENGERT
Associate Professor of Geography,
West Chester University,
West Chester, Pennsylvania

KENNETH S. COOPER
Professor of History, Emeritus,
George Peabody College for Teachers,
Vanderbilt University, Nashville, Tennessee

ROBERT N. SAVELAND
Professor of Social Science Education,
University of Georgia, Athens, Georgia

PATRICIA T. CARO,
Assistant Professor of Geography,
University of Oregon, Eugene, Oregon

SILVER BURDETT COMPANY   MORRISTOWN, NJ
Atlanta, GA • Cincinnati, OH • Dallas, TX • Northfield, IL • San Carlos, CA • Agincourt, Ontario

CONTENTS

UNIT 1 Learning About the Earth

UNIT 2 The United States and Canada

ISBN 0-382-02811-2

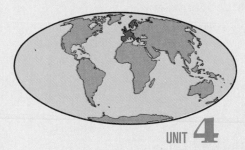

UNIT 5 Eastern Europe and the Soviet Union

UNIT 6 North Africa and the Middle East

UNIT 9 Oceania and Australia

UNIT 10 Taking A World View

MAPS

ATLAS

GRAPHS

GRAPH APPENDIX

DIAGRAMS

TABLE OF COUNTRIES

OTHER TABLES AND TIME LINES

BIOGRAPHIES

A SLICE OF LIFE

END-OF-CHAPTER SKILLS DEVELOPMENT

A LETTER TO YOU FROM THE AUTHORS

Dear Student,

The world is an ever-changing place. There have been changes in the ways people make a living, in the ways they are governed, and in the ways they think. In this book we examine the way the world looks and works today. We try to point out how places are changing — and the reasons why.

You may wonder what is the value of learning about different places and the things that are happening to them. Think about your own community for a moment. What could a new classmate from another state learn from you about playgrounds, areas to explore, or interesting shops? What could you tell your classmate about neighborhoods, about the kinds of people who live in each, and about the kinds of dwellings they live in? What could you tell him or her about the way your community celebrates various holidays, about the kind of weather in your local area, and about the best routes to travel around your community?

In passing on this information, you are explaining the geography of your community. The more you explain, the more your new classmate will feel at home and be able to make good choices about how he or she wishes to participate in community life. It is the same with the world at large. The more you learn about diverse places and peoples, the better you can understand how you fit into the world picture.

In modern geography we study the influence of people on places and regions. Keep this in mind as you read about the various regions of the world. Imagine yourself as a visitor to these places. Ask yourself: Where is this place? What is it like? Why is it like that? What other places is it like? Sometimes these questions are hard to answer. But give it a try. You will soon discover some interesting relationships between the style of life in your community and that of other places. And even though these places will surely change in the near future, you will know some of the reasons why they change.

Sincerely,

Clyde P. Patton

Arlene C. Rengert

Robert N. Saveland

Kenneth S. Cooper

Patricia T. Caro

LEARNING ABOUT THE EARTH

Emphasize to pupils that the study of geography is not only the study of maps and the earth's physical features but also includes climate, natural resources, cities, industries, and how people use the earth.

People and the Earth

When it comes to geography, a great many people have a problem. They try to ignore geography because they think it isn't very exciting. Or they think it doesn't have much to do with their lives. This is too bad, for geography is concerned with two very important subjects—people and the earth.

Today there are about 4.6 billion people in the world. This is more than twice the number there were when your parents went to school. What's more important, by the time you are adults, there are likely to be more than 6 billion people. In a world with so many people, the art of living together has to be learned. A study of geography helps us understand how our neighbors in the world live and work.

To live on the earth, people must learn to live *with* it. Geography helps us identify the different parts that make up the earth and see how the parts fit together. It points out what happens when people start misusing the parts. Geography teaches us how to take better care of our home, the earth.

Maps Represent the Earth

One thing that is special about geography is its use of maps. A good map can show at a glance how one place is like, or different from, another. The maps on the facing page clearly show similarities and differences in temperature and precipitation in the world. What is the average temperature for your part of the United States? How much precipitation falls in your part of the country? In Unit 1 you will learn how to use maps and other visual materials as you study about the world and its people.

The 12 cities shown on the maps below represent the 12 climate regions discussed in detail in Chapter 3, pp. 45–48. You may want to have pupils use the maps showing temperature and precipitation in conjunction with their study of world climate and vegetation regions in Chapter 3.

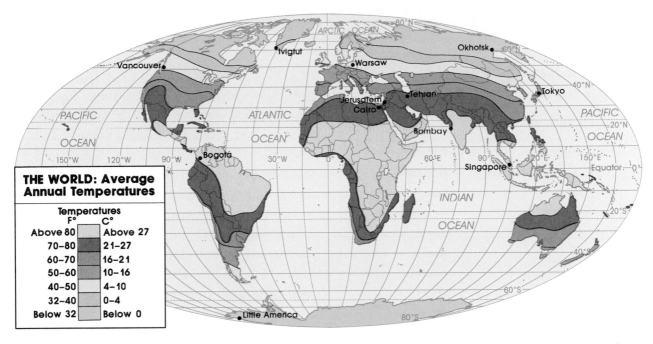

THE WORLD: Average Annual Temperatures

Temperatures	
F°	**C°**
Above 80	Above 27
70–80	21–27
60–70	16–21
50–60	10–16
40–50	4–10
32–40	0–4
Below 32	Below 0

Are the coldest parts of the world near the Equator or near the North Pole and the South Pole? Where are the hottest parts of the world?

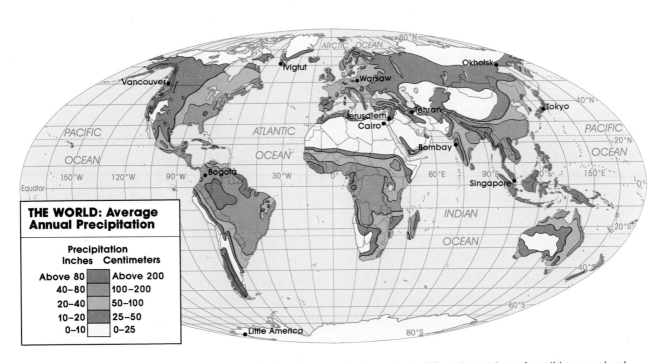

THE WORLD: Average Annual Precipitation

Precipitation	
Inches	**Centimeters**
Above 80	Above 200
40–80	100–200
20–40	50–100
10–20	25–50
0–10	0–25

Precipitation includes rain, snow, sleet, and hail. What do you learn from this map about the amount of rain in lands crossed by the Equator?

Have pupils skim through pp. 4–51 to discover the main ideas presented in Unit 1. Tell pupils to read the main headings and the subheadings, both shown in dark type, and to look quickly at the visual materials. Discuss with pupils their impressions of the unit's content.

The Earth's Physical Features

```
┌─VOCABULARY───────────────────┐
│                              │
│   altitude          mountain │
│   physical features ocean    │
│   canyon            sea      │
│   continent         peninsula│
│   delta             cape     │
│   fjord             plain    │
│   gulf              plateau  │
│   harbor            river    │
│   island            strait   │
│   isthmus           valley   │
│   lake                       │
│                              │
└──────────────────────────────┘
```

Up in balloons   For thousands of years, people did not have the means to fly. The best they could do was watch the birds and dream about what it would be like to look down on the earth from high above. A few people may have tried to imitate the birds. A Greek myth tells the story of Daedalus (ded′ ə ləs), who made two large pairs of wings out of feathers and wax. He and his son Icarus (ik′ ər əs) fastened the wings to their shoulders and flew. But Icarus flew too close to the sun, and his wings of wax melted. So Icarus fell into the sea and drowned.

It was balloons, rather than wings, that first lifted people off the ground. The earliest balloon flights took place in France in 1783. The first balloon to carry passengers was made by two brothers, Joseph and Jacques Montgolfier. They sent up a balloon that carried a duck, a rooster, and a sheep. Soon balloons rose into the air with human passengers. The dream of flying had come true!

Today, people continue to fly in balloons. Balloon racing has become a popular sport. And balloons continue to make history. In 1978, three Americans made the first successful crossing of the Atlantic Ocean in a balloon. The flight of the *Double Eagle II* began at Presque Isle, Maine, and ended 6 days later in a cornfield near Paris, France. It was a journey of more than 3,000 miles (4,837 km). The photograph on the opposite page shows the *Double Eagle II* in flight.

A picture dictionary   At times the *Double Eagle II* floated too high in the air for the balloonists to see the earth below. At other times the balloon descended to a lower **altitude,** or height above sea level. Then the balloonists could see the many different shapes of land and water. (Words in boldface type are in the Glossary, beginning on page 500.)

On pages 6–9 are pictures and descriptions of land and water of different shapes. These are some of the major **physical features** of the earth.

The Double Eagle II *was the first balloon to cross the Atlantic Ocean successfully.*

For more information about the flight of the *Double Eagle II,* ask several pupils to use the *Readers' Guide to Periodical Literature* to locate magazine articles about the event. Have pupils bring the articles to class and give brief oral reports. You may wish to tell the librarian about the activity.

A **canyon** is a very deep valley with very steep sides. Canyons are formed by running water that cuts into the ground over thousands of years. The best-known canyon in the United States is the Grand Canyon in Arizona. In some places the Grand Canyon is over 1 mile (1.6 km) deep.

A **continent** is a huge body of land on the earth's surface. There are seven continents: Africa, Antarctica, Asia, Australia, Europe, North America, and South America. One of the continents is shown at the right. To find out the name of this continent, turn to the map on page 480.

Ask: What continent is shown?
What two oceans are shown in part?

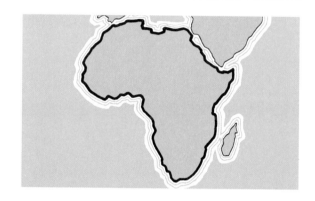

A **delta** is a low plain built up by mud and sand deposited at the mouth of a river. The soil of a delta usually makes rich farmland. Deltas are named for the Greek letter *delta* (Δ) because they have a roughly triangular shape.

A **fjord** (fyôrd) is a long, narrow, often deep inlet of the sea lying between steep cliffs. The word *fjord* is Norwegian in origin. Fjords are found especially along the coast of Norway.

A **gulf** is a part of an ocean or a sea that pushes inland. The Gulf of Mexico, off the southern coast of the United States, is one of the best-known gulfs.

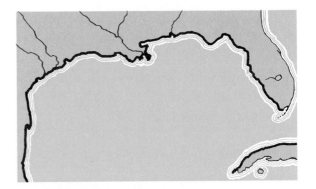

A **harbor** is a protected body of water. It is often protected by an arm of land lying between the harbor and a larger body of water, such as an ocean or a sea. In a harbor, ships and other vessels find shelter from winds and waves. Cities and towns often grow up beside harbors.

An **island** is a body of land with water all around it. It is smaller than a continent. Turn to the map of the West Indies on page 470 and see how many islands you can name.

An **isthmus** (is′ məs) is a narrow strip of land connecting two larger bodies of land. The Isthmus of Panama, shown on the map, connects the continents of North America and South America. The Panama Canal was built across the Isthmus of Panama.

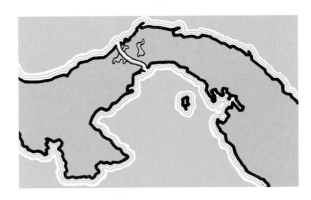

A **lake** is a body of water with land all around it. Lakes can be found in all parts of the world. Find the five large lakes at the northern border of the United States on the map on page 22. What are the names of these lakes?

A **mountain** is a piece of land rising steeply from the land around it. A mountain has a broad base and narrows to a rounded or a pointed top. A group of connected mountains is called a chain or a range. The Rocky Mountains form the longest mountain chain in the United States. Mountains cover a fifth of the earth's land surface.

An **ocean** is a very large body of salt water. About three fourths of the earth's surface is covered by ocean. The four oceans of the world, in order of size, are the Pacific Ocean, the Atlantic Ocean, the Indian Ocean, and the Arctic Ocean. A **sea** is a large body of salt water, but it is not as large as an ocean.

A **peninsula** is a stretch of land with water nearly all the way around it. It is connected to a larger body of land. A **cape** is a piece of land much like a peninsula, only a cape is smaller.

A **plain** is an almost level area that stretches for miles and miles. In Africa large antelope called wildebeest live on the plains. There are large plains in Europe and North America. A **plateau** is an elevated plain.

A **river** is a long, narrow body of water that flows through the land. A river usually begins as a small stream far up in the mountains or hills. As the river flows along, other streams join it and the river becomes larger. The Amazon River, one of the world's longest, starts in the Andes Mountains and flows through the jungles of Brazil to the Atlantic Ocean.

A **strait** is a narrow waterway that connects two larger bodies of water. The Strait of Magellan, outlined on the map with a heavy black line, is located at the tip of South America. This strait connects the Atlantic Ocean and the Pacific Ocean.

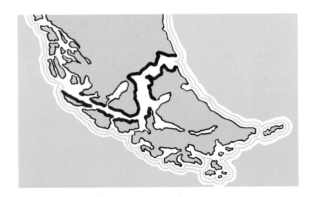

A **valley** is a long, low place between hills or mountains. There is often a river or stream in a valley. There are cities and towns in many valleys.

Arrange a classroom display of the many types of maps that are used in everyday life: road maps; transportation maps; floor plans and seating plans; maps of historical, recreational, and tourist sites; and so on. As a pupil brings in a map, ask him or her to describe how the map was used.

A Guide to Reading Maps

Maps in everyday life   In the world today there are thousands of different maps. Some of them may seem hard to understand. But the map idea itself is really simple. A map is a special kind of drawing to show what the earth or a part of the earth would look like if you viewed it from straight overhead.

At one time, maps were so valuable that they were kept secret. For example, maps showing the trade routes to Asia could make merchants and kings rich. So only a few sea captains were trusted with such information. When the ships returned from a voyage, the maps would be safely locked away. Even today there are maps that are kept secret. Maps containing certain military information are not available to the public.

For the most part, though, maps are plentiful, and people use them daily.

Visitors to the National Arboretum receive a brochure with a map. An arboretum is a place where trees and other plants are grown and displayed to the public.

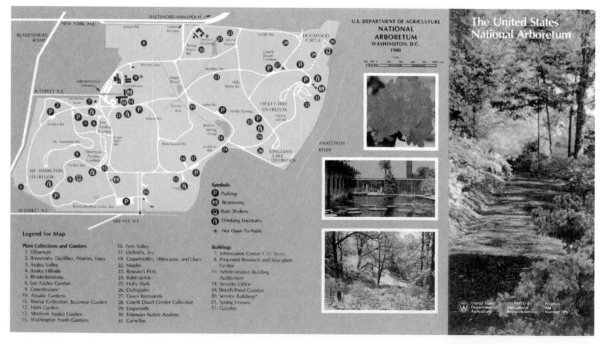

Have pupils list the Vocabulary words in alphabetical order and write a definition for each word before reading the lesson on pp. 10–19. Tell pupils to look up any words they do not know in the Glossary. Point out to pupils that each Glossary term is respelled as well as defined.

THE METRIC SYSTEM OF MEASUREMENT

In this chapter you have learned that one kilometer is equal to a little more than half a mile. A kilometer is a unit of measure in the metric system.

This system is used for measuring distance. It is also used for measuring weight, capacity, and temperature. The metric system is in use or is being introduced in all the major countries of the world except the United States. Someday the United States will probably "go metric" also.

To prepare you for this change, we have used both customary measurements that are in general use in the United States, and metric measurements in this book. When a customary measurement appears, it is followed in parentheses ( ) by the metric measurement that is equal to it. Inches are followed by centimeters (cm), feet and yards by meters (m), miles by kilometers (km), and acres by hectares (ha). Pounds are followed by kilograms (kg), and quarts by liters (L). Degrees Fahrenheit (°F) are followed by degrees Celsius (°C).

Business people use maps to find places to open new stores and offices. Engineers study maps to plan the route of a new highway. Each day thousands of travelers use road maps to plan their trips. You use maps in everyday life, too. A map of the subway will help you find your way in cities such as Boston, Massachusetts, or San Francisco, California. At the zoo in Philadelphia, Pennsylvania, or St. Louis, Missouri, a map will help you find the animals you are most interested in seeing. At Killington, Vermont, or Vail, Colorado, a map of the ski area will help you pick the best trails to ski. No matter what you want to know about a place, there is probably a map to show you that information. How much you really learn from a map, however, depends on how skillfully you can read one.

Scale Fortunately, there are only a few basic things you need to know to read a map successfully. First, you need to keep in mind that maps are drawn to scale. This means that a certain number of inches on a map stands for a certain number of feet or miles on the earth. The scale on the map gives you this information.

Scale may be shown in three different ways. One way is to give scale in words: "One inch stands for 300 miles." Another way is to show scale as a fraction, 1/600, or as a ratio, 1:600. This means that one unit of measurement on the map stands for 600 units on the earth's surface. A third way is to show scale by a straight line with distances marked off on it.

Whichever way scale is shown, it always tells you the relationship between the real distance on the earth and the distance shown on the map.

Notice that the scale bar above shows measurement in both miles and **kilometers** (kil′ ə mē tərz). A kilometer is a measure of distance in the metric system. A kilometer is a little more than half a mile. You can find out more about the metric system in the box above.

11

Cartography as a Career

You won't see many help-wanted ads for **cartographers** (kär tog′ rə fərz), which is what mapmakers are called. There are many more job openings for cooks, engineers, nurses, and salespeople. However, cartography is a satisfying and interesting career, especially for people who like geography. And the demand for skilled cartographers is growing. Many places of business need their services. The maps in this book were prepared by cartographers and cartographic technicians.

A cartographic technician may be a high-school or a technical-course graduate. This person does the actual work of constructing the map after it has been designed by the cartographer. Fine lines must be drawn or engraved on coated plastic. Letters and symbols, usually stored on file tapes and disks, are transferred to sticky-backed clear film. The cartographic technician selects the right style and size of the letter or symbol and carefully positions it on the map by hand. Then the completed map is photographed. Cartographic technicians work with cameras and film as well as with different kinds of instruments and equipment used in mapmaking.

A cartographer usually has at least a four-year college degree. This education helps the cartographer to plan and design a map. Much planning is needed before the map is actually made. This includes research to gather the necessary data and check the accuracy of the information to be shown on the finished map. Each map has a purpose and is intended to communicate certain ideas.

Today, computers may be used by cartographers to construct maps and keep them up-to-date. Computers have the ability to store information and then present the data graphically. Anyone planning a career as a cartographer should also have some knowledge of computers.

There are cartographers at work in state highway departments and local planning agencies in every state. Oil companies, electric companies, commercial map publishing firms, and a wide variety of businesses need the skills of cartographers and cartographic technicians. However, the best employment opportunities in the field of cartography are with the federal government.

This cartographer is scribing, or scratching, lines on coated plastic.

Invite a cartographer or surveyor from the government or from private industry to discuss with pupils (**a**) how maps are made, (**b**) how maps are used in different kinds of work, and (**c**) career opportunities available to people who enjoy working with maps.

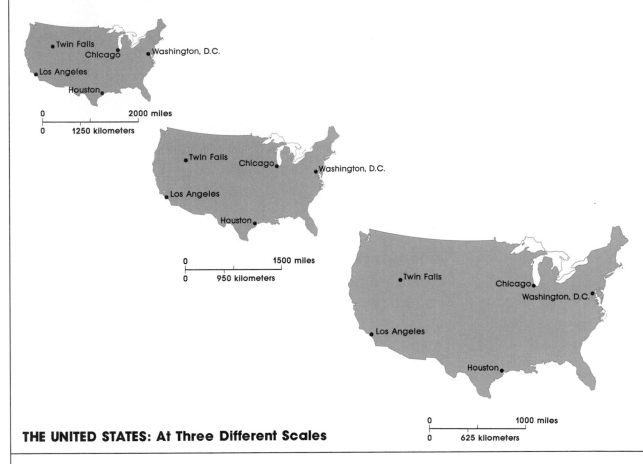

THE UNITED STATES: At Three Different Scales

Map scales tell how to figure distance from one place to another. Map scale is a ratio between distances on the earth's surface and distance on a map.

Measuring scale on maps   A map can be drawn to many different scales. The three maps on this page all show the United States, but each map is drawn to a different scale. Use a ruler to measure the scale line of the left-hand map. You will see that 1 inch stands for about 2,000 miles (1 centimeter stands for about 1,250 kilometers). Now measure how many inches (or centimeters) it is from Twin Falls to Washington, D.C., on the left-hand map above. There is about 1 inch (2.54 cm) between the two cities. To find out how many actual miles (or kilometers) it is between the cities, you multiply 1 times 2,000 (or 2.54 times 1,250). When you have done this, you will see that the distance between Twin Falls and Washington, D.C., is about 2,000 miles (3,175 km). Now go through the same steps with each of the other two maps. You will find that the number of inches to a mile (or centimeters to a kilometer) changes from map to map. However, when you use the scale for each map to figure miles (or kilometers) on the earth's surface, the actual distance between the two cities is always the same.

This photographer is on a plane and is using a special aerial mapping camera.

The numbered buildings on the map of Washington, D.C., are identified as follows: 1—National

Symbols and key   Another thing to know about maps is that they often make use of **symbols.** These may be letters, numbers, lines, colors, or small drawings that stand for real landmarks and places. A star is often the symbol for a state capital. Railroads may be shown as black lines, rivers as blue lines. The map **key** tells you exactly what real features and places the symbols stand for.

The key on one map will not tell you what the symbols on another map mean. On one map a dot may stand for a city. On other maps a dot may stand for 1,000 people, 50 acres (20.3 ha) of corn, or a gold mine. Clearly, then, before you read a map, you should learn the meaning of the symbols on it.

From photograph to map   Most maps today are made from photographs taken from aircraft or even from satellites. The photograph on the facing page was taken from about 9,000 feet (2,743 m) above the earth's surface. The map below it shows what a cartographer can do with such a photograph. The photograph and the map show the same area, but the map shows it in a special way. The cartographer has picked out the most important features of the place in the photograph and has used symbols for them on the map. The key explains what the symbols stand for. Notice, also, that the key shows the scale of the map.

On this map the cartographer has included an additional item. It is a special drawing called a **compass rose**, or a direction marker. It shows where north, south, east, and west are on the map. It also shows the in-between directions: northeast (NE), southeast (SE), southwest (SW), and northwest (NW). A compass rose helps you to determine direction.

Museum of American History; 2—National Museum of Natural History; 3—National Gallery of Art; 4—Department of Agriculture; 5—Hirshhorn Museum and Sculpture Garden; 6—National Air and

On the opposite page is an aerial photograph of Washington, D.C., our national capital. Beneath it is a map of the same area. Notice how the symbols stand for real things.

   Space Museum; 7—Freer Gallery of Art; 8—Rayburn House Office Building; 9—Bureau of Engraving and Printing; 10—Department of Housing and Urban Development; 11—Department of Transportation.

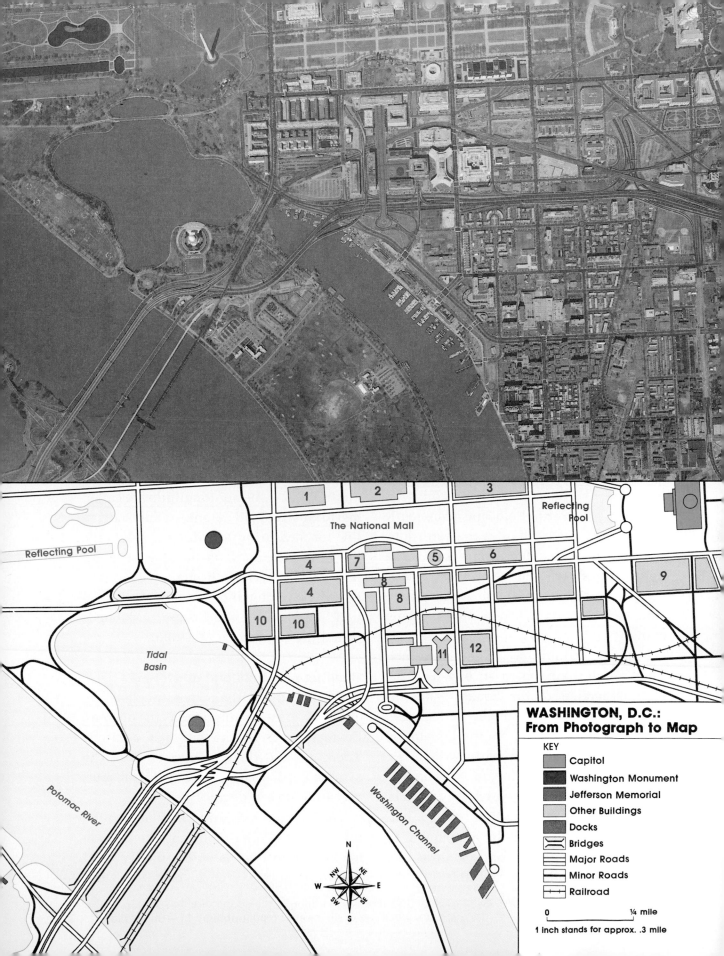

Reflecting Pool

The National Mall

Reflecting Pool

1

2

3

4

7

5

6

9

8

8

4

10

10

11

12

Tidal
Basin

Potomac River

Washington Channel

N
NW NE
W E
SW SE
S

WASHINGTON, D.C.:
From Photograph to Map

KEY

Capitol

Washington Monument

Jefferson Memorial

Other Buildings

Docks

Bridges

Major Roads

Minor Roads

Railroad

0   ¼ mile

1 inch stands for approx. .3 mile

NORTHERN HEMISPHERE

SOUTHERN HEMISPHERE

EASTERN HEMISPHERE

WESTERN HEMISPHERE

THE FOUR HEMISPHERES

The earth can be divided into four different hemispheres.   Ask: Which of these hemisphere maps include the part of the world where you live?

Location by latitude and longitude

You may also use lines of **latitude** and **longitude** for telling directions and locating places. Lines of latitude are a set of lines drawn on maps and globes. They measure distance north and south of the Equator. The Equator is the line midway between the North Pole and the South Pole. The Equator divides the earth into two halves, called **hemispheres**. These hemispheres are the Northern Hemisphere and the Southern Hemisphere. You can see this division on the maps above.

Lines of latitude are called **parallels**. They circle the earth in an east-west direction parallel to the Equator. If you trace a parallel, your finger will always be the same distance from the Equator as it moves around the earth. Parallels never meet no matter how far they are extended. To remember which way lines of latitude go, it may help to think of a ladder. The rungs of a ladder are parallel to each other. Ladder sounds a little like latitude, and both have parallels.

Lines of longitude are another set of lines drawn on maps and globes. They cross the parallels. Since longitude begins with *long*, it may help to think of lines of longitude running the long way, extending from the North Pole to the South Pole. Lines of longitude are called **meridians** (mə rid′ ē ənz). The starting line for measuring longitude is called the Prime Meridian. It is the line of longitude that passes through Greenwich (gren′ ich), England, a town near London. Sometimes the Prime Meridian is called the Greenwich Meridian.

Reading parallels and meridians

Parallels and meridians measure distance. This distance is measured in degrees. Degrees describe the parts of a circle. There are 360 degrees in a circle. The symbol for degrees is °. So 10° is a short way to write *ten degrees*.

The Equator is 0° latitude. The latitude for the North Pole is 90°N and the latitude for the South Pole is 90°S. (For *N*, read the word *north*. For *S*, read the word

Pupils will most likely know that a sphere is something in the shape of a ball or globe. Ask: What, do you think, does the prefix *hemi-* mean? (half)

The Gazetteer, located at the back of the book, includes many of the place-names found in this text. Latitude and longitude are given where appropriate; each entry has a phonetic respelling, a short description, and the page number of a map showing the place. Be sure pupils are familiar with the Gazetteer.

south.) A place that is exactly halfway between the Equator and the North Pole has a latitude of 45°N, while a similar location between the Equator and the South Pole has a latitude of 45°S. The letter N or S tells whether a place is in the Northern or the Southern Hemisphere. You must always use N or S when giving a latitude location.

Meridians measure distances east and west of the Prime Meridian, which is 0° longitude. They go halfway around the world, or 180° from the Prime Meridian. The meridian of 180° lies on the opposite side of the earth from the Prime Meridian and passes through the Pacific Ocean. The 180° meridian and the Prime Meridian form a full circle, which divides the earth into the Eastern Hemisphere and the Western Hemisphere. A place that is exactly halfway between the Prime Meridian and the 180° meridian in the Eastern Hemisphere has a longitude of 90°E. The letter E shows that the place is in the Eastern Hemisphere. What is the longitude of a place exactly halfway between the Prime Meridian and the 180° meridian in the Western Hemisphere?

On a map of a small area, cartographers might show the parallels for every degree of latitude and the meridians for every degree of longitude. However, on world maps they cannot show so many lines. The Atlas map on pages 470–471 shows the parallels and meridians for every 20 degrees.

The Equator is 0° latitude.

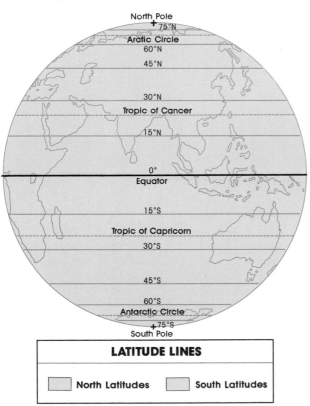

The Prime Meridian is 0° longitude.

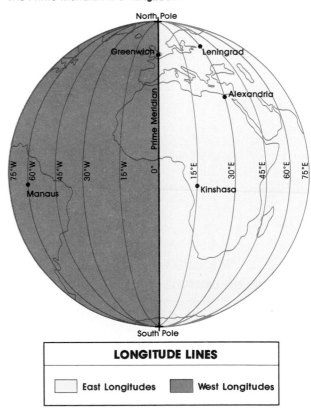

Geographic grid   Parallels and meridians intersect and form a **grid** system. You can see the grid made by these two sets of lines on the map. By using the grid, you can find and describe the location of every place on the earth.

To find the city of New Orleans, Louisiana, on the map, put a finger on the line marked 30° north latitude. Put a finger of your other hand on the line marked 90° west longitude. Now move your fingers toward each other on these lines. The place where these two lines meet is the location of New Orleans. The short way to write the location is 30°N, 90°W. It is not necessary to write 30°N *latitude*, 90°W *longitude,* because only latitude lines are counted north and south, and only longitude lines are counted east and west. Knowing this, you need only learn that Leningrad, in the Soviet Union, is about 60°N, 30°E to find it on the map.

If the parallel or meridian of a place is not shown on a map, then you have to

0° lat./79°W   Mexico City
What is the latitude and longitude of Quito?   What city is located at 19°N, 99°W?

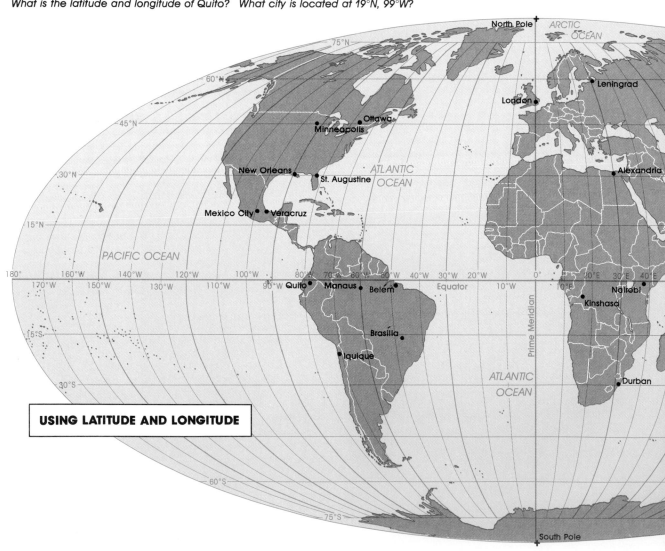

USING LATITUDE AND LONGITUDE

guess its location from the nearest parallels and meridians that are shown. This is called **interpolation** (in tér pə lā′ shən). On the map below, Tokyo, Japan, is located at 140°E and about midway between 30°N and 45°N. By interpolation, you could state that Tokyo's location is about 36°N, 140°E.

CHECKUP

1. What does scale tell us about a map? Name three different ways to show map scale.
2. What do lines of latitude measure? What do lines of longitude measure?
3. Why must the letter *N* or *S* be used after a degree of latitude? Why must the letter *E* or *W* be used after a degree of longitude?

The Round Earth on Flat Paper

VOCABULARY

great circle	elevation
distortion	profile
projection	weather
political map	natural resource
relief map	

A model of the earth   You are probably familiar with a model of a ship, a train, or a doll. Models are small copies of real things, and they are built to scale. Each measurement on a model stands for a larger measurement of the real object. One of the best-known models is a globe. It is a small-scale model of the earth. You may have a globe in your classroom.

Great circles   A **great circle** is the largest circle you can draw on a globe. If you cut a globe along a great circle, the knife would pass through the center of the earth and divide the globe into two equal parts, or hemispheres. The Equator is a great circle because it divides the earth into the Northern Hemisphere and the Southern Hemisphere. Two meridians directly across from each other on a globe also make a great circle. Any number of great circles can be drawn on a globe.

   The important thing to remember about great circles is that they help to measure the shortest distance between two places across the surface of the earth. Ships and airplanes often follow the curve of a great circle. This path is known as a great-circle route. By following great-circle routes, planes and ships use less fuel. And passengers and cargo reach their destination sooner.

One way to find the great circle route is to stretch a string or rubber band tightly between two places on a globe. If you connect Chicago and Tokyo, you will see that the shortest route is over Alaska. You may want to have pupils find the great circle route between a variety of world cities.

Projections   When you try to flatten an orange or a tennis ball, what happens? The sides split, and the shape is changed. The same thing happens when you try to make a world map by flattening a globe onto a piece of paper. It cannot be done without stretching some places. This is called **distortion**. If you ever looked in a funny mirror at an amusement park, you saw an example of distortion. You may have appeared tall and skinny in one mirror and short and fat in another. Your image was distorted, or changed in shape. A similar distortion happens when mapmakers try to transfer the round earth to flat paper.

Cartographers know they cannot make any flat map of the world exactly like a globe. Only on a globe can shape, size, direction, and distance all be shown correctly. But cartographers try to keep some good features of a globe in flat maps. They try to show the continents in their correct shape and size. They also try to show direction and distance correctly. They have learned, however, that they cannot show all four features accurately in a single map. So they must decide which features they want to keep, and which they are willing to lose. Each map **projection** is a different way to show the round earth on flat paper. And each projection shows some, but not all, of the four features correctly. The projection you choose depends on the use you will make of a map.

If you decided to sail across the ocean, you would want to use a map projection invented about 400 years ago by Gerhardus Mercator (je rärd′ əs mėr kā′ tər). The map at the top of the facing page is a Mercator projection. The parallels and meridians are straight lines that cross at right angles. So if north is at the top, then south is straight down, east is directly to the right, and west is directly to the left. This makes it easy to see that Oslo, Norway, is directly west of Leningrad in the Soviet Union. Both are located near 60°N. The Mercator map is also good for finding directions because it shows all directions between places on the map exactly as they are on the globe. However, the Mercator map cannot be used to study size because the size of land and sea areas on the map is not accurate. On a Mercator map, Greenland appears as large as Africa because the size of land areas has been distorted in order to keep directions accurate. A globe shows that Africa is more than 13 times the size of Greenland.

If you want to show land and water sizes accurately, you must use an equal-area projection. This kind of map is shown at the bottom of the facing page. The sizes of places on an equal-area projection are shown true to scale. Equal areas on the map stand for areas of equal size on the earth's surface. Compare the size of Greenland with the size of Africa on this kind of map. You can see the true relationship in size between the two land areas. The Atlas maps on pages 470–473 are equal-area maps.

A wide variety of maps   There are many kinds of maps to show different things about land and people. The Atlas map on page 479 is one familiar kind. It is a **political map** that uses colors to show countries and their boundaries.

If pupils have not already done so, have them turn to the Atlas on pp. 470–488 and examine the maps.
Have pupils compare the information shown on physical maps and political maps. Ask: What is the purpose of a physical map? a political map? Remind pupils to use the Atlas throughout the year's work.

Parallels and meridians cross at right angles and form rectangular shapes on a Mercator projection.

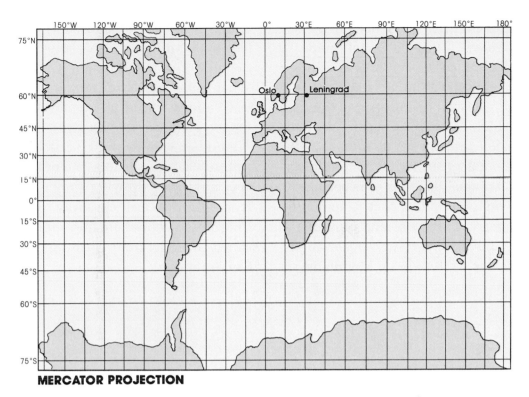

MERCATOR PROJECTION

On a Mercator projection, parallels and meridians are straight lines that cross at right angles.

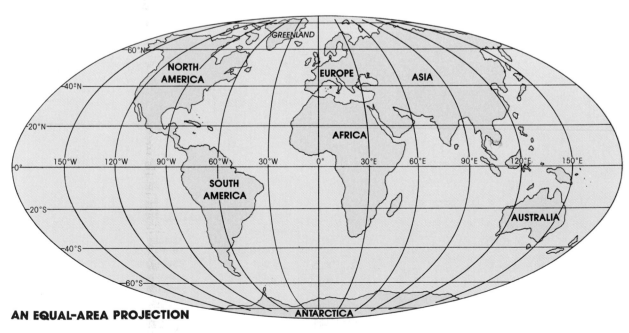

AN EQUAL-AREA PROJECTION

An equal-area projection is good for showing the sizes of land and water areas.

Each meridian runs straight north and south, although they appear as curves on this projection. **21**

Another familiar kind of map is that shown below. It is a **relief map**. It uses different colors to show the differences in the **elevation**, or the height, of the land. Elevation is measured from sea level, which is the average level of the oceans. As you can see by looking at the key, the color green stands for the lowest elevation range. That range is between 0, or sea level, and 1,000 feet (0 to 300 m) above sea level. Browns and pink are the colors used to show higher elevations. Some places in the Rocky Mountains, in the western United States, are over 10,000 feet (3,000 m) above sea level. What is the elevation range for the Great Plains? What is the elevation range for the Central Valley? What is the elevation range for the place where you live?

Another way to show variation in elevation is a cross section, or a **profile**. This special kind of drawing shows an area of land with the earth cut away to sea level. The cross section on the opposite page shows the relief from Washington, D.C., to San Francisco.

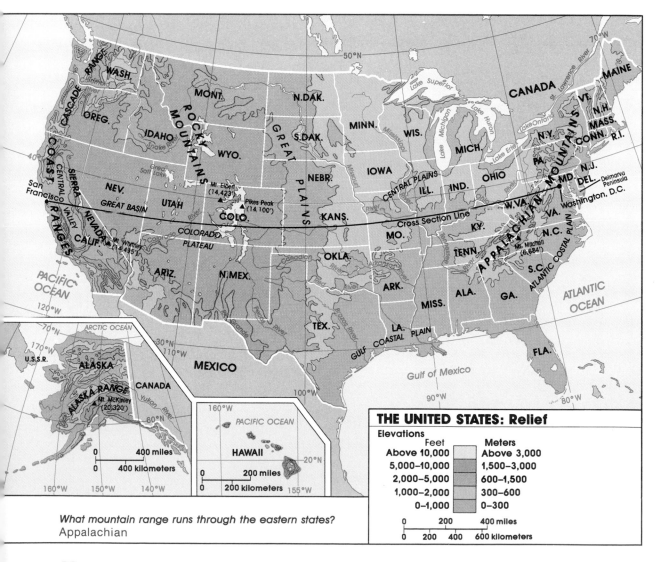

What mountain range runs through the eastern states?
Appalachian

THE UNITED STATES: Relief

Elevations

Feet	Meters
Above 10,000	Above 3,000
5,000–10,000	1,500–3,000
2,000–5,000	600–1,500
1,000–2,000	300–600
0–1,000	0–300

Ask pupils to locate and name the various physical features of the United States shown on this map.

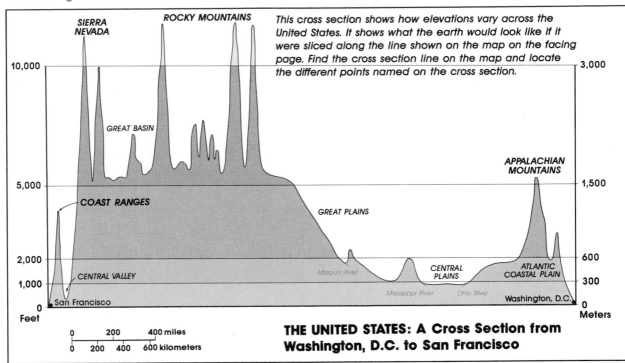

This cross section shows how elevations vary across the United States. It shows what the earth would look like if it were sliced along the line shown on the map on the facing page. Find the cross section line on the map and locate the different points named on the cross section.

THE UNITED STATES: A Cross Section from Washington, D.C. to San Francisco

In drawing a profile, cartographers have to use two different scales. The horizontal scale, shown in miles and kilometers, measures distance along the earth's surface. The vertical scale, shown in feet and meters, measures the height of the land. As you can see, the vertical scale is much smaller than the horizontal one. This causes vertical exaggeration. Vertical exaggeration makes it easy to show hills and mountains on profiles. However, you must remember that the slope of the land is not really as steep as the cross section makes it appear.

Besides political and physical maps, there are many special-purpose maps. One of the best-known is a road map. What is the special purpose of this kind of map? Weather maps give facts about the **weather** in different places on a particular day. Weather is the condition of the air at a certain time: sunny or cloudy, hot or cool, windy or calm, dry or wet. **Natural resource** maps show where things made by nature that people use, such as trees, water, soil, coal, and oil, are found. Other maps may show ski trails, national parks, airplane routes, plant life, or the number of people who live in a place. The title of a map often tells its purpose. To find the special-purpose maps in this book, turn to the front of the book and look at the list of maps in the Contents.

CHECKUP

1. Why is the Equator a great circle?
2. What four features of the earth's surface can be shown correctly together on a globe but not on a flat map?
3. What is the difference between a political map and a relief map?
4. From what point is the elevation of land measured?
5. Give at least three examples of special-purpose maps.

1/CHAPTER REVIEW

KEY FACTS

1. The earth's appearance changes from one place to another because of its different physical features. Among its physical features are mountains, plains, and rivers.

2. Maps show facts about the earth and the people on the earth. Facts are shown with symbols, color, scale, and grid lines.

3. Parallels, or lines of latitude, measure distance north and south of the Equator. Meridians, or lines of longitude, measure distance east and west of the Prime Meridian.

4. The most exact way of locating places on the earth is by latitude and longitude.

5. Only a globe gives a completely accurate view of the earth. It shows size, shape, direction, and distance correctly.

VOCABULARY QUIZ

On a sheet of paper write the numbers of the statements below. Then write the letter of the ending that best finishes each sentence.

1. A stretch of land almost surrounded by water is (**a**) a plain, (**b**) a peninsula.

2. A narrow body of water that connects two larger bodies of water is (**a**) a strait, (**b**) a river.

3. Size or distance on a map is shown by (**a**) symbols, (**b**) scale.

4. Parallels (**a**) cross the Equator, (**b**) run in the same direction as the Equator.

5. The elevation of a place is its (**a**) location on a grid, (**b**) height above sea level.

6. A profile shows (**a**) the varying elevation of an area of land, (**b**) the metric system.

7. Things made by nature that people use are (**a**) projections, (**b**) natural resources.

8. A special drawing that shows direction on a map is (**a**) a key, (**b**) a compass rose.

9. A hemisphere is (**a**) the southern part of the world, (**b**) half of the earth.

10. Different ways to show the earth on paper are called (**a**) projections, (**b**) grids.

REVIEW QUESTIONS

1. Name five physical features that are made up of water, and describe each.

2. Name five physical features that are made up of land, and describe each.

3. What is the 0° line of latitude called? Into which two hemispheres does this parallel divide the earth?

4. How are lines of latitude and longitude used to locate places?

5. What is the difference between a relief map and a cross section, or profile?

ACTIVITIES

1. Make a list of as many physical features in your area as you can. Identify each by name; for example, *Mirror* Lake, *New* River.

2. Find a map of your state in an atlas. What is the latitude and longitude of your state capital? Of your community?

3. Below are the latitudes and longitudes of the largest cities on six of the continents. (There are no cities on the continent of Antarctica.) Use a globe or a world map to locate these cities. On a sheet of paper write the name of each city and the continent on which it is located.

   a. 32°N/122°E   **d.** 24°S/47°W
   b. 30°N/31°E   **e.** 34°S/151°E
   c. 19°N/99°W   **f.** 56°N/38°E

1/SKILLS DEVELOPMENT

USING THE GLOSSARY, GAZETTEER, AND ATLAS

GLOSSARY

This book has some special parts to help you learn about the world and its people. One part is the Glossary. It is arranged alphabetically and defines all the key social studies words. These are the words found in the box at the beginning of each lesson. Turn to the Glossary on page 500. Answer the following questions.

1. What is a glacier?
2. What is the difference between weather and climate?
3. What is permafrost?

GAZETTEER

Another part of the book that is arranged alphabetically is the Gazetteer. It gives information about cities, mountains, rivers, lakes, and other geographic features. For many of these places, the Gazetteer also gives latitude and longitude. The page number at the end of each definition directs you to a map that shows where the place is. Turn to the Gazetteer, starting on page 489, and answer the following questions.

1. What is the latitude and longitude of Mexico City, Mexico?
2. What is the highest peak in the Alps?
3. Where does the Danube River start?

ATLAS

An atlas is a collection of maps. Some atlases form an entire book, and other atlases are just a part of a book. There is an atlas in this book, beginning on page 470. The Atlas contains political and physical maps. As you might guess from its name, a physical map shows the earth's physical features—mountains, plains, and other forms that land and water take. Turn to the physical map of North America on page 476 and answer the following questions.

1. What is the elevation range in meters of the land around the Great Salt Lake?
2. Into what body of water does the Red River flow?
3. What is the name of the large mountain range in the eastern part of the United States?

Turn to the political map of South America on page 479 and answer these questions.

1. What is the national capital of Chile?
2. To what country do the Falkland Islands belong?
3. What is the latitude and longitude of the national capital of Ecuador?

SKILLS PRACTICE

Read each statement below. Use the Glossary, the Gazetteer, or the Atlas to find out if the statement is true or false. If a statement is true, on a sheet of paper write *T* beside the number of the sentence. If a statement is false, rewrite it to make it true.

1. A drought is a long period with no food.
2. Athens, Greece, is located at 65°N, 20°E.
3. The elevation range of the land around Lake Titicaca in South America is 2,000–5,000 feet (600–1,500 m).
4. Australia is the earth's smallest continent.
5. In South America, the Equator passes through the countries of Ecuador, Colombia, and Argentina.

Photographs and Diagrams

┌─ VOCABULARY ─────────────┐

graphic	tradition
montage	satellite
combine	diagram
irrigation	volcano

└──────────────────────────┘

What are graphics? To help you learn about the world, this book uses both the written word and different kinds of **graphics.** Maps are one kind of graphic. Maps show a great deal of information, but it is not written in sentences and paragraphs. You would need several pages of a book to write out all the information that a map gives in a small space. On a map, information is given in both drawings and words. Together, they tell what the earth or part of the earth looks like from overhead. In Chapter 1 you learned how to read a map.

Other kinds of graphics that will be used in this book are photographs, diagrams, tables, graphs, and time lines. They, too, give a great deal of information in a small space. Graphics may use words, numbers, and art. These elements are selected and arranged to convey a special message. Advertisers make great use of graphics in order to call attention to a product and to make people want to buy

it. Over the years you have probably seen hundreds of advertisements in magazines and newspapers. Did any of those ads make you want to buy something?

The people who make textbooks also use many different graphics. Each graphic shows facts about the world in which you live. In this chapter you will find out more about graphics and how to read them.

Photographs tell interesting stories One week a busload of people from the United States stopped at several different cities in Mexico. In each place the passengers took pictures. One person took pictures of a man selling balloons along the street. Another took pictures of a woman and children selling brightly colored decorations. One woman took pictures of a modern museum, and another took pictures of a church. A man took pictures of a potter painting a dish. Several people took pictures of a vegetable market.

The direction in which these people aimed their cameras showed their own interests and ideas. When they returned home, their individual pictures would all give different views of life in Mexico. However, by selecting and arranging the pictures in a **montage** (mon täzh'), or group of pictures, it is possible to have a more well-rounded view of Mexico.

What can you learn about life in Mexico from these pictures?

Make a montage of pictures showing various aspects of life in your community. Then ask pupils to pretend that they know nothing about the community and have them write a description of the community based on what they observe in the montage. Encourage pupils to read their descriptions aloud.

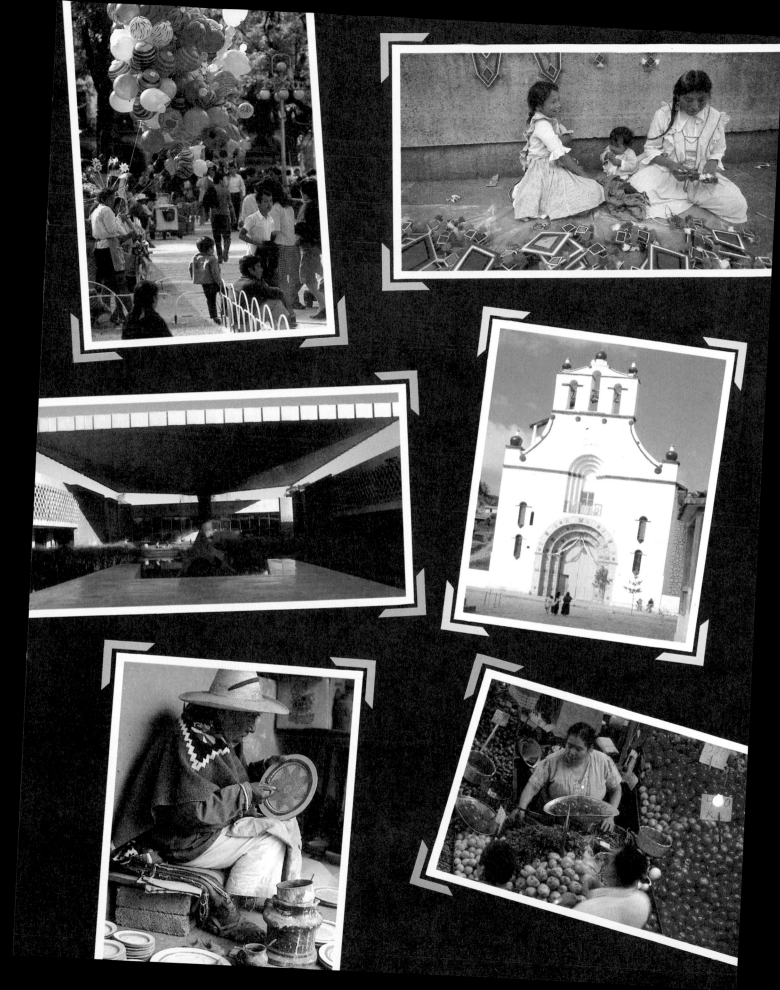

Wheat and rice are two of the world's most important food crops. Wheat is the chief food of the people of the United States and Europe, and rice is the chief food of the people of Asia.

A picture is worth a thousand words

Pictures can bring the world closer to us. But pictures tell their interesting stories only to those who have learned to look at them with a trained eye. In studying any picture in this book, you need to ask questions such as the following: What does the picture show about the land and the people? What makes this place different from where I live? What makes it similar? How does the way people work fit the land in which they live?

Looking carefully at the pictures on this page, you can see some things in the two pictures that are similar and some that are different. Both show farmers at work. Both show stages in growing food. But in one picture a person is harvesting wheat with a huge machine called a **combine**. In the other, someone is planting rice by hand.

The first picture suggests much about the land and the people who live there. The location is Kansas. It appears that farms and fields there are big. In such fields little work can be done by hand. The vast amounts of wheat in the picture must be grown to be sold rather than to be eaten at home. Farming appears to be quite profitable, as the costly machinery indicates.

The other picture was taken in Japan. The farmer is planting rice seedlings, or young plants, in a flooded field. The stooping farmer presses one to six rice stalks into the mud. Fields of rice, called paddy fields, look like bright green lakes when the plants are young. The water points to **irrigation**. Irrigation is the watering of crops, usually by canals, ditches, or pipes. The hand labor may

Have pupils locate the cities of Boston and San Francisco on the Atlas map of the United States on pp. 474–475.

mean that Japanese fields and farms are small. Most of the rice crop may be needed by the farmer's family.

You might look for reasons why things are as they are in these places. You would find that history and trade, **tradition** and markets, all help to explain what you see. Tradition is the way in which people have done things for years and years.

Skill in reading photographs is similar to skill in direct observation of the world around you. In both cases, you need to look carefully at what is there and consider thoughtfully what it means.

Space-age photography   Parts of the earth were first photographed from the air in 1858. This was about 20 years after photography was invented. The cameras were in balloons. During World War I,

The large whitish area in the satellite photograph is the city of Boston, Massachusetts.

This Landsat satellite image shows the San Francisco Bay area. The many bridges of the area are easily seen.

pictures taken from airplanes were used to locate enemy troops. Between 1930 and 1960, large areas of farmland in the United States were photographed from the air. The pictures were then made into maps. Farmers used the maps to improve their use of the land. With the coming of orbiting **satellites** in the 1960s, pictures could be taken from far out in space. Satellites are artificial objects that circle the earth. They carry communications equipment and special cameras.

Space-age pictures give a great deal of detailed information about the earth. Some of these details cannot be seen from the ground. The information is useful to mapmakers and weather forecasters. Scientists use the information for studying pollution, forests, crop growth, and many other subjects. The photographs on this page were taken from space.

29

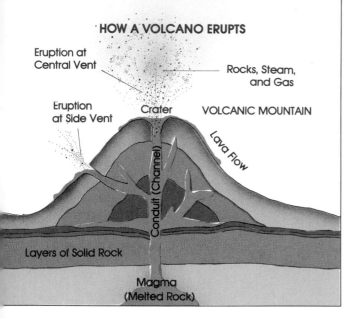

HOW A VOLCANO ERUPTS

Eruption at Central Vent

Rocks, Steam, and Gas

Eruption at Side Vent

Crater

VOLCANIC MOUNTAIN

Lava Flow

Conduit (Channel)

Layers of Solid Rock

Magma (Melted Rock)

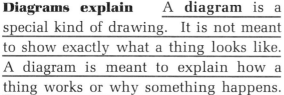

A volcanic eruption is caused by powerful forces within the earth. Magma is pushed upward through the conduit and erupts at the central vent. Sometimes there are eruptions at the side vents, too.

Many of the world's 600 or so active volcanoes are in lands bordering on the Pacific Ocean. A cloud of smoke and ash hangs over the volcano Mount St. Helens in southern Washington. (46°N/123°W; map, p. 53)

Diagrams explain A **diagram** is a special kind of drawing. It is not meant to show exactly what a thing looks like. A diagram is meant to explain how a thing works or why something happens.

The diagram above explains how a **volcano** erupts. A volcano is an opening in the ground out of which melted rock and other materials pour from time to time. As you can see from the diagram, these materials are deep within the earth. The melted rock, called magma, is under great pressure from the weight of the solid rock around it. And this pressure causes the magma to push through a weak spot in the earth's surface. Rocks and great clouds of steam and gas may be thrown high into the air. Red-hot lava may flow down the sides of the volcano for days. Lava, as you can see from the diagram, is the name for the melted rock when it reaches the surface of the earth. What is the name of the hole left at the top of the volcano after an eruption? Crater

To learn more about an active volcano, study the picture on this page. It shows Mount St. Helens, a volcano in the state of Washington. (You will see that the latitude and longitude for a place is often given with its picture. The page number of a map where you can find that place is also given. It will look like this: (46°N/123°W; map, p. 53). You will see this with many of the pictures in your book. It will help you find the places in the pictures.) From 1857 to 1980, Mount St. Helens was quiet. But on the morning of May 18, 1980, the volcano blew its top with a loud boom. The eruption caused great damage, and many people were killed. What details does the picture show that the diagram does not?
Terrain; dense cloud of smoke and ash

CHECKUP

1. What are graphics? Name six kinds of graphics that will be used in this book.
2. What are some things you can observe in photographs?
3. What is the purpose of a diagram?

Tables, Graphs, and Time Lines

```
┌─VOCABULARY──────────────────────┐
│                                 │
│  table            bar graph     │
│  census           line graph    │
│  population       climate       │
│    density        temperature   │
│  pie graph    .   precipitation │
│  pictograph       time line     │
│                                 │
└─────────────────────────────────┘
```

Tables organize facts   A **table** is a list of facts. The facts are arranged in columns and rows to show some relationship. The facts put forth in a table are often numbers, which stand for such things as areas of countries, population, or barrels of oil produced.

Below is a table of facts about the eight largest countries in the world. At the head of each column is a label that shows the information found in that column.

Column 1 lists the names of the countries in order of size.

Column 2 has each country's area, or size.

Column 3 shows the percentage of the total land area in the world represented by each country. (Remember that 100% always stands for the total.)

Column 4 shows population figures. These come from the **census** in each country. A census is an official count of the number of people in a country.

Column 5 shows the **population density** of each country. This tells how closely together people live in a set area of land. The population density figure states the average number of people for each square mile (or square kilometer) of land. To find the population density of each country, divide the total number of people who live in a country by that country's total land area.

THE WORLD'S EIGHT LARGEST COUNTRIES IN AREA				
Country	Area	% World Land Area	Population	Population Density
Soviet Union	8,650,000 sq mi (22,404,000 sq km)	14.9	272,000,000	31 per sq mi (12 per sq km)
Canada	3,840,000 sq mi (9,946,000 sq km)	6.6	24,900,000	6 per sq mi (3 per sq km)
China	3,692,000 sq mi (9,562,000 sq km)	6.4	1,023,300,000	277 per sq mi (107 per sq km)
United States	3,619,000 sq mi (9,373,000 sq km)	6.3	234,200,000	65 per sq mi (25 per sq km)
Brazil	3,286,000 sq mi (8,511,000 sq km)	5.7	131,300,000	40 per sq mi (15 per sq km)
Australia	2,996,000 sq mi (7,760,000 sq km)	5.1	15,300,000	5 per sq mi (2 per sq km)
India	1,269,000 sq mi (3,287,000 sq km)	2.2	730,000,000	575 per sq mi (222 per sq km)
Argentina	1,072,000 sq mi (2,777,000 sq km)	1.9	29,100,000	27 per sq mi (10 per sq km)

Pie graphs show percentages A pie graph is used to show the parts of a whole. The pie graph below gives the percentages as parts of the whole area. This graph is also called a circle graph.

The whole circle stands for the total land area in the world. This equals 100 percent, or the sum of the parts. A slice of the circle, which stands for part of the total land area, shows how the size of that part compares with the total land area. For example, Australia has about 5 percent of the world's total land area. A slice of the circle also shows how the size of the part compares with the other parts. Australia is smaller than Brazil but almost twice as large as India.

The facts shown in this pie graph are the same as the facts shown in Column 3 in the table you just studied. On a pie graph it is easy to see facts and understand how the facts relate to each other.

This pie graph makes it easy to see how parts compare with the whole and each other.

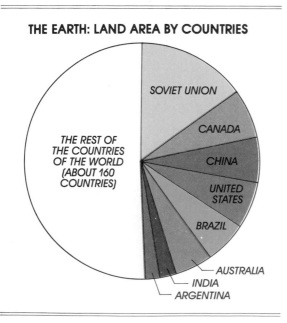

THE EARTH: LAND AREA BY COUNTRIES

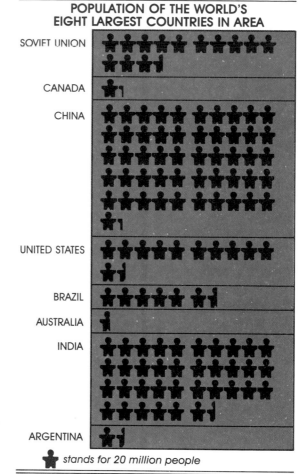

POPULATION OF THE WORLD'S EIGHT LARGEST COUNTRIES IN AREA

👤 *stands for 20 million people*

In the pictograph above, the stick figure is a symbol. What does the symbol represent? About how many people live in the United States?
Population of the United States: about 229 million.

Pictographs use symbols A pictograph uses symbols instead of numbers for fixed amounts of a particular thing. On the graph above, a picture of a person stands for 20 million people. If you are looking for exact numbers, a table is more helpful than a graph. But just a quick look at this graph shows you which country has the largest population and which has the smallest. You can easily see which countries have about the same number of people. To get that kind of information from a table, you have to study the numbers carefully.

Have each pupil select a topic and conduct a poll of his or her classmates. Suggestions for topics include favorite books, movies, sports, hobbies, foods, animals, and school subjects. After pupils have completed their polls, have them display the results of the polls on bar graphs.

Bar graphs show comparisons Each of the bars on a **bar graph** stands for a fact. Since the bars are arranged alongside each other, it is easy to compare these facts. The bar graph on this page shows the elevation of the highest mountain on each continent. The graph gives you an idea of the difference in heights. The names of the continents are shown across the bottom of the graph. The names of the mountains and the places where they are found are shown on the bars of the graph. There are scales on both sides of the graph. One scale measures elevation in feet. The other scale measures elevation in meters. What is the elevation of the highest mountain in the world?

Mount Everest, on the continent of Asia, is about 29,000 feet (9,000 m) high

On which continent is the highest mountain in the world located? About how high is the mountain?

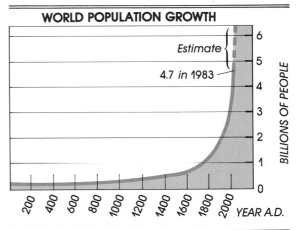

WORLD POPULATION GROWTH

On this line graph you can tell how quickly the world's population grew during any period of years.

Line graphs show change It is also easy to compare things on a **line graph**. A line graph is generally the best kind of graph for showing how things change over a period of time. The graph on this page shows how the world's population has grown. The graph has two scales. The horizontal, or bottom, scale stands for years. The vertical, or side, scale measures the total number of people.

Even a glance at the line shows what happened. For hundreds of years there had been very little change in the population of the world. There were periods during which it probably did not grow at all. When the Declaration of Independence was written in 1776, the world's population was still less than 1 billion. You see, though, that this changed after 1800. From then on, the world's population began climbing faster and faster. It has continued to do so. What is the estimated growth of the world's population from 1983 to about 2000? About how many billion people are estimated to be living in the world by the year 2000?

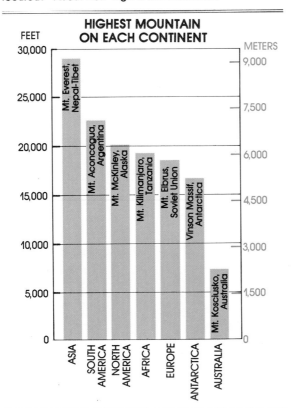

More than 1 billion people from 1983 to 2000
About 6 billion people living in the world by 2000

33

The Fahrenheit thermometer has been used for many years in the United States, but the metric system uses the Celsius thermometer. A temperature on the Celsius thermometer is the same as the temperature directly across from it on the Fahrenheit thermometer.

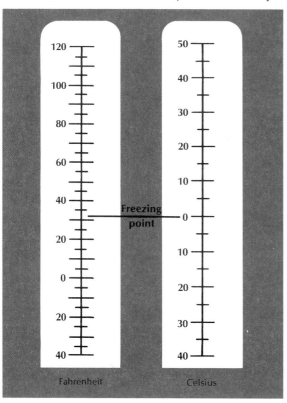

On a Fahrenheit thermometer the freezing point is 32°. What is it on a Celsius thermometer?

Graphs show temperature and precipitation

Bar graphs and line graphs are good ways to show information about **climate**. Climate is the pattern of weather that a place has over a period of time. Two important parts of climate are **temperature** and **precipitation**. Temperature refers to the amount of heat or cold in the air. It is measured on a thermometer in degrees Fahrenheit or degrees Celsius, as shown in the drawing. Precipitation is rain, snow, mist, sleet, and hail.

The graphs below show the average monthly temperature and the average monthly precipitation in Vancouver, Canada. The letters along the bottom of both graphs show the months of the year. On the line graph, the numbers along the left side measure temperature in degrees Fahrenheit. The numbers along the right side measure temperature in degrees Celsius. As you can see, the average tem-

Ask: At what temperature do Fahrenheit and Celsius thermometers have the same reading?

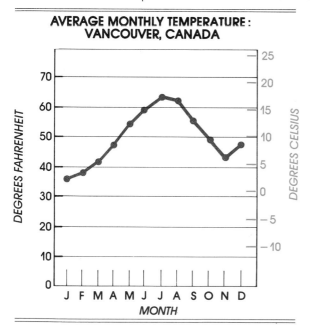

What is the average temperature for April in Vancouver, Canada?

47°F (8°C)

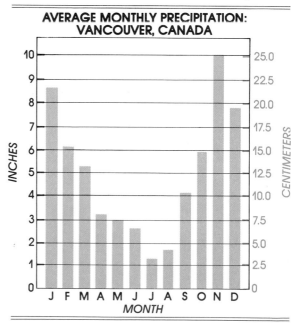

Approximately how many centimeters of precipitation does Vancouver receive on the average in June?

7 cm

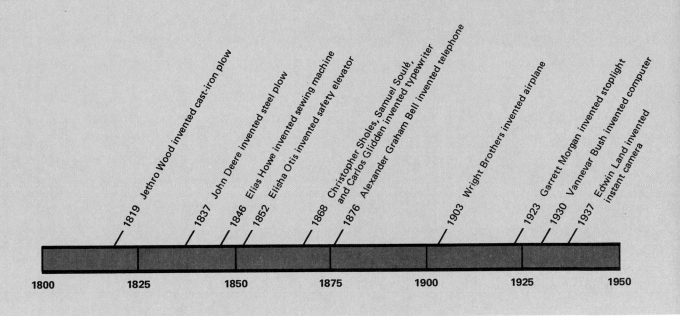

1800	1825	1850	1875	1900	1925	1950

A time line is a special drawing that tells when events took place. When was the safety elevator invented? Who was the inventor?

Safety elevator invented in 1852 by Elisha Otis.

perature for January is 36°F (2°C). This is Vancouver's coldest month. What is the warmest month? What is the average temperature for that month?

July; 63°F (17°C)

On the bar graph, precipitation is measured in inches on the left side and in centimeters on the right side. What is the wettest month in Vancouver? What is the average precipitation for that month? You will use graphs to learn about climate in many places in the world.

November; 10 in. (25 cm)

Time lines show facts about time A <u>time line</u> is a special drawing that tells when events took place. It also shows the length of time between events. A time line, like a map, has a scale. A map scale measures distance; a time line scale measures time.

The time line has a scale that runs from the left of the page to the right. On the time line on this page, each inch stands for 25 years. The whole time line shows 150 years. Along the line are listed some important American inventions and their inventors. Imagine what your life would be like without these inventions.

The time line makes it easy to see the order of events. It shows that the typewriter was invented after the sewing machine and before the telephone. The time line also makes it easy to figure out the length of time between events. How many years passed between the invention of the cast-iron plow and the steel plow? You will find other time lines in this book. They will help you understand ideas about time and the order of events more clearly.

CHECKUP

1. What is a table? How is information arranged in a table?
2. What does a pie graph show?
3. What is a bar graph?
4. What is the advantage of a line graph?
5. What do time lines and maps have in common? What is the purpose of a time line?

Have pupils make a time line that shows some important dates in the history of their community or school. **35**

KEY FACTS

1. Graphics are useful tools for learning about the world. They include maps, photographs, diagrams, tables, graphs, and time lines.

2. Photographs show the similarities and differences between people and places in the world.

3. Diagrams explain how a thing works or why something happens.

4. Tables organize facts in columns and rows to show relationships.

5. Graphs are special drawings that use pictures, circles, bars, or lines to compare one thing with another.

VOCABULARY QUIZ

On a sheet of paper write the letter of the term next to the number of its description. Be careful. Two of the statements describe terms that are not in the list.

a. irrigation   f. montage
b. temperature   g. precipitation
c. pie graph   h. census
d. satellite   i. volcano
e. tradition   j. combine

e **1.** The way in which people have done things for years and years

2. A special drawing that shows when events took place

f **3.** A group of photographs

d **4.** An artificial object that circles the earth, carrying communications equipment and special cameras

g **5.** Moisture that falls on the earth's surface as rain, snow, mist, sleet, or hail

h **6.** An official count of the number of people in a country

i **7.** An opening in the ground out of which melted rock and other materials pour from time to time

c **8.** A graph in the form of a circle that is used to show the parts of a whole

b **9.** The amount of heat or cold in the air, as measured on the Fahrenheit or Celsius scale

a **10.** The watering of crops, usually by canals, ditches, or pipes

11. The average number of people in a given unit of area

j **12.** A farm machine that harvests wheat

REVIEW QUESTIONS

1. Someone once said that a picture is worth a thousand words. Explain this saying.

2. Using the diagram on page 30, explain what happens when a volcano erupts.

3. What is population density? How do you find the population density of the United States?

4. How do line and bar graphs differ?

5. Define the term *climate*.

6. Using the time line on page 35, tell what event took place in 1903.

ACTIVITY

In an almanac find the population of your state for the past ten censuses. Make a line graph to show how the population has changed. Show the number of people along the side and the years across the bottom of the graph. Give your graph a title. If you live in Alaska or Hawaii, make a graph of the United States population instead.

2/SKILLS DEVELOPMENT

READING A DIAGRAM

THE SOLAR SYSTEM

The word *solar* means "of the sun." The solar system includes many different objects that revolve around the sun. Our home, the earth, is one of the planets in the solar system. The planets follow a nearly circular path, or orbit, around the sun. The moon is a natural satellite that circles the earth. The very small, rocky bodies in the solar system are called asteroids. There are also many bodies of dust and frozen gases, which are called comets.

The diagram below shows the solar system. By reading the diagram, you can learn about the relationship of the different objects to the sun and to each other. You can also see the orbit of each planet around the sun.

SKILLS PRACTICE

Study the diagram and answer the questions below. Write on a sheet of paper.

1. What is the center of the solar system?
2. How many planets are in the solar system?
3. Which planet is nearest to the sun?
4. Which planet is farthest from the sun?
5. Which planet is the fourth from the sun?
6. Which two planets travel in orbits that cross one another?
7. Between which two planets is the Asteroid Belt?
8. Which two planets are nearest to the earth?
9. In the diagram, which planet has a moon?
10. Which planet is largest in size?

THE SOLAR SYSTEM

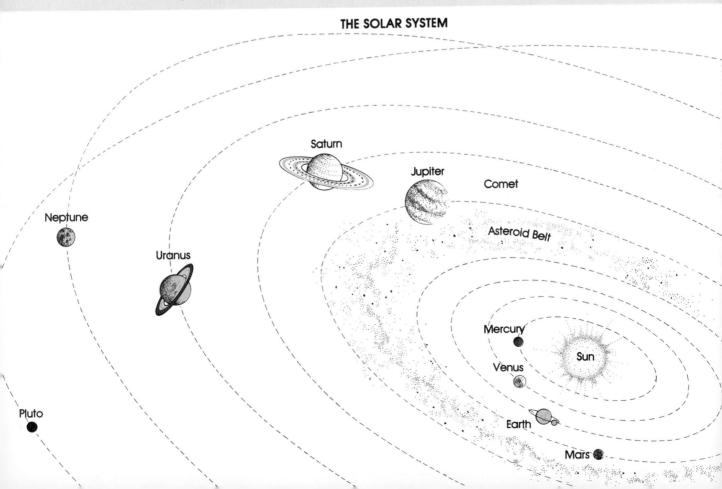

CHAPTER 3 World Patterns

The Earth in Motion

VOCABULARY

petroglyph	Antarctic Circle
revolution	equinox
axis	temperate
Tropic of Cancer	rotation
Arctic Circle	contiguous
solstice	International Date Line
Tropic of Capricorn	ocean current

An ancient stone formation In Chaco Canyon in northwestern New Mexico, scientists have been studying a formation of stones. Three large stone slabs are stacked against the side of a cliff. The slabs are 6 feet (1.8 m) to 9 feet (2.7 m) tall and weigh about 2 tons each. Scientists believe that the stones were carefully arranged against the cliff hundreds of years ago. Until recently, however, scientists did not know why the stones had been placed in this exact position.

The answer was discovered by an artist named Ann Sofaer. In June 1977 she was climbing near the stone slabs, looking for carvings on the rocks. The carvings, called **petroglyphs** (pet′ rə glifs), had been made by the Indians who once lived in the canyon. While Ann Sofaer was looking at two petroglyphs on the cliff wall beside the stone slabs, she saw a dagger of sunlight appear on the larger petroglyph. It took about 12 minutes for the sun dagger to move down through the center of the petroglyph and disappear.

Further studies showed that the sun would shine through the slabs and make a dagger of light on the petroglyphs at particular times of the year. Today, scientists believe that the Indians used the pattern of sunlight on the rock carvings as a calendar. The sun daggers marked the four seasons of the year. In the smaller photograph on the facing page, the sun dagger is marking June 21 on the petroglyph. June 21 is the beginning of summer in the Northern Hemisphere.

The changing seasons The sun daggers mark the seasons of the year because of the earth's movement around the sun. As you saw in the diagram on page 37, the earth revolves around the sun in an oval path called an orbit. It takes 365¼ days for the earth to make one **revolution** around the sun. The revolution of the earth around the sun and the tilt of the earth's **axis** cause the change of seasons. The earth's axis is an imaginary line that goes through the earth from the North Pole to the South Pole. This tilt never changes as the earth revolves around the sun. Ask: Why would ancient peoples need calendars? Encourage pupils to hypothesize.

The inset photograph shows a sun dagger on a petroglyph. The petroglyph is on the cliff wall beside the stone slabs shown in the large photograph. This ancient stone formation is found in Chaco Canyon, New Mexico. (36°N/108°W; map, p. 53)

 Before assigning the lesson, quiz pupils orally on the vocabulary to see how many words are familiar to them. Prepare to give a written vocabulary quiz when the lesson has been completed.

The tropics of Cancer and Capricorn are named for constellations. The position of each tropic was first marked by the fact that each was directly beneath that particular constellation at that time.

Solstices and equinoxes Look at the diagram below and notice the position of the earth on June 21 or 22. The North Pole is tilted toward the sun so that the sun's most direct rays strike the earth at 23½° north latitude. This parallel is called the **Tropic of Cancer.** On June 21 or 22 the sun is in the sky for 24 hours everywhere north of the **Arctic Circle.** The Arctic Circle is a line of latitude at 66½° north. In the Northern Hemisphere, June 21 or 22 marks the summer **solstice.** A solstice is either of the two times in the year when the sun's most direct rays are as far north or south from the Equator as they will ever be. At the summer solstice the Northern Hemisphere re-

ceives the most sunlight, making June 21 or 22 the longest day of the year.

In the Southern Hemisphere, however, June 21 or 22 marks the beginning of winter and is called the winter solstice. At that time the Southern Hemisphere is tilted as far away from the sun as it ever gets, so the sun's rays reach the Southern Hemisphere at a slant. June 21 or 22 is the shortest day of the year in this hemisphere.

After 6 months of revolving, on December 21 or 22, the position of the earth is the opposite of its position on June 21 or 22. Now the sun's rays reach the Northern Hemisphere at a slant. It is the beginning of winter in this hemisphere. In

This diagram shows the seasons for the Northern Hemisphere.

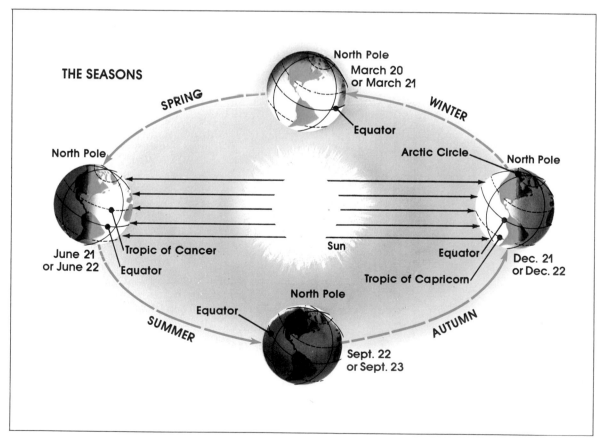

THE SEASONS

SPRING

WINTER

North Pole
March 20
or March 21

Equator

North Pole

Arctic Circle

North Pole

June 21
or June 22

Tropic of Cancer

Equator

Sun

Equator

Tropic of Capricorn

Dec. 21
or Dec. 22

North Pole

Equator

SUMMER

AUTUMN

Sept. 22
or Sept. 23

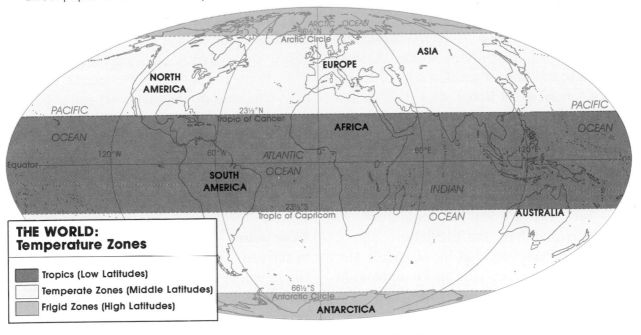

THE WORLD:
Temperature Zones

- Tropics (Low Latitudes)
- Temperate Zones (Middle Latitudes)
- Frigid Zones (High Latitudes)

The low latitudes are located between two special parallels—the Tropic of Cancer at 23 1/2°N and the Tropic of Capricorn at 23 1/2°S. Find these lines of latitude on the map.

the Southern Hemisphere, however, summer is just beginning. The South Pole is tilted toward the sun so that the sun's most direct rays strike the earth at 23½° south latitude. This parallel is called the **Tropic of Capricorn.** Now all places within the Antarctic Circle have 24 hours of daylight. The **Antarctic Circle** is a line of latitude at 66½° south.

The **equinox** marks the beginning of spring on March 20 or 21 and of autumn on September 22 or 23. An equinox is a time of the year when the sun's direct rays are over the Equator. Then there are 12 hours of daylight and 12 hours of darkness everywhere on earth. The term *equinox* comes from two Latin words that together mean "equal night."

Latitude and temperature   The earth can be divided into three temperature zones, as shown on the map above. At one time the low latitudes near the Equator were called the tropical, or very hot, zone. Here the sun's rays are very concentrated, and their heat is spread over a small area. The middle latitudes were called the **temperate** zone. *Temperate* means "not very hot and not very cold." The high latitudes were called the frigid, or very cold, zone. Here the sun's rays reach the earth at a slant, and their warmth is spread over a large area.

The problem with calling these zones tropical, temperate, and frigid is that there are exceptions to these temperature descriptions. Some places in the tropical zone are not always hot, some places in the frigid zone are not always cold, and few places in the temperate zone are really temperate. So it would be better to speak of the low latitudes as being generally warm; the middle latitudes as being changeable in temperature; and the high latitudes as being cool to cold.

Longitude and time   At the same time that the earth is revolving around the sun, it is also rotating, or turning around, on its axis. It takes 24 hours, or 1 day, for the earth to make one **rotation**. This rotation causes day and night.

The earth's rotation also causes differences in time around the world. In one 24-hour period the earth turns from west to east through 360° of longitude. In 1 hour, therefore, the earth turns 15° of longitude (360 divided by 24 equals 15). When the sun is rising in Reno, Nevada (120°W), there has been 1 hour of daylight in Denver, Colorado (105°W); 2 hours in Memphis, Tennessee (90°W); and 3 hours in Trenton, New Jersey (75°W).

In the United States, the 48 **contiguous** (kən tig′ yủ əs), or touching, states extend through more than 45° of longitude between the Atlantic and Pacific oceans. Thus there is a 3-hour difference in time between states on the east coast and states on the west coast. When it is 10 P.M. in New York and North Carolina, it is 7 P.M. in California and Oregon. There is a difference of 5 hours between states on the east coast and Hawaii.

Time zones   If people set their clocks by the sun, they would have to change the clocks whenever they traveled a short distance east or west. To avoid this confusion, most of the countries of the world agreed upon a system of time zones. These are shown on the map below.

The Prime Meridian was chosen as the starting point for the world's time zones.

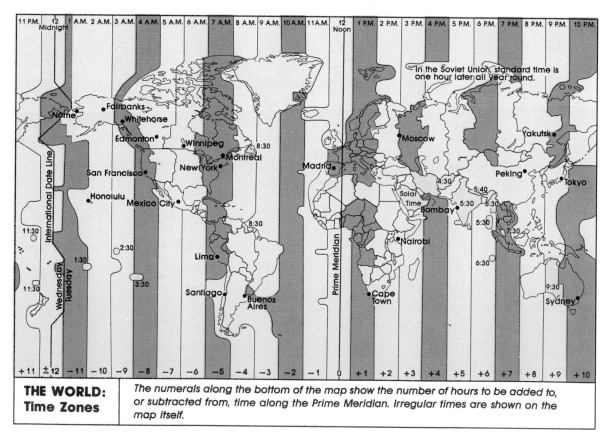

THE WORLD: Time Zones	The numerals along the bottom of the map show the number of hours to be added to, or subtracted from, time along the Prime Meridian. Irregular times are shown on the map itself.

The time zones in Alaska were changed on October 30, 1983, from four zones to two. Ask a pupil to report on why the change was made.

All the other time zones go east or west of the Prime Meridian. There are 24 time zones. Each time zone is centered on a line of longitude. The time zones are 15° apart. As you go east from the Prime Meridian, the time is 1 hour later in each zone. As you go west from the Prime Meridian, the time is 1 hour earlier in each zone.

The map also shows that the boundaries between the time zones are not always straight lines. The boundaries were made to zigzag in places so that certain towns and cities would be in the same zone and would have the same time.

International Date Line   Halfway around the world from the Prime Meridian is the **International Date Line**. This line follows along much of the 180° meridian. It is sometimes called the Sunday-Monday line because it marks the spot where a new calendar day begins. When it is Sunday, April 10, on the eastern side of the International Date Line, a new day—Monday, April 11—has already started on the western side of the line. So when it is Monday in Tokyo, Japan, it is still Sunday in San Francisco.

Ocean currents   The world's oceans are really one continuous body of water, but we divide them into the Pacific, the Atlantic, the Indian, and the Arctic oceans. Within the oceans are strong currents. An **ocean current** is like a river, always flowing in one direction. The winds, combined with the earth's rotation, cause the ocean currents to move in a circular pattern. You can see this on the map of the major ocean currents on page 44.

Matthew Fontaine Maury: Oceanographer

WHEN 19-YEAR-OLD Matthew Fontaine Maury began his first voyage in 1825, he also began his education at sea. The young man saw much of the world during his first years at sea. He sailed across the world's oceans and visited four continents. But his sea-roving days came to a sudden end because of an accident that left him permanently crippled.

Maury had to give up sailing the seas, but he did not give up his study of the sea. He helped develop the science that is now called oceanography. Maury showed that oceanography had practical uses. He became "the pathfinder of the seas" by making maps of ocean winds and currents that enabled sailing masters to cut the time of their voyages. Ships sailing around South America from New York to San Francisco reduced the average trip from 180 to 133 days. Maury directed surveys of the North Atlantic that showed it would be practical to lay an underwater telegraph cable connecting Europe and North America on the ocean floor. When steamships increased in number, Maury proposed that different lanes be set aside for vessels traveling east and west across the Atlantic in order to avoid collisions.

To educate people about science, Maury wrote books, including a series of school geographies. If you had been in school a hundred years ago, you might have used one of his books.

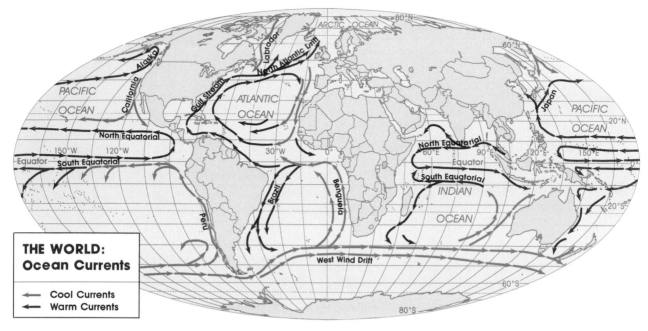

THE WORLD: Ocean Currents

← Cool Currents
← Warm Currents

Major movements of water in the oceans are called ocean currents. Currents that move away from the Equator are warm. Those moving toward the Equator are cold.

Ask: How does the Equator affect water temperature?

Oceans influence temperatures

Oceans and seas moderate, or make less severe, the temperatures on nearby land. This is because water warms more slowly and cools more slowly than land. In the summer the ocean waters often have a lower temperature than the continents, so they cool the nearby lands. In the winter the nearby lands are warmed by the oceans. Places near a large body of water tend to have warmer winters and cooler summers than places that are inland.

The different rates of heating and cooling of land and water produce land and sea breezes. During the day the land heats up more quickly than the water. As a result the air over the land is warmer than the air over the water. Warm air rises and creates a low-pressure center. Cold air sinks and creates a high-pressure center. Air moves from centers of high pressure to centers of low pressure. So the cooler air over the water moves toward the warmer air over the land. During the day the breeze in coastal areas is often from the water to the land. At night the land cools more quickly than the water. The process is then reversed. This daily reversing of the wind happens quite regularly along the coasts.

CHECKUP

1. In what ways does the earth move in space?
2. What is the difference between a solstice and an equinox?
3. Describe the three temperature zones into which the earth can be divided.
4. How does the earth's rotation from west to east affect time in the United States?
5. What is the International Date Line?
6. Describe the general movement of the major ocean currents. Name the four major oceans of the world.

44

Climate Regions of the World

VOCABULARY

drought	desert
economics	steppe
humidity	deciduous
region	coniferous
vegetation	tundra
climograph	permafrost
rain forest	lichen
savanna	iceberg

Weather and economics   Weather is worth money. On a sunny day at the ball park, many more hot dogs and parking spaces will be sold than on a rainy day. In a hot summer, power companies will sell more electricity for air conditioning. In a cold winter, stores will sell more gloves and heavy coats. If farmers have good weather for their crops, they will have more crops to sell and will earn more money to spend for new equipment, clothes, and other goods and services. But if there is a **drought** (drout), or lack of rain, farmers will have to spend money on irrigation and on new plants to replace those that die. You can see that weather is closely related to **economics,** the study of how goods and services are produced and consumed, or used.

Weather and climate   Weather is also a part of climate. Both weather and climate are made up of temperature, precipitation, sunshine, cloudiness, wind, air pressure, and **humidity.** Humidity is the moisture, or wetness, in the air. The difference between weather and climate is that weather is the condition of the atmosphere in a particular place at a particular time. Weather is made up of the day-to-day changes that cannot be forecast more than a few days ahead. Climate, on the other hand, is the average condition of the weather over a wide area for a period of years.

Different types of climate and vegetation   Climate varies over the earth's surface. Sometimes the change in climate is sudden, and sometimes it is gradual. However, there is a regularity and pattern to the changes. There are wide areas within which the climate varies very little. You can see these major climate **regions** on the map on page 46. A region is an area of land that has one or more common characteristics.

A region that has a particular type of climate is likely to have a certain type of natural **vegetation.** Natural vegetation is not the crops that farmers grow in their fields, even though these depend on climate. It is the trees, shrubs, grasses, and mosses that were here long before people appeared on the earth. The different kinds of natural vegetation and the areas in which they are found are shown on the map on page 47.

Now let us look at the different climate regions in the world. For each region there is a **climograph.** It shows both the average temperature and the average precipitation for a certain place over a period of time. The climographs for the different regions appear in the Graph Appendix on pages 511–513. By studying the climographs as you read the text on pages 46–48, you will get a better picture of each climate region.

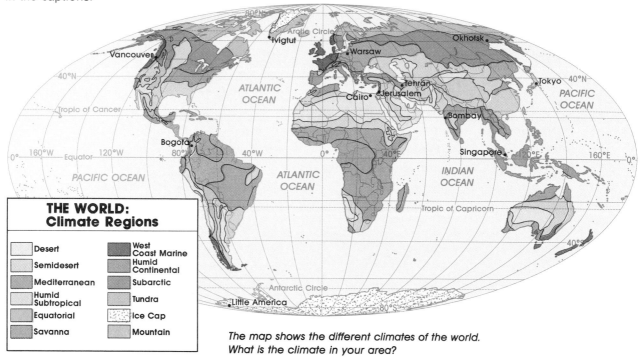

THE WORLD: Climate Regions

- Desert
- Semidesert
- Mediterranean
- Humid Subtropical
- Equatorial
- Savanna
- West Coast Marine
- Humid Continental
- Subarctic
- Tundra
- Ice Cap
- Mountain

The map shows the different climates of the world. What is the climate in your area?

Equatorial   As you might guess, an equatorial climate is found in the low-lands near the Equator. Find this climate region on the map above. Temperatures are high, and rain is heavy all year round. Places in this wet tropical region, such as the Amazon and Zaire river basins, have **rain forests.** A rain forest is a large, very thick growth of trees that usually have large, broad leaves.

Savanna   Lands in this region are in the low latitudes away from the Equator. This climate is sometimes called tropical wet and dry because rainfall is heavy for part of the year and very light for the other part. The temperatures are high throughout the year. Elephants, giraffes, and antelope are some of the animals that make their home among the tall grasses and scattered trees. This kind of natural vegetation is called **savanna.**

Desert   Lands in this region are partly in the low latitudes and partly in the middle latitudes. A **desert** is an area that gets so little precipitation that little vegetation grows. People often think of a desert as a sandy place. Much of the desert, however, is bare and rocky, with a few cacti and other plants that have adapted to the dry conditions. Temperatures vary from hot in the day to very cold at night.

Semidesert   This climate region is on the fringe of the desert. Temperatures are variable throughout the year, and enough rain falls to allow short grass to grow. In the middle latitudes this grassland area is called a **steppe** (step).

Mediterranean   This type of climate is found in places around the Mediterranean Sea. It is also found in places about 35° north or south of the Equator that lie

46

on or near the sea on the western side of the continents. Temperatures are hot in the summer and cool in the winter. Summers are generally dry, and winters are wet.

Humid subtropical Areas in this climate region lie near the east coasts of the continents, about 35° north or south of the Equator. Temperatures are hot in the summer and cool in the winter. There is year-round precipitation, but most of it falls in the summer.

West coast marine Lands in the marine climate region are usually found between latitudes 40° and 60° on the west coasts of the continents. These lands lie directly in the path of winds blowing over warm ocean currents. The ocean has a great influence on this type of climate.

Temperatures are warm in the summer and cool in the winter. There is precipitation all year round, but it is heavier in the winter than in the summer. Grass and broad-leaved trees are the natural vegetation of the marine climate region. Broad-leaved trees are **deciduous** (di sij′ ù əs), which means they lose their leaves in the fall.

Humid continental This climate region is usually found in the same latitude as the marine climate. Unlike the marine climate, however, it is found in the deep interior of a continent or along a continent's eastern edge. The continental climate is found only in the Northern Hemisphere. It has a wide range of temperatures, with warm to unpleasantly hot summers and cold to very cold winters. Precipitation also varies considerably.

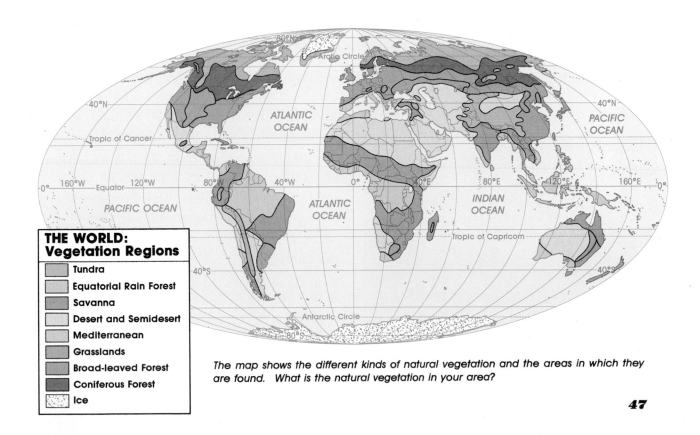

THE WORLD: Vegetation Regions

- Tundra
- Equatorial Rain Forest
- Savanna
- Desert and Semidesert
- Mediterranean
- Grasslands
- Broad-leaved Forest
- Coniferous Forest
- Ice

The map shows the different kinds of natural vegetation and the areas in which they are found. What is the natural vegetation in your area?

Subarctic The subarctic climate is found in the high latitudes. It has short, cool summers and long, severe winters. The total precipitation is generally light, coming as snow in the winter and rain in the summer. But because of the low temperatures, very little of the precipitation evaporates. This means that most of the rain and snow soaks into the soil and washes away minerals that may be there. There is very little farming in this climate. The natural vegetation is **coniferous** (kə nif′ ər əs) trees. These trees produce seeds in cones. They are also evergreen, since they do not shed their thin, needlelike leaves all at once. Great coniferous forests grow in this climate.

In Alaska's short summer, mosses, lichens, and small flowering plants cover the tundra. For a few weeks the tundra is beautiful with the bright colors of these plants.

Tundra North of the coniferous forests is the **tundra,** or barren lands. Temperatures are not as extreme as in the subarctic climate because the nearby oceans moderate the tundra climate. Precipitation is light. No trees grow in this region because the ground below the top layer of soil remains frozen all year. This frozen soil is called **permafrost.** It prevents moisture from soaking through. But mosses, **lichens** (lī′ kəns), and other hardy plants spring up in the short northern summers. A lichen is a plant that has no roots, stems, leaves, or flowers and grows on rocks and other surfaces.

Ice cap This climate is found only in Antarctica and the interior of Greenland. Greenland is a huge island in the North Atlantic Ocean. In these places the average temperature all year round is below freezing, or 32°F (0°C). Precipitation is light. Snow gradually packs until it forms a solid sheet of ice that covers the region. Sometimes a large piece of ice breaks off, falls into the sea, and floats away. This is an **iceberg.** There is no plant life in this frozen polar climate, and no people live here permanently.

Climate does not make us the way we are, but it does affect how we live. In later chapters you will learn how people have adjusted to their particular climate.

CHECKUP

1. How does climate differ from weather?
2. How is natural vegetation different from the crops that farmers grow?
3. What is the difference between deciduous and coniferous trees? Name a climate region where each is found.
4. Describe a tundra climate.

3/CHAPTER REVIEW

KEY FACTS

1. The revolution of the tilted earth around the sun causes the seasons. The rotation of the earth causes day and night.

2. The earth can be divided into three temperature zones. The low latitudes are generally warm, the middle latitudes are changeable, and the high latitudes are cool to cold.

3. The Prime Meridian is the starting point for the world's time zones.

4. Water heats and cools more slowly than land. This has a moderating effect on temperatures on nearby land.

5. The major climate regions of the world may be described in terms of latitude, temperature, precipitation, and natural vegetation.

VOCABULARY QUIZ

Read the following statements. Decide which statements are true and which are false. Write your answers (**T** or **F**) on a sheet of paper. If the statement is false, rewrite it so that it gives the correct definition of the underlined vocabulary term.

T 1. Trees that shed their leaves each year are called <u>deciduous</u> trees.

F 2. An <u>equinox</u> occurs when the sun is at its greatest distance from the Equator.

F 3. It takes 24 hours, or 1 day, for the earth to make one <u>revolution</u>.

F 4. The <u>Tropic of Cancer</u> is a line of latitude located at 66½° north.

T 5. A <u>region</u> is an area of land that has one or more common characteristics.

F 6. <u>Economics</u> is the study of weather and climate.

F 7. <u>Coniferous</u> trees are the natural vegetation of the west coast marine climate.

F 8. <u>Humidity</u> is the weight of air pushing down on the earth.

T 9. The layer of frozen soil found in the tundra climate is called <u>permafrost</u>.

T 10. The <u>International Date Line</u> marks the spot where a new calendar day begins.

REVIEW QUESTIONS

1. Why is it winter in the Southern Hemisphere when it is summer in the Northern Hemisphere?

2. Why is *temperate* a poor name for the climates of the middle latitudes?

3. How many time zones are there in the United States? In the world?

4. How do oceans and other large bodies of water affect temperatures on nearby land?

5. How is weather closely related to economics?

6. Describe the similarities and differences between the following climates: (**a**) equatorial and savanna, (**b**) desert and semidesert, (**c**) west coast marine and humid continental.

7. What is an iceberg?

ACTIVITIES

1. Watch the weather news on television for several days. Make a list of the facts given.

2. Make a chart of the world's climate regions. Describe each region in terms of latitude (low, middle, or high), temperature, precipitation, and natural vegetation. The climographs on pages 511−513 will give you information about the average temperature and average precipitation for each climate region.

3. A wide variety of animals live on the African savannas. Prepare an oral report about some of the animals that you find most interesting.

3/SKILLS DEVELOPMENT

READING CLIMOGRAPHS

TEMPERATURE

On this page there are two special kinds of graphs. They are called climographs because they show temperature and precipitation, two important parts of climate. Each climograph has temperature scales on the left side. They are printed in red. The scale on the outside is for Fahrenheit temperatures. The scale on the inside is for Celsius temperatures. The months of the year are given along the bottom of the graph. The average temperature for each month is shown by a red dot.

SKILLS PRACTICE: PART I

Now use the temperature information on the climographs to answer these questions.
1. Which month is the warmest in New York? In San Diego?

2. Which place is warmer all year round?
3. Is the average January temperature in New York above, or below, freezing (32°F, or 0°C)?

PRECIPITATION

On the right side of each graph are the scales for precipitation. They are printed in blue. Centimeters are given on the inside; inches on the outside. The blue bars show the average monthly precipitation.

SKILLS PRACTICE: PART II

Use the bars to answer the questions.
1. Which place has almost no precipitation from June through September?
2. What is the greatest amount of precipitation for any one month in New York? In San Diego?

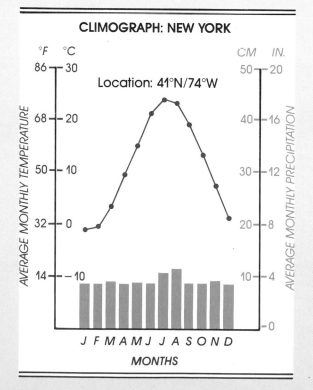

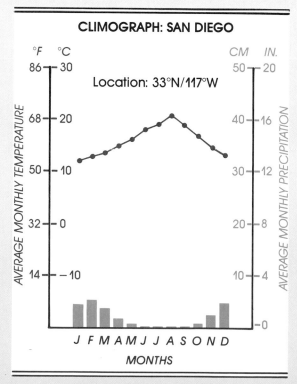

1/UNIT REVIEW

Answer Key in back of book.

READING THE TEXT

Turn to page 16 and read the section "Location by latitude and longitude." Then, on a sheet of paper, answer these questions.

1. Why do people use lines of latitude and longitude?

2. What is the difference between lines of latitude and lines of longitude?

3. Into which two hemispheres does the Equator divide the earth?

4. What are lines of latitude called? What are lines of longitude called?

5. Why is the Prime Meridian sometimes referred to as the Greenwich Meridian?

READING A MAP

Turn to page 46 and look at the map titled "The World: Climate Regions." Note the latitude and longitude lines. Remember that the latitude lines run east and west, and the longitude lines run north and south. On this map, north is at the top, south is at the bottom, east is on the right, and west is on the left.

On a sheet of paper, write the answers to these questions.

Tokyo 1. Which city is located farthest east?

2. In what direction would you be going if
West you traveled from Warsaw to Vancouver, B.C.?

3. In which direction would you be going if
South you traveled from Ivigtut to Little America?

Subarctic 4. In which climate region is Okhotsk?

Desert 5. In which climate region is Cairo?

READING A PICTURE

Turn to page 15 and carefully study the picture of Washington, D.C. Using only the details shown in the picture, decide whether the statements that follow are true or false. On a sheet of paper, write **T** if the statement is true and **F** if it is false.

1. The many buildings in Washington, D.C., are rectangular in shape. F

2. There is no open land or parkland in the city. F

3. Major roads lead in and out of the city. T

4. The sun was shining in Washington when this picture was taken. T

5. Wharves, or docks, jut out into the water along which the city is located. T

READING A GRAPH

Turn to page 33 and look at the graph titled "Highest Mountain on Each Continent." On a sheet of paper, answer these questions about the graph.

1. Which mountain is the highest in the world? Mt. Everest

2. What is the highest mountain in North America? How high is it? Mt. McKinley About 20,000 feet (6,100 m)

3. In which country is Mt. Elbrus located? Soviet Union

4. Is Mt. Kilimanjaro higher or lower than Mt. Aconcagua? Lower

5. On which continent is Mt. Aconcagua located? South America

THE UNITED STATES AND CANADA

At one time in history, a group of Americans wanted the boundary line extended farther north. They used the slogan "Fifty-four forty or fight." (The "forty" refers to 40 minutes. There are 60 minutes in every degree of latitude and longitude.) The people who wanted the more northern boundary did not get it. Nor did they fight.

Table of Countries

COUNTRY	FLAG	TOTAL AREA	POPULATION and POPULATION DENSITY	CAPITAL CITY and POPULATION	WHERE PEOPLE LIVE
Canada		3,840,019 sq mi (9,922,330 sq km)	24,900,000 6 per sq mi (3 per sq km)	Ottawa 304,500	
United States		3,618,770 sq mi (9,372,614 sq km)	234,200,000 65 per sq mi (25 per sq km)	Washington, D.C. 638,000	

Urban ▨   Nonurban ▨   Not Available — ▨

The Longest Peaceful Boundary

The United States and Canada share the longest peaceful boundary in the world. It is almost 4,000 miles (6,436 km) in length. There are no guns or forts along this boundary. You can see this long boundary on the map on the facing page. The longest part of the boundary is a latitude line, the 49th parallel.

Major Landforms of the Region

Besides sharing a boundary, Canada and the United States also share some of the same landforms. The Appalachian Mountains are found in both countries. These low mountains stretch from the Gulf of St. Lawrence into Alabama, a distance of about 1,500 miles (2,410 km). Find the Appalachian Moun-

Table of Countries: Have pupils compare the population of both countries by making a bar graph.

The map includes the following labels:

ASIA, Bering Strait, Bering Sea, ARCTIC OCEAN, Beaufort Sea, QUEEN ELIZABETH ISLANDS, Barrow Strait, Baffin Bay, NUNIVAK ISLAND, BROOKS RANGE, Yukon River, ALASKA, VICTORIA ISLAND, BAFFIN ISLAND, Davis Strait, ALASKA RANGE, Mt. McKinley 20,320 ft (6,194 m), KODAK ISLAND, Gulf of Alaska, YUKON PLATEAU, Mackenzie, Great Bear Lake, Arctic Circle, Hudson Strait, Labrador Sea, COAST MOUNTAINS, CANADIAN SHIELD, Great Slave Lake, Hudson Bay, QUEEN CHARLOTTE ISLANDS, Athabasca River, Lake Athabasca, CANADA, Peace River, Churchill, Nelson River, PACIFIC OCEAN, VANCOUVER ISLAND, Saskatchewan, Saskatchewan R., Lake Winnipeg, NEWFOUNDLAND, Mt. St. Helens, COAST RANGE, ROCKY MOUNTAINS, Saskatchewan, Assiniboine, Columbia River, Snake River, Missouri, LAURENTIAN HIGHLANDS, St. Lawrence River, Ottawa River, Ottawa, NOVA SCOTIA, COAST RANGES, SIERRA NEVADA, GREAT BASIN, Great Salt Lake, GREAT PLAINS, North Platte River, South Platte River, Lake Superior, Great Lakes, Lake Michigan, Lake Huron, Mississippi, Lake Ontario, Lake Erie, APPALACHIAN MOUNTAINS, ATLANTIC OCEAN, Mitchell Peak 10,351 ft (3,155 m), Mt. Whitney 14,494 ft (4,418 m), COLORADO PLATEAU, Chaco Canyon, Mt. Elbert 14,433 ft (4,399 m), Ohio River, CENTRAL LOWLANDS, Washington, D.C., UNITED STATES OF AMERICA, Arkansas River, ATLANTIC COASTAL PLAIN, Red River, Brazos River, Rio Grande, Gulf of California, GULF COASTAL PLAIN, Colorado River, MEXICO, Gulf of Mexico

20°N, HAWAII, 155°W

THE UNITED STATES AND CANADA: Physical

★ National Capitals

0   250   500 miles

0   250   500 kilometers

What is the approximate latitude of the boundary between the western United States and Canada? What is the approximate longitude of the boundary between eastern Alaska and Canada?   49°N; 140°W

Provide pupils with an outline map of the United States and Canada. Have them label on the map the Appalachian

tains on the physical map above.

The interior plains form a lowland area in the central part of the United States and Canada. It includes that part of the United States known as the Great Plains.

Canada's plains stretch from its border with the United States, in the south, to the Arctic Ocean, in the north.

The plains are not level. They rise slowly toward the Rocky Mountains on

Mountains, the Rocky Mountains, the Mackenzie River, the Colorado River, the Missouri River, the Rio Grande, and the Great Plains.

the west. The Rockies extend from northern Alaska through Canada and into New Mexico. In Colorado this mountain chain has peaks that rise more than 14,000 feet (4,300 km).

The Continental Divide runs along the high ridges of the Rockies. It is an imaginary line that is important in relation to the rivers of North America. The rivers to the east of the Continental Divide flow generally toward the east. The rivers to the west of the Divide flow generally west. Many important rivers, including the Mackenzie in Canada and the Colorado, Missouri, and Rio Grande in the United States, have their source in the Rockies.

Along the Pacific Ocean are the coastal mountains. They extend from Alaska into Mexico. The land between these mountains and the Rocky Mountains is known as the intermontane region. *Inter-* means "between." You can guess what *montane* means. The intermontane region is the land between the mountains. The Colorado Plateau and the Great Basin are part of the intermontane region. Find these areas on the physical map.

Reading a Political Map

Now let us look at the political map on the facing page. How is this map different from the physical map? For one thing, the political map shows the boundaries of states in the United States and of provinces and territories in Canada. It is interesting to note how many states of the United States border on Canada. How many states share a land boundary with Canada? Did you count Alaska?

Notice that the lines of latitude and longitude form boxes as they cross one another on the map. These boxes make a grid. On this political map, numbers and letters have been used to label some of the boxes. This grid will help you find places on the map more easily.

Suppose you want to locate the city of Winnipeg. First, find Winnipeg in the list of cities below the map. After *Winnipeg* you see the name of the country in which Winnipeg is located. You also see its location on the map—in box *B-4*. Now find the letter *B* on the right side of the map. Put a finger on *B*. Next find the number 4 at the top of the map. Put a finger of your other hand on 4. Move both fingers, one across and one down, until they meet. They should meet in box *B-4*. That is where you will find the city of Winnipeg. Notice that Winnipeg is almost in box *A-4*. The grid system is used on other political maps throughout this book. It is a helpful tool for finding places on maps.

Reading a Table

On page 52 there is a Table of Countries. It presents a variety of facts about the countries that are discussed in Unit 2. Using these facts, you can discover similarities and differences between Canada and the United States. For example, by comparing the total area of both countries, you learn that Canada is slightly larger than the United States. However, the United States has many more people. Where do most people in both countries live—in urban, or city, areas, or in nonurban areas?

10

THE UNITED STATES AND CANADA: Political

⊛ National Capitals
• Other Cities

Boundaries of States, Provinces, and Territories

0   250   500 miles
0 250 500 kilometers

The cities shown on this map include national capitals and other cities selected on the basis of population. The City Index indicates the population categories. The same criteria are used for showing cities on the political maps in the Introductions to Units 3 through 9.

Cities 100,000 to 499,999
Ottawa (Canada) B-6

Cities 500,000 to 999,999
Baltimore (United States) C-6
Calgary (Canada) A-2
Cleveland (United States) B-5
Columbus (United States) B-5
Dallas (United States) C-4
Edmonton (Canada) A-2
Indianapolis (United States) C-5
Jacksonville (United States) C-5

Memphis (United States) C-5
Milwaukee (United States) B-5
Montreal (Canada) B-6
New Orleans (United States) D-4
North York (Canada) B-6
Phoenix (United States) C-2
San Antonio (United States) D-4
San Diego (United States) C-2
San Francisco (United States) C-1
San Jose (United States) C-1
Toronto (Canada) B-6

Washington D.C.
(United States) C-6
Winnipeg (Canada) B-4

Cities 1,000,000 or more
Chicago (United States) B-5
Detroit (United States) B-5
Houston (United States) D-4
Los Angeles (United States) C-2
New York (United States) B-6
Philadelphia (United States) B-6

Canada and the United States are two of the world's largest countries in area. Canada, however, is a country with few large cities. Which Canadian cities have 500,000 or more people? The United States has six cities with a population of 1,000,000 or more. Locate these cities on the map.

Calgary   Edmonton   Montreal   North York   Toronto   Winnipeg

A Variety of Economic Activities

┌─VOCABULARY─────────────────┐
veterinarian   sustained yield

conveyor   renewable
economic   resource
   activity   spawn
regional   habitat
   specialization
                        deplete
pulp
└────────────────────────────┘

The geography of a hamburger   Who has not had a hamburger at one time or another? Billions of them have been sold. There is probably a hamburger shop near your school or home. Did you ever stop to think about how much work goes into bringing a hamburger to you?

The starting place is a cattle ranch. Thousands of calves are born each year on ranches from Texas to Montana. Much of the land in the Great Plains is too dry or too rugged for farming. The vast grasslands of this region, however, are especially suited to cattle grazing. Cowhands move the calves from one pasture to another so that the grass does not become overgrazed. To keep the calves healthy, **veterinarians** (vet ər ə när′ ē ənz) are called in to check the animals. Veterinarians are doctors who treat animals. At roundup time the cowhands gather the

cattle together and load them onto trains and trucks. Perhaps you have seen trucks loaded with cattle on the highway.

The cattle are taken to farms in the Central Plains for fattening. Here the farmers have planted and harvested crops of corn and hay. These crops are chopped up and stored in tall silos. When it is time to feed the cattle, electric motors in the silo help to bring out a mix of corn and hay. This mix is carried to the cattle on a rubber belt called a **conveyor**.

After the cattle have been fattened, they are sent to the packing plant and killed. Everything in the plant must be kept clean. Large sides of beef are hung in refrigerated rooms. The hides of the animals are sold and made into leather for jackets, handbags, and shoes. Glue is made from the hooves. All parts of the animal are used.

Trucks carry the beef from packing plants to processing plants around the country. Machines grind the meat and form it into hamburgers in the processing plant. Then the hamburger patties are frozen and taken by truck to restaurants and stores, where people buy them.

Grains for bakeries   Many of us like to eat our hamburger on a bun or between two slices of bread. By far the most important ingredient in buns and

Have pupils alphabetize the vocabulary words and define them. After pupils have read the lesson, direct them to check their definitions.

The raising of beef cattle and the processing of the meat are two big industries in the United States.

Pupils could make flowcharts showing the processes that result in hamburgers and buns.

Distribute outline maps of the United States and have pupils label all the states and list the agricultural products mentioned on pp. 58–62 in or near the appropriate states. Tell pupils to save their maps. They will be used again on p. 63.

bread is wheat flour. It is also a main ingredient in piecrust, cake, and other bakery products. Many breakfast cereals are made from wheat, too.

Wheat is a grasslike crop that can be grown on large farms by a few workers operating large machinery. Farmers prepare the fields by driving tractors that pull plows and harrows. These stir and smooth the soil. The wheat seeds are put in the ground by a machine called a drill, which is also pulled behind a tractor. After that, nature does most of the work until harvesttime. If there is good soil and the right amount of sunshine and rain, each plant produces a head of grain.

A large machine called a combine is used to cut the heads of grain from the tops of the plants. At the same time, the combine separates the grain from the chaff. The grain is the wheat kernel, and the chaff is its covering. The machine is called a combine because it does both operations at the same time. The wheat kernels are blown into trucks that drive alongside the combine as it moves through the fields.

A combine costs thousands of dollars, and many wheat farmers cannot afford to buy their own machine. Many of them have to hire harvesters to combine their fields. The harvesters usually start in Texas and Oklahoma because the grain ripens there first. Then they follow the wheat crop northward as it ripens in Kansas, Colorado, and Nebraska. The harvesters haul their combines on trucks and live in vans or motor homes. They may end the season in North or South Dakota or Montana and then head to Florida or California for the winter.

The Wheat Belt The map below shows that wheat is grown widely in the United States. Kansas is the major wheat-producing state. It is in the heart of the winter wheat region. Winter wheat is planted in the fall and harvested in the spring or early summer. North and South Dakota and eastern Montana raise spring wheat. It is planted in the spring. Harvest begins in midsummer.

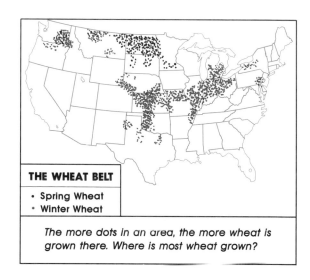

THE WHEAT BELT
- Spring Wheat
- Winter Wheat

The more dots in an area, the more wheat is grown there. Where is most wheat grown?

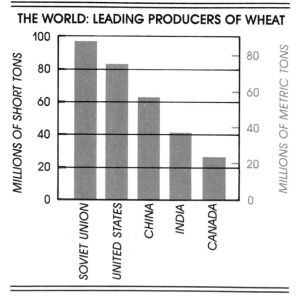

THE WORLD: LEADING PRODUCERS OF WHEAT

Which nation produces the most wheat? About how many tons of wheat does it produce a year?

From storage to supermarket After wheat is harvested, it is taken to a grain elevator. The elevator has machinery for cleaning and storing wheat and other kinds of grain. The wheat is stored in the elevator until it can be shipped to a flour mill. Long trains of wheat cars carry the grain to cities such as Minneapolis, St. Paul, Wichita, and Kansas City, where it is milled into flour. Flour mills turn out sacks and packages of wheat flour that are sent to food stores all over the country.

Regional specialization You have learned that ranching is an important economic activity in the Great Plains region. An economic activity is one that has to do with the production or selling of goods or services. Wheat farming is an important economic activity in the Central Plains region. Ranching and wheat farming are known as regional specializations.

Other parts of the country have developed regional specializations, too. The area around Orlando, in central Florida, is an excellent example. Miles and miles of orange trees cover the countryside. Although oranges grow in other states besides Florida, Florida produces about 80 percent of the orange crop. Oranges grow best in regions with warm summers and mild winters in which the temperature does not go below freezing.

Tree crops There are other tree crops that are associated with certain regions. Cherries grow in the states around the Great Lakes. The state of Washington is known for its apples. South Carolina and Georgia are famous for their peaches. Plums and prunes come mainly from California, as do walnuts and almonds. Pecan trees grow in the humid subtropical climate of the southeastern states. Hawaii specializes in macadamia nuts and pineapples.

Forests Trees are also grown for lumber and wood **pulp.** Hardwood trees such as oak can be used for furniture and flooring. Softwood trees such as pine can be used as two-by-fours in house building or can be ground for pulp. Pulp is a mixture of ground wood and chemicals and is used to make paper. Today there are many paper mills in the southeastern section of the United States, where there are large forests of pine trees. One tenth of the lumber in the United States comes from the state of Washington.

Private landowners may operate tree farms. A tree farm is a place where trees are grown as a business. Millions of acres of trees are owned by the federal government. It gives contracts to lumber companies to allow them to cut trees in the national forests. Only certain areas of mature, or fully grown, trees are opened for cutting each year. In this way there can be a **sustained yield,** or a steady amount of timber produced each year. Forests are a **renewable resource.** This means that although trees in a forest are cut down, new trees may replace them.

Agriculture Some parts of the country are well-known for certain farm products. For example, Aroostook County in northern Maine produces potatoes. Idaho also produces potatoes and is the leading

After pupils have read about Joel, have them discuss the similarities and differences between Joel's life and theirs.

Fishing   Some parts of the country are well-known for fish and other seafood. Shrimp are caught in great numbers off the United States coast from Texas and Louisiana to Georgia and North and South Carolina. The Chesapeake Bay, in Virginia and Maryland, is famous for its oysters and blue crabs. The Georges Bank, off the coast of Massachusetts, has been an important fishing ground for hundreds of years. And some of the best lobsters come from the North Atlantic Ocean off the coast of Maine.

On the Pacific Coast, tuna fishing is important. Large tuna boats, 100 feet

In the United States about 193,000 people work on fishing vessels. This photograph shows a small fishing boat with its catch of tuna. Tuna is an important food fish.

Hawaiian pineapple workers pick the fruit and place it on a conveyor belt. The belt carries the pineapples to a truck.

potato-growing state. Wisconsin ranks first in dairy cattle, and Texas ranks first in beef cattle. Iowa is famous for corn, Kansas is famous for wheat, and Hawaii is famous for pineapples.

California is the leading vegetable-producing state. The Imperial Valley in California is one of the country's richest farming regions. It supplies lettuce and other vegetables to markets across the nation. Because the valley lies in a desert in southern California, farmers must irrigate the land in order to raise crops. Water is brought into the Imperial Valley by canal from the Colorado River.

Joel: Growing Up a Farm Man

Joel Holland wants to be a farmer when he grows up. He lives on a corn and livestock farm in northwestern Illinois. He is the youngest of six children. Only he and his 16-year-old brother, Martin, still live at home with their parents. The house Joel was born in was built by his great-grandfather James, an Irish immigrant. The 245-acre (99-ha) farm has been in the family since 1860.

Joel's mom and dad usually shout into his room to awaken him about 7:30 A.M. He's really not a morning person and has a hard time getting going. In the spring he has to feed the calves before going to school.

The school bus stops on the highway to pick up Joel and the other farm boys and girls who go to school in the town of Scales Mound. The school is a brick building that houses both grade school and high school. There are 235 students, and Joel knows practically everyone in school. Few people leave or move into the community every year, so Joel usually has the same classmates. He is a good student and especially likes the experiments in science.

The first thing Joel does when he gets off the school bus in the afternoon is to take off his sneakers and put on boots. He is no longer a typical teenager. He has farm work, called chores, to do. He has to clean out the farrowing house after a litter of pigs is born. He runs the mixer mill to grind corn for the cattle and hogs.

There is different work at different times of the year. Depending on the season, the corn must be planted, harvested, or stored.

Joel keeps the hogs as a business of his own. Two days after the pigs are born, he squirts serum containing liquid iron into their mouths. Then he cuts their needlelike baby teeth. After that he cuts off their tails and notches their ears to identify them. If the pigs' teeth and tails were not cut, the pigs would chew on each other's tails.

Joel is learning a lot about farming. He would rather live on a farm than in a city. He feels that people don't work together as a family as much in the city as on a farm. He also likes the freedom and the responsibilities on the farm.

But life is not all work on the farm. Joel always has energy left over for sports. He shoots baskets on a backboard nailed to a tree. He plays softball in the spring, goes water-skiing and fishing in the summer, hunts deer in the fall, and rides a snowmobile in the winter.

His mother says the best words to describe Joel are *energetic* and *enthusiastic*. On one summer day he jumped 15 fences, drove farm machinery 25 miles, fed 320 animals, opened and closed 8 gates, walked and ran about 8 miles, jumped on and off the tractor 26 times, lifted 900 pounds of grain and shoveled 4,000 pounds, and ate about 2,600 calories!

Joel's story is told in a good book by Patricia Demuth. The photographs were taken by her husband, Jack. Ask your librarian if you can get a copy of *Joel: Growing Up a Farm Man* (New York: Dodd, Mead & Company, 1982). It tells many more interesting things about Joel, such as how he helped when cows gave birth, and how he built a Fly Zapper that killed bushels of flies.

Many young people join organizations such as 4-H and Future Farmers of America. More than 5 million boys and girls aged 9 through 19 belong to 4-H clubs in the United States and its territories. Nearly 4 million of these members do not live on farms.

(31 m) or more in length, go far out in the Pacific Ocean to look for tuna. The boats may be at sea for weeks at a time. Much of the tuna catch is sent to fish canneries in places such as San Pedro, California, near Los Angeles. Another fish, the salmon, lives in the North Pacific Ocean. Salmon return to the freshwater streams where they hatched in order to **spawn**, or lay their eggs. Many are caught as they come in from the ocean to swim upstream. The Alaskan king crab is also found in the North Pacific. Many people like to eat the meat from the claws of this large crab.

Like forests, fish are a renewable resource. If the fishing grounds are not overfished, there can be a sustained yield. However, if too many fish are taken or if their **habitat** is disturbed by pollution, the fish population will decline. Then there will be fewer fish caught and fewer fish for food. A habitat is the place where an animal or a plant lives or grows naturally. Once the habitat is restored and the catch is limited, the fish population can be restored if the supply has not been **depleted** too much. Some varieties of whales, such as the blue whale, are in danger of being depleted, or reduced to the point where their numbers cannot be increased.

CHECKUP

1. What is the difference between winter wheat and spring wheat? Name the major winter wheat and spring wheat regions in the United States.
2. Name at least one product that is associated with each of the following states: (a) Iowa, (b) Florida, (c) Washington, (d) Wisconsin, (e) California, (f) Texas.
3. Why are forests and fish called renewable resources?

An Industrial Giant

VOCABULARY

industry	nonrenewable resource
smelting	nuclear power
bauxite	acid rain
hydroelectric power	

Riches of the earth   The United States is a world leader in **industry**. One of the meanings of industry is the making, or manufacturing, of goods. Fish canning and lumber milling are two big industries that grew because of the rich supplies of fish and lumber. The United States also has many other valuable natural resources.

Metals are one great resource, and iron is one of the most important. Steel, an iron product, is used to make tools, machinery, and girders for bridges and buildings. It is also used to make rails, locomotives, ships, automobile bodies, and many other products that need a hard, strong metal. Steelmaking is one of the most important industries in the United States.

Steelmaking: a basic industry   Steel is made by refining iron and mixing it with other metals. Iron is found in a kind of rock called iron ore. By using heat from burning coal, the iron can be melted out of the rock. This is called **smelting**.

An important center for the mining of iron ore is the Mesabi Range in Minnesota. About four times more iron ore is mined in Minnesota than in any other state. Much of the iron ore is transported by rail to ports on Lake Superior. The

This Pennsylvania steel mill uses a basic oxygen furnace to produce steel. Pennsylvania is the leading steel-producing state in the country.

Soo Canals between Lake Superior and Lake Huron allow ore boats to travel to the lower Great Lakes. Steel mills were built at Buffalo, New York; Cleveland, Ohio; Detroit, Michigan; Gary, Indiana; and other cities on the Great Lakes.

Coke is another ingredient of steel. Coke is made by placing coal in an oven and heating it until the gases have been removed. The center map on page 65 shows that the United States has abundant coal deposits, especially in Kentucky, West Virginia, Wyoming, Pennsylvania, and Illinois. Pittsburgh, Pennsylvania; Birmingham, Alabama; and Gary, Indiana, are three leading steelmaking cities located near coalfields.

In recent years the steel industry has come upon hard times. One reason is that other metals and plastics have been substituted for steel in many products.

Car manufacturers, for instance, have reduced the amount of steel in automobiles and have produced lighter cars that do not use as much gasoline. Another reason for the hard times in the steel industry is that countries that once bought American steel now have their own steel mills. A third reason is that Americans began to buy more foreign cars. This affected the American automobile industry and the steel mills that supply steel to the car manufacturers. Many people in the automobile and steel industries have lost their jobs.

Other metals The United States also has large amounts of other metals, including gold, silver, copper, lead, aluminum, and uranium.

Aluminum is a lightweight, silver-colored metal that can take many different

Have pupils add locations of coalfields, aluminum-producing areas, and iron and copper mining areas to their outline maps (p. 58). If there is room, you may also wish to have pupils add oil and gas fields to the maps.

63

shapes. It is used to make aircraft parts, pots and pans, chewing gum wrappers, and drink cans. Aluminum comes from an ore called **bauxite** (bôk' sīt). Most of the bauxite in the United States comes from Arkansas. The making of aluminum requires large amounts of **hydroelectric power.** This is electricity produced by moving water. Hydroelectric power is made at dams in rivers. The major aluminum-producing areas in the United States are in the Tennessee Valley and along the Columbia River in the state of Washington.

Copper is a reddish-orange metal that is mainly used in the making of electric wire. This metal was mined on the Upper Peninsula of Michigan as early as 1845. Eventually, the mines went a mile deep. Large amounts of copper ore have also been dug at Butte, Montana, and Bingham Canyon, Utah. Arizona and New Mexico are also important copper-producing states. The map at the top of the facing page shows copper deposits. Is copper mined in your state?

The United States has been fortunate to have abundant supplies of basic metal ores. The richest and most accessible ores are the first to be used. When these are gone, then the lower-grade and less accessible ores are used. In time the mines are worked out, and it becomes necessary to look elsewhere for the ores. Once the ores have been used, they are gone from the earth. Since they cannot be replaced, they are called **nonrenewable resources.** However, some metal products, such as aluminum cans, can be recycled and used again. Perhaps you have collected cans for this purpose.

Petroleum The ability to make gasoline and other fuels for use in motors has brought about a great change in the way people have lived in this century. The Wright Brothers made the first airplane flight at Kitty Hawk, North Carolina, in 1903. About the same time, Henry Ford began to mass-produce his Model T automobile in Detroit, Michigan. Since that time, automobiles and air travel have become available to almost everyone in the United States. The automobile and airplane industries are closely linked to the petroleum industry.

The petroleum that provides the energy to run motors first came from wells in western Pennsylvania. The neighboring states of West Virginia, Ohio, Indiana, and Illinois also developed oil fields. Then, huge oil fields were discovered in Oklahoma, Texas, and Louisiana. California also shared in the wealth that came with oil discoveries. Today the United States is the second largest oil-producing country in the world. Thirty-one states produce oil, as you can see from the bottom map. Some states have both oil and natural gas, another important fuel.

The newest oil fields in the United States were discovered in northern Alaska in 1968. Ice in the Arctic Ocean hindered the shipment of oil by tanker. So a pipeline was built across the state from north to south. The pipeline ended at Valdez, a city on the Gulf of Alaska. Here the oil is pumped onto tankers and carried to oil refineries in California.

The United States is fortunate to have both petroleum and natural gas within its borders. However, more oil is consumed, or used, in this country than can

Discuss the concept of nonrenewable resources. Ask: What can we substitute for some of these resources? Remind pupils that plastics have a petrochemical base, that nuclear energy leaves nuclear waste, that the sun doesn't always shine, and that the wind doesn't always blow.

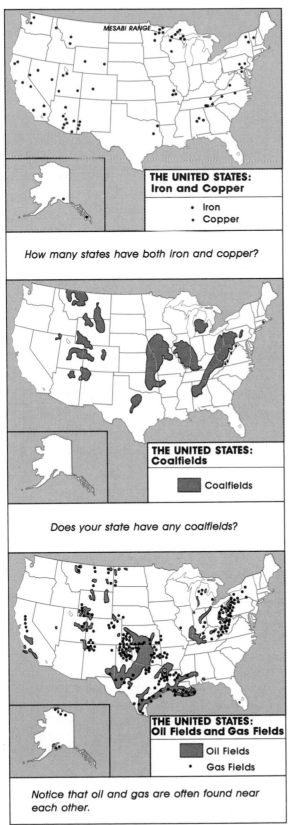

THE UNITED STATES: Iron and Copper

- Iron
- Copper

How many states have both iron and copper?

THE UNITED STATES: Coalfields

Coalfields

Does your state have any coalfields?

THE UNITED STATES: Oil Fields and Gas Fields

Oil Fields
- Gas Fields

Notice that oil and gas are often found near each other.

be produced. So it is necessary for the United States to import oil from other countries, such as Mexico, Venezuela, Nigeria, and Saudi Arabia.

Electricity   Electric power is a form of energy that has come into wide use in this century. The demand for this energy by homes, businesses, and industries has created another important industry— the power industry.

Do you know where the electricity in your home comes from? Along many streets there are power lines running from pole to pole. Sometimes the power lines are underground. If you traced these lines to their source, you would arrive at an electric power plant.

In the power plant large turbine engines turn generators that make electricity. A turbine has fan blades similar to those in the engine of a jet plane. Either waterpower or steam can be used to turn the fan blades.

Petroleum, coal, or **nuclear power** can be used to make steam. Nuclear power is power produced by atomic energy. The process of boiling water to make steam to turn the turbine blades is the same no matter which fuel is used. However, special safeguards must be used in nuclear power plants to prevent radiation from escaping to the surrounding area.

The burning of coal and petroleum to produce power has also created problems. Even though "scrubbers" are used on the smokestacks, various gases and tiny particles of soot go into the atmosphere. A scrubber is a special piece of equipment for washing and cleaning gases. The substances that escape into the air pollute

65

it. The pollutants combine with rain or snow and fall to earth as **acid rain.** In parts of the northeastern United States and southeastern Canada, acid rain has caused freshwater fish to die. Many scientists and business and government leaders in the two countries are trying to solve the problem of acid rain.

Hydroelectric power   A way to produce electricity without burning fuel is to use hydropower. *Hydro-* comes from a Greek word for "water." Hydropower is made by building dams on rivers. Water falls through pipes to spin turbine blades in the power station below the dam. Hydroelectric plants produce about one seventh of the electric power in the United States.

Because no fuels are burned, hydropower is very clean. Hydropower also uses a renewable resource—water. Winds from the oceans bring clouds carrying precipitation. The precipitation adds to the supply of water in the lakes behind the dams.

Unfortunately, the number of good places for building dams is limited. So only a small portion of the electricity that is needed can be produced by hydropower. Another disadvantage of this type of power is that good farmland and wildlife habitats are often flooded when dams are built.

A need for balance   Electricity is vital to the American way of life. The great demand for electric power, however, means that some trade-offs are necessary. Coal mining leaves scars on the land, but there are ways to reclaim land that has been mined. The burning of fuels can cause acid rain. However, American industries cannot operate without huge supplies of electric power. Americans also use a lot of energy at home and enjoy the material goods produced by American industries. Thousands of jobs in the United States depend upon the coal, petroleum, and power industries. The benefits of using nonliving sources of energy always have to be weighed against the cost to the environment.

CHECKUP

1. Name two natural resources that are important in steelmaking. Where are major deposits of each resource found in the United States?
2. What are some uses of aluminum? Of copper?
3. Why are metal ores called nonrenewable resources?
4. What is acid rain?
5. What are two advantages of making electricity with waterpower? What are two disadvantages?

Hoover Dam is located on the Colorado River, on the border between Arizona and Nevada.

Population and Cities

> ┌─VOCABULARY─────────────┐
> │ descendant   petrochemical │
> │ metropolitan │
> │   area │
> └──────────────────────────┘

Population The United States is the fourth largest country in the world in area. Only the Soviet Union, Canada, and China are larger. It is also the fourth largest in the world in population. Only China, India, and the Soviet Union have more people. Find the population of the United States in the table on page 52.

The majority of Americans are **descendants** of people who came from Europe. A descendant is a person born of a certain family or group. A large number of Americans are descendants of people who came from Africa. Only a small number, however, are Indians, the native people of the Americas. In recent years many people have come to the United States from Mexico and other Latin-American countries and from Asia.

Population density The map on page 68 shows where the more than 234 million Americans live. It is a population density map.

When we speak of population density, we are referring to the number of people per square mile or square kilometer in a certain area. Of course, each square mile or square kilometer in that area does not have exactly the same number of people. Population density means the average number of people per square mile or square kilometer. The greater the average number of people to the square mile or square kilometer, the greater the population density.

The map also shows the 25 largest cities in the United States. Six cities have at least 1 million people.

Cities About three fourths of the people in the United States live in or near a city. New York is the most populated city in the country. About 7 million people make their home there. And many more millions of people live in the New York **metropolitan area**. This area includes all the cities and towns around New York. New York is one of the most important business, banking, trading, and manufacturing centers in the world. Two of its largest industries are clothing manufacturing and book publishing. New York is also one of the world's greatest ports. Many ships enter the harbor each year, and millions of tons of cargo are handled.

Central Park, in New York, is a popular place with city residents and visitors. (41°N/74°W; map. p. 68)

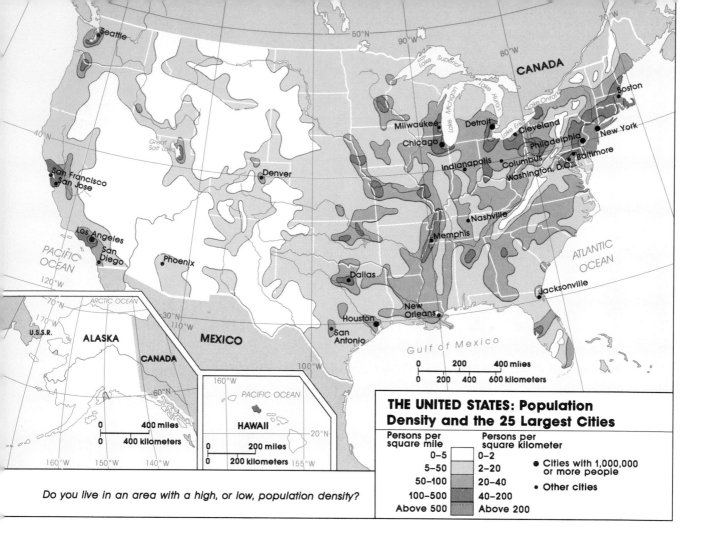

THE UNITED STATES: Population
Density and the 25 Largest Cities

Persons per square mile	Persons per square kilometer	
0–5	0–2	● Cities with 1,000,000 or more people
5–50	2–20	
50–100	20–40	● Other cities
100–500	40–200	
Above 500	Above 200	

Do you live in an area with a high, or low, population density?

Another of the country's largest cities is Chicago. About 3 million people live in the city, and another 7 million live in the Chicago metropolitan area. Chicago is on Lake Michigan. This location has helped the city grow into a major center of business, industry, and transportation. Its port on Lake Michigan is one of the nation's busiest. There are more than 14,000 manufacturers in Chicago, making iron and steel, electrical equipment, machinery, and many other products.

Los Angeles also has about 3 million people. It is by far the largest city on the Pacific Coast. The rich farmland in the area and nearby oil deposits have helped Los Angeles become a most important trade and manufacturing center. Los Angeles is also famous for its motion picture industry.

Philadelphia is the largest city in Pennsylvania and one of six cities in the country with more than 1 million people. Its location on the Delaware River makes it a busy port. The city is famous as the home of the Liberty Bell and Independence Hall, where the Declaration of Independence was signed in 1776.

Houston, the largest city in Texas, has more than 1.5 million people. It is a leader in oil refining, in the manufacturing of parts for oil wells and pipelines, and in

Have pupils study a physical map of the United States and compare it with the population density map. Encourage them to draw conclusions. (Populations are concentrated on coasts, along rivers and lakes, and so forth.)

petrochemicals. A petrochemical is a chemical or synthetic material made from petroleum or natural gas. Like New York, Chicago, and Philadelphia, Houston is an important port city. To reach the port of Houston, ships have to travel through a deepwater channel. The channel connects Houston to the Gulf of Mexico, 50 miles (80 km) away.

Detroit is the largest city in Michigan with a population of about 1.1 million. It is on the Detroit River, between Lake Huron and Lake Erie. Important industries include the making of auto parts, machine tools, iron products, hardware, chemicals, drugs, paint, wire products, automobiles, and trucks. Detroit also has one of the largest salt mines in the United States. The mine is under the city!

The Chicago River flows through downtown Chicago. This section of the city has many skyscrapers and hundreds of stores and offices. (42°N/88°W; map, p. 68)

Washington, D.C., the nation's capital, is a very different city from those you have just read about. Although it ranks seventeenth in size, with over 600,000 people, it is not an industrial city. There are no factories and few big companies in Washington. The city is on the Potomac River, but it is not an important port. It is, however, the most important city in the country. The main business of Washington is the government of the United States. More people in and around Washington work at government jobs than at any other kind. Every year millions of Americans visit their country's capital. Around the city is the pleasant countryside of Maryland and Virginia.

A country of many parts If you look at the back of a dime, you will find these words, E PLURIBUS UNUM. This is a Latin phrase meaning "one out of many." In the center of the dime is a torch, a symbol of freedom. The torch is made from a bundle of rods. Each rod by itself would not have much strength. When bound together, however, the rods make a strong handle for the torch. In the same way the 50 states of the United States, when bound together, make a strong nation.

CHECKUP

1. About how many people live in the United States today?
2. What is population density? What is the population density of the area around Boston, Massachusetts? (Use the map on page 68 to answer this question.)
3. Which six cities in the United States have a population of 1 million or more?
4. What is a metropolitan area?
5. What city is a leader in oil refining?

An oral or written vocabulary quiz will serve as a review for a chapter test.

4/CHAPTER REVIEW

KEY FACTS

1. Different parts of the United States have developed economic activities based on special products. Examples of these activities are orange growing in Florida, cattle ranching on the Great Plains, vegetable farming in the Imperial Valley of California, and fishing on the Georges Bank, off the Massachusetts coast.

2. A rich abundance of natural resources, such as metals, coal, petroleum, and water, has helped to make the United States a world leader in industry.

3. The United States is the fourth largest country in the world in area and population.

4. Approximately three fourths of the people in the United States live in or near a city.

VOCABULARY QUIZ

Match these terms with their definitions. Write your answers on a separate sheet of paper.

a. veterinarian
b. renewable resource
c. deplete
d. habitat
e. bauxite
f. metropolitan area
g. smelting
h. sustained yield
i. pulp
j. industry

g 1. The process of separating a metal from other materials in its ore

c 2. To reduce or exhaust the supply of a natural resource

a 3. A doctor who treats animals

j 4. The manufacturing of goods

e 5. The ore from which aluminum is made

b 6. A resource that can be replaced by nature or people

f 7. An area made up of a large city or several large cities and the surrounding cities, towns, and other communities

d 8. The place where an animal or a plant lives or grows naturally

h 9. A steady amount of a crop produced each year, often helped by controlled harvesting

i 10. A mixture of ground wood and chemicals that is used to make paper

REVIEW QUESTIONS

1. Why is the Great Plains particularly good for ranching?

2. Why don't all wheat farmers harvest their own wheat?

3. Explain the difference between a renewable and a nonrenewable resource. Give an example of each kind of resource.

4. Name the leading coal-producing states.

5. What is the difference between nuclear power and hydroelectric power?

6. Population density in the United States varies from 0 to more than 500 people per square mile (200 per sq km). Where are the areas of greatest population density? Of least density?

7. What city is well-known for clothing manufacturing and book publishing? What city is an important port on Lake Michigan?

ACTIVITIES

1. Steel and petrochemicals are major products of the United States. Look in an encyclopedia to find the kinds of products made from petrochemicals. Then label one sheet of paper Steel Products and another Petrochemicals. List as many items as you can find at home and at school that are made from steel or petrochemicals.

2. On an outline map of the United States, show the 25 largest cities. Use a different symbol for cities of 1 million or more.

READING A MAP: ISOTHERMS

USING ISOTHERMS

Isolines are lines on maps that connect points of equal value. Contour lines, or isohypses, are one kind of isoline. Isohypses connect places of equal elevation. The map on page 22 shows isohypses. Isohyets are another kind of isoline. These lines connect places of equal rainfall. Isotherms are a third kind of isoline. Isotherms connect places that have the same temperature. The word *isotherm* comes from two Greek words—*isos*, meaning "equal," and *therme*, meaning "heat."

Look at the map below. It shows the average January temperatures in Florida. The curving red lines are isotherms. Each isotherm is labeled with a Fahrenheit degree.

SKILLS PRACTICE: Part I

Use the map on this page to answer the following questions. Write on a sheet of paper.

1. What is the highest temperature shown by an isotherm? The lowest?
2. Which city has the warmest average January temperature? Which cities have the coldest average January temperature?
3. Is Orlando warmer or colder on the average than Gainesville?
4. Between which two isotherms is Tallahassee located?
5. Which Florida cities have average January temperatures between 60° and 66°?

SKILLS PRACTICE: Part II

Sometimes color is added between isotherms. Then the map looks like the one on page 3 entitled "The World: Average Annual Temperatures." Use the map on page 3 to answer the following questions.

1. Are the coldest parts of the world near the Equator or near the North Pole and South Pole?
2. Where are the hottest parts of the world?
3. What is the average annual temperature for places in the orange areas on the map?
4. What is the lowest average annual temperature for Australia?
5. What is the average annual temperature for your part of the United States?

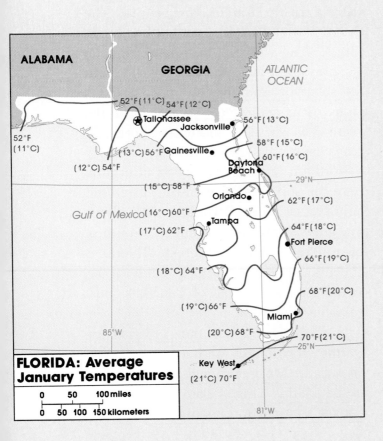

FLORIDA: Average January Temperatures

0   50   100 miles

0   50   100   150 kilometers

Have pupils turn to the table on p. 52 and compare the populations and population densities of the two countries.

Land and Climate

┌─VOCABULARY──────────────────┐
│ province   prairie   │
│ lock   │
└─────────────────────────────┘

A vast country   Canada is the second largest country in the world. Only the Soviet Union is larger. The country of Canada covers most of the northern half of North America, stretching 3,200 miles (5,148 km), from Newfoundland on the Atlantic Ocean to British Columbia on the Pacific Ocean. Canada's land boundaries, in the south and the northwest, are boundaries with the United States.

Canada and the United States are alike in many ways. They share the North American continent. They are similar in size, although Canada is slightly larger. The chief landforms of Canada continue into the United States. Both nations are divided into smaller political units. Canada has ten **provinces** and two territories, as shown on the map on page 83. The provinces are much like the states in the United States and have their own local government. The Canadian territories, on the other hand, do not have enough people to have their own government and are run mainly by the national government. People in both countries speak English, although French is also an official language in Canada. And both nations have been settled largely by people from Europe. But there is at least one outstanding difference between the two countries. Most of Canada is wilderness. Only one twelfth of its almost 4 million square miles (10 million sq km) is used or developed. There are large areas of the country in which no people live. Let us see why this is so.

Climate and vegetation   Large parts of Canada are too cold for most people. The country stretches far inside the Arctic Circle. The world climate map on page 46 shows that most of Canada lies within the subarctic and the tundra climate regions. It is cool or cold for much of the year. The growing season is short, and crops cannot be grown in many places.

Northern Canada is a region of tundra. Here the soil is permanently frozen, and only mosses and a few other small plants can grow in the short summer. South of the tundra is coniferous forest. The pines and firs can stand the long, cold winter. These forests are one of Canada's most valuable resources.

In southern Canada the summers are warmer and longer, and some crops can be raised. Most of Canada's farmland is in the south. This is also where most of Canada's 24 million people live.

The name *Canada* may come from the Iroquois word *kanata*, which means "village" or "community."

Jasper National Park lies in the Rocky Mountains of western Alberta. The Canadian Rockies are part of a mountain chain that extends from New Mexico to Alaska.

The Atlantic Provinces   It is easier to study a large country by regions. Canada's provinces and territories can be divided into five regions.

In the southeastern corner of Canada are the four Atlantic Provinces: New Brunswick, Nova Scotia, Prince Edward Island, and the island of Newfoundland. As you can see on the map, this region borders on the Atlantic Ocean.

The Appalachian Mountains extend into the Atlantic Provinces in the form of low hills. The hills are covered with forests of hardwood and evergreen trees. The short summers of the humid continental climate in this region are well suited to agriculture. Farmers in the valleys raise dairy and beef cattle. They grow potatoes, fruits, cereals, and feed crops.

Most people in the Atlantic Provinces live close to the coast, where hundreds of bays and inlets provide good harbors for fishing boats. The Grand Banks, off the coast of Newfoundland, are one of the world's best fishing grounds. Each year thousands of tons of fish are caught on the Grand Banks and off the coasts of the other Atlantic Provinces.

There are no large cities in the Atlantic Provinces, but Halifax, Nova Scotia, has become an important port. In the winter the St. Lawrence River is frozen. Ships cannot reach such other Canadian cities as Montreal and Quebec (kwi bek'). The harbor at Halifax, however, remains free of ice throughout the winter. Large ships call at Halifax with passengers and cargo in the winter months.

St. Lawrence Valley and Lakes Peninsula   The St. Lawrence River valley and the peninsula that borders on three of the Great Lakes—Lake Ontario, Lake Huron, and Lake Erie—make up an area of lowlands. The gentle relief goes from flatland to rolling hills. Warm summers and fertile soils allow farmers to grow a wide variety of fruits and vegetables. The region also has a number of dairy farms.

The St. Lawrence Valley is mainly in the province of Quebec, and the Lakes Peninsula is in the province of Ontario. More than half of Canada's population lives in this small region. Canada's two largest cities, Montreal and Toronto, are in this region. They are the centers of two metropolitan areas, each of which has a population of nearly 3 million. Montreal, on the St. Lawrence River in southern Quebec, is Canada's chief transportation center. Toronto, on the north-

CANADA: Regions

- Atlantic Provinces
- St. Lawrence Valley and Lakes Peninsula
- Canadian Shield
- Interior Plains
- Cordillera

What is the largest region in Canada?

western shore of Lake Ontario, is a busy lake port and Canada's chief manufacturing center. Ottawa, the capital of the country, is also in this region.

Between Lake Erie and Lake Ontario, the Niagara River plunges over a rocky ledge and forms the famous Niagara Falls. Millions of people come each year to see this spectacular natural wonder. Many people also visit the St. Lawrence Seaway. This water route between the Atlantic Ocean and the Great Lakes was built by both Canada and the United States. The Seaway was opened in 1959. The Great Lakes, the St. Lawrence River, and several canals are part of the Seaway.

The Atlantic Ocean is at sea level. Lake Superior is 600 feet (180 m) above sea level. To make up for the changes in water level, the Seaway has a series of **locks**. A lock is an enclosed area on a canal that raises or lowers ships from one water level to another.

The Canadian Shield

The largest region in Canada is the Canadian Shield. This huge, horseshoe-shaped region curves around Hudson Bay and includes the Arctic Islands, north of Hudson Bay. The Canadian Shield covers large parts of Newfoundland, Quebec, Ontario, Manitoba, and the Northwest Territories. The Shield covers about half of Canada.

This region is largely made up of low hills and lakes. The hills and lakes were formed many thousands of years ago when great sheets of ice moved over the land. The ice scraped away the soil and dug out hollows in the land. Today there is little soil over much of the Shield, so crops are not grown. Few people live in

Henry Hudson: Sea Captain and Explorer

HENRY HUDSON made four trips to North America between 1607 and 1611. He was looking for the Northwest Passage, a water route that early explorers thought would be a shortcut from Europe to Asia. Although Hudson never did find such a route, he explored three waterways that were later named for him — the Hudson River, in New York, and Hudson Bay and Hudson Strait, in Canada.

In 1607, Henry Hudson sailed the small ship *Hopewell* to Greenland and other Arctic islands. On this voyage he sailed to 80° north latitude, farther north than anyone had ever sailed before.

In 1609, Hudson sailed the *Half Moon* for the Dutch East India Company. He explored much of the eastern coast of North America, including the Hudson River. This voyage gave the Dutch a claim to much of the beautiful land along the river.

Hudson's last voyage began in 1610. A group of English merchants hired him to sail the *Discovery*. That year, Hudson entered the strait that bears his name and discovered the huge Hudson Bay. This voyage gave England a claim to much of Canada. Hudson and his crew spent the winter trapped by ice in the bay. The next spring they ran short of food, and the crew turned against its captain. Hudson, his young son, and seven crew members were put into a small boat and cast adrift. They were never seen again.

THE GREAT LAKES-ST. LAWRENCE WATERWAY: A CROSS SECTION

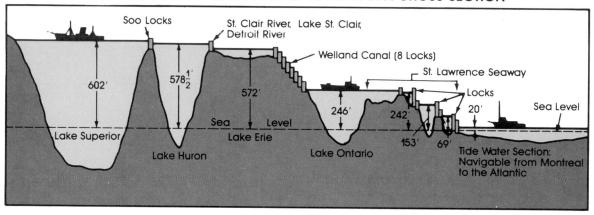

Elevation above sea level is given in feet. (The accent marks after the numbers stand for feet, thus, 602' = 602 feet.) The easternmost locks are near Montreal. The Soo Locks are near Sault (sü) Ste. Marie. Find Sault Ste. Marie and Montreal on the map at the bottom of the page.

HOW A CANAL LOCK WORKS

Passing from a Lower Level to a Higher Level

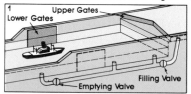

The lower gates are opened to allow the ship to enter the lock.

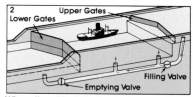

When the ship is in the lock, the gates are closed. The filling valve is opened, and water flows into the lock, lifting the ship.

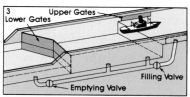

When the ship is at the higher level, the filling valve is closed, and the higher gates are opened to allow the ship to pass out of the lock.

Passing from a Higher Level to a Lower Level

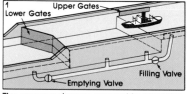

The upper gates are opened to allow the ship to enter the lock.

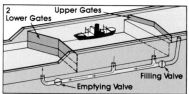

When the ship is in the lock, the gates are closed. The emptying valve is opened, and water flows from the lock, lowering the ship.

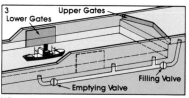

When the ship is at the lower level, the emptying valve is closed, and the lower gates are opened to allow the ship to pass out of the lock.

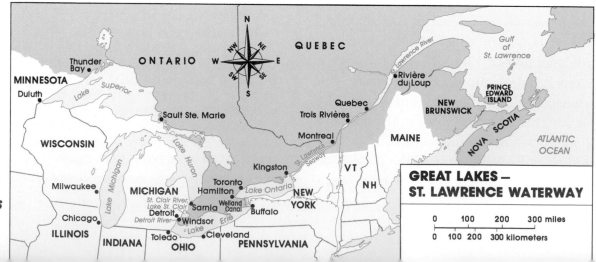

GREAT LAKES — ST. LAWRENCE WATERWAY

0	100	200	300 miles

0   100 200   300 kilometers

the Canadian Shield, because of its poor soil and cold climate. However, the region is very important for its natural resources. It has abundant forests, water, and large deposits of minerals.

The Interior Plains Manitoba, Saskatchewan (sə skach′ ə wən), and Alberta are called the Prairie Provinces. Most of the land in these provinces is in a region called the Interior Plains. The region is an extension of the Great Plains and the **prairies** of the United States. A prairie is a large area of level or rolling land with tall grass and fertile soil. A large part of the prairies of southern Canada has been plowed up and planted with crops such as wheat, corn, and feedstuffs. Canada is one of the world's leading producers of wheat. Most of the wheat is grown on the prairies.

For years the economy of the Interior Plains was based on farming and cattle ranching. With the discovery of large deposits of coal, oil, and natural gas, the region gained a new source of wealth. Alberta has an especially abundant supply of these energy resources. Many people have moved to this region, and manufacturing has developed in the cities. A number of Canada's largest cities, including Winnipeg, Calgary, and Edmonton, are in this region.

The Cordillera The northeastern tip of the province of British Columbia is in the Interior Plains. However, most of British Columbia is in a region called the Cordillera (kôr dəl yār′ ə). This word means "a system of mountain ranges." The Rocky Mountains and the Coast Ranges stretch northward from the United States into British Columbia. The Coast Ranges rise steeply from the ocean, and fjords cut into the rugged coastline. The Canadian Rockies are among the most rugged mountains in the world. Transportation across the mountains is difficult. However, there are a number of passes through which roads and railroads have been built.

Coniferous forests cover much of British Columbia. Many of the province's people work in the lumbering industry. The western mountains are rich in minerals, and mining is another major industry in the province. The rivers of British Columbia are used to produce hydroelectric power. Much of this power is used to refine the ores mined in the mountains. Three of Canada's major rivers have their source in British Columbia—the Columbia, Yukon, and Fraser rivers. The Columbia River flows southward into the continental United States. The Yukon River flows into Alaska. The

Small towns like this one dot the prairies of southern Canada, the country's major wheat-producing region.

Fraser River flows through British Columbia and reaches the Pacific Ocean near the port city of Vancouver. Vancouver is one of Canada's ten largest cities and its most important Pacific port. In Vancouver, Canada exports products such as wheat and lumber and carries on important trade with nations in Asia.

The Territories   The northern part of Canada is divided into the Yukon Territory and the Northwest Territories. The Yukon Territory is largely mountainous, and it is included in the Cordillera region. Most of the Northwest Territories is in the Canadian Shield, although the western part is in the Interior Plains.

The Territories make up more than one third of Canada's land area, but less than one percent of Canada's people live there. Many who live in the cold climate of the Territories are Inuit, as the Eskimos prefer to be called. Minerals have been found in this area, and a few mining towns exist. For the most part, however, this cold Arctic land is undeveloped.

Canada's longest river, the Mackenzie, has its source in the Northwest Territories. The Mackenzie River flows northwest from the Great Slave Lake for about 1,000 miles (1,600 km) to the Arctic Ocean.

CHECKUP

1. Why is most of Canada a wilderness?
2. Name the Atlantic Provinces. What are two ways in which people earn a living in these provinces?
3. Why is the St. Lawrence Seaway important?
4. Name two mountain ranges and four major rivers in western Canada.

Canada's Natural Resources

```
┌─VOCABULARY────────────────────┐
│  zinc              reserve      │
│  alloy             tar sands    │
│  radioactive       saturate     │
│  nickel            pitchblende   │
│  asbestos          uranium       │
└───────────────────────────────┘
```

Mineral wealth   Although large parts of Canada may have little value for farming or lumbering, they offer rich mineral deposits. **Zinc**, lead, and copper are abundant in the very old rock of the Canadian Shield. Zinc, a shiny, blue-white metal, is applied to other metals, such as iron and steel, to prevent them from rusting. Food cans may be plated with zinc if the cans are made from steel. Zinc is also joined with copper to make brass. Brass is an **alloy** (al'oi), or mixture of two or more metals. It is one of the most decorative and useful metals. Canada is the world's leading supplier of zinc.

Lead is a very heavy but soft metal that has many uses. A lead layer is used in hospitals and clinics to protect doctors and technicians who operate X-ray machines. Lead is also used in nuclear plants to prevent leaks of **radioactive** materials. Such materials give off harmful rays. Lead is used to make ammunition for guns, type for large printing machines, and some kinds of paint.

When the Canadian-Pacific Railroad was being built north of Lake Huron in 1883, a large deposit of copper and **nickel** was discovered near Sudbury, Ontario. At that time, nickel was believed to be worthless. The copper-nickel deposit in Ontario was not developed until

Canada is the world's leading exporter of minerals.

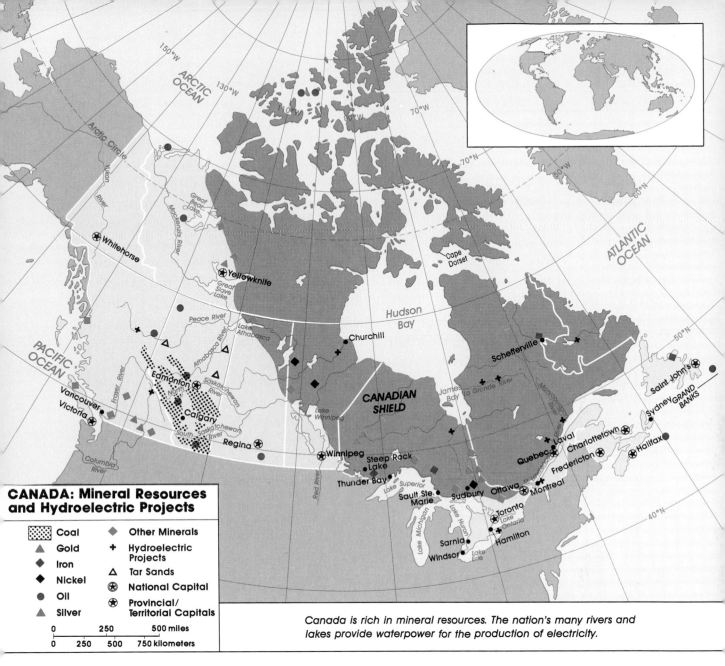

CANADA: Mineral Resources and Hydroelectric Projects

Coal
Gold
Iron
Nickel
Oil
Silver
Other Minerals
Hydroelectric Projects
Tar Sands
National Capital
Provincial/Territorial Capitals

0   250   500 miles
0   250   500   750 kilometers

Canada is rich in mineral resources. The nation's many rivers and lakes provide waterpower for the production of electricity.

new smelting methods, or ways of separating the two ores, were invented. Today, nickel is a very important metal that is used for coins and as an alloy of steel. About one third of the world's nickel comes from Sudbury, Ontario.

The world's largest deposits of **asbestos** outside of the Soviet Union are found in Canada. The chief deposits are in eastern Quebec south of the St. Lawrence River. Other deposits are found in New-foundland, Ontario, British Columbia, and the Yukon Territory. Asbestos does not burn or conduct heat. It has been used for insulation and roofing shingles. Unfortunately, asbestos fibers have been found to cause cancer in humans. Asbestos was used in the ceilings of many schools and has had to be removed. The findings about the connection between asbestos and cancer have hurt the asbestos industry.

Direct pupils' attention to the map. Ask specific questions, such as these: What resource is abundant in the Calgary-Edmonton area? (Coal) Near what city are there nickel deposits? (Sudbury)   **79**

Iron ore is one of the most important resources of the Canadian Shield. Canada had iron ore deposits around Lake Superior. Like those in the Mesabi Range of the United States, however, some of the better grades of ore around Lake Superior in Canada have been depleted. Fortunately, a very rich iron ore deposit was discovered at the bottom of Steep Rock Lake, Ontario. It was necessary to pump the lake dry and take away 60 to 200 feet (18 to 61 m) of mud to get to the main body of the ore. This is one of the richest iron deposits in the world. Another deposit of high-grade iron ore has been developed on the border between Quebec and Labrador. A railroad was built from the St. Lawrence River below the city of Quebec to the ore fields. Ore from Schefferville in northern Quebec can be shipped to steel mills around the Great Lakes and along the Atlantic coast, and even to steel mills in Europe. Hamilton and Sault Ste. Marie, in Ontario, and Sydney, in Nova Scotia, are steelmaking cities.

Gold, silver, and platinum are also smelted from ores found in the Canadian Shield. These precious metals are mostly used in making jewelry, but they have industrial uses, too.

Energy resources Canada is fortunate to have an abundant supply of energy resources. Most of its petroleum comes from oil fields in Alberta. Pipelines carry the crude oil to refineries in Vancouver, British Columbia, and Toronto and Sarnia, Ontario. Canada's Arctic oil **reserves** may be greater than those in northern Alaska. Reserves are supplies of fuel or other things that are available or set aside for future use.

In addition to its rich oil fields, Alberta has large supplies of **tar sands**. These sands, which are **saturated**, or filled, with oil, are in the central part of the province. The oil is very thick and sticky, so the sand clings to it. To get the oil, the sand has to be dug up, too. Then the oil and sand are separated, but only about 10 percent of the thick oil can be removed from the sand. This is an expensive way of getting oil. A large plant for removing oil from the sand has been built near the Athabasca tar sands. As the oil fields begin to run dry, the tar sands may become an important source of oil.

Which nation is the leading producer of nickel? About how many tons of nickel does Canada produce yearly?

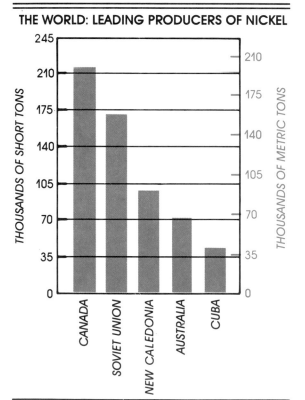

THE WORLD: LEADING PRODUCERS OF NICKEL

Have a pupil do research on the methods used to remove oil from tar sands and report to the class.

Lumbering is one of Canada's most important industries. Trucks transport the largest number of logs to mills.

Canada also has large deposits of **pitchblende**. This is a brownish-black mineral that is the main source of **uranium**. Uranium is a metal that is used to produce nuclear energy.

Canada's chief source of power is its thousands of lakes and rivers. There are many lakes in the Canadian Shield. The lakes are the source of many rivers. Within the Shield and at its edge, these rivers break into waterfalls and rapids. The waterfalls and rapids are used to produce hydroelectric power for many of Canada's industries, including the large aluminum industry.

Refer pupils to the map on p. 79 and have them locate the hydroelectric projects.

The wealth of the forest Great softwood forests are one of Canada's most important natural resources. Lumber, pulp, and paper are some of the leading forest products. Canada produces more newsprint, the paper used for newspapers, than any other country. Lumbering has developed in areas that can be reached by land or water transportation. The island of Newfoundland is a major source of lumber and pulp. Lumber is also floated down the many rivers that flow from the Canadian Shield to the St. Lawrence River. Then the lumber is processed into pulp, paper, plywood, and other wood products at mills in Quebec. The United States and many European countries buy large amounts of Canadian pulp for their own paper industries.

CHECKUP

1. Canada is a leading source of many minerals. Name at least five of these minerals.
2. Where is most of Canada's petroleum found?
3. What are tar sands? Why might these sands be of great value one day?
4. What is Canada's chief source of power?

Population and Government

Indians and Inuit The native peoples of Canada are the Indians and the Inuit, or Eskimos. The Indians lived on the prairies and in the subarctic forest. The Inuit settled on the tundra along the Arctic Coast. Both groups lived mainly by hunting and fishing. The Indians hunted fox and deer and fished in the rivers and lakes. They gathered wild rice and berries. The Inuit hunted seals, walrus, and polar bears.

Today most of the Indians and the Inuit live in well-insulated houses in villages and towns. Some of them still hunt and fish for a living. Others work for oil companies and mining companies. Some work in transportation, and others work for the government. Of the 24 million people in Canada today, the Indians and the Inuit make up less than two percent of the country's population.

European ancestry   Most Canadians are descendants of people who came from Europe. Today, about 45 percent of Canada's people are of British descent. Early settlers from Great Britain built homes in what is now New Brunswick, Nova Scotia, Prince Edward Island, and Newfoundland. Some of the earliest English-speaking people to come to Canada were from the United States. When the American colonies gained their independence in the American Revolution, Great Britain kept control of Canada. After the American Revolution, some British settlers who had been living in the United States wanted to remain British citizens. Many of these people moved to Canada.

About 26 percent of Canada's people are of French descent. When French settlers began coming to Canada in the early 1600s, they built farms and villages in the St. Lawrence Valley. Most of Canada's more than 6 million French Canadians live in the province of Quebec.

During the 1800s, English, Irish, and Scottish people continued to settle in Canada. Beginning in the late 1800s, people began moving to Canada from other European countries. These new-

comers settled mostly in the new industrial cities and on the farmland of the prairies. Europeans continued to come to Canada until World War I began in 1914.

The next great wave of **immigration** came in the years after World War II. Immigration is the movement of people from one country to another country to live permanently. Between 1946 and 1961 about 2 million immigrants came to Canada from Europe. These people were German, Dutch, Italian, Polish, and Scandinavian. Their descendants and about 35,000 black people and over 150,000 Asians make up most of the rest of Canada's population today.

Independence and self-government   In 1867, Great Britain passed the British North America Act. It created a new government for Canada, which became known as the Dominion of Canada. Under this act, Canada was divided into provinces. In 1867 there were four provinces—New Brunswick, Nova Scotia, Ontario, and Quebec. The time line on page 86 shows when the other provinces and the two territories were added. In 1931, Canada became an independent and self-governing nation.

Canada, like the United States, has a **federal** form of government. This means that power is divided between the national government and the governments of the political units. In the United States these units are the states; in Canada they are the provinces and territories. The head of the government of Canada is the prime minister. However, Queen Elizabeth II of Great Britain is recognized as queen of Canada.

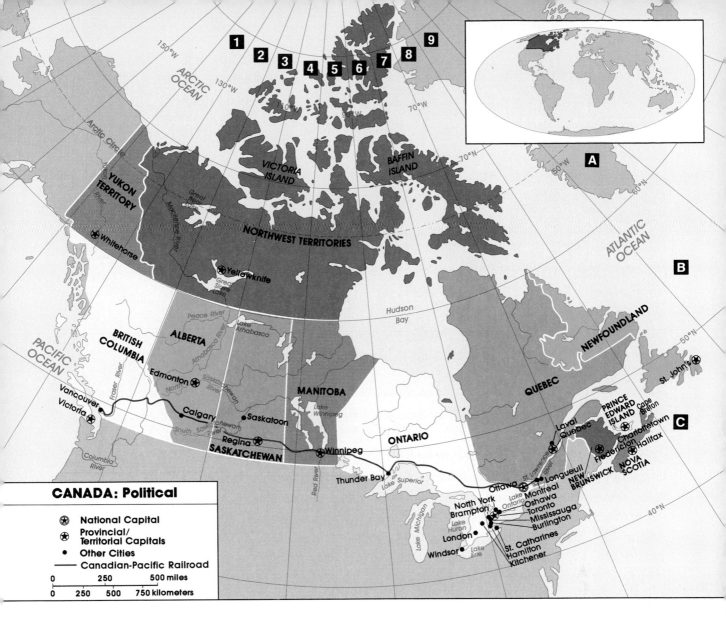

CANADA: Political

- ⊛ National Capital
- ⊛ Provincial/Territorial Capitals
- • Other Cities
- — Canadian-Pacific Railroad

```
0        250        500 miles
0    250     500   750 kilometers
```

Cities with less than 100,000

Charlottetown, P.E.I.	C-8
Fredericton, N.B.	C-8
St. John's, Newf.	C-9
Victoria, B.C.	C-2
Whitehorse, Y.T.	A-1
Yellowknife, N.W.T.	A-3

Cities with 100,000–499,000

Brampton, Ont.	C-7
Burlington, Ont.	C-7

Halifax, N.S.	C-8
Hamilton, Ont.	C-7
Kitchener, Ont.	C-6
Laval, Que.	C-7
London, Ont.	C-6
Longueuil, Que.	C-7
Mississauga, Ont.	C-7
Oshawa, Ont.	C-7
Ottawa	C-7
Quebec, Que.	C-7
Regina, Sask.	B-4
St. Catharines, Ont.	C-7

Saskatoon, Sask.	B-4
Thunder Bay, Ont.	C-6
Vancouver, B.C.	C-2
Windsor, Ont.	C-6

Cities with 500,000–999,000

Calgary, Alta.	B-3
Edmonton, Alta.	B-3
Montreal, Que.	C-7
North York, Ont.	C-7
Toronto, Ont.	C-7
Winnipeg, Man.	B-5

Most of Canada's cities and most of the people are in the southern part of the nation. Which cities have 500,000 or more people? Which capitals have less than 100,000 people?

At this point you may wish to provide pupils with extra practice in using grid coordinates.

Montreal, Quebec, located between the St. Lawrence River and Mount Royal, is the largest French-speaking city in the world after Paris. (47°N/90°W; map. p. 83)

Commonwealth The **Commonwealth** is made up of independent countries that were once ruled by Great Britain. The countries in the Commonwealth include Australia, New Zealand, and India, among others. The countries of the Commonwealth share their ideas on topics such as trade, education, food production, and health. The Commonwealth countries try to work together.

Have a pupil investigate what it means for a country to have two official languages.

Two languages There are two official languages in Canada—English and French. Although English is the language of most Canadians, French is the chief language in the province of Quebec, where most French Canadians live. Some French Canadians, called **Separatists,** want the province of Quebec to separate from Canada and become an independent country. The Separatists have different ideas about such things as business

dealings and the way to run the schools. They also have a different view of many of the laws that govern the country. Only a small number of French Canadians hold these views. In 1980 the people of Quebec voted against separating from the rest of the nation.

Despite the differences between the English-speaking and French-speaking peoples, Canada's future is very promising. As the resources of its provinces and territories continue to be developed, Canada's wealth and power will increase.

CHECKUP

1. Who are the native peoples of Canada? Where did they live? Where do they live today?
2. Of what descent are most Canadians?
3. Why did English-speaking people from the United States settle in Canada after the American Revolution?
4. What form of government does Canada have?
5. What is the Commonwealth?

Ask: Where else have you read about Separatists? (In United States history—the Pilgrims)

Ask a pupil to make a chart listing the members of the Commonwealth of Nations. The chart could be keyed to a world map.

KEY FACTS

1. Because of the cold climate in most of Canada, a major part of the population lives along the southern border of the country.

2. The Lakes Peninsula and the St. Lawrence Valley is the most densely populated region in Canada. It has the two largest cities, Montreal and Toronto, and much of the manufacturing industry.

3. Minerals, forests, and water are the most valuable resources of the Canadian Shield.

4. The Prairie Provinces are the rich wheat-growing lands of Canada.

5. Canada is a leading source of many minerals, including zinc, nickel, asbestos, iron ore, and pitchblende, the chief source of uranium.

6. Most Canadians are descendants of people who came from Europe. The native Canadians, the Indians and the Inuit, make up a very small percentage of the country's population.

7. Canada is an independent nation composed of ten provinces and two territories.

VOCABULARY QUIZ

Match these terms with their definitions. Write your answers on a sheet of paper.

a. province   f. immigration
b. lock   g. prairie
c. asbestos   h. radioactive
d. zinc   i. uranium
e. federal   j. alloy

g 1. A large area of level or rolling land with tall grass and fertile soil

d 2. A shiny, blue-white metal applied to other metals to prevent them from rusting

h 3. Giving off harmful rays

e 4. Having to do with a form of government in which power is divided between national government and the governments of the political units

f 5. The movement of people from one country to another country to live permanently

b 6. An enclosed area on a canal used for raising or lowering ships from one water level to another

j 7. A mixture of two or more metals

i 8. A metal found in pitchblende that is used to produce nuclear energy

c 9. A mineral that does not burn or conduct heat

a 10. A division of a country

REVIEW QUESTIONS

1. List the five regions of Canada and the provinces or territories that make up each region.

2. What effect has climate had on Canada's population?

3. On what three lakes is the Lakes Peninsula located?

4. Name Canada's longest river. What two bodies of water does this river connect?

5. In what way does Quebec differ from the other provinces of Canada?

ACTIVITIES

1. For one week collect newspaper articles about Canada. How many different topics are included in your articles? How many articles deal with problems? Is one problem mentioned more often than others?

2. Prepare a report on the Separatist movement in Canada. Tell why some French Canadians think the province of Quebec should become an independent country.

USING TIME LINES

PRACTICE IN THINKING ABOUT TIME

Making a time line is one way to organize historical information. On a time line, events are arranged in the order in which they happened. Events that happened longest ago are farthest left on most time lines. Events that happened closer to the present are farther right.

The time line on this page shows some events that are important in the history of Canada. The date or dates before an event state when it took place. Study the time line carefully. It gives you all the information you need to do the following exercise.

SKILLS PRACTICE

Use the information in the time line to decide if the statements below are true or false. Write your answers on a sheet of paper.

T **1.** The Dominion of Canada was established in 1867.

F **2.** Prince Edward Island joined the Dominion before British Columbia.

T **3.** The Northwest Territories became a part of Canada after the Yukon Territory.

T **4.** Alberta and Saskatchewan joined the Dominion in the same year.

T **5.** Newfoundland was the last province to be established in Canada.

T **6.** Canada became independent of Great Britain in 1931.

F **7.** Canada's independence from Great Britain came 75 years after the Dominion of Canada was formed.

T **8.** The building of the St. Lawrence Seaway took 5 years.

F **9.** The Canadian-Pacific Railroad and the Trans-Canada Highway were completed before the St. Lawrence Seaway.

T **10.** The most recent event in Canada's history, as shown on the time line, was the end of Britain's control over Canada's constitution.

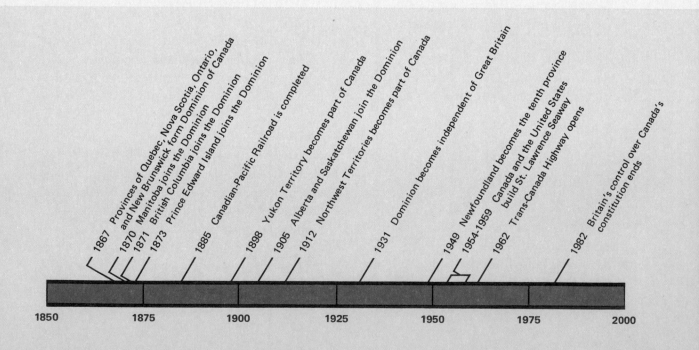

2/UNIT REVIEW

Answer Key in back of book.

READING THE TEXT

Turn to page 72 and read the section "A vast country." Then, on a sheet of paper, write the answers to these questions.

1. Why is Canada described as a "vast country"?

2. Which boundaries does Canada share with the United States?

3. What is the difference between a province and a territory in Canada?

4. In what ways are Canada and the United States alike?

5. What is one outstanding difference between Canada and the United States?

READING A MAP

Turn to page 68 and look at the map titled "The United States: Population Density and the 25 Largest Cities." When we speak of population density, we are referring to the average number of people per square mile or square kilometer in a certain area. The higher the average number of people per square mile or kilometer, the higher the population density.

On a sheet of paper, write the answers to these questions.

1. Do more people live in the eastern half of the country or in the western half? eastern

2. What is the population density of Denver as measured in persons per square mile? 50 to 100

3. Which of the following three cities has the highest population density? (a) Nashville, (b) Dallas, (c) Boston. Boston

4. Which of the 25 cities on the map has the lowest population density? Phoenix

5. What two things do Los Angeles and Philadelphia have in common?
   1. more than 1 million people
   2. population density above 500

READING A PICTURE

Turn to page 84 and study the picture of Montreal, Canada. Using the details that you see in the picture, answer the following questions on a sheet of paper.

1. Where is Montreal located? on a river

2. Is Montreal built around a mountain? yes

3. Does Montreal have a large harbor? yes

4. Is Montreal a center for business, trade, and transportation? yes

5. Is Montreal one of the largest cities in Canada? yes

Now write a paragraph describing Montreal to someone who has never seen a picture of Canada's largest city.

READING GRAPHS

Study the graphs on pages 58 and 80. Then answer these questions on a sheet of paper.

1. Which two countries are leading producers of both wheat and nickel? Canada and the Soviet Union

2. Approximately how much nickel does Canada produce, measured in short tons? 210,000

3. Which country produces about half as much wheat as the United States produces? India

4. Which country is the third leading producer of nickel in the world? New Caledonia

5. Does China produce more, or less, wheat than India? more

LATIN AMERICA

Prepare a guide for a "walking tour" through Latin America. Start at Tierra del Fuego or the Rio Grande and "walk" pupils through the geography as shown on the map. Have pupils locate landforms by country, by latitude and longitude, or any other means that you feel will capture their interest. Have them name rivers, mountains, highlands, and plains as they "cross" them.

A Long Region

In Unit 2 you learned about the Americans of the United States and Canada. Now you will learn about the over 300 million Americans who live in Latin America, the group of countries that lie south of the United States.

Latin America stretches about 6,000 miles (9,650 km) from about 30°N to about 55°S. This is as far as the distance between Texas and Antarctica.

The most northern country in Latin America is Mexico. Latin America also includes the whole continent of South America as well as the countries between Mexico and South America. The narrow strip of land between Mexico and South America is called Central America. The islands of the Caribbean Sea are part of Latin America, too.

A high mountain range runs most of the length of Latin America. The Andes of South America are a huge range of mountains. This mountain range is much higher and narrower than the ranges in the western part of the United States. Find the Andes on the map on the facing page.

The mountains continue north through most of Central America to Mexico. In Mexico they divide into two mountain ranges. One range goes along the east coast of Mexico; the other along the west coast.

Latin America also has lowlands. The lowlands of Latin America are hotter and wetter than the lowlands of Canada and

What are Mexico's two mountain ranges? Find the meaning of oriental and occidental in a dictionary. What mountain range runs almost the entire length of South America?

Sierra Madre Oriental and Sierra Madre Occidental. *Occidental* means "western"; *oriental,* "eastern." The Andes

120°W   110°W   100°W   90°W   80°W   70°W   60°W   50°W   40°W   30°W

UNITED STATES

Gulf of Mexico

ATLANTIC OCEAN

30°N

Tropic of Cancer

SIERRA MADRE OCCIDENTAL

SIERRA MADRE ORIENTAL

MEXICO

20°N

Nassau ★

BAHAMAS

Havana ★

CUBA

GREATER ANTILLES

DOMINICAN REPUBLIC

PUERTO RICO (U.S.)

VIRGIN IS. (U.S.)
VIRGIN IS. (U.K.)

BERMUDA (U.K.)

Mexico City ★

Yucatán Peninsula

Citlaltépetl
18,700 ft (5,700 m)

HAITI

Port-au-Prince ★

San Juan ★

Santo Domingo ★

Basseterre ★ **ST. CHRISTOPHER–NEVIS**
St. Johns ★ **ANTIGUA AND BARBUDA**

Belmopan ★

BELIZE

GUATEMALA

JAMAICA

Kingston ★

MONTSERRAT (U.K.)
GUADELOUPE (FR.) ★ Roseau
DOMINICA

HONDURAS

Tegucigalpa ★

Caribbean Sea

MARTINIQUE (FR.)
Castries ★ **ST. LUCIA**

Guatemala ★

San Salvador ★

EL SALVADOR

NICARAGUA

NETHERLANDS ANTILLES

Kingstown ★ **ST. VINCENT AND THE GRENADINES**
★ **BARBADOS**

LESSER ANTILLES

10°N

Managua ★

ARUBA (NETH.)

CURAÇAO (NETH.)
★Bridgetown

San Jose ★

COSTA RICA

Panama ★

St. George's ★ **GRENADA**

Caracas ★

★ **TRINIDAD AND TOBAGO**
Port of Spain ★

PACIFIC OCEAN

PANAMA

Maracaibo

Orinoco River

GUYANA

Georgetown ★

LLANOS

VENEZUELA

Paramaribo ★

SURINAM

• Cayenne

Bogota ★

FRENCH GUIANA

Tolima
18,425 ft (5,616 m)

GUIANA HIGHLANDS

COLOMBIA

0°

Equator

Magdalena River

Quito ★

Cotopaxi
19,347 ft (5,897 m)

ECUADOR ▲

Chimborazo
20,561 ft (6,168 m)

Amazon River

ANDES

PERU

Huascarán
22,205 ft (6,768 m)

BRAZIL

10°S

Lima •

BRAZILIAN HIGHLANDS

BOLIVIA

La Paz ★

Lake Titicaca

Sucre ★

★ Brasilia

Lake Poopó

20°S

Tropic of Capricorn

CHACO

PARAGUAY

Asunción ★

Río Salado

CHILE

Aconcagua
22,834 ft (6,960 m)

ARGENTINA

Santiago ★

Uruguay River

URUGUAY

30°S

PAMPAS

Buenos Aires ★

Montevideo •

Colorado River

ANDES

40°S

PATAGONIA

LATIN AMERICA: Physical

★ National Capitals

• Other Cities

TIERRA DEL FUEGO

FALKLAND IS. (U.K.)

50°S

0   500   1,000 miles

0   500   1,000   1,500 kilometers

SOUTH GEORGIA (U.K.)

60°S

the United States. This is because much of Latin America lies close to the Equator.

The lowlands in parts of Latin America are very hot and often very wet. Thick tropical rain forests grow here. Latin America has one of the most famous rain forests in the world—the Amazon rain forest.

The Amazon River is one of the most important in the world. The river starts in the Andes Mountains and flows across the South American continent into the Atlantic Ocean. The Amazon and its many tributaries drain a land area of over 2,375,000 square miles (6,150,000 sq km).

A Land of Contrasts

The map on the facing page shows that Latin America is a region of many countries. Some, like Brazil and Mexico, are large, and some, like El Salvador and Haiti, are small. Most of these countries have things in common. Latin America today, however, is also a land of great contrasts.

Latin America is a land of old cultures and empires. The early farmers were the first people in the world to grow potatoes, corn, and tomatoes. These first farmers often were part of great empires. The largest empires were the Aztec in northern Latin America and the Inca in southern Latin America.

Some people still live the very old lifestyle of the early Indians. Others work in some of the most modern and newest cities in the world. Four of the largest cities in the world—Mexico City, São Paulo, Rio de Janeiro, and Lima—are in Latin America. Many people in the cities have good jobs and enough money to spend on books, cars, and vacations. Other people, however, are not able to find jobs that will give them enough money for a diet of bread and vegetables. One of the main problems facing the Latin American region today is that there is not enough work for the people seeking jobs.

One of the largest and richest nations in Latin America is Mexico. Mexico, the countries of Central America, and the is-

Cities less than 100,000

Basse-Terre (Guadeloupe)	C-6
Basseterre (St. Christopher-Nevis)	C-6
Belmopan (Belize)	C-4
Bridgetown (Barbados)	C-7
Castries (St. Lucia)	C-6
Charlotte Amalie (Virgin Islands)	C-6
Fort-de-France (Martinique)	C-6
Hamilton (Bermuda)	A-6
Kingstown (St. Vincent)	C-6
Plymouth (Montserrat)	C-6
Port of Spain (Trinidad and Tobago)	D-6
Road Town (British Virgin Islands)	C-6
Roseau (Dominica)	C-6
St. George's (Grenada)	C-6
St. Johns (Antigua)	C-6
Sucre (Bolivia)	F-6
Willemstad (Netherlands Antilles)	C-6

Cities 100,000-499,999

Brasilia (Brazil)	F-8
Georgetown (Guyana)	D-7
Kingston (Jamaica)	C-5

Nassau (Bahamas)	B-5
Panama (Panama)	D-5
Paramaribo (Surinam)	D-7
Port-au-Prince (Haiti)	C-5
San José (Costa Rica)	D-4
San Juan (Puerto Rico)	C-6
San Salvador (El Salvador)	C-4
Tegucigalpa (Honduras)	C-4

Cities 500,000-999,999

Asunción (Paraguay)	G-7
Barranquilla (Colombia)	C-5
Belém (Brazil)	E-8
Cali (Colombia)	D-5
Cuidad Juárez (Mexico)	A-2
Cordoba (Argentina)	H-6
Curitiba (Brazil)	G-8
Fortaleza (Brazil)	E-9
Guatemala (Guatemala)	C-3
Guayaquil (Ecuador)	E-5
La Paz (Bolivia)	F-6
León (Mexico)	B-2
Managua (Nicaragua)	C-4
Maracaibo (Venezuela)	C-5

Netzahualcóyotl (Mexico)	C-3
Nova Iguaçu (Brazil)	G-8
Pôrto Alegre (Brazil)	G-7
Quito (Ecuador)	E-5
Rosario (Argentina)	H-6
Santo Domingo (Dominican Republic)	C-6

Cities 1,000,000 or more

Belo Horizonte (Brazil)	F-8
Bogotá (Colombia)	D-5
Buenos Aires (Argentina)	H-7
Caracas (Venezuela)	C-6
Guadalajara (Mexico)	B-2
Havana (Cuba)	B-4
Lima (Peru)	F-5
Medellin (Colombia)	D-5
Mexico City (Mexico)	C-3
Monterrey (Mexico)	B-2
Montevideo (Uruguay)	H-7
Recife (Brazil)	E-9
Rio de Janeiro (Brazil)	G-8
Salvador (Brazil)	F-9
Santiago (Chile)	H-5
São Paulo (Brazil)	G-8

Latin America includes all the countries in the Western Hemisphere from Mexico to the tip of the South American continent. The population of all of Latin America is more than 375 million. Which nation has five cities with 1,000,000 or more people?

No other river has a larger drainage area than the Amazon.

LATIN AMERICA: Political

- ⊛ National Capitals
- ★ Other Capitals
- ● Other Cities

0   500   1,000 miles

0   500   1,000   1,500 kilometers

1   2   3   4   5   6   7   8   9

120°W 110°W 100°W 90°W 80°W 70°W 60°W 50°W 40°W 30°W

A   B   C   D   E   F   G   H   I

UNITED STATES

Ciudad Juárez

Gulf of Mexico

Hamilton ★ BERMUDA (U.K.)

ATLANTIC OCEAN

Tropic of Cancer

SIERRA MADRE OCCIDENTAL

SIERRA MADRE ORIENTAL

Monterrey

MEXICO

Guadalajara   León

Mexico City

Netzahualcóyotl

Yucatán Peninsula

BAHAMAS

Nassau

Havana

CUBA

GREATER ANTILLES

DOMINICAN REPUBLIC

PUERTO RICO (U.S.)
VIRGIN IS. (U.S.)
VIRGIN IS. (U.K.)
Road Town

BELIZE

Belmopan

GUATEMALA

Guatemala

HONDURAS

Tegucigalpa

San Salvador

EL SALVADOR

NICARAGUA

Managua

HAITI

Port-au-Prince

Santo Domingo

San Juan

Charlotte Amalie (US, VI)

ANTIGUA AND BARBUDA

Basseterre   St. John's

ST. CHRISTOPHER—NEVIS

Plymouth

MONTSERRAT (U.K.)

Basse-Terre

GUADELOUPE (FR.)

Roseau

DOMINICA

Fort-de-France

MARTINIQUE (FR.)

Castries

ST. LUCIA

BARBADOS

Bridgetown

ST. VINCENT AND THE GRENADINES

Kingstown

GRENADA

St. George's

LESSER ANTILLES

JAMAICA

Kingston

Caribbean Sea

NETHERLANDS ANTILLES

CURAÇAO (NETH.)

Willemstad

ARUBA (NETH.)

Maracaibo

Barranquilla

Managua

San José

COSTA RICA

Panama

PANAMA

Medellín

Cali

Bogotá

COLOMBIA

Lake Maracaibo

Caracas

VENEZUELA

Orinoco River

TRINIDAD AND TOBAGO

Port of Spain

GUYANA

Georgetown

Paramaribo

SURINAM

Cayenne

FRENCH GUIANA

GUIANA HIGHLANDS

PACIFIC OCEAN

Equator

Quito

ECUADOR

Guayaquil

Belém

Amazon River

PERU

ANDES

Lima

Lake Titicaca

BOLIVIA

La Paz

Sucre

Lake Poopó

BRAZIL

BRAZILIAN HIGHLANDS

São Francisco River

Fortaleza

Recife

Salvador

Brasília

Belo Horizonte

Nova Iguaçu

São Paulo

Rio de Janeiro

Curitiba

Tropic of Capricorn

Atacama Desert

CHACO

PARAGUAY

Asunción

Paraguay River

CHILE

ANDES

Rio Salado

Paraná River

Uruguay River

ARGENTINA

Córdoba

Rosario

PAMPAS

Santiago

Buenos Aires

URUGUAY

Montevideo

Porto Alegre

Rio de la Plata

Colorado River

PATAGONIA

FALKLAND IS. (U.K.)

TIERRA DEL FUEGO

S. GEORGIA (U.K.)

30°N 20°N 10°N 0° 10°S 20°S 30°S 40°S 50°S 60°S

Rio Grande

lands of the Caribbean Sea are all part of what we call Middle America. There are 13 countries on the continent of South America. The two largest South American countries are Brazil and Argentina.

The countries of Latin America all share one experience. For some time they were ruled by countries far away in Europe. This colonization by Europeans is very important to the history of Latin America. Most of the Latin American countries today combine the cultures of native peoples and of the European colonizers. Most of Latin America was colonized by Spain. Spanish is spoken by most Latin Americans. The Spanish language developed from Latin. This is one reason why we call this region Latin America.

People of other areas have also come to Latin America. There are black people of African ancestry; white people from other European countries; and Asian people from Japan and China.

This diagram shows the elevations of the climate zones in Latin America. Land below the mountain peaks and above tierra fría is used mainly for grazing.

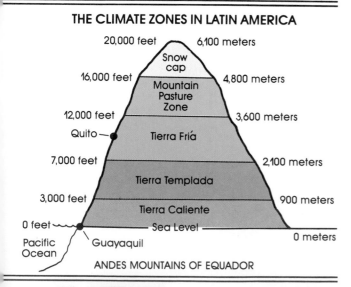

THE CLIMATE ZONES IN LATIN AMERICA

ANDES MOUNTAINS OF EQUADOR

A Region of Many Climates

Latin America has all types of climates. Except for the highland areas, most places near the Equator are warm, even hot, during all months of the year. We call this kind of climate tropical.

We use words from the Spanish language for the names of the three climate zones that are found in the tropical lowlands of Latin America. These zones are the tierra (tyer′ ə) caliente (ka lyen′ tə), the tierra templada (tem′ plä də), and the tierra fría (frē ə). Find them in the diagram on this page.

Tierra means "land." *Caliente* means "hot" or "warm." The tierra caliente is the zone of hot or warm land in Latin America. In this zone the weather is warm all year long. Usually it rains, in general about once a day, all year long. The hot, moist weather is ideal for growing bananas and sugarcane, two of the main crops of Central America and the islands of the Caribbean Sea.

Farther up the mountain slope is a climate zone called the tierra templada. *Templada* means "temperate," or "mild." The temperatures of the temperate lands are something like spring temperatures in the United States. It is not hot, but it usually is not cool enough for a sweater, except perhaps at night. The temperature is average, and so is the rainfall. Corn grows well in this climate, and so does coffee.

The tierra fría is a colder land. Toward the higher parts of this climate zone it is so cold that sometimes it is hard to find crops that will grow. Farmers are most likely to grow potatoes or to raise sheep.

Have pupils describe the climate zones of Latin America. Ask: In what ways might life in Guayaquil differ from life in Quito? (Pupils should mention the differences in climate and agriculture.)

LATIN AMERICA

COUNTRY	FLAG	TOTAL AREA	POPULATION and POPULATION DENSITY	CAPITAL CITY and POPULATION	WHERE PEOPLE LIVE
Antigua and Barbuda		171 sq mi (442 sq km)	100,000 585 per sq mi (226 per sq km)	St Johns 22,000	
Argentina		1,072,067 sq mi (2,776,654 sq km)	29,100,000 27 per sq mi (10 per sq km)	Buenos Aires 2,908,000	
Bahamas		5,380 sq mi (13,934 sq km)	200,000 37 per sq mi (14 per sq km)	Nassau 101,500	
Barbados		166 sq mi (431 sq km)	300,000 1,807 per sq mi (696 per sq km)	Bridgetown 9,000	
Belize		8,867 sq mi (22,965 sq km)	200,000 23 per sq mi (9 per sq km)	Belmopan 3,000	
Bolivia		424,162 sq mi (1,098,581 sq km)	5,900,000 14 per sq mi (5 per sq km)	La Paz 654,500 and Sucre 63,500	
Brazil		3,286,470 sq mi (8,511,957 sq km)	131,300,000 40 per sq mi (15 per sq km)	Brasília 272,000	
Chile		286,396 sq mi (741,766 sq km)	11,500,000 40 per sq mi (16 per sq km)	Santiago 3,448,500	
Colombia		455,355 sq mi (1,179,369 sq km)	27,700,000 61 per sq mi (23 per sq km)	Bogotá 4,294,000	
Costa Rica		19,653 sq mi (50,901 sq km)	2,400,000 122 per sq mi (47 per sq km)	San José 259,000	
Cuba		44,218 sq mi (114,524 sq km)	9,800,000 222 per sq mi (86 per sq km)	Havana 1,925,000	
Dominica		290 sq mi (751 sq km)	100,000 345 per sq mi (133 per sq km)	Roseau 18,000	

Urban ▆ Nonurban ▆ Not Available – ▆   **93**

Be sure pupils understand the terms *urban* and *nonurban*. Discuss possible reasons why information about where people live is not available. (No census taken; small populations; isolated areas; and so on)

LATIN AMERICA

COUNTRY	FLAG	TOTAL AREA	POPULATION and POPULATION DENSITY	CAPITAL CITY and POPULATION	WHERE PEOPLE LIVE
Dominican Republic		18,704 sq mi (48,443 sq km)	6,200,000 331 per sq mi (128 per sq km)	Santo Domingo 1,318,000	
Ecuador		105,685 sq mi (273,724 sq km)	8,800,000 83 per sq mi (32 per sq km)	Quito 743,000	
El Salvador		8,124 sq mi (21,041 sq km)	4,700,000 579 per sq mi (223 per sq km)	San Salvador 406,500	
French Guiana		35,135 sq mi (91,000 sq km)	67,000 2 per sq mi (1 per sq km)	Cayenne 34,000	
Grenada		133 sq mi (344 sq km)	100,000 752 per sq mi (291 per sq km)	St. George's 27,000	
Guatemala		42,042 sq mi (108,889 sq km)	7,900,000 188 per sq mi (73 per sq km)	Guatemala City 836,000	
Guyana		83,000 sq mi (214,969 sq km)	800,000 10 per sq mi (4 per sq km)	Georgetown 187,500	
Haiti		10,714 sq mi (27,750 sq km)	5,700,000 532 per sq mi (205 per sq km)	Port-au-Prince 306,000	
Honduras		43,277 sq mi (112,088 sq km)	4,100,000 95 per sq mi (37 per sq km)	Tegucigalpa 274,000	
Jamaica		4,244 sq mi (10,991 sq km)	2,300,000 542 per sq mi (209 per sq km)	Kingston 112,000	
Mexico		761,601 sq mi (1,972,547 sq km)	75,700,000 99 per sq mi (38 per sq km)	Mexico City 8,988,000	
Nicaragua		57,143 sq mi (148,000 sq km)	2,800,000 49 per sq mi (19 per sq km)	Managua 623,000	

94

Urban ▣   Nonurban ▣   Not Available – ▣

Ask specific questions that require pupils to read the Table of Countries. For example, ask: Which country has more people per square mile, the Dominican Republic or Mexico? (Dominican Republic)

LATIN AMERICA

COUNTRY	FLAG	TOTAL AREA	POPULATION and POPULATION DENSITY	CAPITAL CITY and POPULATION	WHERE PEOPLE LIVE
Panama		29,306 sq mi (75,903 sq km)	2,100,000 72 per sq mi (28 per sq km)	Panama City 460,000	
Paraguay		157,047 sq mi (406,752 sq km)	3,500,000 22 per sq mi (9 per sq km)	Asunción 513,500	
Peru		496,222 sq mi (1,285,216 sq km)	19,200,000 39 per sq mi (15 per sq km)	Lima 2,862,000	
Puerto Rico		3,435 sq mi (8,897 sq km)	3,400,000 990 per sq mi (382 per sq km)	San Juan 433,000	
St. Christopher-Nevis		104 sq mi (261 sq km)	60,000 577 per sq mi (230 per sq km)	Basseterre 15,500	
St. Lucia		238 sq mi (616 sq km)	100,000 420 per sq mi (162 per sq km)	Castries 17,500	
St. Vincent and the Grenadines		150 sq mi (388 sq km)	100,000 667 per sq mi (257 per sq km)	Kingstown 22,000	
Surinam		63,251 sq mi (163,820 sq km)	400,000 6 per sq mi (2 per sq km)	Paramaribo 151,500	
Trinidad and Tobago		1,980 sq mi (5,128 sq km)	1,200,000 606 per sq mi (234 per sq km)	Port of Spain 62,500	
Uruguay		68,548 sq mi (177,539 sq km)	3,000,000 44 per sq mi (17 per sq km)	Montevideo 1,238,500	
Venezuela		352,143 sq mi (912,050 sq km)	18,000,000 51 per sq mi (20 per sq km)	Caracas 1,754,500	

Urban ▮ Nonurban ▮ Not Available – ▮

95

Have pupils make a variety of graphs using information from the table: 5 largest (smallest) countries in area; 5 largest (smallest) countries in population; 5 countries with greatest (smallest) population density.

Landscapes and Resources

> **VOCABULARY**
>
> import   developing
> export   country
>   rain shadow

A bridge between two worlds   Mexico is part of the continent of North America. In many ways, Mexico is a bridge between English-speaking America and Latin America. To the north of Mexico is the United States. Many Mexicans live in the United States. There are also many people from the United States who live in Mexico.

Mexico and the United States exchange products as well as people. Mexico trades more with the United States than with any other country. In 1980 over 65 percent of the products Mexico bought from other countries came from the United States. The products one country buys from another are **imports**. Over 60 percent of the products Mexico sold to other countries were bought by the United States. The products sold by one country to another are **exports**. You will learn about some of the products Mexico sells to the United States later in this chapter.

Mexico is one of the richest countries in Latin America. Life has become easier for many Mexicans in recent years. Most people have decent food, clothing, and shelter. There are doctors and hospitals to care for the sick. There are enough schools to educate most of the children. It has not always been this way. For many years, Mexico was a **developing country**. A developing country is one that is not highly industrialized. It is a country whose wealth is in the hands of only a few and in which there are many poor people. Most of the countries in Latin America are still developing countries. Today, Mexico is a leading country of both Latin America and the world.

The countries of English-speaking America are rich nations. Most countries of Latin America are poor nations. Mexico is somewhere between. In this way, too, Mexico bridges two worlds.

Location and shape   Mexico is a good place for world trade because it lies between two oceans. Except for two peninsulas most of the country is shaped like a long cone. One peninsula is Baja (bä′ hä) California on the west. Baja California is long and narrow. It hangs south of California like a string bean. *Baja California* means "lower California" in Spanish.

The other peninsula is the piece of land that sticks into the Caribbean Sea from the southern coast of Mexico. It is called

Aztec ruins, a colonial church, and modern buildings are symbols of Mexico's past and present. This plaza is in Mexico City. (19°N/99°W; map, p. 91)

This plaza is called *Plaza de las Tres Culturas*—the Plaza of the Three Cultures.

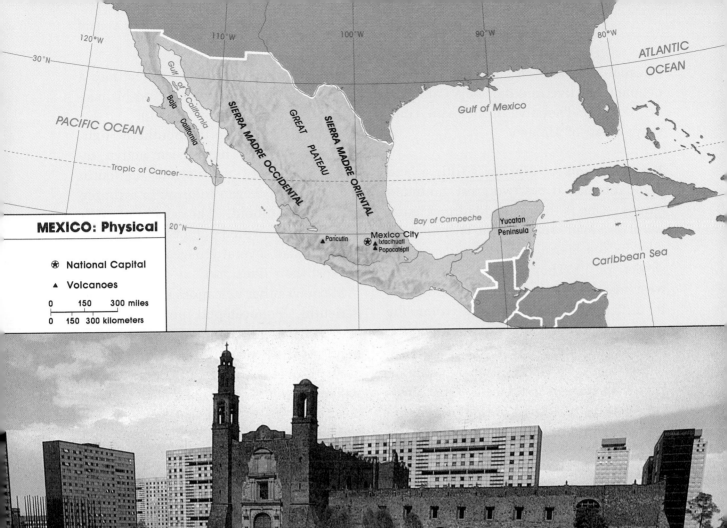

PACIFIC OCEAN

Gulf of California

Baja California

SIERRA MADRE OCCIDENTAL

GREAT PLATEAU

SIERRA MADRE ORIENTAL

Gulf of Mexico

ATLANTIC OCEAN

Tropic of Cancer

Bay of Campeche

Yucatán Peninsula

Caribbean Sea

Paricutín

Mexico City
Ixtacihuatl
Popocatéptl

⊛ National Capital

▲ Volcanoes

0   150   300 miles

0   150   300 kilometers

Yucatán (yü kə tan′). Most Mexican people don't live in either Baja California or Yucatán. They live in the main, cone-shaped part of Mexico.

A rugged land   Mexico is truly a land of mountains. It has two great mountain ranges. One is the Sierra Madre Oriental (sē er′ ə mäd′ rē ōr ē en täl′) and the other is the Sierra Madre Occidental (äk sə den täl′). They follow the east and west coastlines. These long ranges make it difficult to travel inland from the oceans. Find the mountain ranges on the map on page 89.

Between Mexico's two mountain ranges is the Great Plateau. The Mexicans call the main part of this plateau the Mesa Central. *Mesa* is the Spanish word for "table."

The Great Plateau of Mexico is high enough that its climate is fairly cold. It is also dry. Since the plateau is between the Sierra mountains, it is not easy to go from one coast to the other. The mountains make it expensive to build roads and railroads.

The mountains are even more of a problem in southern Mexico. The Sierra Madre Oriental and the Sierra Madre Occidental meet in the Southern Highlands. The mountains here are much more difficult to cross. They are higher and there are many more of them.

Smoking mountains   Many mountains in Mexico are old volcanoes. When the fire, smoke, and melted rock are still making the volcano, it is active. When things cool down and the volcano is no longer active, it becomes an ordinary mountain, but a high one. Sometimes a volcano will, after a long period of inactivity, become active once again.

Some volcanoes in the Southern Highlands of Mexico have been active recently. In 1943 the volcano Parícutin (pə rē′ kə tēn) began to grow in a simple mountain cornfield. The ashes and melted rock soon covered up not only the cornfield but also several villages. Some people lost their lives, too.

Mexico's other volcanoes are older than Parícutin. Popocatépetl (pō pə kat′ ə pet əl), the "smoking mountain," and Ixtaci-huatl (ēs tä sē′ wät əl), the "white lady," are both over 17,000 feet (5181 m) above sea level. Some of the old volcanoes have been quiet for so long that farmers have started growing crops on their steeply sloped sides.

Not many rivers   If Mexico had many rivers, travel within the country would be easier. But Mexico has only a few rivers and they do not flow through heavily populated areas.

The best known river is the Rio Grande. This river separates the United States and Mexico. Most of the travel is across the river rather than down the river to the sea. Can you find the Rio Grande on the map on page 89?

Have pupils review the diagram on p. 92.

Many different climates   Mexico has many types of climates because it lies in the tropics and yet has high mountains. The lowlands in the tropics are in the region called the tierra caliente. The mountaintops are very cold. In the highest mountains, there is snow on the ground all year.

Discuss with pupils the cost of building and maintaining railroads and highways. Ask: What are the needs of a developing country? (Schools, transportation, health care, and so forth.) Discuss the difficulty of meeting all these needs at the same time.

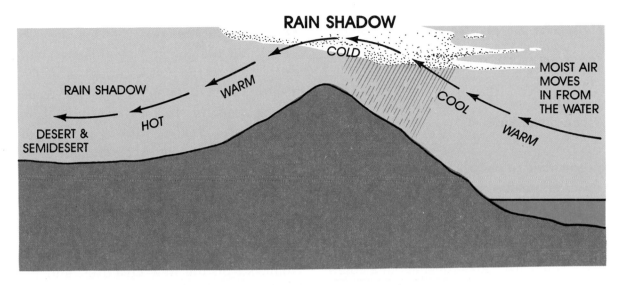

RAIN SHADOW

COLD

RAIN SHADOW

WARM

HOT

DESERT &
SEMIDESERT

COOL

MOIST AIR
MOVES
IN FROM
THE WATER

WARM

The winds have lost most of their moisture by the time they pass over the mountains.
Have pupils locate these climate areas on a display map as they are being discussed in class.

Most of the land in Mexico is so dry that good farming is possible only when the land is irrigated. Water for irrigation comes from rivers or lakes. But Mexico does not have enough rivers and lakes in the right places to irrigate all the dry land.

The lowland areas near the eastern coast do get rain. The trade winds that blow onto Mexico from the Caribbean Sea carry moisture with them. When the winds hit the Sierra Madre Oriental and the Southern Highlands, the moist air rises. The air cools as it rises. As the winds blow over the mountains from the east, they lose most of their moisture. The rain falls on the eastern side of the mountains. This creates rich farmland. On the southern part of the coast, which is closest to the Equator, tropical rain forests have developed. Here the rains are heavy for many months of the year.

The western coast of Mexico, on the other hand, is dry. In fact, the driest parts of Mexico are in the north and the west. This is because the air from the trade winds has very little moisture left to offer

as rain by the time it passes over the Sierra mountains. These lands are said to be in a **rain shadow**. The mountains shut out the rain just as a building shuts out the sun and causes a shadow.

The Great Plateau, especially in the north, is quite dry. In many places it is a desert. Few people live here, and there is little farming. Most of Baja California is a desert. Another large desert is the Sonora Desert in northwestern Mexico.

Mexico has deserts, frozen highlands, and tropical rain forests. Most of the rest of the country is cool rather than cold. This is the region called the tierra templada. There is enough rainfall here to allow people to grow crops. Most Mexicans live in this region.

CHECKUP

1. Why can Mexico be called a bridge between English-speaking America and Latin America?
2. Where are Mexico's two main mountain ranges? What are their names?
3. What is the area between the mountain ranges called?
4. Which coast of Mexico gets the most rain? Why?

99

People and Places

VOCABULARY

culture
civilization
conquistadores

mestizo
adobe

Importance of culture It is said that a country's greatest resource is its people. If that is true, then Mexico is very rich indeed. It ranks tenth in the world in population today.

We can learn a great deal about a country by studying its people and their way of life, or their **culture.** This is true for all countries, but it is even more so for Mexico, where several cultures have blended.

Early Indian civilizations The first people who lived in what is now Mexico were Indians. They came to Mexico about 10,000 B.C. Long before they had any contact with Europeans, the Indians built great cities. Rich farmlands surrounded these cities, and Indian farmers grew enough food to feed the city people.

In the cities there were great temples and other public buildings. There were warehouses and schools, beautiful palaces for the rich and simple housing for the poor. City dwellers did many different kinds of work. Some made fine ornaments from crystal and metal. Others studied science and mathematics, and kept records of their discoveries in books. All of these are signs of a **civilization.** Two of the most important early Indian civilizations are the Maya (mä' yə) of the Yucatán and the Aztec (az' tek) of central Mexico.

The Spanish conquest One day, in A.D. 1519, traders and soldiers brought news back to the Aztec capital city, Tenochtitlán (tä näch tē tlän'), that some strange creatures had arrived by boat on the eastern coast of Mexico. Some of these creatures were people, although they were strange-looking and spoke a language that no one understood. They had other creatures with them that had four legs; strange, hard feet; and swishing tails. They were huge! The odd people would sit on the new creatures, and together they could travel faster than even the swiftest soldier could run.

These strange people were **conquistadores** (kon kēs tə dor' ēs), soldiers from Spain, a country in Europe. *Conquistadores* means "conquerors." They had beards and pale skin. They spoke Span-

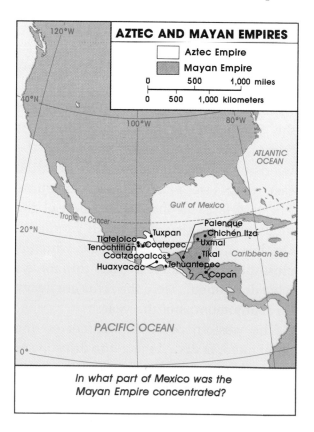

AZTEC AND MAYAN EMPIRES

☐ Aztec Empire
▓ Mayan Empire

0   500   1,000 miles
0   500   1,000 kilometers

ATLANTIC OCEAN

Gulf of Mexico

Tropic of Cancer

Palenque
Chichén Itzá
Tuxpan
Tlatelolco
Tenochtitlán
Coatepec
Uxmal
Coatzacoalcos
Tikal   Caribbean Sea
Tehuantepec
Huaxyacac
Copán

PACIFIC OCEAN

In what part of Mexico was the Mayan Empire concentrated?

Emphasize that Mexican culture is a blend of Indian and European, especially Spanish, cultures.

ish. They brought horses with them. The horse was an animal the Aztecs had never seen before. The conquistadores also brought gunpowder, steel swords, cannons, and armor. They had come to fight and to stay. The Spanish culture became the second important culture in Mexico.

The Spanish had several reasons for coming to the Americas, which they called the New World. One was a spirit of adventure. Another was the desire for new land. To the Spanish, land was wealth. There was not enough good farmland in Spain. The conquistadores saw the fine farms run by the Aztecs. This was land that was already organized for crops. A third reason was the desire for mineral wealth. The Spanish had never seen such gold and silver! Furthermore, the powerful Aztecs already had large numbers of workers trained to work in the mines.

The Spanish decided to replace the Aztec rulers with their own. Since they had horses, superior weapons, and a person helping them who spoke the Aztec language, the Spanish quickly took over. By the early 1520s, they had captured Tenochtitlán. They destroyed the capital and built a new one in its place. Later the capital was named Mexico City.

When Hernando Cortes and the conquistadores came, there were 25 million Indians in Mexico. Many died from sicknesses they caught from the Spanish. Others were killed in battle. Others died because they had little food and the Spanish made them work too hard. After 100 years of Spanish rule, only 3 million Indians were left.

Malinche: A Woman of Two Worlds

ONE OF THE MOST FAMOUS WOMEN in Mexican history is known by two names. The woman who helped Cortes defeat the Aztec nation is known as Malinche to people of Indian heritage. To those of Spanish heritage, she is Doña Marina. To one people, she is a betrayer, almost a traitor. To the other, she is a hero.

Malinche was born an Aztec princess. When her father died, her mother remarried and began a new family. So that her new son could have the family title and riches, Malinche's mother sold her into slavery. Malinche was a slave to a Mayan-speaking group on the east coast of Mexico when Cortes landed there in 1519.

Although he had an interpreter who spoke Mayan, Cortes had no knowledge of Nahuatl, the Aztec language. He also was ignorant of the customs of the Aztecs. As a speaker of both Nahuatl and Mayan, and as one who had been raised in the Aztec court, Malinche became Cortes's interpreter and adviser. She learned Spanish quickly and worked with Cortes in deciding how to deal with the Aztecs. Spanish writers have called her the brains behind the capture of Tenochtitlán. She headed off several attempts to unseat Cortes once he was in power. The Spanish called her Doña as a mark of respect. She became a rich landowner after the conquest and never again had to worry about being a slave.

Portraits of historical figures often present a problem. Sometimes the only available portraits are ones that were done long after the subject's death. The drawing above is a modern representation of Malinche. No one today knows what she really looked like.

Present-day Mexicans Most Mexicans today have ancestors who were Europeans and ancestors who were Indians. People of this mixed ancestry are called **mestizos** (mes tē′ zōz). The mestizo population has a culture that is both Spanish and Indian. Although most of the mestizos speak Spanish, they take pride in their Indian history. About 90 percent of the people who live in Mexico are mestizos.

Mexico still has some Indian groups. They are the groups the Spanish left alone. They live high in the mountains, especially in southern Mexico. Others live in the lowland jungles of the Yucatán Peninsula. All in all, Indians make up less than 10 percent of Mexico's population. Many of them speak Mayan or Nahuatl (nä′ wä təl), the ancient language of the Aztecs.

There are several other groups of people in Mexico, who together form a small percentage of the population. There are blacks, many of them descendants of Africans who were first brought to work as slaves in the fields. There are Europeans and Americans who came to Mexico on business or for vacation and have stayed to live. There are also older Americans who wanted to live in a pleasant climate after they retired.

It is probable that by 1985 there will be about 85 million people in Mexico. This number is twice the population of 25 years ago. One reason for the rapid population growth is the high birthrate in Mexico. Most Mexicans today are under 20 years of age. There are signs, however, that the rate of growth is beginning to slow down.

Where Mexicans live Most of the Mexican people live in the Great Plateau. The two largest cities of Mexico, Mexico City and Guadalajara (gwäd ə lə här′ ə), are on the Great Plateau.

There are also many small farms in this area. Farming is good here because there is rich soil and generally enough rainfall to grow a variety of crops. The Great Plateau was once the home of the Aztecs and it has remained the heartland of the country.

Fewer people live in northern Mexico. Here the land is too dry for farming, except in places where there is irrigation. There are cities along the border with the United States. Two of these are Ciudad Juárez (sē ü dad′ (h)wär′ ez), just south of Texas, and Tijuana (tē ə wän′ ə), just south of California. The Rio Grande supplies them with water, and there are jobs for people in factories or offices. Some people work in shops that are visited by people from the United States. Another important city is Monterrey. This industrial city is often called the Pittsburgh of Mexico.

Still other Mexicans live along the coast of the Gulf of Mexico. The cities of Tampico and Veracruz are important ports. It is here that the products that Mexico exports to other countries around the world leave the country. Many imports to Mexico also come through these port cities. The farmland of the Gulf region includes the lowlands of the Gulf states and the Yucatán Peninsula. Much of the land that lies in the lowlands of the Gulf Coast is too wet for farming. There are forests in this area, however, that provide work in the lumber industry.

Ask: What are some synonyms for *heartland*? Does *center of the country* mean the same thing? Does the United States have a heartland similar to Mexico's?

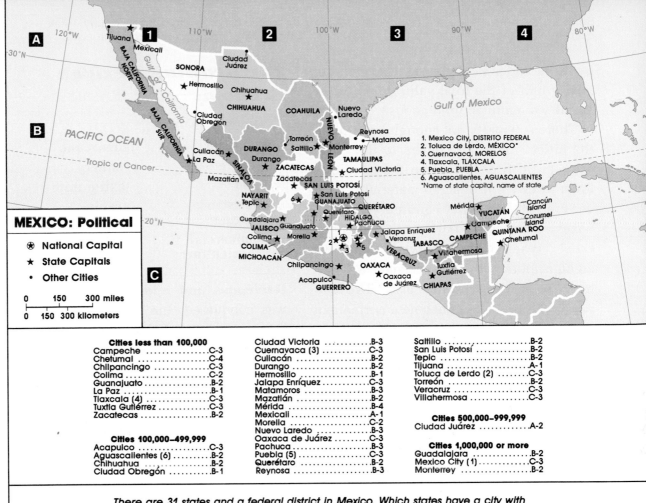

MEXICO: Political

- ⊛ National Capital
- ★ State Capitals
- • Other Cities

0   150   300 miles
0   150   300 kilometers

1. Mexico City, DISTRITO FEDERAL
2. Toluca de Lerdo, MÉXICO*
3. Cuernavaca, MORELOS
4. Tlaxcala, TLAXCALA
5. Puebla, PUEBLA
6. Aguascalientes, AGUASCALIENTES
*Name of state capital, name of state

Cities less than 100,000

Campeche	C-3
Chetumal	C-4
Chilpancingo	C-3
Colima	C-2
Guanajuato	B-2
La Paz	B-1
Tlaxcala (4)	C-3
Tuxtla Gutiérrez	C-3
Zacatecas	B-2

Cities 100,000–499,999

Acapulco	C-3
Aguascalientes (6)	B-2
Chihuahua	B-2
Ciudad Obregón	B-1

Ciudad Victoria	B-3
Cuernavaca (3)	C-3
Culiacán	B-2
Durango	B-2
Hermosillo	B-1
Jalapa Enríquez	C-3
Matamoros	B-3
Mazatlán	B-2
Mérida	B-4
Mexicali	A-1
Morelia	C-2
Nuevo Laredo	B-3
Oaxaca de Juárez	C-3
Pachuca	B-3
Puebla (5)	C-3
Querétaro	B-2
Reynosa	B-3

Saltillo	B-2
San Luis Potosí	B-2
Tepic	B-2
Tijuana	A-1
Toluca de Lerdo (2)	C-3
Torreón	B-2
Veracruz	C-3
Villahermosa	C-3

Cities 500,000–999,999

Ciudad Juárez	A-2

Cities 1,000,000 or more

Guadalajara	B-2
Mexico City (1)	C-3
Monterrey	B-2

There are 31 states and a federal district in Mexico. Which states have a city with populations of 1,000,000 or more?   Jalisco—Guadalajara Neuvo León—Monterrey

Village Mexico   Most farmers live in villages and walk to their fields every day. Those who can afford them use horses, oxen, or burros. Very few village families own tractors or cars.

The type of houses people live in varies with the climate. Villages in dry areas have houses made of **adobe** (ə dō′ bē), sun-dried brick made of mud. Those in the wetlands have houses made of wood or bamboo with grass or palm-leaf roofs.

People of the cities   Most people who do not live in villages live in the large cities. The map on this page shows where many of these cities are.

Mexico City is by far the largest city in the country. It is growing larger every day. In the early 1980s it was the second largest city in the world. If it keeps grow-ing the way it has, it soon could be the largest city. It is the capital of Mexico and is in a federal district like the District of Columbia in the United States. This spot has been the center of government since the days of the Aztecs.

Mexico City is also a cultural, educa-tional, and industrial center. There are about 25,000 factories in Mexico City. Automobiles, chemicals, clothing, tex-tiles, drugs, iron, steel, and machinery are the major products. The goods produced by the factories in Mexico City account for nearly half of the total value of all of the country's manufactured goods.

There is usually not enough housing in the cities. The newcomers to the cities often build tiny houses on the edge of a town or city out of scrap material. They use any materials they can find—wooden boxes, cardboard, burlap, flattened tin cans! When they find work and have enough money, they either make a better house or move somewhere else. The temporary houses often become a permanent part of many cities.

City life   The rich and middle-class people live close to the center of the city. They are teachers, office workers, salespeople, and lawyers, and live just like people in cities the world over. Downtown Mexico City has tall, shiny skyscrapers; busy streets; and fancy stores just like New York, Chicago, or Los Angeles.

In almost any Mexican city, regardless of its size, you will find a park with a central area called a plaza. This comes from their Spanish heritage. On weekend nights, teenagers go to the park to meet their friends. Often there is a place for a band in the center of the park. On Sunday afternoons there is music and people selling balloons and refreshments. The parks are happy, active places that both rich and poor can enjoy.

CHECKUP

1. Name the two main groups of people that are most important to Mexican culture.
2. Name the largest city in Mexico. What was the name of an earlier city in the same place?
3. How are people in many Mexican cities solving their housing problem?

104

The Growing Mexican Economy

┌─ VOCABULARY ─────────────────┐

hacienda	sugarcane
land reform	refinery
ejido	textile mill
subsistence farmer	arable
commercial agriculture	fertilizer
	tourist

└──────────────────────────────┘

Haciendas and ejidos   After Mexico was conquered, the king of Spain gave huge portions of land there to some nobles and officers as a reward for services to the crown. In time most of this land was turned into very large farms called **haciendas.** Most farmers in Mexico worked on the haciendas for little or no pay. They were usually given a small portion of the total crop or were allowed to farm a small plot for their own use.

Independence from Spain in 1821 did not change this way of owning land. The hacienda system lasted until the 1920s. A new government took control of the country. One of the first things it did was to start **land reform**—that is, it changed the way land was owned. Land was taken from the few wealthy landlords and divided into smaller farms.

These farms were called **ejidos,** (ā hē' dōs). The ejidos were owned and worked by several families, or, sometimes, by the whole village. In some cases, the farmers would share in all the work and all the profits. On other ejidos, farmers would work only their own plots of land. This land reform allowed the people who were really farming the land to own it.

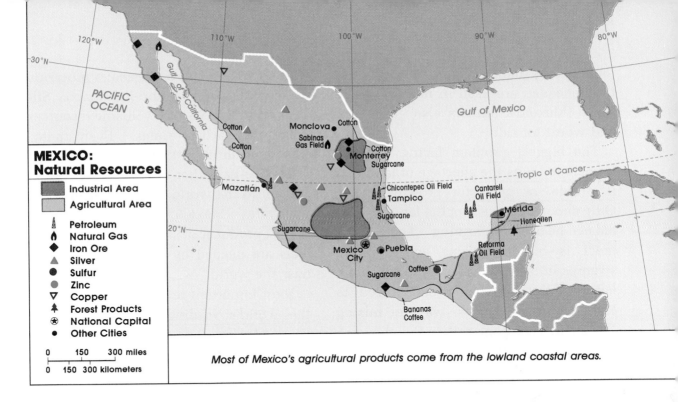

MEXICO: Natural Resources

- Industrial Area
- Agricultural Area
- Petroleum
- Natural Gas
- Iron Ore
- Silver
- Sulfur
- Zinc
- Copper
- Forest Products
- National Capital
- Other Cities

0   150   300 miles
0   150 300 kilometers

Most of Mexico's agricultural products come from the lowland coastal areas.

Farming in Mexico Many Mexicans are still **subsistence farmers.** Subsistence farmers are only able to grow enough for their family's use. They are not able to make extra money for things like books, farm machinery, or indoor plumbing. Small farms are usually subsistence farms.

Other farmers have more land and are able to grow crops for sale. This is called **commercial agriculture.** In southern Mexico, where the lowland has a tropical climate, many farms grow **sugarcane.** Sugarcane is a tall stalk that is used to make sugar. The stalk is crushed to make a juice. The juice is then boiled and made into sugar.

Sugar is an important product because growing and selling sugarcane is a way for farmers to earn money. Then, making sugar out of the sugarcane gives work to other people. Sugar is made from sugarcane in a factory called a **refinery.**

In the early 1970s there were 90,000 farms in Mexico that grew sugarcane. The country had 66 sugar refineries that gave work to 45,000 people. That is a lot of people earning money from sugar! There are even more if we count the people working in factories that use sugar to make candy, chewing gum, or soda.

In northern and central Mexico, vegetables and cotton are important crops. Farmers who grow food for sale have learned that the United States is a good market for fresh vegetables. During the winter months, airplanes carry vegetables such as tomatoes to restaurants and stores in cities in the United States. Fresh fruits such as perishable strawberries are also sent by airplane.

Farmers who grow cotton usually sell the cotton to factories that make it into cloth. These factories are called **textile mills.** Sometimes the cotton is sold to textile mills in other countries. Cotton is an important Mexican export.

Coffee, bananas, and oranges are other important Mexican crops. The henequen (hen' ə kin) plant is, too. The leaves of the henequen are used in making strong rope. Mexico's farmers also grow corn and wheat for sale.

The biggest problem facing Mexican farmers today is the shortage of land that is **arable**, or good for growing crops. Only about 10 percent of the land in Mexico can be used for farming. The government is building dams and draining swamps in order to make more farmland. Farmers are also being encouraged to learn the most modern ways of raising crops and saving the soil so that they can get more from their land.

Some Mexican farmers raise animals on land that is not suited to raising crops. The animals most commonly raised for sale are cattle. Most cattle are beef cattle. Some farmers raise pigs, hogs, goats, and chickens. Some raise bees. Mexico exports more honey than any other country in the world.

Thatch-roofed cabanas will shelter visitors as they enjoy the beach on Cancún. (21°N/86°W; map, p. 103)

Some special resources: minerals
Many minerals are found in Mexico. Silver and gold have been valuable resources since the earliest times. Even today, Mexico is an important source of silver.

Mexico has other minerals that are important to the world—copper, lead, zinc, and sulfur. Mexico is the world's second largest producer of sulfur. Mexico's minerals are needed by many industries all over the world.

Most important of all, Mexico is one of the world's leading sources of petroleum. No one knows how much petroleum Mexico has, since new discoveries are made every year. It is estimated that Mexico has petroleum reserves of 31 billion barrels. Most petroleum has come from areas in the eastern part of the country along and near the coast. These oilfields lie mainly in the states of Chiapas, Tabasco, and Veracruz. Find these and other oilfields on the map on page 105. Recently deposits have been found on the west coast of Mexico, too.

Some other special resources: trees and beaches Mexico's tropical forests are full of valuable trees. Rubber, vanilla, and chicle (for chewing gum) come from these trees. Valuable woods such as mahogany, which is used to make fine furniture, also come from Mexico's forests. These resources have been important for a long time.

Mexico has beautiful beaches on both the Atlantic and Pacific oceans. These beaches are important to the country because many people take vacations there. Beautiful beaches in pleasant climates are a resource worth a great deal.

Industrial Mexico　Today many Mexicans work in factories. You have already read about sugar refineries and textile mills. There are also flour mills and meatpacking plants.

Mexico is also lucky to have both iron and coal. These resources are used to make steel. The earliest steel mills were near the city of Monterrey in the north, but today there are steel mills in other places in Mexico as well. The steel is used in factories in Mexico to make products such as automobiles, heavy machines, bicycles, motors, refrigerators, and even pins.

The chemical industry uses petroleum, sulfur, and other minerals to make paints and plastics. Another important product of the chemical industry is **fertilizer**. Fertilizer is something that farmers can add to the soil that will help plants grow faster and bigger.

Tourist Mexico　A **tourist** is someone who travels to a place on vacation. Many tourists come to Mexico from many parts of the world. They spend a lot of money when they are there. Tourists are very important to Mexico's economy.

The tourists do not buy refrigerators or fertilizer. They often buy things people have made by hand to remind them of their visit. A tourist might buy a bracelet made of silver, a doll made of wood, or a purse made of fine leather. Mexico has people who know how to make beautiful things from silver, wood, and leather. These people can earn money because of tourists. People who work in hotels, restaurants, and airports can earn money, too.

Mexico tomorrow　Earlier in this chapter you learned that Mexico has become a leading country of Latin America. It is no longer a developing country. Now that you have learned about some of the products of Mexico, you can understand why the country is growing richer. Yet Mexico, like many other countries today, is also having economic problems.

Mexico is spending much of its new wealth on education. Until recently, many Mexican children had no schools to attend. They grew up without learning how to read and write. Now there are schools for almost all of the children in the country and even for many of the adults who had never been to school.

Mexico also has some fine universities and colleges. Here, people learn to be doctors, teachers, scientists, and geographers. Mexico is using some of its new wealth to have geographers plan places for new factories and industries. Scientists are being asked to find better ways of growing crops. And the Mexican government is sending doctors and teachers to poor villages so that the people there have health care and basic schooling.

Things are getting better for Mexico. They will be even better tomorrow.

CHECKUP

1. Name three plants Mexican farmers grow for sale. Which plant is not something people eat?
2. What kinds of animals bring money to Mexico's economy?
3. What resources are used in making steel? What are some things steel is used for?
4. What are three of Mexico's valuable minerals? What other kinds of resources does the country have?
5. Why are tourists important to Mexico?

KEY FACTS

1. Mexico is one of the richer nations in Latin America.

2. Most of Mexico's trade is with the United States.

3. The many mountains in Mexico make transportation difficult.

4. Much of Mexico's land is not good for farming. It is too dry or too steep.

5. Many Mexican farmers are subsistence farmers.

6. Mexico City, the capital of Mexico, may soon be the largest city in the world. It is also an industrial, cultural, and economic center.

7. The steel, chemical, and petroleum industries are important to Mexico's economy.

VOCABULARY QUIZ

Choose the word or words from the list that best complete each of the sentences below. Write your answers on a sheet of paper.

imports	subsistence farmers
tourists	adobe
culture	rain shadow
ejidos	mestizos
refinery	conquistadores
exports	developing country

1. Spanish soldiers, called __conquistadores__, came to Mexico in 1519.

2. The products that Mexico buys from the United States are called __imports__.

3. We can learn a great deal about Mexico by studying its people and their way of life, or their __culture__.

4. The products that Mexico sells to the United States are called __exports__.

5. Village houses in dry areas are often made of __adobe__, sun-dried brick made of mud.

6. An area in a __rain__ __shadow__ does not get much rain because it is on the protected side of high mountains.

7. Most of Mexico's people are __mestizos__, people who are part Indian and part Spanish.

8. A __refinery__ produces sugar from sugarcane.

9. Many villages in Mexico are __ejidos__, which means that the village people own the land as a group.

10. The Mexican economy is helped by __tourists__, people who travel to a place on vacation.

REVIEW QUESTIONS

1. Why is travel difficult in Mexico?

2. What is a developing country?

3. How did the land reform movement in the 1920s change the way land is owned in Mexico?

4. What is the difference between subsistence farming and commercial agriculture?

5. Where is sugarcane grown? Why is it an important crop for Mexico?

6. What are some products the United States buys from Mexico?

ACTIVITIES

1. Do research to find out more about either the Maya or Aztec Indians. Imagine that you are a Spanish conquistador reporting to the king. Write a letter to the king telling about the Indians you find.

2. If someone you know has visited Mexico, interview that person about the trip. Prepare a report to present to the class.

3. Write a one-page description of life in the United States that will tell someone your age in a Mexican classroom about our culture.

LEARNING WORD ORIGINS

WORDS FROM SPANISH

Words have histories. And sometimes, studying the history of words can teach you quite a bit about the history of people and places. Take the word *tomato*, for example. If you study the origin of that word, you will learn something about what happened in the 1500s in the area we call Mexico.

The Aztecs grew many fruits and vegetables. Among them was a red, not terribly firm fruit the Aztecs called tomatl (tə mä′ təl). The Spanish took the fruit back to Europe with them and called it tomate (tō mä′ tə). We call it tomato.

The Spanish settled throughout Latin America and in what is today the southern part of the United States, particularly the southwest. The English language, especially as it is spoken in the United States, is full of Spanish words.

SKILLS PRACTICE

Did you know that the Spanish word for "fried" is *frito*? Does your house have a patio? Have you ever played a guitar?

Some Spanish words that have become part of the English language are listed below. Definitions are listed in the next column. On a sheet of paper write the letter of the correct definition next to the number of the word. You may use a dictionary if you wish.

d **1.** rodeo   a **8.** pueblo

i **2.** fiesta   m **9.** plaza

n **3.** machete   f **10.** mosquito

l **4.** lariat   e **11.** quirt

j **5.** adobe   k **12.** ranch

h **6.** arroyo   c **13.** vigilante

b **7.** mesa   g **14.** avocado

a. town or settlement

b. table; large, flat-topped hill

c. watchman; someone who acts outside the law to punish criminals

d. performance in which cowboy skills are displayed

e. whip

f. biting fly

g. vegetable

h. gully

i. festival

j. sun-dried brick

k. large farm where horses and cattle are raised

l. rope

m. town square

n. large, heavy knife

You would probably understand some Spanish words even if you have never studied the language. Study this list of Spanish words. Write down what you think these words mean.

1. aeroplano		**6.** familia
2. oficina		**7.** civilización
3. mapa		**8.** educación
4. fútbol		**9.** petróleo
5. crema		**10.** sopa

Be careful with *sopa*. You do not wash your hands with it. It is something you eat.

Spanish is a Romance language. This means that Spanish has developed from the language the Romans spoke—Latin. Do you know why you know what most of the words on the list mean? Most of the words have their origin in Latin. There are many, many Latin words in English. We share this heritage with Spanish-speaking people.

Landscapes and Climate

VOCABULARY

coral

The importance of location   Between North America and South America lie many small countries. Some of these countries are islands. Others are on the isthmus that connects North and South America.

The isthmus is called Central America. How, do you suppose, did the area get that name? The most northern country in Central America is Guatemala (gwät ə mäl′ ə). Find Guatemala on the map on page 112. What country is north of it?

Now look at the Caribbean Sea on the map. The Caribbean Sea is a part of the Atlantic Ocean. It lies between North and South America. There are many islands in the Caribbean Sea. Cuba is the largest island in the Caribbean. What country lies just north of it?

The small countries of Central America and the Caribbean are located between two important continents. They are also located between two large oceans, the Atlantic and the Pacific. A waterway through the isthmus of Central America connects these two oceans. It is at the southern end of Central America.

A mountainous landscape   The islands in the Caribbean Sea form a ring of mountains. The islands are the tops of a mountain range that begins under the sea. Many of these islands were active volcanoes a long time ago. Not all of the islands, however, are the tops of volcanoes. Some are older mountains under the sea that have new tops made of **coral**. Coral is a hard, chalky, rocklike material that is made of the shells of sea animals called coral polyps. When coral polyps are alive, they live in bunches in warm seawater. The polyps attach to any base they can find, such as old mountaintops under the sea. When the polyps die, they leave their shells behind as a rocky covering. Then, new polyps attach to this covering. After hundreds of years a large number of coral polyps have come and gone. The result is a coral island. Many of the smaller islands in the Caribbean are coral islands.

There are also many mountains in Central America. Here too most of the mountains are old volcanoes. Some of the volcanoes in the long range of mountains that covers the length of Central America are still active. In the middle of the last century, the city of San Salvador was completely destroyed by the eruption of a volcano. There have been a number of eruptions in this century, too.

Discuss with pupils how the formation of coral islands is a good example of cause and effect.

Yachts anchor in the shelter of the Tobago keys. A key is a low coral island or reef.

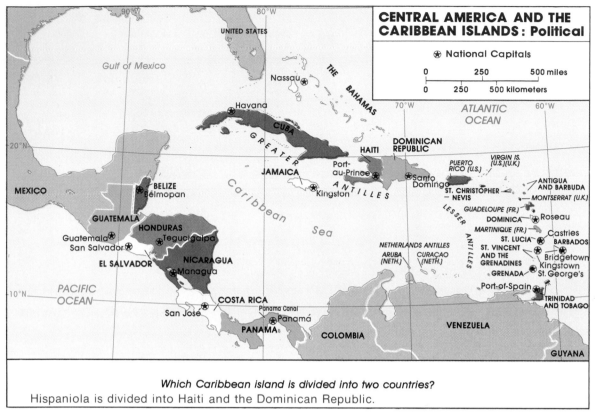

CENTRAL AMERICA AND THE CARIBBEAN ISLANDS: Political

⊛ National Capitals

Which Caribbean island is divided into two countries?
Hispaniola is divided into Haiti and the Dominican Republic.

Even when volcanoes are not active, they are a problem because they are high mountains. You can see from the map on this page that it is a short distance from ocean to ocean in Central America. That short distance, however, is up and down several high mountains and is a very difficult trip. A section of the Pan American highway, about 1,555 miles (2,500 km) long, is the only road that links all the Central American countries. There are towns that can be reached only by plane, mule, oxcart, or on foot. Transportation is one of the most difficult problems that the countries of Central America have to solve.

Climate   The countries of Central America and the Caribbean are close enough to the Equator that their lowland areas are very warm. They are in a tropical climate, a climate that is never cold. Almost all of these countries have mountains. And, as you remember, the highest parts of mountains are often cold.

Most of the countries in Central America have all three climate zones— the tierra caliente, the tierra templada, and the tierra fría. Most of the islands in the Caribbean, however, are not high enough above sea level to have a tierra fría.

CHECKUP

1. What is the name of the isthmus that connects North and South America?
2. Name two ways the islands of the Caribbean Sea have been formed.
3. What are the three climate zones found in Central America?

112

People and Places

VOCABULARY

Arawak	colony
Carib	independent nation
conuco system	

Lands of many cultures   In Chapter 6 you learned that Mexico was a blend of two main cultures, the Indian and the Spanish. We cannot describe the culture of Central America and the Caribbean islands so simply. It is true that there were early Indian civilizations in most of the countries in the area. But many of the countries were also colonized by Spain. Others were colonized by other European countries. In addition, large numbers of black people from Africa have contributed to the culture of the area.

Early Indian cultures   Before the arrival of the Europeans, parts of the region were ruled by several groups of Indians. The area was not divided into the countries of today. Instead, much of the land of northern Central America was part of the Mayan kingdom. Other Indian groups lived on the islands of the Caribbean. The most important of these were the **Arawak** (ä′ rä wäk) and the **Carib** (kar′ ib). The Caribbean Sea is named after the Caribs.

You read about the Mayas in Chapter 6. They were important in southern Mexico. Their civilization, however, began in Guatemala. From Guatemala, the kingdom spread north to Mexico and to other parts of Central America.

Mayan civilization was at its peak around A.D. 800. At that time three of the most important Mayan cities were Copán, Palenque, and Tikal. Today, Tikal is in Guatemala; Palenque is in Mexico; and Copán is in Honduras.

Arawaks and Caribs   The Arawaks were the farming people of the Caribbean islands. They knew how to grow tobacco and cotton. They learned how to irrigate when the climate was dry. They invented a good system for farming many crops. In this system, called the **conuco system**, several types of crops are grown together in mounds of earth. First there would be a plant grown for its roots, such as the sweet potato or the peanut. Second would be plants of different heights that provide a crop from their stalk or leaves. Corn is an example of this kind of plant. Finally, something that grows on vines would be added. Usually this was squash.

The conuco system might seem strange, but it worked. It kept the soil from being washed away. The different plants produced more food than they would have if they had been grown by themselves in separate fields. Each kind of plant added something to the soil that one of the other kinds of plants could use. Some farmers on the islands today still use this system. Carl Sauer, a famous geographer, has called the conuco system one of the best ever. He says that the Arawak people, given the number of farmers and the kinds of tools they had, produced more food this way than they could have using any other system.

The Caribs, the other main group of island Indians, were warriors. Although they did do some farming, they were

113

better at conquering other tribes. The Caribs came from South America and traveled from island to island in the Caribbean in large canoes. Each canoe could hold 40 to 50 people. The canoes had sails made of cotton. The Caribs wove the sails from cotton that they grew. They also grew fruits and other crops. The Caribs ate the fruits and vegetables that they farmed. The Caribs also ate fish.

Today both the Carib and the Arawak are gone. They did not survive the Spanish conquest. Mayas, however, are still found in parts of Central America.

The Spanish colonizers   The Spanish were the first Europeans to come to the Caribbean islands and Central America. The first European to land in the region was sailing for Spain, but actually came from Italy.

Columbus claimed the places where he landed as the property of the king and queen of Spain. Between 1492 and 1502 he made four trips from Spain to the Americas. He landed on more than ten islands and in parts of Central America. Columbus left people behind in many of these places to start **colonies.** A colony is a place that is settled at a distance from the country that governs it. The Spanish built forts and began to take over the land.

What happened to the Indians? Many were killed in the conquest. Others died of new sicknesses, such as smallpox. Still others died because they no longer had land on which to grow food. The land had been divided among the new governors from Spain. Often these governors, or local rulers, were soldiers who had helped in the conquest.

The Spanish governors tried to change the Indian cultures, especially the religion. The Spanish were Christian and thought all people should be Christians. They brought in priests to teach the Indians to follow the Christian religion. They also taught the Indians the Spanish language, and to be loyal to the king and queen of Spain.

The coming of other rulers   Spain had established its rule in Central America and the Caribbean islands by the middle of the 1500s. Pirates from England and France began attacking Spanish ships and towns in the Spanish colonies. The pirates would attack the Spanish ships that were carrying gold and silver back to Spain. The pirates sometimes were encouraged by the rulers of England and France. During the 1500s, England and France were often at war with Spain. One of the most successful pirates was Sir Francis Drake of England. The English people thought he was a hero!

Spanish power in Central America and the Caribbean was weakened by wars in Europe. In the 1600s, many small islands in the Caribbean were taken over by England, France, and the Netherlands. In addition, England captured the large island of Jamaica. Most of the Caribbean islands, however, remained under Spanish rule for a very long time. So did most of the isthmus of Central America.

The countries today   Although most of the countries of Central America and the Caribbean islands are no longer colonies, they still show the influence of the countries that had ruled them. Some of

Houses, which look very much like those that can be seen in any Dutch city, stand near the harbor of Willemstad, in the Netherland Antilles. (12°N/68°W; map, p. 112)

the houses and churches in Jamaica look like buildings you would see in England. English is the main language. French is still spoken in the countries that were colonized by France. Spain, however, has had the greatest influence.

Beginning in the 1800s the European colonies in Central America and the Caribbean began to seek their independence. The people wanted to have their own government rather than to be ruled by the countries of Europe. <u>Most countries in the region are **independent nations** today.</u> An independent nation has its own government. Some of the nations have had success in governing themselves. Others have had problems. The small size of many of the countries has been one problem. Some countries have had additional problems because bigger countries want their resources.

CHECKUP

1. In which Central American country did the Mayan civilization begin?
2. Who were the farming Indians of the Caribbean islands?
3. What religion did the Spanish bring to the Indian peoples?
4. Why aren't all the people in the Caribbean islands Indian, Spanish, or mestizo?
5. Are any of the Central American and Caribbean island countries still colonies of the European countries?

Ask pupils to use the map on p. 112 to locate places that are still colonies.

Some Island Nations

Cuba, an important nation   You can see on the map on page 112 that Cuba is the largest of the Caribbean islands. Cuba was a colony of Spain until the Spanish-American War in 1898.

Cuba is of special interest to our country because it has a Communist government. Miami, Florida, is only about 200 miles (321 km) from Havana, the capital city of Cuba. The United States and the Soviet Union nearly went to war over Cuba in 1962.

Cuba's main product is sugar. Cuba has some of the best land in the world for growing sugarcane. Many countries buy Cuban sugar. Nickel, a metal important to industry, is also a leading product of Cuba. Only four countries in the world produce more nickel than Cuba.

Hispaniola, island of two countries
Another large island, Hispaniola (his pən yō′ lə), was originally colonized by Spain, just as Cuba was. French pirates began to use the western end of Hispaniola as a base. In 1697 the western third of the island became a colony of France. It was called Haiti. The French started **plantations** to grow sugarcane, coffee, cotton, and other tropical crops. A plantation is a large farm that grows one special crop. Haiti became one of the richest colonies in the French empire. In time the people of Haiti revolted against French rule and Haiti became the first black republic in the Western Hemisphere.

French is the official language of Haiti, but most people speak **Creole**. Creole is a language that combines the French language and African languages. The ancestors of most Haitians came from Africa. There are also many Haitians who have both French and African ancestors.

Most people in Haiti are very poor. There is not enough work for people who need it. There are some factories in the capital city of Port-au-Prince. A textile industry is starting to grow in Haiti. Copper and bauxite (bôk′ sīt), an ore used in making aluminum, are mined in Haiti and then sent to refineries in the United States.

Most people live on the small farms that replaced most of the plantations.

Toussaint L'Ouverture, born a slave, led the successful revolution in Haiti. He was a very able general and proved to be a wise leader as well. Haiti enjoyed a good deal of prosperity during his rule.

Some coffee and sugarcane are grown for export. The country is very mountainous and has little land that has not already been used for better farming. In recent years many Haitian people have left Haiti to live in other countries, including the United States.

Dominican Republic, the eastern part of Hispaniola What of the other part of Hispaniola? It remained under Spanish rule for most of the time until 1844, when it became an independent nation called the Dominican Republic. Today the capital city, Santo Domingo, is one of the more attractive cities of the Caribbean. Over 600,000 people live there. It is the oldest city founded by Europeans in the Western Hemisphere.

Most people in the Dominican Republic still farm. The climate there is warm and tropical all year. There is a broad, fertile plain between the mountains that is good for growing sugarcane and tropical fruits. Refining sugarcane is the leading manufacturing industry in the Dominican Republic. Sugar is the leading product. Bauxite, gold, gypsum, and marble are among the country's resources.

Jamaica, land of bauxite and beaches Jamaica, the third largest Caribbean island, lies about 90 miles (145 km) south of Cuba. In the 1650s the island was captured by Great Britain.

The British founded Kingston, the present capital. Coffee and sugarcane were grown on huge plantations and shipped back to England. Thousands of Africans were brought in as slaves to work on the plantations. Today almost all of the Jamaican people are the descendants of those slaves. They speak English and follow British customs and traditions. Jamaica remained a British colony until 1962.

Jamaica is a mountainous island without a great deal of good farmland. Only 10 to 15 percent of the land can be farmed. Sugarcane, bananas, and coffee are the main export crops. If it were not for two special resources, however, Jamaica would be a very poor country. Jamaica has been blessed with bauxite and beaches.

Jamaica has some of the most important bauxite deposits in the world. It is the country's main export, the most important contributor to its economy.

Tourism is the second most important contributor to the Jamaican economy. There are many beautiful beaches in Jamaica. Well over half a million people, many from the United States, visit Jamaica as tourists each year.

Puerto Rico, territory of the United States Puerto Rico (pwert ə rē′ kō) has the same early history as most of the other Caribbean islands. It was a Spanish colony for a longer time than many of the other islands. During the time of Spanish rule, many Africans were brought to the island as slaves to work on sugar and other plantations. Today many Puerto Ricans are black. Others are of European or Indian ancestry. Some, as in other Latin American countries, have mixed backgrounds.

Puerto Rico's later history is quite different from that of the other Caribbean islands. In 1898, instead of becoming an

117

independent nation, it became a territory of the United States. Although Puerto Rico is not a state, its people are citizens of the United States. Many Puerto Ricans now live in the United States.

Today most of Puerto Rico's wealth comes from industries rather than from farming. Even though over half of Puerto Rico is farmland, most people live in cities and towns rather than on farms. They work in factories and office buildings. The factories make textiles and clothing, chemical and metal products, and processed food.

Some people work in hotels and restaurants visited by tourists from the United States and other countries. Tourism is an important part of the Puerto Rican economy. Over one million people visit Puerto Rico each year.

Visitors to Puerto Rico like the pleasing differences between the old and new buildings that they see in the cities. San Juan, the capital, has the gleaming, modern office buildings and the exciting nightlife of any American city. But in Old San Juan the red tile roofs and white stucco walls of early Spanish houses give a feeling of the early history of Puerto Rico. It is possible to visit a fortress built by the Spanish over 400 years ago and learn of the time when Europeans thought of Puerto Rico as the gateway to the Spanish New World.

CHECKUP

1. Which is the largest island in the Caribbean Sea?
2. Which two Caribbean countries share the same island? Which one was a colony of France?
3. Name two important resources of Jamaica.
4. Which island is part of the United States?
5. Are most Puerto Ricans farmers?

Central America: Seven Small Countries

VOCABULARY

fertile	earthquake
volcanic ash	canal

The Central American isthmus   Central America is divided into seven small countries. Find them on the map on the facing page. Only Nicaragua (nik ə räg′ wə) is larger than the island of Cuba. All of the countries put together do not have as much land area as the state of Texas. Most of the countries are poor. They do not have much industry.

Guatemala and Belize   Guatemala is a rugged land of mountains and plateaus. The mountains are in the southern part of the country. They stretch almost from coast to coast. Because of the mountains and because Guatemala lies entirely in the tropics, it has all three climate zones: the tierra fría, the tierra templada, and the tierra caliente.

The highest mountain in the Caribbean and Central American region is in Guatemala. Tajumulco (tä hü mül′ kō) is 13,850 feet (4,200 m) above sea level. Like the other high Guatemalan mountains, it is an old volcano. Western Guatemala is a region of old volcanoes called Los Altos, which means "The High Ones." Only crops such as corn and potatoes grow well at the higher elevations [above 5,500 feet (1,670 m)] of the tierra fría.

In between the high mountains are valleys. Many are in the tierra templada. There is often quite **fertile** soil in these

Have pupils divide a sheet of paper into columns and list the resources given in the map key, one to a column. Using the map as a source, have pupils list the country or countries where that resource can be found. You may wish to extend the activity to include agricultural products.

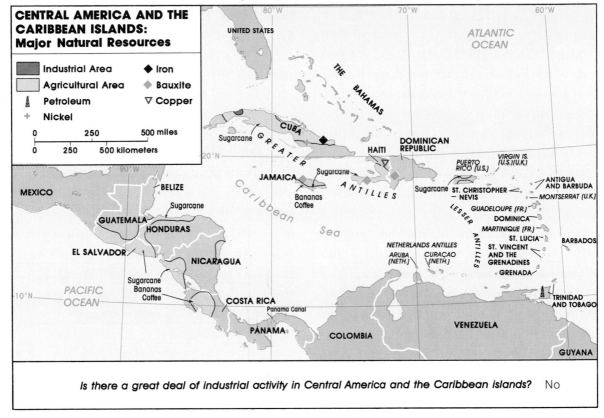

CENTRAL AMERICA AND THE CARIBBEAN ISLANDS: Major Natural Resources

Key:
- Industrial Area
- Agricultural Area
- Petroleum
- Nickel
- ◆ Iron
- ◆ Bauxite
- ▽ Copper

0   250   500 miles
0   250   500 kilometers

Is there a great deal of industrial activity in Central America and the Caribbean islands? No

valleys. Fertile soil is earth that has the minerals that plants need to grow well. In earlier times, when the volcanoes were active, the land was covered with ash from the volcanoes. **Volcanic ash** makes soil more fertile because it adds minerals to the soil.

Coffee is grown in the mountain valleys and on the mountain slopes. Coffee is Guatemala's main export crop. Most of the coffee is grown on the western, or Pacific, slopes of the Los Altos region. Coffee needs mild temperatures and does not grow well in the tierra caliente.

The tierra caliente is a dry zone on the west coast. Cattle and cotton are raised here. On the east coast, where more rain falls, the land is more likely to be used for banana plantations. One area in the tierra

caliente, the region in northern Guatemala called the Petén (pe ten'), is not good for farming. However, it does have valuable trees.

The rain forest of Petén continues eastward to the Caribbean. Because of an accident of history, the area east of Guatemala's Petén is a separate country, called Belize (bə lēz'). British sailors were shipwrecked there in the 1600s and made the land a British colony. It was called British Honduras until 1981, when it became an independent country. More people in Belize speak English than Spanish or the Indian languages.

The people of Guatemala, on the other hand, are Indians and mestizos. Many of the mestizos live in Guatemala City, the capital. Guatemala City, the largest city

119

in Central America, is located in a mountain basin.

More than half of the Guatemalans today are Indian. Most are descendants of the Mayas. Many speak an Indian language rather than Spanish. The Guatemalan Indians tend to live in the highlands of the Los Altos region and to raise food crops and sheep. They also practice handicrafts that they learned from their ancestors. Often they come to the cities to sell these products in open markets.

El Salvador, Honduras, and Nicaragua These three countries are the same in many ways. They were ruled by Spain during colonial times. Spanish is the official language in all three countries today.

The populations of El Salvador, Honduras, and Nicaragua are growing rapidly. Many people live in the cities. The capital cities of San Salvador, Tegucigalpa (tə gü sə gal′ pə), and Managua (mə näg′ wə), each have a population of around 400,000.

Most of the people in all three countries, however, live in the countryside. Farming is the most important part of the economy of each country. All three countries have plantations or large estates along their coasts and on the lower mountain slopes. The main crops are coffee from the mountain slopes, bananas and sugarcane from lowland areas that have a lot of rainfall, and cotton from the drier areas. The best land is used for these export crops.

Land that is not as good for farming is left for the subsistence farmers. Most of these people have very small plots of land, plots too small to make a living. The farmers work very hard to get as much food as they can from their small plots. They know that most of the good land is used to grow export crops.

Some of the volcanoes in the three countries are still active. People live in fear not only of a volcano erupting but also of **earthquakes**. An earthquake is a shaking of the earth caused by movement beneath the earth's surface. Serious earthquakes are not unusual in regions where there are volcanoes. In this century several cities in Central America and the Caribbean islands have been destroyed or badly damaged by active volcanoes or earthquakes.

This cut sugarcane will be taken to a factory where it will be made into raw sugar. The stubble left in the field will produce another crop.

Columbus brought the first sugarcane plants to the Western Hemisphere in 1493.

Costa Rica   Ever since colonial times, Costa Rica has been somewhat different from the other Central American countries. It was settled by Spanish families who farmed the land themselves rather than using African or Indian workers. Costa Ricans today are mestizos or are of European ancestry.

Costa Rica's most valuable resource is the fertile soil. Bananas, coffee, sugar, and beef are important farm products. Fewer people are subsistence farmers than in other parts of Central America. Costa Ricans are usually well educated. Many work in offices or have factory jobs. The leading products are furniture, leather goods, and textiles.

Panama   Panama, in the south of Central America, was a part of Colombia, its neighbor country in South America, until 1903. Now an independent nation, Panama is the narrowest country in Central America. Its location and shape have made it a very special place. It is where the **canal** connecting the Atlantic and Pacific oceans was built. A canal is a waterway made by people rather than by nature. Can you imagine digging a ditch big enough and deep enough for large ships to pass through? Moving ships from one place to another quickly has to be very important for people to go to the cost and work of building a canal. Before the Panama Canal was built, ships going from New York to San Francisco had to travel all the way around the southern tip of South America. This took weeks.

Since 1914 the United States has controlled the land near the canal, a strip called the Canal Zone. In 1978 the

It took 10 years and $380 million to build the Panama Canal. Thousands of workers, using heavy machinery as well as picks and shovels, cut the nearly 53-mile (83-km) long canal through hills, swamps, and jungles.

United States agreed to a plan to return this land, and eventually the canal itself, to Panama. The canal is Panama's most important resource.

The Panama Canal is also important to the world's economy. Today it is used by over 20,000 ships a year. The ships come from all parts of the world. Some people are already talking of building a second canal, either in Panama or in some other Central American country.

CHECKUP

1. In what country is the highest mountain in Central America?
2. Why is volcanic ash good for soil?
3. Which Central American country used to be a British colony?
4. Which country has the fewest subsistence farmers?
5. In which country was a canal across the isthmus built?

Extra Credit: A pupil might like to build a model of a lock or draw a cross-section of the Panama Canal.

7/CHAPTER REVIEW

KEY FACTS

1. The location of Central America and the Caribbean islands is important.

2. Mountains are the major landform in this region. Many of the Caribbean islands are the tops of mountains that begin on the seafloor.

3. Bananas and sugarcane grow well in the hot, moist climate of the lowlands; coffee is an important crop in the more temperate climate zone.

4. The early Indian cultures of this region were the Maya in Central America and the Arawak and the Carib in the Caribbean.

5. Most of the countries in this region were once colonies of Spain.

VOCABULARY QUIZ

On a sheet of paper write **T** if the statement is true or **F** if it is false. If the statement is false, rewrite it so that it gives the correct definition of the underlined word.

T 1. Some Carribbean islands are made of coral.

T 2. The Arawak Indians were good farmers.

T 3. The conuco system is a way of farming.

T 4. Volcanic eruptions can cause earthquakes.

T 5. Volcanic ash adds minerals to soil.

F 6. Creole is a language spoken in Cuba. **Haiti**

T 7. Fertile soil is rich in minerals.

T 8. A plantation is a large farm where one crop is grown. **is governed by a distant country**

F 9. A colony is a country that governs itself.

F 10. A canal to connect the Atlantic and Pacific oceans was built in Guatemala. **Panama**

REVIEW QUESTIONS

1. What is important about the location of Central America and the Caribbean islands?

2. Describe the climate zones in this area. Name a crop that can be grown in each one.

3. Describe the way of life of two early Indian groups that lived in the Caribbean region. What modern countries were once part of the Mayan kingdom?

4. What besides farming is important to the economies of some of the Caribbean islands?

5. Why is the Panama Canal so important to the entire world?

ACTIVITIES

1. Pick any of the smaller Caribbean islands not described in this book. Using an encyclopedia or other reference material, find out (a) how many people live on the island; (b) what country (if any) colonized it and whether it is still a colony; (c) what one or two of its main products are.

2. Draw an imaginary island that has elevations ranging from 0 to 8000 feet above sea level. Make contour lines showing the elevations. Use one contour line for 0', another for 1000', and so on up to 8000'. You will have nine contour lines.

Pretend your island is in the Caribbean Sea and decide what crops will be planted there. Would you plant bananas? Where? Make tiny banana symbols on that part of your island or simply write the word *bananas* over your banana-growing area. Would you plant coffee? Where? You could use tiny coffee cups or beans to show your coffee-producing zone. Would you plant corn? Squash? Sugarcane? Cover your whole island with crops. Now, give your island a name that sounds Spanish. The Spanish word for "island" is *isla* (ēs' lə). Create a legend for your map that provides the name of the island and an explanation of any symbols you may have used.

COFFEE FROM BERRY TO POT

Read the following material carefully. Notice especially the sequence, or order, in which coffee is produced.

Coffee grows as berries on fairly low-growing trees. There are machines that can harvest the berries, but most coffee berries are still picked by hand. Then the berries are dried. Sometimes they are spread out in the sun, but they can also be dried by machine.

During the next step a machine removes the two beans that are inside each coffee berry. It sorts them according to size, shape, and color. Then the beans are graded. A person called a "cupper" tastes coffee made from each type of bean and decides how good it is. After the sorting and testing, the coffee beans are bagged. Most of the coffee is exported.

Manufacturing is usually done in the country where the coffee will be sold. The coffee is roasted in large ovens at high heat. The various beans are blended and then ground. The coffee is packed into vacuum tins or bags and is shipped to markets.

SKILLS PRACTICE

Place the following statements in the sequence in which they happen.

2   The berries are dried and cured.   B
5   The beans are roasted at high heat.
1   Coffee beans are picked by hand.   A
4   The beans are graded and tested.   C
3   Machines remove the beans from the berries and sort them.
6   The coffee is ground and packed in tins. D

These pictures show parts of the coffee-making process. On your paper write the letter of each picture next to the statement that it illustrates.

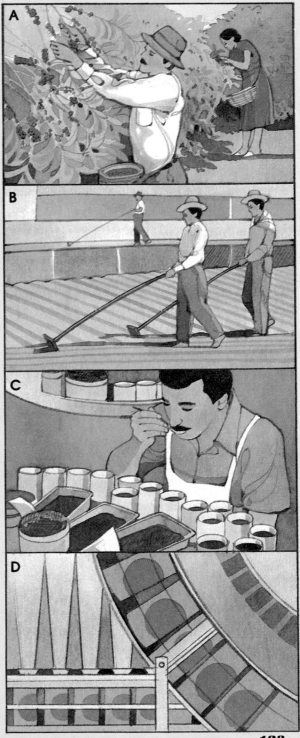

8 South America

Landscapes and Resources

┌─ VOCABULARY ─────────────────┐
| frontier   altiplano |
| tributary   tropics |
└──────────────────────────────┘

Great in size   South America is a very large continent. There are two large countries on the continent, Argentina and Brazil, and ten smaller ones. There is also one colony on the mainland, French Guiana (gē an′ ə). The Falkland Islands lie about 300 miles (480 km) off the southern coast of Argentina. The Falklands are governed by Great Britain.

South America is shaped like a long triangle, with the narrow point near the South Pole and the wide part to the north. The wide part is very close to the Equator.

The Andes in South America are the longest mountain range in the world. One of the largest rivers in the world, the Amazon, is also found on the continent. South America is one of the few places in the world where there are still **frontiers**, places with room for more settlement. Some of these frontiers are in the tropical lowlands around large rivers.

The rivers   The Amazon is an enormous river! It carries more water than any other river in the world, and it has a wide expanse of **tributaries**. A tributary is a stream or a river that flows into a larger body of water. The river basin of the Amazon and its tributaries is part of six countries: Brazil, Venezuela, Colombia, Peru, Ecuador, and Bolivia. Find these countries on the map on page 91. The Amazon River basin drains over one half of the South American continent.

Some other important rivers in South America are the Orinoco (or ə nō′ kō) River and the Magdalena (mag dä′ lā′ nä) River in the north, and the Paraná (par ə nä′) River and the Río de la Plata in the south. Although these rivers are much smaller than the Amazon, they are important to the economy of the region.

The mountains   The Andes Mountains run the entire length of the west coast of South America. This high range has always been a barrier between eastern and western South America.

Much of this rugged land cannot be farmed, because it is either too high or too steep. Some mountain valleys, however, have fertile farmland. The largest mountain flatland is a wide plateau called the **altiplano** (äl ti plä′ nō). *Altiplano* means "high plain."

The altiplano is a plateau of flat or rolling land in the middle of the Andes. It lies in the tierra fría. You can find the

Have pupils use the map on p. 91 to make an alphabetized list of South American countries. They can check their work by comparing their lists with the table on pp. 93–95.

Just by looking at this picture of mountain peaks in southern Chile, you can understand how the Andes can be a barrier between eastern and western South America.

These peaks—the Payne Horns—are in Payne National Park in Chile. The park was named for a nineteenth-century British naturalist and mountain climber.

altiplano on the map on page 89 by looking along the border between Bolivia and Peru until you find Lake Titicaca (ti tē′ kä kä). Lake Titicaca is on the altiplano. The world's highest large lake, it is 12,500 feet (3,810 m) above sea level.

Several other highland areas in addition to the Andes are important to South America. The Brazilian Highlands dominate the eastern part of the continent. The Guiana Highlands separate the Orinoco and Amazon river basins in the north. And in the southern part of Argentina is a high region known as Patagonia (pat ə gō′ nyə).

The landscape of South America consists generally of high mountains and plateaus, except for places where rivers have carved out lowlands. The coastal lowlands are often very narrow because the highlands rise steeply close to the sea. Most settlement has been along the narrow coastland.

Many environmental regions   Look at South America on the map on page 127. Notice that the continent extends from above 10° north latitude, above the Equator, to nearly 60° south latitude, close to Antarctica. Most of the continent lies in the **tropics**, the zone between the Tropic of Capricorn and the Tropic of Cancer. The middle latitudes begin south of Bolivia, and the climate gets cooler. The middle latitudes of South America have changing seasons. Unlike North America, however, the coolest months are June, July, and August. The warmest time of year is around the end of December. In the far south the temperature ranges from cool to cold. The southern tip of South America is about as far from the South Pole as southern Alaska is from the North Pole.

The lowlands near the Equator are in the tierra caliente. The land is usually rain forest. It can rain here nearly every day, sometimes resulting in over 100 inches (254 cm) of rain a year. Other lowland areas are desert, especially along the west coast. Some places in the desert go for years at a time without rain.

The highland slopes are in the tierra templada. Some of the mountain tops of the Andes, which are in the tierra fría, are cold enough to be covered with snow throughout the year.

The Brazilian and Guiana highlands are high plateaus with seasonal dryness. The land is covered with grass and scattered small trees. This is an example of savanna vegetation. This land can be used for grazing cattle. Because of the long dry season, however, it cannot be used as farmland—to grow crops—unless it is irrigated.

Resources of South America   The mineral resources of South America helped to build strong civilizations long before the Europeans came to the continent. South America has rich deposits of silver, iron, bauxite, copper, tin, and petroleum. Animals are an important resource, too. The ocean off the west coast of South America offers some of the best fishing in the world. Fish are especially important to the economy of Peru. Other countries of South America, Argentina and Uruguay in particular, are important producers of cattle and sheep.

SOUTH AMERICA:
Natural Resources

| | Agricultural Area |
| Manufacturing Area |

🐂 Cattle	◇ Diamonds
▽ Copper	🐟 Fish
◆ Iron	▲ Gold
⚑ Petroleum	🌲 Forest Products
◇ Bauxite	
+ Manganese	🐑 Sheep
▲ Tin	
▼ Nitrates	
✪ National Capitals	
• Other Cities	

0   250   500   750 miles
0   250 500 750 kilometers

ARUBA (NETH.)   CURAÇAO (NETH.)

Barranquilla
Caribbean Sea
Bananas
Maracaibo
Lake Maracaibo
Cacao
Coffee
Sugarcane
Caracas
VENEZUELA
Orinoco River
Caura River
GUYANA
Georgetown
Paramaribo
SURINAM
Cayenne
FRENCH GUIANA
Sugarcane
Kaieteur Falls
Medellin
Coffee
Bogotá
COLOMBIA
Buenaventura
Cali
Coffee
Cauca River
Magdalena River
GUIANA HIGHLANDS
ATLANTIC OCEAN
Quito
ECUADOR
Cacao
Bananas
Guayaquil
Manaus
Amazon River
Belém
Cotton
Fruit
Fortaleza
Sugarcane
PERU
BRAZIL
Recife
ANDES
Lima
Callao
Cotton
Lake Titicaca
Lake Poopó
BOLIVIA
La Paz
Sucre
Potosí
BRAZILIAN HIGHLANDS
São Francisco River
Cacao
Sugarcane
Salvador
Sugarcane
PACIFIC OCEAN
Coffee
Belo Horizonte
Bananas
Coffee
Sugarcane
Nova Iguaçu
São Paulo
Santos
Rio de Janeiro
Chaco
PARAGUAY
Ascunción
Paraná River
Curitiba
Antofagasta
Atacama Desert
Tropic of Capricorn
Salado River
Tucumán
Uruguay River
Grain
Pôrto Alegre
Córdoba
Rosario
Buenos Aires
San Justo
URUGUAY
Montevideo
Valparaíso
Santiago
Grapes
CHILE
ARGENTINA
Pampas
Río de la Plata
Grain
Colorado River
ANDES
Patagonia
Comodoro Rivadavia
Strait of Magellan
FALKLAND IS. (U.K.)
TIERRA DEL FUEGO
Equator

Some unusual animals are exported from South America. The rare snakes, lizards, and monkeys that you see in zoos often come from the rain forests of South America. Unusual snakes and other animals that are valuable are sometimes smuggled out of South America.

CHECKUP

1. How many countries are there in South America? What are the names of the two colonies?
2. What is the name of the mountain range that runs along the west coast of South America?
3. Identify Amazon, Titicaca, and altiplano.
4. What are three important South American resources?
5. What is the warmest time of the year in the middle latitudes of South America?

The People of South America

┌─VOCABULARY─────────────────┐
│ llama   liberator   │
│ terrace   Quechua   │
└────────────────────────────┘

The Incas: the first colonizers The early peoples of South America lived in small settlements and villages. There was almost no contact between one settlement and another. Each small group had its own customs and language.

For a long time the Incas were one of these small groups. They lived high in the Andes Mountains, in an area that is today part of Peru. The Incas lived by herding **llamas** (lä′ məs). A llama is a woolly animal that is bigger than a donkey and smaller than a camel. Like the donkey and the camel, it is used for carrying goods. Its wool, like sheep's wool, can be used to make cloth.

Have pupils trace the extent of the Inca empire on a modern political map. They should note the countries that were part of the empire.

About 700 or 800 years ago the Incas began to spread their influence among neighboring groups. By 1438 the Incas had established an empire. Look at the map on the next page to see the extent of the Inca empire.

How the Incas lived The Incas had a well-organized society that had a ruler and noble classes who governed the common people. The common people had to obey the ruler, but in return they always had as much land and food as they needed. When a child was born, the government gave extra land to the family for its support. The Incas even had laws that punished officials who let the people for whom they were responsible go hungry.

The Incas were good farmers who knew about fertilizer and irrigation. They were the first to grow potatoes, peanuts, tomatoes, and lima beans. The Incas also knew how to make **terraces** on the steep slopes of the mountains so that the land could be farmed. Terraces are flat shelves of land, arranged like wide steps on a mountainside. Stone walls at the edge of the terraces keep the soil from washing away.

Some of the Incas mined gold, silver, and copper, which were made into fine jewelry by skilled craftworkers. Inca artists made beautiful pottery and wove fine cloth from wool and cotton. The Incas studied geography and even made maps, using clay symbols for geographic features. They used the maps to make plans for keeping their empire strong.

The Incas also were good builders. They could build stone walls that held together without cement. The Inca rulers and the rich lived in great stone palaces.

The Incas also built bridges and fine roads, even in the rugged mountains. One long mountain road connected what is now Colombia to the northern part of what is now Bolivia.

With their roads and their central government, the Incas colonized most of western South America. They treated the tribes they conquered well. Some of the tribes were asked to become part of the Inca empire. The Incas protected all the people under their rule.

Pizarro is a good subject for an oral report.

The Spanish: conquerors of the Incas

In 1531 a Spanish adventurer named Francisco Pizarro (pə zär′ ō) crossed the isthmus of Central America and began a journey into western South America. He had heard rumors of the rich Inca empire. Pizarro and his people took over the Inca

These are buildings in the Inca city of Machu Picchu, high in the Andes Mountains. (13°S/72°W; map, p. 129)

empire. They pretended to come in friendship and then killed the Inca ruler. Soon other Spanish people followed. Some came for land and riches, some to add to the power of Spain, and others to bring Christianity to the Indians.

By 1600 the Spanish were rulers of all of northern and western South America. Their governors divided the best land into haciendas. The Indians on this land had to work as farmhands, servants, or miners. They had to become Christian and obey the laws of the Spanish governors. Other Indians were able to hide in the high Andes or deep in the rain forest, where the Spanish left them alone. On the good land and near the mines, however, the Spanish imposed their language and culture on the Indians. Many Spanish men married Indian women so that today many people of South America are mestizos.

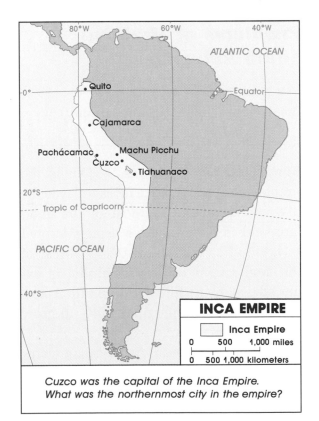

Cuzco was the capital of the Inca Empire. What was the northernmost city in the empire?

Cuzco was the capital of the Inca empire. In Quechua, *cuzco* means "navel [center] of the world."

Other European colonizers   Shortly after Pizarro began the conquest of western South America for Spain, Portugal began conquering and colonizing eastern South America. There were fewer Indians in the eastern lands. The land was well suited to plantation crops such as sugarcane. The Portuguese brought in Africans to work on their plantations and in their mines. Today in eastern South America there are many black people whose ancestors were brought from Africa as slaves. The land that was ruled by Portugal is now the country of Brazil.

Three other European countries had small colonies in South America. Later you will learn about French Guiana, British Guiana, and Dutch Guiana.

Independence   European countries ruled South America for about 300 years. During the 1800s, courageous leaders, following the example of the people of Haiti and Mexico, began to organize armies to fight for independence.

The most famous of these **liberators**, or leaders of a movement for independence, was Simón Bolívar (sē mōn' bo lē' vär). He wrote the constitution for Bolivia, a country named in his honor. Through his efforts and those of other liberators, such as José de San Martín in Argentina and Bernardo O'Higgins in Chile, most Spanish rule in South America had ended by 1824. Brazil became independent during this time, too.

People today   The majority of people in South America today are mestizos. However, many descendants of the original Indians remain in the high mountains and the river basins of the interior. Some still speak **Quechua** (kech' wä), the language of the Incas. People of African descent also live in many parts of South America, especially along the coasts. In more recent times, immigrants from other countries, such as Italy, Japan, and Germany, have come to South America.

Particularly to Brazil and Argentina

South America is a blend of many cultures and races. The Spanish and Portuguese heritage dominates, however. It gives the people of the different countries a great deal in common.

CHECKUP

1. How did the Incas farm on the sides of the mountains?
2. Name four European countries other than Spain that have or had colonies in South America.
3. Who was Simón Bolívar?

Problems of Modern South America

> **VOCABULARY**
>
> latifundia   dual economy
> minifundia

Some common problems   One of the problems South America faces today is the distribution of land. Most of the good farmland is held in large estates known as **latifundia** (lat' ə fun' dē ə). Most of the food grown on the latifundia is exported. Many people within South America need food or the opportunity to grow food for themselves.

Some of the South American governments have begun land reform. Land is taken from the large estates and given in small parcels to farming families. These

Discuss with pupils why the manufacture of industrial products creates a healthier economy
than the export of unfinished materials.

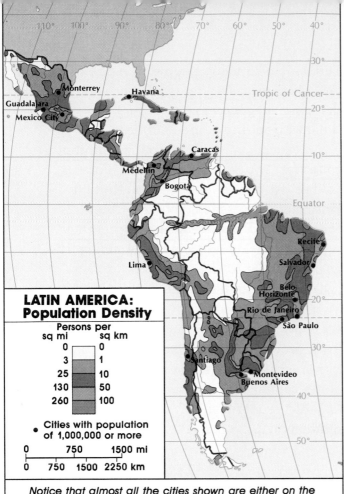

LATIN AMERICA: Population Density

Persons per	
sq mi	sq km
0	0
3	1
25	10
130	50
260	100

• Cities with population of 1,000,000 or more

0	750	1500 mi
0	750	1500 2250 km

Notice that almost all the cities shown are either on the coast or on navigable rivers that connect them with the coast.

Ask: How many cities in South America have a population of 1,000,000 or more?

small farms are called **minifundia.** Mini-fundia allow the farming families to grow food for themselves. However, mini-fundia cannot produce enough food to feed the people of the cities, too.

South American cities today are grow-ing very rapidly. They are crowded with people who cannot find work. Many of the people looking for work have come from the countryside, where they had no land and no opportunity to make a living on a farm. When they come to the cities, they live in makeshift houses, such as those you learned about in Chapter 6.

Twice as many people live in South America today as did in 1955. Jobs in the cities and farmland are not keeping up with this rapid growth. Advances in technology and land development as well as a drop in the rate of population growth may help solve these problems.

Export products Most of the South American nations have an economy that is based on one or two main exports. These are agricultural products and min-eral resources that are used as materials in factories in other countries. If the factories that used the mineral resources were in South America, there would be more jobs for the people who live there. The South American economies suffer because their exports bring in less money than the countries must spend for manu-factured goods that must be imported.

Dual economy A **dual economy** is one in which a few people are very rich and most people are very poor. There are not many people in between the rich and the poor in a dual economy. Without more and better jobs and without more land for the people, it is difficult for a middle class to develop. This is especially true if the number of poor people continues to increase.

The problems of rapid population growth, very little industry, and a dual economy are common to developing countries. Most of the countries in South America are developing countries.

CHECKUP

1. What is the difference between latifundia and minifundia?
2. Is the population of South America growing or shrinking?
3. What is a dual economy?

131

The Countries of South America

Northern South America Along the Caribbean and Atlantic coasts of South America are two large countries, Colombia and Venezuela (ven əz wā′ lə), and three smaller ones once known as the Guianas. Tropical lowlands and bustling ports are the major features of the northern parts of these countries. To the south, away from the ports of the Caribbean and Atlantic coasts, are highlands. The Guiana Highlands make up the southern parts of these countries. The northern part of the Andes extends into Colombia and western Venezuela.

Venezuela and Colombia were colonized by Spain; the Guianas by other European countries. French Guiana remains a colony of France. British Guiana and Dutch Guiana are now the independent nations of Guyana (gī an′ ə) and Surinam (sur′ ə nam).

All three of the former Guianas have large areas of rain forest vegetation and plantation crops. They export tropical woods and other forest products. In addition, Guyana and Surinam are important sources of bauxite.

French Guiana, Guyana, and Surinam each has a population of fewer than 1 million people, and room for more. Most of the people are blacks, whose ancestors were slaves on the colonial plantations.

There are also many people of Asian origin who are descendants of the workers the colonial governments brought to the Guianas from India and Indonesia.

Venezuela is one of the wealthiest countries in South America. Caracas (kə rak′ əs), the capital, is a beautiful city. Petroleum is the main source of Venezuela's wealth. Iron is also an important source. Venezuela is using the money it gets from exporting oil, iron ore, and agricultural products to develop industry. Money that is used to develop a country's economy is called **capital**. Capital is used to improve farmland and to build factories, schools, roads, and housing. Some of the capital in Venezuela is being used to build modern cities where industrial products will be made.

The largest known oil deposits in South America are under and around Lake Maracaibo. (10°N/71°W; map. p. 127)

An island off the coast of French Guiana was notorious as a prison. Few escaped from Devil's Island.

Colombia, the other large country of northern South America, is only slightly larger than Venezuela. However, it has twice as many people. Population growth is a greater problem for Colombia than for Venezuela.

Most Colombians are farmers. Coffee is Colombia's leading export. Grown in cool mountain valleys in the tierra templada, Colombian coffee is some of the best in the world. Colombia also produces petroleum, although it does not have as much as Venezuela.

Colombia is a mountainous country in which the Andes Mountain range fans out, or forks, to form western, central, and eastern ranges. Bogotá (bō gə tô'), Colombia's capital and largest city, is in a valley of the eastern range. Medellín (med əl ēn'), the second largest city and an important center of textile manufacturing, is located across the central range from Bogotá.

Not many people live in the interior of Colombia and Venezuela. These backlands are the wide plains, called **llanos** (län' ōz), of the swampy Orinoco River. During the rainy season, the llanos are flooded. During the dry season, grass dries up and small streams have no water. With enough capital the llanos could be developed into productive farmland.

Coastal countries of the Andes Ecuador (ek' wə dôr) and Peru lie just south of Colombia. The Andes are the major landform in these countries. There are also lowland areas on the eastern and western sides of the mountains. For many years not many people have lived in the eastern lowlands. The recent dis-

Quito is the only national capital located on the Equator. The climate, however, is springlike throughout the year. Why? (0°/78°W; map, p. 91)

covery of rich oil deposits in the eastern regions has helped the two countries' economies. Ecuador, especially, has gained a great deal of capital from the export of oil.

Agriculture is well developed on the western side of the Andes. The fertile tropical lowlands of western Ecuador produce bananas and **cacao** for export. The cacao seed is used to make cocoa and chocolate. Peru's coastal lowlands are dry, but cotton and sugarcane are grown in irrigated areas.

Lima (lē' mə), Peru's capital and one of the largest cities of western South America, is located near the coast. Ecuador's capital of Quito (kē' tō) is located in the mountains at an altitude of over 9,000 feet (2,740 m). Ecuador's largest city, however, is Guayaquil (gwī' ə kēl), located on the coast. Clearly, the coast is important to the economies of Ecuador and Peru.

133

Hermalinda: Urban Worker of Peru

The family farm could not support Hermalinda and her whole family. So when she was 9 years old, she went to Lima with an aunt to find work as a household servant. Most girls and women without schooling can find work only as servants. At age 29, Hermalinda was still a servant. She lived in a shantytown on the edge of Lima. There she met an American anthropologist named Elsa Chaney, who gave the following description of Hermalinda's life:

Hermalinda lives in a reed hut without a roof. It is on a sandy hill where no trees, grass, or flowers can be seen. The house has neither electricity nor piped water. Hermalinda pays for water to be delivered weekly to a barrel outside the house. She and her two children share one bed. There is a rickety table, a couple of chairs, and a two-burner kerosene stove. They have no refrigerator, no bathroom, and no clock. She keeps track of time with a transistor radio.

Each day, Hermalinda gets up at 5 A.M. Before she sets out on her 1-hour bus journey to work, she gets her children ready for their day. Her son attends school. Her daughter, a 10-year-old named Sonia, works mornings as a servant to earn money for school expenses. In the afternoon she attends school. But Sonia is behind in school because for many years she had to stay home to care for her brother while her mother worked. Until recently, Sonia had two younger brothers, but one of them died of malnutrition.

Hermalinda does not get home until about 8 P.M. She earns the equivalent of a dollar a day. Sonia earns about $10 a month. It may not be much income, but it is more money than they could earn in the village. And at least Sonia and her brother can attend school and may be able to get good jobs later on.

The waters off Peru are an important fishing area because of a cool ocean current, the Humboldt Current. A fish that is exported in large quantities is the anchovy, which many people like to eat in salad or on pizza.

Fish also provide a fertilizer that is exported—fish meal. Fish meal is a dry fish powder made from less popular fish. It can be used both as a food and a fertilizer.

Chile, to the south of Peru, produces another kind of fertilizer—**nitrate**. Nitrate is a valuable mineral that is also used in explosives. Some of the world's richest nitrate deposits are found in the Atacama (ät ə käm′ ə) Desert in northern Chile. Chile's most important export is copper. Copper from the mines of northern Chile makes up over 70 percent of the country's exports.

Chile is a long, narrow country. It extends 2,400 miles (3,862 km) from Peru to the southern tip of South America. It is only 190 miles (306 km) wide at its widest point. The Andes are an important feature. There are three distinct geographical regions in Chile. In the north is a desert and important mineral deposits. The middle has rich farmland and large

The Humboldt Current is named for Alexander von Humboldt. See p. 140.

cities. The south is cool, rugged sheep country. Few people live here. Ninety percent of the people in Chile live in the middle region, which begins at about 30° south latitude. This middle-latitude location allows a wide variety of crops to be grown, including the fine grapes for which Chile is known. Most people in this part of Chile live in cities, and especially in Chile's large capital, Santiago (sant ē äg′ ō). Santiago has a larger population than Chicago or Los Angeles.

Argentina and its neighbors Argentina has more cities than any other South American country except Brazil. Buenos Aires (bwā nə sar′ ēz), which is the capital and chief port, has a population of over 3 million. Other port cities are Rosario and Santa Fe. The western ranchland

area is served by the cities of Córdoba (kôrd′ ə bə), Tucumán, and Mendoza.

Over 80 percent of Argentina's 29 million people live in cities. Most Argentines are of European origin. There are not many Indians or mestizos in the country. Most of the people are of Spanish descent, but large numbers of Italians and Germans have also settled in Argentina.

Argentina can be divided into four regions: the Andes, the Chaco, the Pampas (pam′ pəz), and Patagonia. Find them on the map on page 127. The most distinctive region is the Andes. These mountains rise like a wall in western Argentina. Rivers that start in these mountains help irrigate land in the foothills, or **piedmont** area, making it possible to grow sugarcane and grapes. The Chaco is in the northern part of the country.

There are many cattle ranches in the Pampas. The colorful, hardworking Argentinian gaucho is like the North American cowboy or vaquero.

Much of the land is forested, but there are also savannas and grasslands. Some cotton is grown here. The seasonal rainfall, resulting in floods in the summer and very dry winters, makes farming very difficult. The Pampas region, on the other hand, is the agricultural heartland of Argentina. The soil is good. The summers are hot, and the winters are mild. The rolling plains of the Pampas are covered with grass. Beef cattle, sheep, and other livestock and many crops, including vegetables, are raised in the Pampas. In contrast, Patagonia is a dry, windswept plateau. Summer never comes to the most southern part of the Patagonian region. Most of the land is used for grazing sheep that produce a very fine, expensive wool.

Two of Argentina's neighbors are **landlocked.** They are countries without seacoasts. The term landlocked calls attention to how important water transportation is to trade with other countries, and thus to a growing economy. Countries without a seacoast are locked in by the countries around them. They are also often locked into being poor.

So it is with the landlocked countries of Bolivia (bə liv′ ē ə) and Paraguay (par′ ə gwī). Find these countries on the map on page 91. Paraguayans and Bolivians are among the poorest people in South America. It is difficult to see how the countries can get enough capital for development.

Paraguay has two unusual forest products, a kind of tea called maté (mä tā′) and **tannin,** an extract from the quebracho (kä brä′ chō) tree. Tannin is used in tanning leather. Most of Paraguay's agricultural products cannot be exported because of the high cost of transportation.

Bolivia has some of the world's most productive tin mines. However, most Bolivians are subsistence farmers. Bo-

Mining is the most important industry in Bolivia. Over 13 percent of the world's supply of tin comes from Bolivia.

livia is beginning to develop its eastern lowlands. Oil has been discovered in the foothills of the Andes Mountains. There are also deposits of many other minerals. The poor transportation system makes it very difficult to get to the areas where these resources are found.

Uruguay is the smallest independent nation in South America. Most people live in cities, especially the capital, Montevideo (mänt ə və dā′ ō). Montevideo is a popular place for tourists to visit and an important industrial center. Uruguay exports wool and cattle products, such as meat and leather.

Uruguay is the one country in South America that lies entirely outside of the tropics. It lies in the middle latitudes, the zone between 30°S and 60°S.

Brazil, the sleeping giant   The fifth largest nation in the world, Brazil takes up one half of the South American continent. It is larger than the United States if Alaska is not included. As you can see from the map on page 91, Brazil has a common border with every country in South America except Chile and Ecuador.

Brazil truly is a giant land with many resources. It is a country of many environments. It has the largest rain forest in the world. It also has cool plateau lands, middle-latitude temperate regions, and desertlike dry land.

For its size, Brazil has relatively few people. Most of them live near the coast. Brazil is still discovering its "wild west," the sparsely settled lands of its interior. Because there is a lot of room for growth and new development in Brazil, some people say this giant country is "sleeping."

It is actually very much awake and constantly changing.

Brazil is rich in minerals, many still waiting to be used. The gold and diamonds that attracted the Portuguese so long ago are still being mined. Brazil has other minerals, such as manganese, and has energy resources of petroleum and waterpower. However, since it has the world's richest iron deposits, the greatest hope for Brazil's future lies with this resource, and with steel made from the iron.

Brazil also has many unused resources in the Amazon rain forest. Valuable woods are exported now. Some tropical animals and fishes are also valuable. There are many possibilities for increased wealth from the tropical forests.

Brazil's farmland in many climate regions produces a wide variety of crops. In addition to coffee, Brazil is an important producer of sugarcane, cacao, cotton, soybeans, bananas, and oranges. Brazilians also raise tobacco, corn, wheat, rice, and both cattle and sheep.

The export of most of these products provides capital to develop industry. Large iron and steel factories are located near Rio de Janeiro (rē′ ō dā zhə ner′ ō). The nation's capital from 1763 to 1960, Rio de Janeiro today is an important government center and an industrial leader. It has one of the world's most beautiful harbors, which is visited by many tourists every year. São Paulo is an even larger industrial city. It is the home of Brazil's growing automobile industry and the center of the coffee-producing region. These two cities are the largest cities in South America.

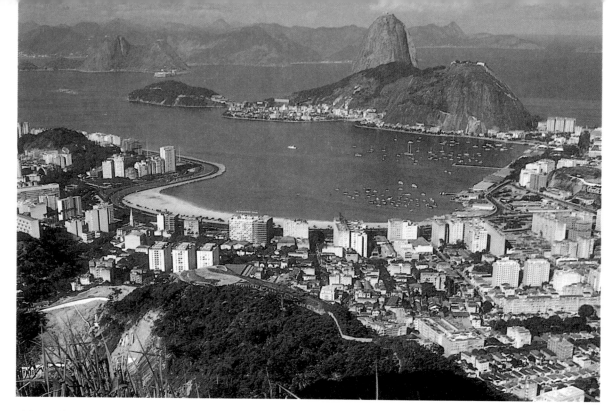

A beautiful natural harbor helps make Rio de Janeiro a busy seaport. (23°S/43°W; map, p. 127)

You will notice on the map on page 91 that most of Brazil's cities are on or near the coast or on major rivers. The only major city in the interior of the country is Brasilia (brə zil′ yə). Brasília did not exist before the 1950s. It was a planned city. It was designed to be the national capital. In 1960 it replaced Rio de Janeiro as the capital of Brazil. Highways linking Brasília to other cities are helping to open up the interior of Brazil to industry and commercial farming.

Perhaps the most interesting part of Brazil is the Amazon Basin. It is alive with 2,500 kinds of trees, 2,000 kinds of fishes, many rare animals and birds, and very few people. Some of these people are Indians who would like to be left alone. Others are people from other parts of Brazil and from other countries, who are trying to find ways to make profits in this frontier area. Even today the interior of Brazil is largely unexplored.

The rain forest land of the Amazon River basin is constantly warm, humid, and rainy. It has an average temperature of 80°F (26°C) and rainfall of 60–80 inches (152–203 cm) yearly. The heavy rains leach, or wash away, important minerals from the soil and make it infertile. So far, farmers have not found a way to grow good crops in the Amazon Basin. Brazil is seeking new and better ways to use this vast area.

CHECKUP

1. What resource is bringing new capital to Venezuela, and also to Colombia, Peru, and Ecuador?
2. What country has coffee as its leading export?
3. In what country is tin mined? Copper?
4. Name two landlocked countries in South America.
5. In what country are the Pampas located?
6. What is unusual about the capital of Brazil?

Sugarloaf Mountain, a landmark in Rio's harbor, is 1,325 feet (404 m) high and is the result of millions of years of erosion. Ask a pupil to investigate how it got its name.

KEY FACTS

1. The Andes are the longest mountain range in the world.

2. The Amazon River basin drains over one half of the South American continent.

3. Major mineral resources of South America are petroleum, bauxite, copper, tin, and nitrate.

4. The South American countries that lie in the tropics export agricultural products such as coffee, cacao, and bananas.

5. The South American countries located in the middle latitudes export beef, wool, and sometimes grains such as wheat or corn.

VOCABULARY QUIZ

Use the words listed below to complete the descriptions of the lives of children from seven South American countries. Write your answers on a sheet of paper.

altiplano	llanos
cacao	tributary
landlocked	tropics
liberator	

1. María lives in a small house in Brazil by the Purus River, which feeds into the Amazon. The Purus River is a __tributary__ of the Amazon.

2. José helps his family raise sheep high in the Andes of Bolivia on a wide plateau known as the __altiplano__.

3. Luz, a Colombian teenager, likes to read about Simón Bolívar, the man who led the fight to make Luz's country an independent nation. Simón Bolívar was a __liberator__.

4. Lucila lives in the flat backlands of Venezuela far from other people. Part of the year there is very wet and part is very dry. Lucila lives in the __llanos__.

5. Francisco lives on a small farm in Ecuador, one of that country's minifundia. There is enough land to have a few __cacao__ trees, which produce seeds used to make chocolate.

6. Carolina lives in the lowlands of Guyana, where it never gets cold. Her country is located between the Tropic of Capricorn and the Tropic of Cancer, a zone which is called the __tropics__.

7. Emilio earns his living by picking maté tea leaves in Paraguay. Paraguay has no seacoast; it is __landlocked__.

REVIEW QUESTIONS

1. What two geographic features dominate the South American continent?

2. Who were the first colonial rulers in South America? How big was their empire?

3. Name one South American country that you would expect to export each of the following: bauxite, cacao, coffee, copper, fish or fish meal, tannin, tin, wool, and beef.

ACTIVITY

Make a puzzle. Begin by drawing the outlines of the countries of South America on a piece of tracing paper. You can use the map on page 91. Using carbon paper, transfer your outlines onto cardboard or heavy paper. Neatly label each country and color or paint it if you wish.

Now cut out the countries along their borders to form a 13-piece puzzle. Use the puzzle to learn the location of the countries of South America. You can also use the puzzle as a game. With a timer or stopwatch, see which of your friends, classmates, or family members can put the puzzle together the fastest.

139

8/SKILLS DEVELOPMENT

USING CONTEXT CLUES

ALEXANDER VON HUMBOLDT
(1769-1859)

Alexander von Humboldt was a German scientist and geographer. He spent 5 years exploring Central America and northern South America. He traveled over 40,000 miles (64,360 km) during this time. He studied the Latin American landscape and civilizations. Humboldt spent 35 years writing about what he had learned in Latin America and other parts of the world.

SKILLS PRACTICE

Read these descriptions written by Humboldt. As you read, notice the words listed below. Try to define the words as they are used. Write your definitions on a sheet of paper. Use a dictionary to check your definitions. How close were you to the correct meaning of these words?

passage	fording
uninhabited	stupendous
stratum	freestone
crevices	fortification
vegetation	riveted
deluge	

The mountain of Quindío is considered the most difficult passage in . . . the Andes. It is a thick, uninhabited forest. . . . Not even a hut is to be seen. . . .

. . . In this part of the Andes, as in almost every other, the rock is covered with a thick stratum of clay. The streamlets which flow down the mountains have hollowed out gullies about twenty feet deep. Along these crevices, which are full of mud, the traveler is forced to grope his passage, the darkness of which is increased by the thick vegetation that covers the opening above. . . .

We traversed [crossed] the mountain of Quindío in the month of October, 1801, on foot, followed by twelve oxen which carried our collections and instruments, amidst a deluge of rain to which we were exposed during the last three or four days in our descent. . . . The road passes through a country full of bogs and covered with bamboos. Our shoes were so torn by the prickles which shoot out from the roots of these gigantic grasses that we were forced . . . to go barefooted. This circumstance, the continual humidity, the length of the passage, the muscular force required to tread in a thick and muddy clay, the necessity of fording deep torrents of icy water render [make] this journey extremely fatiguing. . . .

. . . there still exist wonderful remains of the great road of the Incas, that stupendous work by means of which communication was maintained among all the provinces of the empire along an extent of more than 1,000 miles. On the sides of this road, and at nearly equal distances apart, there are small houses built of well-cut freestone. These buildings . . . answered the purpose of stations. . . . Some are surrounded by a sort of fortification; others were . . . baths and had arrangements for the conveyance [carrying] of warm water. . . . While we journeyed onward for the distance of about four miles, our eyes were continually riveted on the grand remains of the Inca road, which was more than twenty feet wide. This road had a deep understructure and was paved with well-hewn blocks of . . . porphyry [volcanic rock containing crystals]. None of the Roman roads which I have seen in Italy, in the south of France, and in Spain appeared to me more imposing than this work of the ancient Peruvians. . . .

Taken from *Stars, Mosquitoes, and Crocodiles* by Millicent E. Selsam (New York: Harper and Row, 1962).

Use the source citation to point out the difference between primary and secondary sources. This selection was taken from a secondary source—an edited version of Humboldt's work.

3/UNIT REVIEW

Answer Key in back of book.

READING THE TEXT

Turn to pages 130–131 and read the paragraphs under the heading "Problems of modern South America." Then, on a sheet of paper, write the answers to these questions.

1. How has land reform affected some of the latifundia in South America?
2. Why are South American cities growing so rapidly?
3. What are the two main types of exports of most South American countries?
4. What is a dual economy?
5. What problems do most developing countries have in common?

READING A MAP

Study the map on page 112. On a sheet of paper, write the answers to these questions.

1. Which island located directly east of the Dominican Republic is a territory of the United States? Puerto Rico
2. Which two Central American nations do not have coasts on both the Pacific Ocean and the Caribbean Sea? Belize and El Salvador
3. Which island in the Netherlands Antilles is at 70°W? Aruba
4. Between what degrees of latitude do most of the countries of Central America and the Caribbean Sea lie? 10°N and 20°N
5. About how many miles is it between the capital cities of Cuba and Panama? 1,000 miles

READING A PICTURE

Turn to page 97 and carefully examine the picture. Then, on a sheet of paper, write the words that best complete the description of the picture.

The Plaza of the Three Cultures is in Mexico City. Two of the three cultures shown here are from Mexico's past. The platform and steps are remains of the culture of the (1) Aztecs . These people used (2) stones as building material. The building just behind the ruins is a (3) church . It is a symbol of (4) Spanish culture. The culture of modern Mexico is symbolized by the (5) tall buildings in the background of the picture.

READING A DIAGRAM

Study the diagram of the temperature zones on page 92. Then, on a sheet of paper, answer these questions.

1. In which of these zones is the temperature most likely to be neither too hot nor too cold? tierra templada
2. Which temperature zone is found above 2,100 meters? tierra fría
3. Which city shown on the diagram is more likely to have a higher annual temperature? Guayaguil
4. In which range of elevation is the tierra caliente? between 0 and 3,000 ft. (0–900 m)
5. What effect does the elevation of a place have on its temperature? Temperature decreases as elevation increases.

UNIT
4

WESTERN EUROPE

Point out to pupils that Europe is a large peninsula with many smaller peninsulas on the landmass of Eurasia. Have pupils look at the physical map of Eurasia in the Atlas on pp. 482–483. If pupils sailed from the Black Sea in southeastern Europe to the Barents Sea in northern Europe, they would sail around all sides of Europe except one. Next have pupils look at the map on the facing page. They can see the smaller peninsulas on the larger European peninsula. Have pupils locate the following: Balkan Peninsula, Italy, Iberian Peninsula, Jutland Peninsula, Scandinavian Peninsula.

A Small Tip of the Largest Continent

If you look at the map on the facing page, you will notice that there is no obvious barrier, such as an ocean, separating Western Europe from the rest of the continent. Europe is just the small western tip of a triangular landmass called Eurasia. The small tip has all of the major landforms of Asia. But in Europe they are squeezed together in a narrow space. That explains why the scenery changes so quickly when you travel through Europe. The pictures in Unit 4 show some of the changes in landscape.

Language, religion, and customs are just as varied as the landscape. Food and drink, clothing, the hours that stores are open, the way beds are made, and the kinds of curtains in the windows may change completely as you pass into a different region or country.

Many Migrations and Languages

Many groups of people have moved into Europe from Asia and Africa. Each group spoke its own language and had a different way of making a living. We know little about the earliest people, but about 5,000 years ago, people who grew crops and lived in villages began to live in the Mediterranean part of Europe. About a thousand years later, invaders came from the north. They conquered the native people and slowly took on some of their customs. These newcomers were known as Indo-Europeans because they all spoke related languages that spread as far east as India and as far west as Europe. In time the related languages of the Indo-Europeans developed into many of the modern European languages, including Italian, Greek, and English. You will learn more about languages in this unit.

142 **INTRODUCTION**

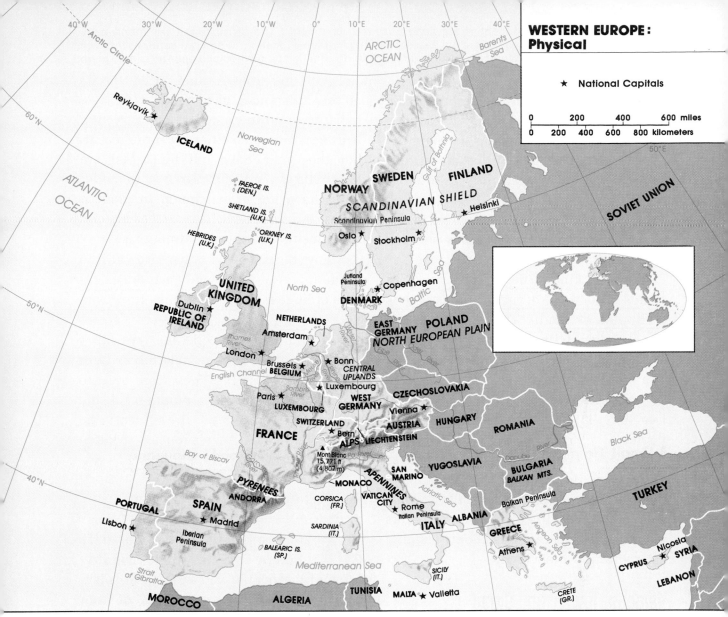

Many countries in Western Europe are islands or peninsulas. Among Western Europe's island countries are the United Kingdom, the Republic of Ireland, and Iceland. In the north Norway and Sweden make up the Scandinavian Peninsula.

Fields and Farms

Many kinds of field patterns and farming communities can be seen in Europe today. They show the different ways of farming of the past and present.

One of the most common field patterns in rural Europe is called open field. It is called open because no fences or hedges mark the edges of farm plots. The farmers usually work many tiny and scattered plots. The farmers and their families live in villages, and they have to walk long distances to work their many fields. Since World War II many farmers have wanted to use farm machinery, but there have been problems. Most of the plots are too small for tractors. Roads need to be built on the farmland so that the farmers can reach each field with their machinery.

The irregular shape of the European continent means that many parts of Western Europe are close to the sea. Remind pupils of what they learned in Chapter 3 about the effect of large bodies of water on climate.

Many governments have tried to rearrange the plots so that each family has a single piece of land. This is not easy because all of the owners must agree on the new farm boundaries. Still, some farmers have moved out of their villages to modern farmsteads located in the middle of their fields. This is a big change in the way people live, but the fields are still open, without hedges or fences.

A second kind of field pattern is called enclosed field. An enclosure surrounds each plot of land. The enclosures are often hedges with trees or stone fences. The farmers with enclosed fields often live on isolated farms.

European farmers generally prefer to live in villages rather than smaller settlements. Most farming villages were founded centuries ago. Many villages arose from the need for friendship and defense. European farmers enjoy the traditional village life that their ancestors knew. They are cautious about changing the pattern of their land.

Villages, Towns, and Cities

Villages in Europe are not all the same. Some are long strings of houses stretched out on both sides of a single street. Some are clustered around a church that faces a central square. Other villages have a starlike shape. The buildings are different, too. In southern Europe, people build mainly with stone. If they use bricks, they cover the bricks with mortar. In northwestern Europe, brick houses and barns are common. Wood is used in Scandinavia and in parts of central Europe.

Towns and cities are also varied. Some of the differences have to do with age. Most Mediterranean towns are very old. Northern European cities are more recent, but they may have buildings that are hundreds of years old. Some of the older cities have not grown much in modern times, and some have been kept as historic monuments and tourist attractions.

Many older towns have grown into modern cities. Rome and Paris are examples of huge modern cities that grew from very old beginnings. There are also industrial cities in Europe that are fairly new. Finally, there are new towns built since World War II. They were built to house the overflow population of the crowded older cities. Britain and the Netherlands have been pioneers in planning new towns.

A Small Area, But Many Nations

Many people have tried to unify Europe into a single country. Most of the people and their local rulers thought that they were so different from their neighbors that they could not live under common rule. This view, called nationalism, has become very strong in the last 200 years.

Many disputes and wars have taken place to decide what the territory and government of each nation will be. These conflicts have created the present countries of Western Europe. Some countries, such as Denmark, France, and Switzerland, are more than 600 years old. Others are much more recent. Germany and Italy did not become unified countries until the 1800s.

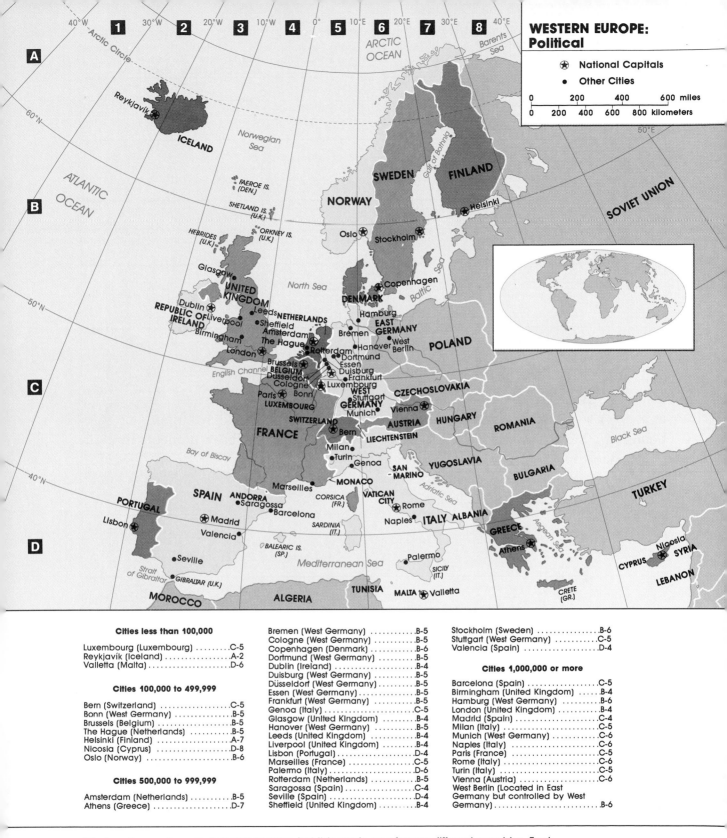

WESTERN EUROPE: Political

⊛ National Capitals

• Other Cities

Cities less than 100,000		
Luxembourg (Luxembourg)	....	C-5
Reykjavík (Iceland)	....	A-2
Valletta (Malta)	....	D-6

Cities 100,000 to 499,999

Bern (Switzerland) C-5
Bonn (West Germany) B-5
Brussels (Belgium) B-5
The Hague (Netherlands) B-5
Helsinki (Finland) A-7
Nicosia (Cyprus) D-8
Oslo (Norway) B-6

Cities 500,000 to 999,999

Amsterdam (Netherlands) B-5
Athens (Greece) D-7

Bremen (West Germany) B-5
Cologne (West Germany) B-5
Copenhagen (Denmark) B-6
Dortmund (West Germany) B-5
Dublin (Ireland) B-4
Duisburg (West Germany) B-5
Düsseldorf (West Germany) B-5
Essen (West Germany) B-5
Frankfurt (West Germany) B-5
Genoa (Italy) C-5
Glasgow (United Kingdom) B-4
Hanover (West Germany) B-5
Leeds (United Kingdom) B-4
Liverpool (United Kingdom) B-4
Lisbon (Portugal) D-4
Marseilles (France) C-5
Palermo (Italy) D-6
Rotterdam (Netherlands) B-5
Saragossa (Spain) C-4
Seville (Spain) D-4
Sheffield (United Kingdom) B-4

Stockholm (Sweden) B-6
Stuttgart (West Germany) C-5
Valencia (Spain) D-4

Cities 1,000,000 or more

Barcelona (Spain) C-5
Birmingham (United Kingdom) B-4
Hamburg (West Germany) B-6
London (United Kingdom) B-4
Madrid (Spain) C-4
Milan (Italy) C-5
Munich (West Germany) C-6
Naples (Italy) C-5
Paris (France) C-5
Rome (Italy) C-6
Turin (Italy) C-5
Vienna (Austria) C-6
West Berlin (Located in East
Germany but controlled by West
Germany)..........................B-6

Western Europe is a small region in area, but it is made up of many different countries. Each country has its own government, laws, money, and traditions.

Provide an outline map of Western Europe and have pupils label the countries in the region and the national capitals.

WESTERN EUROPE

COUNTRY	FLAG	TOTAL AREA	POPULATION and POPULATION DENSITY	CAPITAL CITY and POPULATION	WHERE PEOPLE LIVE
Andorra		175 sq mi (453 sq km)	28,000 160 per sq mi (62 per sq km)	Andorra la Vella 13,000	
Austria		32,374 sq mi (83,849 sq km)	7,600,000 235 per sq mi (91 per sq km)	Vienna 1,517,000	
Belgium		11,781 sq mi (30,513 sq km)	9,900,000 840 per sq mi (324 per sq km)	Brussels 144,000	
Cyprus		3,572 sq mi (9,251 sq km)	700,000 196 per sq mi (76 per sq km)	Nicosia 117,000	
Denmark		16,629 sq mi (43,069 sq km)	5,100,000 307 per sq mi (118 per sq km)	Copenhagen 499,000	
Finland		130,120 sq mi (337,009 sq km)	4,800,000 37 per sq mi (14 per sq km)	Helsinki 483,000	
France		211,208 sq mi (547,026 sq km)	54,600,000 259 per sq mi (100 per sq km)	Paris 2,300,000	
Germany (West)		95,934 sq mi (248,468 sq km)	61,500,000 641 per sq mi (248 per sq km)	Bonn 288,000	
Greece		50,944 sq mi (131,944 sq km)	9,900,000 194 per sq mi (75 per sq km)	Athens 867,000	
Iceland		39,769 sq mi (103,000 sq km)	200,000 5 per sq mi (2 per sq km)	Reykjavik 84,000	
Ireland		27,136 sq mi (70,283 sq km)	3,500,000 129 per sq mi (50 per sq km)	Dublin 525,500	
Italy		116,314 sq mi (301,253 sq km)	56,300,000 484 per sq mi (187 per sq km)	Rome 2,830,500	
Liechtenstein		61 sq mi (157 sq km)	25,000 410 per sq mi (160 per sq km)	Vaduz 4,500	

Urban ■   Nonurban ☐   Not Available – ■

Assign each pupil a different country in Western Europe. Have pupils prepare a fact sheet that includes information about chief products, government, educational system, and other topics of interest to pupils.

WESTERN EUROPE

COUNTRY	FLAG	TOTAL AREA	POPULATION and POPULATION DENSITY	CAPITAL CITY and POPULATION	WHERE PEOPLE LIVE
Luxembourg		998 sq mi (2,586 sq km)	400,000 401 per sq mi (155 per sq km)	Luxembourg 79,000	
Malta		122 sq mi (316 sq km)	400,000 3,279 per sq mi (1,266 per sq km)	Valletta 14,000	
Monaco		0.58 sq mi (1.49 sq km)	26,000 44,828 per sq mi (17,450 per sq km)	Monaco 1,700	
Netherlands		15,892 sq mi (41,160 sq km)	14,400,000 906 per sq mi (350 per sq km)	Amsterdam 701,000	
Norway		125,182 sq mi (324,219 sq km)	4,100,000 33 per sq mi (13 per sq km)	Oslo 452,000	
Portugal		35,553 sq mi (92,082 sq km)	9,900,000 278 per sq mi (108 per sq km)	Lisbon 830,000	
San Marino		24 sq mi (61 sq km)	21,000 875 per sq mi (344 per sq km)	San Marino 5,000	
Spain		194,885 sq mi (504,750 sq km)	38,400,000 197 per sq mi (76 per sq km)	Madrid 3,159,000	
Sweden		173,732 sq mi (449,964 sq km)	8,300,000 48 per sq mi (18 per sq km)	Stockholm 647,000	
Switzerland		15,941 sq mi (41,288 sq km)	6,500,000 408 per sq mi (157 per sq km)	Bern 145,500	
United Kingdom		94,251 sq mi (244,108 sq km)	56,000,000 594 per sq mi (229 per sq km)	London 6,696,000	
Vatican City		0.17 sq mi (0.44 sq km)	1,000 5,882 per sq mi (2,273 per sq km)		

Urban ▇ Nonurban ▇ Not Available —▇   **147**

CHAPTER

9 The British Isles and Scandinavia

The British Isles

Two governments and five peoples
The British Isles are made up of two main islands, Great Britain and Ireland. Great Britain is about one third the size of Texas. Great Britain includes England, Wales, and Scotland. Ireland is about half as large as New England. It includes Northern Ireland and the Republic of Ireland, or Eire (ar′ ə). There are other islands in the British Isles that are much smaller. All together, the British Isles are almost the same size as New Mexico. The map on page 150 shows you where all these parts of the British Isles are located. Be sure to look at the scale so that you can tell how far it is from one place to another.

The British Isles are ruled by two governments. The larger of the two political states is known as the United Kingdom of Great Britain and Northern Ireland— often shortened to either United Kingdom or Great Britain. It includes England, Wales, Scotland, and Northern Ireland. Its capital is London. Great Britain is a member of the Commonwealth of Nations. The other political unit is the Republic of Ireland. It includes most of Ireland, and its capital is Dublin. The areas and populations of the political units that make up the British Isles are shown in the table on pages 146–147.

Five major groups of people live on these islands—the English, the Welsh, the Scots, the Irish, and the North Irish. The English, numbering about 46 million, live in England. This country is located in the southern part of the island of Great Britain. The people all speak English and most of them are Protestants who belong to the Church of England.

There are nearly 3 million Welsh who live in Wales, located on a western peninsula of Great Britain. Almost all the Welsh speak English, but about one fifth of them speak Welsh, one of the Celtic (sel′ tik) languages. Celtic languages were once spoken all over the British Isles, but now they are spoken only in a few remote areas. The Welsh are almost all Protestants who belong to the Methodist Church.

The Scots live in the northern part of Britain, which is called Scotland. Almost all of the 5 million Scots speak English, but about 90,000 still speak the Celtic language called Scottish Gaelic (gā′ lik). Most Scots belong to the Presbyterian Church. When we speak of the English, Welsh, and Scots as a single group, we call them the British.

London is a large historic city. Millions of tourists visit each year to see such landmarks as the famous Clock Tower of the Houses of Parliament. (52°N/0° long; map, p. 150)

The Commonwealth of Nations is a group of independent countries and other political units that were once ruled by the British. The Commonwealth covers about one fourth of the earth's land and has about one fourth of its population.

THE BRITISH ISLES: Physical-Political

✪ National Capitals
• Other Cities

Great Britain and Ireland are the two largest islands of the British Isles group.

Highland and Lowland Britain The British Isles are divided into two clearly different landform regions. These regions are the highlands and the lowlands. In the highlands are mountains with gentle slopes and rounded tops. The highest point in the British Isles is the Scottish mountain called Ben Nevis. It is only 4,406 feet (1,343 m) above sea level. Nevertheless, these highlands stand out against the gently rolling lowlands of southeastern England. The border between the highlands and the lowlands is shown by the red line on the map on this page. The area north and west of the line is called High-

One of Europe's most scenic areas is the rugged Highlands of northern Scotland. Deep blue lakes provide some of the most beautiful scenery. Shown here is Loch Assynt, a lake in northern Scotland.

Ireland is divided by two groups who have different histories and religions. Most of Ireland is inhabited by the more than 3 million Irish. Three quarters of them speak English, and the rest speak the Celtic language called Irish Gaelic. Almost all of these Irish are Roman Catholics. In the northeastern corner of Ireland, there are a million Protestants. They are known as the North Irish. Almost all of them are descendants of English or Scots who moved to Ireland starting in the seventeenth century. There are also half a million Catholic Irish who live in the same area.

150

The huge gray stones of the ancient Stonehenge monument, located in Wiltshire, England, form a circle about 97 feet (30 m) in diameter. (51°N/2°W; map, p. 150)

land Britain, but it contains a few lowlands of its own. Much of Ireland is a lowland. So is the central part of Scotland, which is called the Scottish Lowlands.

On the borders between Highland and Lowland Britain are found the major coal deposits of the British Isles. The most important coalfields are in southern Wales, along the edges of the Pennines, and in the Scottish Lowlands. Unfortunately for Ireland, it has no important coal deposits. Its only local source of fuel is **peat.** Peat is made up of partly rotted plants and moss that are found in bogs or swamps. When peat is dried, it can be used to produce electricity, but it does not have the heating power of coal. For this reason, peat is not a good fuel for use in industries.

The landscape of Lowland Britain is made up of low ridges with broad lowlands in between. Several thousand years ago, people used these ridges as routes of travel because the lowlands were often marshy or covered by dense forests. The five main ridges of southeastern England meet at one point, and this is where Stonehenge was built about 4,000 years ago. Stonehenge is in ruins today, but it was once a ring of enormous, rough-cut stones. Scholars think that ancient people built the structure in order to study astronomy, a science that deals with the heavenly bodies and their motions. People probably came from far away to take part in special ceremonies at Stonehenge. That may explain why Stonehenge was built at the intersection of those major routes of travel.

The monument at Stonehenge may have served as an accurate astronomical calendar, capable of predicting the seasons of the year and the eclipses of the sun and moon.

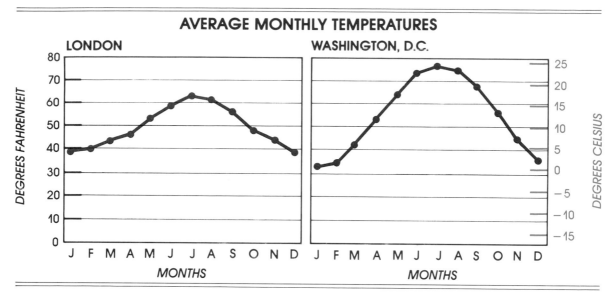

AVERAGE MONTHLY TEMPERATURES

LONDON — DEGREES FAHRENHEIT — MONTHS: J F M A M J J A S O N D

WASHINGTON, D.C. — DEGREES CELSIUS — MONTHS: J F M A M J J A S O N D

Use these graphs to compare the average monthly temperatures of London and Washington, D.C.

A marine climate   The climate of the British Isles is very unusual for a place so far north. Northern Scotland is almost as far north as southern Alaska, and London is in the same latitude as the southern shore of Hudson Bay. However, Great Britain and Ireland are much warmer in winter than those places. In January, London is as warm as Washington, D.C., which is almost 900 miles (1,450 km) farther south. Yet British summers are cool. In July, London is 15°F (8°C) cooler than Washington, D.C. Why is that? The main reason is that the Gulf Stream and the west winds bring marine air from the Atlantic Ocean to the British Isles. The graphs above show the average monthly temperatures for London and Washington, D.C.

The Gulf Stream is an ocean current that flows north and east from the warm waters of the Gulf of Mexico. When the Gulf Stream changes direction from northward to eastward, it is called the North Atlantic Drift. In winter the air blowing off this ocean current warms up the British Isles and the rest of northwestern Europe, so winters there are very mild. Other places in the world that are as far north in latitude have very cold winters with temperatures that are below freezing and harbors that are clogged by ice. In summer the air over the Gulf Stream is still warm, but it is cool compared to air that heats up over the land. The result is that northwestern Europe is cooler in summer than other places in the same latitude. A climate that is neither very cold in winter nor very hot in summer is called marine because it has temperatures that are affected by the ocean.

CHECKUP

1. Name the two governments of the British Isles.
2. What is the capital of the United Kingdom?
3. What are the two landform regions of the British Isles?
4. Why are the winters in the British Isles warmer than those in most places in the same latitude?

To further reinforce the effect of the Gulf Stream on London temperatures, have pupils record the daily temperatures in London, given in their local newspaper. Contrast these temperatures with those in other northern cities, such as Warsaw.

People on the Land

Celtic, Roman, and Germanic Invaders

The people who built Stonehenge were followed by other settlers. About 800 B.C. a tribe of Celts, whom we call the Britons, appeared. They gave their name to the British Isles and brought farming and ox-drawn plows to Britain. From the air you can still see traces of their fields and of the fantastic chalk pictures they drew on hillsides. The names of many rivers and mountains, such as the Thames (temz) and the Pennines, are Celtic. So are the names of some modern cities, such as London, Dublin, and Liverpool. These cities were only small fortified villages in Celtic times.

The Romans ruled England for the first four centuries of the Christian **Era** (ir′ ə). An era is a period of years counted from a set point in time. The Romans introduced Christianity to the Celts. They also built towns, roads, and forts. The Roman name for "fort" was *castrum*, and the English gradually changed the sound to *chester*. English cities whose names end in *-chester*, such as Manchester, started out as fortified Roman camps. Roman roads and towns, however, did not survive the invasion of the Germanic tribes who began to raid England around A.D. 450.

The Angles, Saxons, and Jutes were the Germanic tribes who crossed the North Sea to the British Isles. These people came for plunder and later stayed as settlers. They pushed the Celts west into Wales and north into Scotland. In time the largest part of Britain was renamed for these people. It was called Angleland or England. From these groups came the English people and the English language. They also set up small farming villages. The names of many places in Great Britain come from this period. A common ending of place-names is *-ham*, as in Birmingham. In early English, *ham* meant "home." Birmingham may have started out as the home village of a farmer whose name sounded like *Birming*.

Scandinavians also invaded Britain. The most famous invaders were the Normans, who invaded England in 1066 under William the Conqueror. They came from Normandy, in France, where they had adopted French speech and customs.

William the Conqueror was a strong and brave fighter. Few warriors showed greater bravery in battle. This tapestry section shows William with sword in hand.

A manor was like a village with its large fields, orchard, farm buildings, and church.

Labels on image: Third field (fallow), Pasture, Serfs' houses, Second field, Church, Water mill, Barn, First field, Sheep meadow, Manor home, Inn, Well, Lord's oven

Under the Normans, the **manor** became the center of life in Britain. The manor was a small farming village surrounded by open fields and pastures, and separated from the next manor by large forests or woodlands. Each manor raised barely enough to feed the villagers and the household of the lord of the manor.

Some of the people who worked on the manor were **serfs.** They lived in the village and farmed land on the manor, but they were not free to leave without the permission of the lord of the manor. Besides working in the fields, the serfs took care of the lord's home and livestock. The life of a serf was hard, but it was the life led by many people in **medieval** times. *Medieval* refers to the period from about 500 to about 1450 that is known as the Middle Ages.

Changes in the land—the Enclosure Movement and the Industrial Revolution By 1300 this medieval system of working the land changed. Lords of the manor began to have serfs pay rent for the land they used rather than work for the lord. The serfs became tenant farmers and paid rent by giving the lord a large share of the crops they grew. A few farmers even owned their own land.

In part, these changes came about because of a growth in trade—particularly the exchange of English wool for cloth made in Flanders (a part of modern Belgium). It became more profitable for some landowners to raise sheep for wool than to grow wheat or other food. More space was needed for sheep and less for crops. This meant that fewer farmers were needed, so some of them were forced

Have pupils research the differences between serfs (who worked for the land without wages and who belonged to the land) and slaves (who worked without wages and who could be sold because they were the property of a master).

either to find new farmland or to move to towns and cities. The open fields now used for grazing were surrounded by fences or hedges to keep the sheep enclosed. This change in the use of the land is called the **Enclosure Movement.** It began in the 1300s and continued for the next 500 years.

In the 1700s, still another great change took place in England. This time the change was brought about by the invention of machines. They were not worked by hand. The new machines ran on waterpower and steam power. These power-driven machines and the workers to run them were brought together in factories. Soon most people worked in factories instead of making things in their own homes as they had before. Factories and workers moved from the countryside to cities. Cities also began to grow up around the factories. In addition, the population began to grow much more rapidly than before, and the land could no longer feed everyone. Many people moved from their farms to the coal-mining areas on the edge of Highland Britain. Coal was much in demand as a source of power for the factories. As the number of factories grew, the number of machine-made goods increased.

As you can see, the way English people lived and worked changed greatly during this period. England had become a nation of industries and factory workers instead of agriculture and farmers. This period of great change from an agricultural to an industrial society is called the **Industrial Revolution.** And England was a pioneer in the Industrial Revolution. The steam engine, railroads, textile machinery, and methods of making steel were all invented or first developed in England.

British trade and empire   The Industrial Revolution stimulated trade and made it more important than ever. The factory owners needed raw materials such as wool, cotton, and iron. They also needed markets in which to sell their manufactured goods. Fortunately, Great Britain had a huge colonial empire that included Australia, Canada, India, and large parts of Africa. These colonies provided raw materials and markets for British-made goods. The British built up the largest merchant fleet and the most powerful navy in the world. Today most of Britain's former colonies are independent nations belonging to the Commonwealth of Nations.

During the nineteenth century, trade within the British Empire and with other countries became as important as industry to the economy of Great Britain. Britain became the trading and financial capital of much of the world. British banks, such as the Bank of England, and insurance companies lent money and insured goods all over the world.

Many British people moved to other parts of the empire such as Canada, Australia, New Zealand, and South Africa. Quite a few, including most of the **emigrants** from Ireland, went to the United States. An emigrant is someone who leaves one country to settle in another. The English language and other aspects of British life, such as government, law, and education, were spread to the far corners of the world.

Discuss the historical meaning of the word *revolution* (a process of rapid and significant change).

155

The British economy today   In 1900, Great Britain was the leading industrial, trading, and financial country in the world. But the country became poorer after World War I ended in 1918. It was a costly war. Many men, a large part of the merchant fleet, and huge sums of money were lost. The focus of world trade shifted from Britain to the United States and Japan.

Since the end of World War II in 1945, Britain has faced more economic problems. Britain gave up most of its colonies and had to live on its own resources. Many of its coal mines, steel mills, and textile factories are old and no longer efficient. Many people are without jobs in the coal-mining and shipbuilding regions. A few businesses are still prosperous, however. Sheffield steel, woolens from Yorkshire, and high-quality British ceramics are still being sold abroad. British ships still carry the goods of other countries. Newer industries, such as the making of airplane engines, cars, trucks, and machine tools, help pay for the food and raw materials that Britain has to import.

The brightest spot in the present British economy is the North Sea. Here Britain controls nearly half of the underwater oil and natural gas fields. The map on this page shows some of these newly discovered resources, of which Britain and Norway share the largest part.

Turmoil in Northern Ireland   For centuries, historical and religious differences have caused serious problems in Ireland. In the Middle Ages, England took over Ireland, and for hundreds of

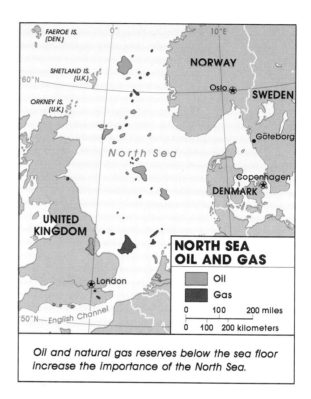

Oil and natural gas reserves below the sea floor increase the importance of the North Sea.

years, Ireland was under British rule. The people of Ireland fought back, but they were unable to overthrow the British. Beginning in the seventeenth century, people from Scotland and England moved to Ireland. These people were Protestants, while most people in Ireland were Catholics. When Britain gave Ireland its independence in 1921 and the Republic of Ireland came into being, most Irish were happy. However, the northeastern corner of Ireland remained in the United Kingdom. This was the home of a million Protestants as well as many Catholics. Some Irish were unhappy with this division and demanded that all of Ireland become part of the republic.

The British gave this new territory of Northern Ireland many local rights. However, the bitter feelings between Catholics and Protestants remained and became worse after World War II. The textile and shipbuilding industries in Northern Ireland lost work, and many workers lost their jobs. Unemployment was particularly high among Catholics. Riots were followed by killings on both sides. In 1972 the British government took over direct rule of Northern Ireland and brought in soldiers. But acts of terrorism against both religious groups and against British troops have continued.

The Republic of Ireland   Ireland's economy has long depended on the raising of cattle, sheep, and pigs. Only the northeast—that part which later became Northern Ireland—developed industries like those of Britain. Nevertheless, the population of Ireland was very large and it kept growing. This meant that the land had to support more and more people. In 1841, Ireland was more densely populated than Britain, despite the fact that Ireland had no large cities and very little industry.

In the 1840s, disease destroyed the potato crop in Ireland. This caused a **famine,** or great shortage of food, because the potato was the basis of the Irish farmer's diet. Some people died, and many Irish left their homeland. In the 10 years after the famine, one sixth of the total population of Ireland came to live in the United States. Between 1841 and 1901 the population of the island decreased from 8 million to 4 million.

Today, Ireland is slowly gaining population again. It is still a farming country, sending food to Britain and the rest of Europe. Ireland has few resources, but it has been able to attract some foreign businesses with its low taxes.

A typical view of the green Irish countryside is shown below. Many of the Irish people live in small villages and work on the land.

The Tower of London, located on a bank of the Thames River, was formerly a combination fort, prison, and royal home. Today the Tower of London is one of the major tourist attractions of England.

London—still a world capital   The Celts built a small fortified settlement on the Thames River, and the Romans made it a government center of Britain. London almost completely disappeared during the Anglo-Saxon invasions. Late in the eleventh century, the son of William the Conqueror built a combination fort, prison, and royal home on the north bank of the Thames. It later became known as the Tower of London. A church was built a few miles to the west. In between, merchants and bankers lived and traded close to the river, where seagoing ships loaded and unloaded at small wharfs. This was the real beginning of London. Its growth after that closely followed the growth of England and the development of the Brit-

ish Empire. In the seventeenth century, London already had more than half a million people, and by 1800 it had passed the million mark. It then had twice as many people as Paris, which was the next largest European city. Half the world's trade in such things as coffee, tea, sugar, and gold went through the port of London. As the British Empire grew during the 1800s, so did London. In 1900 it had more than 6 million people and had become the world's most important commercial and financial center, as well as the most populated city on the earth.

Today quite a few cities have grown to be as large as, or larger than, London. And some of them have become more important as industrial, trading, or banking centers. London is still a world capital, however. Its trade with the rest of the world continues to be very large. Almost every kind of manufacturing industry—including clothing, furniture, machines, chemicals, and foodstuffs—is found in London. London's port is one of the busiest in the world. Its airport is also busy. And the number of banks, insurance companies, and other financial institutions in London is second only to that of New York.

CHECKUP

1. What did the Celts contribute to the British Isles? How did the Angles, Saxons, and Jutes change the land?
2. Why did sheep raising become more important than farming in the 1300s?
3. What effect did the Industrial Revolution have on where the people of Britain lived?
4. How did the two world wars change Britain?
5. What two groups live in Northern Ireland?
6. Why did the population of Ireland decline in the 1800s?

Point out one reason the Tower of London has endured in such good condition for so long: It has very thick walls that have provided solid protection against entire armies of invaders.

Scandinavia—The Countries of the North

Four distinct landform regions The Scandinavian countries—Iceland, Norway, Denmark, Sweden, and Finland—have many things in common, but the landscape of each country is very differ-ent. On the map, you can see the four landform regions of Scandinavia.

The oldest landform is the **Scandinavian Shield** which covers most of Sweden and all of Finland. The Shield is made up of the oldest rocks in Europe. They have been eroded for more than 600 million years, leaving a flat land of hard rocks and thin soils. The main resources of this region are iron ore deposits, forests, and waterpower from the streams.

The mountains of Norway are another landform region. These mountains are high and rugged in places. There are few lowlands that are good for farming.

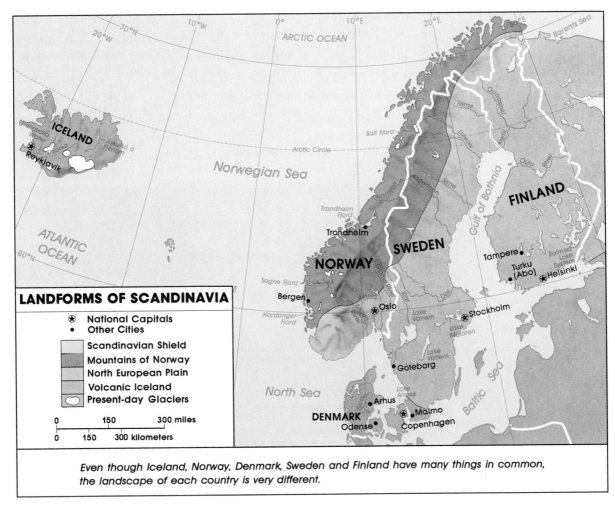

LANDFORMS OF SCANDINAVIA

⊛ National Capitals
• Other Cities

Scandinavian Shield
Mountains of Norway
North European Plain
Volcanic Iceland
Present-day Glaciers

0   150   300 miles
0   150   300 kilometers

Even though Iceland, Norway, Denmark, Sweden and Finland have many things in common, the landscape of each country is very different.

Using the above map as their information source, have pupils make a chart showing the capital city **159** and predominant landform found in each of the Scandinavian countries.

Denmark and the southern tip of Sweden are parts of the **North European Plain.** Here the land is flat and low. There are few mineral resources and the streams are too slow-moving to produce hydroelectricity. This is electricity developed from waterpower. The soils of this region are good, however, and this part of Europe has been farmed for more than 3,000 years.

The fourth landform is Iceland. It has the youngest rocks in Europe. Iceland is made up of volcanic lava and ash that are still pouring out of craters and cracks in the earth. One useful resource produced by volcanic action is the **geyser** (gī′ zər). A geyser is a fountain of steam and water that has been heated by the hot lava and forced above ground by volcanic gases. Reykjavík (rāk′ yə vēk), the capital of Iceland, uses water from geysers to heat its buildings and homes.

How glaciers affected the land During the last million years, Scandinavia was repeatedly covered by ice thousands of feet thick. The ice sheet, or **glacier,** advanced and retreated, or melted, at least four times. The ice started its last retreat 10,000 years ago. Today only a few small glaciers are left in the mountains of Norway and in Iceland.

In earlier times, when the glacier was moving forward, it scraped the land like rough sandpaper on soft wood. The scraping made the Shield even flatter and smoother. But in places where the rocks were soft, the glacier cut grooves that today are filled by lakes. On the map, you can see the many lakes of Sweden and Finland. In the Norwegian mountains the ice deepened and widened the river valleys and even scooped out long, narrow troughs below sea level. Water from the Atlantic Ocean later filled the

Only a few small glaciers are left in the mountains of Norway. Glaciers such as this one carved deep fjords that were later filled by the sea.

troughs. These beautiful inlets that look like water-filled canyons are fjords.

Denmark was also scraped by the glacier, but the land was shaped more by the melting ice. When a glacier melts, it has to dump all of the rock, sand, and fine clay that it has scraped up during its advance. Denmark is made up of material left behind by retreating glaciers. The soil that developed from these glacial deposits can grow good crops and pasture if it is carefully farmed.

Mild climates and rugged ones Scandinavia is a northern region. Much of it is in the same latitude as the Yukon Territory. But Scandinavian winters are mild compared to those in northern Canada because the Gulf Stream flows past the coasts of Iceland and Norway. In January, the southwestern coast of Iceland and the central coast of Norway are as warm as New York, which is 1,500 miles (2,400 km) farther south. Both Iceland and Norway have average winter temperatures just above freezing. Summers in Scandinavia are cool, however. The Norwegian coast is almost 18°F (10°C) cooler than New York in July, and Iceland is even cooler. Some of the coastal areas of Scandinavia get over 60 inches (152 cm) of rain a year, and snowfall is quite heavy in the highlands.

The marine climate changes as you cross the Norwegian mountains into Sweden and Finland. The influence of the Gulf Stream is less, and therefore winters are colder. Stockholm, Sweden, is 8°F (4°C) colder than Bergen, Norway, in January, and Helsinki, Finland, is 5°F (3°C) colder than Stockholm. The northern part of the

Finland is known for its natural beauty. Thick forests cover more than half of the land. The forests make it possible for Finland to have a thriving forest-products industry.

Baltic Sea freezes over every winter. Many of the Baltic ports are blocked by ice for many months. In summer the **interior** is a few degrees warmer than the Atlantic coast. The interior is the part of a region or country that is away from the coast or the border. Rainfall decreases rapidly east of the Norwegian mountains, particularly in the north. Northern Sweden and Finland get less than 20 inches (51 cm) of rain a year. Snowfall is not very heavy, but snow covers the ground for several months.

Repeat the activity described in the annotation on p. 152, but this time have pupils record and compare the daily temperatures in Copenhagen and Moscow.

TABLE OF NUMBERS FROM ONE TO FIVE

English	Dutch	German	Danish	Swedish	Norwegian	Icelandic	Finnish
one	een	eins	en	en	en	einn	yksi
two	twee	zwei	to	tva	to	tveir	kaksi
three	drie	drei	tre	tre	tre	thrír	kolme
four	vier	vier	fire	fyra	fire	fjórir	neljä
five	vijf	fünf	fem	fem	fem	fimm	viisi

Similarities and differences among the peoples of Scandinavia Who are the Scandinavians? Two thousand years ago they spoke a Germanic language that they shared with other groups. *Germanic* does not mean "German." German is only one of many languages in the Germanic language family. English, Dutch, and the present-day Scandinavian languages are also part of the Germanic language family.

When the ancestors of the Scandinavians moved north into Denmark, Sweden, and Norway, they lost touch with their Germanic cousins to the south. They began to change their habits and customs, and their language. As the Scandinavians themselves became different from each other, four languages replaced the single Scandinavian tongue of earlier years. Iceland kept the old language. Danish, Swedish, and Norwegian changed more than Icelandic, but they changed in many of the same ways because of close contact among the countries. Although Danish, Swedish, and Norwegian are separate languages, the people who speak them can usually understand each other. Only the Finns do not speak a Scandinavian language. Finnish belongs to a different language family.

Habits, customs, and ways of living changed right along with language, but the common Scandinavian heritage remained strong. One of the ways to measure this closeness is to look at the modern languages. The table of numbers from one to five shows how similar the Scandinavian languages are. You can also see the family resemblance between the Scandinavian and other Germanic languages, and how different Finnish is from the languages in the Germanic family.

Language is not the only thing that most Scandinavians have in common. Most of them, including the Finns, belong to the Lutheran Church. All the countries have developed democratic governments in modern times. In each country, overpopulation and poverty became problems in the 1800s. Large numbers of people emigrated to North America at that time. Between 1880 and 1910 a million and a half Scandinavians came to the United States alone. However, during the last 80 years the standard of living has risen steadily in each country. Today, Scandinavians are among the healthiest, best-educated, and most well-to-do people in the world. The income per person in each of the five countries ranks among the top twenty in the world.

162

Note that the language of Finland is not part of the Scandinavian language group. Another way to classify the five countries in this region is to describe them as *Nordic*.

Stacked in this Norwegian lumberyard is some of the country's lumber supply.

Finland shares most of these characteristics, but its history has been different. Finland was a colony of Sweden for 500 years, until 1809. From 1809 until 1918, Finland was part of the Russian Empire. When the Russians built railroads, the tracks were the same width as those in Russia. Finnish trains, even today, cannot travel on the narrower European tracks. Finland became independent in 1918, and since then it has had to develop very careful relations with the Soviet Union. Today, Finland's standard of living and its democratic government, just like its religion, link it to Scandinavia.

Five countries and their economies
The five Scandinavian countries are all trading nations, and they all have very high standards of living. In other ways, their economies are different.

Iceland has to import almost everything it uses. Farming is limited by very cool summers. The island has few mineral resources and no trees. Iceland's wellbeing depends on the rich fishing grounds that surround the island. The cod-fishing industry is especially important to Iceland.

Norway also depends on the sea for its livelihood. Norway catches more fish than any other European country. The Norwegian merchant fleet is one of the largest in the world. In recent years, Norwegian rigs have been taking oil and natural gas from the floor of the North Sea. On land, Norway leads the world in the production of electricity. Part of Norway's hydroelectric power is used to make aluminum. Norway also has a steel industry based on its own iron ore deposits. Wood is another resource, but the forests in Norway can no longer supply enough wood pulp for the country's paper industry. Wood pulp is shredded wood that has been treated to make it into a soft paste. This wood pulp becomes the raw material for making paper and cardboard. As you can see, Norway's economy is similar to Iceland's. However, Norway has much more industry, and it has the North Sea oil fields.

The original inhabitants of Finland were a nomadic people, known as the Lapps, who now occupy the extreme northern part of Scandinavia, called Lapland.

Copenhagen is an important trading and industrial center. (56°N/13°E; map, p. 159)

Sweden is the most industrialized of the five countries. The Scandinavian Shield contains minerals such as lead, copper, and iron. The rivers can be dammed where they come out of the mountains to make hydroelectric power. The land is covered by forests of pine and spruce. The Swedes have used these three resources very skillfully. Sweden was one of the first countries to develop better ways of refining iron ore so that it could be used to make steel. Sweden exports some of its high-grade iron and also exports manufactured products, such as ball bearings and automobiles. Sweden was also one of the first countries to find ways to send electricity over long distances, from the northern rivers to the southern factories. The forests of Sweden make it a leading producer of paper, pulp, and cardboard. Sweden's best farmland is in the southern part of the country, where the land and the climate are like those of Denmark. As you can see, Sweden is much more industrial than Iceland or Norway. It also has more farming, but it does not depend as much on the sea.

Denmark's wealth comes from farming, manufacturing, and a good location for trade. Notice on the map that the Danish peninsula and the many islands almost cut off the Baltic from the North Sea. To get in or out of the Baltic Sea, ships have always had to pass close to Copenhagen. Copenhagen, the capital of Denmark, has been an important trading center and naval base since medieval times. Denmark produces many industrial products, such as diesel engines, but the country is best known for its agriculture. Some of its main exports are butter, meat, and eggs. Years ago the Danish government decided that the country should specialize in these farming products. So the government set up farmers' **cooperatives** for buying feed and selling the final products.

The above photo includes a view of Copenhagen harbor, where the famous statue *The Little Mermaid* is found. This statue represents a character from a fairy tale by Hans Christian Andersen.

You may want to contact a local travel agency to request posters and brochures that illustrate the cities and countryside of Scandinavia.

Finland's traditional resource is its forests. However, the Finns have greatly increased their production of manufactured goods, such as machinery, textiles, and chemicals. The invasion of Finland by the Soviet Union in 1940 prompted this economic change. After Finland lost the war, it had to take in many Finns who had lived in the lands given up to the Russians. It also had to pay the Russians in goods and money. To solve its problems, Finland made jobs in industry for the displaced Finns. The goods produced also helped to pay off Finland's debt to the Soviet Union. Finland's economy today is linked to the Soviet Union by very close trade connections.

Cities, towns, and hamlets   Scandinavian settlements share some strong similarities. Copenhagen, the capital of Denmark, and Stockholm, the capital of Sweden, are good examples. They are the two largest cities in Scandinavia. Each one has over a million people in the city and its suburbs. Both cities have canals and waterways in the oldest section of town. In both cities, crowded nineteenth-century buildings surround a modern business center. Still, there are differences. Stockholm is a city of tall buildings; Copenhagen's are lower and more spread out. The Swedish high-rise suburbs are like isolated trees rising out of a land of lakes and bare rock. The Danish suburbs look like rose gardens across meadowland. Both cities are clean and beautiful; both are obviously Scandinavian. But they are not alike.

Oslo and Helsinki, the capitals of Norway and Finland, and Göteborg, Sweden's main port, are only half the size of Stockholm and Copenhagen. Nevertheless they have the same sorts of likenesses and differences. Even the smaller towns, which are numerous in Sweden, show the same thing.

Rural settlements also differ from one country to the next. Danish farmers used to live in compact villages, but the Danish government moved many farmers out of their villages and into scattered farmsteads. Today in Denmark you have to go to villages to see old farmhouses and out into the fields to see new ones. Southern Sweden looks like Denmark, except that the farmers still live in villages. In northern Sweden, homes are scattered over the land. Norwegians prefer **hamlets**, groupings of houses, barns, and stables that belong to two or three families. In Finland and in Iceland scattered settlements are the most common.

Throughout Scandinavia old buildings and newer buildings are made of wood. Even in Denmark, where wood is scarce, the farmhouses are often half-timbered. This gives Scandinavia an appearance that is very different from the rest of Europe.

CHECKUP

1. What areas does the Scandinavian Shield cover? What resources are found in the Shield?
2. How did glaciers affect the land in Norway? How did they affect the land in Denmark?
3. What languages are spoken in Scandinavia? Which languages are very similar?
4. How is Finland like other Scandinavian countries? How is it different?
5. Which Scandinavian countries depend on the sea for their livelihood? Which country is the most industrialized? Which one has the most farming?

9/CHAPTER REVIEW

KEY FACTS

1. The United Kingdom is made up of England, Wales, Scotland, and Northern Ireland.

2. Religious differences between its people have caused serious problems in Northern Ireland.

3. The Industrial Revolution made Great Britain a world leader in trade, colonization, and manufacturing in the nineteenth century.

4. The newly discovered oil and gas fields under the floor of the North Sea have aided Britain's economy.

5. The Scandinavian Shield and the North European Plain are distinct landform regions in Scandinavia, and they both provide important natural resources.

6. The peoples of Scandinavia share many common characteristics of history, economy, government, language, and religion.

VOCABULARY QUIZ

Write each word in the list on a sheet of paper. Match each word with the correct meaning below.

a. peat	**f.** geyser
b. emigrant	**g.** interior
c. famine	**h.** cooperative
d. serf	**i.** hamlet
e. manor	**j.** era

j **1.** A period of years counted from a set point in time

i **2.** A grouping of farm buildings that belongs to several families

b **3.** A person who leaves one country to settle in another

a **4.** A fuel resource of Ireland

g **5.** The part of a region or country that is away from the coast or the border.

h **6.** An organization in Denmark that buys feed and sells farm products.

f **7.** A fountain of water and steam that has been heated by hot lava and forced above ground by volcanic gases

d **8.** A person who lived and worked on a manor

e **9.** A small medieval farming village

c **10.** A great shortage of food

REVIEW QUESTIONS

1. The British Isles and western Scandinavia both have a marine climate. How would you describe this type of climate?

2. What impact did the Industrial Revolution have on the United Kingdom?

3. Why is Ireland divided today?

4. What are the major natural resources of each country in Scandinavia?

5. How are the five Scandinavian economies different? How are they similar?

ACTIVITIES

1. Trace a map that shows the political boundaries of Scandinavia and the British Isles. Then choose five colors: one each for Lutherans, Presbyterians, Methodists, Church of England, and Roman Catholics. Color each country appropriately. If a country has two main religions, make stripes of the two colors. Then answer the following questions. How many religions are there **(a)** in Scandinavia, **(b)** in the Republic of Ireland, **(c)** on the Island of Great Britain, and **(d)** in Northern Ireland?

2. When you visit a supermarket, make a list of the things you can find that were made in the British Isles and in Scandinavia. Do the same thing in a toy or hobby store.

9/SKILLS DEVELOPMENT

USING PRIMARY SOURCES

WHAT IS A PRIMARY SOURCE?

In the middle and late 1800s, millions of immigrants came to live in the United States. As you know, many of them came from Ireland. Below are two reports about the conditions in Ireland in 1847. These reports are called primary sources. A primary source is something written by someone who either saw or took part in an event.

TO HELP YOU READ

There are certain rules to keep in mind when you read primary-source material. Sometimes words are shown in brackets [like this]. Words in brackets are put in by the editor to make the meaning of the passage clearer. Words that appear in brackets are not part of the primary-source material.

If the editor decides to leave words out of the source material, three periods mark the place where the words were. This is called an ellipsis (i lip′ sis). If the ellipsis is at the end of a sentence, a fourth period is added.

FIRST REPORT

Out of this population of 9,800 souls . . . there are at this moment over 7,000 in the greatest state of misery and distress, out of which 5,000 have not . . . a single meal to provide for their wants tomorrow. This has arisen from the total failure of the potato, upon which the people solely relied, and also . . . the [poor] oat crop last harvest, in these districts.

SECOND REPORT

I accompanied a Captain of one of her Majesty's steamers. . . . He, too, could scarcely believe the accounts of the famine, until I brought him to their hovels, and showed five or six lying in fever, huddled together on the damp, cold ground, with scarce a wisp of straw under them; and, in another cabin, four or five unfortunate beings just risen from fever, crouched over a small pot of seaweed boiling on the fire, that one of them had crawled to the shore, to collect for their dinner.

(Taken from *Immigration as a Factor in American History* by Oscar Handlin. Englewood Cliffs, N.J.: Prentice-Hall, Inc., 1959, pp. 21–22.)

SKILLS PRACTICE

The questions below are about the two reports that you have just read. Answer the questions on a sheet of paper. Number your answers.

1. What does the first report say had happened in Ireland?
2. Out of the population of 9,800, how many people, according to the report, did not have food for the next day?
3. What caused the misery and distress among the people that is described in these reports?
4. The potato crop failed. The harvest of another crop was poor. What was this crop?
5. Why, would you say, did many people in Ireland want to move to the United States?
6. What do you think the word *hovel* means? Refer to a dictionary and write the dictionary definition of the word on your paper.
7. Why did one of the people have to crawl to the shore to find food for dinner?
8. What do you think would be a good title for each of these reports?
9. If you had been living in Ireland in 1847, do you think you might have wanted to move to the United States? Write your answer in a paragraph. Be sure to give some reasons for your answer.

1. A major famine 2. 5,000 3. Crop failure 4. Oats 5. Hunger and quest for a better life 6. A shed or open-roofed shelter 7. To collect seaweed 8. Answers will vary. 9. Answers will vary.

France—Where Northern and Southern Europe Meet

┌─ VOCABULARY ──────────────┐
vineyard   technology
basin   tourism
└───────────────────────────┘

A varied land   France is the largest European country west of the Soviet Union. Mountains of the Alpine system are in southern France. The Alps form the boundary with Italy. The Jura Mountains form the boundary with Switzerland, and the Pyrenees form the boundary with Spain. The Alps are the country's highest and most rugged mountains, yet they have passes which can be used to get from France to Italy.

The northern boundaries of France lie in the middle of the North European Plain. This flat area stretches southward as far as the foothills of the Pyrenees. The deep and fertile soils of this lowland make up some of the best farming areas in the country.

France has several hills and low mountains. These make up the Central Uplands. You can see the location of these uplands on the map on page 171. France's major coalfields and iron ore deposits are on the edge of the most northerly of these uplands, the Ardennes.

France also has a varied climate. The western half of the country has a marine climate. Southern France has a Mediterranean climate. The northeastern corner of France has a continental climate.

Celts, Romans, and Franks   Three groups of people helped to create modern France. The first of these groups was the Celts. The Celts who lived in France called themselves Gauls. The Romans conquered the Gauls 2,000 years ago. By A.D. 400 the Gauls had become very much like the Romans. They had given up their Celtic language for Latin. They also became Christians when the Romans did. And they adopted Roman farming practices. Many of the Gauls lived in towns and cities like those of the Romans.

When the power of Rome declined in the fifth century A.D., Gaul was overrun by Germanic tribes. The most important were the Franks, who settled in northern France. They ruled much of France and gave their name to the country. The Franks brought their own farming practices. They quickly adopted Christianity. They gave up their Germanic language and began to speak French. French was a new language that was developing from Latin. They also adopted the Roman system of law. It is still the basis of French law.

Children in wheelchairs view the mountains in a section of the French Alps, the country's highest mountain range.

The concept of natural law originated with the Romans and was a key factor in the development of democracy in both France and the United States in the eighteenth century.

FRANCE AND THE LOW COUNTRIES: Political

⊛ National Capitals
• Other Cities

0 100 200 miles
0 100 200 kilometers

North Sea

NETHERLANDS
IJsselmeer
Haarlem
The Amsterdam
Hague Utrecht
Rotterdam
Maas

WEST
GERMANY

UNITED KINGDOM

Antwerp
Ghent
⊛ Brussels
BELGIUM Liège
Charleroi
Scheldt
Sambre
Meuse
Rhine
Moselle

English Channel
50° N

Luxembourg
LUXEMBOURG

Le Havre

Seine

Paris ⊛

Strasbourg

Loire

Nantes

FRANCE

Saône

SWITZERLAND

Bay of Biscay

Lyons
Saint-Étienne

Grenoble

Rhône

ITALY

Bordeaux

Garonne

MONACO
Nice

Toulouse

Marseilles

SPAIN

ANDORRA

Mediterranean Sea

France is a large country. The Low Countries are much smaller than France. All together the Low Countries are not much larger than the state of West Virginia.

Each of the three groups—Celts, Romans, and Franks—has had a strong influence on France. The people, customs, law, religion, and language of France are all a result of their combined influences.

The fields and farms People in France have farmed the land for more than 2,000 years. Traces of this long farming past can be seen in the modern agriculture of France.

Roman influence was strongest in the southern part. Here Mediterranean plants, such as grapes, olives, and figs were grown. These are still the leading crops of this part of France.

The Romans did not enclose their fields. Even today there are few fences or hedges in southern France. Straight rows of trees have been planted, not as fences, but as a protection against the wind. Many of the farmers in southern France now live in hamlets. Others live in clustered villages or scattered farms.

Northern France was less affected by the Romans. Only a few of the Mediterranean crops, mainly wheat and grapes, could be grown there. The Romans planted **vineyards** (vin′ yərdz), or fields of grapevines, all over the Paris Basin. A **basin** is a low area almost entirely surrounded by higher land. The grapevines lasted until the nineteenth century, when the vineyard owners faced competition from the more productive grape-growing areas of the south. But wheat has always been the major crop in the Paris Basin. When the Franks came, they brought their own form of open fields and clustered villages. Fences were not allowed on their fields. They wanted free movement for farmers and animals. Even though the Paris Basin is now an area of modern, mechanized farming, open fields and clustered villages can still be seen there.

In northwestern France the soil is not very fertile, and the land is hilly. Much of the land has been planted in pastures and orchards. Many of the farmers live in hamlets. Around the tiny settlements are fields that are enclosed by rows of thick hedges and trees. The hedges were grown centuries ago to keep the animals in the pastures and out of the orchards.

On an outline map of France, and with the above map as a reference, have pupils draw and label the rivers of France and the Low Countries. Use this map to accompany and reinforce the Activity on p. 180.

Population change   In 1700, France had one fifth of the total population of Europe, excluding Russia. France had more people than any other European state. The soil, climate, and farming system of France made it one of the most densely populated and richest countries in Europe. In the 1800s, however, the large farming population of France began having smaller families. France then grew much more slowly than its neighbors. Today, France has only one tenth of the population of Europe. France has fewer people than West Germany, Italy, or the United Kingdom, which are all much smaller in area.

Agriculture today   Since World War II, French agricultural production has increased greatly. In some ways, however, farming in France has changed very little. Grapes, olives, and citrus fruits are still grown in the south. Wheat, sugar beets, and other high-yield crops are grown mainly in the Paris Basin. Western France is still a land of pastures and orchards. Almost all parts of the country produce dairy products, particularly cheese.

The farming population of France is now only one third as large as it once was. The average size of each farm has increased. The average size is now more than 60 acres (24 ha). Many farms, however, are much smaller. These smaller farms are often made up of many tiny, separate plots of land. The French government has arranged for many of these tiny plots to be combined into larger plots. Production often goes up by 25 percent when this is done.

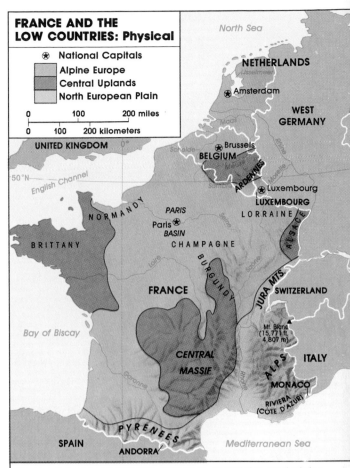

France is a varied land with beaches, mountains, and plains. Belgium, Luxembourg, and the Netherlands are named the Low Countries because they do not have much high land.

Business and industry today   It is often said that France is a nation of small shopkeepers. The average French village has its own baker, and its own butcher, grocer, and café or restaurant. Many people work in small retail stores, but the economic strength of France depends on its industry. The small retail shops are found everywhere, but the industries are concentrated in just a few regions.

The most important region is Paris and its suburbs. This region employs the most workers and produces the most valuable goods. Paris produces everything

Henri, Albert, and Pierre of France

Twelve-year-old Henri, Albert, and Pierre are playing in their schoolyard. They are talking about the test that all 12-year-olds in France must take at the end of the year. The test determines who will go to a trade school, a business school, or an academic high school that prepares students for the university.

The test is written in Paris, and a person must be able to read and write French well to pass the test. Henri, Albert, and Pierre live in Alsace, where most people speak a dialect of German called Alsatian.

The three boys grew up in the same village, but they do not always speak the same language. They speak Alsatian when they play together. Alsatian is a spoken language, not a written language.

Alsatian is the only language spoken in Albert's home. In fact, Albert first learned French when he began school at the age of 6. He uses French only in the classroom. Albert is not worried about the test because he does not want to continue school after he is 15. He wants to go to work instead.

Henri likes his friends, but he feels uncomfortable speaking Alsatian. His parents do not let him use Alsatian at home. He learned Alsatian only in the schoolyard. Henri wants to do well enough on the test to enter an academic high school next year. He would later like to study at the Sorbonne, a part of the University of Paris.

Pierre likes both Alsatian and French. Both are spoken at home by his parents. Pierre also understands German because his grandparents speak German. He often visits his grandparents, who live next door, to watch television. His grandparents watch only the German television stations because their French is poor and there are no programs in Alsatian. Pierre wants to enter a business school next year. Someday he would like to own a shop that would attract tourists from various countries.

Contrast the French national qualifying examination with the lack of similar national standards in the United States.

from high-fashion clothes to steel. It makes more than half of all the cars and planes made in France.

In northern France and the Central Massif, industry started as a result of the coalfields and iron ore deposits. Besides iron and steel, these regions make textiles. In recent years these regions have had economic problems. The machinery in many plants is out-of-date, and people are out of work.

In southern France some industries have grown because of new **technology**. Technology is the knowledge and skill people use to make things. The aircraft industry of the city of Toulouse produces the Concorde jet. In Grenoble many new industries have developed that use hydroelectric power from the Alps. An industrial zone near Marseilles refines imported oil and sends it by pipeline to other parts of France.

Tourism is another important industry in France. The tourism industry is made up of businesses that encourage tourists to come to an area and businesses that take care of tourists' needs once they have arrived. Visitors have long flocked to Paris and to the beaches and resorts of the French Riviera. New interests such as skiing have created other tourist areas, particularly in the Alps. To the south, along the valley of the Loire River, people visit the palaces built by the French kings and nobles more than 400 years ago. Millions of tourists each year spend money in France. The income from tourists is important to the French economy.

The standard of living in France has risen sharply. It is now higher than Britain's and almost as high as West Germany's. There are more television sets and cars per person in France than in any other country in Europe.

Thousands of tourists enjoy the beaches and coastal waters of France every year, as do these people sailing in the Mediterranean, off the French Riviera.

The Concorde, a supersonic transport (SST) aircraft was built jointly by France and Great Britain. Notice the tremendous length of the Concorde — 203 feet 9 inches (62 m).

The Louvre Palace, on the bank of the Seine River in Paris, houses one of the world's largest art museums and the offices of the French Ministry of Finance.

Paris—center of the French world
Imagine that all of Chicago's bus terminals, railroad yards, and its airports were added to the outskirts of New York City. Then move all of Washington's government buildings to New York City. Now move Harvard University and the University of California to New York. Add some of Pittsburgh's steel mills and half of Detroit's automobile plants to the suburbs. Add Seattle's Boeing plant and the stockyards of Kansas City. Throw in Hollywood's movie studios and Hawaii's tourist trade. Maybe now you can begin to imagine just how large Paris is and how important it is to France.

Paris has more than ten times the population of any other French city. Almost one fifth of France's population lives in Paris and its suburbs. Any economic activity, except farming, is greater in Paris than in any other place in France. The same is true of government, education, and the arts in Paris.

All this activity has made Paris a very important and crowded city. The government has encouraged people and industries to settle in other parts of the country. However, the area in and around Paris has continued to grow because its attraction is more than economic. Paris is the center of French life because the French people want it to be. Most French people admire Paris, with its broad avenues and stately buildings and its magnificent historical monuments. They enjoy its restaurants and its activity. They are proud that Paris is the home of many famous writers, painters, and musicians. For almost all French people, and for many French-speaking people outside of France, Paris is the center of the world.

CHECKUP

1. Who were the three groups of people who had a strong influence on France and, therefore, helped to create modern France?
2. What kinds of industrial regions does France have?
3. In what ways is Paris the center of France?

Paris has been nicknamed City of Light because, at night, the abundant use of floodlights enhances its magnificent palaces and monuments.

The Low Countries—the Netherlands, Belgium, and Luxembourg

VOCABULARY

dike	Walloon
polder	tariff
reservoir	European
Fleming	Economic Community

Low uplands The Netherlands, Belgium, and Luxembourg are called the Low Countries because they are in the lowest part of the North European Plain. Half of the Netherlands is below sea level. Most of Belgium is not much higher than the Netherlands. The elevation rises above 600 feet (200 m) only in the Ardennes. This forested region is not very high or very large. However, it provides Belgium with coalfields at its northern edge and Luxembourg with iron ore deposits at its southern edge.

Rivers, dunes, and deltas Rivers are among the most important resources of the Low Countries. The areas below sea level would have been invaded by the North Sea if the rivers had not helped to make sand dunes and new land. The Rhine, Meuse, and Schelde rivers have been carrying and depositing large amounts of sediment for thousands of years. They deposit most of this material where they meet the sea. In this way, deltas have been formed. Much of the western section of the Low Countries is made up of the deltas of the Rhine, Meuse, and Schelde rivers. These rivers have also supplied the sand that coastal currents have moved and deposited along the shore. These deposits have formed sand dunes. The dunes are not very high and they are interrupted by the rivers. However, they form the natural walls that have often kept the salt water of the North Sea from invading the farmland of Belgium and the Netherlands.

The rivers have also made the Low Countries a major transportation center of Europe. The Rhine is the busiest waterway in the world, and the Meuse and the Schelde also have heavy barge traffic. Rotterdam is the largest port in the world, and Antwerp is the sixth largest port.

Climate The Low Countries have a marine climate. The winters are mild and cloudy, and the summers are cool. Each month about 2.5 inches (6.4 cm) of rain falls, which is about the same as in northern France and a little more than in southeastern England.

Heavy barge traffic travels along the Rhine River, one of the busiest waterways in the world.

Use the map on p. 170 to reinforce pupil awareness of the contrast in size between France and the Low Countries.

The Dutch fight against the sea The Dutch have fought the sea for 2,000 years. Their land is not only low, it is slowly sinking. Because of the sinking land, the North Sea storms have often broken through the protecting dunes, and the storm waters have destroyed villages and farmland. A big storm took place in 1953. Almost 2,000 people died, and 375,000 acres (152,000 ha) of land were flooded.

Around A.D. 500 the Dutch put their farms on large mounds that had been built to rise above the water. Later they built **dikes** between the mounds. A dike is a wall of sand, clay, and stone that holds back water. Then they pumped out the

salt water from inside the dikes. Land reclaimed from the sea and protected by dikes is called a **polder.** In the thirteenth century the idea for windmills was brought back from the Near East by returning crusaders. Windmills made pumping water much easier. However, the polders remained very small until steam power became available in the middle of the last century. Today many windmills have been replaced by engines, which work more regularly than the old windmills.

Between 1200 and 1900 the Dutch gained almost 2,000 square miles (5200 sq km) of land by diking along the seacoast or by draining salty lakes. This gain was equal to one sixth of the total area of the Netherlands. But storms caused the sea to invade almost 2,200 square miles (5700 sq km). The Dutch had been working hard, but they were losing ground! They decided to fight back with three big projects. First, they shut off the Zuider Zee from the North Sea by building a 20-mile (32-km) dam across the northern end of the Zuider Zee. This turned it into a freshwater lake, called IJsselmeer (ī′ səl mer). Inside the new lake the Dutch built polders. These polders added about 1,000 square miles (2600 sq km) of new farmland to the Netherlands. The second project sealed off the Rhine Delta from the North Sea. Dams were built to join the outer edges of the islands that make up the lowest part of the delta. This was done to keep the sea storms from doing great damage, as in 1953. The dams also created a freshwater **reservoir** (rez′ ər vwär) that was needed for the fastgrowing Dutch population. A reservoir is a place

In the lowlands of the Netherlands, these farmers are gathering grass. Farmers sometimes wear wooden shoes because the soil is often wet.

where water is collected and stored for use. The third project is still being planned. This project will create another freshwater lake in the northern part of the country by joining the dunes on many unconnected islands into one long dike.

The Dutch have also dealt with the sea in more usual ways. They have been sailors and traders since the beginning of their history. In the sixteenth century half of the ships that traded in the Baltic seaports were Dutch. In the seventeenth century the Dutch colonial empire stretched from New Amsterdam, in North America, to the East Indies, in Asia. Today the Dutch merchant fleet is the tenth largest in the world. It has the biggest fleet of river barges in Europe. Dutch barges carry more than half the goods that move on the Rhine. This shipping activity has made the Netherlands one of the great trading nations of the world.

During the time when there were Dutch colonies, the Dutch imported raw materials to be processed at home. Amsterdam became famous for diamond cutting. Haarlem was known for growing tulips, which were originally imported from Persia. Other towns made such things as chocolate, cheese, cigars, and rum. These goods and others are still made and exported by the Dutch. The Dutch cities have become more important as centers of commerce, finance, and transportation. Nine tenths of the Dutch people are city dwellers, and the zone from Amsterdam to Rotterdam is one of the world's most densely populated urban regions. The fast-changing Dutch have kept their windmills and wooden shoes mainly as souvenirs of the past.

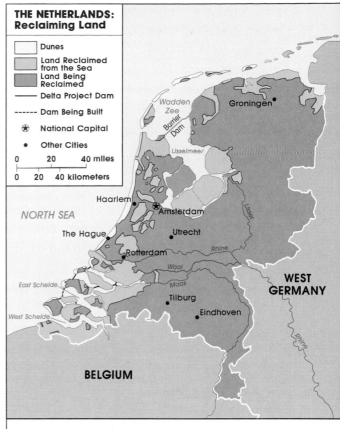

The people in the Netherlands have had to move the sea back from the land.

The divided Belgians Belgium is a troubled country. The **Flemings**, who speak Dutch, live in northern Belgium. The **Walloons**, who speak French, live in the south. The two groups have been on bad terms since Belgium became a country in 1830.

In the nineteenth century the Walloons were as numerous as the Flemings. The Walloons had most of the wealth and positions of high rank. They also had coal mines that made their region very rich. The region produced coal and steel.

The Flemings were farmers in the nineteenth century. They were poor and had large families. They could not get good jobs because they spoke Dutch. They hated the Walloons for treating them as second-class citizens.

In the twentieth century the Walloon coal mines began to run out of coal. New industries were developed, but they were placed mainly in the north, around Antwerp. Both parts of Belgium produce steel and grow crops for food and textiles. However, the Flemish region is now Belgium's richest area, and the Flemings outnumber the Walloons. These changes have made the Flemings demand rights for themselves and their language.

Belgium is now a country divided into two equal but separate parts. French and Dutch are both official languages, but only in Brussels do people of both languages mix. They do not mix happily. Language, economics, and different ideas about religion still divide these peoples.

Belgium's economy Dairy farming and the cultivation of vegetables, wheat, and other grain crops are carried on in

Fiber flax, as shown in this Belgian field, is used to make linen, one of Belgium's textile products.

This night view of Brussels' Grand' Place, the main square, captures the beauty of its lovely buildings.

Belgium. Manufacturing industries are also very important to Belgium.

The most important industry in Belgium is iron smelting and steelmaking. Belgium has an annual production of about 13 million tons (12 million t) of steel a year. The textile industry is also important in Belgium. Belgium has long been famous for its linen, woolen, and cotton cloths.

Luxembourg—tiny but rich Luxembourg is the smallest of the Low Countries. Its capital is the city of Luxembourg. Luxembourg is a tiny country with a strong sense of independence. For 500 years it was ruled by others, but in 1866 it gained its independence. It was invaded and occupied by Germany in both world wars. Both the French and German languages are spoken in this tiny country.

Although Luxembourg is smaller than Rhode Island, it is a very rich country. It has excellent soils that provide for good

In Luxembourg cities and villages are nestled between the rolling hills and mountains.

farming. Its greatest wealth, however, comes from its iron ore deposits. In all of Western Europe, only France, Sweden, and Britain produce more iron than tiny Luxembourg. Luxembourg's wealth is shared by a very small population. The income per person is one of the highest in the world.

A Western Europe unification agreement The most recent and most successful attempt to unite the countries of Western Europe began soon after World War II. In 1948, Belgium, Luxembourg, and the Netherlands decided to allow coal and steel to be shipped across each other's borders without **tariffs** (tar′ ifs). A tariff is a tax on imports or exports. This group of countries called itself Benelux. Can you guess why? Belgium had almost all the coal; Luxembourg had all the iron ore; and the Dutch owned the barges that carried the coal, iron, and steel from one country to the other. In 1950, France, Italy, and West Germany joined Belgium, Luxembourg, and the Netherlands in this agreement. Seven years later the **European Economic Community**, often called the European Common Market, was born. Denmark, Ireland, and the United Kingdom became members in 1973, and Greece became a member in 1981.

The purpose of the European Common Market is to allow goods and workers of the member countries to move freely across each other's borders. This causes some problems for member countries. France and Italy are no longer allowed to protect their own industries by giving them government payments and by taxing manufactured goods made in other countries. West Germany, Britain, and the Low Countries can no longer protect their own agriculture in the same way. Despite such drawbacks, most people in the member countries enjoy the overall benefits of a common market. Prices are lower because of the free competition of so many producers, and buyers can now find products that were not easily available before. A Belgian coal miner can now buy Italian peaches, and a French wheat farmer can buy a Dutch television set. These purchases would have been too expensive before the removal of tariffs.

CHECKUP

1. In what ways have rivers been important to the Low Countries?
2. What are the recent Dutch projects to protect the land of the Netherlands?
3. In what ways were the Flemings and the Walloons different in the nineteenth century? How are they different now?
4. How did the Common Market begin? What are the main advantages for the member countries now?

Because of its central location, Brussels is the headquarters of the European Economic Community.

KEY FACTS

1. France is the largest European country west of the Soviet Union.

2. France has three agricultural regions, which differ in crops and field patterns.

3. Industry has become more important in the French economy than farming or retailing.

4. Paris is the center of most of the economic and cultural activities in France.

5. The Dutch have had to use various means to protect their low land from the North Sea.

6. Conflict between the Walloons and the Flemings has troubled Belgium since 1830.

7. Luxembourg is a rich country because of its iron ore deposits.

VOCABULARY QUIZ

On a sheet of paper write the numbers of the statements below. Next to each number write the letter of the word or words that best fill in the blank in the statement.

a. polder   g. dike
b. vineyard   h. European
c. tourism   Economic
d. tariff   Community
e. basin   i. reservoir
f. Walloon   j. Fleming

1. An industry that encourages people to come to an area is the __tourism__ industry.

2. A __vineyard__ is a field of grapevines.

3. A __dike__ is a wall of sand, clay, and stone that holds back water.

4. A low area mostly surrounded by higher land is called a __basin__.

5. A piece of low land that has been reclaimed from the sea or other body of water and is protected by dikes is called a __polder__.

6. The __European Economic Community__ is an organization of European countries whose goods and workers are free to pass across each other's borders without paying tariffs.

7. A Dutch-speaking person living in the northern part of Belgium is known as a __Fleming__.

8. A __tariff__ is a tax on imports or exports.

9. A __reservoir__ is used to collect water and store it for later use.

10. A French-speaking person living in the southern part of Belgium is known as a __Walloon__.

REVIEW QUESTIONS

1. What group of people gave France its name?

2. What is the most important industrial area in France?

3. What is a polder? How long have polders been in existence?

4. What is the source of Luxembourg's wealth?

5. What countries started the European Common Market? Name the ten countries that now belong.

ACTIVITY

Some of the world's important rivers, such as the Garonne, Loire, Meuse, Rhine, Rhone, and Saône, are in France and the Low Countries. Use an encyclopedia to find the length of these rivers in miles and kilometers. Then use the figures given in miles to make a bar graph to compare the length of the rivers. Use the figures given in kilometers to make a second bar graph.

READING A TABLE

WHAT IS POPULATION DENSITY?

An important part of geography is the study of where people live. Population density is a figure that tells how many people live in a certain area of a specific size. Population density refers to the number of people per square mile or square kilometer in a certain area, such as a state or a country. In the United States, we usually speak of the population density per square mile. In Europe and in other parts of the world, people speak of population density per square kilometer. It is important to notice in which unit the population density is given, because a square mile is more than two and a half times as large as a square kilometer. (You divide the density per square mile by 2.6 to get the density per square kilometer.)

Population density represents the average number of people per square mile or square kilometer. Each square mile or square kilometer in a certain area does not have exactly the same number of people. Population density also usually varies within a country.

SKILLS PRACTICE

Use the table below to compare the population figures of some European countries. The figures given in the table show the populations that lived within the present-day borders of each country. In 1980, which country had the largest population?

From the information given in the table, figure out the population density of the Netherlands in 1820, 1880, 1940, and 1980. To do this, divide each population figure by the area of the Netherlands, as given in the table on page 147. List each date and the population density on a piece of paper. Round each population density figure to the largest whole number. Use your list to answer the following questions about the Netherlands.

1. By how much did the population density increase between 1820 and 1880? 107 per sq ml

2. During which periods did the density more than double?

3. When did the population density of the Netherlands become greater than the 1980 population density of the United Kingdom? 1960

2. 1800–1900; 1860–1920; 1900–1960; 1920–1980

	Belgium	Netherlands	France	United Kingdom	West Germany
POPULATION CHANGE 1800–1980					
1800	3,100,000	2,100,000	27,500,000	11,400,000	10,800,000
1820	3,900,000	2,400,000	31,000,000	15,100,000	13,800,000
1840	4,200,000	2,900,000	34,800,000	20,000,000	17,600,000
1860	4,700,000	3,300,000	37,300,000	24,200,000	20,500,000
1880	5,600,000	4,100,000	39,000,000	30,600,000	25,200,000
1900	6,800,000	5,200,000	40,200,000	37,800,000	31,400,000
1920	7,500,000	6,900,000	38,800,000	43,800,000	38,100,000
1940	8,400,000	8,900,000	41,000,000	47,900,000	43,500,000
1960	9,100,000	11,600,000	45,500,000	52,500,000	55,600,000
1980	9,900,000	14,100,000	53,700,000	55,900,000	61,600,000

CHAPTER
11 Central Europe

West Germany

Two Germanys   The Germany of today is divided into two separate political units. They are West Germany and East Germany. At the end of World War II, Germany was divided into four zones of occupation. The three western zones, or sections, were controlled by the United States, the United Kingdom, and France. These three sections gained their independence in 1949 and became the Federal Republic of Germany. The Federal Republic of Germany is commonly known as West Germany. It has a democratic government. It also has basically a capitalistic economy. **Capitalism** is an economic system in which people or groups of people own land, factories, and other means of production. They compete with one another to produce goods and services for profit. The United States has a capitalistic economic system.

The eastern zone was controlled by the Soviet Union. It is now known as the German Democratic Republic and is commonly referred to as East Germany. East Germany has a Communist form of government and economy. In a Communist economy the state owns, controls, and manages all means of production. East Germany has close ties with the Communist government of the Soviet Union. Today the two Germanys continue to be divided by different ideas about government and economic organization.

Invisible lines that divide   Invisible language boundaries divide Germany into a northern, a central, and a southern part. In northern Germany, people speak one **dialect** of German, and in southern Germany they speak another. A dialect is a form of speech that is used in a certain area. The people of central Germany speak a dialect that is in between the other two. Standard German is used in schools, in books and magazines, and on television. However, many people still speak a dialect. The three dialect regions are still very important in Germany.

An invisible dividing line also separates the Catholics from the Protestants in West Germany. In most European countries a single religion is dominant. West Germany is evenly divided, however. It has about 28 million Catholics and 27 million Protestants out of a total population of 61 million people.

Climate   The climate of West Germany is continental. The land away from the sea has colder winters and warmer summers than that near the sea. Most of the

Much of Germany is noted for its scenery, partly made possible by the mild climate.

Examples of United States dialects (heard on tapes, records, and on television) can help pupils to better understand what a dialect is.

SIX REGIONS IN WEST GERMANY

⊛ National Capital
• Cities

0   50 miles

0   50 kilometers

West Germany is a leading industrial country with industrial cities located throughout the six regions.

The third region is central West Germany. The city of Frankfurt is an important banking and financial center in this region. Germany's largest airport is located in Frankfurt. Central West Germany is also a fast-growing region.

The fourth region is the Rhineland. It is an area of contrasts. It has vineyards along the Moselle and Rhine rivers. These rivers are lined by many lovely old towns. But it also includes the Ruhr, an important industrial area. Here is found one of the world's heaviest concentrations of industrial cities, mines, and factories. Bonn, the capital of West Germany, is also located in this region. Bonn is the major center of government and politics.

The northern part of West Germany is the fifth region. It is different from the rest of the country. Buildings are often made of brick, and the land is flat. Some of the warehouses and homes of medieval traders still stand in many of the river and coastal cities. Some of these cities, such as Hamburg and Bremen, are now huge modern ports. The city of Wolfsburg, near Hanover, is known for its automobile industry. This is where Volkswagens—one of today's most popular automobiles—are made.

Finally, there is the city of West Berlin. When Germany was divided into two countries after World War II, Berlin was divided into two parts. Only half of the city is a part of West Germany. The other half is a part of East Germany. The Berlin wall divides the city. West Berlin is a part of West Germany, but it is completely surrounded by East Germany. West Berlin, a cultural and industrial center, is West Germany's largest city.

rain in West Germany comes as summer thundershowers. Winters are colder than winters in France or the Low Countries.

Six regions in West Germany   Within West Germany there are six distinct areas. Bavaria is probably the most distinctive area. Munich (myü′ nik), the capital of Bavaria, is one of the fast-growing cities in West Germany. It is famous for its fall festival, the Oktoberfest. Munich is also a large manufacturing center.

The second region is the southwest. It has many important industrial cities. The largest city is Stuttgart (stət′ gärt), where automobiles are made. The southwest is one of the fastest-growing areas in West Germany.

184   The Munich Oktoberfest is one of the world's largest fairs. The sixteen day celebration of the harvest includes street fairs, a costumed procession, and other festivities.

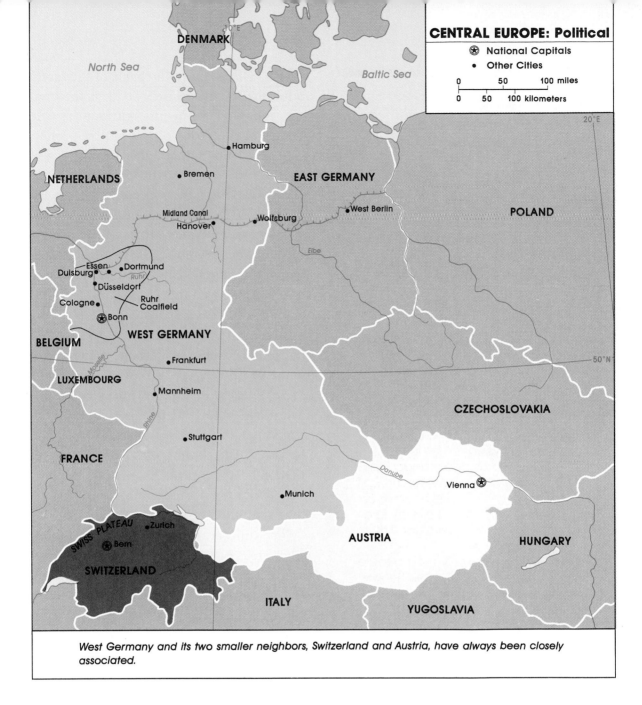

West Germany and its two smaller neighbors, Switzerland and Austria, have always been closely associated.

The Ruhr—mainstay of West German industry

The Ruhr is a small river in a narrow valley. It flows into the Rhine midway between the city of Cologne and the Dutch border. Before the 1840s the Ruhr Valley was a farming region of little importance. By 1900 it had become the center of the world's greatest industrial region.

The Ruhr industrial region is small. It stretches for only 40 miles (64 km) along the Rhine River, from Cologne to Duisburg. It covers about the same distance along the Ruhr Valley. Within this area of about 1000 square miles (2600 sq km) live 12 million people. There are 9 cities of more than 250,000 people, and 14 cities of more than 100,000 people.

Albert Einstein: Scientist

ALBERT EINSTEIN was one of the world's great scientists. He was not the kind of scientist who works in a laboratory, surrounded by test tubes. He worked in a book-lined room, and pencils and paper were his tools. Einstein was a theoretical physicist. This means he spent nearly all of his time thinking of theories, or explanations, of the ways that physical things in the universe work with or against each other. After he thought of a theory, he thought of a way to prove it. Einstein's work on the laws governing atomic energy laid the groundwork for the development of the atomic bomb.

Albert Einstein was what most people would call a genius. Yet when he was a boy, his teachers thought him backward and slow. He was not even very good in mathematics. All this changed as he got older.

Germany was Einstein's birthplace. He was born in 1879. His parents moved to Switzerland when he was a child. Einstein moved back to Germany in 1914. By that time he was a famous university professor. He won the 1921 Nobel Prize for Physics. He left Germany in 1933, when the Nazis came to power, and came to the United States to Princeton University. He became an American citizen in 1940. Albert Einstein died in 1955, a man of great learning who was honored by people all over the world.

Rich coalfields are the basis of the many industries of the Ruhr. At first the coal was removed from the surface of the ground at the sides of the valley. Later, deep shafts were dug below the surface of the ground to reach the richer coal deposits. Coal production continued to increase. Then, in the 1960s, it became cheaper to import coal than to dig deeper shafts. Nearly 300,000 coal miners lost their jobs between 1960 and 1980. Even so, local coal remains important as a fuel for the Ruhr's industries.

Large ironworks and steelworks, smelting plants, and various factories cover much of the western part of the Ruhr Valley. Smaller plants are strung out toward the east. There is also industry along the Rhine River in cities such as Duisburg, Düsseldorf (dü′ səl dörf), and Cologne. Factories that make textiles and metal utensils are on the fringe of the Ruhr region.

The Ruhr is an old industrial region. Other areas of West Germany have started to catch up with it. New industries such as oil refining, chemicals, and car manufacturing have moved into the Ruhr area. Nevertheless, there were 600,000 fewer jobs in the region in 1980 than in 1960. The fastest-growing industrial area in West Germany is now the southwest. This area has many jobs to offer people.

CHECKUP

1. What is the common name for the Federal Republic of Germany? What is the common name for the German Democratic Republic?
2. What are some invisible lines that divide the people of Germany?
3. What resource makes the Ruhr Valley such an important industrial center? Why is the southwest growing fast today?

Einstein was never well-to-do and was never concerned about money. He turned down many financial offers involving huge sums. He had a great love for music and a keen interest in world affairs.

Switzerland

A lowland between mountains Switzerland is a small, mountainous country. The Alps cover most of the southern part of Switzerland. The Alps are high and have many beautiful valleys that were carved out by glaciers. The Rhine and the Rhone rivers each have their source in the Alps. Along these two rivers are towns in which most of the people in the Alps live. There are few people elsewhere in the Alps. Many Alpine farmers have left their farms in the last century.

North of the Alps is the Swiss Plateau, a low but hilly region that contains almost all of the Swiss cities and farmland. The Swiss Plateau serves as a corridor, or route, between eastern and western Switzerland.

In northwestern Switzerland are the Jura Mountains, which are lower than the Alps. Most of this region is covered by forests and pastures. Long valleys with villages and hamlets lie between the ridges of the mountains.

A continental climate Switzerland has a continental climate that varies with the elevation of the land. Snow falls year round in the mountains. On the Swiss Plateau, however, summers are warm, and winter temperatures are just below freezing. The southern side of the Alps and the Jura Mountains gets much more sunshine than the northern side. Crops such as corn and grapes are grown on the slopes of the Rhone Valley that face south. Forests and pastures cover the slopes that face north.

Manufacturing, banking, and tourism Industry is the basis of the Swiss economy. Rivers are Switzerland's main natural resource. Therefore, many industries in Switzerland use hydroelectric power to operate their factories. Chemicals, tools, and electrical equipment are made in the factories of the Swiss Plateau. Watches are made in the Jura Mountains. Switzerland does not have many mineral resources. Most of the materials needed for making goods are imported. The Swiss people produce expensive, high-quality goods for export.

Switzerland is one of the world's banking centers. Many Swiss cities, but especially Zurich (zür′ ik), are the home of

The climate of Switzerland is good for growing hay. Here a hay farmer is working in the field. Most of the crops are raised on the Swiss Plateau.

It is useful to note that the Swiss use of hydroelectricity, rather than coal or oil, to power their factories helps keep their busy industrial centers free of smoke.

187

Sonja of Switzerland

Foreigners often notice that the people of Switzerland like to speak foreign languages. The German-speaking Swiss in particular have a great desire to learn foreign languages. Their own language is made up of many dialects. Each small region has words and sounds that make its speech unique. The Swiss enjoy their different dialects because their dialects are like badges that identify their home region.

The German-Swiss use their own local dialect when they talk to other German-speaking Swiss. Since the dialects are not written languages, the German-Swiss people have to write in standard German. Many of them view German as a foreign language. German is easy for them to learn but uncomfortable to use. French is also a foreign language. However, many German-Swiss people take pride in learning French well. Knowing French well is a mark of culture, and it is Switzerland's second language.

Sonja Rutli is a 16-year-old girl from Bern, Switzerland. Sonja is spending a *Welschenjahr* in a small village in French Switzerland. The *Welschenjahr* is a year to become acquainted with the language and culture of the Welschen, or the French-Swiss. Sonja lives in a boarding school with 12 other German-Swiss girls. This is their last year of school. Most of them hope to begin their working careers at age 17. To do this, they must be accepted for 3 years of apprenticeship in a place such as a bank, a business, or a hotel. The girls are taking mostly business courses now.

From the first day that Sonja and the other girls began their *Welschenjahr,* they have been allowed to speak only French. The headmistress of the school is fair but strict. She wants the girls to become fluent in French as soon as possible. When the headmistress is not around, the girls speak to each other in their dialects. However, they eat all their meals with the headmistress, and she goes with them on all their outings. The girls are learning French very fast.

Sonja likes French, but she feels pressured under the constant watch of the headmistress. Sonja also finds it hard to adjust to the strict rules at the school.

For the past 10 years, each class at Sonja's school has been smaller. The cost of living in Switzerland has risen sharply. It has become harder for middle-class families to afford the cost of a *Welschenjahr.*

important international banks. People from many countries deposit money in Swiss banks. Switzerland is a **neutral** country. A neutral country is one that does not take sides in a war or a dispute. Because Switzerland is neutral, many people think Swiss banks are the safest in the world. During all the wars in Europe over the past 100 years, Switzerland has remained a neutral country.

Switzerland was one of the first countries to make tourism a well-paying business. Many ski and health resorts have been built in the Alps. Summer tourism

Point out that in keeping with their policy of neutrality, the Swiss have no army or regular military force. They rely on a militia, or citizens' army, for which all men receive training.

is important on the Swiss Plateau. Visitors come here to admire some of Europe's finest architecture.

A diverse nation lives in peace   Switzerland is known as a country where different peoples live in harmony. The people of Switzerland have four languages and two main religions, but each group has a strong sense of being Swiss.

The Swiss people live peacefully with each other because they have two traditions. Each group protects its own interests by defending its own territory, and each group keeps to itself. Switzerland now consists of 26 **cantons.** A canton is a small political unit. A canton corresponds to one of our states, but is much smaller. The cantons have always been very important. Each canton has its own history, customs, and even its own way of speaking.

Each of the four major language groups of Switzerland has its own territory. Seventy-two percent of the Swiss speak a dialect of German, 19 percent speak French, 8 percent speak Italian, and 1 percent speak Romansh (rō mansh'). Romansh is a language similar to Latin. The language of each area is used in the schools and for all official business. If a Swiss person moves to another language area, he or she must learn the language of that area.

The existence of four language groups makes the functioning of business and government complicated. The Swiss, however, are proud that they have so many languages. Switzerland is a country where a variety of people make up a rich and very independent nation.

Switzerland's scenic mountains and villages have helped to make it a well-known country attracting thousands of visitors each year.

As is true for West Germany, about half of the Swiss people are Catholic, and about half are Protestant. In the past there have been many religious disputes. Today, religion does not affect daily life as much as it did in the past. **Migration** has mixed the Protestants and Catholics to some extent. Migration is the movement of people from one place to another. Religion, unlike language, is not officially assigned to a territory. Although the Catholics and Protestants have different views on many issues, these differences do not cause problems in Switzerland today.

Swiss democracy has one important weakness: Most women do not have a voice in local government. Women have been allowed to vote in national elections only since 1971. How does this situation compare with the United States?

The Swiss way of life   The Swiss are united by their way of life. Each language and religious group keeps alive its customs and holidays. The Swiss people vote on every issue that affects their hometown, their canton, and their country. They believe that their way of life is the best in the world, and that it gives them their high standard of living.

The Swiss way of life owes much to centuries of freedom, independence, and neutrality. Few of its people, cities, and resources have been destroyed by wars.

CHECKUP

1. Where do most of the people in the Alps live?
2. What are some of the industries in Switzerland?
3. What are the languages of Switzerland?
4. How do the people of different cantons differ?

Austria

┌─VOCABULARY─────────────
raw material
└─────────────────────────

The Alps and their fringe   Austria is about twice the size of Switzerland. It too is a mountainous country. Most of Austria is covered by the Alps. The Alps stretch in an east-west direction for nearly 350 miles (550 km). They are highest in the west. They get lower toward the east, finally becoming low hills near Vienna. The Danube River flows along the northern edge of the Alps. The city of Vienna is on the Danube. In Austria the Alps have two main ridges. Valleys are located between these ridges. Several important rivers flow eastward through the valleys. These rivers eventually join the Danube.

Most of Austria's cities and transportation routes are found along the river valleys. Vienna is the capital and largest city. Austria is divided into nine provinces. Three of these provinces are along the Danube.

The climate of Austria is much like Switzerland's. Austria's winters have freezing temperatures. The high mountains of the west make summer temperatures fairly cool. In the low-lying Vienna Basin, summers are hot, and precipitation is fairly low.

Resources   During World War II there was industrial growth in Austria. Industry in the western parts of Austria has continued to grow since the war. Their growth has been helped by three kinds of resources. The most important is Austria's swift-moving rivers. Hydroelectric plants powered by these rivers produce most of the nation's electricity. Austria exports much of this hydroelectric power to West Germany. A second resource is minerals. The major ones are the iron ore and the salts that support Austria's steel and chemical industries. The coal, gas, and oil deposits in Austria have almost been used up. The third resource is scenery. Western Austria is one of the most beautiful parts of Europe. Many tourists and skiers are attracted to its mountains and countryside every year. Over one sixth of Austria's income comes from tourism.

The economic boom that has taken place in western Austria has raised the standard of living for the whole country. Today Austria has one of the strongest economies in Western Europe.

Vienna—the old and the new   Vienna is an old city. The Romans built one of their major forts there. In the fifth century, Germanic invaders destroyed the city. Later it was rebuilt, and it regained importance. Eventually, Vienna became the capital city of the Hapsburgs. The Hapsburgs were the ruling family of the Austro-Hungarian Empire, a large and powerful European empire.

Why was Vienna often chosen as a place for an important settlement? One reason is its excellent position. Vienna is on an old north-south route that skirts the Alps on its way to the Mediterranean. Moreover, the city lies on the Danube River, which allows easy movement in an east-west direction.

The Danube has always been the major transportation route of central and southeastern Europe. It is nearly 1800 miles (2900 km) long. Half of this long river flowed through lands of the Austro-Hungarian Empire. In those days, Vienna was an important river port. **Raw materials** came up the Danube to Vienna. Raw materials are goods that are used to make manufactured or finished products. Manufactured goods were sent downstream to southeastern Europe. In the nineteenth century, Vienna was the largest city in central Europe.

Vienna became less important after World War I. The Austro-Hungarian Empire fell after that war. Today, Vienna continues to lose population, but the Viennese are better off than they have ever been. This is partly due to the economic boom Austria experienced after World War II. Vienna now employs many people in the banking and insur-

Vienna, a cultural center of Europe, is truly a city of the old and the new, as you can see from this view through the Hofburg Gates. (48° N/16° E; map, p. 143)

ance businesses. It has also become a center for international conferences. Vienna is gaining back some of its importance as an international city.

CHECKUP

1. Where are most of Austria's cities and transportation routes located?
2. What are the modern resources of the Austrian Alps?
3. Why has Vienna been a good place for a settlement throughout history?

A major tourist attraction in Vienna is the Schönbrunn Zoo, which was established in 1752 and is the oldest zoo in the world.

KEY FACTS

1. The Germany of today is divided into two separate political units—West Germany and East Germany.

2. Invisible lines divide West Germans into language and religious groups.

3. The Ruhr is a West German region of concentrated industrial activity based on coal.

4. The Swiss Plateau is a lowland that lies between the Alps and the Jura Mountains.

5. Switzerland is a very rich country where industry, banking, and tourism have become very important.

6. Switzerland has four language groups and two main religious groups.

7. Switzerland is a neutral country.

8. Settlement and transportation in Austria follow the river valleys.

9. The economy of western Austria has grown since World War II.

10. For centuries, Vienna has been an important extension of western Europe into central and eastern Europe.

VOCABULARY QUIZ

On a sheet of paper write the letter of the word or group of words that correctly completes each statement.

1. An economic system in which people or groups of people own land, factories, and other means of production is called (**a**) commercialism, (**b**) communism, (**c**) capitalism, (**d**) industrialism.

2. A (**a**) quarry, (**b**) code, (**c**) dialect, (**d**) diphthong is a form of speech that is used in a certain area.

3. If a country is neutral, it (**a**) has a Communist government, (**b**) has territory in many parts of the world, (**c**) does not take sides in a war or a dispute, (**d**) is a member of the European Common Market.

4. The Protestants and Catholics in Switzerland are mixed to some extent. This is partly due to (**a**) migration, (**b**) colonization, (**c**) organization, (**d**) irrigation.

5. Goods that are used to make manufactured or finished products are called (**a**) raw materials, (**b**) consumer goods, (**c**) synthetics, (**d**) renewable goods.

REVIEW QUESTIONS

1. What kind of government does West Germany have? East Germany?

2. What is the main language of West Germany, Switzerland, and Austria? Does everyone speak the language in the same way?

3. What are three important industries in Switzerland? Why have these industries developed in Switzerland?

4. How have the Alps affected transportation and settlement in Austria?

5. Today the city of Vienna has regained some of its importance as an international city. In what businesses are many people in present-day Vienna employed?

6. What do the industries of West Germany, Switzerland, and Austria have in common? Where is the main industrial area in each country?

ACTIVITY

Almost all of the countries in the world are members of the United Nations. The United Nations is an organization of countries that works for world peace. Use an encyclopedia to find out when Austria and West Germany joined the United Nations and why Switzerland never joined the organization.

II/SKILLS DEVELOPMENT

INTERPRETING SYMBOLS/READING A MAP

SKILLS PRACTICE: PART I

Europeans must have an oval sticker on the back of their car. The sticker has one, two, or three letters. The letter or letters are a symbol for the name of the country in which the car is registered. Below are five of these symbols. What European country do you think each of these symbols represents? (Hint: The table on pages 146−147 will help you.) Write your answers on a sheet of paper.

1. DK **2.** GR **3.** IRL **4.** N **5.** NL

Denmark **Greece** **Ireland** **Norway Netherlands**

SKILLS PRACTICE: PART II

European cars also have license plates that identify the city or region in which the car is registered. It is fun to look at license plates to see where cars are from. For example, Switzerland uses two letters to indicate which canton the car is from. The first letter is always the same as the first letter of the canton. The canton often has a big city with the same name as the canton name. Use the list of cantons below to name the canton the cars with the following license plates are from.

1. GE 12749 **2.** ZH 31178 **3.** BE 71423

Geneva **Zurich** **Bern**

SKILLS PRACTICE: PART III

Imagine that you are in the city of Rome, Italy. You have spotted two of the three license plates. You know the home region of the cars, but you want to know what route the cars will take home. Use the map on page 143 and answer true or false to the following statements. Write your answers (**T** or **F**) on a sheet of paper.

For the car BE 71423:

1. To get directly home, this car must cross one or more major ranges of the Alps. **T**

2. The direct route home crosses the Rhone River. **T**

Now imagine that you are in the city of Vienna, Austria. You have spotted the license plate below. Use the map on page 185 to answer the following questions true or false.

For the car ZH 31178:

3. The most direct route home crosses Poland. **F**

4. Going directly home, this car will pass within 50 miles of the city of Frankfurt. **F**

5. The direct route home is mostly through Austria and West Germany. **T**

CANTONS IN SWITZERLAND

Aargau	Fribourg	Neuchâtel	Ticino	Zug
Appenzell-Inner	Geneva	Saint Gall	Nidwalden	Zurich
Appenzell-Outer	Glarus	Schaffhausen	Obwalden	
Basel-City	Graubünden	Schwyz	Uri	
Basel-Country	Jura	Solothurn	Valais	
Bern	Lucerne	Thurgau	Vaud	

12 Mediterranean Europe

Three Peninsulas and Their Islands

VOCABULARY
out-migration
temporary migration
host country

A hand, a leg, and a head   Three peninsulas of Europe extend southward into the Mediterranean Sea. They are the Iberian, the Italian, and the Balkan peninsulas. Greece forms the southern tip of the Balkan Peninsula. Greece has the most complex shape of the three peninsulas. Greece also has hundreds of islands. The mainland has narrow extensions that reach out into the sea like the fingers of a hand. The mainland of Italy is shaped like a leg in a lady's boot. Italy also has two large islands, Sicily and Sardinia, with mostly straight coasts. The Iberian Peninsula, shaped like a head, is occupied by Spain and Portugal. The coastline has few indentations, except in the northwest.

Rugged hills and mountains of the Alpine system cover large parts of each peninsula. Earthquakes are frequent in these areas. The famous eruption of Mt. Vesuvius (və sü′ vē əs), on the Bay of Naples, Italy, occurred in A.D. 79. The eruption covered the town of Pompeii (päm pā′) near the foot of the mountain with 60 feet (20 m) of volcanic ash. Mt. Etna, on the island of Sicily, erupted in 1981 and ruined much farmland. These events are a reminder that the land is constantly changing and that mountains are still being formed in some parts of the world.

All three peninsulas have a Mediterranean climate over most of their land. Winter temperatures are mild or even warm. Winter is also the rainy season. The summers are dry, and the summer temperatures are hot.

Phoenicians, Greeks, and Romans Early colonizers from advanced civilizations in the eastern Mediterranean brought important ideas and techniques to the Mediterranean's western shores. Around 1000 B.C. the Phoenicians sailed from their homeland in present-day Lebanon and Syria to colonize the western Mediterranean. Their largest colony, Carthage (kär′ thij), had almost a million people. The Phoenicians founded other towns such as Cadiz (kə diz′) and Málaga (mal′ ə gə), in Spain, and Palermo (pə lər′ mō), in Sicily. They introduced such things as trading, banking, using an alphabet, and steering ships by the stars.

Barbaric warriors from the north invaded Greece about the time that the Phoenicians were developing trade

You might want to find illustrations of the excavations of Pompeii and display them for your pupils to make the understanding of the eruption of Vesuvius and its results more vivid.

About one fifth of Greece is made up of islands. Shown here is a view of the island of Thíra, located on the south side of the Aegean Sea.

throughout the Mediterranean. The invaders gradually adopted Mediterranean ways and became city dwellers, traders, and seafarers. By 500 B.C. these people, whom we call Greeks today, had developed a civilization in which art, science, philosophy, and literature were highly prized. They spread this civilization throughout the Mediterranean and founded many cities, including Marseilles, in France, and Naples, in Italy.

By A.D. 100 the Romans had conquered all of the Mediterranean lands. The western Mediterranean, particularly Spain, Portugal, and Italy, was completely converted to Roman laws, Romance languages, and Roman Catholicism. In the eastern part of the Mediterranean, however, Greek civilization was strong enough to keep out Roman influences. The Greek language and the Greek Orthodox form of Christianity dominated the eastern part of the Roman Empire.

Some north-south contrasts in Europe
There are some major differences between the Mediterranean part of Europe and the part north of the Alps. The rivers of the Mediterranean region are often dry in the summer. These rivers have never been important transportation routes, and settlements do not cluster along the rivers as they do in the north. In the Mediterranean area many settlements are on hilltops, away from the marshy lowlands. Almost all of the people live in clustered villages. Some villages have as many as 20,000 people. They are crowded and compact. Many houses are painted white to reflect the heat, and the roofs serve as porches.

Olives, grown mostly in countries bordering the Mediterranean Sea, require careful picking and processing.

Agriculture is different south of the Alps. Irrigation is often necessary during the dry summer. Tree crops such as figs, grapes, olives, and citrus fruits are often more important than field crops such as wheat, rice, corn, and vegetables. Sheep, goats, donkeys, and mules are much more common than cattle or horses. The people in the north and the south eat different foods, too. Southern Europeans eat less meat, fish, and milk than northern Europeans. Wheat and olive oil are important in the south, while potatoes and butter are important in the north.

Lands of continuing out-migration
The Phoenicians and the Greeks were the earliest Mediterranean people to leave their overcrowded homelands to find easier living in distant lands. In the past 400 years, many Portuguese and Spaniards have gone to Latin America. And since the late 1800s, many Italians and Greeks have come to North America.

Topics on ancient Greece are good choices for reports, both because of the accessibility of resource material and because of the significance of this material to Western history. You might have your pupils report orally to share their findings.

Movement from one region to another region is called **out-migration**.

Since World War II, **temporary migrations** have become common. These are migrations that are for a limited time only. Millions of people from the Mediterranean area have migrated to northern Europe to work in the cities. These workers are allowed to stay in the **host country**, or country that received them, for only a few years. Many of these people send money home to their families, who have stayed behind in Mediterranean Europe. The Mediterranean countries get an important part of their national income this way.

The European Sun Belt   Tourism is another major source of income for the Mediterranean countries. These countries have always attracted tourists from northern Europe and North America. The climate is appealing. The art and architecture of the Greek, Roman, and medieval periods makes the Mediterranean countries like indoor and outdoor museums.

The Mediterranean coasts are now the major tourist attractions. Campgrounds and fancy resort hotels share the Mediterranean coastline and serve the demands of the huge and growing tourist industry.

CHECKUP

1. When is the rainy season in Mediterranean Europe?
2. What contributions did early civilizations in the eastern Mediterranean make to lands in the western Mediterranean?
3. How do agriculture and rural settlements in the Mediterranean differ from those in northern Europe?
4. How are the incomes of the Mediterranean countries being helped by temporary migrations to northern Europe?

The Iberian Peninsula— Spain and Portugal

VOCABULARY

tungsten   reconquest

Spanish uplands and Portuguese lowlands   Spain is separated from the rest of Europe by the long, straight mountain range called the Pyrenees. There are few passes through the Pyrenees. All the major transportation routes go around the mountains, along either the Mediterranean or the Atlantic coast. The other major range of the Alpine system, the Sierra Nevada, is in the southern part of Spain. In between is the Meseta, a plateau that is between 1,500 and 2,500 feet (500 and 800 m) in elevation. This plateau extends into northern Portugal. Southern Portugal and nearby parts of Spain are lower.

Most of the Iberian Peninsula has a Mediterranean climate, but there are local

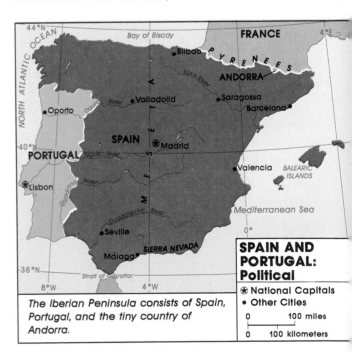

SPAIN AND PORTUGAL: Political
⊛ National Capitals
• Other Cities
0   100 miles
0   100 kilometers

The Iberian Peninsula consists of Spain, Portugal, and the tiny country of Andorra.

197

climate variations. Northwestern Spain has very rainy winters and cool summers. The southern half of Portugal is a little less rainy and warmer in the summer. The Meseta is the driest part of Europe. The Meseta is also colder in the winter than the rest of the Iberian Peninsula. In southern Spain, summers are very hot.

The mineral resources of the Iberian Peninsula are varied. Spain has some coal and iron ore and is the world's leading source of mercury. Mercury is used in thermometers and in making paint and paper. There are other less important resources, such as **tungsten** in Portugal. Tungsten is a hard, heavy metal that is used to make steel hard and strong. It is also used to make the filaments in electric light bulbs. Some hydroelectric power is produced in the rainy northwest of the peninsula. Although many trees have been cut down, there are still large forests of cork oak in Spain and Portugal. Cork comes from the bark of the cork oak tree. Many products you use are made from cork. Floats for fishing nets, bottle stoppers, insulation, floor and wall coverings, engine gaskets, bulletin boards, hot-dish pads, and shoe soles are some of the many items made from cork.

Romans, Goths, and Moors   The Iberian Peninsula was a part of the Roman Empire. Except for Italy itself, the Iberian Peninsula was the most Romanized part of the Mediterranean. Even now, Roman

Olives are grown throughout the Mediterranean region. It takes 15 years for olive trees to mature and produce fruit. The tree and the fruit provide many useful products.

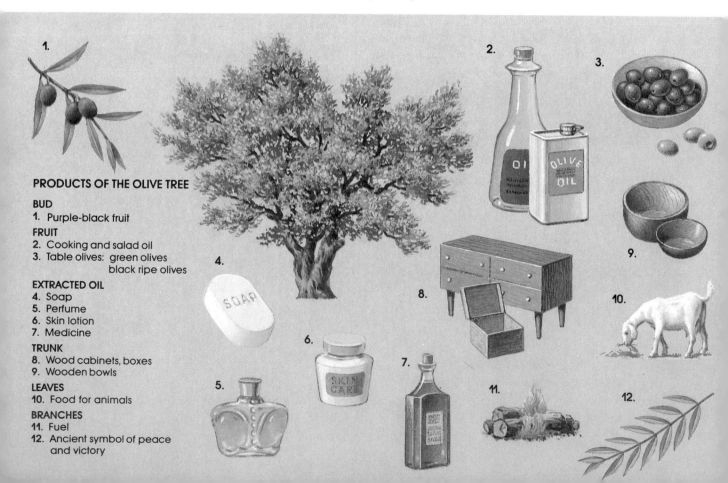

PRODUCTS OF THE OLIVE TREE

BUD
1. Purple-black fruit

FRUIT
2. Cooking and salad oil
3. Table olives: green olives
      black ripe olives

EXTRACTED OIL
4. Soap
5. Perfume
6. Skin lotion
7. Medicine

TRUNK
8. Wood cabinets, boxes
9. Wooden bowls

LEAVES
10. Food for animals

BRANCHES
11. Fuel
12. Ancient symbol of peace
    and victory

You might want to display newspaper or magazine articles about the Basque independence movement. Compare this movement to the campaign for independence in Northern Ireland studied in Chapter 9.

aqueducts, stadiums, walls, and statues can be seen all over southeastern Spain.

The Germanic Goths came as conquerors, but they gave up their own language and many of their customs for the language and customs of the Romans. Soon after, a new group of people, the Moors, invaded the Iberian Peninsula. The Moors ruled most of the peninsula for 700 years. They changed the land and the society greatly.

The Moors were North Africans who had been converted to Islam (is' ləm) and had adopted Arabic ways. The Moors started schools of science and medicine that were later copied by Europeans. They improved the Roman irrigation systems in southern Spain. They introduced crops from the Near East, such as sugarcane, citrus fruits, and rice. These crops are now very important in other parts of the Mediterranean as well.

The Moors made Spain a rich country in which Moslems, Christians, and Jews were allowed to live together in peace. In the far north, however, several small Christian kingdoms stayed independent of the Moors. They fought to take back the peninsula. The Christians regained Portugal first, and by 1492 almost all of Spain had been reconquered. During this long **reconquest,** or regaining, the Iberian people adopted new ways of living as a result of their long fight against the Moors.

The Basques (basks), who had not been conquered by the Romans or the Goths, were conquered by the Spanish during the reconquest. More than a million Basques live in the western part of the Pyrenees. Most of them live in Spain, but some live in France. Half of them speak a language known as Basque. The Basques do not share many of the ideas of the Spanish and have tried to become as independent of Madrid as possible. Spain's largest minority group is the Catalans. They make up one fifth of the population of Spain. The Catalans also have tried to gain local independence from Madrid. Neither group has had much success until very recently.

Modernization of Spain and Portugal

Many great movements, such as the Industrial Revolution, had very little effect on Spain and Portugal. The changes in the land, people, settlements, industry, and government that were taking place in northern Europe did not pass south of the Pyrenees. So the modernization of Spain and Portugal began very late. Before World War II these two countries were among the most backward in Europe. After the war, life in Spain and Portugal began to improve. Recently, some of the demands of the Basques and the Catalans have been met. Spain has taken some giant steps to become more like the rest of Western Europe. Public health and schooling has improved, and the Spanish standard of living has gone up. Portugal, however, has made less progress.

CHECKUP

1. What is the Meseta? What landforms border it?
2. In what ways did the Roman Empire have a long-lasting effect on Spain?
3. What did the Moors introduce to the Iberian Peninsula?
4. In what ways, until recently, have Spain and Portugal been less developed than other parts of Western Europe?

Italy

---VOCABULARY---
in-migration

Mountains and plains   Much of Italy is covered by mountains. The whole northern border of Italy is covered by the Alps. Glaciers formed many passes through these high mountains. For a long time, people have used northern Italy as a passageway from the Mediterranean to northern Europe. Today, railroads and superhighways follow the passes to make travel between Italy and neighboring countries easier. The Italian Alps have become a tourist center. They attract visitors to their beautiful lakes in the summer and to their ski slopes in the winter. The Alps also provide Italy with a source for hydroelectric power.

The Po Valley is Italy's largest lowland. South of the Po Valley are the Apennine Mountains. This mountain range stretches from the French border to the toe of the Italian boot. The Apennines are much lower than the Alps, but they are rugged and more extensive.

On the west side of the Apennines are three important lowlands. The most northern is Tuscany, with its old cities of Florence and Pisa. In the center of Italy is the lowland area of Latium (lā′ shē əm), with its principal city, Rome. Farther south is the third lowland, Campania, around the city of Naples.

Italy includes two large islands in the Mediterranean, Sardinia and Sicily. Sicily is mountainous, with narrow lowlands along the coast. Sardinia is a rugged plateau with steep sides and a small amount of flat land.

Climate   The climate of Italy south of the Po Valley is Mediterranean. The climate of the Po Valley is in between Mediterranean and continental. The summers are very warm and have more rain than the winters. The winters have near-freezing temperatures. The summer climate and fertile soils of the Po Valley have made it Italy's best agricultural area.

Three regions in Italy   There are three distinct regions in Italy—the north, the center, and the south. The northern region is all of the Po Valley and the coastal area around the city of Genoa. The center begins at the northern edge of the Apennines and goes south to about halfway between Rome and Naples. The southern region is made up of the rest of the mainland and the islands of Sicily and Sardinia. The history, economic devel-

Naples, the third largest city of Italy, lies on the west coast. Naples is an area of volcanic activity. Volcanic Mount Vesuvius is shown in the background.

opment, and standard of living of these three regions is very different.

The center is the region where economic development and the standard of living are about average for Italy. The past achievements of this region are spectacular. Rome was the center of Europe's largest and best-organized empire. Later it became the center of the Roman Catholic world. The city of Florence, in Tuscany, was a leading European center of art and science in the fifteenth and sixteenth centuries. When Italy became a unified nation in the 1860s, Rome was chosen as the capital. Rome remains the dominant Italian city today.

The south is the poorest part of Italy. It once was an important center of Greek civilization, and its importance continued until the early Middle Ages. Today it is a farming region with only one large city, Naples, and a small amount of industry. Much of the land is in large estates, which are farmed by peasants who do not own the land. Many farmers own land around Naples, but their farms are tiny. It has been difficult growing enough food for all of the people. There are too many people and too few jobs. Millions of people from the south have migrated to northern Italy or the Americas.

The north is the most prosperous region. It has many large cities and produces 70 percent of the country's industrial products. About a century ago, when Italy became a country, much of Italy's money was used to build dams, railroads, and factories in the north. As a result, northern Italy is now an area of **in-migration**. In-migration is movement into a region or community. Much of

ITALY: Three Regions

⊛ National Capital
• Other Cities

North
Center
South

0   75   150 miles
0   75   150 kilometers

Cities less than 100,000:	Catania	Cities 500,000 to 999,999:
Pisa	Florence	Genoa
Vatican City	Messina	Palermo
Cities 100,000 to 499,999:	Padua	**Cities 1,000,000 or more:**
Bari	Taranto	Milan
Bologna	Trieste	Naples
Brescia	Venice	Rome
Cagliari	Verona	Turin

As you can see from the map, Italy consists mainly of a long, narrow peninsula.

northern Italy is urban and industrial. Farming in the Po Valley is mechanized and has a very high yield. The industrial activity and good farming have helped make the standard of living in the north higher than in the center or the south.

The present economy Italy has few mineral resources. Large amounts of mercury and sulfur are mined there. But Italy does not have much coal, iron ore, oil, or natural gas, so most of these items are imported. Since the Common Market has helped lower the price of coal and iron

Briefly discuss Florence as the center of the Renaissance. Show pictures of Renaissance art and architecture.

ore, manufacturing has greatly increased. The living standards of all three regions of Italy have risen, but improving the economy of the south is still a problem. The government created a fund to be used to improve the economy of the south, and billions of dollars have already been spent. The money has been used for such things as irrigation, fertilizer, land reclamation, land reform, and building industrial plants. The south is now richer than it was, but many people continue to migrate from the region.

Rome—the Eternal City Rome is called the Eternal City because it has always played a leading role in the history of Europe. It was the capital of the Roman Empire for 700 years. The Roman capital had more than a million people and was full of magnificent buildings. Two of the most impressive ruins are those of the Forum and the Colosseum. The Forum

These ruins of the Roman Forum show some of the architecture that was characteristic of the buildings.

was Rome's great public meeting area and marketplace. It covered 60 acres (25 ha) and was surrounded by temples and public buildings. The Colosseum was Rome's largest stadium. Various kinds of games and fights were held there for entertainment. The Roman invention of concrete made it possible to build thousands of large buildings. The size of the Roman buildings is impressive even today.

When the Roman Empire fell, Rome lost much of its importance and its population. It remained one of the largest cities in Europe, however, because it was the center of Roman Catholicism and the home of the pope. The Vatican, home of the pope and headquarters of the Roman Catholic Church, is on the edge of Rome in Vatican City, an independent state. Because Vatican City is located within Rome, Rome could be called a religious capital as well as a political capital.

When Rome became the capital of modern Italy in 1871, it began to regain the population it had lost in the Middle Ages. New monuments, palaces, government offices, foreign embassies, and other buildings were built. These added to the earlier symbols of Rome's power and importance. Today, Rome is one of the major cities of the world. It has more than 3 million people, and it is the center of Italian culture and politics.

CHECKUP

1. What are the lowlands of Italy? How is each one important?
2. Why is southern Italy an area of out-migration? What has the government done to improve the economy of the south?
3. What are some of the things that have helped to make Rome a major city of the world?

Greece—Exporter of Ideas and People

┌─VOCABULARY─────────────────┐
│ archipelago   │
│ population exchange   │
└─────────────────────────────┘

Mountain fingers extending into the sea
The Balkan Peninsula, occupied by Greece, is the most mountainous of the three Mediterranean peninsulas. Most of the land in Greece is covered by rugged hills or mountains that extend to the coastline. The few lowlands are small and scattered. Neither the mainland nor the islands have much agricultural potential. There are few rivers in Greece. Most are short mountain streams. The climate of Greece is Mediterranean.

Modern Greece includes most of the many islands in the Aegean Sea. A group of islands, such as the Aegean islands, scattered through the sea is called an **archipelago** (är kə pel′ ə gō). It is a Greek word meaning "chief sea." The term originally applied to the Aegean Sea. The Ionian Islands, which lie off the west coast of Greece, are also a part of Greece. Crete is the largest of the Greek islands. It lies across the southern entrance to the Aegean Sea. To the east of Crete, off the coast of Turkey, is Rhodes (rōdz). Northwest of Rhodes is a group if islands known as the Cyclades (sik′ lə dēz).

There are few mineral resources in Greece. The most important is bauxite, from which aluminum is made. Greece produces five percent of the world's supply of bauxite and is Europe's second largest producer of the mineral. Greece has no coal or oil.

Greece has hundreds of islands. Crete is the largest island. East of Crete is the island country of Cyprus.

The changing role of Greece in the world The ancient Greek language and civilization were spread widely. Even under the Romans, Greek was the most important language in much of the Middle East. The eastern part of the Roman Empire was so important that in A.D. 330 the capital was moved from Rome to Constantinople, Istanbul in present-day Turkey. The language spoken in the new capital was Greek. Constantinople became the center of Greek life and the most important city in the Mediterranean. It was the home of the eastern branch of Christianity, the Eastern Orthodox Church. The center of Greek life remained outside present-day Greece for more than 1500 years. The Turks took over Greece in the fifteenth century, and it remained a Turkish territory until the 1800s.

In 1829 the Greeks regained their independence from the Turks. But many Greeks continued to live under Turkish

Greek soils are so poor that a humorous Greek legend tells that, during creation, God sifted the earth through a strainer, and all the discarded rock with no worth became Greece.

rule. After World War I, Greece and Turkey agreed to a **population exchange.** The Turks living in Greece were moved to Turkey in exchange for the Greeks living in Turkey.

Greece today   The economy of modern Greece has many things in common with that of ancient Greece. The land does not produce enough to feed the people, and the resources for industry are limited. Because the population of Greece is growing, many Greeks have had to emigrate to find a living elsewhere. The modern Greeks, like their ancestors, depend heavily on trade. Greek ships make up the sixth largest merchant fleet in the world. Greece also depends on tourism for part of its income.

The capital of Greece is Athens. It is the leading manufacturing city of the country. Many tourists are attracted to Athens by the beauty of its historic ruins. Remains of the Parthenon and other famous buildings are located on a hill in Athens called the Acropolis.

Cyprus   East of Crete is the island of Cyprus. It, too, has a Mediterranean climate. About half of the people are farmers. Irrigation has helped the farmers to overcome the dry summers. Such crops as carrots, potatoes, lemons, oranges, grapefruit, olives, and grapes are grown on Cyprus. Asbestos and copper are also important in Cyprus. Asbestos can be made into a cloth that will resist heat.

About a fifth of the people of Cyprus are descendants of the Turks who came to Cyprus when it was under Turkish rule.

The ruins of the Parthenon, an ancient Greek temple built for the goddess Athena, stand on the Acropolis in Athens, Greece. (38°N/23°E; map, p. 203)

The other four fifths are of Greek descent. Each group has kept its own language and religion.

In the late 1800s, Cyprus became part of the British Empire. In 1960 it became an independent republic. Some of the Greeks living on Cyprus wanted to unite with Greece. But this was resisted by the Turks living on the island. In 1974 the northern part of Cyprus was invaded by Turkey. The island is now divided into a Turkish part and a Greek part. United Nations troops are helping to prevent further conflict between the two parts of the island. The United Nations is an international organization that tries to bring peace to the world.

CHECKUP

1. What are the natural resources of Greece? What important resources does Greece lack?
2. Where was the center of Greek life after A.D. 330?
3. To what church do the Greeks belong?
4. Name two sources of income for modern Greece.

The historic ruins of Athens have particular meaning because they are the vestiges of the center of an ancient civilization on which our traditions of justice, individual freedom, and democracy are based.

KEY FACTS

1. The peninsulas of Mediterranean Europe have similar climates and landforms. These peninsulas also have rugged mountains and frequent earthquakes.

2. First the eastern Mediterranean, and then the western Mediterranean, were the homes of Europe's great early civilizations.

3. The people of the eastern Mediterranean lands were not influenced by Rome as much as the people of the western Mediterranean lands.

4. The Mediterranean countries earn much of their income from tourism and from their own citizens who live and work in other countries.

5. The Moors started schools, improved irrigation systems, and introduced crops that changed Spain and the Spanish people in many long-lasting ways.

6. Spain and Italy have become more modern and industrialized in recent decades.

7. Italy is made up of three distinct regions. Each region has its own history, economic development, and standard of living.

8. Tourism and trade are modern Greece's major sources of income.

VOCABULARY QUIZ

On a sheet of paper write the numbers of the statements below. Next to each number write the letter of the word that best fills in the blank in the statement.

a. tungsten
b. temporary migration
c. in-migration
d. out-migration
e. archipelago

1. A hard, heavy metal that is used to make steel hard and strong is called ___tungsten___ .

2. Movement from one region to another is called ___out-migration___ .

3. ___Temporary migration___ from the Mediterranean area to host countries in northern Europe is common.

4. Industrialization in northern Italy has caused much ___in-migration___ into the area.

5. A group of islands scattered through the sea is often referred to as an ___archipelago___ .

REVIEW QUESTIONS

1. What is the Meseta and where is it located?

2. What roles do tourism and out-migration play in the economies of the Mediterranean countries?

3. What are the problem areas in Spain today?

4. What is the problem area in Italy today? What are some of the specific problems of this area?

5. What are two of the best-known and most impressive ruins of Rome? How was each used by the people of Rome?

6. What does the economy of modern Greece have in common with that of ancient Greece?

ACTIVITY

Almonds, figs, raisins, and olive oil are among the most important exports of the Mediterranean countries. Look at the labels on these products at your local supermarket. Make a list of the products in a column. List both American products and those from Mediterranean countries. In a second column write the name of the country from which each product came. In a third column record the price of each product. Compare the prices. Is there a difference in price between the American products and the same products from the Mediterranean countries?

INTERPRETING GRAPHS

READING A POPULATION PYRAMID

A population pyramid is a special kind of bar graph that shows different facts about the population of a country. A pyramid shows the population by age groups. Some pyramids also show the number of males and females. One of the pyramids below shows the population of the United States in 1979. It shows what percentage of the population in different age groups was male, and what percentage was female.

Each horizontal bar on the pyramids below represents a 5-year time period. For example, the bar at the base of each pyramid shows how many children there were up to 5 years of age. The next bar shows the number of children from age 5 to age 10. The horizontal bars often get shorter as they go up because they represent older people.

The vertical line in the center of the pyramid divides the population into males and females. The number of males is shown on the left, and the number of females on the right.

A population pyramid tells a lot about the history of a place. For example, many 20- to 35-year-old men are killed in wars. This causes the male side of the bar representing that age group to be shorter than the female side. Temporary migration mostly affects people from 20 to 40 years of age. In-migration makes the pyramid bulge out, while out-migration makes it go in. An event such as a baby boom also causes the pyramid to bulge out.

SKILLS PRACTICE

Trace the pyramid of Portugal shown below. For each cause listed below, label the part of the pyramid that is the result of that cause.

Causes in Portugal

1. Out-migration of workers, mostly men
2. Low birthrate caused by the depression in the 1930s
3. Women living longer than men
4. High birthrate of a rural population between 1962 and 1967

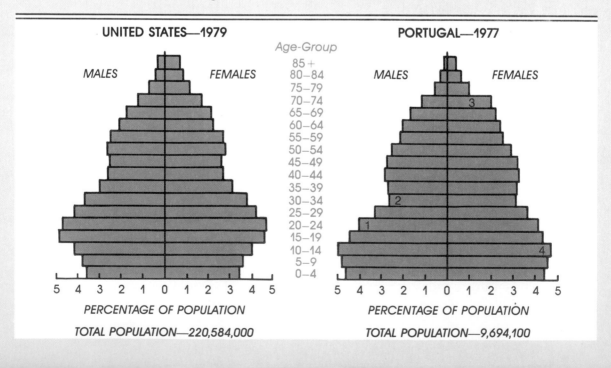

UNITED STATES—1979

MALES   FEMALES

PORTUGAL—1977

MALES   FEMALES

Age-Group

85+
80–84
75–79
70–74
65–69
60–64
55–59
50–54
45–49
40–44
35–39
30–34
25–29
20–24
15–19
10–14
5–9
0–4

5 4 3 2 1 0 1 2 3 4 5

PERCENTAGE OF POPULATION

TOTAL POPULATION—220,584,000

5 4 3 2 1 0 1 2 3 4 5

PERCENTAGE OF POPULATION

TOTAL POPULATION—9,694,100

4/UNIT REVIEW

Answer Key in back of book.

READING THE TEXT

Turn to page 163 and read the section "Five countries and their economies." Then, on a sheet of paper, answer these questions.

1. What two things do the economies of all five Scandinavian countries have in common?
2. On what industry is Iceland's economy mainly dependent?
3. In what area of production does Norway lead the world?
4. Which Scandinavian country has the highest level of industrialization?
5. Which Scandinavian country has the closest economic ties with the Soviet Union?

READING A MAP

Turn to page 171 and look at the map titled "France and the Low Countries: Physical." Study the key and notice the scale bar.

On a sheet of paper, write the answers to these questions.

1. Name the mountain chain in the extreme south of France. On what other country does this region of France border?
2. Name the river that flows in the southwestern part of France. In which direction does this river flow?
3. Using the scale bar, give the approximate distance in miles between Paris and the capital city of Belgium. And the capital city of the Netherlands.
4. What type of landform is found in most of the Netherlands? In most of Luxembourg?
5. What region is in the far west of France? What river flows through this region?

READING A PICTURE

Turn to page 183 and carefully examine the picture of a West German village in the Rhine Valley. On a sheet of paper, answer these questions.

1. Identify two ways in which the river is being used as a means of transportation. What other type of transportation is shown?
2. What indication can you find that this part of Germany has a mild climate?
3. What evidence do you see that there is a Christian community in this village?
4. What type of terrain does the region in the picture have?
5. Do you think the village shown in the picture would be popular with tourists? Write a paragraph explaining why you think it would or would not be popular.

READING A CHART

Turn to page 198 and study the chart titled "Products of the Olive Tree." On a sheet of paper, answer these questions about the chart.

1. Name the part of the olive tree from which home furnishings are made.
2. What two parts of the olive tree are part of the human diet?
3. Name the part of the olive tree from which cleansing and beauty products are made.
4. Name the part of the olive tree that has symbolic meaning. What symbol does it represent?
5. Name the part of the olive tree that provides food for animals.

EASTERN EUROPE AND THE SOVIET UNION

After pupils have read the section titled "From sea to sea," provide them with outline maps of the region. Have them label the main physical features of Eastern Europe and the Soviet Union, including the following: Arctic Ocean, Baltic Sea, Adriatic Sea, North European Plain, Ural Mountains, Carpathian Mountains, Caucasus Mountains, Balkan Mountains, Volga River, Lena River, Danube River. You may wish to have pupils include other physical features shown on the physical map of the region.

From Sea to Sea

Eastern Europe and the Soviet Union make up a huge region that stretches from the Baltic Sea to the Pacific Ocean, a distance of about 6,000 miles (9,654 km). As you can see from the map on the facing page, this region extends almost halfway around the world—from approximately 10° east latitude to 170° west latitude.

Much of this region is an extension of the North European Plain, which you read about in Unit 4. This plain continues eastward across Eastern Europe and the Soviet Union into Siberia. The North European Plain is interrupted by a range of low mountains called the Urals. These mountains are often regarded as the boundary between Europe and Asia.

The North European Plain has been an important east-west route for centuries. Many invasions from Asia into Europe have taken place in the southern part of this lowland known as the steppe. This semiarid, treeless grassland was the home of nomadic people, such as the Huns, the Mongols, and the Turks. You will read about these people in this unit.

Most of the other landforms in the region have been barriers to easy movement. In the central part of Eastern Europe are the hook-shaped Carpathian Mountains. Farther south are several different Alpine ranges. Much of the southern border of the Soviet Union is made up of very high and rugged Alpine mountains. North of them, in central Asia, is a huge desert.

As the map shows, the Soviet Union spans two continents. It stretches from Eastern Europe to the Pacific Ocean. The Ural Mountains form the east-west divide between Asia and Europe.

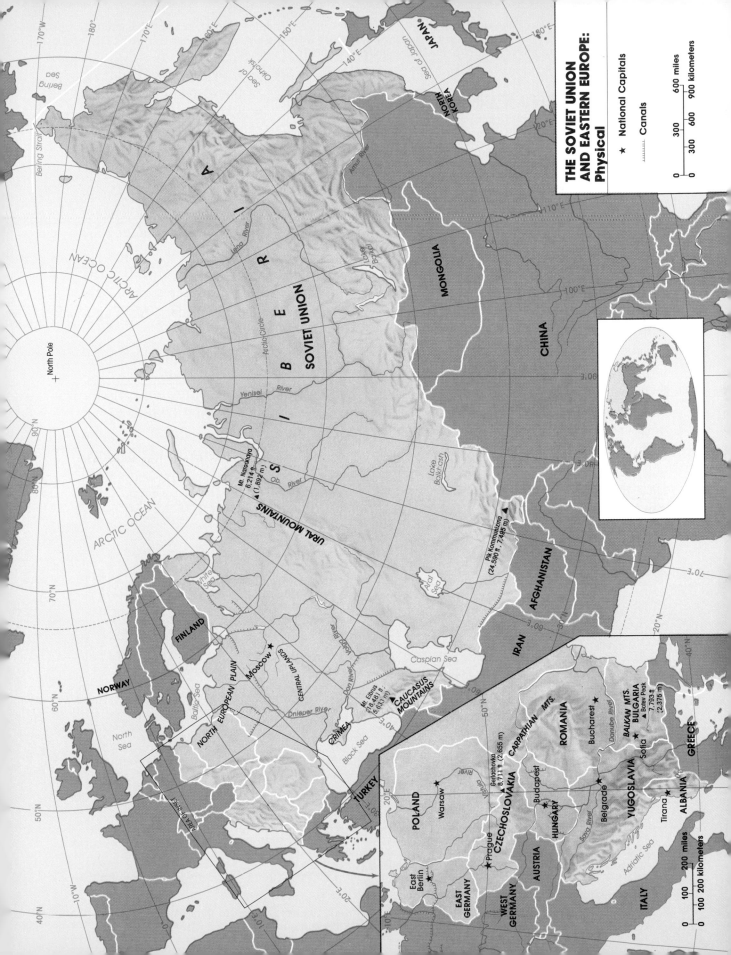

THE SOVIET UNION AND EASTERN EUROPE: Physical

★ National Capitals

.... Canals

0   300   600 miles
0   300   600   900 kilometers

North Pole

ARCTIC OCEAN

Bering Strait

Bering Sea

Sea of Okhotsk

JAPAN

Sea of Japan

NORTH KOREA

Amur River

Lena River

SIBERIA

SOVIET UNION

MONGOLIA

CHINA

Lake Baikal

Lake Balkhash

Yenisei River

Ob River

Mt. Narodnaya
6,214 ft.
(1,894 m)

URAL MOUNTAINS

Arctic Circle

ARCTIC OCEAN

White Sea

FINLAND

NORWAY

North Sea

Baltic Sea

NORTH EUROPEAN PLAIN

Moscow ★

CENTRAL URAL LANDS

Volga River

Don River

Dnieper River

CRIMEA

Black Sea

Caspian Sea

Mt. Elbrus
18,481 ft.
(5,633 m)
CAUCASUS MOUNTAINS

Aral Sea

Pik Kommunizma
24,590 ft. 7,495 m.

AFGHANISTAN

IRAN

TURKEY

GREECE

AREA OF INSET

POLAND

Warsaw ★

EAST GERMANY

East Berlin ★

WEST GERMANY

Prague ★ CZECHOSLOVAKIA

AUSTRIA

Gerlachovka
8,711 ft. (2,655 m)

Vistula River

CARPATHIAN MTS.

HUNGARY

Budapest ★

Belgrade ★

YUGOSLAVIA

Sava River

ROMANIA

Bucharest ★

Danube River

BALKAN MTS.
BULGARIA
Botev Peak
7,793 ft.
(2,375 m)

Sofia ★

Tirana ★

ALBANIA

Adriatic Sea

ITALY

0   100   200 miles
0 100 200 kilometers

Old Empires and Twentieth–Century Nations

The region of Eastern Europe and the Soviet Union was once part of large empires. The Mongols ruled most of Asia in the thirteenth century, and their empire included southern Russia. In the 1500s the Turks took control of all of southeastern Europe, as far north as Hungary and Romania. By the 1800s the Austro-Hungarian Empire stretched over a large area and included much of the land formerly held by the Turks. The Russian empire included many parts of Eastern Europe and Asia between the sixteenth and twentieth centuries. The German empire extended into parts of northeastern Europe.

World War I destroyed the empires that had controlled much of the region. In 1917 the Russian empire was replaced by the Union of Soviet Socialist Republics, often called the U.S.S.R. or the Soviet Union. Small independent countries took the place of the old empires in Eastern Europe. From the Baltic Sea to the Mediterranean Sea, these countries formed a zone that was supposed to be a buffer between Russians and Germans.

After World War II, the Soviet Union took back most of the territory in Eastern Europe that had once been part of the Russian empire. It also set up Communist governments in the rest of Eastern Europe. Today the Soviet Union has control over all of Eastern Europe except for Yugoslavia and Albania.

The Soviet Union and the Eastern European countries have economic and military ties. All of these countries except for Yugoslavia have joined COMECON, an organization that was formed to make trade easier among the member nations. Most of these countries have a defense agreement called the Warsaw Pact. In it they have promised to help each other in case of war.

Cities 100,000 to 499,999
Tirana (Albania) F-13

Cities 500,000 to 999,999
Alma-Ata (Soviet Union) C-6
Barnaul (Soviet Union) B-7
Dresden (East Germany) E-13
Frunze (Soviet Union) C-6
Irkutsk (Soviet Union) B-9
Izhevsk (Soviet Union) B-4
Karaganda (Soviet Union) C-6
Kazan (Soviet Union) B-3
Khabarovsk (Soviet Union) C-12
Kishinev (Soviet Union) C-1
Krasnodar (Soviet Union) C-2
Kraków (Poland) E-13
Krasnoyarsk (Soviet Union) B-8
Krivoi Rog (Soviet Union) C-2
Leipzig (East Germany) E-13
Łódź (Poland) E-13
Lvov (Soviet Union) C-1
Novokuznetsk (Soviet Union) B-7

Perm (Soviet Union) B-4
Poznan (Poland) E-13
Riga (Soviet Union) B-1
Rostov (Soviet Union) C-2
Saratov (Soviet Union) B-3
Togliatti (Soviet Union) B-3
Tula (Soviet Union) B-2
Ufa (Soviet Union) B-4
Vladivostok (Soviet Union) C-12
Volgograd (Soviet Union) C-3
Voronezh (Soviet Union) B-2
Wrocław (Poland) E-13
Yaroslavl (Soviet Union) B-2
Zaporozhye (Soviet Union) C-2
Zagreb (Yugoslavia) F-13

Cities 1,000,000 or more
Baku (Soviet Union) D-4
Belgrade (Yugoslavia) F-14
Bucharest (Romania) F-14
Budapest (Hungary) F-13

Chelyabinsk (Soviet Union) B-5
Donetsk (Soviet Union) C-2
Dnepropetrovsk (Soviet Union) C-2
East Berlin (East Germany) E-13
Gorki (Soviet Union) B-3
Kharkov (Soviet Union) C-2
Kiev (Soviet Union) B-2
Kuibyshev (Soviet Union) B-4
Leningrad (Soviet Union) B-2
Minsk (Soviet Union) B-1
Moscow (Soviet Union) B-2
Novosibirsk (Soviet Union) B-7
Odessa (Soviet Union) C-2
Omsk (Soviet Union) B-6
Prague (Czechoslovakia) E-13
Sofia (Bulgaria) F-14
Sverdlovsk (Soviet Union) B-5
Tashkent (Soviet Union) C-5
Tbilisi (Soviet Union) C-3
Warsaw (Poland) E-14
Yerevan (Soviet Union) C-3

The map shows the Soviet Union and the eight nations that make up Eastern Europe. What is the capital city of the Soviet Union? On which river is Poland's capital located? Which countries have a national capital with a population of 1,000,000 or more?

Although both Yugoslavia and Albania are Communist countries, Yugoslavia often deals with non-Communist countries of the West, while Albania has little contact with any part of the world.

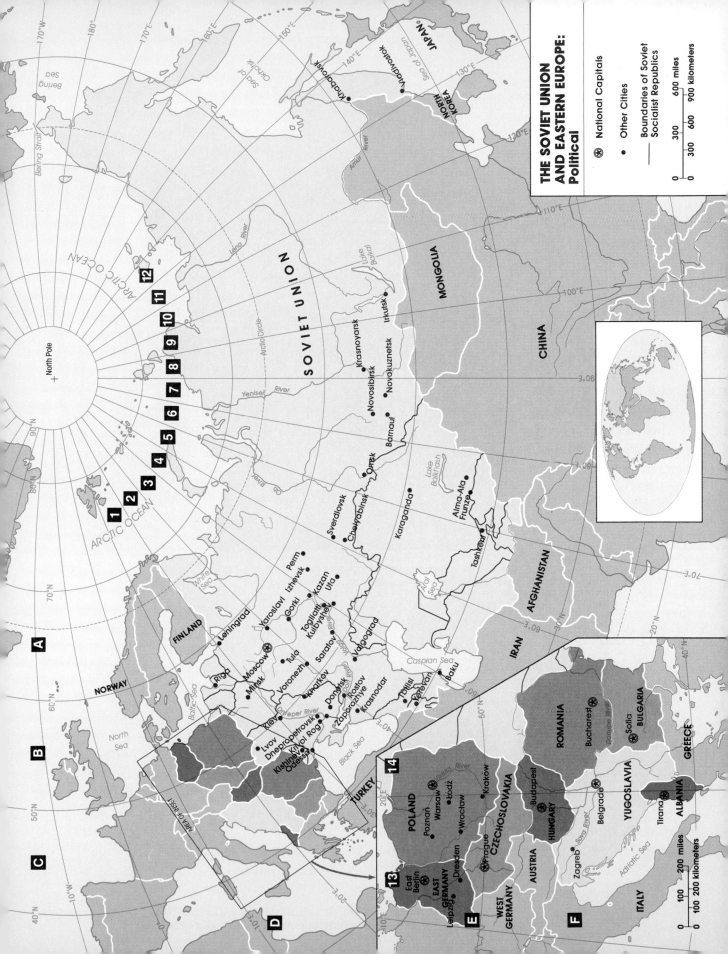

THE SOVIET UNION AND EASTERN EUROPE: Political

- ⊛ National Capitals
- • Other Cities
- — Boundaries of Soviet Socialist Republics

0   300   600 miles
0   300   600   900 kilometers

Map labels

ARCTIC OCEAN

North Pole

SOVIET UNION

FINLAND
NORWAY

Leningrad
Riga
Minsk
Moscow
Tula
Yaroslavl
Gorki
Izhevsk
Perm
Kazan
Ufa
Togliatti
Kuibyshev
Saratov
Voronezh
Kharkov
Donetsk
Rostov
Zaporozhye
Krasnodar
Volgograd
Kiev
Dnepropetrovsk
Krivoi Rog
Odessa
Kishinev
Lvov

Sverdlovsk
Chelyabinsk
Omsk
Barnaul
Novokuznetsk
Novosibirsk
Krasnoyarsk
Irkutsk
Karaganda
Alma-Ata
Frunze
Tashkent
Baku
Tbilisi
Yerevan

Khabarovsk
Vladivostok

JAPAN
NORTH KOREA
MONGOLIA
CHINA
AFGHANISTAN
IRAN
TURKEY

Caspian Sea
Black Sea
Baltic Sea
North Sea
White Sea
Bering Sea
Sea of Japan
Sea of Okhotsk
Bering Strait
Aral Sea
Lake Balkhash
Lake Baikal

Lena River
Yenisei River
Ob River
Amur River

GREECE
ITALY
WEST GERMANY
AUSTRIA
YUGOSLAVIA
ALBANIA
Tirana
Belgrade
Zagreb
Adriatic Sea
Sava River

POLAND
Warsaw
Poznań
Łódź
Wrocław
Kraków
East Berlin
EAST GERMANY
Dresden
Leipzig
Prague
CZECHOSLOVAKIA
Budapest
HUNGARY
ROMANIA
Bucharest
BULGARIA
Sofia
Danube River
Vistula River

0   100   200 miles
0   100   200 kilometers

AREA OF INSET

Grid: A B C D (rows); markers 1–14

These Russian schoolchildren know that education can bring success in their country. They are graded on their behavior and leadership as well as on their schoolwork.

The Peoples and Their Common Backgrounds

There are about 400 million people in Eastern Europe and the Soviet Union. Their world is mainly Slavic and Eastern Orthodox, but there are many other languages and three other main religions. Slavic languages, such as Russian and Polish, are spoken by three fourths of the people. Nearly 100 million speak other languages, such as Hungarian or Romanian.

Many of the people of this region have common religious backgrounds. Eastern Orthodoxy was the state church in Russia, Romania, and parts of Yugoslavia. Poland, Czechoslovakia, and Hungary are largely Roman Catholic. East Germany is Protestant. Albania and many parts of the Soviet Union are Moslem. Today, members of religious groups are hard to count because each government officially discourages religious worship. However, in every country of the region, religious groups continue to exist.

Table of Countries: Ask: What is the largest country in area in Eastern Europe? (Poland) The smallest? (Albania) Which country in the region has the greatest population density? (East Germany)

EASTERN EUROPE AND THE SOVIET UNION

COUNTRY	FLAG	TOTAL AREA	POPULATION and POPULATION DENSITY	CAPITAL CITY and POPULATION	WHERE PEOPLE LIVE
Albania		11,100 sq mi (28,748 sq km)	2,900,000 261 per sq mi (101 per sq km)	Tirana 192,000	
Bulgaria		42,823 sq mi (110,912 sq km)	8,900,000 208 per sq mi (80 per sq km)	Sofia 1,048,000	
Czechoslovakia		49,371 sq mi (127,869 sq km)	15,400,000 312 per sq mi (120 per sq km)	Prague 1,182,500	
Germany (East)		41,768 sq mi (108,178 sq km)	16,700,000 400 per sq mi (154 per sq km)	Berlin (East) 1,152,500	
Hungary		35,919 sq mi (93,030 sq km)	10,700,000 298 per sq mi (115 per sq km)	Budapest 2,062,000	
Poland		120,725 sq mi (312,677 sq km)	36,600,000 303 per sq mi (117 per sq km)	Warsaw 1,611,500	
Romania		91,699 sq mi (237,500 sq km)	22,700,000 248 per sq mi (96 per sq km)	Bucharest 1,861,000	
Soviet Union		8,649,500 sq mi (22,402,000 sq km)	272,000,000 31 per sq mi (12 per sq km)	Moscow 7,831,000	
Yugoslavia		98,766 sq mi (255,804 sq km)	22,800,000 231 per sq mi (89 per sq km)	Belgrade 1,445,000	

Urban ■ Nonurban ■ Not Available – ■   **213**

Have pupils make a bar graph showing the population of the nine countries in the region.

East Germany and Poland—Countries of the North European Plain

> **VOCABULARY**
>
> lignite   collective
>
> Berlin wall   Solidarity
>
> per capita   satellite
> income

The land   The North European Plain covers most of East Germany and Poland. The northernmost part of the plain has lakes and low hills. Here the main resources are the ports on the Baltic Sea.

River valleys are an important part of the central North European Plain. The Elbe River forms East Germany's chief water route. The Oder River and its tributary, the Neisse, form the boundary between East Germany and Poland. The Vistula (vis′ chə lə) River is Poland's own river. It crosses no national boundaries. These river valleys are farming areas.

The southernmost parts of East Germany and Poland are in the Central Uplands. There are many minerals, including coal, in these parts. Poland has very important coalfields in Silesia (sī lē′ zhə). The coal in East Germany is not of high quality. East Germany has large deposits of **lignite,** or brown coal. Lignite is a coal of low quality. Although lignite is useful as a fuel, much more of it must be burned than hard coal to produce heat.

The southern parts of East Germany and Poland also have excellent loess soils. Farmers grow mainly wheat and sugar beets here. North of the loess lands, where the soil is poorer, farmers grow crops such as rye and potatoes.

The climate   The climate of East Germany and Poland is continental. Summers are fairly cool in the north and warmer toward the south. The average temperature in January is just below freezing. Winters are slightly warmer along the Baltic coast. The winters in Poland are longer and colder than in East Germany. The Polish harbors are usually blocked by ice during the winter, and snow covers the land.

East Germany after World War II East Germany was separated from the rest of Germany in 1945 and put under Russian military occupation. In 1954 it became an independent country, and East Berlin was made its capital. Many difficulties faced the new nation. Parts of its cities were in rubble after the bombings during the war. The Russians had moved many East German factories to the Soviet Union.

The name Poland means "the land of the plain." Most of the country lies in the North European Plain and is quite flat. Wheat is grown in the better soils of southern Poland.

Note that East Germany does not have the variety of landscape that West Germany has. While it does have some mountainous areas in the south, it lacks the drama of the Black Forest or the majesty of the Bavarian Alps.

EASTERN EUROPE: Landforms

Lowlands

Central Uplands

Alpine Mountains

0   250   500 miles
0   250   500 kilometers

Poland is the largest country in Eastern Europe. The North European Plain covers most of Poland.

At first there was great uncertainty in East Germany. Living conditions were bad. Most of the people did not want to live under a Communist government, and many people left. Between 1945 and 1961 more than 2.5 million East Germans escaped to West Germany. The Communist government of East Germany was determined to stop this movement of people. First the government placed 600 miles (965 km) of barbed wire and lookout towers along the country's border with West Germany. But the East Germans were still able to escape in the city of Berlin. To stop this movement, the East German government built a concrete wall through the city of Berlin in 1961. It is known as the **Berlin wall.** It consists of two walls that are 11 feet (3.5 m) high and separated by 100 yards (100 m) of empty space. It is topped with glass and barbed wire. The 28-mile (45-km) wall separates Communist East Berlin from West Berlin. The wall is guarded by 10,000 East German police.

East Germany today   The population of East Germany declined for 30 years after World War II. The population is now beginning to grow again. The country's industry and agriculture have made great progress. East Germany has become the leading industrial country of Eastern Europe. The cities of Dresden and Leipzig (līp′ sig) are the major industrial centers.

East Germany's standard of living is now high. Its **per capita income** is higher than that of any other Eastern European country. Per capita income is the amount of income each person in a country would have if the country's total income were divided equally among all of its people.

A memorial to those who have died trying to cross the Berlin wall is shown on this section of the wall in West Berlin. (53°N/13°E; map, p. 185)

Poland's changing borders   As you can see on the map, Poland's borders have been moved many times.   At the end of World War I, after more than 100 years of rule by Russia, Germany, and Austria, Poland regained its independence.   There were many problems in setting the new boundaries of Poland. Among other decisions it was determined that Poland would be given land along the coast so that the country would not be cut off from the Baltic Sea.   This made the Germans unhappy because the German province of East Prussia was separated from the main part of Germany. The Germans and Poles continued to argue about what territory was rightfully theirs.

In 1939, Germany and Russia agreed to divide the land of Poland between themselves.   On September 1, 1939, Germany invaded Poland.   Then France and Britain declared war on Germany.   This was the beginning of World War II.   In a short time, Germany conquered Poland.   Poland was also invaded from the east by Russia.   Poland was divided between Germany and Russia.   Then, in 1941, Germany attacked Russia and took all of Poland.   After World War II, new borders were drawn, and Poland's boundaries changed again.

The economy of postwar Poland   Poland wanted to build up a modern economy after World War II.   It had a low standard of living.   Two thirds of its people were farmers.   Its economy depended on the export of raw materials such as coal and grain.   Wartime destruction added to its problems.   Cities, industries,

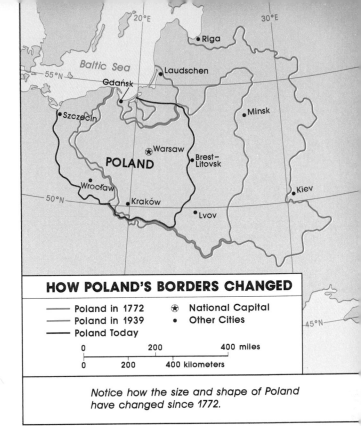

HOW POLAND'S BORDERS CHANGED

——— Poland in 1772   ✴ National Capital
——— Poland in 1939   • Other Cities
——— Poland Today

0   200   400 miles
0   200   400 kilometers

Notice how the size and shape of Poland have changed since 1772.

and the transportation system had to be rebuilt.

After some rebuilding, the Poles turned to building new industries.   The land that had been taken from Germany already had industries, but other areas needed factories.   New chemical plants were started.   Factory towns were built on the Silesian coalfields.   Automobile and tractor plants were started in the city of Warsaw.   The ports on the Baltic Sea were expanded.   Gdańsk (gə dänsk´) became the main port of Poland's goods. Szczecin (shchet´ sēn) became the main port for the goods of landlocked Czechoslovakia.   Shipbuilding became important, and Poland built up a large merchant marine.

Agriculture has been a problem in Poland.   There were large landholdings in prewar Poland, and these were broken up

EASTERN EUROPE: Natural Resources

Coal   ⚑ Petroleum   ★ National Capitals
◇ Bauxite   • Other Cities

0   250   500 miles
0   250   500 kilometers

Poland is the fourth largest coal producer in the world. Poland's most important coalfields are in the region of Silesia.

It still has a large debt it must pay back.

In the mid-1970s, when the government decided to raise the price of meat and other foods, Poles rioted in many cities. They wanted lower prices. In 1980, workers in various Polish cities went on strike. Besides asking for higher pay, the Polish workers wanted the government ·to allow them to form unions free from government control. Many Polish workers joined an organization of free trade unions called **Solidarity**. Solidarity was a labor organization that was independent of the Communist party. This organization demanded some freedoms that the government leaders would not allow. Many of the leaders feared that the Communist government of Poland was being threatened by Solidarity. In 1981 many of the Solidarity leaders were arrested. In October 1982 the government outlawed Solidarity.

Poland dislikes being a **satellite** of the Soviet Union. A satellite is a country that claims to be independent but is actually controlled by a more powerful country. Poland is a country devoted to Roman Catholicism. Its people are very proud of their country and its history. For the last 200 years, they have struggled against foreign rule. Many of the Poles support Communism, but would like to have an economy not so closely tied to the needs and desires of the Soviet Union.

into smaller holdings. At first the Communist leaders tried to turn all of the farmland into **collective** farms. Such farms are operated by groups of people, who grow and share the crops. But the Polish farmers resisted strongly. Today 85 percent of the farmland in Poland is privately owned. Most of these farms are small and poorly equipped. The country has not been able to produce enough food to meet both its own needs and those of its trading partners. The government has introduced more modern farm methods, and farm production has begun to rise.

Modernizing the Polish economy has been costly. Poland borrowed money from the Soviet Union and from the West.

CHECKUP

1. What landform covers most of East Germany and Poland?
2. What did the East German government do to keep people from leaving the country?

Discuss the ways a satellite country differs from an independent country. Using the map above, point out other East European countries that are satellites of the Soviet Union.

Two Landlocked Countries — Czechoslovakia and Hungary

VOCABULARY

depopulate   fodder

Mountains and lowlands of central Europe   Czechoslovakia and Hungary are neighbors, and both countries are landlocked. However, both are very different from each other.

Czechoslovakia is more mountainous than Hungary. Bohemia, the western part of the country, is made up of a lowland surrounded by low, heavily forested mountains. Farther east, in Slovakia (slō väk′ ē ə), the land is more rugged. Between Bohemia and Slovakia is a lowland area called Moravia (mə rā′ vē ə).

Hungary is a flatter country. It is a large lowland plain bordered mostly by Alpine mountain ranges. Some low hills cross Hungary, but almost all of the country is between 300 and 400 feet (90 and 120 m) above sea level.

Grass is the natural vegetation in Hungary. The grass-covered plains are called steppes. The steppes have very good soils, and the hot summers of the Hungarian Plain allow grapes, corn, and wheat to grow.

The people of Czechoslovakia   In the past, three groups lived in what is now Czechoslovakia. The largest group was the Czechs. They spoke Czech and lived in Bohemia and Moravia. In medieval times their region was one of the most important parts of central Europe.

It had mines, industries, and prosperous agriculture. It was also an important part of the Holy Roman Empire, a medieval union of German states. The Czechs' capital city, Prague (präg), was one of the largest in the empire.

The second group was the Slovaks. Their region, Slovakia, was a part of Hungary until 1918. The Hungarians used Slovakia as a source of food and cheap labor. They did not develop the region, and it remained poor and rural.

The third group of people was the Germans. German miners and farmers moved into Bohemia from the northwest as early as the thirteenth century. Some also moved into northern Moravia.

Czechoslovakia was formed as an independent state in 1918. It included 7 million Czechs and 3.5 million Germans, who were called Sudeten Germans. Adolf Hitler, Germany's leader, invaded Czechoslovakia in 1938. After World

Prague, the capital of Czechoslovakia, is a city of many beautiful old palaces. (50°N/14°E; map, p. 218)

War II the Sudeten Germans were expelled from the country. This allowed Czechs and Slovaks to move into the emptied areas of Bohemia and Moravia. These areas were some of the main industrial zones of the country.

The economy of Czechoslovakia today
After World War II, Czechoslovakia had the most advanced industry of any Eastern European country. In 1948 the Communists took over. Czechoslovakia became a satellite of the Soviet Union. Czechoslovakia immediately became the leading industrial supplier of the Communist world. Today, Czechoslovakia exports trucks, cars, coal, textiles, and various precision-made goods. Its glass industry recently invented soft contact lenses.

Czechoslovakia does not produce enough food to feed its people. Sugar beets and wheat are grown in the lowlands of the west. Slovakia produces rye and oats. The country has to export industrial goods so that food and raw materials can be imported.

Despite its good start, the Czechoslovak economy has slowed down, compared to the economies of the other Eastern European countries. Many Czechs blame the tightly controlled government for this lack of progress.

The Hungarians The Magyars (mag' yärs) were the ancestors of the modern Hungarians. They spoke a language that we call Hungarian. It is still the language of Hungary. The Magyars settled in the Hungarian Plain and became the ruling class of a powerful kingdom. Turkey later took most of this area from the Hungarians, and many settlements on the steppes were **depopulated**. This means that they lost their inhabitants. The Hungarians moved to safer areas. In the eighteenth century the steppes were settled again, mostly by Hungarian nobles and peasants. When the Austro-Hungarian Empire was broken up in 1918, Hungary was reduced to its present size.

Agriculture and industrial strength
At one time the economy of Hungary was based mostly on agriculture. Most of the land was divided into large estates. Hungary had enough grain and animals for the rest of the Austro-Hungarian Empire. Most of the people lived in very large farming villages of over 10,000 people.

A Communist government was set up in Hungary after World War II. Hungary was a rural and agricultural country at that time. One fourth of the farmers did not own any of the land. The government took the large estates and divided

This worker in a glass factory in Czechoslovakia gives his full concentration as he works.

Wine grapes are one of Hungary's chief crops.

uranium, and small gas and oil fields. Most of these resources are in the hilly region. Much of the new industry has been located in Budapest, the capital of Hungary, and its suburbs. Budapest has become a supplier of such things as locomotives and tractors to the COMECON countries. COMECON stands for the Council for Mutual Economic Assistance. This economic community was formed in 1949 and is made up of the Soviet Union and most of the Communist countries of Eastern Europe.

the land among the farmers who did not own any land. Most people were happy with this division of land. But in the 1950s the government began to take back the private land to create collective farms. This and some other unpopular programs were resisted by the Hungarians. In 1956 the Hungarians revolted. The revolt was harshly put down by Russian troops. Afterward the government went back to the system of collective farms.

Today most of the land is in collective farms. Wheat and corn are the major crops. In Hungary, corn is used to make **fodder**, a coarse food fed to livestock. Fodder is a mixture of hay and cornstalks with their leaves. Hungary exports a large amount of pork and beef to the Soviet Union. Although industry is growing in Hungary, most people still farm.

Industry has become important in Hungary only since the Communist takeover. First the country's natural resources were developed. Hungary has Europe's largest bauxite deposits. It now supplies much of this raw material to the aluminum industry of other Communist countries of Eastern Europe. Hungary also has lignite,

CHECKUP

1. Where are the lowlands of Czechoslovakia?
2. What is the natural vegetation of the steppes?
3. Why was the region inhabited by the Czechs important in medieval times? Why did Slovakia remain poor and rural?
4. Who were the Magyars?
5. When did industrialization begin in Hungary?

The Balkans

┌─ VOCABULARY ─────────────────────
  ethnic group
└─────────────────────────────────

The land and the climate In southeastern Europe between the Mediterranean, Adriatic, and Black seas lies the Balkan Peninsula. Much of the peninsula is covered by two groups of Alpine mountains. In the west, in Yugoslavia and Albania, the Dinaric Alps run along the coast of the Adriatic Sea. Farther east are the Carpathian and Balkan mountains.

Between the mountains are several lowlands. Part of the Hungarian Plain is included in these lowlands. Another important lowland covers southern Romania. It is called Walachia (wä lā′ kē ə).

The climate in the Balkans varies. The Adriatic coast of southern Yugoslavia and Albania has a Mediterranean climate. The Dinaric Alps are very wet. In the lowland basins the climate is continental and dry.

The people   The Balkan Peninsula was settled by people of different languages, religions, and ways of life. By A.D. 700, Slavic-speaking farmers had settled most of the peninsula. Later, invaders from the east moved across the steppes of Walachia and Hungary.

In the fifteenth and sixteenth centuries, the Balkans were invaded by the Turks. The Turks brought their religion, Islam, to the peninsula, and many people in the Balkans converted to Islam. Today about 5 million people in this region are Moslems, as people who practice Islam are called. Another 35 million people in the Balkans are Eastern Orthodox Christians, and 5 million are Roman Catholic.

The harvesting of corn on a state farm in Romania is shown here. Corn is one of Romania's leading crops.

The regions of Romania   Romania has distinct regions that have different landforms, people, and economic resources. First there is Walachia, the historical and economic heart of Romania. It is a large lowland basin that slopes gently southward from the Carpathian Mountains to the Danube River. It has the best farmland in the country and is covered by fields of wheat and corn. Near the mountains are the Ploieşti (plô yesht′ ē) oil fields, Eastern Europe's largest oil fields. In the center of Walachia is Bucharest (bü′ kə rest), the capital and only large city of Romania. Northeast of Walachia is a similar lowland called Moldavia (mäl dā′ vē ə).

The Carpathian Mountains are a second region of Romania. Forests cover the higher elevations, but there are pastures and orchards in the valleys. The government has begun to encourage the use of the region's mineral resources and the use of waterpower there for producing electricity.

Transylvania, a third region, is a hilly lowland northwest of the Carpathian Mountains. Most of Transylvania is rural. Fruits and vegetables are the main crops. The region belonged to Hungary until 1918. It has had a mixed population of Romanians, Hungarians, and Germans since the Middle Ages. The population of Transylvania is less diverse now, because many Germans left after World War II.

The regions of Bulgaria   The mountains of Bulgaria divide the country into uplands and lowlands. The country's most important lowland area, south of the Balkan Mountains, is made up of many

Maria of Bulgaria

Maria is a 13-year-old girl who lives in the Gypsy ghetto in Sofia. Maria is the Slavic name that she must use in school and must have on her passport. At home and in the ghetto, she is known as Atidze (ä tē′ djā). The Balkans have about 2 million Gypsies. All of the Gypsies must make compromises between their citizenship and their Gypsy ethnicity.

Gypsy life has changed greatly in the past 40 years. The Nazis killed more than half of Europe's Gypsies during World War II. Most of the remaining Gypsies found their way to the Balkans. They used to be nomadic, traveling through Europe in horse-drawn wagons. But the postwar governments have tried very hard to make the Gypsies settle into permanent homes and jobs. Ghettos for Gypsies have sprung up in cities of Eastern Europe. This has happened because the Gypsies want to be together and because they are not welcome in other neighborhoods. Some of the ghettos even have walls around them, but Atidze's does not. Atidze lives in a block of apartment buildings in an industrial section of Sofia. Atidze's father works in a nearby factory, and her mother works as a street cleaner. These are typical jobs for urban Gypsies. Most of Atidze's neighbors dislike their jobs and the ghetto. The older men in her apartment building often talk about the days when they traveled around as tinsmiths, musicians, or horse traders. The older women still talk about the days when they were fortune-tellers.

In some ways, Atidze is like any other Bulgarian girl. She reads, writes, and speaks Bulgarian. She goes to public school and wears the required pinafore over her dress. But being a Gypsy makes her different. At home she speaks Romany, the Gypsy language. Like the other Gypsy women of Moslem background, Atizde wears Turkish pants around the ghetto. And, like all 13-year-old Gypsy girls—whether Moslem, Orthodox, or Catholic—she is already thinking about marriage.

Atizde's wedding plans involve many people. Her four sisters have begun to collect gifts for her wedding. Soon her parents will select a Gypsy boy and will show these gifts to his family. If his family approves, Atidze will marry him in about 2 years and then move into his father's house.

Atidze feels secure when she is following Gypsy customs rather than Bulgarian ones. She is glad that Gypsies are still allowed to celebrate their weddings in a traditional way. The wedding will consist of 5 days of music, dancing, and feasting. Hundreds of her friends and relatives will join in the activities. For those 5 days they will forget about the compromises that they must usually make in Bulgarian society.

Note that, while the Gypsies probably originated in India, their tradition holds that they came from a place in the Middle East called Little Egypt. The word *Gypsy* is a shortened version of *Egyptian*.

separate valleys. Sofia, the capital city, is in the westernmost valley.

The Rhodope (räd′ ə pē) Mountains form the southern border of Bulgaria. They are rugged and have few settlements. Beyond the mountains, in Greece and Yugoslavia, are groups who speak Bulgarian, the language of Bulgaria. Bulgaria claims these areas, which causes strained relations between Bulgaria and Greece and Yugoslavia.

The land and people of Yugoslavia
Yugoslavia has a variety of landforms. The Alps extend into the northwestern part of the country. The Hungarian Plain, which is centered on the Danube River, covers the rest of northern Yugoslavia. But most of Yugoslavia is made up of the Dinaric Uplands. The highest part of the Dinaric Uplands is called the Dinaric Alps.

Yugoslavia has many kinds of people. At the end of World War I, many nations were joined to form the state of Yugoslavia, which means "land of the southern Slavs." These groups distrusted each other because of their different languages, religions, and histories.

Yugoslavia now has a federal form of government. The country is divided into federal units called republics. Each of the six main **ethnic groups** has its own republic. An ethnic group is made up of people who share many traits and customs. The six republics—Serbia, Croatia, Slovenia, Macedonia, Montenegro, and Bosnia-Herzegovina—are of unequal size and resources. But each ethnic group is allowed its own territory and freedom to make decisions. One exception is the Albanians, a Moslem group that lives in part of the republic of Serbia. Each republic also has its own combination of language and religion.

Today about half of the people of Yugoslavia live in cities. Belgrade is the capital and largest city. Zagreb (zäg′ reb) is the country's second largest city. In addition to these two cities, there are seven cities that have more than 100,000 people. In one of these cities, Sarajevo (sär′ ə ye vô), tourists can find the site of the 1984 Winter Olympics.

Dubrovnik, Yugoslavia, is a major port and tourist attraction. (43°N/18°E; map, p. 218)

The Balkans under Communism

The Communist governments that came to power after World War II have changed the economies of Romania and Bulgaria in similar ways. The people did not object to the formation of collective farms, and today most of the land is used this way. Industry has grown. Romania's industry is mainly chemical, based on its oil and natural gas. Bulgaria has fewer natural resources, but it has received aid from the Soviet Union. Bulgaria now produces steel and farm machinery.

The Communism of Yugoslavia is independent of the Soviet Union. The economy of Yugoslavia has many ties with the West. A million Yugoslavs work as temporary migrants in high-paying countries of Western Europe. The income they save and the money they send back home allows Yugoslavia to pay for goods imported from both Eastern and Western European countries.

Most of the land in Yugoslavia is privately owned. The Hungarian Plain is the breadbasket of the country, producing wheat, corn, and sugar beets. The government has had a greater hand in planning the country's industrial growth. Lignite, natural gas, iron ore, and bauxite have allowed Yugoslavia to build steel mills, car factories, and aluminum plants.

The Danube The Danube River used to be the major transportation route between the Austro-Hungarian Empire and its trading partners in the Balkans. But differences between Communist and non-Communist countries have reduced this trade. As a result the Danube has become less important.

The largest dam on the Danube is the Iron Gate Dam, between Yugoslavia and Romania. (45°N/23°E; map, p. 216)

The Balkan countries are working on several projects that will increase the importance of the Danube in the future. Romania is building a canal to shorten the distance from the Danube to the Black Sea. Romania and Yugoslavia are also developing the Danube farther to the west, on the border of their countries. The Danube flows through a gap between the Carpathian and Balkan mountain ranges. The gap is known as the Iron Gate. One of the world's largest hydroelectric dams has been built here. Locks have been built to allow large barges to go all the way from the Black Sea to the Yugoslav capital of Belgrade.

CHECKUP

1. What are the main ethnic groups in Romania and Bulgaria.
2. What are the three regions of Romania described in this lesson?

Stress the uniqueness of Yugoslavia among Eastern European countries in its independent relationship with the Soviet Union. This achievement is largely attributable to Tito, who was Yugoslavia's president from 1943 to 1980.

KEY FACTS

1. The North European Plain covers most of East Germany and Poland; Czechoslovakia has many upland areas.

2. Since World War II the economic growth of Czechoslovakia has been slower than that of the other Eastern European countries.

3. In recent years economic problems in Hungary, Czechoslovakia, and Poland have led to protests.

4. Poland's boundaries have been changed many times by other countries.

5. For centuries the Czech region of Czechoslovakia has been more developed than the Slovak region.

6. The fertile, grass-covered lowland plains of Hungary are called steppes.

7. The people of Hungary are similar, while the Balkans are a meeting ground of different ethnic groups.

8. Romania and Bulgaria have many zones of agricultural lowland and rugged upland.

9. Each of the six main ethnic groups in Yugoslavia has its own republic.

10. The economy of Yugoslavia has many ties with the West.

VOCABULARY QUIZ

Match the terms in the list with their definitions. Write your answers on a sheet of paper.

a. per capita income
b. depopulate
c. Berlin wall
d. landlocked
e. collective
f. ethnic group
g. lignite
h. fodder
i. satellite
j. Solidarity

g 1. A coal of low quality, called brown coal

d 2. Having no outlet to the sea; surrounded on all sides by land

c 3. A concrete wall that divides the city of Berlin into East and West Berlin

a 4. The amount of income each person in a country would have if the country's total income were divided equally among all of its people

e 5. Operated and worked by a group

j 6. A Polish labor organization

i 7. A country that claims to be independent but is actually controlled by another country

b 8. To reduce the population of an area

h 9. A coarse food fed to livestock

f 10. A group of people who share many traits and customs

REVIEW QUESTIONS

1. What are the main resources of the northernmost parts of East Germany and Poland?

2. In Hungary today what kind of farms are most common? What are the major crops in this country?

3. How does Czechoslovakia obtain the food needed to feed its people?

4. Which Eastern European country has a different ethnic group in each of its republics?

5. What is unusual about Yugoslavia's Communist government?

ACTIVITY

The size of a foreign country is easier to visualize when it is compared to that of one or more states in the United States. For example, Czechoslovakia (49,371 sq mi or 127,869 sq km) is about the same size as New York (49,576 sq mi or 128,402 sq km). Pick any three other Eastern European countries and compare them to states in the United States. Use your own state in some of the comparisons.

USING THE LIBRARY

A SOURCE OF INFORMATION

Most of the peoples of Eastern Europe speak one of the Slavic languages. Perhaps you would like to know more about these languages. Or maybe you would like to know more about the first Slavs, who lived more than 5,000 years ago in Eastern Europe.

Information such as this can be found in your school or public library. A large amount of material is available in the library, but do you know how to find the information that you need? To find information, you must know something about how books and other materials are organized in the library.

REFERENCES

In the reference section of the library, you will find encyclopedias, almanacs, atlases, dictionaries, and other books of general information. If you do not know very much about a topic that you wish to research, it is a good idea to start with an encyclopedia.

The *Readers' Guide to Periodical Literature* is also found in the reference section of most libraries. This guide tells you whether any magazine articles have been written about the topic you have chosen. Many libraries have magazines of general interest. Specialized magazines such as *National Geographic Magazine*, *Smithsonian*, and *Natural History* may be especially helpful when you are researching social studies topics.

CARD CATALOG

Do you know how to find a book that has the information you need? One way is by using the card catalog. The card catalog is a listing of all the books in the library. Each book is listed in the card catalog alphabetically by subject, title, and author's last name. Looking under the subject area of your topic is a good way to find out how many books the library has on that topic.

VERTICAL FILE

Collections of pictures, illustrations, and maps are kept in most libraries. These are kept in a file called a vertical file. Some libraries also have files of pamphlets and newspaper articles. These are also kept in the vertical file. These materials are usually stored alphabetically by subject.

SKILLS PRACTICE

Now it is time for you to use your library skills. Listed below are topics relating to the Eastern European countries that you read about in this chapter. Pick a topic from the list or choose a topic of your own. Using the books, articles, and other materials that you find in the library, research and write a short report on your topic. At the end of your report, be sure to list the library resources you used.

Holy Roman Empire	Budapest
Austro-Hungarian Empire	Council for Mutual Economic Assistance
Hapsburg family	Cyrillic alphabet
Adolf Hitler	Ploieşti
Berlin wall	karst
Iron Curtain	Belgrade
Solidarity	Zagreb
Thaddeus Kosciusko	lignite
Magyars	Sofia
Silesian coalfields	Danube River
Czechs	
Slovaks	

14 The Soviet Union

The Natural Environment of the Soviet Union

┌─ VOCABULARY ─────────────┐
internal   chernozem
  drainage
taiga
└──────────────────────────┘

A huge country of large lowlands The Soviet Union is the largest country in the world today. It covers about a sixth of all the land area in the world. The Soviet Union is larger than Canada, the United States, Mexico, and Central America put together. It stretches for more than 6,000 miles (10,000 km) from west to east. Most of the Soviet Union lies in the high northern latitudes.

The Soviet Union is made up of four enormous lowland regions—European Russia, Western Siberia, Central Siberia, and Soviet Central Asia. European Russia makes up the western part of the country. It stretches all the way south to the Caucasus Mountains and east to the Ural Mountains. The Ural Mountains are the highest part of European Russia, but the range is low when compared to other mountains in the Soviet Union.

The second major lowland is Western Siberia. It stretches from the Urals to the Yenisei (yen ə sā′) River and from the Arctic Ocean to the low hills at the north-ern edge of Soviet Central Asia. Most of the land is low and marshy. This lowland has very few people except along its southern edge.

A third lowland is Central Siberia. It stretches from the Yenisei to the Lena River. It is higher than the other low-lands and not marshy. But it is an empty land with little possibility for farming because of the severe climate.

The fourth of the great lowlands is known as Soviet Central Asia. This low-land region is much warmer than the other three regions. This region has large, salty inland lakes. The rivers of this region drain into these lakes.

The highlands Rugged mountains make up the southern border of the coun-try. The Caucasus Mountains are the most important mountain chain in the west. They are considered the southern boundary between Europe and Asia. They form a high, straight barrier that runs between the Black and Caspian seas.

Farther east are the highest mountains in the country, the Tien Shan (tē en′ shän′) and The Pamirs (pə mirz′). They are in central Asia, on the borders with Afghanistan (af gan′ ə stan) and China. They are very high and rugged, and they have few passes. The highest peak is Pik Kommunizma (pēk′ käm ū nēz′ mə), or

Moscow is the heart of the vast country of the Soviet Union. Moscow's Kremlin walls sur-round palaces, churches, museums, and government offices.

To strengthen your pupil's appreciation of the size of the Soviet Union, point out that it is larger than four of the continents—South America, Antarctica, Europe, and Australia.

Communism Peak. It is 24,590 feet (7,495 m) high.

Most of eastern Siberia, beyond the Lena River, is a region of many separate mountain ranges. There is one important lowland, the valley of the Amur River. The Amur River forms the border between the Soviet Union and China for over 1,200 miles (2,000 km).

Rivers, lakes, canals Some of the longest rivers in the world are in the Soviet Union. One of the longest rivers is the Volga, which flows into the Caspian Sea. Most of the large rivers of the Soviet Union flow either north or south. Because of this, the rivers of the Soviet Union do not provide a continuous water route across the country. But the Russians used the European rivers, such as the Dnieper (nē′ pėr), Don, and Volga, for transportation in early days.

To the east of the Ural Mountains are the Ob, Lena, and Yenisei rivers. The Lena River is the longest river flowing within the Soviet Union. It begins its northward course near Lake Baikal, the world's deepest lake.

Most of the rivers of Asiatic Russia flow to the Arctic Ocean. The Arctic Ocean is frozen over and closed to navigation for much of the year. Therefore, the rivers of Asiatic Russia are not used much for transportation today. But the southern stretches of the rivers were the principal means of crossing Siberia until the twentieth century.

The Caspian Sea, a salt lake mostly in southern Russia, is the world's largest inland body of water. East of the Caspian Sea is an area of rivers that do not have

This Russian fishing crew on the Volga River gather fish for caviar, a food made from fish eggs.

ocean outlets. They drain into the Caspian Sea or other inland lakes. This is a region of **internal drainage**, drainage into inland bodies of water.

The Russians have made many east-west connections between some of their European rivers. For example, a canal connects Moscow and the Volga River. The Don and Volga rivers flow close to each other near the city of Volgograd. A canal connects the rivers at this point. This allows barges from the Volga to reach the Black Sea.

Water transportation is difficult in the Soviet Union because the rivers and canals freeze over in the winter. Nevertheless, water traffic is very important. Soviet canals and navigable rivers total nearly 100,000 miles (about 160,000 km) and connect the White, Baltic, Caspian, and Black seas. This enormous canal system carries a huge amount of freight.

Point out that the quest for a warm water port is one of the key historic reasons for Russian expansionism.

Compare the building of the Siberian pipeline shown in the photograph below with the building of the Alaskan pipeline in North America.

The climate   The Soviet Union has a continental climate, even though there is water on three sides of the country. In the winter, the northern waters are frozen over. Even the Pacific Ocean is covered with ice for several hundred miles off the coast of eastern Siberia. The icy waters cannot warm the land, so winter temperatures are bitterly cold. The coldest temperatures and the longest winters occur in northeastern Siberia.

The frozen waters also leave the Soviet Union with few ice-free ports. Strangely enough, one of the most important ice-free ports is Murmansk, far north of the Arctic Circle. This port is the only one lucky enough to receive the warm waters of the North Atlantic Drift in the winter.

In the summer the cold waters of the Arctic Ocean affect the climate in the wrong way. They keep summer temperatures down. But the cold waters do not cool the air as far south as Soviet Central Asia. Here, summer temperatures often reach 100°F (38°C).

Most of the Soviet Union is so far from unfrozen seas that there is little moisture for rainfall. Over most of European Russia, the precipitation is moderate—between 20 and 24 inches (51 and 61 cm) a year. In the southeast the climate is much drier. In Soviet Central Asia less than 10 inches (25 cm) of rain falls a year. Most of it falls in the winter.

Soils and vegetation   Climate is partly responsible for the kind of soil and natural vegetation found in an area. Tundra is found all along the coast of the Arctic Ocean. Summer is too short and cool for trees to grow. Small flowers bloom for a short time in the summer, but the vegetation is mostly mosses and lichens. The soils of the tundra are permanently frozen just a few feet below the surface. This permafrost greatly limits the use of the land for farming and mining. Building roads and railroads is almost impossible because the ground buckles when the top of the soil melts in the summer and freezes in the winter.

South of the tundra is the world's largest area of forest. This forest is called the **taiga** (tī′ gə). It is made up of conifers. A conifer is a cone-bearing tree with soft wood. The pines, firs, spruces, and larches of the taiga are not very tall or very close, but they cover an area larger than all of Canada. The soils of the taiga are not very good for farming.

There are also hardwood forests in the central part of European Russia. Here, conifers grow near broad-leaved hardwoods, such as birches, oaks, and maples. Most of this forest has been cleared for farming. The soils of the hardwood forest

Weather conditions cause hardships for workers such as these working on a pipeline from Siberia to the Urals.

The vegetation regions of the Soviet Union are dependent on the climate.

are more fertile than the taiga soils. The most common plants grown are potatoes, rye, and grasses for hay. Find the two different forest areas on the map above.

South of the forest is the belt of treeless grasslands called the steppes. Here much of the rainfall evaporates because of the hotter summers. This leaves too little moisture in the soil for trees. But there is enough for grasses. The steppes are a major resource because the soils that form under the grasses are deep and very fertile. These soils are called **chernozem** (cher′ nə zem). The word means "black earth" in Russian. The rich black soils are ideally suited to grain crops. This is one of the largest wheat-growing areas in the world. The only problem is the dry climate in which chernozem soils are found. In very dry years, winds blow away the topsoil and make farming im-

possible. The Soviet government has tried to find ways to expand farming in the chernozem zone of central Asia.

Desert vegetation and desert soils are found south of the steppes. The vegetation is mostly low bushes that are widely spaced. The desert soils can be quite good for farming, but they need irrigation to grow crops. The oases of the desert produce semitropical trees such as figs and citrus.

CHECKUP

1. What are the four main lowland areas of the Soviet Union? What landform is found along the southern border of the Soviet Union?
2. The world's largest inland body of water is in the Soviet Union. What is the name of this body of water?
3. How do seas and oceans affect the climate of the Soviet Union?
4. Where is the coldest part of the country? The hottest part?

To reinforce pupils' comprehension of soil/vegetation zones, have them write the names of the zones listed in the map key on this page and accompany each with a definition.

A State of Many Different Peoples

┌─VOCABULARY─────────────┐
Mongol	socialism
kremlin	secede
tsar	
└────────────────────────┘

The beginnings of the Russian state
Sometime around A.D. 500, Slavs moved into what is now European Russia. Slavs were among the first tribes of people to live in the hills and plains of Eastern Europe. By A.D. 900 the first Russian state was founded. The state was centered around Kiev, a prosperous city located on the Dnieper River. Many Russians feel that the Slavs formed this state. It is also believed that the Vikings played a large role in setting up the state of Kiev.

Around 1000, missionaries from the Balkans converted the Russians to the Eastern Orthodox form of Christianity. With the new religion came the Bible, written in an alphabet that had been developed for the Slavic languages. The Cyrillic alphabet is still used by Russians today.

The Mongols invade   The state of Kiev lasted about 300 years. It was destroyed by **Mongols** in the thirteenth century. The Mongols were a group of nomadic people from Mongolia, a dry and rugged land in the heart of Asia. The Mongol Empire was the largest empire the world has ever known.

The Mongols were the leaders in this empire, but it also included many groups who spoke Turkic languages. These groups moved into what is now the Ukraine, the Caucasus Mountains, and Soviet Central Asia. Most of these people were converted to the Islamic religion, and their descendants are Moslems today.

When the Turkic invaders took over the steppes of southern Russia, the Russians were forced out. They moved to the north, where Finnic-speaking people were living. The Finnic-speaking people were converted to Eastern Orthodox Christianity and to the Russian language.

The rise of Moscow   The Russians had to pay taxes to the Mongol overlords. Some Russians in the forestlands of central Russia were able to keep some of their freedom. One Russian prince made his headquarters in a small settlement called

The Communists have made museums out of many churches in the Soviet Union.

Moskva. *This small settlement was the beginning of Moscow.* Moskva *means "the bear's den" in Finnic. It is the origin of the use of a bear as a symbol of the Russians.* The Russians built a wall around the Eastern Orthodox church and the residence of the prince. This kind of fort was called a **kremlin** by the Slavs. Moscow's Kremlin was only one of many such fortresses. But it became the center of Russia's government. When people speak of the Kremlin today, they usually mean the Soviet government.

Ivan the Great became prince of Moscow in 1462. In 1480 he put an end to Mongol domination by refusing to pay the money that the Mongols demanded each year. The prince of Moscow became the **tsar** (zär) of Russia. The word *tsar* is sometimes spelled *czar*. It is the Russian form of the name Caesar.

A young tsar known as Peter the Great came to power around 1700. He worked to bring Western ways and learning to Russia. He had an interest in ships and boats and established Russia's first navy. He was also interested in spreading his empire. After defeating Sweden in war, he gained a piece of the Baltic seacoast from Sweden. Peter the Great decided to build a new capital city as a port on the Baltic Sea. He called it St. Petersburg. Today it is known as Leningrad. It is the second most populated city in the Soviet Union.

Peter the Great died in 1725. Catherine II, also known as Catherine the Great, was the next ruler who helped bring Western ways to Russia. Catherine also expanded the territory of Russia. Under Catherine the Great, Russia reached the Black Sea and took a large part of Poland.

This kremlin wall is typical of those in various Russian cities.

In the last half of the nineteenth century, the Russian empire gained a large part of central Asia. Many Turkic-speaking Moslems lived in this area. These people were the descendants of the Turkic invaders who had been part of the Mongol Empire. The Russians also pushed the borders of Russia to the Amur River and the Pacific coast north of Korea. The Chinese and Koreans already living in this area were soon outnumbered by the Russians.

The Russian Revolution The existence of many languages and religions affected the way the vast territory of the Russian empire was organized after the Communist revolution of 1917. Russia had suffered a great defeat in World War I, and the tsarist government was blamed for the problems the people experienced. Hungry people rioted, and in 1917, rule by the tsar came to an end. A powerful leader named Nikolai Lenin decided that this time of weakness was the right time to introduce **socialism** into Russia. Lenin believed that land and industry should be owned and controlled by the government rather than by individuals. He wanted a revolution that would take land, factories, and other businesses away from those who owned them. Lenin's followers came to be called Communists, and their ideas became known as communism. The Communists were only a small group in 1917, but in November of that year the Communists and their supporters overthrew the Russian government. They gained control of Moscow and made it the capital. By 1922 the Communists had control of the country. After the

Catherine the Great: A Strong Ruler

CATHERINE II, also called Catherine the Great, ruled Russia from 1762 to 1796. She came to Russia in 1742 as a 13-year-old German princess who was eager to marry into the imperial family. She gave up many of her German ways and began to adopt those of her new country. She learned the Russian language and became a member of the Russian Orthodox Church. Catherine had a strong desire to be accepted by the Russians because she intended to rule the country some day.

When Catherine was 33, she became empress of Russia. There were some questions about her right to rule. But soon she made many welcome changes. Catherine promoted the building of many hospitals and canals. She also promoted the education of women. During her rule the first schools for girls were opened in Russia. Catherine's real love, however, was art and culture. She sent Russian artists and writers to western Europe. She also brought many French writers and philosophers to her court in St. Petersburg.

Catherine also expanded the Russian empire. During her reign, Russia reached the Black Sea and acquired most of Poland. Catherine made Russia powerful and more respected culturally, but she kept all democratic ideas out of her empire. She ruled Russia as a dictator until her death in 1796.

Point out that Lenin's ideas were adapted from those of Karl Marx (1818–1883), who first formulated the modern Communist theory.

The Soviet Socialist Republics of the Soviet Union are shown on this map. Today there are 15 republics.

revolution, the country was renamed the Union of Soviet Socialist Republics. The name is often shortened to Soviet Union or U.S.S.R. People sometimes speak of the whole country as Russia.

Republics The Union of Soviet Socialist Republics was organized as a federation of republics, much as the United States is a federation of states. Today there are 15 republics. Each republic represents the home territory of an ethnic group. The map above shows the republics. Notice that the borders of the republics have been drawn in peculiar ways. Each republic has a border on the sea or with a neighboring country. This was done because the Soviet Union's constitution gives these republics the right to **secede,** or withdraw, from the union. However, none of the republics are able to take this right to secede seriously.

THE SOVIET SOCIALIST REPUBLICS OF THE SOVIET UNION

Republic	Comparable Area in the United States
Russian Soviet Federated Socialist Republic	Twice the United States
Ukraine	Texas
Uzbekistan	California
Kazakhstan	United States less Texas and Alaska
Belorussia	Kansas
Azerbaijan	Kansas
Georgia	West Virginia
Moldavia	Massachusetts, Connecticut, Rhode Island
Tadzhikistan	North Carolina
Kirgizia	Nebraska
Lithuania	West Virginia
Armenia	Massachusetts, Connecticut
Turkmenistan	Utah, Nevada
Latvia	West Virginia
Estonia	Vermont, New Hampshire

You may wish to use this description of Soviet republics as an opportunity to review the relationship between the 50 states and the federal government in the United States. Secession is unconstitutional.

You may wish to use the Activity described on p. 245 at this time.

Ethnic groups Each republic is named for an important group of people. In most republics the majority of the people belong to that group. About half of the people in the Soviet Union are Russians. The next two largest groups of people are the Ukrainians and the Uzbeks. Today the Soviet Union recognizes more than 100 ethnic groups within its territory. Slavic groups compose about 75 percent of the population. Non-Slavic groups represent about 25 percent of the population. The various groups are identified mainly by the languages they speak. The most common language is Russian, the official language of the country. Besides Russian there are six other Slavic languages. Turkic is the most common non-Slavic language family, and there are about 25 different Turkic languages. Within the Soviet Union more than 100 different languages are spoken.

Most of the Slavic people of Russia have the same religion. They are followers of the Russian Orthodox Church,

Keeping the traditional culture alive, this song and dance group perform in Kiev. (50°N/31°E; map, p. 236)

the largest religious group in the country. The Moslems form the second largest religious group. Although the Moslem group is smaller, it is growing more rapidly than the Russian Orthodox Church.

CHECKUP

1. Who converted the Russians to Christianity?
2. What is the origin of the use of a bear as a symbol of the Russians?
3. What does the word *kremlin* mean?
4. What was the outcome of the Communist revolution of 1917?
5. How many republics make up the U.S.S.R.? What do they represent?

The Soviet Union Under Communism Today

┌─VOCABULARY─────────────────────┐
| heavy industry | consumer good |
| light industry | kulak |
└────────────────────────────────┘

The economy and two world wars The Communists who overthrew the Russian government in 1917 set out at once to change the economy. But some plans for building new industries and changing the farming system had to wait. It took many years for the country to rebuild after World War I. Then World War II came to the Soviet Union in 1941. Twenty million Soviet citizens lost their lives. After the war the Soviet Union placed Communist governments in most of the countries of Eastern Europe. Trade with these countries helped the Soviet Union to recover from the damages of war. With its great wealth of resources, the Soviet Union today is one of the world's most powerful industrial nations.

Refer your pupils to the Graph Appendix in the back of this text to determine the five leading countries in the production of each resource described in the section below.

Resources   A country as large as the Soviet Union has a big share of the world's natural resources. In addition to fertile soils and huge forests, the Soviet Union has large deposits of petroleum, coal, iron ore, and other minerals. Unfortunately, the forests and many other resources are in Siberia. Severe climate and great distance make it difficult to use some of the country's natural wealth.

The Soviet Union is the world's leading producer of oil. Large petroleum fields are in the Caucasus Mountains. The Baku (bä kü') field is the oldest of these. Today, however, the major oil-producing region is in the Ural Mountains. Coal deposits found in the Ukraine and Siberia make the Soviet Union the world's second largest coal-producing country. More than one third of all the coal mined in the Soviet Union comes from the Donets Basin, in the Ukraine. Iron ore also is mined in the Ukraine, Siberia, and the Ural Mountains. The Soviet Union leads the world in the mining of iron ore. Locate these natural resources on the map on page 239.

The Soviet Union is also rich in natural gas, chromium, aluminum, nickel, lead, zinc, gold, silver, and tungsten. The Soviet Union leads the world in the production of manganese, a metal needed to make steel. The Soviet Union's great supplies of almost every resource needed for industry mean that the country does not have to import many natural resources.

Automobile factories benefit from the country's vast supply of iron ore, used to make steel.

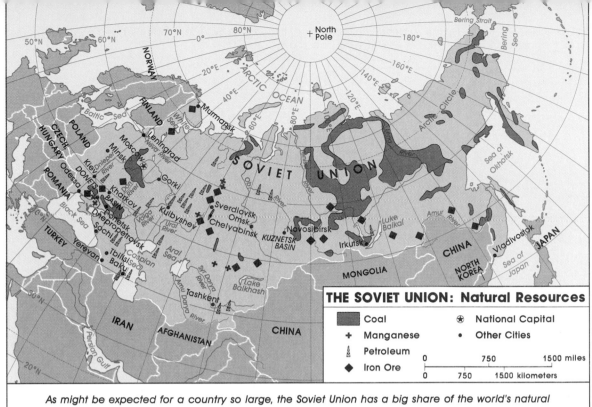

As might be expected for a country so large, the Soviet Union has a big share of the world's natural resources.

A planned economy   The basic ideas of a Communist economy are government control and planning. In the Soviet Union, small groups of Communist leaders prepared a series of five-year plans. The plans applied to the whole country. They were lists of tasks to be done, such as building factories, opening up mines, making machines and tools, and building fertilizer and power plants. Each plan set the economic goals for a specific 5-year period. For example, the Fourth Five-Year Plan (1946–1950) was a plan for rebuilding the country after World War II.

From the beginning the plans put **heavy industry** first. They called for more workers and raw materials to increase the production of petroleum, coal, steel, electric power, and heavy machinery. The products made by heavy industry are used by other industries to make different goods. In contrast, the five-year plans gave little attention to **light industry**, that is, industry that makes products for use by consumers. **Consumer goods** are things like food, clothes, appliances, and books. They use up raw materials but cannot be used to produce other goods.

Agriculture and consumer goods suffered because of the attention given to heavy industry. The government paid for industrialization by buying food at low prices from the farmers and selling it at high prices to the city dwellers. This system kept both the farmers and the city dwellers from having money left over to buy consumer goods. It also meant that the government had money to put into industry and needed projects such as schools and hospitals.

This section affords an excellent basis for a class discussion of the advantages and disadvantages of a planned economy versus a free enterprise system.

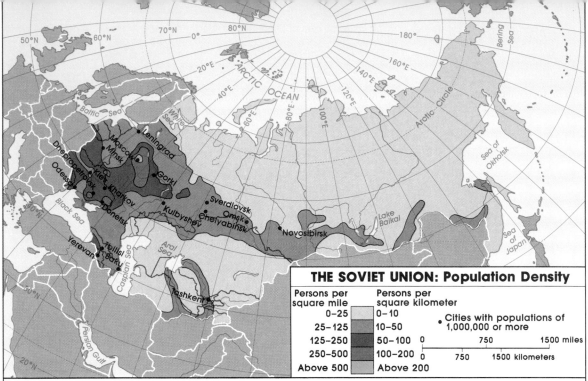

THE SOVIET UNION: Population Density

Persons per square mile	Persons per square kilometer
0–25	0–10
25–125	10–50
125–250	50–100
250–500	100–200
Above 500	Above 200

• Cities with populations of 1,000,000 or more

0   750   1500 miles
0   750   1500 kilometers

The Soviet Union is the largest country in the world. The population of the Soviet Union is about 272 million. About 62 percent of these people live in cities. There are 18 cities in the country with 1 million or more people.

The Communist government turned a rural country into one of the leading industrial countries in the world. The main effort was directed toward developing new industries. New sources of raw materials were found in the Urals and Siberia, and huge industrial centers were built around them. In the process millions of people were moved from the countryside to industrial cities. Today the Soviet Union has 18 cities with 1 million or more people.

This rapid change cost the Soviet Union a great deal. The people's standard of living stayed low because the money for industry came from savings on agriculture and consumer goods. The government told the people that this sacrifice was necessary for the time being. Many people were willing to give up decent food and housing in return for the promise of a better future. But most were unwilling to move to the new industrial centers in Siberia. The new centers were in a faraway place with a cold climate and poor housing conditions. So beginning in the 1930s the government forced many people to move.

Industry The increase in production was spectacular in the early days, and it still remains impressive. Between 1960 and 1980, steel production more than doubled, the output of crude oil and electric power became four times greater, and the production of natural gas became ten times greater.

The most important industrial area in the Soviet Union is Moscow. The capital city and nearby towns produce more than half of all the textiles made in the Soviet Union. The area also makes automobiles, electric motors, farm machinery, and similar goods.

The second most important industrial area in the country is centered around the coalfields of the Donets Basin, in the Ukraine. Half the iron ore and a third of the coal in the Soviet Union come from here. These resources are used to make much of the steel and many of the tractors and machine tools manufactured in the Soviet Union.

The third industrial area is the city of Leningrad. It is an important manufacturer of machinery and other metal products. Leningrad is also a major shipbuilding center and the leading seaport of the Soviet Union. Modern ships called icebreakers are now able to keep the harbor open for most of the winter.

There are two other major industrial areas in the country. One is on the border between European Russia and Siberia, in the Ural Mountains. This area was one of the first to be developed by the Communist government. The southern part of the Urals has large mineral deposits, including oil and natural gas. Factories, such as the world's largest tractor factory, at Chelyabinsk, were built in the Urals in the 1930s. The area produces such things as steel, paper, chemicals, and cars.

The last of the major industrial areas is centered around the Kuznetsk coalfields, in Siberia. It is a new manufacturing area, developed entirely since the 1930s. As a result it has large reserves of coal and natural gas. The cities in this new area have grown rapidly since 1930. Novosibirsk, the largest city in Siberia, has more than a million inhabitants today.

Transportation The Siberian industrial centers are located very far from other places. Shipping goods in and out is a problem because there are few transportation routes. In 1891 the Russians began building a rail line across Siberia, the Trans-Siberian Railway. *Trans-* means "across" or "over." This line connects Moscow with Vladivostok, on the Pacific coast. It is Siberia's major railroad. In Siberia the railroad network is made up of only a few long lines. There is much rail traffic, and it sometimes takes a long time for goods to be loaded. The road network is even worse, so there is not much truck traffic. Building roads and railroads over thousands of miles in faraway places and a severe climate is difficult. Recent five-year plans have begun to pay more attention to transportation.

The Trans-Siberian Railroad, Siberia's major railroad, covers a distance of about 5,600 miles (9,000 km).

241

The policies of Stalin in the 1930s were as devastating to human life as those of Hitler in Nazi Germany.

Agriculture under communism

Much of the Soviet Union is too cold or too dry to be good farmland. However, the country is one of the world's leading crop producers. About one tenth of the country is farmed.

The Communist government of the Soviet Union has viewed agriculture as a way to raise money to develop industry and to make some farmers become factory workers. To serve these purposes the government has tried to control the farmers and the farmland.

After the Russian Revolution, in 1917, the Communists forced the farmers to combine their individual plots of land in large collective farms. The members of a collective farm worked the land together. But food production fell off sharply, so the government allowed private ownership of land among farmers. In 1930, however, the Soviet leader Stalin ordered all farms to become collective farms again.

This order was opposed by many people, but especially by **kulaks** (kü läks'). A kulak was a farmer who owned enough land to make a living from it. The kulaks hated the idea of losing their own farms. They killed their livestock rather than give the animals to the government.

Stalin decided to get rid of the kulaks. A million and a half kulaks were sent to prison camps in Siberia in the first 6 months of 1930 alone. More people went later, and many were killed. So many farmers were unwilling to work for the government that food production fell. Five million people died of starvation. Many who died were farmers. Each year the government took the same amount of food from each farm. In the years of bad harvests, many farmers did not have enough food left to feed themselves and their families.

Three kinds of Soviet farms　Today there are three kinds of farms in the Soviet Union. About half of the farmland is in state farms, and a little less is in collective farms. Only three percent of the land is privately owned.

The state farms are completely owned by the state. The farmers get a salary from the government and are treated like any other worker. A typical state farm is very large. It might have about 600 workers on it. These are the best-equipped farms in the Soviet Union. They are also the most specialized. Many are dairy farms or cattle ranches. Some of them are huge vegetable farms near large cities.

The collective farms are half as large as the state farms. They are less well

Here grain is being harvested on a state farm. The state farms are typically large and well equipped.

equipped and less specialized. On the collective farms, the harvests of all the farmers are combined and sold at a set price. From the money earned, each farmer is paid according to the amount of time he or she worked. Few people want to work on collectives, and most of the workers are the sons and daughters of older collective farmers. Collectives are the most common kind of farms in Soviet Central Asia and in the southern part of European Russia.

The private farms are not true farms. They are small plots that are worked by the owners in their spare time. They work hard on their private plots because they are allowed to sell their produce for a profit. They specialize in such things as vegetables and eggs, which can be sold for high prices. These private plots produce 30 percent of the food in the Soviet Union, even though they take up only 3 percent of the farmland. The government allows private farms because their high output is necessary to feed the nation.

Crops and output today   Grains are the basis of Soviet farming. Barley, oats, and rye are important, but wheat is the main crop. The best grain-growing area is the zone of chernozem soils. Most of the Soviet farmland is inside a triangle whose corners are Leningrad, Odessa, and Irkutsk. A few outlying places, such as the Caucasus and the oases of central Asia, produce fruits and vegetables.

Other important crops are found in more specific areas. The steppes grow half of the world's sunflowers. Their seeds are used mostly for cooking oil.

Near Sochi, a seaport town on the Black Sea, these workers are picking tea leaves. (44°N/40°E; map, p. 239)

The steppes also grow a third of the world's sugar beets. Cotton is grown in the irrigated valleys of central Asia. The Soviet Union and the United States are the world's two leading producers of cotton.

In general, Soviet agriculture has never been very productive. Crop production has gone up mostly when new lands have been opened up for farming. Even now the yield per acre is only a third as high as that in Western Europe, and production per farmer is only one sixth of that in the United States. The unfavorable climate of the Soviet Union is partly responsible. But part of the difference is due to the five-year plans. They sacrificed agriculture in order to industrialize the country. Better tools, fertilizers, and farming methods are needed. Recently the Soviet government has begun to pay attention to these needs.

Point out that, because of the low productivity of Soviet agriculture, there is a vital dependence on grain imports in the Soviet Union. A large percentage of these imports comes from the United States.

243

Your pupils might enjoy learning that after-school activities are required of Russian children. One of these activities, in which all must take a turn, is cleaning and repairing the school.

Life in the Soviet Union

The Communist party, which took over the country in 1917, still rules it. It is the only political party that the government allows. The most important leaders are always members of this one party. Although elections are held in the Soviet Union, they are very different from elections in Western Europe or the United States. There is only one name for each office on the ballot. That name is always someone approved by the Communist party. People can only vote for or against the party's choice. People have no chance to vote for anyone who opposes the Communists.

The people in the Soviet Union also have limited freedom of religion, speech, and press. They are not allowed to practice many of their religious traditions. Although people read a lot, they may read only those materials approved by the government. The government owns the publishing businesses, so anything written against the Communists or the government is not printed. The Communist party publishes *Pravda*, the country's leading newspaper. *Pravda* is the official voice of the government. It gives only the news that the party wants the people to read. The government has similar control over the country's radio and television stations.

For the ordinary Soviet citizen, the standard of living has been rising. More consumer goods are available, but often there is a shortage of certain goods, such as meat and other foods.

The Communists believe in the value of education, and the schools in the Soviet Union have very high standards. The government makes the decisions about what subjects are taught in the schools and which books are used. Schools stress science and mathematics, and many students follow careers in those fields. Special trade schools also train young people to become skilled workers in industry and agriculture. In all schools, students are taught to be loyal to the Communist government.

In much the same way as Americans, the Russians are interested in space travel. Students looking toward aerospace careers must study science and mathematics.

CHECKUP

1. What is a five-year plan? Why have agriculture and consumer goods suffered under the five-year plans?
2. What are the five main industrial regions of the Soviet Union?
3. Who were the kulaks? What are the three kinds of farms in the Soviet Union today?

KEY FACTS

1. Most of the Soviet Union is made up of four enormous lowlands bordered by high mountains on the south.

2. The climate differs from one part of the Soviet Union to another, but, in general, it is a continental climate.

3. Much of the natural vegetation of the Soviet Union is tundra, taiga, and steppe.

4. The Russian empire was the home of many different ethnic groups.

5. The Soviet Union is composed of 15 republics. Each republic is the home territory of an ethnic group.

6. The Soviet Union is one of the world's richest nations in both the quantity and the variety of its mineral resources.

7. The Soviet five-year economic plans have stressed the development of heavy industry.

8. In the Soviet Union there are two kinds of large farms: state-owned farms and collective farms. Small plots of land worked by individuals make up only three percent of the farmland, yet they provide much of the food.

VOCABULARY QUIZ

Choose the term from the list below that best completes each sentence that follows. Write your answers on a sheet of paper.

a. tsar
b. kremlin
c. taiga
d. consumer goods
e. kulak
f. secede
g. internal drainage
h. chernozem
i. socialism
j. heavy industry

1. The fertile black soils of the steppes are called __chernozem__.

2. Moscow grew up around an old fortress called a __kremlin__.

3. Industries in the Soviet Union make some __consumer goods__, such as clothing and housewares.

4. __Socialism__ is a system that calls for ownership of land and industry by the government.

5. The Soviet Union's constitution gives the republics the right to __secede__ from the union.

6. __Tsar__ was the title given to the rulers of the Russian empire.

7. The world's largest area of forest is called the __taiga__.

8. The products made by __heavy industry__, such as steel and large machinery, are used by other industries to make different goods.

9. In 1930 a Soviet farmer who owned enough land to make a living from it was called a __kulak__.

10. An area of __internal drainage__ is one in which rivers flow into lakes rather than into oceans.

REVIEW QUESTIONS

1. What is the Soviet Union's most important industrial area? What major industrial area has developed since the 1930s?

2. Why has the development of railroads in the Soviet Union been slow?

3. How are state-owned farms different from collective farms? Why are the individual plots of land important in the Soviet Union?

4. What role does the government play in education in the Soviet Union?

ACTIVITY

Using an encyclopedia or other reference material as a source, list the language and religion of the majority ethnic group of each republic in the Soviet Union. Which republics have similar languages?

IDENTIFYING MAIN IDEAS

WHAT IS A TOPIC SENTENCE?

As the name suggests, a topic sentence states the topic, or main idea, of a paragraph. Usually the first sentence in a paragraph is the topic sentence. In some cases, however, the first sentence of a paragraph does not state the main idea, and the second or third sentence may be the topic sentence. The other sentences in a paragraph supply details that support the main idea. They are called supporting sentences.

Some topic sentences try to cover more than can be developed in one paragraph. They try to tell everything in one sentence. A good topic sentence states a subject or idea that can be properly developed in one paragraph.

SKILLS PRACTICE

In the passage below, the paragraphs have been run together purposely. Read the passage and decide where you would divide it to make three paragraphs.

The Volga

The Volga River rises in the Valdai Hills, to the northwest of Moscow, and after a course of 2,300 miles (3,701 km), it enters the landlocked Caspian Sea. It is a wide, slow-flowing river, and from the earliest times it has been used for navigation. A thousand years ago it carried the trade between the peoples around the Baltic Sea and China and India. Small boats were carried downstream by wind and current, and on the return voyage they were rowed. Today things have greatly changed. A series of dams have been built, and the great river has been transformed into a succession of lakes that drop like gigantic steps from the Valdai Hills to the Caspian. No longer does one hear the melancholy song of the rowers; it is the shrill whistle of a ship's siren and the beat of stern paddle and screw. The Volga is busier than ever before. It carries much of the internal trade of the Soviet Union: coal and oil, lumber, and cement and building materials. It is also joined by canal with other rivers. But some of the problems that confront the modern riverboats and their tows are the same as those faced on the Volga in the past. During the long Russian winter, the river is frozen, and shipping comes to a halt. In the spring the snows melt, and the current is swift. In the fall the water level is low, and navigation is difficult except on the lakes. Still the Volga continues its long tradition of serving as an important trade route.

Write the title of the passage on a sheet of paper. Then write the topic sentence of each paragraph. Does each of the sentences you chose state the main idea of the paragraph? For each topic sentence write a short explanation telling why you think the sentence does or does not state the main idea. Copy the entire passage as three separate paragraphs on your paper. After you have copied the passage in paragraphs, answer the following questions.

1. What are some of the details given in the supporting sentences of the first paragraph? Write two words from the first paragraph that describe the Volga River.
2. What does the second paragraph describe?
3. How many supporting sentences are there in the third paragraph? What kinds of details do they give?

5/UNIT REVIEW

Answer Key in back of book.

READING THE TEXT

Turn to page 242 and read the section "Agriculture under communism." On a sheet of paper, write **T** if the statement is true and **F** if it is false.

1. The Soviet Union is not a leading producer of agricultural products. **F**
2. The collective farms established in the Soviet Union after 1917 were not very productive. **T**
3. The Soviet government wanted to use profits from agriculture to develop industry. **T**
4. Stalin ordered all farms to become collective. **T**
5. The kulaks were private farmers who fought against the collective farms. **T**

READING A MAP

Turn to page 239 and study the map titled "The Soviet Union: Natural Resources." On a sheet of paper, write **T** if the statement is true and **F** if it is false.

1. The Soviet Union has discovered important petroleum deposits in the area northeast of the Caspian Sea. **T**
2. There are no significant iron ore deposits on the Lena River. **T**
3. Leningrad is the site of major coal deposits. **F**
4. There are no major iron ore deposits east of Sverdlovsk. **T**
5. The Soviet Union has coal deposits near the border with Afghanistan. **F**

READING A PICTURE

Turn to page 224 and carefully examine the picture of the city of Dubrovnik, Yugoslavia. On a sheet of paper, write **T** if the statement is true and **F** if it is false.

1. Most of the buildings shown in the picture have a modern design. **F**
2. The buildings on the water probably served as a fortress against invasion at an earlier time in history. **T**
3. The people who live in the houses shown in the picture probably make their living by farming. **F**
4. From the picture, it is clear that the people of Dubrovnik enjoy leisure activities on the water. **T**
5. The picture shows that Dubrovnik is a major trading and shipping center. **F**

READING A TABLE

Turn to page 213 and study the table that opens Unit 5. On a sheet of paper, write **T** if the statement is true and **F** if it is false.

1. Hungary has the smallest area of all the countries listed on the table. **F**
2. Albania has fewer people than any other Eastern European or Soviet country. **T**
3. Albania has the lowest population density of all the countries listed on the table. **F**
4. Bucharest is the second largest capital city in Eastern Europe and the Soviet Union. **F**
5. The population of Romania is almost equally balanced between urban and non-urban peoples. **T**

NORTH AFRICA AND THE MIDDLE EAST

On an outline map of the region, have pupils outline and label the main physical features of North Africa and the Middle East. Use the physical map on the opposite page as a source. Give special emphasis to the Tigris, Euphrates, and Nile rivers and discuss the historical and present-day importance of these river valleys.

The Character of the Land

In this unit you will learn that the countries of North Africa and the Middle East are similar in many ways. One similarity is in the character of the land. Most of the region has a desert climate. There is very little rain even in the highest parts of the Arabian plateau. Farming is possible only along rivers that can supply water for irrigation.

Not all of the region is a desert, however. The northernmost parts of North Africa are dry in the summer, but they get quite a bit of rain from the winter storms that cross the Mediterranean Sea from west to east. The same thing is true in the mountainous lands of Turkey and Iran.

Ancient Civilizations

Some of the oldest and most important civilizations in human history began in the eastern Mediterranean area. One civilization grew up between the Tigris and the Euphrates rivers. The land between these rivers was called Mesopotamia. Five thousand years ago (before 3000 B.C.), there were cities in Mesopotamia. They were most likely the first cities in the world.

City life developed in Mesopotamia because the people had learned how to breed animals and plant crops. The domestication (də mes ti kā′ shən) of plants and animals meant that people could live in settled villages and raise enough food. A dependable food supply freed some peo-

In this photograph an Algerian farmer tends his vegetable garden in the Sahara. An underground spring provides the water necessary to raise these few crops.

Point out that while the countries of North Africa occupy the same continent as those of Africa south of the Sahara, they have more in common with the countries of the Middle East.

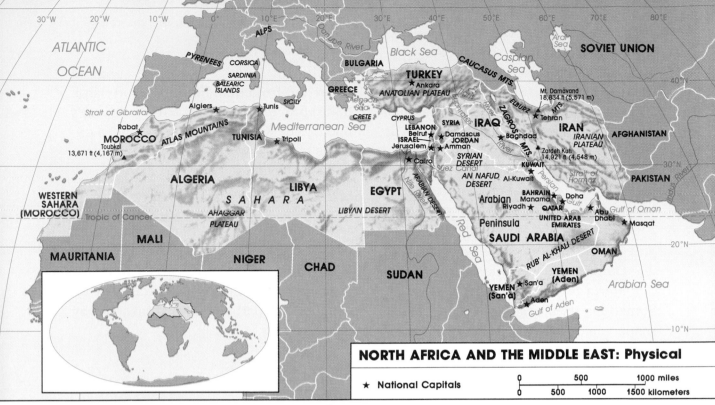

NORTH AFRICA AND THE MIDDLE EAST: Physical

★ National Capitals

0	500	1000 miles
0	500	1000	1500 kilometers

North Africa and the Middle East are located in the middle of a great mass of land formed by the continents of Africa, Asia, and Europe. You can see this if you look at the small inset map of the world above.

ple in the villages to do other things besides farming. Some people became potters or weavers. Others became merchants or traders. In time, some of the villages in Mesopotamia, such as Babylon and Ur, grew into great cities.

It was in Mesopotamia that the world's oldest form of writing was developed. Around 4000 B.C. a people called the Sumerians began to use a system of writing called cuneiform (kyü nē′ ə fôrm). *Cuneiform* means "wedge-shaped." The Sumerians used a stick to make wedge-shaped characters in soft clay. When the clay hardened, the writing could be preserved for a long time.

At about the same time that Mesopotamia was being settled, another group of people were building a civilization along the Nile in Egypt. The river supplied water for irrigation in this desert land. It also provided new soil with each year's flood. The Kingdom of Egypt (3000 B.C.– 300 B.C.) grew wealthy from agriculture.

The ancient Egyptians developed a new form of writing called hieroglyphics (hī ər ə glif′ iks). Each picture symbol stood for a word. Many of the hieroglyphics that were written thousands of years ago still exist because they were carved in stone. However, most of the writing was done on papyrus, a paperlike material invented by the Egyptians.

Three Religions

The Jews, another group living in the region, made an important contribution to the world. They developed a religion, called Judaism (jü′ dē is əm), that is one of the oldest religions still practiced today. Judaism was the first religion to teach belief in one God. Christianity, which developed from Judaism, also teaches belief in one God. Judaism and Christianity started in Palestine. *Palestine* is an old name for the region between the Mediterranean Sea and the desert, in what is today Israel and Jordan.

The Arabs, another group of people in North Africa and the Middle East, developed and spread the third religion to come from this region. That religion is Islam.

Some Common Problems

The countries of North Africa and the Middle East share some common problems today. One of them is the un-

Iran and Saudi Arabia

Which of the world's leading producers of petroleum are located in the Middle East?

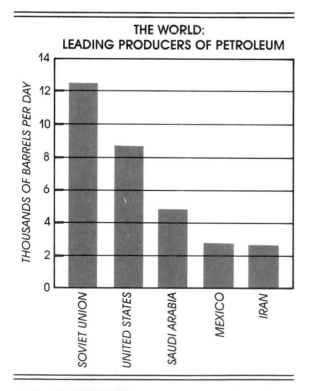

THE WORLD:
LEADING PRODUCERS OF PETROLEUM

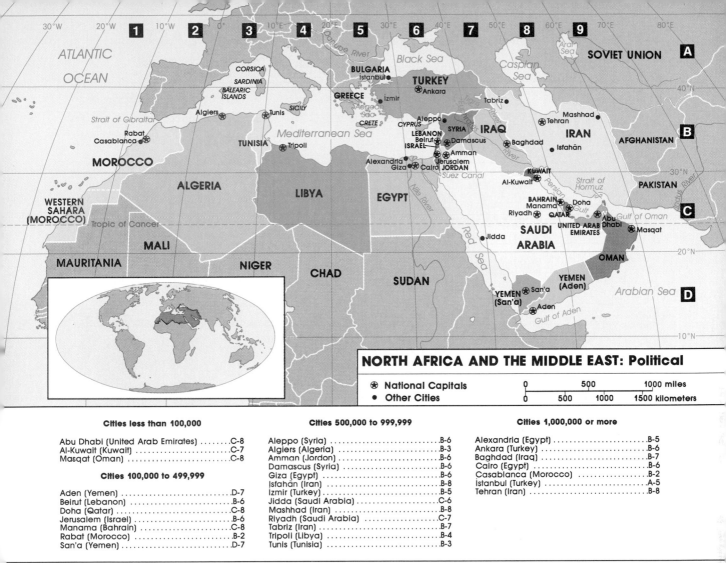

NORTH AFRICA AND THE MIDDLE EAST: Political

⊛ **National Capitals**
• **Other Cities**

0		500	1000 miles
0	500	1000	1500 kilometers

Cities less than 100,000

Abu Dhabi (United Arab Emirates) C-8
Al-Kuwait (Kuwait) C-7
Masqat (Oman) C-8

Cities 100,000 to 499,999

Aden (Yemen) D-7
Beirut (Lebanon) B-6
Doha (Qatar) C-8
Jerusalem (Israel) B-6
Manama (Bahrain) C-8
Rabat (Morocco) B-2
San'a (Yemen) D-7

Cities 500,000 to 999,999

Aleppo (Syria) B-6
Algiers (Algeria) B-3
Amman (Jordan) B-6
Damascus (Syria) B-6
Giza (Egypt) B-6
Isfahán (Iran) B-8
Izmir (Turkey) B-5
Jidda (Saudi Arabia) C-6
Mashhad (Iran) B-8
Riyadh (Saudi Arabia) C-7
Tabriz (Iran) B-7
Tripoli (Libya) B-4
Tunis (Tunisia) B-3

Cities 1,000,000 or more

Alexandria (Egypt) B-5
Ankara (Turkey) B-6
Baghdad (Iraq) B-7
Cairo (Egypt) B-6
Casablanca (Morocco) B-2
Istanbul (Turkey) A-5
Tehran (Iran) B-8

The region of North Africa and the Middle East stretches from Morocco in the west to Iran in the east, and from Turkey in the north to the two Yemens on the southern part of the Arabian Peninsula.

equal distribution of natural resources, particularly oil. A number of the countries in this part of the world have become rich in recent years, but others have remained poor. Most of the poor countries have low oil production. The graph on the facing page shows the world's leading producers of petroleum. Which producers are located in this region?

A second common problem is the conflict between countries in the region. Since 1948 there have been four Arab-Israeli wars. Fighting and terrorist acts are part of daily life in many Middle Eastern countries.

A third problem shared by the countries of this region is the increase in population. This can be explained in large part by higher birth rates and lower death rates. As you study this unit, you will learn how different countries deal with their population problem.

Appoint a current-events committee of volunteers whose responsibility it will be to keep the class informed of day-to-day developments in this region as you are studying it with the class.

NORTH AFRICA AND THE MIDDLE EAST

COUNTRY	FLAG	TOTAL AREA	POPULATION and POPULATION DENSITY	CAPITAL CITY and POPULATION	WHERE PEOPLE LIVE
Algeria		919,595 sq mi (2,381,741 sq km)	20,700,000 23 per sq mi (9 per sq km)	Algiers 903,500	
Bahrain		240 sq mi (622 sq km)	400,000 1,667 per sq mi (643 per sq km)	Manama 89,000	
Egypt		386,662 sq mi (1,001,449 sq km)	45,900,000 119 per sq mi (46 per sq km)	Cairo 6,818,500	
Iran		636,296 sq mi (1,648,000 sq km)	42,500,000 67 per sq mi (26 per sq km)	Tehran 4,498,000	
Iraq		167,925 sq mi (434,924 sq km)	14,500,000 86 per sq mi (33 per sq km)	Baghdad 1,745,500	
Israel		8,019 sq mi (20,770 sq km)	4,100,000 511 per sq mi (197 por sq km)	Jerusalem 398,000	
Jordan		37,738 sq mi (97,740 sq km)	3,600,000 95 per sq mi (37 per sq km)	Amman 732,500	
Kuwait		7,768 sq mi (20,118 sq km)	1,600,000 206 per sq mi (80 per sq km)	Al-Kuwait 78,000	
Lebanon		4,015 sq mi (10,400 sq km)	2,600,000 648 per sq mi (250 per sq km)	Beirut 475,000	
Libya		679,362 sq mi (1,759,540 sq km)	3,300,000 5 per sq mi (2 per sq km)	Tripoli 551,500	

Urban ■ Nonurban ▢ Not Available — ▢

Have pupils add to the tables on these pages by using an almanac to find the major natural resources and the GNP of each country listed. Ask: Is there any connection between these two items? (Yes, oil and high GNP)

NORTH AFRICA AND THE MIDDLE EAST

COUNTRY	FLAG	TOTAL AREA	POPULATION and POPULATION DENSITY	CAPITAL CITY and POPULATION	WHERE PEOPLE LIVE
Morocco		172,414 sq mi (446,550 sq km)	22,900,000 133 per sq mi (51 per sq km)	Rabat 367,500	
Oman		82,030 sq mi (212,457 sq km)	1,000,000 12 per sq mi (5 per sq km)	Masqat 5,000	
Qatar		4,247 sq mi (11,000 sq km)	300,000 71 per sq mi (27 per sq km)	Doha 50,000	
Saudi Arabia		831,313 sq mi (2,153,090 sq km)	10,400,000 13 per sq mi (5 per sq km)	Riyadh 667,000	
Syria		71,498 sq mi (185,180 sq km)	9,700,000 136 per sq mi (52 per sq km)	Damascus 836,500	
Tunisia		63,170 sq mi (163,610 sq km)	6,800,000 108 per sq mi (42 per sq km)	Tunis 550,500	
Turkey		292,261 sq mi (756,953 sq km)	49,200,000 168 per sq mi (65 per sq km)	Ankara 2,203,500	
United Arab Emirates		32,278 sq mi (83,600 sq km)	1,400,000 43 per sq mi (17 per sq km)	Abu Dhabi 22,000	
Yemen (Aden)		128,560 sq mi (332,968 sq km)	2,100,000 16 per sq mi (6 per sq km)	Aden 285,500	
Yemen (San'a)		75,290 sq mi (195,000 sq km)	5,700,000 76 per sq mi (29 per sq km)	San'a 448,000	

Urban ■ Nonurban ■ Not Available – ■ **253**

Have pupils group the countries on the tables into those that are predominantly urban and those that are predominantly nonurban.

CHAPTER

15 North Africa

The Physical Environment

VOCABULARY

dry farming	oasis
fallow	caravan
oasis agriculture	

Mountains and desert   North Africa extends from the Atlantic Ocean on the west to the Red Sea and the Suez Canal on the east.   The Red Sea and the Suez Canal separate the continent of Africa from the huge Arabian Peninsula, which is part of Asia.   North Africa also borders on the Mediterranean.   Five countries make up the region.   From west to east the countries are Morocco, Algeria, Tunisia, Libya, and Egypt.   Find these countries on the map on page 249.

As you look at the map, find the Atlas Mountains of Morocco, Algeria, and Tunisia.   These mountains, the most important in North Africa, are part of the Alpine system.   The mountains contain useful minerals for industry.   There are oil deposits south of the mountains in Algeria and Libya.   Most of North Africa, however, is low and flat, and its rocks are not very rich in natural resources.

North Africa is on the northern edge of the world's largest desert.   This desert stretches more than a quarter of the way around the world, from the Atlantic Ocean to Pakistan.   The African part of this dry land is called the Sahara.   It covers all of Egypt, almost all of Libya, and large parts of Tunisia, Algeria, and Morocco.

Two kinds of climate   Most of North Africa has a desert climate.   Look at the climograph for Cairo on page 511.   It shows a desert climate.   South of the Atlas Mountains, the land is very dry and gets less than 4 inches (10 cm) of rain a year.   Summer temperatures are very hot.   The hottest temperature ever recorded was at a place called Azizia, a few miles south of Tripoli, the capital of Libya.   Here the temperature in the shade reached 136°F (58°C) on September 13, 1922.

The lands between the Mediterranean Sea and the Atlas Mountains have a Mediterranean climate.   Summers are sunny, dry, and hot.   Winter storms from the sea bring much rain to the coastal lands, especially in Morocco and Algeria.   The world climate map on page 46 clearly shows that only a very small part of North Africa has a Mediterranean climate.

Farming in dry lands   The high temperatures in most parts of North Africa cause much of the rainfall and groundwater to evaporate.   This makes farming difficult in most of the region.   Only two kinds of agriculture are possible.   In the

A goat herd tries to graze at the foot of a huge sand dune in the Sahara.

To clarify pupils' understanding of North Africa as a distinct region, use a map to point out that the African continent can be divided into two widely contrasting cultural regions that are separated by the Sahara.

PRODUCTS OF THE DATE PALM TREE

BUD
1. Cabbage-shaped vegetable

FRUIT
2. Date
3. Sugar
4. Food for animals

SEEDS
5. Medicine
6. Cooking oil

TRUNK
7. Sandals, bowls

LEAVES
8. Baskets, mats

FIBERS
9. String, rope

STALKS
10. Fuel

The date palm tree supplies a variety of products to the people of North Africa.

Atlas Mountains and along the Mediterranean coasts of Morocco and Algeria, **dry farming** is practiced. Farmers who practice dry farming try to make up for low rainfall by growing only certain kinds of crops and by using farming methods that save moisture in the soil. Often a crop is planted only every other year. During the years in between, the land remains unused, or **fallow**. This helps the soil store up moisture. The crops usually grown by dry farming are wheat, barley, grapes, and tree crops such as olives and citrus fruit. However, even this kind of farming requires some rain. Dry farming can be practiced only in places that get more than 12 inches (30 cm) of rain a year.

The other kind of farming is called **oasis agriculture**. An **oasis** is a place in the desert that has enough water for trees and plants to grow. Farmers in the desert region of North Africa can grow many different crops if water is provided for irrigation. One of the most important crops is the date fruit that comes from palm trees. The diagram above shows some of the many uses of the date palm.

The most important oasis in North Africa is the valley and delta of the Nile River in Egypt. The Nile is the longest river in the world. It flows north from the highlands of East Africa into the Mediterranean Sea near Alexandria, Egypt. Other North African countries also have river oases, but they are much smaller. Some oases are just a piece of farmland around a well in the desert. In the past these were very important settlements that supplied food and water along **caravan** routes. A caravan is a group of people traveling together. For thousands of years, people have crossed the Sahara by camel caravan. The small oases around wells are still important stopping places for caravans. However, these oases do not produce as much food as the river oases or the areas of dry farming in the uplands.

CHECKUP

1. In which African countries does the Sahara lie?
2. Why does the coast of North Africa receive more rainfall than inland areas?
3. What is dry farming?
4. What is an oasis? Where is the most important oasis in North Africa?

The Nile River provides irrigation for over 10,000,000 acres of farmland in Egypt and the northern Sudan.

The People of North Africa

┌─VOCABULARY─────────────┐

Arabize   nomad

Bedouin   Berber

fellahin   Copt

└────────────────────────┘

The Arabs   Many groups of people came into North Africa. However, few groups made as great an impact on the region as the Arabs. From A.D. 640 to 710, they spread their language and faith to all parts of North Africa. Arabic replaced all other languages, and Islam became the major religion. There has been no major change in the language and religion of North Africa since that time. Although dialects of Arabic have developed and slightly different forms of Islam have appeared, the basic language and religion have bound the people of North Africa together.

North Africa did not become completely **Arabized** (ar′ ə bīzd), however. Many local customs have survived. Quite a few people kept their own language, and some even kept their old religious beliefs.

At the beginning of the Arab conquest, the people of North Africa could be divided into two groups, the **Bedouins** (bed′ ủ inz) and the **fellahin** (fel ə hēn′). The Bedouins were **nomads** who moved from place to place to find pastureland for their sheep or goats. The fellahin were crop-raising farmers. Many of the conquering Arabs were Bedouins. By overgrazing, their animals destroyed the farmland in many parts of North Africa. Many of the fellahin opposed the Arab Bedouins. In time, however, most people in North Africa adopted Arab ways.

The **Berbers** were one group that kept many of their old ways. Even now, 12 million Berbers still live in the plateaus and mountain valleys of Morocco and Algeria. The **Copts**, or Coptic Christians, of Egypt were another group that resisted adopting Arab ways. Today, Egypt has about one million Copts. The Copts in modern Egypt are the descendants of an early Christian group whose center was the city of Alexandria. The language the Copts use in church and in religious matters is related to the Berber language. The language of the Copts is the only survivor of ancient Egyptian, which was spoken before the Greek, Roman, and Arab invasions.

The Arab conquest of North Africa influenced where cities grew up in the region. Before the Arabs arrived, most of the cities were on the Mediterranean coast. The sea was the chief route between the many busy trading centers. The Arabs, however, established inland cities that could serve the land-based caravan trade. As the inland cities grew, the cities and trade on the Mediterranean coast became less important. Alexandria was replaced by Cairo as the principal city of Egypt, for example.

Colonialism in North Africa   The history of the region since the Arab conquest has been one of conflict between local people and foreign rulers. There has always been friction between Arabs and Berbers. Most of the Arabs were not descendants of the conquerors who had come from Arabia in the eighth century. They were local people who had become Arabized by speaking Arabic and prac-

257

ticing Islam. These Arabs were not foreigners, but the Berbers disliked them anyway. They often rebelled against their "foreign" rulers.

In the sixteenth century all of North Africa, except Morocco, was conquered by the Turks. They ruled for nearly 300 years. During this time there was little economic or scientific progress, and North Africa did not prosper.

Except for a few cities held by Spain and Portugal, there were few Europeans in North Africa. European rule really began with the French conquest of Algeria in the 1830s. By the 1880s the French

The fortress in Oran, a port city in Algeria, was the scene of many battles between Algerians and invaders. The French government, using soldiers of the Foreign Legion, conquered Algeria in the 1830s.

also controlled Tunisia, and the British ruled Egypt and the Suez Canal. Morocco became French, and the Italians took Libya just before World War I. Independence came to all of North Africa after World War II.

European rule changed North Africa in many ways. Some social and economic conditions improved. Schools and railroads were built. Medical care became available to the North Africans. Cities grew, and agriculture became more productive. But many Europeans moved to North Africa in order to form a small ruling class. The local people usually could not get good jobs at good pay. Sometimes the local people rebelled, and the European powers often put down these rebellions with armies. From this the North Africans learned to hate foreign rule. They also learned to fight for their independence.

In Algeria there were more than a million French in 1960. They made up only about one tenth of the population, but they had almost all of the political power. They also controlled most of the good farmland. There were bitter feelings between the Algerians and the French. A long war between the Algerians and the French finally ended in 1963 when France gave Algeria its independence. As a result, most of the French in Algeria moved to France.

CHECKUP

1. How did the Arabs change North Africa?
2. Define *Arabize*. Which groups in North Africa have not been completely Arabized?
3. When did Europeans begin to colonize North Africa? What improvements did the Europeans make in the region? What problems arose?

North Africa Today

> **VOCABULARY**
> Maghreb
> phosphate

Neighboring countries   Egypt and Libya are neighboring countries that share several traits.   Both countries lie mostly in the Sahara.   Arabic is the language and Islam is the religion of each country. The majority of Egyptians and Libyans are farmers.   Both countries were Turkish colonies for centuries before being ruled by Europeans.   The differences between the two nations, however, are much more important than these similarities.

Egypt   Egypt has more people than any other Arab nation.   It has 14 times as many people as Libya, even though it is only half as large.   Most of the people live on a narrow strip of land along the Nile River and its delta.   Cairo, the capital of Egypt and the most populated city in Africa, is located on the Nile.   Alexandria, the second most populated city in Egypt, is located on the edge of the Nile Delta.

The Nile Valley has rich soil.   Most of Egypt's farmland lies along the course of the river.   Cotton is Egypt's most important crop.   Egypt is one of the world's leading producers of cotton.   Other important crops include oranges, beans, corn, sugarcane, and wheat.   Farming is Egypt's main source of income.   The Nile River is Egypt's chief natural resource.

Egypt has tried to modernize, but it has many problems.   There are some deposits

Anwar El Sadat: Egyptian Leader

MOHAMMED ANWAR EL SADAT was an outstanding Egyptian leader.   He was born in a small town in the Nile Delta in 1918.   Sadat went to a local religious primary school, but had to move to Cairo to attend secondary school.   In 1936 he was admitted to the Egyptian Military Academy and met future leaders of Egypt. One of them, Gamal Abdel Nasser, became the leader of the groups that were trying to free Egypt from British control.

In 1952 the British left, and Egypt became a republic.   Nasser became president, and Sadat joined him in the new government.   In 1970, Nasser died, and Sadat succeeded him as president.   At first, Sadat worked for unity and cooperation among the Arab nations.   This often meant taking a strong stand against Israel.   However, after the Arab-Israeli War of 1973, Sadat tried to find a peaceful solution to the problems of the Middle East.

Unlike other Arab leaders, Sadat was willing to deal with Israel peacefully.   He visited Jerusalem in 1977 to show his goodwill.   These efforts, supported by President Jimmy Carter, resulted in a treaty of peace between Egypt and Israel.   Sadat was given the Nobel Peace Prize in 1979.   He continued to work for his goals of peace and modernization.   In 1981, however, he was assassinated by people who disagreed with his ideas.   The world lost an able leader and peacemaker.

Explain that the Nobel Prize originated with Alfred Nobel, the Swedish chemist who invented dynamite.   He hated its use in war, which he had not intended.   The prizes were designed to promote international peace.

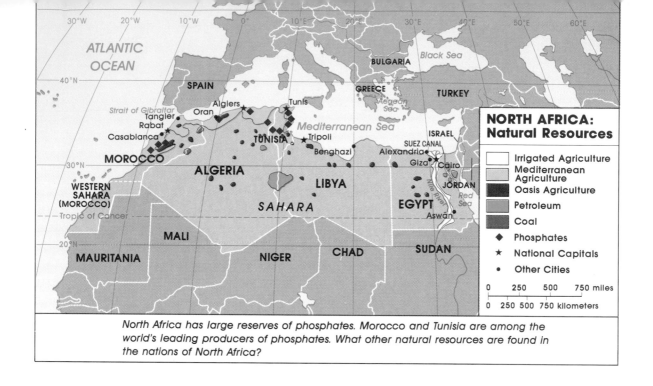

North Africa has large reserves of phosphates. Morocco and Tunisia are among the world's leading producers of phosphates. What other natural resources are found in the nations of North Africa?

of oil and other minerals, but these resources are not very great for a country of 46 million people. Although Egypt is an agricultural country, it has to import food. Egypt's growing cities and industries have taken over land once used for farming. It is now against the law in Egypt to put an industrial building on land that can be used for crops. Egypt imports machinery, motor vehicles, and other industrial goods, but it exports few manufactured goods. The result is that Egypt spends much more on imports than it receives from exports. The country has to borrow money to make up most of the difference.

The Aswān dam The Egyptian government has borrowed money for projects that will develop the country's economy. In 1970 a huge dam across the Nile was completed at Aswān. The Nile River behind the Aswān dam forms a lake 300 miles (483 km) long. The lake provides irrigation water for new cropland. The dam also prevents the Nile from flooding the valley below the dam. The high dam provides hydroelectric power, which in turn means more industries and jobs. The income from this power has paid for the cost of the dam.

The Aswān dam has been good for Egypt in some ways, but it has also caused some problems. The dam has not improved Egypt's agriculture as much as people had expected. At first, irrigation water from the lake behind the dam helped to create farmland out of desert land. Within 2 years, about 1,500 square miles (3,885 sq km) of desert land were reclaimed. But the costs were so high that the government ended the irrigation projects in 1972. In other ways the Aswān dam actually hurt Egypt's agriculture. After the dam was built, it shut off much water from the lower course of the Nile. This meant that the river could no longer carry large amounts of mud and sand to

You might wish to briefly discuss the concept of an ecosystem. Use the Aswan Dam as an example of a human-made change in the environment that disturbed the ecological balance.

deposit at its mouth. Thus the river could no longer build its delta out into the Mediterranean. Now the sea has begun to destroy parts of the delta, and salt water has started to build up in the soil.

The Suez Canal One of Egypt's most important assets is the Suez Canal. In normal times the Suez Canal is a steady source of income for Egypt. Ships passing through the canal pay a toll.

The canal cuts across an isthmus between Africa and Asia. The Isthmus of Suez separates the Red Sea from the Mediterranean and is 75 miles (121 km) wide. Several attempts were made to cut a canal to join the two seas. But it was not until 1854 that a French engineer named Ferdinand de Lesseps (də les' eps) got Egypt's permission to build a canal across the Isthmus of Suez. It took years to dig the Suez Canal. When the canal was completed in 1869, a water route connecting the Far East, Europe, and East Africa crossed through the isthmus.

The canal was closed as a result of war in 1956. It was closed again in 1967 during the Arab-Israeli War, but was reopened in 1975. Among the ships that use the canal are oil tankers bound for Europe and North America from the Persian Gulf.

Libya In contrast to Egypt, Libya has only a little farming and no great river like the Nile. The country's farmland is along the Mediterranean coast, where there is just enough rain for certain crops to grow. Libya's two major cities, Tripoli, the capital, and Benghazi (ben gäz' ē), are on the coast.

Libya's greatest source of wealth is its oil. In the last 20 years, Libya has become the world's ninth leading producer of petroleum. Libya was once a poor country, but the discovery of oil there has brought quick riches. The government invests much of the income from oil in irrigation systems and other economic projects.

Maghreb The area of mountains, plateaus, and coastal valleys that lies in the western part of North Africa between the Sahara and the Mediterranean is called the **Maghreb** (məg' rəb). It receives more rain than any other part of North Africa. Tunisia, Algeria, and Morocco are the three countries of the Maghreb. Each of these countries also extends into the Sahara.

In Algerian villages, farmers from the country sell their products in open-air markets.

Tunisia   Tunisia is the smallest of the three countries. In some ways, Tunisia is like Egypt. It has some petroleum, but much less than its neighbors. It has to import food and manufactured goods, and it has few exports to pay for its imports. But Tunisia is not nearly as poor as Egypt. It has more usable farmland and almost as many mineral resources as Egypt. Tunisia is a leading producer of **phosphates** (fos′ fāts). Phosphates are materials that are used to make fertilizers and detergents.

Most of the people in Tunisia live in the northern part of the country. This is also where most of the cities are located, including the capital, Tunis. At its northern tip, Tunisia is only about 85 miles (137 km) from Sicily, a part of Europe.

Morocco and Tunisia are two of the world's leading producers of phosphates. How much does each nation produce?

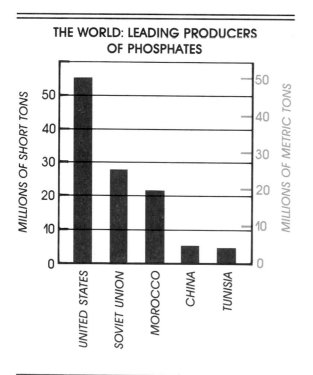

THE WORLD: LEADING PRODUCERS OF PHOSPHATES

Thousands of visitors come from Europe to lie on Tunisia's sunny Mediterranean beaches and to visit the ruins of ancient cities. Tourism is a big business in Tunisia.

Algeria   Algeria is one of the world's largest countries, but 90 percent of its land is desert. The Sahara, however, provides Algeria with one of its main resources—oil. Algeria's oil production is not as great as Libya's, but oil and natural gas make up 97 percent of Algeria's income from exports. The income from oil and natural gas pays for all of Algeria's imports.

The population density of Algeria is only 23 people per square mile (9 per sq km). This low figure, however, is very misleading. As in all of the North African countries, most of the land in Algeria is uninhabited, and people are crowded into a few small areas. The narrow coastal strip where most of the cities are located covers only two percent of Algeria, but it is where more than half of the people in Algeria live. The population density there is about 400 people per square mile (154 per sq km). Algiers, the capital and largest city, lies on the Mediterranean Sea.

When Algeria was under French rule, much of the best land was owned and farmed by French settlers. They grew grapes for wine, wheat, olives, and citrus fruit. Most of what they raised was exported to France. Algerian farmers were angry that their best land was in foreign hands, and they did not like the idea of growing grapes to make wine. Algerians practice the Islamic religion, which forbids the drinking of alcohol.

Agriculture in Algeria changed after the country became independent in 1963. French landowners had to give up their land. Today the Algerian government owns half the farmland in the country. The government has favored the growing of wheat and other food crops, and it has reduced the amount of land used for growing grapes. Even so, Algeria has to import food because its population is growing fast. Like Libya, Algeria is lucky to have oil exports to pay for imports.

Morocco Morocco is a little different from the other North African countries. The Arabs never really took over the upland valleys and plateaus of Morocco. The Berbers who live there were able to resist adopting Arab ways. Today there are 7 million Berbers in Morocco. In the lowlands, on the other hand, the people changed to Arabic speech and Arab ways long ago.

In the early 1900s, Morocco was ruled by France and Spain. But few Europeans came to settle in Morocco, as they had in Algeria.

Morocco is fairly rich in natural resources. It has two thirds of the world's supply of phosphates. It has more agricultural land than other North African countries. Morocco also has rich fishing grounds in the Atlantic Ocean.

Despite these advantages, Morocco is a poor country. Its population is rising, so it has to import more food. Morocco also has to import oil, and the price of oil keeps going up. Morocco's exports can no longer pay for its imports. Most of the developing countries that have to import oil have this problem.

In Moroccan cities most people live in adobe houses on narrow winding streets. People dress as their ancestors did.

Another reason for the poverty of Morocco is its ongoing war with the people of the Spanish Sahara. This coastal stretch of Africa was given up by Spain in 1976. The area, now called the Western Sahara, borders Morocco, Algeria, and Mauritania (môr ə tā′ nē ə), a country in East Africa. Morocco and Mauritania agreed on a division of land that gave Morocco most of the phosphate mines. But many of the Berbers who lived in the area wanted independence rather than rule by Morocco. Algeria supported the Berbers. The result has been a long, costly war between Morocco and troops supported and supplied by Algeria.

CHECKUP

1. In what ways has the Aswān dam helped Egypt? What problems has the dam caused?
2. How are Tunisia and Egypt alike? How are they different?
3. How has agriculture in Algeria changed since 1963?
4. What are Morocco's chief natural resources?

You might wish to review the differences between developing countries and developed countries.

KEY FACTS

1. The Sahara Desert takes up much of North Africa.

2. Dry farming is practiced only in places where there is more than 12 inches (30 cm) of rain a year.

3. The Nile Valley is the most important farming area in North Africa.

4. The Arabs introduced the Arabic language and Islamic religion to North Africa.

5. The Berbers resisted adopting Arab ways with greater success than other North African groups.

6. Egypt has few resources to support its growing population.

7. Oil has made Libya a wealthy country.

8. Morocco, Algeria, and Tunisia are the countries of the Maghreb.

VOCABULARY QUIZ

Match the terms in the list with their definitions. Write your answers on paper.

a. dry farming
b. fallow
c. fellahin
d. caravan
e. phosphate

f. Bedouin
g. Maghreb
h. Copt
i. Arabize
j. nomad

h 1. A member of a Christian group whose church language is ancient Egyptian

a 2. A method of farming in which only certain crops are grown and the moisture in the soil is conserved

b 3. Not used or planted for a season or more

c 4. A group of crop-raising farmers who opposed the Bedouin herders

d 5. A group of people traveling together

j 6. A person who moves from place to place

e 7. A mineral used in making fertilizers and detergents

f 8. A wandering Arab herder

g 9. A region covering part of Morocco, Tunisia, and Algeria that receives more rain than any other part of North Africa

i 10. To make to adopt Arab ways

REVIEW QUESTIONS

1. What are the names of the major desert and the major mountain range in North Africa?

2. Describe the two kinds of farming possible in the dry lands of North Africa.

3. In what ways is the Nile Valley the center of life in Egypt?

4. What caused cities to grow up in the inland areas of North Africa?

5. Why has there always been friction between Arabs and Berbers in North Africa?

6. What happened in Algeria to cause a war with France?

7. Why does Egypt, an agricultural country, have to import food?

8. Why did the Algerians dislike the growing of grapes by the French in Algeria?

9. What group of people lives in the upland valleys and plateaus of Morocco?

ACTIVITIES

1. Look up the following words in a dictionary or encyclopedia: *mummy, papyrus, pharaoh, sphinx.* What does each of these words tell us about the ancient civilization of the Nile Valley?

2. Look up the Rosetta stone in an encyclopedia. Write a brief report on what it is and why it is important in understanding ancient Egypt.

LOOKING FOR CAUSES

ASK *WHAT* THE FACTS ARE AND *WHY* THEY ARE TRUE

When we learn about a subject, we want to know *what* the facts are and *why* they are true. The first four exercises give some facts that are mentioned in Chapter 15. Each fact is followed by three statements. Each of the three statements is true, but only one tells why the fact is true. Only that statement gives the cause or the reason why the fact is true.

SKILLS PRACTICE: Part I

On a sheet of paper, write the letter of the statement that completes the sentence and tells why the fact is true. The page number following the fact tells where the fact is presented in the chapter.

Example: Tunisia is a richer country than Egypt because (page 262)

  a. it has more usable farmland.

  b. it was once a French colony.

  c. it is part of the Maghreb.

Both **b** and **c** are true statements, but only **a** tells why Tunisia is richer than Egypt.

1. Arabs established inland cities rather than seaports because (page 257)

  a. they were more interested in inland caravan trade.

  b. the Roman Empire had come to an end.

  c. the religious centers of Islam were inland cities.

2. Algeria's low population density figure is misleading because (page 262)

  a. it was much lower 50 years ago.

  b. it is lower than Morocco's population density figure.

  c. most of Algeria is uninhabited.

3. Moroccan Berbers were able to resist adopting Arab ways because (page 263)

  a. there are 7 million of them today.

  b. the Arabs did not take over the upland valleys and plateaus where the Berbers lived in Morocco.

  c. the Berber language is related to ancient Egyptian.

4. The Suez Canal is one of Egypt's most important assets because (page 261)

  a. the canal was completed in 1869.

  b. it took years to dig the canal.

  c. ships passing through the canal pay a toll.

SKILLS PRACTICE: Part II

The questions in this part of the exercise are about facts presented in Chapter 15. You are to answer each question with a complete sentence that tells what the fact is and why it is true. Your sentences will probably include such words as *because, in order that,* or *so that.* The page number after each question tells where the fact is stated.

Example: Why is Morocco poor when it is fairly rich in natural resources? (page 263)

A complete sentence telling what the fact is and why it is true might read: *Morocco is a poor country because its exports do not pay for the food and oil it has to import.*

Write your answers to the following four questions on a sheet of paper.

1. Why is land often left fallow in dry farming? (page 256)

2. Why did Algerians have bitter feelings toward the French in Algeria? (page 258)

3. Why does the Libyan government have money to invest in economic projects? (page 261)

4. Why does Egypt spend more on imports than it gets from exports? (page 260)

16 The Middle East

The Physical Environment

```
┌─VOCABULARY──────────────────┐
│  rift valley        fault line  │
└──────────────────────────────┘
```

Plateaus, mountains, and plains   The lands of southwestern Asia that stretch from the Mediterranean Sea to the highlands of central Asia are often called the Middle East.   The people of Europe gave the name Middle East to these lands because they are located east of Europe. Other lands in Asia, such as China and Japan, are farther east of Europe and are often called the Far East.   The map on page 249 shows that the Middle East is where Europe, Africa, and Asia meet.

The Arabian Peninsula covers much of the southern part of the Middle East. Highlands of the Alpine system ring the northern edge of the Middle East.   The Taurus Mountains in Turkey are relatively low, although Mount Ararat (ar′ ə rat) reaches 16,945 feet (5,165 m).   The mountains of Iran are higher.   Mount Damā-vand (dam′ ə vand) in the Elburz (el burz′) Mountains is 18,834 feet (5,571 m) above sea level.   Mount Damāvand is the highest mountain in the Middle East.   The Zagros (zag′ rəs) Mountains run along the western edge of the Iranian Plateau. These mountains separate Iran's highlands from the low plain of the Tigris and Euphrates rivers.   The plain was once known as Mesopotamia, "the land between two rivers."   The plain was part of the Fertile Crescent, an area of rich, irrigated farmland.   In ancient times great cities flourished in Mesopotamia.

A rift valley   To the west of the Arabian Peninsula is the Red Sea.   Find this long, narrow body of water on the map. The sea occupies a part of the earth's crust that looks like an enormous canyon. This canyon is a **rift valley**.   The sides of the rift valley are two **fault lines,** or cracks in the earth's crust.   Millions of years ago pressure below the earth's surface caused part of the earth to drop down between the two fault lines.   This formed the canyonlike valley that is the Red Sea.   The rift valley continues even beyond the Red Sea.   It extends northward to include the Dead Sea and the Jordan River.   The rift valley also extends southward into East Africa.   You will read more about the rift valley in Chapter 17.

Climate   Most of the Middle East, including nearly all of the Arabian Peninsula, has a desert climate.   However, the coastal parts of Turkey, Syria, Lebanon, and Israel have a Mediterranean climate. The climograph for Jerusalem on page 512 shows this kind of climate.

In this picture of Jerusalem, you see the ancient walled city, the Old City, beyond the Damascus Gate.   Jerusalem, a holy city to Jews, Christians, and Moslems, is the capital of Israel.   (32°N/35°E; map, p. 251)

On the map on p. 270, point out that ancient Mesopotamia occupied the area of modern-day Iraq, eastern Syria, and southeastern Turkey.

Other places in the Middle East that get rain are either mountainous or near mountains. As the warm, moist air rises over the mountains, it cools. As the moist air cools, it drops rain or snow. The water that falls in the mountains forms the rivers in the Middle East.

Farming in the Middle East The climate and landforms of the Middle East combine to form three kinds of agricultural environments. In the uplands and mountain valleys, there is enough rainfall for dry farming. Even so, the upland streams are often used for irrigation because there is not much rain in the summer. Most of the farming in the Middle East takes place along the valleys of

For thousands of years the people of Iraq have sailed the Tigris River in small boats. And just as their ancestors did, people irrigate their fields with river water.

the major streams and rivers. Like the Nile Valley in Egypt, the Tigris and Euphrates valleys in Iraq are important river oases. In the desert, farming is limited to small oases around wells and springs.

CHECKUP

1. How did the lands of southwestern Asia get the name Middle East?
2. What is a rift valley?
3. Where does most of the farming in the Middle East take place?

The People of the Middle East

┌─VOCABULARY─────────────────┐

hegira	Sunni
Shiite	revenue

└────────────────────────────┘

The spread of Islam Three of the world's major religions—Judaism, Christianity, and Islam—began in the Middle East. Islam, the most recent of the three religions, was founded by Mohammed (mu ham' əd). He began to preach around the year A.D. 610 in the city of Mecca. Mecca is on the western side of the Arabian Peninsula. At that time people in Arabia believed in many gods and goddesses. However, Mohammed taught there was only one God and that he was God's messenger. When Mohammed told people in Mecca about his religious messages, many of the city leaders thought he was dangerous. So Mohammed left Mecca in A.D. 622 and went to Medina, another city on the Arabian Peninsula. The trip from Mecca to Medina is called the **hegira** (hi jī' rə). Moslems number

Moslem pilgrims travel from all parts of the world to visit the Kaaba (kä′ bǝ), the most sacred shrine in all of Islam. The Kaaba is in Mecca. (21°N/40°E; map, p. 251)

their years from the hegira, that is, from the year A.D. 622 by the Christian calendar. By the time of Mohammed's death in 632, he had brought almost all of Arabia under his rule. In the next 100 years, Islam spread across North Africa into Spain and throughout the Middle East.

The Islamic religion has always had close ties with the Arabic language. Arabic is the language of the Koran, the holy book of Islam. As Islam spread, so did Arabic. The Arabic language soon replaced all others in the region.

Islam did not spread as a single religion, however. Two main branches developed. About one fifth of the Moslems, as followers of Islam are called, are **Shiite** (shē′ īt) Moslems. Most people in present-day Iran and Iraq are Shiites. But the great majority of Moslems are **Sunni** (sun′ ē) Moslems. The Sunnis are found in the rest of the Islamic lands of the Middle East and North Africa, as well as in other parts of the world.

Although Islam became the chief religion of the Middle East, some groups kept their old religion. Most of these groups were Christian, but there were also small Jewish communities.

In the middle of the 1200s, Mongols invaded the Middle East. The Mongols were nomadic people from Mongolia in Asia. Under their rule the Middle East declined in power. It was no longer a leader in art, science, architecture, and industry. The Middle East became a backward region and remained that way for centuries.

Turkish and European influences
As the power of the Mongols weakened, Turkey gained control over a large area. In time the Turkish empire, which is known as the Ottoman Empire, stretched from Hungary into the Middle East and North Africa. But Turkey slowly began to lose power. By the end of World War I, the Ottoman Empire was gone.

After World War I, the French and British divided up the former Turkish possessions between themselves. The people of the Middle East, however, wanted their own government. Eventually all of the Middle East regained its independence from European control.

Europeans also influenced the economy of the Middle East. The Middle East has huge amounts of oil. Half of the world's known oil reserves are found

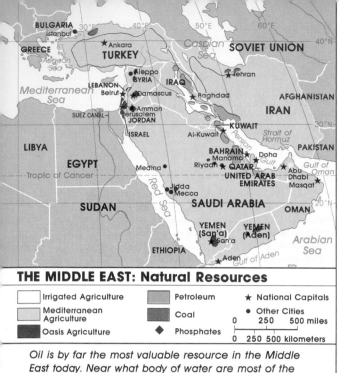

THE MIDDLE EAST: Natural Resources

☐ Irrigated Agriculture		▨ Petroleum		★ National Capitals
☐ Mediterranean Agriculture		▨ Coal		• Other Cities
■ Oasis Agriculture		◆ Phosphates		

0   250   500 miles
0   250 500 kilometers

Oil is by far the most valuable resource in the Middle East today. Near what body of water are most of the region's oil deposits found?

here. British business people first developed the oil fields in what is now Iraq, Iran, and the countries of the Arabian Peninsula. Soon after, companies from other countries moved in to pump, refine, and export the region's oil. Today eight foreign oil companies control almost all of the oil production in the Middle East. Five are American companies (Exxon, Texaco, Chevron, Mobil, and Gulf), one is British (British Petroleum), one is British and Dutch (Royal Dutch Shell), and one is French (Total). Today these companies have to share their oil **revenue**, or income, with the governments of the oil-producing countries.

CHECKUP

1. Who was Mohammed?
2. What effect did the Mongol invasions have on the Middle East?
3. How did the Europeans influence the economy of the Middle East?

The Arab Lands of the Middle East in the Twentieth Century

┌─VOCABULARY─────────────────┐
OPEC   conservative
└────────────────────────────┘

The Arabian Peninsula The last 30 years have changed this peninsula greatly. One could say that the people of Arabia have gone from camels to Cadillacs in one generation. The peninsula is still largely uninhabited, even though many cities have sprung up in the desert. Much of this change has taken place because local oil fields and oil refineries were developed. The change has also come about because the rising price of oil has brought more money to the oil-producing countries.

Not everyone in Arabia owns a big new car, however. Not every country has developed its oil resources. And some countries have no oil at all. Moreover, the profits from oil have not been divided evenly among all of the people of the oil-rich countries.

Saudi Arabia, a leader in the Arab world Saudi Arabia is by far the largest country on the Arabian Peninsula. It has three fourths of the land and half of the population. Riyadh (rē (y) äd′), its capital, and Jidda, its major port on the Red Sea, are both modern cities with more than 500,000 people. Saudi Arabia has become one of the leaders in the Arab world. It has played an important role in the Organization of Petroleum Exporting Countries, or **OPEC**. The countries that make up OPEC play a big role in determining the price of oil in the world. Saudi Arabia has also been a leader in spending oil revenues for schools and hospitals, and for the general economic development of the country. And Saudi Arabia has been willing to loan money to its Arab neighbors to help them develop their own countries.

Resources bring wealth   If the wealth of the countries in the world is measured by the average income of the people in each country, then four of the five richest countries in the world are in Arabia. They are Saudi Arabia, Kuwait (kə wät′), Qatar (kät′ ər), and the United Arab Emirates (ə mir′ its). These four countries all have well-developed oil resources. Two other countries of Arabia, Bahrain (bä rān′) and Oman (ō män′), are not quite as rich. However, the average income of the people in those two countries is quite high.

The other two countries of Arabia, both named Yemen (yem′ ən), have no oil resources and rank among the poorest countries in the world. In fact, they have very few resources of any kind, and their populations are increasing rapidly. These two countries have had to borrow money to buy the imports they need. They owe a great deal of money.

Change versus tradition   As you have learned there are some countries in Arabia, such as Saudi Arabia, that are wealthy. Others, such as the two Yemens, are poor. Most of the countries in Arabia are trying to develop their economies, and most of them are modernizing. But many of the people in these countries

are very **conservative.** They want to keep things as they are or as they were in the past. So old ways continue even in countries that have become very rich in the last few years. In Saudi Arabia, for example, women cannot leave their air-conditioned houses without wearing veils. They are not allowed to drive the family car. Girls cannot go to the same schools as boys, even in the universities of the country. And thieves are punished for repeated stealing by having their hands cut off.

Jordan, Syria, and Iraq   On the northern edge of the Arabian Peninsula are the three other Arab and Moslem states in the Middle East. They are Jordan, Syria, and Iraq.

Jordan was part of a large Turkish province before World War I. After the war the southern part of the province was given to Britain. The British divided this territory into two parts. The part west of

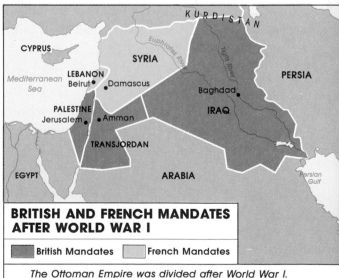

BRITISH AND FRENCH MANDATES AFTER WORLD WAR I

■ British Mandates   □ French Mandates

The Ottoman Empire was divided after World War I. Britain and France were given a mandate or the right to govern parts of the Middle East.

In Syria one sees many mosques, Moslem places of worship, and beautiful handicraft, such as rugs, textiles, glassware, and metalwork.

the Jordan River was known as Palestine; the part east as Transjordan. Transjordan was a desert land with few people. In 1948 it became the independent state of Jordan. Amman, Jordan's capital, had fewer than 20,000 people before World War II. Its present population is nearly 700,000. Jordan has remained a poor land with few resources. It has some minerals, but no oil. Frequent warfare with its neighbor Israel has made Jordan even poorer. Jordan has also quarreled with its neighbors Syria and Iraq.

Syria and Iraq make up the northern part of the old Turkish lands. Their histories are rich and long, but the whole region lost its wealth and activity after the Mongol invasion. By the time the region was added to the Ottoman Empire, Syria and Iraq were backward provinces. Many of the important cities had disappeared. Today there are only a few big cities in the two countries, but they have grown greatly in the last 50 years. Iraq, for example, has only one large city, Baghdad (bag′ dad). But Baghdad has more than 3 million people. Syria has two large cities, Damascus (də mas′ kəs) and Aleppo (ə lep′ ō). Damascus, the capital, has more than a million people, and Aleppo is only a little smaller.

Iraq and Syria are alike in some ways. They are chiefly Arabic-speaking, Moslem countries. The governments of both countries have similar views. Iraq and Syria are strongly anti-Israel. *Anti-* is a prefix that means "against." Both countries receive money and arms from the Soviet Union that have been used to fight Israel. Iraq and Syria also have some important differences, and they generally do not get along with each other. Iraq has oil, and most Iraqis are Shiite Moslems. Syria has very little oil, and most of its people are Sunnis.

CHECKUP

1. In what ways has Saudi Arabia become a leader in the Arab world?
2. What are the oil-rich countries of Arabia?
3. What are the important cities of Jordan, Syria, and Iraq today?
4. In what ways are Syria and Iraq alike? Different?

You might use the Activity on p. 279 to aid pupils' understanding of the individual nations that make up the Middle East.

Non-Arab Lands of the Middle East

VOCABULARY	
Kurdistan	PLO
Zionist	kibbutz
Palestinian	

Turkey   The central part of Turkey is the Anatolian Plateau. High mountain ranges, part of the Alpine system, cut the plateau off from the Black and Mediterranean seas. The rest of Turkey faces the sea. The country has a long coastline. Turkey controls the Bosporus (bäs′ prəs) and the Dardanelles (därd ən elz′). These two straits and the Sea of Mamara connect the Black Sea and the Aegean Sea. It is easy to see the importance of this waterway. Whoever holds it, holds the water gateway to a large part of Eastern Europe. The land on either side of the gateway is part of Turkey. Istanbul, Turkey's largest city, is a major port on the Bos-

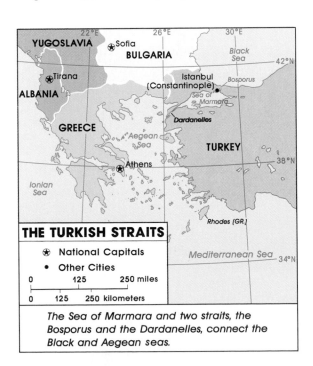

THE TURKISH STRAITS

⊛ National Capitals
• Other Cities

0   125   250 miles
0   125   250 kilometers

The Sea of Marmara and two straits, the Bosporus and the Dardanelles, connect the Black and Aegean seas.

porus. Istanbul, once called Constantinople, has a history that goes back many centuries. In 1919, however, Ankara was chosen to be the capital of Turkey. Although it is a fairly new city, it already has 2 million people.

Atatürk's changes   Turkey is a Moslem nation, but it follows the ways of Western Europe more than the other Moslem countries of the Middle East. Turkey became more Western in its way of life after 1919 under the leadership of Mustafa Kemal Atatürk (mùs tä fä′ kə mäl′ ä tä turk′). Before that the country had been governed by Moslem laws, and its schools were entirely religious. Atatürk wanted the people of Turkey to give up their old ways and to become more modern. So he brought about many changes.

Atatürk wanted his people to think of themselves as Turks rather than Moslems. The government made laws that limited the powers of religious leaders. It closed religious schools and opened schools run by the government. The Roman alphabet replaced the Arabic alphabet. Atatürk also wanted to make men and women equal in Turkey. He said that women must no longer wear veils to hide their faces. In the past, girls had not gone to school in Turkey. Atatürk ordered them to do so. Women were given the right to take jobs in business and government. There were changes in Turkey's economy, too. Roads and railroads were built, and many factories were started.

Turkey today   Modern Turkey has many problems. It has a large and growing population. There are not enough

273

jobs for all its people. Many Turks have gone to work in Western Europe. For the past 15 years, the government of Turkey has not been stable. Its army has sometimes taken over and ruled the country.

Kurdistan Another problem that Turkey must deal with is **Kurdistan** (ker' də stan). Kurdistan, a region of about 75,000 square miles (194,000 sq km), lies in Turkey, Iraq, Iran, and Syria. Most of the 15 million people of Kurdistan are Islamic Kurds. Of all the people in the world, the Kurds are the largest group without a country of their own.

The Kurds are often treated harshly. The Turkish government has exiled Kurdish leaders, put soldiers in many Kurdish cities, and made the use of the Kurdish language illegal. Turkey does not even call the Kurds by their name. They are called "Mountain Turks" instead. For a time the Kurds of Iraq and Iran were treated a little better. In an effort to make trouble for the other's government, Iraq and Iran each supported the Kurds in the other's country. But this aid stopped in 1976, and the Kurdish hope for an independent state remains a dream.

But the Kurds are stubborn. They continue to speak Kurdish, even though there are no schools in their language. Despite the attitude of the countries in which they live, the Kurds continue to hope for independence.

Iran, an ancient country Iran was known as Persia for many years. Iran has a great history that goes back 2,500 years. Both Iran and Persia are old names, but Iran has been the official name of the country since 1935. The language of the people of Iran is still called Persian.

The old religion of the Persian Empire was replaced by Islam. This happened in the seventh century when the Arabs con-

Although Iran has become rich from the sale of oil, for many people life has not changed.

Childhood in an Iranian Village

Mohammed is an 8-year-old boy who lives in a small village in the province of Khorāsān. Mohammed's grandfather Reza likes to tell him about how hard life was years ago. Like most of his friends in those days, Reza went to work weaving carpets when he was 8 years old.

The children worked under a master weaver from daybreak to sunset. Their only day off was Friday, the holy day of the Moslems. The carpet-weaving shop was owned by a man from Tehran. He made a big profit by paying low wages and by exporting the famous carpets of Khorāsān to many parts of the world. The children did not like to work so hard for someone else, but there was little else for them to do. The only school in the village was run part-time by a local Moslem priest, called a mullah (mul' ə). The mullah tried to teach the children how to read the Koran in Arabic, but he didn't know the language very well himself.

Much has changed in the villages of Iran in the last 20 years. The government has established schools, and schoolteachers make sure that small children do not work in carpet-weaving shops. Mohammed goes to such a government school. The teacher is paid by the Iranian government and comes from a nearby city. He teaches mainly reading, writing, and arithmetic; and he gives the children 2 or 3 hours' worth of homework every night. Mohammed likes his school, even though the work is hard. He often tells his little sister, Mariam, all about his day. Mariam is looking forward to going to the girls' school in the village. But her parents aren't sure that she needs an education, and there may be no school for her anyway. As part of its effort to return to older Islamic ways, the government of the Ayatollah Khomeini is talking about closing down the girls' schools.

quered the region. In the sixteenth century the shah, or ruler, of Persia made his subjects switch from Sunni to Shiite Islam. He did this because many people of Persia were Turks. The shah wanted to make all the people in his country feel different from the Turks. Iran is still a Shiite country, and Turkey remains a Sunni country.

Iran is one of the largest countries in the Middle East and North Africa. It is larger than any country in Europe, except the Soviet Union. Much of Iran is desert, so its farmland is limited. Iran does not produce enough food to feed all of its people today because its population has grown so rapidly in recent years. Almost half of the people in Iran now live in cities and towns. Many of these people work in the country's oil industry. Iran is one of the world's leading producers of oil. The government of Iran now owns the oil industry in the country.

Recent events in Iran Political problems have upset Iran in recent years. Many Iranians, particularly Moslem religious leaders, opposed the ruling shah. In

Point out that the shah governed Iran as a dictator. His government **275** denied freedom of speech and civil rights.

1979 a revolution overthrew the shah's government. A Moslem religious leader, Ayatollah Khomeini (ī yä tō′ lä kō mā′ nē), took control of the country. His government did away with many of the modern changes the shah had introduced. Many people in Iran do not like Khomeini's efforts to go back to old Islamic ways. Iran also has groups of people, such as the Turks and the Kurds, who think that Khomeini has little tolerance for anyone who is not a Persian-speaking Moslem.

On top of all this, Iran has been fighting a war with Iraq. Both countries claim control of the waterway through which the Tigris and Euphrates rivers flow into the Persian Gulf. The Iranian people have spent a lot of money for weapons. To make things worse, the war is being fought in Iran's chief oil-producing area.

The birth of modern Israel   Israel came into being out of the land called Palestine (pal′ ə stīn). Over the years, Palestine was ruled by the Jews, the Romans, the Arabs, and finally by the Turks. When Turkish rule ended in 1918, Britain promised to allow Jews to return and make a homeland in Palestine. A small number of Jews moved to Palestine and bought land from the Arabs who lived there. These Jews were **Zionists** (zī′ ə nists). They believed that a Jewish state should be formed as a homeland for Jews.

In the 1930s, Germany's dictator, Adolf Hitler, declared that all Jews were enemies of the state. Because of this, many Jews fled from Germany and the countries that Germany controlled. Many went to live in Palestine. Those Jews who did

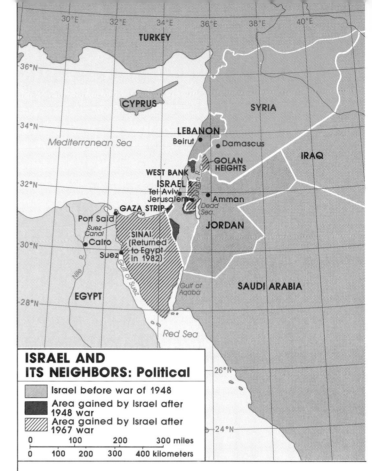

The state of Israel was created out of the part of the Middle East once known as Palestine.

not escape were put in slave labor camps or killed. After World War II many more Jews went to Palestine. The Jewish population in Palestine grew from 50,000 in the 1930s to 650,000 in 1948. By then, Jews made up about 40 percent of the total population of the area. Britain could no longer govern both Jews and Arabs peacefully. The United Nations proposed that Palestine be divided. In 1948, Israel became an independent country. The Arab **Palestinians** claimed that the new country was created on their land. Israel was immediately attacked by its Arab neighbors, who believed that Israel had no right to lands once held by Arabs.

The population of Israel has continued to grow, so that the estimated 1984 population is well over 4 million.

On a kibbutz, children are raised together in a common home and visit with their parents each day.

Israel tried to strengthen itself against its neighbors by building a strong army and air force. Israel also encouraged as much in-migration as possible. By 1972 there were more than 3 million Jews in Israel. Since the first war in 1948, Israel and its Arab neighbors—Syria, Jordan, Lebanon, and Egypt—have been involved in three other wars. In each war, Israel has defeated the Arabs and gained land from them. In 1979 a peace treaty was signed by Egypt and Israel. It is hoped that this treaty will prevent another war from breaking out.

Each time that Israel has gained Arab land, the number of displaced Palestinians has grown. Now that their homes and soil are part of Israel, these Arabs feel angry and uprooted. Some of these Palestinians have formed an organization whose aim is to retake Palestine by force. This is the Palestine Liberation Organization, known as the **PLO**. It is an army that is supported by Arab countries and allowed to operate in some of those countries, such as Syria and Lebanon.

Israel today Israel is a small country, and much of it is desert. With irrigation, farmers have turned much of the desert into farmland. Israel grows about three fourths of its own food and exports crops such as oranges and other citrus fruit. Some farms are privately owned, but many Israeli farmers belong to a community called a **kibbutz** (ki büts′). In a kibbutz the people work together and share all the property and income.

Israel has no great deposits of minerals, but it has done well with what it does have. The salty water of the Dead Sea has minerals in it. The Israelis have built a plant that evaporates the salty water and leaves the minerals behind.

Much of Israel's economy, however, has little to do with the land. Its leading import, for example, is rough diamonds and its leading export is worked diamonds. These are diamonds that have been cut and polished for industrial uses or for jewelry. Israel also has factories that make such products as shoes, textiles, tires, and machinery.

Today Israel is the richest Middle Eastern country that has no oil. The Israelis have shown that hard work and careful planning can overcome the lack of many natural resources. Israel has received help from Jewish groups outside of Israel and from friendly governments such as that of the United States.

Farmers in Israel have learned to grow crops that do best in Israel's soil and climate. Today, Israel is a leading producer of oranges.

This is a salt bed in Lebanon. When the seawater evaporates, crude salt is left.

Lebanon   When France took over part of the old Ottoman Empire, it divided its share of the land into several parts. One was called Lebanon, and it became an independent country in 1943. The new country was very small, and its population was only 1 million. Its religious makeup was more complicated than that of any other Middle Eastern country. A little more than half the Lebanese were Christians. About 45 percent of the population was Moslem, but it was divided. Nearly half were Sunnis, and a slightly smaller number were Shiites.

The government of Lebanon was formed in such a way as to keep a balance among all the groups. The president of Lebanon must be a Maronite Christian, the prime minister must be a Sunni Moslem, and the president of the legislature must be a Shiite Moslem. The legislature itself must be made up of 54 Christians and 45 Moslems. This ratio is based on the number of people in each religious group in 1932. No census has been taken since then because new figures would make new political problems. But every-

one in Lebanon knows that there are now 60 Moslems for every 40 Christians.

In 1975 a civil war broke out between Moslem and Christian groups in Lebanon. This war caused much destruction in Beirut (bā rüt'), the capital city. Other Arab countries sent troops into Lebanon to try to stop the fighting. In 1982 the Lebanese government asked France, Italy, and the United States to send soldiers to Lebanon to help keep the peace. Israel also became involved in the fighting. Beirut was attacked, and more of the city was left in ruins. The destruction of Beirut and the fighting in Lebanon have seriously hurt the country's economy. And the troubles in Lebanon threaten the future of all the Middle East.

CHECKUP

1. What changes did Mustafa Kemal Atatürk make in Turkey?
2. Where is Kurdistan? Why is it a problem area?
3. Why is Iran a Shiite Moslem country?
4. How was the modern country of Israel created?
5. Who are the Palestinians? What is the PLO?
6. What are the religious groups of Lebanon? How does religion affect government there?

One of the key factors in the Lebanese civil war is conflict over religious differences. Compare the situation in Lebanon to other areas in today's world where similar conflicts over religion are occurring.

16/CHAPTER REVIEW

KEY FACTS

1. Most of the Middle East has a desert climate.

2. The spread of the Arabic language throughout the Middle East is closely linked to the spread of Islam.

3. The oil fields of the Middle East were developed by Europeans after World War I.

4. The countries of the Middle East that are rich today are those that have developed their oil resources.

5. Jordan, Syria, and Iraq are poor countries that have often quarreled with each other and warred with Israel.

6. Turkey is the most modern and Western of the Moslem countries of the Middle East.

7. Iran is a Persian-speaking country that has political and economic problems.

8. Jews from different lands went to Palestine to build a homeland, which is now the state of Israel.

VOCABULARY QUIZ

On a sheet of paper write the term that correctly fills in the blank in each statement.

a. rift valley
b. fault line
c. Shiite
d. Sunni
e. conservative
f. OPEC
g. PLO
h. Zionist
i. revenue
j. Kurdistan

1. Most of the ___Shiite___ Moslems are found in Iran and Iraq.

2. The great majority of Moslems in North Africa and the Middle East follow the ___Sunni___ branch of Islam.

3. The organization established by a group of Palestinians to retake Palestine by force is called the ___PLO___.

4. The 15 million people of ___Kurdistan___ hope that their large region will someday be independent.

5. The organization that plays a big role in setting oil prices in the world is ___OPEC___.

6. Each long side of the Red Sea is a ___fault line___.

7. A Jew who wishes to make a homeland in Palestine is called a ___Zionist___.

8. A canyonlike hollow that was made when the earth's surface pulled apart is a ___rift valley___.

9. People who want to keep things as they are or as they were in the past are ___conservative___.

10. The foreign oil companies in the Middle East have to share their oil ___revenue___ with the governments of the various oil-producing countries in the region.

REVIEW QUESTIONS

1. What countries make up the Middle East?

2. What mountain ranges are found in the Middle East? Name the important rivers of the region. Which seas touch the coast of the Middle East?

3. What three major religions began in the Middle East? Which religion is practiced by most people in the region?

4. Why has life changed so greatly for many of the people living on the Arabian Peninsula?

5. What is the Bosporus? The Dardanelles? Why are they important?

ACTIVITY

Make a chart showing the following information for the countries of the Middle East: (a) area, (b) population, (c) capital city, (d) chief imports, (e) chief exports.

PLACE NAMES

USING MAPS

It is often easier to learn facts about the geography of a country from a map than from a written description. Listed below are statements about countries of the Middle East. In each statement there are blanks, each with a letter in it.

SKILLS PRACTICE

Using the maps on pages 249 and 251, find the correct words to go in the blanks. On a sheet of paper, complete each statement by writing the missing place names or figures after the letter of the blank. For example, the first answer is as follows:

1. **a.** Aden **b.** Arabian

1. The Red Sea flows south into the Gulf of **a.** _Aden_, which empties into the **b.** _Arabian_ Sea.
2. **a.** _Baghdad_, the capital of Iraq, is on the **b.** _Tigris_ River, which flows into the **c.** _Persian_ Gulf.
3. The capital of Iran is **a.** _Tehran_. If you went straight west from this city, you would reach the country of **b.** _Iraq_. If you went straight east, you would reach **c.** _The Soviet Union_.
4. Saudi Arabia has more neighbors than any other country in the Middle East. Its boundaries touch those of the following countries: **a.** _Jordan_, **b** _Iraq_, **c.** _Kuwait_, **d.** _Qatar_, **e.** _United Arab Emirates_, **f.** _Oman_, **g.** _Yemen (Aden)_, and **h.** _Yemen (San'a)_.

5. **a.** _Abu Dhabi_ is the capital of the United Arab Emirates. **b.** _Masqat_ is the capital of Oman. Which city is farther east? **c.** _Masqat_.
6. Turkey's boundaries touch three countries: **a.** _Syria_, **b.** _Iraq_, and **c.** _Iran_.
7. Traveling west from Turkey, you would reach the **a.** _Aegean_ Sea. If you continued traveling west across the sea, you would reach the country of **b.** _Greece_.
8. The **a.** _Elburz_ Mountains are located in northern Iran. They separate the **b.** _Iranian_ Plateau from the **c.** _Caspian_ Sea. The highest mountain peak is Mount **d.** _Damāvand_, with an elevation of **e.** _18,834_ feet, or **f.** _5,571_ meters.
9. The Strait of Hormuz is a narrow body of water connecting the **a.** _Persian_ Gulf and the Gulf of **b.** _Oman_.
10. **a.** _Beirut_, the capital of Lebanon, is north of **b.** _Jerusalem_, the capital of Israel, and west of **c.** _Damascus_, the capital of Syria.
11. Countries of the Middle East that border on the Mediterranean Sea are **a.** _Turkey_, **b.** _Syria_, **c.** _Lebanon_, and **d.** _Israel_.
12. Bahrain is a small island nation located in the **a.** _Persian_ Gulf. Its capital city is **b.** _Manama_.
13. Zardeh Kuh is the highest peak in the **a.** _Zagros_ Mountains. These mountains extend along and across the border between **b.** _Iran_ and **c.** _Iraq_.
14. The latitude and longitude of **a.** _Al-Kuwait_, the capital of Kuwait, is **b.** _29°N,48°E_. What capital city is located at 36°N, 51°E? **c.** _Tehran_.

6/UNIT REVIEW

Answer Key in back of book.

READING THE TEXT

Turn to page 257 and read the section "The Arabs." Then, on a sheet of paper, write the answers to these questions.

1. Name two important features of the Arab way of life that had great impact on North Africa.

2. Who were the Bedouins? Why did they migrate throughout North Africa?

3. Who were the fellahin? Why did they oppose the Bedouins?

4. How did the Berbers and the Copts react to Arab rule?

5. Why did the Arabs establish inland cities in North Africa?

READING A MAP

Turn to page 270 and study the map titled "The Middle East: Natural Resources." Then, on a sheet of paper, answer these questions.

1. In what area of the Middle East are most of the petroleum deposits found?

2. According to the map, what resource is found in the two countries of the Middle East called Yemen?

3. In which countries of the Middle East are coal deposits found?

4. Near which national capitals are phosphates found?

5. Name the country in the Middle East that has extensive irrigated agriculture.

READING A PICTURE

Turn to page 267. Study the picture and read the caption. Then, on a sheet of paper, write the answers to the following questions.

1. What is the name of the city shown in the picture?

2. Of which Middle Eastern country is this city the capital?

3. List the three major religious groups for which this city is a holy place.

4. Name the gate that serves as an entrance to the old section of this city.

5. How do you think people get from place to place in the old city? Explain your answer.

READING A TABLE

Turn to pages 252—253 and study the table, titled "North Africa and the Middle East." On a sheet of paper, answer these questions.

1. Name the largest country in North Africa and the Middle East.

2. Name the country in North Africa and the Middle East that has the largest population.

3. Name the country in North Africa and the Middle East that has the highest population density.

4. List the capital cities of North Africa and the Middle East that have populations over 1 million.

5. Which capital city in North Africa and the Middle East has the lowest population?

UNIT 7

AFRICA SOUTH OF THE SAHARA

To reinforce the many physical and cultural variations on the African continent, divide the class into committees. Assign each committee a country of sub-Saharan Africa on which to prepare an oral report. Specify that each committee include climate, vegetation, temperature range, natural resources, form of government, language, religion, GNP, and trade patterns in its research. Have each committee give its report when the chapter that deals with their country is studied.

A Large and Varied Region

Africa is the second largest continent. It is more than three times the size of Europe. Most of the 9 million square miles (14,480,000 sq km) of Africa lies south of the desert called the Sahara. This is sub-Saharan Africa, or Africa south of the Sahara.

Contrasts in the land and climate of Africa south of the Sahara are great. There are rain forests, grasslands, and deserts. The Equator crosses Africa. There are parts of Africa with hot, tropical climates where as much as 50 inches (127 cm) of rain falls each year. There are desert areas where little or no rain falls. In some parts rain falls every day; in other parts there are wet and dry seasons.

The climate affects the plant life of Africa south of the Sahara. Tall trees grow in the rain forests around the Equator. The ground is always wet because of the almost daily rainfall.

The savanna region lies to the north and south of the rain-forest region. Here the rainfall becomes more seasonal. The ground is covered with coarse grasses, and the trees tend to grow in thick clumps where water is most plentiful. The trees become more scattered as the land rises.

Grassland, semidesert, and desert form the next bands of vegetation to the north and south. Here the rainfall becomes less and less, and the land reflects the increasing lack of water.

Much of Africa south of the Sahara is more than 2,000 feet (610 m) above sea level. This elevated region is a plateau that rises from the sea. There are high mountains on the plateau, and there is also a deep valley. The Great Rift Valley runs north and south through the eastern side of the plateau. Many of Africa's most

AFRICA SOUTH OF THE SAHARA: Physical

★ National Capitals

| 0 | 400 | 800 miles |
| 0 | 400 | 800 | 1,200 kilometers |

Africa south of the Sahara is larger than the continent of North America. Most of Africa lies between the Tropic of Cancer and the Tropic of Capricorn. The southernmost tip of Africa is Cape Agulhas, where the Atlantic Ocean meets the Indian Ocean.

famous lakes are in the Great Rift. One of these lakes is a source of the Nile River. Find it on the map above.

Except for the Nile, all of Africa's major rivers are south of the Sahara. They all begin on the plateau and descend either east to the Indian Ocean or west to the Atlantic. Because they begin so far above sea level, there are many rapids and waterfalls on these rivers. Victoria Falls, on the Zambezi River, is twice as high and nearly twice as wide as Niagara Falls.

Point out that the Sahara is the world's largest desert. It is almost as large as the entire United States.

An excellent source to use with your pupils to highlight the early African kingdoms is Basil Davidson's beautifully illustrated book for young people, *African Kingdoms*.

Kingdoms Become Colonies

Africa may have been the first home of people. From what scholars have been discovering, it is possible that people existed in Africa long before they lived anywhere else. These people lived by hunting wild animals and gathering wild plants. Some of these early people knew how to use fire and simple tools. They were nomads. They moved from place to place gathering food crops.

Africans were farming about 10,000 years ago. Different groups at different times made the discovery that they could grow their food. Settlements developed, and people gave up the nomadic life.

Some of the settlements grew into powerful kingdoms. The kingdom of Ghana lasted for almost 700 years. At its most powerful, the kingdom included the territory of modern Mali and Mauritania. The kingdom of Ghana was replaced by the kingdom of Mali, which covered even more of West Africa. Arab merchants started to trade products from the east coast of Africa for goods from China and India. Eventually, city-states were established on the African coast. The kingdom of Kongo and the kingdom of Monomotapa, in what are now Mozambique and Zimbabwe, had highly organized systems of government. These kingdoms were also very advanced in the arts, especially in music and sculpture.

For a long time Africa was not known to Europeans except as a place that had to be sailed around on the way to Asia. The Europeans knew the African coastline. They did not care to brave the interior to learn about the rest of it.

One reason the Europeans did not explore the interior had to do with the African plateau. The rise to the plateau from the coast was a barricade that kept outsiders from coming in. The steep slope up to the highlands was, and still is, difficult to climb. It was, and is, even more difficult to travel inland by water. Can you imagine sailing up a waterfall?

Trade with Europe Begins

Although the Europeans rarely entered the interior, they did set up trading posts along the coasts. At first the Europeans were only interested in Africa for trade in slaves, some tropical products, and metals. The continent was difficult to enter and was well protected by the powerful African kingdoms. In addition, most of the land was too dry or too wet for Europeans to farm easily.

By the 1800s many different European countries had trading posts on the African coastline. Each European country claimed the land around and inland from each of its trading posts. To hold onto their claims, they sent Europeans to settle and to live on the land. The colonies that Europeans established did not follow the boundaries of the kingdoms of the African people. Sometimes Africans whose ancestors were enemies were grouped together in a colony. Sometimes a boundary between two colonies would separate people from friends and family in nearby towns. Breaking up the historic groupings of the African people made it more difficult for them to fight against the European invasion.

Slowly almost all places in sub-Saharan

Have pupils find definitions of the words *nation* and *state*. Discuss the difference between them. Point out that a colony is a political unit much like a state. Note that the European-drawn colonial boundaries in Africa divided African nations.

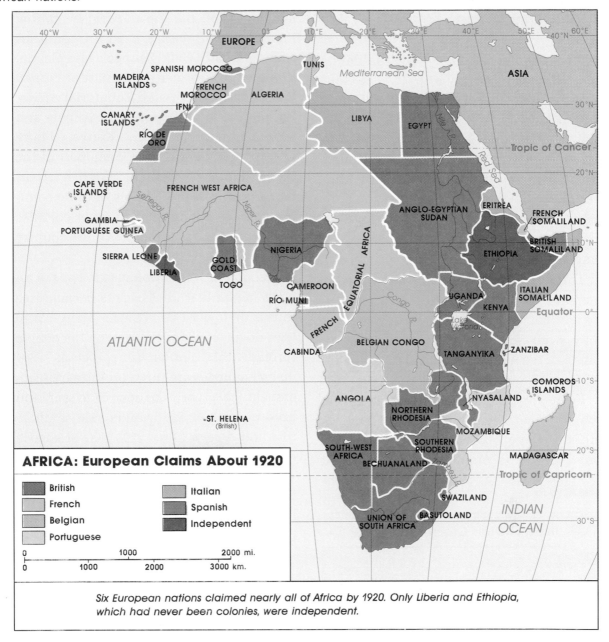

AFRICA: European Claims About 1920

- British
- French
- Belgian
- Portuguese
- Italian
- Spanish
- Independent

0   1000   2000 mi.
0   1000   2000   3000 km.

Six European nations claimed nearly all of Africa by 1920. Only Liberia and Ethiopia, which had never been colonies, were independent.

Africa became part of one or another European empire. When European countries had wars with each other, the African lands sometimes changed hands. Germany lost all its African colonies after World War I.

Look at the map on this page. It shows how Africa was divided among France, Great Britain, Belgium, Italy, Portugal, and Spain in 1920. Notice how mixed-up everything was! Not only were African groups divided in strange ways, but different European countries ruled neighboring colonies. This was a different experience from Latin America where, as you learned in Unit 3, only two countries— Spain and Portugal—did most of the colonizing.

Using the map on p. 285 as a source, have pupils list the colonies of Africa in categories according to the European countries that claimed them.

Independent Nations Emerge

The names of many African lands have changed since 1920. The Gold Coast is now Ghana. The Belgian Congo has become Zaire. Nyasaland is Malawi. Many cities that had European names now have African names. Salisbury, which was the capital of Southern Rhodesia, is now Harare, the capital of Zimbabwe. Léopoldville, named for the Belgian king who made the Congo part of his empire, is now called Kinshasa.

These changes in place-names were made as the nations of Africa became independent. The changes showed that they were no longer European colonies. Some of the new names came from the old African kingdoms.

Even though European countries no longer rule Africa, European influences are still there. The language of the colonial power is often one of the official

Most countries in Africa became independent within the past 30 years.

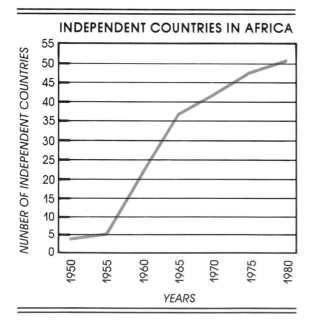

INDEPENDENT COUNTRIES IN AFRICA

YEARS

NUMBER OF INDEPENDENT COUNTRIES

languages of the new African nation. French is still being used in countries such as Chad, Mali, Senegal, and Gabon. These countries were once part of French West Africa and French Equatorial Africa. Portuguese is still spoken in Angola and Mozambique. Zambia, Kenya, Sierra Leone, and Nigeria were once part of the British Empire in Africa. English is still being taught in the schools of these countries today. Many of the former colonies also keep trade relations with the country that once ruled them.

Freedom from European rule has not always meant that all Africans became free to run their own countries. Many countries do have leaders chosen by the people through the democratic process. But many countries are ruled by military leaders who have used the armies to gain and hold power. Some leaders rule as dictators and do not allow freedom of speech or press. There are also some countries where the European part of the population, even though it is a minority, has not been willing to let black Africans take part in government. South Africa is an example of this situation.

The independent nations of Africa present a varied picture. Nigeria has a population of 84 million people. Equatorial Guinea has fewer than 500,000. The Sudan covers more than 967,500 square miles (2,505,825 sq km). São Tomé e Príncipe is only 372 square miles (964 sq km) in size. Ethiopia has been an independent nation for over 2,000 years. Zimbabwe became independent in 1980. Today there are over 50 independent nations in Africa. No other continent has that many.

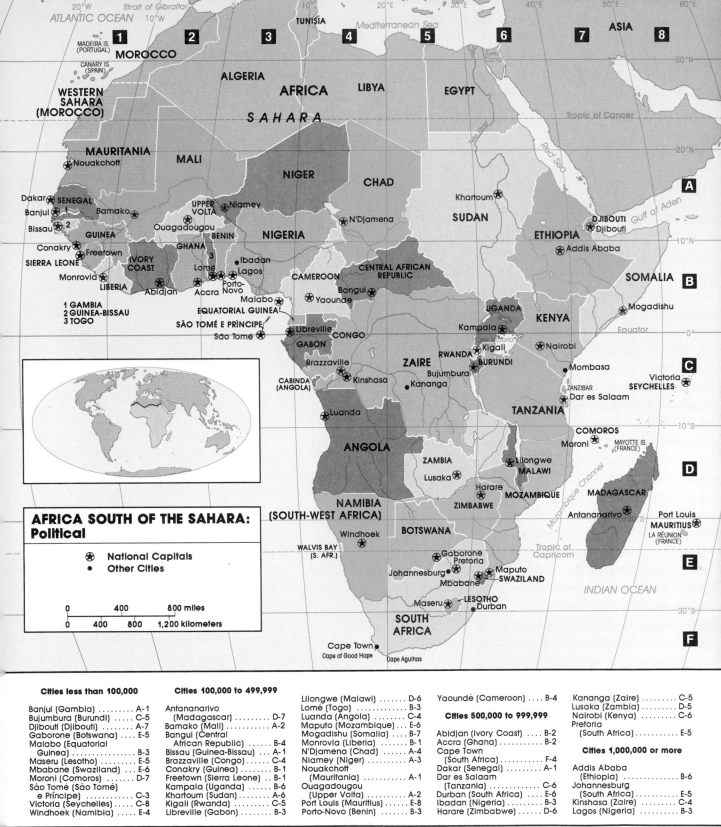

AFRICA SOUTH OF THE SAHARA: Political

★ National Capitals
• Other Cities

| 0 | 400 | 800 miles |
| 0 | 400 | 800 | 1,200 kilometers |

Cities less than 100,000

Banjul (Gambia) A-1
Bujumbura (Burundi) ... C-5
Djibouti (Djibouti) A-7
Gaborone (Botswana) E-5
Malabo (Equatorial
  Guinea) B-3
Maseru (Lesotho) E-5
Mbabane (Swaziland) ... E-6
Moroni (Comoros) D-7
São Tomé (São Tomé
  e Príncipe) C-3
Victoria (Seychelles) ... C-8
Windhoek (Namibia) E-4

Cities 100,000 to 499,999

Antananarivo
  (Madagascar) D-7
Bamako (Mali) A-2
Bangui (Central
  African Republic) B-4
Bissau (Guinea-Bissau) . A-1
Brazzaville (Congo) C-4
Conakry (Guinea) B-1
Freetown (Sierra Leone) . B-1
Kampala (Uganda) B-6
Khartoum (Sudan) A-6
Kigali (Rwanda) C-5
Libreville (Gabon) B-3

Lilongwe (Malawi) D-6
Lomé (Togo) B-3
Luanda (Angola) C-4
Maputo (Mozambique) ... E-6
Mogadishu (Somalia) ... B-7
Monrovia (Liberia) B-1
N'Djamena (Chad) A-4
Niamey (Niger) A-3
Nouakchott
  (Mauritania) A-1
Ouagadougou
  (Upper Volta) A-2
Port Louis (Mauritius) E-8
Porto-Novo (Benin) B-3

Yaoundé (Cameroon) B-4

Cities 500,000 to 999,999

Abidjan (Ivory Coast) B-2
Accra (Ghana) B-2
Cape Town
  (South Africa) F-4
Dakar (Senegal) A-1
Dar es Salaam
  (Tanzania) C-6
Durban (South Africa) .. E-6
Ibadan (Nigeria) B-3
Harare (Zimbabwe) D-6

Kananga (Zaire) C-5
Lusaka (Zambia) D-5
Nairobi (Kenya) C-6
Pretoria
  (South Africa) E-5

Cities 1,000,000 or more

Addis Ababa
  (Ethiopia) B-6
Johannesburg
  (South Africa) E-5
Kinshasa (Zaire) C-4
Lagos (Nigeria) B-3

Most African countries south of the Sahara became independent of their European rulers between 1957 and 1980. Ethiopia, however, became independent more than 2,000 years ago. Find the nation of Ethiopia on the map above.

Have pupils find and record the independence date for each of the countries shown on the above map, using a world almanac as their source.

AFRICA SOUTH OF THE SAHARA

COUNTRY	FLAG	TOTAL AREA	POPULATION and POPULATION DENSITY	CAPITAL CITY and POPULATION	WHERE PEOPLE LIVE
Angola		481,354 sq mi (1,246,700 sq km)	7,600,000 16 per sq mi (6 per sq km)	Luanda 475,500	
Benin		43,484 sq mi (112,622 sq km)	3,800,000 87 per sq mi (34 per sq km)	Porto-Novo 119,000	
Botswana		231,805 sq mi (600,372 sq km)	900,000 4 per sq mi (1 per sq km)	Gaborone 33,000	
Burundi		10,747 sq mi (27,834 sq km)	4,500,000 419 per sq mi (162 per sq km)	Bujumbura 79,000	
Cameroon		183,569 sq mi (475,442 sq km)	9,100,000 50 per sq mi (19 per sq km)	Yaoundé 274,500	
Cape Verde Islands		1,557 sq mi (4,033 sq km)	400,000 257 per sq mi (99 per sq km)	Praia 21,500	
Central African Republic		240,535 sq mi (622,984 sq km)	2,500,000 10 per sq mi (4 per sq km)	Bangui 302,000	
Chad		495,755 sq mi (1,284,000 sq km)	4,700,000 10 per sq mi (4 per sq km)	N'Djamena 281,000	
Comoros		838 sq mi (2,171 sq km)	400,000 477 per sq mi (184 per sq km)	Moroni 12,000	
Congo		132,047 sq mi (342,000 sq km)	1,700,000 13 per sq mi (5 per sq km)	Brazzaville 310,000	
Djibouti		8,494 sq mi (22,000 sq km)	300,000 35 per sq mi (14 per sq km)	Djibouti 62,000	
Equatorial Guinea		10,830 sq mi (28,051 sq km)	300,000 28 per sq mi (11 per sq km)	Malabo 37,000	

288

Urban ■ Nonurban □ Not Available — ▨

Using the tables on these pages as a source, ask which country has the highest population (Nigeria); the highest population density (Seychelles); the greatest area (Sudan).

AFRICA SOUTH OF THE SAHARA

COUNTRY	FLAG	TOTAL AREA	POPULATION and POPULATION DENSITY	CAPITAL CITY and POPULATION	WHERE PEOPLE LIVE
Ethiopia		471,778 sq mi (1,221,900 sq km)	31,300,000 66 per sq mi (26 per sq km)	Addis Ababa 1,242,500	
Gabon		103,347 sq mi (267,667 sq km)	700,000 7 per sq mi (3 per sq km)	Libreville 186,000	
Gambia		4,361 sq mi (11,295 sq km)	600,000 138 per sq mi (53 per sq km)	Banjul 45,500	
Ghana		92,100 sq mi (238,537 sq km)	13,900,000 151 per sq mi (58 per sq km)	Accra 564,000	
Guinea		94,926 sq mi (245,857 sq km)	5,400,000 57 per sq mi (22 per sq km)	Conakry 197,500	
Guinea-Bissau		13,948 sq mi (36,125 sq km)	800,000 57 per sq mi (22 per sq km)	Bissau 109,500	
Ivory Coast		124,504 sq mi (322,463 sq km)	8,900,000 71 per sq mi (28 per sq km)	Abidjan 560,000	
Kenya		224,961 sq mi (582,646 sq km)	18,600,000 83 per sq mi (32 per sq km)	Nairobi 835,000	
Lesotho		11,720 sq mi (30,355 sq km)	1,400,000 119 per sq mi (46 per sq km)	Maseru 45,000	
Liberia		43,000 sq mi (111,369 sq km)	2,100,000 49 per sq mi (19 per sq km)	Monrovia 171,500	
Madagascar		226,658 sq mi (587,041 sq km)	9,500,000 42 per sq mi (16 per sq km)	Antananarivo 400,000	
Malawi		45,747 sq mi (118,484 sq km)	6,800,000 149 per sq mi (57 per sq km)	Lilongwe 103,000	

Urban ▮   Nonurban ▮   Not Available – ▮   **289**

Have pupils who can draw prepare regional posters for East and Equatorial, West, and Southern Africa highlighting the flags of the countries in each region. Display for the class.

AFRICA SOUTH OF THE SAHARA

COUNTRY	FLAG	TOTAL AREA	POPULATION and POPULATION DENSITY	CAPITAL CITY and POPULATION	WHERE PEOPLE LIVE
Mali		478,767 sq mi (1,240,000 sq km)	7,300,000 15 per sq mi (6 per sq km)	Bamako 404,000	
Mauritania		397,956 sq mi (1,030,700 sq km)	1,800,000 5 per sq mi (2 per sq km)	Nouakchott 135,000	
Mauritius		790 sq mi (2,045 sq km)	1,000,000 1,266 per sq mi (489 per sq km)	Port Louis 144,500	
Mozambique		302,330 sq mi (783,030 sq km)	13,100,000 43 per sq mi (17 per sq km)	Maputo 354,500	
Namibia (South-West Africa)		318,251 sq mi (824,292 sq km)	1,100,000 3 per sq mi (1 per sq km)	Windhoek 64,700	
Niger		489,191 sq mi (1,267,000 sq km)	6,100,000 12 per sq mi (5 per sq km)	Niamey 225,500	
Nigeria		356,669 sq mi (923,768 sq km)	84,200,000 236 per sq mi (91 per sq km)	Lagos 1,061,000	
Rwanda		10,169 sq mi (26,338 sq km)	5,600,000 551 per sq mi (213 per sq km)	Kigali 117,500	
São Tomé e Príncipe		372 sq mi (964 sq km)	100,000 269 per sq mi (104 per sq km)	São Tomé 17,500	
Senegal		75,750 sq mi (196,192 sq km)	6,100,000 81 per sq mi (31 per sq km)	Dakar 799,000	
Seychelles		108 sq mi (280 sq km)	100,000 926 per sq mi (357 per sq km)	Victoria 23,000	
Sierra Leone		27,669 sq mi (71,740 sq km)	3,800,000 137 per sq mi (53 per sq km)	Freetown 214,500	

Urban ▉ Nonurban ▉ Not Available — ▉

AFRICA SOUTH OF THE SAHARA

COUNTRY	FLAG	TOTAL AREA	POPULATION and POPULATION DENSITY	CAPITAL CITY and POPULATION	WHERE PEOPLE LIVE
Somalia		246,201 sq mi (637,657 sq km)	5,300,000 22 per sq mi (8 per sq km)	Mogadishu 400,000	
South Africa		471,445 sq mi (1,221,037 sq km)	30,200,000 64 per sq mi (25 per sq km)	Pretoria 544,000	
Sudan		967,500 sq mi (2,505,813 sq km)	20,600,000 21 per sq mi (8 per sq km)	Khartoum 334,000	
Swaziland		6,704 sq mi (17,363 sq km)	600,000 89 per sq mi (35 per sq km)	Mbabane 24,000	
Tanzania		364,900 sq mi (945,087 sq km)	20,500,000 56 per sq mi (22 per sq km)	Dar es Salaam 852,000	
Togo		21,622 sq mi (56,000 sq km)	2,800,000 129 per sq mi (50 per sq km)	Lomé 229,500	
Uganda		91,134 sq mi (236,036 sq km)	13,800,000 151 per sq mi (59 per sq km)	Kampala 330,500	
Upper Volta		105,869 sq mi (274,200 sq km)	6,800,000 64 per sq mi (25 per sq km)	Ouagadougou 168,500	
Zaire		905,568 sq mi (2,345,409 sq km)	31,300,000 35 per sq mi (13 per sq km)	Kinshasa 2,444,000	
Zambia		290,586 sq mi (752,614 sq km)	6,200,000 21 per sq mi (8 per sq km)	Lusaka 641,000	
Zimbabwe		150,804 sq mi (390,580 sq km)	8,400,000 56 per sq mi (22 per sq km)	Harare 686,000	

Urban ■   Nonurban ■   Not Available – ■

291

Land and Water

VOCABULARY
geologic history

Snow in the middle of Africa Look at the map of Africa on page 283. Notice how much of Africa lies within the boundaries of the tropics and near the Equator. It is possible to assume that the continent is a hot, steamy jungle. Some parts of Africa, however, even places near the Equator, have snow.

Mount Kenya is right on the Equator, but because it is over 17,058 feet (5,199 m) high, its top has constant snow. Mount Kenya is in the country of Kenya. Nearby in the country of Tanzania (tan zə nē′ ə) is an even higher mountain, Mount Kilimanjaro (kil ə mən jär′ ō).

Most of eastern Equatorial Africa is either plateau or mountains. Other parts of Equatorial Africa are lower and have the hot, humid climate that is usual in the tropics.

Great Rift The history of the formation of the earth's surface is called **geologic history**. East and Equatorial Africa have a landscape created by a special event in geologic history. Millions of years ago a break, or rift, occurred in the plateau in the area now called East Africa. It created the Great Rift Valley.

Volcanoes Many centuries after the rift occurred, volcanoes erupted at places in the Great Rift Valley. Two of these are Mount Kilimanjaro and Mount Kenya.

The volcanoes have been a mixed blessing for East Africa. On one hand, the steep slopes and high elevations of the volcanoes make transportation and farming difficult. On the other hand, volcanic soil is rich in minerals. This means that areas in East Africa that do have flat farmland often have fertile soil.

The great lakes of Africa Almost all of Africa's large lakes are in East Africa. One of these, Lake Tanganyika (tan gən yē′ kə), is over 4,700 feet (1,430 m) deep. It is the second deepest lake in the world. A stone thrown into the lake would drop for nearly a mile before reaching bottom. Lake Victoria, the largest in Africa, is a shallow lake.

Lake Tanganyika is Africa's second largest lake. Lake Malawi (mə lä′ wē), in southern Tanzania and eastern Malawi, is the third largest lake in Africa.

The lakes have contributed to the economies of the East African countries in several ways. The land around the lakes is some of the best farmland in Africa.

The Nile River The Nile River is the longest river in the world. From its source in East Africa, it travels over

Mount Kilimanjaro is one of the scenic wonders of Africa. (3°S/37°E; map, p. 283)

4,000 miles (6,600 km) through the countries of Sudan and Egypt to its mouth at the Mediterranean Sea. Two branches combine to form the Nile. The branch which begins in the lakes of Uganda and Tanzania is called the White Nile. The Blue Nile has its source in Ethiopia.

For centuries the waters of the White Nile and the Blue Nile have been used to irrigate farmland. In Sudan the White Nile helps to create a vast, marshy area known as the Sudd. In recent times, dams have been built in many places along the rivers to control the flow of the water. Many people think these dams are necessary for irrigation and for hydroelectric energy. Other people worry that the dams may cause harm to plant and animal life, and even to farmland. In addition, governments have had serious disagreements over who controls the water and its use. Water is a valuable resource in the dry lands of East and North Africa.

The other great river   The Nile flows out of East Africa to the north. Another great river, the Zaire River, flows out of East Africa to the west. It flows through the lower land of central Equatorial Africa, through Africa's main rain forest area. The modern country of Zaire contains most of the river basin. You will learn more about the river when you study Zaire later in this chapter.

CHECKUP

1. Why are there cold places in Equatorial Africa?
2. What valley was formed by a break in the plateau in the area now called East Africa?
3. Where are the sources of the Nile River?

Resources of East and Equatorial Africa

┌─**VOCABULARY**─────────────────┐
copal   industrial diamond
cobalt
└──────────────────────────────┘

The land as a resource   For a long time, Africa was important to Europeans as a place for trade. There was trade in slaves and precious metals. Eventually, Europeans began to settle in Africa to take advantage of another African resource— the land. Forests were cleared, and plantations were started. The plantations produced cacao, palm nuts, rubber, and coffee. The highlands of Kenya attracted many Europeans. The climate there was better than in the lowlands. There were fewer disease-bearing insects.

The rain forests   The forests of Equatorial Africa are both a plus and a minus in the economy of the area. Valuable hardwoods, such as ebony and sandalwood, are found in the rain forests. **Copal**, a tree resin used in varnish, is also a product of the rain forest. Rubber and oil palm trees can also be cultivated in the equatorial climate. Palm oil is used in making soap and margarine. Equatorial Africa is one of the world's leading sources of palm oil.

Mineral resources   Most of the countries of East and Equatorial Africa lack mineral resources. The major exception is Zaire, which supplies most of the **cobalt**, diamonds, and much of the copper used throughout the world. Cobalt is a mineral used in producing a special, very hard steel.

Have pupils prepare a chart outlining the natural resources of the countries of eastern and equatorial Africa. Use the map on the facing page as the source of data.

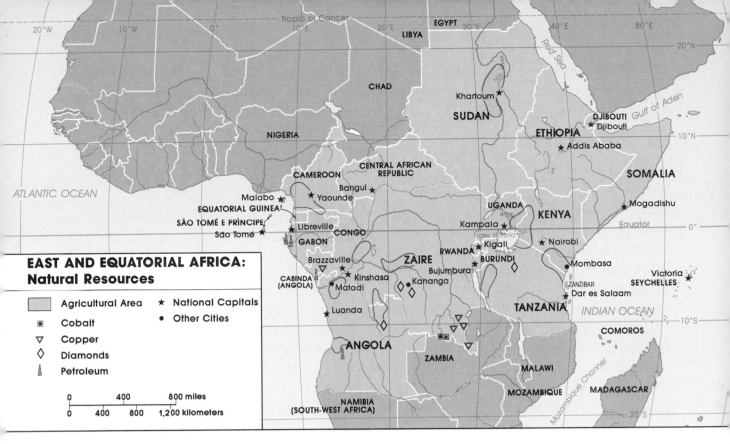

EAST AND EQUATORIAL AFRICA: Natural Resources

Agricultural Area
★ National Capitals
• Other Cities

▣ Cobalt
▽ Copper
◇ Diamonds
⚑ Petroleum

0   400   800 miles
0   400   800   1,200 kilometers

Many African countries have not yet begun to develop their rich mineral resources.

The diamonds that come from Zaire are not used in jewelry. They are **industrial diamonds.** The diamonds are very hard stones used in grinders, drills, and phonograph needles. Tanzania also produces industrial diamonds.

Other resources   The animal life of East and Equatorial Africa is another resource. Many valuable and unusual animals, from the antelope to the zebra, live there. They are exported to zoos all around the world. Tourists come to this region to see the animals.

Large national parks, like Tsavo National Park in Kenya, give the animals protection, yet allow people to see them in their natural environment. Tsavo covers an area of about 8,000 square miles

(20,720 sq km). The park is larger than the state of New Jersey. The land is high plateau country, broken here and there by a mountain peak. The vegetation is mostly brush that merges into scrub growth in the northern part of the park. This makes it possible for many different kinds of wild animals to live here. The existence of parks like Tsavo will protect many wild species that are scarce or in danger of extinction.

CHECKUP

1. What two plantation crops are important exports from East Africa today?
2. What country is the source of most of the world's supply of cobalt?
3. What is palm oil used for?
4. What would tourists go to Tsavo Park to see?

If there is a zoo in your area, invite a representative to visit your class and discuss the zoo's policy of acquisition and treatment of animals. Discuss the broader question of animal conservation.

East Africa

The East African landscape The large countries of Tanzania and Kenya, and the smaller countries of Uganda, Rwanda, and Burundi are often grouped together and called East Africa. Two other eastern countries are Ethiopia and Somalia. Find all these countries on the map on page 295.

The highland plateau rises very quickly just inland from the Indian Ocean coast. The lowland coastal strip, some 10 to 40 miles (16 to 64 km) wide, is the only rain forest in East Africa. The rest of the region has the range of climates you learned about when you studied about Latin American climates.

Cattle are a very important part of Tanzania's largely agricultural economy.

The land often is dry in East Africa. Much of the region has savanna vegetation. You remember that savanna is grassland with wet and dry seasons. Without irrigation the savanna land is difficult to farm. Cattle herding often is the best way to earn a living.

The Indian Ocean is also important to East Africa. The currents of the Indian Ocean made early trade between East Africa and Asia possible. When the winds blew west, the trading ships came to East Africa. When the winds blew east, the trading ships returned to Asia. Trade between Asia and East Africa still goes on today.

Tanzania in earlier years Tanzania was once two separate nations, Tanganyika and Zanzibar. Zanzibar was the island headquarters of the traders who sailed between Asia and Africa in pre-European times. The Arab traders brought the Islamic religion and Arabic architecture to East Africa. They also brought many Arab and Indian people to Africa. The descendants of these people are part of the East African population today. Many East African people, especially on the islands and coast, are of mixed Asian and African background. The **Swahili** language, which is spoken widely in East Africa, has many Arabic, Persian, and Indian words.

Zanzibar eventually became a British colony. Tanganyika was originally a colony of Germany, but after World War I it too came under British control. The British ruled these two countries until the early 1960s. After independence, Zanzibar joined Tanganyika to form Tanzania.

The slopes of Mount Kilimanjaro and Mount Kenya are major agricultural areas of Kenya and Tanzania. The cooler temperatures in these highland areas are well suited to the cultivation of coffee.

Agriculture in Tanzania For their own food, farmers in Tanzania grow cassava, beans, and grains such as corn, millet, and wheat. When they have enough land, they also grow some crops for sale. Depending on the climate, these crops might be coffee, cotton, tobacco, tea, or **pyrethrum** (pī rē′ thrəm). The flowers of the pyrethrum plant are used in making insecticides. Another special Tanzanian crop is **cloves**, a spice of very high value. Most of the world's cloves come from the Tanzanian islands.

Ethiopia and Kenya These are two of Africa's most important countries. Ethiopia has a long history of independence. Its rugged landscape helped protect it from foreign invasion. Ethiopia has been a kingdom since the fourth century A.D.

Africa Hall in Addis Ababa (ad ə sab′ ə bə), Ethiopia's capital city, is an important building. It is the headquarters of the Organization of African Unity, to which over 40 African nations belong.

Kenya is an important coastal country. The landlocked countries of Uganda, Rwanda, and Burundi use its ports. The railroad that carries goods from these interior countries to Kenya's port of Mombasa is famous because it has a very steep roadway. It travels from high altitudes to sea level. On its way from the rich farmlands near Lake Victoria to the Indian Ocean, it passes through Nairobi (nī rō′ bē), Kenya's largest city.

How far inland is Nairobi from Mombasa? How much higher is it?

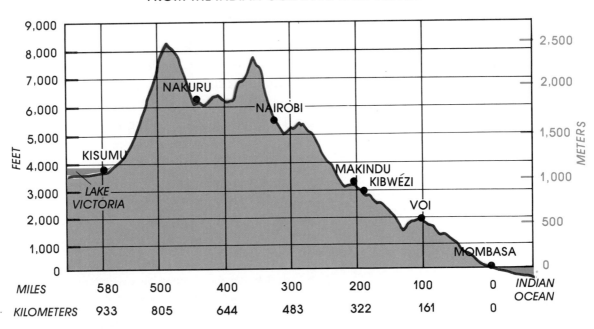

A CROSS SECTION OF KENYA'S RAILROAD ROUTE:
FROM THE INDIAN OCEAN TO LAKE VICTORIA

Jomo Kenyatta: African Leader

JOMO KENYATTA was one of the leaders who fought for independence in Africa. He was born in the late 1880s in what later became part of the British colony of Kenya. Kenyatta's grandfather was a respected leader of the Kikuyu people.

Kenyatta received a modern education. He first attended a mission school. Later he lived in England for 15 years. He studied anthropology and wrote an influential book, *Facing Mt. Kenya.* It is about Kikuyu life and customs.

The more Kenyatta traveled and studied, the more convinced he became that Africans should rule their own countries. In 1946 he returned to Kenya and became a leader of the nationalist movement. Many Africans joined in the fight for independence from Great Britain. Some fought with violence and terrorism. Others fought with words. All of them viewed Kenyatta as a leader. The British government imprisoned Jomo Kenyatta for many years.

Finally, in the early 1960s, the British freed both Kenyatta and the country he loved so dearly. Kenya became an independent nation, and Kenyatta became its first president. He worked hard to equalize opportunities for black and white Kenyans. Jomo Kenyatta was known as the "grand old man" of African independence. He died in 1978.

Other East African countries The countries of Uganda, Rwanda, and Burundi are poor even though they are located in the Great Rift Valley with its rich, volcanic farmland. They are Africa's most densely populated countries. Somalia, far to the east on the "horn" of Africa, is large in size but has fewer people than either Rwanda, or Burundi. Most of the people are nomadic herders who live on the dry, scrubby land.

Problems to overcome There are two serious problems in East Africa today. One is the presence of diseases such as malaria and sleeping sickness. These diseases weaken people. The countries of East Africa do not have enough money to provide medical care for all the people who need it. It is also very difficult to control the spread of these diseases. Malaria is carried by mosquitoes, and sleeping sickness is carried by the tsetse fly. The tsetse fly also carries a disease that kills cattle and other livestock.

The other problem is the need for education. The people of East Africa are still suffering from the lack, in earlier times, of opportunities for schooling. The countries are trying to overcome this problem. Tanzania, for example, spends about a fifth of its budget on education. But there is still a long way to go before all 12- and 13-year-old children will be able to attend school.

CHECKUP

1. How did the currents in the Indian Ocean help early trade between East Africa and Asia?
2. What is Swahili?
3. Where is the headquarters of the Organization of African Unity?

Children in East African countries are not required to go to school. Education is highly prized and students are very competitive.

It has taken over 12 years to build the entire Inga hydroelectric project. It is one of the largest in the world. Zaire is able to export electricity to surrounding countries as a result of this project.

Zaire and Its Neighbors

VOCABULARY	
navigable	bureaucrat
Bantu	exploitation

A large forest country   Zaire is the main country of Equatorial Africa. It is a large country with as much land as the United States east of the Mississippi River. It is sparsely populated, however, and has only as many people as live in the states of New York and Pennsylvania.

About half of the country is rain forest. In the equatorial lowlands it rains heavily all year round. Vegetation is thick, especially along the rivers. For a long time these thick rain forests helped keep the Europeans who explored the rivers from learning much about the land.

Higher and drier land is found in eastern and southern Zaire. In some places it is mountainous, and in others it is hilly or flat. Coffee, tea, and cotton are produced in these nontropical areas.

A giant of a river   The Zaire River, the world's seventh longest, swings through the country, crossing the Equator twice. As you can see from the map on page 295, the Zaire River has three main branches, each extending into different parts of the country. The three branches have thousands of islands, hundreds of waterfalls, and a rich supply of fish.

In spite of its waterfalls, the Zaire is an important river for transportation. Long stretches of the Zaire are **navigable**—able to be traveled by boat—and offer very good transportation because the water flows evenly and steadily throughout the year.

The waterfalls of the rivers are important as sources of hydroelectric power. Because it is a valuable source of energy for producing electricity, a waterfall is sometimes called "white coal." Zaire has more sources for hydroelectric power than any other country in the world. Some of the greatest places for hydroelectric power occur in the 200 miles (320 km) of the Zaire River between Kinshasa (kin shäs′ ə) and Matadi (mə täd′ ē), where the river is full of waterfalls and rapids. Zaire is still developing this power.

Early kingdom of the Bantu-speakers
The country and the river of Zaire both used to be called the Congo. *Congo* or *Kongo*, were the European spellings of the name of a powerful kingdom that traded with the Europeans from the 1500s to the 1800s. The Kongo was one of

The Inga Dam near Matadi will help develop Zaire's great hydroelectric potential. (6°S/14°E; map, p. 295)

The original inhabitants of Zaire were the Pygmies, a nomadic food-gathering people who were dispersed by the migration of the Bantu into the area.

several kingdoms of the **Bantu**-speaking peoples. Bantu is a family of African languages. Most native peoples of sub-Saharan Africa speak one of the Bantu languages.

About 2,000 years ago the center of the Bantu civilization was in part of what is now Zaire. At that time the Bantu-speaking people began to travel from Zaire throughout sub-Saharan Africa, making new settlements. The Bantus knew how to make iron and how to farm. In the rain forests they became farmers of yams. In the better farmland near Lake Victoria, they grew bananas. And in dry lands too poor for farming, they learned to herd animals such as cattle and sheep. The best use of the land was made in each area. Each group of people was organized under a government, which was usually headed by a king.

The kingdom of the Kongo was one of the largest Bantu nations. The king,

called the Mani Kongo, was believed to have god-given powers. He ruled over a highly organized government of six provinces, each with its own governor. Under the governors were province supervisors, district **bureaucrats**, and village leaders. A bureaucrat is a person in charge of a government department or bureau.

Colonial development   For several centuries European countries traded with the African kingdoms and sent missionaries there, without attempting to conquer the kingdoms. During the 1800s, however, European rulers were influenced by adventurers who braved the African interior and wrote exciting reports about what they saw.

King Leopold II of Belgium was one of these rulers. He hired Henry Stanley, an explorer who knew Africa well, to claim an African kingdom for him. Stanley tra-

This illustration shows an old map of the city of Lovango in the Kongo kingdom. *Do you think the Europeans were impressed by this city in the ancient kingdom of Kongo?*

veled along the Zaire River and claimed the area south of it for King Leopold. It was called the Congo Free State. Later it became the Belgian Congo.

The land to the southwest of the Belgian Congo was a colony of Portugal for many years. Today it is the independent nation of Angola. The lands to the north of Zaire were colonies of France. Today they are independent countries called Congo, the Central African Republic, Gabon, and Cameroon.

For the African people the colonial period was painful. Some people say that the European countries helped the Africans by building railroads, bridges, ports, and cities, all of which made greater trade possible. However, the colonizers took away the rulers and governments of the early African kingdoms.

People, problems, and prospects Since 1960, when it became independent, Zaire has had problems developing a strong government. Some foreign companies seek to take products from Zaire at a large profit for themselves leaving little for the people of Zaire. This is called **exploitation.** Most of Zaire's people still lack schooling. Many people who want to work cannot find jobs. Governments have a hard time governing well when problems such as these exist.

Zaire is a land of great resource wealth. In addition to some of the world's richest supplies of hydroelectric power, copper, cobalt, and industrial diamonds, it has zinc, tin, and uranium. The drier and higher lands produce high-quality coffee, tea, and cotton. The forest lands produce bananas and rice.

Most people in Zaire are still subsistence farmers. The food that comes from small farms often is not enough to support a large family. Many families have sons and daughters who have moved to other places to try to make a living.

Today 30 percent of the people in Zaire live in cities. Kinshasa, with over 2 million people, is one of the large cities of Africa. It is a busy port.

Neighboring countries Zaire's neighbors also have gained independence recently. Angola, the largest of these, did not become independent from Portugal until 1975. It is a large country, much larger than Texas and California combined. Angola has petroleum deposits that are bringing in new capital.

Gabon, the Republic of the Congo, Cameroon, and the Central African Republic gained independence in 1960. They are countries with many tropical forests. Some of the tropical trees are valuable exports. Gabon is a large exporter of wood from the okoume (ō kə mā′) tree, which is used in making plywood. Gabon also has important petroleum deposits.

These countries export other tropical products such as coffee, cacao, cotton, and bananas. They use the large port cities of Libreville in Gabon, Pointe-Noire (pwant nə wär′) in Congo, and Douala (dů äl′ ə) in Cameroon.

CHECKUP

1. What is Zaire's "white coal"?
2. Name three European countries that had colonies in this part of Africa.
3. What resource is a source of wealth for Angola and Gabon?

Belgium did not prepare the Africans of Zaire sufficiently for self-government. For example, when independence came, there were only 30 university graduates in the entire country.

301

17/ CHAPTER REVIEW

KEY FACTS

1. The Nile River and the Great Rift Valley are two important physical features in East Africa.

2. The exports of East and Equatorial Africa are largely agricultural or forest products.

3. Zaire is a leading source of the world's supply of cobalt, industrial diamonds, and copper.

4. National parks protect African wildlife and are tourist attractions.

5. Most of the native peoples of sub-Saharan Africa speak one of the Bantu languages.

6. There were several powerful pre-colonial kingdoms in this part of Africa.

7. Most of the countries of East and Equatorial Africa were colonies of European countries until quite recently.

VOCABULARY QUIZ

On a sheet of paper write the letter of the term next to the number of its definition.

a. exploitation	f. navigable
b. geologic history	g. Bantu
c. cobalt	h. bureaucrat
d. industrial diamonds	i. pyrethrum
e. copal	j. cloves

d 1. Hard stones used in grinders and drills

g 2. A family of African languages

a 3. Taking too large profits from a nation

j 4. A spice

h 5. A person in charge of a government department

c 6. A mineral used in making a very hard steel

e 7. A tree resin used in varnish

i 8. A plant used in making insecticides

b 9. The history of the formation of the earth's surface

f 10. Able to be traveled by boat

REVIEW QUESTIONS

1. What special event in geologic history took place in East Africa?

2. What kind of mountains are Mount Kilimanjaro and Mount Kenya?

3. The waterfalls on the Zaire River are both good and bad for the country. Name one way in which the waterfalls are helpful and one way in which they are harmful.

4. To what language family do the languages spoken by most people in Zaire and neighboring countries belong?

5. Name the European countries that colonized (a) Zaire, (b) Angola, and (c) Zanzibar (now a part of Tanzania).

6. Name the two serious diseases that affect people in Tanzania and other parts of tropical Africa.

ACTIVITIES

1. You have learned about many different countries in this chapter. Pick one of them and learn more about it by using reference books in your library. Write a one-paragraph report that tells something about the country you chose and that gives the source in which you found your information.

2. Each of these people was important to the history of one of the countries in this chapter: Julius Nyerere, Patrice Lamumba, Henry Morton Stanley, Jomo Kenyatta, Haile Selassie, David Livingstone. Write a report about one of them.

3. On separate sheets of paper, trace the outlines of three of the countries you have studied in this chapter. Use the map on page 295 as a guide. Then see whether your friends and classmates can guess the name of each country from your outline maps.

WHAT A MAP SHOWS

A vegetation map shows the plant-life patterns of an area. A map can show quite specific types of vegetation for a small area. Or it can show a general pattern for a large area, such as a continent. These large-scale patterns are worldwide. Approximately the same vegetation appears in approximately the same latitudes. The distribution of vegetation depends on landforms, soil, and climate.

There are three basic types of vegetation: forests, grasslands, and deserts. There are many variations within each basic type. Rain forests have broad-leaved evergreen trees. The temperature is high all year round, and there is a great deal of rainfall. A savanna is a type of grassland. The grass in a savanna, however, grows in clumps rather than in stretches of tall or short grasses. There are also trees scattered over a savanna. The rainfall is very seasonal; there are long periods of little or no rain. The climate in the Mediterranean zone is temperate and produces a mixed vegetation of various types of trees, plants, and grasses. Deserts get so little rainfall that vegetation is very sparse.

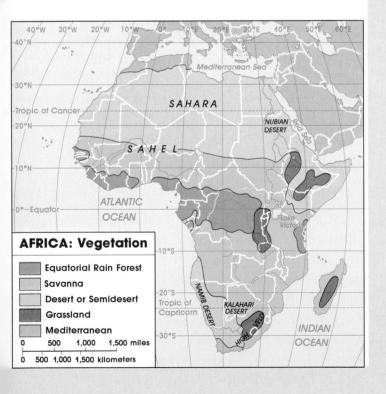

AFRICA: Vegetation

- Equatorial Rain Forest
- Savanna
- Desert or Semidesert
- Grassland
- Mediterranean

0   500   1,000   1,500 miles
0   500 1,000 1,500 kilometers

SKILLS PRACTICE

Look at the map on this page to identify the vegetation patterns in Africa.

1. List the types of vegetation found in Africa and after each write the key color that identifies each type.
2. Where are the two areas of Mediterranean vegetation in Africa? Do you think the same types of crops can be grown in both places?
3. Along which line of latitude is the major rain forest area in Africa?
4. What are the two largest vegetation areas in Africa?
5. Which one borders the rain forest area?
6. Which vegetation area lies outside the tropic zones?
7. Are the vegetation zones north and south of the Equator similar?
8. What other kind of map would be useful in studying vegetation? Why?

303

18 Southern Africa

Landscape and Resources

High land and low land   The African plateau covers most of Southern Africa. It is especially high in the southeast, where altitudes range from over 4,000 feet to 6,000 feet (1,219 to 1,828 m) above sea level. The plateau drops sharply to the low land near the sea. The steep **escarpment**, or slope, makes it difficult to travel inland. This escarpment curves around the southern tip of the African continent like a fortress wall.

Most of the land in Southern Africa is either high, on the plateau, or low, near sea level. The upland grassland is called the **High Veld**. The term comes from the Dutch, who were the first Europeans to come to Southern Africa to stay. The High Veld is similar to the Great Plains of the United States.

Different climates   The southernmost tip of Southern Africa lies in the middle latitudes rather than in the tropics. The climate here was healthier for Europeans than that in tropical Africa and was good for growing European-type fruits, vegetables, and grains. This climate is similar to that of Mediterranean Europe. Not all of Southern Africa can be cultivated, however. The Namib (nə mib´) Desert on the west coast gets less than 5 inches (13 cm) of rain a year. Often the rain evaporates before it reaches the ground. Very little plant life is possible. Farther inland the land is higher and a little wetter. There is enough rain for grasses to grow, and even for scrubby forests. This is the Kalahari (kal ə här´ ē). It is often called a desert, but actually is an example of semidesert climate and vegetation. Find these areas on the map on page 283.

Semidesert, or semiarid, and savanna   On the edge of the desert and reaching through the central part of Southern Africa, almost to the east coast, is a climate zone known as semidesert, or semiarid. *Arid* means "dry." *Semiarid* means "partly dry." The land in this climate zone is too dry to grow good crops. Rainfall ranges from 10 to 20 inches (25 to 50 cm) a year.

Little grows here except clumps of short grass, cacti, and small, woody bushes. Often the steppe land can be made productive if irrigation is possible. So far the countries of Southern Africa with large areas of steppe have not been able to afford modern irrigation. Namibia (nə mib´ ē ə) and Botswana (bot swän´ ə) are two of these countries.

The African plateau rises sharply behind the city of Cape Town near the Cape of Good Hope at the southern end of Africa. (34°S/18°E; map, p. 283)

Have pupils check the daily temperature range of Pretoria listed in the local newspaper. Contrast this temperature range with the listing for a tropical African city, such as Dakar. Ask: How might these contrasting temperatures help explain the pattern of European settlement in Africa?

The country of Zimbabwe (zim bäb' wē) also has some semidesert land. However, most of Zimbabwe is savanna land. Zimbabwe, Zambia (zam' bē ə), and the northern part of Malawi (mə lä' wē) are dominated by highland savanna. The savanna in upland areas in Southern Africa has mild temperatures, even during the rainy season.

The rains in savanna lands come down so fast and hard that they erode the rich soil. Sometimes they damage crops. During the dry season the earth dries out and cakes in a hard, warped surface. Plants turn brown, and windy dust storms sweep up loose particles of soil. Food can be scarce until the next rainy season.

Rivers   Three main rivers cut through the plateau in Southern Africa. The Orange River flows from South Africa westward to the Atlantic Ocean. The Limpopo River flows eastward from Botswana and Zimbabwe to the Indian Ocean. It forms the border between those countries and South Africa. The Zambezi River begins in Angola and flows east and south through the countries of

The Zambesi River forms part of the border between Zambia and Zimbabwe. This bridge over a gorge cut by the river links the two countries.

Have each pupil prepare a chart listing the countries of southern Africa shown on the map below together with the mineral resources found in each of these countries.

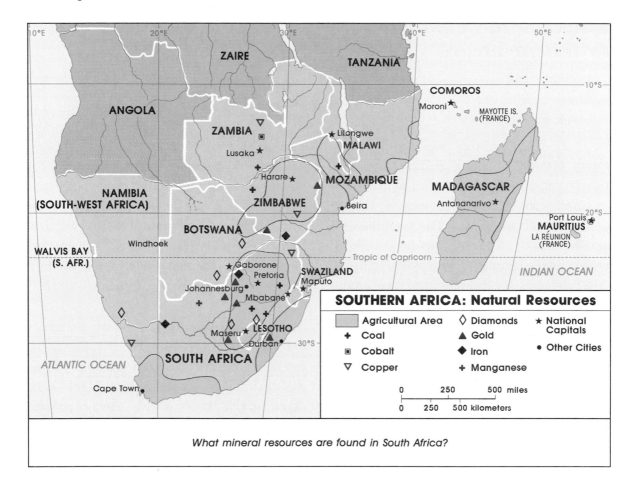

SOUTHERN AFRICA: Natural Resources

- Agricultural Area
- + Coal
- ▣ Cobalt
- ▽ Copper
- ◇ Diamonds
- ▲ Gold
- ◆ Iron
- + Manganese
- ★ National Capitals
- ● Other Cities

0   250   500 miles
0   250   500 kilometers

What mineral resources are found in South Africa?

Zambia and Mozambique (mō zəm bēk′) to the Mozambique Channel in the Indian Ocean.

The Zambezi is one of Africa's large rivers. It is 2,200 miles (3,540 km) long. Unfortunately, like the other African rivers, it is not navigable in many places. There are many dangerous rapids and waterfalls. Victoria Falls is very beautiful. Many tourists visit the falls each year.

The Kariba (kə rē′ bə) Dam was Africa's first hydroelectric project. It is on the Zambezi River on the border between Zambia and Zimbabwe. Kariba Lake, created by the building of the dam, is one of the largest of its type in the world.

Mineral wealth Some countries of Southern Africa have mineral wealth. Zambia is a leading source of copper and cobalt. Zimbabwe has important coal deposits. South Africa has a wide variety of valuable minerals and gems. It is the world's leading supplier of diamonds and gold. South Africa also has supplies of platinum, manganese, chromium, asbestos, coal, and uranium.

CHECKUP

1. What part of Southern Africa is in the middle latitudes?
2. Name two countries with a large amount of savanna land.
3. Name three minerals that Southern Africa has in large amounts.

Point out that South Africa occupies only about 4 percent of Africa's area but has almost 50% of the continent's mineral wealth. **307**

You might want to assign Activity 1 on p. 314 at this time.

Kingdom to Colonies to Independence

> **VOCABULARY**
> **Boer**
> **black nationalism**

Early history   Long before the Europeans came, there was one large kingdom in Southern Africa. It was a highly developed civilization. The people were skillful farmers. They knew how to work with metal. Some of the stone temples and fortresses built during the time of the Zimbabwe kingdom are still standing.

The Europeans came   Portuguese sailors looking for a route to India were the first Europeans to see South Africa. This was in 1488. It was nearly 200 years later that the first European settlers arrived. The Dutch East India Company founded a colony at what is now Cape Town to serve ships going to and from the East Indies.

By 1795 the colony had a population of 60,000. Twenty thousand were whites. The rest were black Africans, slaves, and people of mixed ancestry. These early Dutch settlers in South Africa were known as **Boers**, which is Dutch for "farmers." The British took over the colony in 1814. South Africa became independent in 1931.

The colonial period   The British became more and more interested in the rest of Southern Africa as they became aware of the riches of the area. By 1900, Cecil Rhodes, an Englishman, had expanded English rule well into the interior of Southern Africa.

During the twentieth century many white people came to farm the land and to direct the mines. Black Africans provided the labor for the European farms and mines. White families had control of the good farmland. They enjoyed good schools, health care, and large houses.

Colonial policies were different for blacks and whites. The policies favored the white settlers. Gradually, however, Great Britain softened these policies. Black people in its colonies were treated more fairly. In the 1950s, Great Britain began to cooperate with blacks.

New independence   One of the forces behind the independence of many African countries is **black nationalism.** Black nationalism is the idea that black Africans ought to control their nations. Black nationalists fought very hard in many of these countries to end colonial rule. In countries where white Europeans remained in control after independence, the black nationalists had to fight again to gain power. Today the countries of Zimbabwe, Zambia, Malawi, Mozambique, and Madagascar (mad ə gas′ kər) are independent nations.

Sometimes black nationalists do not agree on how a country should be run. Sometimes they make mistakes. Sometimes they fight each other. As independent nations, these countries are young and still learning and growing.

CHECKUP

1. What was the name of the precolonial kingdom in Southern Africa?
2. Who were the Boers?
3. What is black nationalism?

The word *Zimbabwe* means "house of stone." People who lived in this early African kingdom were skilled at constructing stone buildings.

South Africa and Its Neighbors

> VOCABULARY
>
> apartheid
>
> protectorate

Land of factories and farms Both manufacturing and agriculture are important to the South African economy. The chief manufactured goods are clothing, processed foods, chemicals, and metal items, including iron and steel products. As you can see from the list, South African factories can fill the needs of the country for manufactured goods. South Africa does not have to depend on other countries for these items. Most of the factories in South Africa are in or near the cities of Pretoria, Johannesburg, Durban, Port Elizabeth, and Cape Town. Find these cities on the map on page 481.

South Africa has some of the best farmland in the world. Many kinds of crops are grown here. This is because there are several different climates in South Africa.

The first type of climate and farmland is Mediterranean agriculture. The Mediterranean climate is good for growing fresh fruit, especially grapes, and for wheat. The wheat is grown in the winter months of June and July. Most of this kind of farming is done within 100 miles (160 km) of the coast, where rainfall is plentiful. It is quite dry farther inland. Here sheep and cattle are raised.

The second type of climate and farmland is the subtropical sugar lands. They are in the coastal area near the city of Durban. Behind the coastal lowland is the Drakensberg escarpment, where the bold, peaked edge of the African plateau is at its highest. Moist winds blowing inland from the Indian Ocean rise abruptly at the Drakensberg escarpment, losing their moisture in the form of rain.

The upland hilly grassland of the plateau in Southern Africa is the High Veld. It is the third type of climate and farmland. The rainfall is seasonal, but the High Veld has a good underground water supply. Windmills pump the water from wells. Farmers of the High Veld grow most of the corn in South Africa. They feed the corn to beef cattle.

The High Veld first became an important farming area in the 1800s. At that time, people of Dutch ancestry had serious disagreements with newly arriving British settlers and fled to the High Veld. The High Veld might have remained only a farming area if two discoveries had not been made there in the 1860s and 1870s.

Farms on the High Veld tend to be large, with many acres of open fields. Crops such as corn, wheat, and hay are as easily grown here as they are on the Great Plains of the United States.

South Africa's farms are able to produce all of the food needed by the country's people.

Nearly 2 million pounds (almost 1 million kg) of ore must be processed to produce 1 gold bar that weighs approximately 27.5 lb (400 troy oz) and is slightly smaller than a building brick.

Fine gems and metals   The discovery of diamonds and gold quickly brought fortune hunters, mining camps, and British capital to the High Veld.   Today, South Africa is the world's leading supplier of gold and diamonds.   Almost all the gold comes from the High Veld, especially from a region called The Rand. Johannesburg, the most populated city in sub-Saharan Africa, is in The Rand.   So is Pretoria, another important South African city.

The gold and diamonds allowed South Africa to pay for many things that have turned it into a modern, industrial nation. Other important minerals, such as uranium and chromium, which were discovered later, also contributed to the growth of South Africa.   The country can afford the costly building of railroads and roads from the seacoast up the great escarpment.   It can pay for expensive irrigation systems for dry farmland.   It has capital to support good schools and universities. It is able to construct good houses with electricity and modern plumbing.   Some South Africans live a comfortable life.

Apartheid—a forced separation   As you learned earlier, Europeans, particularly the Dutch, have lived in South Africa for hundreds of years.   They think of themselves as Africans.   For generations their families have known no other homeland.   The white Africans control the government of South Africa.   They are afraid that if the black nationalist movement takes hold in South Africa, they will lose their homes and everything they and their ancestors have given to South Africa.

Casting melted gold into bars is the last step in a process that begins with crushing the mined ore into small particles.   These bars are nearly 100 percent pure gold.

As an example of South Africa's wealth and modernization in comparison with the rest of Africa, note that this country has about half of the telephones in all of Africa.

South African law enforces **apartheid** (ä pärt' hāt). Apartheid is the forced separation of nonwhites and whites. By law they cannot attend the same schools or live in the same places. They are paid different wages. The law does not allow black families to buy houses in white cities. Instead, black families who work in white cities live in fenced-off communities outside the cities. Soweto (sō wə' tō), one of these black urban areas, has a population of about a million people.

In recent years the government has assigned many South African black people new places to live. It calls these places black homelands. The homelands make up 13 percent of South Africa's land.

The homelands are areas of poor land. They do not have modern transportation or housing or jobs. Since there are no jobs in the homelands, the wage earners of a family, usually the parents, have to seek work in South Africa's cities and mines. The children remain in the barren homelands. The South African government claims that it is helping black Africans become independent by making them live in these separate places.

South Africa's neighbors   Botswana, Lesotho (lə sō' tō), and Swaziland (swäz' ē land) are three of South Africa's neighbors. Find them on the map on page 307. Until recently they were British **protectorates**. A protectorate is an area under the control of another country. It is different from a colony in that it is expected to become an independent nation after a period of time. Botswana, Lesotho, and Swaziland became independent black nations in the late 1960s.

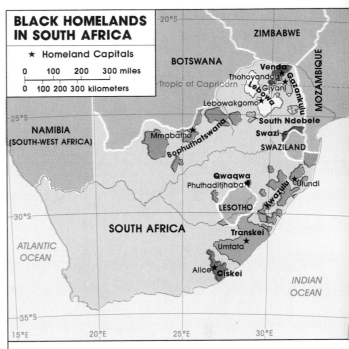

BLACK HOMELANDS IN SOUTH AFRICA

★ Homeland Capitals

0   100   200   300 miles

0   100 200 300 kilometers

There are ten homelands. Imagine the difficulty of forming strong nations from scattered land areas.

These three countries are landlocked. They have few opportunities for trade with other nations. They are poor countries. Many of their citizens work in South Africa. Botswana does have some important diamond mines. Swaziland has a variety of farmland and exports agricultural products.

Another of South Africa's neighbors still is not an independent nation. Namibia used to be called South-West Africa. The country is a protectorate of South Africa. It is trying to gain independence.

CHECKUP

1. Name three resources of the High Veld.
2. What is apartheid?
3. Name three landlocked neighbors of South Africa.
4. Which country in Southern Africa is still not independent?

The African chief Moshesh built a fortress in the hills of Lesotho and successfully overcame attacks of the Boers and British throughout the first half of the nineteenth century.

Zimbabwe and Its Neighbors

┌─VOCABULARY─────────────┐
│ sisal   │
│ Malagasy   │
└────────────────────────┘

The new Zimbabwe   In 1980 a new government came to power in Southern Rhodesia. The people gave their country the name of the old African kingdom— Zimbabwe. The new government faces many problems. Within the country's boundaries are people who were at war with each other before colonial times. Among the citizens of the country are white people whose ancestry is British but whose families have lived on their African farms for generations.

Zimbabwe has many resources but very little capital with which to develop them. The country is landlocked. Zimbabwe has to pay high transportation costs to participate in world trade.

Zimbabwe is working to make improvements. Coal from the rich deposits in western Zimbabwe is used to fuel new industries. Factories are clustered in Harare, the capital city, and in Bulawayo. There is an iron and steel plant at Que Que. The Zambezi River continues to be a good source of hydroelectric power.

There is good farmland in the high plateau country. Tobacco, beef, and grain are important farm products. Zimbabwe has most of the resources it needs for development. Its biggest worry is the newness of its government.

Zambia and Malawi   Zambia lacks good farmland. Much of its land is too swampy to farm or is infested with the tsetse fly. You remember from an earlier chapter that the tsetse fly carries serious diseases that harm people and animals.

Zambia's most important resource is copper. Huge deposits of this mineral, possibly as much as one fourth of the world's copper supply, are found in a region of Zambia called the Copper Belt. Ninety percent of the money Zambia gets from exports comes from copper. When other countries pay a high price for copper, the Zambian economy benefits. From time to time, however, the world copper price falls. This brings unemployment and hard times to the Zambian

Which country shown on this graph is most dependent on the export of a single item? What is the resource? What problems might this country have in the future?

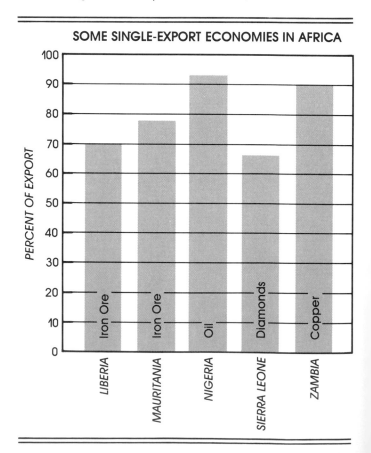

SOME SINGLE-EXPORT ECONOMIES IN AFRICA

PERCENT OF EXPORT

- LIBERIA — Iron Ore
- MAURITANIA — Iron Ore
- NIGERIA — Oil
- SIERRA LEONE — Diamonds
- ZAMBIA — Copper

Among the other single-export economies in sub-Saharan Africa are Burundi (coffee comprises 88 percent of its exports); Ghana (cocoa, 75 percent); Chad (cotton, 62 percent); Somalia (livestock, 68 percent).

people. Whenever a country has only one major resource, its people are always in a state of uncertainty about the future.

Malawi is another landlocked country with an uncertain future. Malawi is a narrow, mountainous country. Farming is the basis of the country's economy. Malawi exports tobacco and tea. Without many mineral resources and with little industry, Malawi is one of this region's poorest countries.

Mozambique and Madagascar Mozambique is a coastal country with lowlands near the coast. The land rises to plateaus in the west. Most of the country has a tropical climate with rainy and dry seasons.

Mozambique was a colony of Portugal until 1975. It became independent only after a long period of warfare between the colonial government and black nationalist fighters.

Mozambique is a poor country. Many of its people travel to South Africa to work in the mines of the High Veld. Farmers in Mozambique grow cashew nuts and **sisal** (sis′ əl). Sisal is used to make rope and twine. Farmers also grow crops for the local food markets.

Mozambique's two important ports of Maputo (mə püt′ ō) and Beira (bā′ rə) are often used by the landlocked countries of the region. Maputo is also an important port for the Transvaal area of South Africa.

Madagascar, also known as the Malagasy Republic, is different from the other countries you have been studying. It is an island nation. Located 250 miles (400 km) off the coast of Mozambique in

It takes about 100 pounds (45 kg) of sisal to make 4 pounds (2 kg) of fibers 20–50 inches (50–127 cm) long.

the Indian Ocean, it is the fourth largest island in the world. It is almost 1,000 miles (1,600 km) long.

A ridge of rugged mountains runs the length of Madagascar. Sometimes the slopes are terraced for rice farming. Rice is the main food of the people of Madagascar. Most of the people are subsistence farmers. Madagascar produces more vanilla than any other country. There is little mineral wealth on the island. The few small industries produce tobacco, food products, and some textiles and leather goods.

Madagascar became independent from France in 1960. French is one of the official languages of the country. The other is **Malagasy.** This language is different from the other African languages. It is related to Malay and Indonesian.

CHECKUP

1. Name one problem the new government of Zimbabwe faces.
2. On what does the Zambian economy depend?
3. How is Madagascar different from other African countries?

Madagascar has a large Indonesian population, which can trace its history on the island back to ancient times.

18/CHAPTER REVIEW

KEY FACTS

1. The African plateau covers most of Southern Africa.
2. The Kalahari and Namib are desert-like areas in Southern Africa.
3. The Zambezi River cuts through the African plateau and is a source of hydroelectric power.
4. Three types of agriculture are practiced in South Africa.
5. Many parts of Southern Africa are rich in mineral resources.
6. Great Britain, France, and Portugal had colonies in Southern Africa. Their colonies are all independent nations now.

VOCABULARY QUIZ

Read the following statements. Decide which are true and which are false. Write your answers (**T** or **F**) on a sheet of paper.

F 1. Sisal is a breed of African cattle.

T 2. A plantation is a large farm where cash crops are raised.

T 3. Black nationalism led to the independence of many colonies in Africa.

T 4. Apartheid is a South African policy that keeps groups of people separated.

F 5. Malagasy is an important mineral resource in Mozambique.

T 6. The High Veld is a farming area in South Africa.

F 7. The Boers were early French settlers in South Africa.

T 8. An escarpment is a side of a plateau that drops sharply to sea level.

F 9. A protectorate is a part of the country set aside for the black population in South Africa.

F 10. The tsetse fly is a constant danger to Africans who live in the semidesert areas.

REVIEW QUESTIONS

1. Why was Southern Africa a good place for European settlement?
2. Name three kinds of climates found in Southern Africa.
3. What are three agricultural products of Southern Africa? What are three important mineral resources?
4. Name two discoveries made in South Africa's High Veld.
5. What are the black homelands?
6. When did most of the colonies in Southern Africa get their independence?

ACTIVITIES

1. Cecil Rhodes was a very important person in African history. Look in an encyclopedia or other reference book to learn what he did in Africa. Write a report about Rhodes from the point of view of a British imperialist (a person who believes colonies are a good thing) or from the point of view of a black nationalist.

When you have finished writing your report, you and a classmate who took the opposite view could have a debate on the topic "Resolved: Cecil Rhodes was good for Africa."
2. Collect stories about the African countries in this chapter from recent newspapers and magazines. Prepare a report that summarizes the articles. You may wish to include a map.
3. Prepare ten true-false questions about the material in this chapter. Exchange questions with a classmate.
4. Make a list of the ways the following can be used: gold, copper, chromium, asbestos.
5. Write a story about how the discovery of gold in the High Veld affected a Boer, an English person looking for gold, and a black African.

MAKING A GRAPH FROM A TABLE

STUDYING URBAN GROWTH

A city's size is measured by the size of its population. Growth in a city's size is called urban growth.

Until recently, Africa had few large cities. Most people lived in rural areas and farmed the land. Today most families in Africa still live in rural areas. But now when the children grow up, they move to cities to seek work.

Africa's cities are growing very rapidly. About every 10 years each country takes a census. The number of people who live in each place is counted. This table shows the census figures from 1940 to 1980 for seven African cities. You can see how the cities have grown by studying the figures. You can also make a graph showing the growth of the cities' population. A graph allows you to see the pattern of growth quickly and easily.

SKILLS PRACTICE

If possible, use graph paper to do this activity. You may use regular lined or unlined paper if graph paper is not available. Near the bottom of the paper, make a horizontal line at least 5 inches long. Then make a perpendicular line at least 9 inches long that joins the horizontal line at the left-hand side. Divide the horizontal line into five equal parts and label each section with a date—1940 to 1980. Divide the perpendicular line into 18 equal parts. Label these sections with numbers starting with 100 and ending with 1,800. Under the horizontal line write *YEAR* and along the perpendicular line write *THOUSANDS OF PEOPLE*. Now plot the urban growth of the cities listed in the table. Above each year, place a dot that indicates the size of the population in that year.

When you have marked all the dots for one city, connect them with a line. To plot the growth history of the different cities, use a different color or line pattern for each. Be sure you make a key identifying the city that each color or line pattern represents. Add a title to your graph. Make your work as neat as possible.

GROWTH PATTERN OF SEVEN AFRICAN CITIES					
City	1940	1950	1960	1970	1980
Johannesburg, South Africa	286,000	880,000	1,111,000	1,152,000	1,772,000
Lagos, Nigeria	180,000	230,000	449,000	875,000	1,168,000
Cape Town, South Africa	187,000	594,000	746,000	807,000	1,476,000
Addis Ababa, Ethiopia	150,000	402,000	449,000	684,000	1,668,000
Nairobi, Kenya	100,000	112,000	267,000	535,000	1,275,000
Harare, Zimbabwe	51,000	120,000	270,000	390,000	863,000
Kano, Nigeria	89,000	100,000	119,000	190,000	289,000

CHAPTER
19 West Africa

The Physical Region

VOCABULARY

mangrove   commerce
Sahel

Location   Look at the map of Africa on page 283. Notice how the western side of the continent bulges out into the Atlantic Ocean. This bulge is the region we call West Africa. It lies between the Sahara and the Gulf of Guinea, which is part of the Atlantic Ocean. Also notice that there are many countries in this West African region.

Coastal wetlands   The West African coast is in the rainy, tropical climate zone. Rain forests cover much of the land. The soil there is leached by heavy, frequent rains.

Part of the coastal region is **mangrove** swamps. These are areas of very dense vegetation. Mangrove wood is used for fuel, and tannin comes from the bark. The mangrove tree has a very unusual root system. Part of it is above the water. These roots are hard and stiff. They look like bare tree branches. The rest of the roots go deep into the soil below the water. They keep the soil from washing away. A mangrove swamp can be drained and can become very good farm-

land. However, the countries in this part of the world are too poor to be able to drain very much of this swampland and thus add to the food supply.

Interior dry lands   The interior part of West Africa is a plateau. It is higher and drier than the coast. Savannas replace the thick vegetation of the rain forest. The temperature is still hot, but the rain is less and falls mainly in the summer. This is because the winds bringing rain blow from the Atlantic only in the summer. In the winter the winds blow from the direction of the Sahara. The closer the land is to the desert, the drier it is.

Between the savanna lands and the desert is an area called the **Sahel** (sə hel'). The Sahel has a semidesert climate. The rainy season is too short for good crop production. Drought is a constant danger in this area. Vegetation will die out forever if a drought lasts long enough. Then there is nothing to hold the soil, which blows into dust and sand. This happened in the Sahel in the late 1960s and early 1970s. The sands of the Sahara began to drift southward into the Sahel since there was no vegetation to hold them back. Between 1970 and 1980 the Sahara moved 75 miles (120 km) farther south.

The trees in the rain forest form a continuous cover that allows very little light to filter down to the forest floor. In certain delta regions of western Africa, the rain forest gives way to coastal mangrove swamps.

Have pupils prepare for a spelling bee based on the names of the countries to be studied in this chapter and those studied in the previous two chapters.

Using an outline map, have pupils draw in and label the rivers of West Africa. Point out that, except for the Niger, the rivers are fairly short and flow directly from the interior plateau to the sea.

Rivers and ports The Niger River is one of Africa's important rivers. Find it on the map on page 283. Notice that it flows north and then south through a large part of West Africa. The Niger has been used for hundreds of years as a river of **commerce.** Commerce is trade and business between people. For many centuries, merchants from the northern dry lands would exchange salt and dates for products from the southern rain forests.

Shorter rivers flow from the plateau area to the south or west coast. One of the most important of these is the Volta River. Its waters are used to make hydroelectric power.

On the coast are a number of ports. Most are modern. Freetown, in Sierra Leone (sē er ə lē ōn′), has one of the world's perfect natural harbors. Other ports are Dakar (də kär′), in Senegal (sen i gôl′); Accra (ə krä′), in Ghana (gän′ ə); and Lagos (lā′ gäs), in Nigeria (nī jir′ ē ə). Railroads have been built from the ports into the interior of the countries to bring goods to the coast.

Resources Ghana used to be called Gold Coast. This name tells how important one of West Africa's resources was. Some gold is still being mined there. Other resources that were valuable trading items were ivory, spices, and ostrich

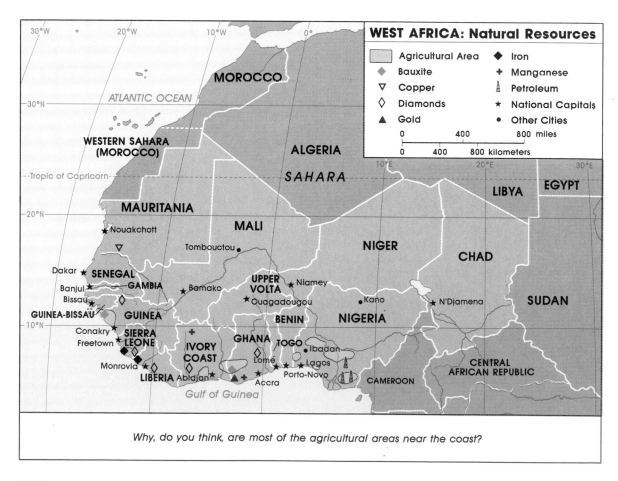

WEST AFRICA: Natural Resources

Why, do you think, are most of the agricultural areas near the coast?

The search for more oil goes on in Nigeria. Instruments that measure seismic waves locate underground formations that could be petroleum deposits.

The People of West Africa

The nations of West Africa The word *nation* can mean "a group of people who have the same language and traditions." People in a nation see themselves as belonging together. By this definition there are hundreds of nations in West Africa.

The country of Nigeria is a good example of how these nations have become part of the modern West African countries. People have been living in what is now Nigeria for at least 10,000 years. Scientists have found iron-smelting furnaces in Nigeria that date from the fourth century B.C. They belonged to the Nok people. The Nok made tools and other objects from stone and clay, as well as metal. They were a farming people.

Other groups came later. The Yoruba (yō′ rü bä) organized territory west of the Niger River into city-states around A.D. 1000. The Yoruba were **artisans,** or craftworkers. They worked in brass and bronze that they imported from North Africa. The Ibo (ē′ bō) lived on the delta of the Niger River. They were a farming people. The river was a barrier between them and the Yoruba. The Hausa (hou′ sä) lived in the northern part of what is now Nigeria. They were linked by trade to North Africa rather than to the ports on the coast. They were Moslems and thought of themselves as quite separate from the people to the south. There are still Yoruba, Ibo, and Hausa today. They

feathers. Another resource that was a popular trading item in the fourteenth century and is still traded today is the kola nut. In the past, people chewed it; today it is used to flavor soft drinks.

The newest resource for development is oil. Other important West African mineral resources are bauxite, iron ore, and diamonds. Phosphate, used in fertilizer, tin, uranium, and manganese are exported by West African countries.

Most of the wealth of West Africa, however, comes from its farms and forests. You will learn more about the West African economy later in this chapter.

CHECKUP

1. Where are the rain forests of West Africa?
2. What is the Sahel?
3. Why is the Niger River important?
4. Name three mineral resources of West Africa.

In the traditional society, Africans passed down their history orally. A historian at the French Institute for Black Africa stated that when an old man in Africa dies, it is as if a library has been burned.

are the three major groups among the over 200 nations of modern Nigeria.

If you look at a map of modern West Africa, such as the one on page 318, you will see that Nigeria is one of 16 countries. Where are the hundreds of nations in West Africa?

The European colonizers   The Europeans came to West Africa for the same reason they came to the rest of the continent—trade.   Portugal was the first country to trade with nations in West Africa.   In the 1700s, England and France built trading posts on the coast.   The names they gave these areas—Ivory Coast, Gold Coast, and Slave Coast—tell what was traded.   Eventually the Europeans moved into the interior and established colonies.

The colonies ignored the African nations.   Different nations, or groups that had nothing in common—neither language nor customs—were included in one colony.   Sometimes the African population of a colony would consist of nations that had been at war with each other.   The nations within a colony often were held together only by the fact that they were a colony.   The only language they had in common was the language of the colonizer.   The map on page 285 shows which European country controlled which colonies.

The new African states   When the colonies became independent, they became states.   A state is a political unit with definite recognized boundaries.   Many of the old problems still exist in these new states.   The many nations must still learn to live together, to share power, and to give up some of their traditions in order to build good governments and strong states.

Living and working in West Africa
The cities of West Africa are very much like cities in other parts of the world. This is true even of cities such as Tombouctou (tōm bük tü'), or Timbuktu, in Mali; and Kano, in Nigeria.   These cities were important commercial centers long before the Europeans came.

Men and women in West African cities today dress the same as business people anywhere in the world.   People wearing traditional clothing are also a common sight in the cities.   The roads are filled with the traffic of cars, buses, and bicycles.   People are speaking English or French or one of the national languages.

People in West African urban areas work in factories, offices, and stores. Many shopkeepers are women.   Women are also often the sellers in the open-air markets that exist in many West African cities.   As the chances for higher education improve for women, more women are also becoming doctors, scientists, and government officials.

The basis of the economies of the West African countries is agriculture.   Many people are farmers.   In the wet coastal areas, farmers build houses with frames of wood or bamboo plastered with mud. Roofs are grass or tin.   Food crops are usually root-crops such as yams.   The cash crops—cacao, palm oil, and rubber—come from trees.   Farms are small.

Farmers learned long ago that soil in wetlands could be made richer by adding

SLASH-AND-BURN FARMING

1. Trees and brush are cut down.
2. The area is burned.
3. Seeds are planted.
4. Crops are grown.
5. The forest takes back the land.

Slash-and-burn farming is also called shifting cultivation. Can you guess why?

wood ashes. They developed **slash-and-burn farming.** In this system of farming, farmers cut, or slash, tree branches and other plant growth, and let it dry so that it will burn. Then they burn the dried vegetation, clearing the ground and enriching the soil at the same time. After this they plant crops, using whatever tools they have. In modern times their tool is usually a metal hoe, but in earlier times it was a simple digging stick.

After several years the soil loses its fertility, and the farmers clear and burn a new piece of land. Wild vegetation is allowed to grow in the used-up field. In 10 or 20 years, the soil has new nutrients,

and people return to farm the land. The slash-and-burn system works well for simple farming as long as there is enough new land. In most places, however, land is not plentiful.

In the north, houses are usually made of mud bricks, which last a long time in this area of little rainfall. The food crops are grains such as millet and corn. Peanuts, called groundnuts in Africa, and cotton are the major cash crops.

The peanut is the only nut that grows underground.

CHECKUP

1. Who were the Nok people?
2. Why are English and French important languages in West Africa?
3. What are groundnuts?

Have pupils describe and discuss the process of slash-and-burn farming. Ask: What problems do farmers who practice this type of farming face? (Limited crops, few tools, and lack of land are possible answers.)

The Countries of West Africa

---VOCABULARY---
| lagoon |

Nigeria <u>More people live in Nigeria than in any other African country. It has a variety of resources. Petroleum is an especially important one.</u> Nigeria has several large cities and 13 universities. To visit Nigeria is to visit a diverse and growing country.

Nigeria has swamps along its coast, then rain forests farther inland, and savanna lands in its interior. In the far north the savanna lands become semi-arid land, or steppe.

Southeast of Nigeria are the Cameroon Mountains, and the country of Cameroon that you read about in Chapter 17. To the west are the small countries of Benin (bə nin') and Togo.

More people live in southern Nigeria than in the northern part of the country because the land in the south has more moisture for farming. The south also is where many of Nigeria's large cities are located.

In 1980 there were over 1 million people living in Lagos, the capital of Nigeria. Many of them have moved there recently from farming villages. They have come to look for work in one of the many factories of the growing city, or in the shipyards. Lagos handles most of Nigeria's international commerce.

The name *Lagos* comes from a Portuguese word meaning **"lagoon."** A lagoon is a large, shallow body of water near a larger body of water. The city of Lagos is located on an island in the large lagoon off the Nigerian coast. This location hinders the growth of the city since it limits the places where new houses can be built. People crowd together in tiny houses to be able to live near their jobs in the city. Supplying a growing population with housing, fresh water, and sewage removal is a major problem.

All Nigerian cities have modern stores and other business buildings. They also have open marketplaces where sellers arrange their goods on the ground or on simple tables. These city markets are the original shopping malls—that is, places that offer a wide variety of goods and where people go as much to look as to buy. The markets are lively, happy places where families see their friends and exchange news.

International trade is very important to the economy of busy modern Lagos. (6°N/3°E; map, p. 287)

Miryam: Subsistence Farmer of Africa

Planting, weeding, hoeing, walking, carrying—this is how African subsistence farmers, many of whom are women, must spend their days. The work of the farm must be done by hand.

Miryam is the farmer in her family. She has three children. Her younger son is still a baby. She wraps him in a long cloth that she ties around her body so that she can carry him on her back as she works in the fields. The fields are far from the house. Miryam's older son and daughter must work there with her.

Hoeing and digging in dry earth is hard work. The back-breaking work of planting and weeding is harder still. Food is scarce and there is little protein in the diet. Miryam and her family are hungry all day long.

People in subsistence farming villages must process their own food. They must grind and cook the grain they have grown. Wood fuels the cooking fire. Finding wood is the hardest part of Miryam's day. Often she must walk many miles from the village to find fallen branches. She carries bundles of branches on her head all the way back to her house. Wood becomes more and more scarce, since even young trees are cut for fuel.

No water is piped into Miryam's village. She and her children must carry all the water the family uses from a distant spring.

When there is work from dawn to dusk, there is little spare time in the day of a subsistence farmer.

The desert "shore" The countries to the north of Nigeria are not so fortunate. They are part of the Sahel. *Sahel* is an Arabic word meaning "shore." The Sahel is the "shore" of the great desert. Waves of aridity, or dryness, sweep over the villages of the Sahel without warning. Even in the best of years, the land is so dry that most farmers can never grow enough to live comfortably.

The Sahel is part of the large West African countries of Chad, Niger, Upper Volta, Mali, and Mauritania (môr ə tā′ nē ə), and of the smaller countries of Senegal, Gambia, and Cape Verde. Together these countries form an area about two thirds the size of the United States. They are sparsely populated. Only about 30 million people live in this large area.

The countries of the Sahel are poor, and most people are simple farmers. Farmers grow groundnuts, cotton, and food crops. Some people are nomads, tending herds of cattle and goats in a continual search for grass.

Life in the Sahel has always been difficult. People there spend a great deal of their time searching for water, digging for water, and carrying water from wells to their crops and animals. When every drop of water used has to be hand-carried in buckets and bowls, it takes a lot of strength and steady work just to stay alive.

A great drought hit the Sahel between 1968 and 1973. Water holes dried up. Grass died. Nomads had to watch their animals get thinner and thinner as they

In traditional West African society, men were hunters or herders. Today it is common for men to go to the cities for work. **323** wandered in search of grasslands that they never found. Many nomads, as well as their animals, died of thirst and starvation. Without water, farmers could not grow crops. Without food, many farmers died. It was a time of famine, when large numbers of people died for want of food.

Normal rains began again in 1974. Still, the water resources of the Sahel are not enough to support all of the people and animals that live there. The threat of drought and famine is still present.

Landlocked, poor countries   Today, Mali, Niger, Chad, and Upper Volta are among Africa's poorest countries. They are landlocked and must ship their goods through other countries to the coast. If they were on the coast, they could market palm oil, groundnuts, and mineral resources much more economically.

Niger has large uranium reserves. Reserves are natural resources that have not yet been used. Mali has reserves of bauxite, iron ore, copper, and phosphate. Chad also has uranium and iron ore. The mineral wealth of Chad was one reason why Libya invaded that country in 1981.

Strong economies to the south   Both Ghana and Ivory Coast have the variety of resources that leads to a strong economy. They have good agricultural land as well as mineral resources. They have hydroelectric power. With the recent building of artificial harbors, both have good ports. Many people are moving to Ghana and Ivory Coast in search of work.

Ghana's mines still supply gold and diamonds, which have been mined for centuries. Bauxite is even more impor-

Elmina Castle in Accra was built during the days of the slave trade. Trading forts were the start of European colonial rule. (5°N/0°; map, p. 318)

tant to the modern economy of Ghana. Both Ghana and Ivory Coast have large aluminum-smelting industries.

Ghana and Ivory Coast have rich farmlands. They are among the world's leading producers of cacao. Ivory Coast also exports large amounts of coffee.

Most of the cacao, coffee, and aluminum is exported through new ports, such as Tema near Ghana's capital of Accra. The coastal cities have large modern downtown areas. Some of the forts and castles of early trading days still stand amidst the modern buildings. Elmina Castle in Accra was one of these early trading forts. Today it is used as a government office building, but it is a reminder of Ghana's early trade in slaves, gold, ivory, and spices.

CHECKUP

1. What is unusual about the city of Lagos?
2. How do most people in the Sahel make a living?
3. Why are Niger, Chad, Mali, and Upper Volta among the poorest African countries?
4. Which two West African countries have aluminum-smelting industries?

19/CHAPTER REVIEW

KEY FACTS

1. There are many countries in the region of West Africa.
2. There are wet rain forests on the West African coast and drier savanna to semiarid steppe lands in the interior.
3. The Sahel is a physical feature of many West African countries.
4. There are many modern cities in West Africa.
5. Even though West Africa is rich in mineral resources, the basis of the region's economy is agriculture.

VOCABULARY QUIZ

On a sheet of paper write the letter of the word or words that correctly complete each sentence.

1. Farmers in wetlands use a traditional method of farming called (a) cash cropping, (b) slash-and-burn, (c) contour plowing.
2. In West Africa the land area between the savanna region and the great northern desert is called the (a) Sierra, (b) Sahara, (c) Sahel.
3. A political unit with definite, recognized boundaries is a (a) neighborhood, (b) state, (c) company.
4. A craftworker can also be called an (a) artisan, (b) architect, (c) alchemist.
5. A tree that grows in swamps is a (a) mongoose, (b) migrant, (c) mangrove.
6. A group of people who have the same language and traditions can be called a (a) nation, (b) notion, (c) notation.
7. A period of no rainfall is a (a) draft, (b) drought, (c) drift.
8. Unused natural resources are (a) reverses, (b) reveres, (c) reserves.
9. A large shallow body of water near a larger body of water is a (a) harbor, (b) dock, (c) lagoon.
10. Commerce is (a) a way of farming, (b) trade and business between people, (c) the capital of a West African country.

REVIEW QUESTIONS

1. Why did the Europeans come to West Africa? How did this affect the African nations?
2. What countries were the main colonial powers in West Africa?
3. Name one important resource of Nigeria.
4. Name three exports from Ghana and Ivory Coast.

ACTIVITIES

1. Pick a country from this list of West African countries.

Benin	Mali
Chad	Mauritania
Gambia	Niger
Guinea	Senegal
Guinea-Bissau	Sierra Leone
Ivory Coast	Togo
Liberia	Upper Volta

What questions would you like to ask about that country? Make a list of five questions. Use an encyclopedia and other reference materials to find the answers to your questions.

2. The size of another country becomes more meaningful when you compare it to the size of states in the United States. Choose three countries from the list above and find their land areas in the table on pages 288–291. Using an almanac, find states in the United States that are of similar size. Write a sentence for each country, comparing it to smaller or larger states.

325

MAKING A TIME LINE

WHAT A TIME LINE SHOWS

A time line shows when events took place. The events shown on a time line are put in the order, or sequence, in which they occurred. The breaks in the time line on this page indicate the passage of more time than can be shown on the scale. At this point you may wish to review what you learned about time lines in Chapter 2.

SKILLS PRACTICE

The map and the table on this page show when the countries of Africa gained their independence. Use this information to make a time line.

On a sheet of paper draw a time line like the one below. Make your time line larger, but be sure to keep the correct scale in showing the time periods. You will also have to decide how to show several events for the same date in a clear, concise fashion. When you have finished the time line, answer the following questions.

1. Did Ethiopia become an independent country before, or after, Egypt?

2. In what year did 17 African countries become independent?

3. Which country became independent first, Liberia or South Africa?

4. Which African country became independent most recently?

5. Did most African countries become independent in the first, or second, half of the twentieth century?

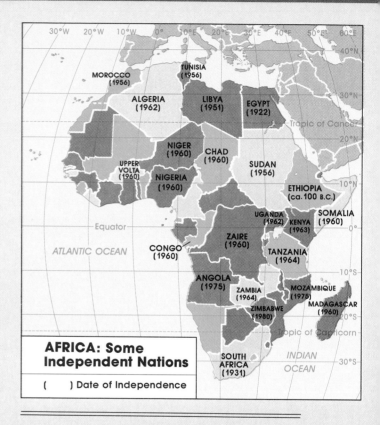

AFRICA: Some Independent Nations

( ) Date of Independence

SOME INDEPENDENT AFRICAN COUNTRIES

Country	Date	Country	Date
Benin	1960	Ivory Coast	1960
Botswana	1966	Lesotho	1966
Burundi	1962	Liberia	1847
Cameroon	1960	Malawi	1964
Cape Verde	1975	Mali	1960
Central African Republic	1960	Mauritania	1960
Comoros	1975	Mauritius	1968
Djibouti	1977	Rwanda	1962
Equatorial Guinea	1968	São Tomé e Príncipe	1975
Gabon	1960	Senegal	1960
Gambia	1965	Seychelles	1976
Ghana	1957	Sierra Leone	1961
Guinea	1958	Swaziland	1968
Guinea-Bissau	1974	Togo	1960

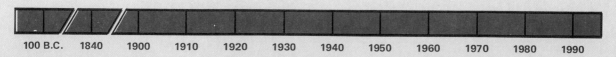

| 100 B.C. | 1840 | 1900 | 1910 | 1920 | 1930 | 1940 | 1950 | 1960 | 1970 | 1980 | 1990 |

7/UNIT REVIEW

Answer Key in back of book.

READING THE TEXT

Turn to page 323 and read the section "Miryam: Subsistence Farmer of Africa." Then read the statements below. On a sheet of paper, write **T** if the statement is true and **F** if it is false.

1. Many subsistence farmers in Africa are women. **T**
2. Miryam grows enough to sell her surplus in the market. **F**
3. There is little protein in the diet of Miryam and her family. **T**
4. Wood is scarce and gathering it is hard work. **T**
5. Miryam's village is well supplied with water. **F**

READING A MAP

Study the map on page 283. On a sheet of paper, write the answers to these questions.

1. What capital city of what country is near the junction of the Blue Nile and the White Nile rivers?
2. How high is Mount Kilimanjaro?
3. Into what body of water does the Zambesi River flow?
4. What three countries border Lake Chad?

5. What is the name of the southernmost cape in Africa?

READING A PICTURE

Turn to page 321 and examine the illustration carefully. On a sheet of paper, write the answers to these questions.

1. What is the subject of this series of drawings?
2. What is the natural vegetation in an area such as that pictured here?
3. What kinds of tools are being used?
4. Is the land being cleared permanently for farming?
5. Are people who practice this kind of farming more likely to be subsistence farmers?

READING A GRAPH

Study the graph on Single-Export Economies on page 312 and, on a sheet of paper, answer these questions.

1. What is a single-export economy?
2. Which country is most dependent on a single export?
3. What is Sierra Leone's major export?
4. Which country's major export is copper?
5. What problems can be caused by a single-export economy?

SOUTH ASIA AND EAST ASIA

Have pupils find the following on the map on p. 329: two plains, two plateaus, a desert, a basin, a gulf, a strait, and the three named mountain peaks. (North China Plain and Manchurian Plain; Mongolian Plateau and Plateau of Tibet; Gobi Desert; Tarim Basin; Gulf of Siam; Strait of Malacca or Korea Strait; Pobeda Peak, Ulugh Muztagh, and Mt. Everest)

A Region of Opposites

What words come to mind when you think of Asia? Some of them should be *large, small, rich, poor, high, low, most, least, wet,* and *dry.* This list of adjectives includes several opposites because Asia is a region of many contrasts. It is a large region, larger than North and South America combined. Two of the world's largest countries are in Asia. But some of the world's smallest nations are also there.

Among Asia's nations are one of the world's richest and one of the world's poorest. The highest mountains in the world and some of the lowest delta lands are in Asia. It has both cold and hot regions, some regions that are very wet, and some that are very dry.

Important Geographical Features

The Himalayas are Asia's best-known landform. Mount Everest, the highest peak in the world, is a famous challenge to mountain climbers. Asia has 13 other mountains that are more than 25,000 feet (7,620 m) high. In addition to the Himalayas, some other mountain ranges are the Kunlun Shan, Tien Shan, and Hindu Kush. They spread out like spokes of a wheel from a mountain center called the Pamir Knot. Can. you find these mountains on the map on the next page?

Since Asia is so large, it should be no surprise to learn that many large and important rivers are found there. Four of Asia's rivers—the Hwang, the Yangtze, the Amur, and the Mekong—are longer than the Mississippi River.

Some of the world's highest mountains and longest rivers are in South Asia and East Asia.

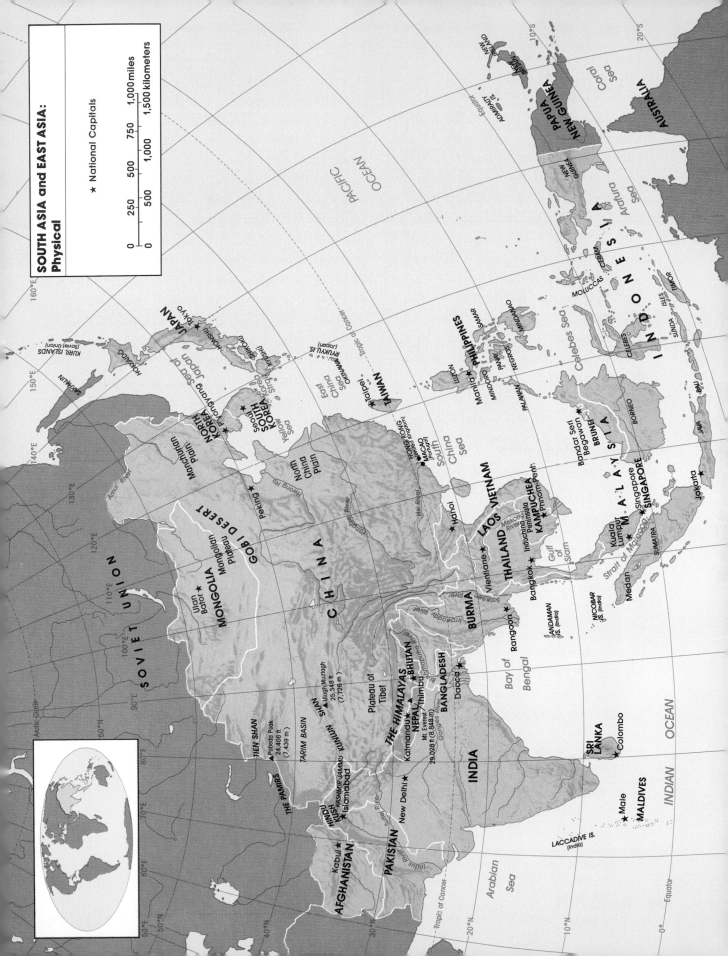

Scale:
0   250   500   750   1,000 miles
0   500   1,000   1,500 kilometers

KURIL ISLANDS
(Soviet Union)

SAKHALIN

SOVIET UNION

Arctic Circle

Amur River

HOKKAIDO

Sea of Japan

JAPAN

TOKYO
HONSHU
SHIKOKU
KYUSHU

Manchurian Plain

NORTH KOREA
PYONGYANG

SOUTH KOREA
Seoul

Yellow Sea

RYUKYU IS.
(Japan)

East China Sea

OKINAWA

Tropic of Cancer

PACIFIC OCEAN

Equator

ADMIRALTY IS.

NEW IRELAND
NEW BRITAIN

PAPUA NEW GUINEA

NEW GUINEA

Coral Sea

AUSTRALIA

Arafura Sea

CERAM

MOLUCCAS

CELEBES

Celebes Sea

I N D O N E S I A

SUNDA ISLES

TIMOR

BALI

JAVA

Jakarta

BORNEO

SUMATRA

Strait of Malacca

Medan

SINGAPORE
Singapore

Kuala Lumpur

M A L A Y S I A

BRUNEI
Bandar Seri Begawan

PALAWAN

MINDANAO

PANAY
NEGROS

PHILIPPINES
Manila

SAMAR

MINDORO

LUZON

Taipei

TAIWAN

HONG KONG
(United Kingdom)

MACAO
(Portugal)

South China Sea

Hsi River

Hanoi

VIETNAM

LAOS
Vientiane

Mekong River

KAMPUCHEA
Phnom Penh

Indochina Peninsula

THAILAND
Bangkok

Gulf of Siam

BURMA
Rangoon

Salween River

Irrawaddy River

ANDAMAN IS.
(India)

NICOBAR IS.
(India)

Bay of Bengal

Yangtze River

Peking

North China Plain

Huang Ho
(Yellow River)

C H I N A

GOBI DESERT

Mongolian Plateau

MONGOLIA
Ulan Bator

Plateau of Tibet

TIEN SHAN
Pobeda Peak
24,406 ft
(7,439 m)

TARIM BASIN

SHAN
Ulugh Muztagh
25,348 ft
(7,726 m)

KUNLUN

THE PAMIRS

KASHMIR-JAMMU

THE HIMALAYAS

BHUTAN
Thimbu

NEPAL
Katmandu

Mt. Everest
29,028 ft (8,848 m)

BANGLADESH
Dacca

Brahmaputra River

Ganges River

INDIA

New Delhi

Sutlej River

Indus River

HINDU KUSH

Islamabad

PAKISTAN

Kabul
AFGHANISTAN

Tropic of Cancer

Arabian Sea

LACCADIVE IS.
(India)

Male
MALDIVES

SRI LANKA
Colombo

INDIAN OCEAN

Equator

The People of Asia

Asia is the home of some of the world's oldest cultures. Inventions and ideas that were developed here have influenced all the world. Europeans learned about gunpowder and printing from the Chinese. Two great religions—Hinduism and Buddhism—developed in India.

Japan continues to amaze the world with its technical development. Its industrial output has given it one of the world's leading economies. This high level of development is due partly to the creation of new ways to use workers efficiently in industry.

Despite the intense industrialization in some areas, most Asians are still rural people who work on farms. They live in farming villages or fishing communities. Most farms are small, although there are large plantations in some areas.

Asia has more of the world's largest cities than any other region. Some cities, such as those in Japan, have a large middle class and look very modern. Most cities in other parts of Asia have a large number of very, very poor people living in them. Count the cities in the Index on this page that have a population of 1,000,000 or more. Many of these cities are larger than Chicago or Los Angeles.

When you realize how many big cities Asia has and also that most people in Asia live in rural areas, you will appreciate how many people live in Asia. Today over 3 billion of the world's 5 billion people live in Asia.

There are 53 cities with more than 1,000,000 people.

Cities less than 100,000
Bandar Seri Begawan
  (Brunei) F-5
Islamabad (Pakistan) . .B-2
Male (Maldives) B-5
Phnom-Penh
  (Kampuchea) E-4
Thimbu (Bhutan) C-3

Cities 100,000 to 499,999
Katmandu (Nepal) C-3
Kuala Lumpur
  (Malaysia) E-5
New Delhi (India) B-3
Ulan Bator (Mongolia) . .E-1
Vientiane (Laos) E-4

Cities 500,000 to 999,999
Agra (India) B-3
Amagasaki (Japan) H-2
An-shan (China) G-1
Ch'ang'ch'un (China) . .G-1
Ch'ang-sha (China) F-3
Cheng-chou (China) . . . F-2
Chiba (Japan) I-2
Ch'i-ch'i-ha-erh (China) .G-1
Chittagong
  (Bangladesh) D-3
Colombo (Sri Lanka) . . .C-5
Faisalabad (Pakistan) . . .B-2
Foochow (China) F-3
Hangchow (China) G-2
Higashiosaka (Japan) . .H-2
Hiroshima (Japan) H-2
Howrah (India) C-3

Huai-nan (China) F-2
Hyderabad (Pakistan) . .A-3
Inch'ön (South Korea) . .G-2
Indore (India) B-3
Jaipur (India) B-3
Kabul (Afghanistan) A-2
Kirin (China) G-1
K'un-ming (China) E-3
Kwangju (South Korea) .G-2
Kuel-yang (China) E-3
Lan-chou (China) E-2
Lo-yang (China) F-2
Lucknow (India) C-3
Madurai (India) B-5
Medan (Indonesia) D-6
Multan (Pakistan) B-2
Nagpur (India) B-3
Nan-ch'ang (China) F-3
Okayama (Japan) H-2
Palembang
  (Indonesia) E-6
Pao-t'ou (China) E-1
Pen-ch'i (China) G-1
Poona (India) B-4
Quezon City
  (Philippines) G-4
Rawalpindi (Pakistan) . . .B-2
Semarang (Indonesia) . .F-6
Sendai (Japan) I-2
Shih-chia-chuang
  (China) F-2
Su-chou (China) G-2
Su-chow (China) F-2
Taejön (South Korea) . . .G-2

T'ai-chung (Taiwan) G-3
T'ainan (Taiwan) G-3
T'ang-shan (China) F-2
Tsinan (China) F-2
Tzepo (China) F-2
Varanasi (India) C-3
Wu-hsi (China) G-2

Cities 1,000,000 or more
Ahmadabad (India) B-3
Bandung (Indonesia) E-6
Bangalore (India) B-4
Bangkok (Thailand) E-4
Bombay (India) B-4
Calcutta (India) C-3
Canton (China) F-3
Ch'eng-tu (China) E-2
Chungking (China) E-3
Dacca (Bangladesh) . . .D-3
Delhi (India) B-3
Fukuoka (Japan) H-2
Fu-shun (China) G-1
Haiphong (Vietnam) E-3
Hanoi (Vietnam) E-3
Harbin (China) G-1
Ho Chi Minh City
  (Vietnam) E-4
Hong Kong
  (United Kingdom) F-3
Hyderabad (India) B-4
Jakarta (Indonesia) E-6
Kanpur (India) C-3
Kao-hsiung (Taiwan) G-3
Karachi (Pakistan) A-3

Kawasaki (Japan) H-2
Kitakyushu (Japan) H-2
Kōbe (Japan) H-2
Kyōto (Japan) H-2
Lahore (Pakistan) B-2
Lu-ta (China) G-2
Madras (India) C-4
Manila (Philippines) G-4
Mukden (China) G-1
Nagoya (Japan) H-2
Nanking (China) F-2
Osaka (Japan) H-2
Peking (China) F-2
Pusan (South Korea) G-2
P'yöngyang
  (North Korea) G-2
Rangoon (Burma) D-4
Sapporo (Japan) I-1
Seoul (South Korea) G-2
Shanghai (China) G-2
Sian (China) E-2
Singapore (Singapore) . .E-5
Surabaja (Indonesia) . . .F-6
Taegu (South Korea) G-2
Taipei (Taiwan) G-3
T'ai-yuan (China) F-2
Tientsin (China) F-2
Tokyo (Japan) H-2
Tsingtao (China) G-2
Wu-han (China) F-2
Yokohama (Japan) H-2

All but one of the countries of South and East Asia are north of the Equator. Which country is located right on the Equator? Name the capital of that country. Indonesia; Jakarta

Have pupils name the major islands that make up Indonesia. (Sumatra, Java, Celebes, Timor, and parts of Borneo and New Guinea)

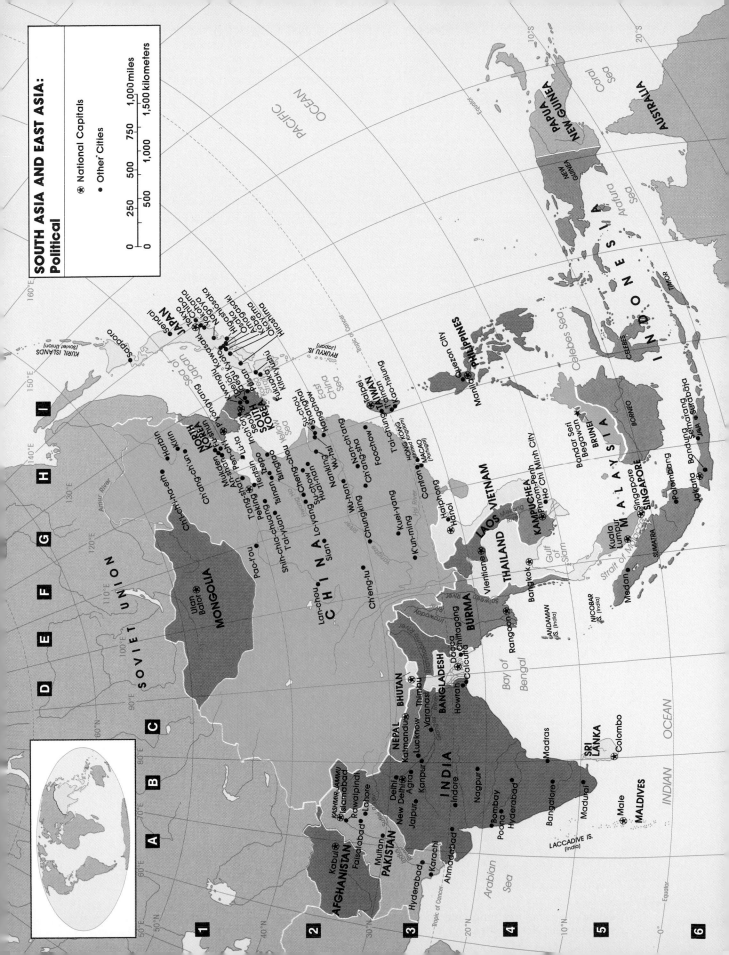

SOUTH ASIA AND EAST ASIA:
Political

⊛ National Capitals
• Other Cities

0	250	500	750	1,000 miles	
0	500	1,000	1,500 kilometers		

SOUTH ASIA AND EAST ASIA

COUNTRY	FLAG	TOTAL AREA	POPULATION and POPULATION DENSITY	CAPITAL CITY and POPULATION	WHERE PEOPLE LIVE
Afghanistan		250,000 sq mi (647,497 sq km)	14,200,000 57 per sq mi (22 per sq km)	Kabul 913,000	
Bangladesh		55,598 sq mi (143,998 sq km)	96,500,000 1,736 per sq mi (670 per sq km)	Dacca 1,679,500	
Bhutan		18,147 sq mi (47,000 sq km)	1,400,000 77 per sq mi (30 per sq km)	Thimbu 9,000	
Brunei		2,226 sq mi (5,765 sq km)	200,000 90 per sq mi (35 per sq km)	Bandar Seri Begawan 37,000	
Burma		261,218 sq mi (676,552 sq km)	37,900,000 145 per sq mi (56 per sq km)	Rangoon 2,055,500	
China		3,691,523 sq mi (9,561,000 sq km)	1,023,300,000 277 per sq mi (107 per sq km)	Peking 9,230,500	
India		1,269,346 sq mi (3,287,590 sq km)	730,000,000 575 per sq mi (222 per sq km)	New Delhi 302,000	
Indonesia		578,119 sq mi (1,497,320 sq km)	155,600,000 269 per sq mi (104 per sq km)	Jakarta 4,576,000	
Japan		145,711 sq mi (377,389 sq km)	119,200,000 818 per sq mi (316 per sq km)	Tokyo 8,646,500	
Kampuchea (Cambodia)		69,898 sq mi (181,035 sq km)	6,000,000 86 per sq mi (33 per sq km)	Phnom-Penh 394,000	
Korea (North)		46,540 sq mi (120,538 sq km)	19,200,000 413 per sq mi (159 per sq km)	P'yŏngyang 1,500,000	
Korea (South)		38,025 sq mi (98,484 sq km)	41,300,000 1,086 per sq mi (419 per sq km)	Seoul 8,366,500	
Laos		91,429 sq mi (236,800 sq km)	3,600,000 39 per sq mi (15 per sq km)	Vientiane 176,500	

Urban ▮ Nonurban ▯ Not Available – ▨

Have some pupils rearrange the countries in order from smallest to largest. Have other pupils rank them by population.

SOUTH ASIA AND EAST ASIA

COUNTRY	FLAG	TOTAL AREA	POPULATION and POPULATION DENSITY	CAPITAL CITY and POPULATION	WHERE PEOPLE LIVE
Malaysia		127,316 sq mi (329,749 sq km)	15,000,000 118 per sq mi (46 per sq km)	Kuala Lumpur 938,000	
Maldives		115 sq mi (298 sq km)	200,000 1,739 per sq mi (671 per sq km)	Male 29,500	
Mongolia		604,250 sq mi (1,565,000 sq km)	1,800,000 3 per sq mi (1 per sq km)	Ulan Bator 402,500	
Nepal		54,362 sq mi (140,797 sq km)	15,800,000 291 per sq mi (112 per sq km)	Katmandu 333,000	
Pakistan		310,404 sq mi (803,943 sq km)	95,700,000 308 per sq mi (119 per sq km)	Islamabad 201,000	
Philippines		115,831 sq mi (300,000 sq km)	52,800,000 456 per sq mi (176 per sq km)	Manila 1,454,500	
Singapore		224 sq mi (581 sq km)	2,500,000 11,161 per sq mi (4,303 per sq km)	Singapore 2,500,000	
Sri Lanka		25,332 sq mi (65,610 sq km)	15,600,000 616 per sq mi (238 per sq km)	Colombo 586,000	
Taiwan		13,885 sq mi (35,961 sq km)	18,900,000 1,361 per sq mi (526 per sq km)	Taipei 2,220,500	
Thailand		198,457 sq mi (514,000 sq km)	50,800,000 256 per sq mi (99 per sq km)	Bangkok 4,870,000	
Vietnam		128,402 sq mi (332,559 sq km)	57,000,000 444 per sq mi (171 per sq km)	Hanoi 2,571,000	

Urban ▉ Nonurban ▨ Not Available – ▨

333

Have pupils look in almanacs to find other kinds of information
and use the data to make their own tables.

CHAPTER
20 China and Its Neighbors

Refer pupils to the table on p. 31 to find the countries that are larger than China.

Land of Varied Regions

VOCABULARY

| tableland | double cropping |

A giant country   There are only two countries that are larger in land area than China. Some of the highest mountain ranges in the world are part of China's borders. There are valleys in China that are at a higher elevation than the tops of mountains in some other countries.

China also has a long seacoast. If China were on the North American continent, it would extend from the northern latitude of Newfoundland or southern Alaska to south of Mexico City.

Geographically this vast country can be divided into three regions.

The western interior—dry plateaus and mountains   Southwestern China is a region of high plateaus surrounded by even higher mountain ranges. Just north of the Himalaya Mountains is the plateau of Tibet [Xizang], an enormous, high **tableland**. *Tableland* is another word for "plateau." The Tibetan plateau has an average elevation of 15,000 feet (4,500 m). Mountains rise another 10,000 feet (3,000 m) above this tableland. The Tibetan plateau has always been a barrier to trade and transportation. Except for travel through the narrow valleys formed by rivers that drain toward the east and south, travel in and out of the region is difficult. Only a few people live here, mostly in villages in the valleys. The valleys in this region are very isolated from each other.

To the north the Tibetan plateau drops like a giant stairstep to the somewhat lower, but larger Sinkiang [Xinjiang] plateau. The Sinkiang plateau is an area without much vegetation. Hills and low mountains bring some variety to the landscape. The Tarim Basin is part of this region. It is very dry. The few rivers here never reach the sea. They flow into shallow lakes, where the water evaporates into the dry air.

Throughout most of China's history, this area south of the Tarim Basin has been the chief route for trade and commerce. Animal caravans traveled along the chain of oases ringing the Takla Makan (täk lə mə kän´) Desert. This was called the Great Silk Road. It was through this area that Marco Polo traveled more than 700 years ago on his famous trip to China. Recently the Chinese government has been building railroads and highways to this area to make it less isolated.

Southeastern and central China   The central part of China's coastland is the economic heart of the country. Here the

To many people the Great Wall is a symbol of China. It was built to guard the northern frontier from invaders. There are towers every 200 to 300 yards (180 to 270 m).

The Great Wall is actually a series of walls that were connected during the reign of the first Chinese emperor, Shih Huang Ti. The top of the wall is wide enough to permit mounted troops to ride along it.

mountains are lower, and there are wide stretches of lowland along the coast. The most extensive lowlands are the Hwang and Yangtze river valleys. The Hwang Ho [Hwang He] and the Yangtze (yan′ sē) [Chang] are rivers that wind between the mountains. The huge deltas that have formed at the mouths of the rivers are the largest lowland areas of the entire country. Many of the great cities of China are in the valleys or on the deltas of one of these two great rivers. This is where the largest clusters of China's population are located.

The southern part of eastern China is mostly a rugged landscape. Some of the best farmland in China is in this southeastern region. It is in the small river valleys and the coastal plains. The warm climate of the south makes it possible to grow crops throughout the year. Farmers can grow two crops of rice. One is grown in the summer and another in the mild winter. In between these two crops, farmers squeeze in a planting of vegetables. In addition to rice and vegetables, farmers in southern China grow sugarcane, cotton, sweet potatoes, tea, and peanuts.

Other farmers in this region also grow more than one crop a year by combining summer rice with winter wheat. The practice of planting twice a year is called **double cropping**. These farmers also grow soybeans and vegetables. Cabbage is an important vegetable in China. It can be dried for use all year long. It is not unusual to see cabbage drying on rooftops, in courtyards, and hanging from the sides of buildings.

Northeastern China This section of China is often called Manchuria. It is a large lowland plain with mountainous borderlands. The northeast has no dominating river like the Yangtze or the Hwang.

This region is rich in mineral resources. There is coal, iron ore, and a major petroleum field in the north. It has the best railway network in China. In this cooler climate, farmers grow soybeans, grain sorghum, potatoes, and sugar beets. Sugar beets are a root crop that can be processed

---

THE PINYIN SYSTEM

As you read this chapter, you will notice that the names of places in China are followed, in most cases, not only by a respelling for pronunciation in parentheses but also by another word in brackets. Find the word *Tibet* on page 334. The word [*Xizang*], which follows *Tibet*, is from the Pinyin system for spelling and pronouncing Chinese words.

In the 1950s the Chinese government introduced the Pinyin system for writing Chinese words in English or in any other language that uses the Roman alphabet. The Chinese feel that the Pinyin spelling comes closer to the correct pronunciation of standard Chinese.

The system that has been in use until the introduction of Pinyin was developed by two Englishmen around the turn of the century. This is the system that most people recognize: *Peking* instead of *Beijing*, *Canton* instead of *Guangzhou*. Some words, but only a few, do not change from one system to the other. *Shanghai* is one such word. It will take a long time for people to change—to think of *Zhongguo* instead of *China*.

Chinese writing is not based on an alphabet; characters represent things or ideas. There are about 50,000 separate characters in modern Chinese writing. Spoken Chinese has developed into many different dialects, often almost different languages. Written Chinese has remained constant.

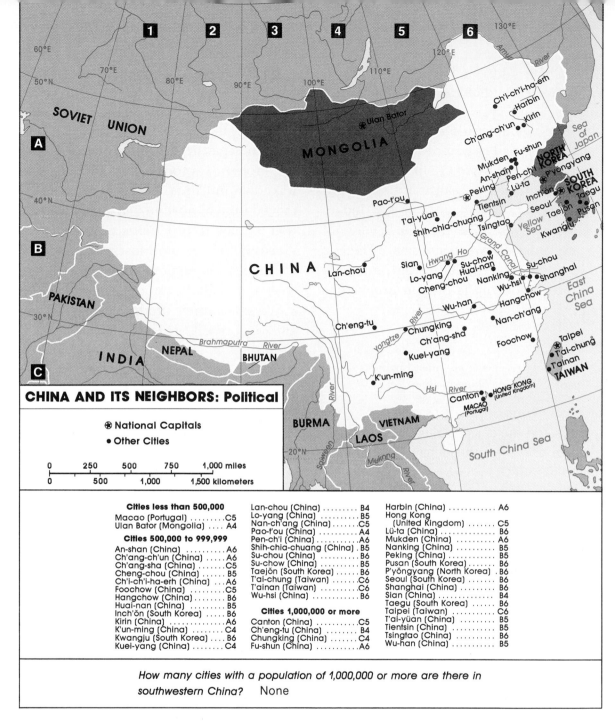

CHINA AND ITS NEIGHBORS: Political

⊛ **National Capitals**

● **Other Cities**

```
0     250    500    750    1,000 miles
0      500       1,000      1,500 kilometers
```

Cities less than 500,000

Macao (Portugal) C5
Ulan Bator (Mongolia) A4

Cities 500,000 to 999,999

An-shan (China) A6
Ch'ang-ch'un (China) A6
Ch'ang-sha (China) C5
Cheng-chou (China) B5
Ch'i-ch'i-ha-erh (China) . . . A6
Foochow (China) C5
Hangchow (China) B6
Huai-nan (China) B5
Inch'ŏn (South Korea) B6
Kirin (China) A6
K'un-ming (China) C4
Kwangju (South Korea) B6
Kuei-yang (China) C4

Lan-chou (China) B4
Lo-yang (China) B5
Nan-ch'ang (China) C5
Pao-t'ou (China) A4
Pen-ch'i (China) A6
Shih-chia-chuang (China) . B5
Su-chou (China) B6
Su-chow (China) B5
Taejŏn (South Korea) B6
T'ai-chung (Taiwan) C6
T'ainan (Taiwan) C6
Wu-hsi (China) B6

Cities 1,000,000 or more

Canton (China) C5
Ch'eng-tu (China) B4
Chungking (China) C4
Fu-shun (China) A6

Harbin (China) A6
Hong Kong
  (United Kingdom) C5
Lü-ta (China) B6
Mukden (China) A6
Nanking (China) B5
Peking (China) B5
Pusan (South Korea) B6
P'yŏngyang (North Korea) . B6
Seoul (South Korea) B6
Shanghai (China) B6
Sian (China) B4
Taegu (South Korea) B6
Taipei (Taiwan) C6
T'ai-yüan (China) B5
Tientsin (China) B5
Tsingtao (China) B6
Wu-han (China) B5

How many cities with a population of 1,000,000 or more are there in southwestern China? None

This is an excellent opportunity for pupils to work extensively with the grid system on the map.

into sugar. China, like the United States, gets most of the sugar it does not import from sugar beets rather than sugarcane.

Many large cities Only about 30 percent of China's population lives in cities. There are, however, so many people in China that about 15 Chinese cities have a population of more than 1 million. Look at the map on this page to locate these cities.

Some cities, like Canton [Guangzhou] and Shanghai, are busy ports. Peking (Beijing), the capital, is on the great plain in northern China. A number of cities in Manchuria and on the steppe bordering Mongolia are growing into large industrial and manufacturing centers.

China has had large cities for many hundreds of years. Marco Polo was very impressed with their wealth and size. But rapid modern urban growth has led to many problems. The cities have very old or very simple sewage systems. There is not enough piped water for the large populations. Housing is often a problem as well.

CHECKUP

1. What part of China is the most isolated?
2. Name two major Chinese rivers.
3. What was the Great Silk Road?

Land of Many Resources

Mineral resources for industry   China has a great variety of mineral resources. It is richer in resource wealth than many countries. China has large supplies of manganese, mercury, and tungsten. These are very important because China is growing as an industrial power.

Coal is China's greatest source of energy. The country ranks third in the world in both coal reserves and coal mining. The largest coal deposits are in the Hwang Ho valley. About two thirds of the nation's total reserves are here. This is one of the major coalfields in the world. China has at least a little coal in each of its provinces.

There is iron ore in many parts of China, but most of it is of low quality. The main iron-ore mining areas are near the coalfields of the northeast and along the Yangtze River in central China.

Petroleum production was almost unknown in China until recently. China moved from almost no petroleum production in 1950 to producing most of the oil it uses in the 1970s. Most of the oil fields are in the Sinkiang region of the far northwest and in the far northeast.

When a country produces what it needs and, as a result, does not have to import a product it uses, it is said to be **self-sufficient** in that product. In 30 years, China went from almost no production of petroleum to national self-sufficiency. This is truly a major accomplishment.

The discovery of petroleum has led to the development of a flourishing petrochemical industry in China.

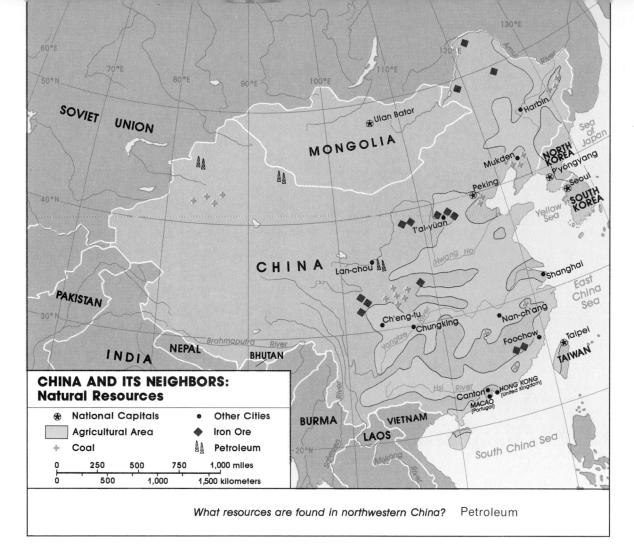

**CHINA AND ITS NEIGHBORS:
Natural Resources**

⊛	National Capitals	•	Other Cities
▨	Agricultural Area	◆	Iron Ore
+	Coal	♨	Petroleum

0   250   500   750   1,000 miles
0   500   1,000   1,500 kilometers

What resources are found in northwestern China?   Petroleum

Water and soil resources   Two of the largest rivers in the world are in China. Both the Yangtze River and the Hwang Ho are extremely important for irrigation. They also serve as transportation avenues to China's interior. The Yangtze is navigable for 1,000 miles (1,600 km). It also has huge potential for hydroelectric power. China is rapidly building the dams that will use this potential.

The Hwang Ho is a different kind of river. Its water moves slowly. It is weighed down by particles of soil called **silt.** The Hwang Ho is a shallow river. It changes course and floods frequently. The floods bring disaster to the people who live on the **flood plain.** A flood plain is the flat land around a river that can be flooded.   During floods, homes are washed away, and crops are destroyed. The flooding river leaves behind rich, fertile soil. So in years when there is no flood, the crops are bountiful.

These rivers have their sources in the snow-covered mountains of the Tibetan plateau. The edge of this plateau is also the source of the Hsi [Xi] River. This is an important river in the south. Over 15 million people live on its rich delta, many in the large city of Canton. The main importance of the Hsi River is its delta soil.

The Hwang used to be labeled the *Yellow River* on many maps. *Hwang* means "yellow"; the river got its name because the soil particles give it a yellowish cast.

Rice grows lushly in the fertile alluvial soil of the Hsi River plain. These fields are near the city of K'un-ming. (25°N/102°E; map, p. 331)

Delta soil and other soil that has been carried by water and deposited in new places is called **alluvial.** The alluvial soils of the river deltas and flood plains of China make up some of the most fertile farmlands in the world.

Soil carried by wind is called **loess** (lō′ is). China is unusual in having some of the world's largest deposits of loess. Fine, yellow-brown loess covers much of north China. There are deposits as thick as 250 feet (75 m). This is also very rich farmland.

CHECKUP

1. Why is coal an important resource in China?
2. What is a flood plain?
3. What is loess? Why is it an important resource?

The story of the "Peking Man" (actually partial skeletons of several people—male and female) would make an interesting report.

A Very Old Country Moves into Modern Times

┌─ VOCABULARY ─────────────────┐
dynasty	Confucianism
Taoism	barbarian
philosopher	commune
└──────────────────────────────┘

Home of early people Scientists have discovered that people existed in China 500,000 years ago. Bones of humans who lived at that time were found in a cave near the city of Peking. Scientists know very little about these people. They do know that people who lived in China 50,000 years ago were hunters of elephant and rhinoceros. They also know that people who lived in China 5,000 years ago crafted pottery and made tools from stone. These people lived in villages and practiced slash-and-burn farming.

China is a very old civilization. There are written records of Chinese history beginning around 2000 B.C. They describe a series of **dynasties,** or families of rulers.

A nation develops The dynasty that gave the country the name by which we know it was the Ch'in. In 221 B.C. a Ch'in emperor brought together several warring kingdoms into one strong, central government. The Chinese empire lasted in one form or another for the next 2,000 years. There were many dynasties. There were wars and famines. Even so, sometime during the period of the Sung dynasty (960–1279), China's population reached 100 million. In the early 1200s, China was invaded by outsiders. The Mongols, led by Genghis Khan, conquered the Chi-

This Ch'in emperor was the one buried with the life-size clay army. See *National Geographic,* April 1978, pp. 440–459.

nese. Kublai Khan (kü' blə kän') was the grandson of Ghengis Khan. He was the emperor of China at the time of Marco Polo's visit. Kublai Khan much prefered the Chinese way of life to that of the Mongol. He chose Chinese officials to carry on the business of his large empire. As a result, the rule of the Mongol emperor was much like that of the earlier Chinese emperors. The Mongol conquerors adopted the ways of the people they conquered. Thus the Chinese civilization went on.

One reason for this was the development of two religions in China during the Chou dynasty (1100–250 B.C.). **Taoism** urges people to live in harmony with nature. It is based on the writings of the philosopher Lao-Tzu (lou' dzü'). A **philosopher** is someone who searches for truth by reasoning or thinking. **Confucianism** is based on the ideas of Confucius (con fyü' shəs). He felt that it was very important that society be well-ordered and that only superior people rule. Respect for the past and one's ancestors is also important in Confucianism. The philosophy of Confucius influenced the government of China even to modern times.

Chinese contributions   The Chinese have made contributions to the rest of the world. They invented the compass. They were the first to weave silk into cloth, to make paper, and to turn clay into fine porcelain. The Chinese also developed the idea of printing. Carved wooden blocks were inked and then pressed on paper. This was at a time when books in Europe were still being copied by hand.

By the time that Marco Polo visited China in the thirteenth century, the Great Wall and the Grand Canal had been built. The Great Wall stretches 1,500 miles (2,400 km) across northern China. It has been called the largest structure ever built.

This jade shroud of a Han dynasty (202 B.C.–A.D. 220) prince was found in an ancient tomb in 1970. The pieces of jade are sewn together with fine silver wire.

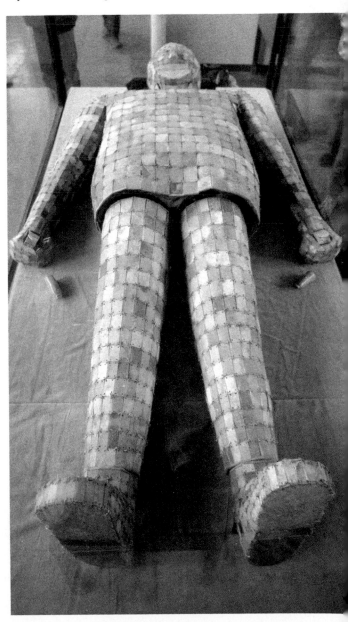

Ask pupils to speculate about how things would be different if the Chinese had not invented paper, gunpowder, porcelain, or the compass.

If such a wall were built in the United States, it would reach halfway across the country. The Grand Canal is a series of waterways. By A.D. 605 it connected the Yangtze and Hwang rivers. The Grand Canal is still being used today. It is one of the longest waterways ever built. It extends for more than 1,000 miles (1,600 km).

A closed country When Europeans visited China, they saw a well-organized, self-sufficient, strong civilization. The Chinese viewed these quaint foreign visitors as **barbarians**. They thought their dress and habits were crude. They saw little value in the products that Europeans offered them in exchange for the silk, fine

Matteo Ricci is a good subject for an oral report.

china, and tea that Europeans wanted from China. The Chinese insisted on being left to themselves. Foreigners were not allowed to leave the port cities so that they would not be a bad influence on the civilized Chinese.

Much later, after a series of wars in the 1800s, Europeans won trade agreements with China. By that time, Europe had grown in industry and wealth. China, which had closed its doors to Europe's inventions, had fallen behind in technology and military might. Foreign countries were able to influence the Chinese government.

Early in the twentieth century, China had about 40 years of civil war. Rival rulers struggled for power. Japan tried

The Grand Canal, also once called the Imperial river, connecting Hangchow (30°N/120°E; map, p. 331) and Peking (39°N/116°E; map, p. 331) has been in use for over 1,000 years.

Assign several pupils to work in pairs to create dialogue between a reporter and one of the following: a Taoist, a barbarian from Europe, to take China over. In 1945, when the Japanese occupation ended, the once strong country of China was a war-torn shambles.

The Chinese Revolution   The Chinese farmer in the 1940s was one of the most unfortunate people in the world. All land was controlled by wealthy landowners who rented small parcels to farming families for high prices. The families also had to pay high taxes. There was no welfare system or social security for older people. When there was a bad harvest or a serious illness, the family had to borrow money or food at high interest rates. If they could not pay, their sons or daughters would become slaves to the landowner.

Two groups were struggling for power during this time, the Nationalists and the Communists. In 1949 the Communist Chinese defeated the Nationalist Chinese. They took control of the government. The Nationalists retreated to the island of Taiwan (tī wän′), off the southern coast of China. Taiwan remains under a separate government today. It developed a strong trading partnership with the United States.

Revolutionary changes   The new China, under Communist rule since 1949, is known as the People's Republic of China. There have been major changes in the way Chinese society is organized. The new government follows the Communist philosophy that all people should have a tolerable life before anybody has a better life. There are no wealthy landowners; their land was taken away. Farm families work together on shared land in

Workers in small tubs float among the water chestnuts in order to harvest them. This is the Tian Ling commune near Nanking. (32°N/118°E; map, p. 331)

a village system called a **commune**. People in the commune share in decision-making, work, and profit.

China is becoming a modern nation very rapidly. Modern industries are developing. New universities are training scientists, language specialists, and engineers. Farm production is large enough to provide food for the people in the growing cities.

If China has a worry, it is that its population will grow too fast to be cared for properly. Limiting population growth is a serious concern for a country that already has over a billion people—one quarter of the world's population.

CHECKUP

1. What is a dynasty?
2. What religions developed in China?
3. Name three Chinese inventions or discoveries.
4. When did the Communists take over the Chinese government?

a Confucianist, a Nationalist Chinese from Taiwan, a member of a commune. Ask the pairs of pupils to make up short dialogues to share with the rest of the class. The others can attempt to identify each person being interviewed.

China's Neighbors

┌─VOCABULARY──────────────┐
│ demilitarized zone │
└─────────────────────────┘

Mongolia   The country of Mongolia is landlocked between China and the Soviet Union. It is controlled by the Soviet Union. In land area, Mongolia is nearly twice as large as Texas. However, its population density is about three people per square mile (one per sq km). The land is rugged. There are plateaus and mountains. Mongolia shares the Gobi Desert with China. The Mongols were once nomadic herders. Livestock raising is still the major source of income. Most herds of cattle or goats are now raised on livestock farms.

North and South Korea   Locate the Korean peninsula on the map on page 337. You will notice that there are two countries there. This division came about after World War II. North and South Korea had a major war in the 1950s. They are still not at peace. There is a strip of land between them that is a **demilitarized zone**— an area where there are no troops or weapons. This keeps the two countries separate.

North Korea is somewhat larger than South Korea but has only about half as many people. It has a Communist government. About 65 percent of the population lives in cities. North Korea has been the chief industrial region of the peninsula, and its industrial growth is continuing. Rivers provide hydroelectric power. Graphite and magnesium are important mineral resources. Rice is the most important agricultural product.

Over half of the 41 million people in South Korea live in urban areas. Its capital of Seoul (sōl) is one of the world's largest cities. There was very little industry in South Korea in 1948, when the peninsula was divided. The country has had remarkable industrial growth since that time. The graph on this page, which shows the growth of the important shipbuilding industry, can be seen as an example of the growth of all industry in South Korea. Manufacturing is very important. The chief products are chemicals, machinery, and textiles. Agriculture is still very important. Rice production here is still greater than in North Korea.

Hong Kong   One of the world's largest cities is the tiny but important city of Hong Kong. It is a British colony about 90 miles (140 km) southeast of Canton.

South Korea is now the second largest exporter of ships in the world.

SOUTH KOREAN SHIPBUILDING INDUSTRY

Year	Ships (each symbol = 250,000 gross tons)
1973	🚢
1974	🚢🚢🚢🚢🚢 (about 4½)
1975	🚢🚢🚢🚢🚢 🚢🚢🚢🚢 (about 9½)
1976	🚢🚢🚢🚢🚢🚢 🚢🚢🚢🚢🚢🚢 (about 11½)
1977	🚢🚢🚢🚢🚢🚢 🚢🚢🚢🚢🚢 (about 11)
1978	🚢🚢🚢🚢🚢🚢 🚢🚢🚢🚢🚢 (about 11)
1979	🚢🚢🚢🚢🚢🚢 🚢🚢🚢🚢🚢 (about 11)
1980	🚢🚢🚢🚢🚢🚢 🚢🚢🚢🚢🚢 (about 11)

The shipyards in Kao hsiung on Taiwan are an important part of the island's modern industrial growth. (22°N/120°E; map, p. 331)

It is made up of a small island and a tiny part of the Chinese coast. It has a land area of about 400 square miles (1,000 sq km). Most of Hong Kong's 5 million people work in factories. Many make textiles and clothing for American and European markets. Many residents of Hong Kong came there as refugees from one or the other of China's governments.

Taiwan The Nationalist Chinese set up their government, the Republic of China, on the island of Taiwan. It is south of Hong Kong and about 90 miles (140 km) off the Chinese coast. Taiwan is mountainous and thickly forested. There are few mineral resources. Financial aid from foreign countries such as the United States has helped to change Taiwan from an island of poor farmers to a modern, industrial nation. Many forest products such as bamboo, plywood, lumber, and paper are exported. Other exports are cement, fertilizer, plastics, chemicals, textiles, and canned foods. Taiwan is one of China's most important neighbors. It is also the one with which China is least friendly.

CHECKUP

1. Is Mongolia controlled by China?
2. Which country has the greater population, North or South Korea?
3. What is the name of the British colony off the Chinese coast?
4. What is the name of the government on Taiwan?

Create a word puzzle that uses all the vocabulary words introduced in this chapter. Put the puzzle on a duplicating master and distribute copies to your pupils.

KEY FACTS

1. China is the third largest country in land area and the largest in population.

2. High mountains and plateaus, great deserts, and vast river valleys are part of China's landscape. Until recently the western interior of China was isolated from the rest of the country.

3. There is a great variety of mineral resources in China, which vary in quality.

4. The frequent flooding of the Hwang Ho has created a flood plain of rich alluvial soil.

5. China is a very old country that has governed itself for almost 4,000 years.

6. The Communist Chinese government has changed the way people live and work.

7. China and the neighboring countries are becoming more industrial.

VOCABULARY QUIZ

On a sheet of paper write each definition given below. Next to each definition write the term that best fits each definition.

a. commune	**f.** flood plain
b. dynasty	**g.** barbarian
c. double cropping	**h.** self-sufficient
d. loess	**i.** silt
e. tableland	**j.** philosopher

j 1. One who searches for truth by reasoning

g 2. A person crude in dress and habits

b 3. A family of rulers

e 4. Plateau

d 5. Windblown soil

a 6. Village system in which people share work and profits

i 7. Particles of soil in water

c 8. Planting twice a year

h 9. Producing enough to fill one's needs

f 10. Flat land around a river

REVIEW QUESTIONS

1. What are the Yangtze and the Hwang?

2. Describe the landscape of the western interior of China.

3. What are three sources of energy in China today?

4. What are Taoism and Confucianism?

5. What is the People's Republic of China?

6. What happened in Korea in 1948?

7. Which of China's neighbors is the least modern and industrialized?

8. Which has become very highly industrialized since 1949?

ACTIVITIES

1. Write a one-paragraph report on one of the following people.

Sun Yat-sen	Li Po
Richard Nixon and	Confucius
Communist China	Lao-tzu
Chiang Kai-shek	Empress Dowager
Mao Tse-tung	Tzu Hsi
(Mao Zedong)	Syngman Rhee
Kublai Khan	Teng Hsiao-P'ing
Marco Polo	(Deng Xiaoping)
Pearl Buck	

2. Most Chinese farm products are also grown in the United States. Where in this country is each of the following products grown?

a. Soybeans	**c.** Rice
b. Sugar beets	**d.** Cotton

3. Two products of early China that attracted European traders were silk and tea. Pick one of these products and write a report that tells how it was produced in the past; how and where it is produced today; and, in the case of silk, what it is used for.

USING HISTORICAL MAPS

MARCO POLO'S JOURNEY

Marco Polo was one of the few Europeans to travel across Asia during the Middle Ages. He reached China in 1275, when Kublai Khan was emperor. Marco Polo spent 17 years in China.

After Polo returned home, he wrote a book telling the people of Europe about East Asia. The book became very popular. People thought his stories about far-off lands were interesting, but they did not always believe them. People in Europe knew so little about China at that time that they found it hard to believe Marco Polo's stories about a great empire in the East. But Marco Polo said he had not told half of the wonders he had seen.

Today we know that Marco Polo gave accurate descriptions of what he had seen. He was not so dependable when he told of places and wonders he had only heard about.

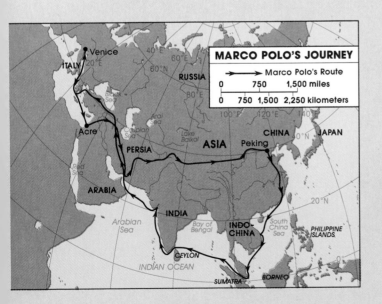

SKILLS PRACTICE

All maps show facts about places. Historical maps show facts about places at a particular time. Look at the map of Marco Polo's journey. Notice the names of countries. How many of these names, do you think, are the same on a map today? Look at the map on pages 484—485 in the Atlas to see how accurate you are.

Answer the following questions, using the map on this page.

1. What do the black arrows show?
2. From what city did Marco Polo begin his journey?
3. Did Polo begin his journey on land or sea?
4. To what Chinese city did he travel?
5. You learned in this chapter that Marco Polo traveled on the Great Silk Road. Did he travel this route on his way to China?
6. Near what degree of latitude is the Silk Road?
7. Did Marco Polo visit Japan? Russia? Borneo?
8. If Polo described a city that was at 80°E and 20°N, would you believe all that he told you? Why or why not?
9. Measure the distance that Marco Polo traveled on his journey to the court of the Chinese emperor in Peking. A piece of string laid along the route and then measured on the map scale will give you a reasonably accurate figure. Do the same for Polo's journey home. Which was the longer journey in distance?
10. Which journey, do you think, took more time?

Landscape and Resources

VOCABULARY

dormant	fish farm
typhoon	

The Japanese islands   A group of is- lands is called an archipelago (är kə pel′ ə go). The Japanese archipelago has over 3,000 islands. They sweep 1,500 miles (2,250 km) along Asia's east coast. Find Japan on the map on page 329.

The most northern of the four large is- lands of Japan is the island of Hokkaidō (hä kīd′ ō). Slightly smaller than the state of Maine, it is Japan's second largest island. The largest island, Honshū (hän′ shü), is just south of Hokkaidō. It is slightly larger than Minnesota. The large cities of Tokyo and Ōsaka (ō säk′ ə) are on this island. The southern part of Honshū curves around the smallest of Japan's four main islands, Shikoku (shi kō′ kü). Still farther south is Kyūshū (kē ü′ shü), which is about the size of Connecticut and Mas- sachusetts combined.

If all of Japan's islands were combined in one landmass, Japan would be smaller than either Montana or California. Yet only 24 million people live in California as compared to the 120 million people who live in Japan. Japan is a very densely populated country.

A mountainous land   The Japanese islands are very hilly and mountainous. They are part of a long volcanic fringe that extends from the Aleutians, in the North Pacific, through Japan, the Philippines, and Sumatra into Java, in Indonesia. Some people call this the "Ring of Fire." Find the places on the map on page 470.

A long chain of mountains runs down the middle of Japan's islands. There are flat plains of alluvial soil near the coast. The largest is the Kanto Plain of Honshū, which is the area around Tokyo Bay. Other, smaller plains are found on Hok- kaidō and Honshū. Most of Japan's land surface is steep slopes and narrow val- leys. Most of the rivers are too steep for large boats to sail.

Centuries ago Japanese farmers began to terrace the mountain slopes. The steep slopes were turned into farmland. Even with these spectacular terraces, only one sixth of Japan's land can be farmed.

Volcanic eruptions and earthquakes have been frequent throughout Japanese history. There has not been a serious earthquake since 1923. Mild earthquakes occur in Japan nearly every day. There are over 60 active volcanoes in Japan. That is ten percent of all the active vol- canoes in the world. Volcanic mountains make a beautiful landscape. Mount Fuji (fyü′ jē), the most famous of Japan's many

Mount Fuji, the highest mountain in Japan, is on Honshū island near Tokyo. The last eruption of Mount Fuji took place in 1707. (35°N/138°E; map, p. 357)

The train in the foreground is part of the *Shinkansen,* or New Trunk Line, one of the world's fastest train services. The line serves 12 of the 13 largest cities in Japan. Between 1964, when it started, and 1980, the Shinkansen has carried more than a billion passengers.

dormant, or inactive, volcanoes, rises over 12,300 feet (3,700 m) above sea level. It is topped with snow all year long.

Volcanoes benefit Japan as a source of beauty and rich volcanic soil. They also provide an unusual resource—hot water. Underground water is heated by volcanic activity. It comes from the ground as hot springs. Japan is world famous for its mineral hot springs. Hot springs resorts are popular vacation spots. People relax by soaking in the healthy natural waters.

Climate made mild by water   Japan is in the middle latitudes, where the climate is temperate. Japan's winter climate is generally warmer than places at similar latitudes on the continents. Japan's summer climate is not as hot as mainland areas of similar latitude.

The reason for this mildness of climate is that Japan is an island nation. As you remember, land near water is cooler in the summer and warmer in the winter. Japan has a marine climate.

No part of Japan is too dry for agriculture. In Hokkaidō and the northern third of Honshū, however, crops can be grown only during the summer. Farmers plant grains, soybeans, potatoes, sugar beets, and middle latitude fruits such as apples and pears. The heavier snowfall in this part of Japan makes it a wonderful area for winter sports. People come from all over the world to the annual sports festival at Sapporo (sə pōr′ ō), on Hokkaidō. The Winter Olympic Games were held here in 1972.

On southern Honshū, Kyūshū, and Shikoku, the climate is warmer. Winters are very mild; and summers are long, hot,

and humid. Farmers can grow many subtropical crops. In the most southern areas, they can even use double cropping for rice.

One special feature of Japan's climate, which is also a result of its island location, is the constant threat of **typhoons** (tī fünz′). A typhoon is a violent, hurricanelike storm. Typhoons are common in central and southern Japan, as well as in other Asian island nations and parts of China. They do heavy damage to crops and buildings every year. This is especially true in central Japan, where so many people live.

Resources from the sea   The sea is very important to Japan's economy. The Inland Sea, which separates Shikoku from Honshū, is a sheltered waterway dotted with hundreds of small islands. Find the Inland Sea on the map on page 357. There are many fishing villages hidden in little coves on the shores of its hilly, forested islands.

Ski jumping was an exciting event at the 1972 Winter Olympics in Sapporo. (43°N/141°E; map, p. 357)

Ships and boats of all sizes are part of Japan's fishing fleet of over 400,000 vessels. Japan has the world's largest fishing industry.

The Inland Sea and the seas that surround Japan are rich in fish. The archipelago is located where cold ocean currents from the north meet warm ocean currents from the south. Fish such as sardines, tuna, mackerel, herring, cod, and salmon thrive in these waters. The warm waters of southern Japan also produce many shellfish, such as oysters.

The Japanese also raise many fish in small ponds and shallow bays near their homes. Most of the fish raised on **fish farms** are carp, which are used for food. But Japan also is an important producer of goldfish, which are shipped to pet stores around the world.

Other resources The forests that cover 65 percent of Japan's land area provide lumber for many industries. The waters of Japan's mountain streams and rivers are an important resource. They are the source of much-needed hydroelectric power. Japan has only small amounts of coal and iron ore. Of all the important raw materials for industry, Japan is self-sufficient only in limestone and sulfur.

CHECKUP

1. What is an archipelago?
2. What effect does Japan's island location have on its climate?
3. What is Mount Fuji?
4. Why is the sea important to Japan?

The Japanese Experience

> **VOCABULARY**
>
> | | |
> |---|---|
> | hearsay | social reform |
> | shogun | compulsory education |
> | figurehead | illiteracy |

A separate development Japan has always been linked with the Asian continent by trade. The Korean peninsula is only 125 miles (200 km) away, and China lies just beyond it. But the same stretch of sea that has given Japan a historical link with the rest of Asia has also kept it separate. Point out similarity to Great Britain.

Japan's story is one of a country that developed apart from other countries. It was never a colony. Except for one period very early in its history, when it sought and used many ideas from China, and a second period that is more recent, Japan has remained alone.

Japan's history is long and complicated. A study of four different years—1000, 1603, 1868, and 1945—will give you some idea of the variety of experiences Japan has had. It will help you to understand the reasons that Japan is such a strong country today. You will also learn why there have been so many changes in Japan in its recent history.

The civilization of early Japan Early Japanese civilization was at a high point about A.D. 1000. At that time, Paris and London were small towns with muddy streets and simple houses. But Japan's capital, Kyōto, was a city of half a million people. A university there was already 100 years old. One of the world's greatest novels—*The Tale of Genji*, by Lady Murasaki (mù rä sä′ kē)—was written about that time. This work is still being published and read today.

Japan began to trade regularly with China around A.D. 300. From China and neighboring Korea, the Japanese had learned metalworking, tanning, shipbuilding, and weaving skills. They also had adopted the Chinese style of writing. Until this time the Japanese had no written language. The Japanese learned of the teachings of Confucius. They also studied the Chinese system of government. As a result they organized the Japanese government around a strong emperor. The emperor was believed to be a direct descendant of the sun goddess. Japanese leaders tried to use only those Chinese ideas and products that would strengthen Japan. Even though the Chinese influence on Japan was great, by 1000 the Japanese had a distinctly Japanese culture, a separate identity.

This Shinto shrine is in Kyōto. Shinto is a very ancient Japanese religion. (35°N/135°E; map, p. 357)

People put slips of paper bearing wishes for themselves or others on a tree or bush near a shrine.

The Tokugawa shogunate   Europeans first learned about Japan through the writings of Marco Polo. Japan was one of the places that Polo learned of and described by **hearsay**, by what he was told. He never actually saw Japan. His descriptions of a land of gold and other riches interested Europeans. Reaching Japan by sea was one of the goals of explorers during the Age of Exploration. Portuguese sailors were the first to reach Japan. They arrived in 1543. They were followed by Catholic missionaries. After them came traders and merchants from England and the Netherlands.

By the 1600s there was considerable European influence in Japan. By this time too the nation had a different kind of government. For several hundred years, Japan had been ruled by **shoguns** (shō′ gunz). A shogun is a military ruler. His government is called a shogunate. The shoguns ruled in the name of the emperor, who had become a **figurehead**—a leader with no real power. In 1603 a very powerful shogun began to rule. His family, the Tokugawas (tō kủ gä′ wäz), ruled for the next 250 years. The first shogun of his family did not like all the foreign influence in Japan. He did not like the religions that the foreigners were spreading. He did not like the weapons they were willing to trade for Japanese goods. He decided to banish all foreign influence from Japan. No Japanese were allowed to travel abroad. And, except for a few Dutch and Chinese traders who were allowed on one island, no foreigners were allowed to visit Japan. As a result, Japan was cut off from the rest of the world for several centuries.

The island was in the harbor of Nagasaki.

Hitotsubashi was the last Tokugawa shogun. He resigned in 1867 turning his powers over to the emperor.
Japan had been ruled by shoguns for 700 years.

The Meiji Restoration   In 1868, Japan had a new government. In 1854, Americans led by Commodore Matthew C. Perry had persuaded the Japanese to sign treaties of friendship. These had been expanded into trade agreements. Japan had begun new trade and communication with other countries.

The new government that replaced the Tokugawa shogunate in 1868 restored, or returned, power to the emperor. This emperor was called Meiji (mā′ jē). The Meiji Restoration was more than a change in government. It was also a change in Japan's attitude toward foreign governments. The new Japanese government had been impressed with American steamships and with other inventions developed by Europeans and Americans. With great energy the Japanese entered into world trade. They moved the capital from Kyōto, which was inland, to Tokyo,

Commodore Perry impressed the Japanese officials with a display of armed force and personal dignity.

along the coast, so that trade would be easier. Every effort was made to become an industrial trading nation as rapidly as possible.

The Meiji Restoration also brought **social reforms.** A social reform is a change made for the good of the people. In 1872, **compulsory education** was started in an effort to remove **illiteracy** (i lit′ ər ə sē). Compulsory education means that the government provides free schools and requires that all children attend them. Illiteracy is not knowing how to read or write. Soon most children in the country were learning to read and to write. Many went on to become college graduates. The Meiji government encouraged scientists and business owners to travel to other countries to learn new ideas.

New businesses and industries grew rapidly. Iron and steel, textiles, railroad equipment, and other products soon were produced in Japan as efficiently as they were in Europe and the United States.

One of the main products Japan began to make was military equipment.

The end of World War II and a new beginning Japan was successful in becoming a strong, industrial nation. Still fearful of domination by foreigners, Japan decided instead to dominate them. Japan conquered many new lands. Sometimes Japan feared the greater strength of other nations. Sometimes Japan wanted new lands to supply raw materials for use in Japanese factories.

During World War II Japan was at war with the great powers. It fought with China, Great Britain, France, the Soviet Union, and the United States. It had won many battles and had conquered large parts of Asia. It had bombed the American military base at Pearl Harbor, in Hawaii.

By 1945, Japan was forced to surrender. Japan was seriously weakened by the war. Large cities, factories, and schools had been destroyed. Two million Japanese had been killed. The United States helped Japan begin again. American advisors lived in Japan and worked with Japanese officials. Japan changed from a nation of military might to a nation of industrial and educational strength.

CHECKUP

1. From what country did the Japanese borrow a style of writing?
2. Who were the first Europeans to arrive in Japan?
3. How did the Tokugawa shogunate affect Japan's relations with other countries?
4. What important social reform was made during the Meiji Restoration?
5. With whom did the Japanese fight in World War II?

Townsend Harris, the first representative to Japan of the United States government, is an interesting subject for a report.

Japan in the 1980s

┌─ VOCABULARY ───────────────┐
| gross national   life expectancy |
| product   juku |
| populous |
└────────────────────────────┘

Country of high income   A country's **gross national product** (GNP) is the total value of all the goods and services it produces. The gross national product of each country is figured in dollars so that different countries' GNPs can be compared. Japan's 1980 GNP was nearly a trillion dollars. Only the gross national products of the United States and the Soviet Union are higher.

Such a large GNP is unusual for a country with so few natural resources. Japan's economy is based on world trade, not on use of its own resources. It imports, or brings in, raw materials such as fuel, metals, lumber, and cotton. It uses these as raw materials in its factories. Japanese factories produce high-quality, costly items such as automobiles, cameras, tape recorders, computers, and scientific instruments. Japan also has a very active shipbuilding industry. The goods produced in Japan are exported all over the world.

Country of healthy people   Japan is the seventh most populous nation in the world. **Populous** means "having a large number of people." Ninety percent of the people live on the lowland plains. Look at the table on page 332 to find the percentage who live in urban areas. In the large cities there is little open space and houses are small.

Still, Japanese people are healthier than people in most other countries. One way to measure good health is to look at how long people live. This measure is called **life expectancy**. Men in Japan can expect to live to age 73, on the average, and women to age 79. The Japanese life expectancy is higher than that of most other countries. In the United States life expectancy is 69 for men and for women it is 77.

Manufacturing is the most important part of the Japanese economy. It employs nearly 25 percent of the work force. Forty percent of these workers are women.

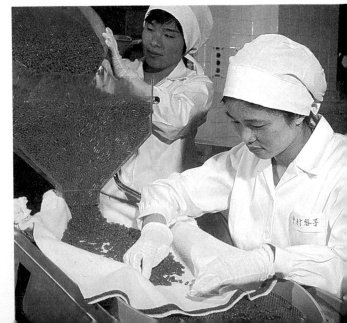

Tatsuhiko of Tokyo

When Tatsuhiko passed the exams that allowed him to enter the lower secondary school, he felt that he had jumped the biggest hurdle of his life! Now, at age 14, he has two more years before the next series of exams—this time to see whether he will qualify for three years of upper secondary school. Tatsuhiko is already starting to prepare for those exams.

He is one of many pupils who attend a juku after the regular school day. The juku gives pupils extra lessons to help them prepare for exams. Tatsuhiko's parents encourage him to study hard. They are willing to pay for the juku because they want him to be able to attend a good university. They are hoping he will study to be either a scientist like his mother or an engineer like his father.

Tatsuhiko also takes piano and violin lessons, and he is on a baseball team. When he does especially well in school, his parents sometimes reward him by taking him to a baseball game or to a concert.

During vacations and on weekends, Tatsuhiko takes time off from studying to watch television, to go to the movies, or to go bicycling in the park. He also likes to listen to rock music. His parents would rather he didn't; noises from his radio can be heard throughout their tiny apartment.

Twice a year Tatsuhiko and his family take a vacation. One of their favorite vacations is to go to a resort in the central mountains. Here, warm mineral hot springs fill large pools, called baths. The public bath is an old Japanese custom. Modern Japanese families like the baths as a soothing change from their usual active lifestyle.

Several times Tatsuhiko's family have visited another country on vacation. They like to visit strange lands where people speak different languages and have different customs. Of these foreign lands, Tatsuhiko liked the United States best because the people there like baseball almost as much as they do in Japan.

Country of educated people Education is important in Japan. <u>Almost 100 percent of all young children attend school.</u> Visiting teachers go to the homes of children too sick to attend school.

Almost 95 percent of all children go on to high school. But first they must pass difficult examinations. To have a better chance of passing, most Japanese middle-school children attend a second school after regular school hours. This school for cramming is called a **juku** (jü′ kü).

The juku gives children extra lessons that will better prepare them for regular school exams and for exams for higher levels of schooling. Children do homework from both schools.

Japan has 450 colleges and universities and over 500 junior colleges. The college entrance examinations are very difficult. Education is so valued, though, that students who have failed to be accepted into the college they wish to attend sometimes have committed suicide. Japan has the world's highest suicide rate for young people.

Japan's rigorous educational system has produced many excellent engineers, poets, writers, photographers, biologists, mathematicians, and geographers. Japanese tourists can be seen in countries all over the world. They enjoy the new experiences that travel brings. They are eager to learn from other people.

Country of city people Most Japanese live in cities. Over 8.5 million people live in Tokyo. It is the third most populous city in the world. Tokyo was the largest city in the world in 1700. But then it had only a million or so people.

Present-day Japan has nine other cities of over a million people. Find these cities on the map on this page. Two of them, Yokohama (yō′ kə häm′ ə) and Kawasaki (kä wə säk′ ē), blur with Tokyo into a giant supercity of 25 to 30 million people. This is the major industrial and manufacturing area in Japan.

Among Japan's other important cities are Ōsaka; Nagoya (nə goi′ ə), known especially for textile manufacturing; and Kōbe (kō′ bē). Kōbe is the country's main shipbuilding center and one of its busiest ports.

Another important city, a city of over 2 million people, is Kyōto. It was Japan's capital from 794 to 1869. Kyōto has many shrines and temples, places of traditional Shinto and Buddhist worship. People in Kyōto are likely to work in crafts and small businesses. Large factories cannot be built in Kyōto. The people want to keep it as it was in the past.

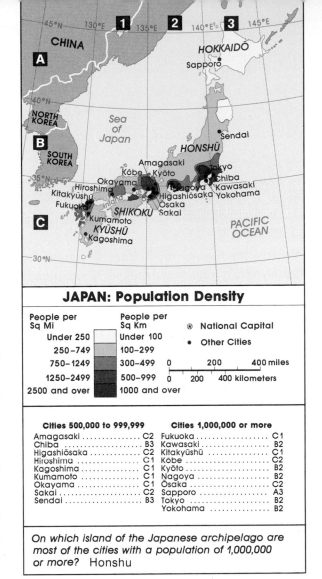

JAPAN: Population Density

People per Sq Mi	People per Sq Km
Under 250	Under 100
250–749	100–299
750–1249	300–499
1250–2499	500–999
2500 and over	1000 and over

⊛ National Capital
• Other Cities

0   200   400 miles
0   200   400 kilometers

Cities 500,000 to 999,999		Cities 1,000,000 or more	
Amagasaki	C2	Fukuoka	C1
Chiba	B3	Kawasaki	B2
Higashiōsaka	C2	Kitakyūshū	C1
Hiroshima	C1	Kōbe	C2
Kagoshima	C1	Kyōto	B2
Kumamoto	C1	Nagoya	B2
Okayama	C1	Ōsaka	C2
Sakai	C2	Sapporo	A3
Sendai	B3	Tokyo	B2
		Yokohama	B2

On which island of the Japanese archipelago are most of the cities with a population of 1,000,000 or more? Honshu

People from all parts of Japan visit Kyōto to stay in touch with the past. The Japanese have a modern economy, and they are educated world travelers, but they still value the old traditions. They are proud of their past and their nation's special culture.

CHECKUP

1. What do the initials GNP stand for?
2. Where does Japan get most of the raw materials used in its factories?
3. What is a juku?
4. What is Japan's largest city?

KEY FACTS

1. Japan is a very mountainous island country; only one sixth of its land is arable.

2. Japan is in a zone of volcanic eruptions and earthquakes.

3. From the time of the Tokugawa shogunate until 1868, Japan was isolated from foreign countries.

4. Under the Meiji Restoration, Japan began a new push for industrial development.

5. Japan was seriously weakened by World War II.

6. Only the United States and the Soviet Union have a gross national product larger than Japan's.

7. Most Japanese live in cities.

VOCABULARY QUIZ

On a sheet of paper write the letter of the word or phrase that correctly completes each statement.

c **1.** The average length of time people live is (**a**) gross national product, (**b**) life insurance, (**c**) life expectancy.

c **2.** A violent, hurricanelike storm is (**a**) an atomic bomb, (**b**) a shogun, (**c**) a typhoon.

a **3.** A group of islands is (**a**) an archipelago, (**b**) a fish farm, (**c**) a continent.

c **4.** A school that helps students prepare for examinations is called a (**a**) middle school, (**b**) test school, (**c**) juku.

a **5.** Another word for an inactive volcano is (**a**) dormant, (**b**) marine, (**c**) vacant.

c **6.** Not knowing how to read or write is (**a**) hearsay, (**b**) illegal, (**c**) illiteracy.

a **7.** An example of a social reform is (**a**) compulsory education, (**b**) a dance class, (**c**) a shogun.

b **8.** The total value of all the goods and services a country produces is its (**a**) life expectancy, (**b**) gross national product, (**c**) bank account.

c **9.** A military ruler of early Japan was (**a**) a president, (**b**) a prime minister, (**c**) a shogun.

b **10.** A leader without power is a (**a**) typhoon, (**b**) figurehead, (**c**) shogun.

REVIEW QUESTIONS

1. What are the names of the four largest Japanese islands?

2. How is Japan's climate affected by its island location?

3. What effect did each of the following have on Japan: (**a**) China, (**b**) Tokugawa shogunate, (**c**) Meiji Restoration.

4. How do we know Japan is a wealthy country?

5. Name three important Japanese industries.

ACTIVITIES

1. Find three advertisements for products made in Japan in a magazine or a newspaper.

2. Politeness and courtesy have a high value in Japanese culture. Children usually address their parents and teachers with terms of respect, such as "Ma'am" and "Sir." For one day use nothing but politeness toward your parents and teachers, and address each of them at least once as "Ma'am" or "Sir." Write an essay describing this experience, including how easy or difficult it was for you and people's reaction to your behavior.

3. Ask someone who remembers World War II what she or he can remember hearing of Japan's attack on Pearl Harbor. People who were adults then often remember where they were and what they were doing.

21/SKILLS DEVELOPMENT

READING PIE GRAPHS AND TABLES

UNITED STATES—JAPANESE TRADE

Both the pie graphs and the tables on this page tell you about Japan's trade with the United States. They give information about what Japan imports from the United States, and what Japan exports to the United States. Only the major categories of products are given. Both the graphs and the tables tell you the percentages in each category, and the tables also give you the actual dollar amounts that are used to figure the percentages.

1980 JAPANESE EXPORTS TO THE UNITED STATES

	Millions of dollars	Percent
Foodstuffs	245	.8
Textiles and clothes	593	1.9
Chemical and non-mineral products	1,231	3.9
Metals and metal products	4,167	13.3
Machinery and equipment	23,021	73.4

1980 JAPANESE IMPORTS FROM THE UNITED STATES

	Millions of dollars	Percent
Foodstuffs	5,171	21.2
Lumber	2,170	8.9
Soybeans	1,248	5.1
Other raw materials (cotton, scrap iron)	2,965	12.2
Mineral fuels	2,098	8.6
Chemical products	2,536	10.4
Machinery and equipment	5,015	20.5

An "Other" category was not included in the tables and graphs. As a result, percentages do not add up to 100.

SKILLS PRACTICE

The two pie graphs give you the same information that the two tables do. The pie graphs are easier to understand at a glance because they give you proportions in pictures.

Study the graphs and tables and then answer the questions below. After each answer, write *graph* or *table*, depending on which you used to find your answer.

1. What is Japan's main type of export to the United States? Machinery and equipment
2. What is Japan's main type of import? Foodstuffs
3. Does Japan buy machinery and equipment? Yes
4. Does the United States buy foodstuffs from Japan? Yes
5. How many millions of dollars worth of soybeans did Japan buy in 1980? $1,248,000

1980 JAPANESE EXPORTS TO THE U.S.

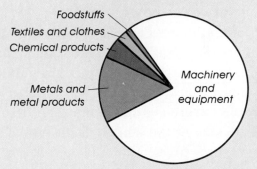

1980 JAPANESE IMPORTS FROM THE U.S.

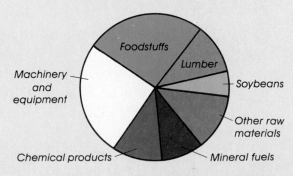

The South Asian Landscape

┌─ VOCABULARY ─────────────┐
subcontinent   monsoon
└──────────────────────────┘

Region of seven countries India is part of a region called the South Asian **subcontinent.** It is called a subcontinent because while it is a large part of the Asian continent, it is set apart from most of it. High mountain ranges separate the subcontinent from the rest of Asia.

South of the mountain ranges are wide valleys. They have been created by rivers. South of these wide river plains, the Indian Peninsula juts into the Indian Ocean. On the west is the Arabian Sea, and on the east is the Bay of Bengal. Just south of the Indian Peninsula is the large island nation of Sri Lanka (srē′ läng′ kə).

India is the largest country on the subcontinent in both land area and number of people. Only slightly more than one third the size of the United States, India has over three times the population of the United States. And India's population is still growing rapidly. China is the only country in the world with more people than India. Look at the graph on page 520 showing the most populous countries.

Two other populous countries lie to the east and west of India. Pakistan (pak ə stan′), to the west of India, is the world's ninth largest country. Bangladesh (bäng glə desh′), to the east, has the world's eighth largest population. Pakistan and Bangladesh each have close to 100 million people.

Afghanistan is a remote, mountainous country to the west of Pakistan. In size, it is a little smaller than Texas. There are about 60 people per square mile (23 per sq km). Most of the people are farmers or herders. Afghanistan has good mineral resources, but they are mostly undeveloped. In 1979, the Soviet Union invaded Afghanistan in support of the pro-Communist government. The government was in danger of being overthrown by rebels.

To the north, in the Himalayas (him ə lā′ əz) between India and China, are two smaller, landlocked countries. Nepal (nə pôl′) is the larger of the two. One of the wonders of the world—Mount Everest—is in Nepal. The Nepali call the mountain Sagarmatha (säg ər′ mä thə). Most people in Nepal and in smaller Bhutan (bü tan′) live in the valleys and plateaus between the mountains. In both countries most people make their living by farming or herding.

Sri Lanka, the island nation, was called Ceylon (sə län′) for many years. It is a country of plantations, which produce coconuts, rubber, or tea depending on the elevation.

Bathing in the Ganges, a holy river to the Hindus, is an act of purification. Here the Ganges flows past the city of Varanasi, also a holy place. (25°N/83°E; map, p. 371)

Tell pupils to skim the headings of the paragraphs in this lesson. Have them make lists of what they think the lesson is about.

Varanasi, formerly called Banares, is a holy city to other religions as well as to the Hindu religion. Note the floral offering in the foreground.

South Asia's four greats   South Asia has a complicated landscape that is easier to learn about if you think of it as having four greats. It has great mountains, great rivers, a great plateau, and a great wind.

You have already read something about the great range of the Himalayan mountain system. This highest of mountain ranges joins others to form a giant wall that separates the Indian subcontinent from the rest of Asia. The Pamir (pə mir') Knot, in north India, is a place where many mountain ranges meet. It is sometimes called the roof of the world.

These giant mountain ranges are a barrier to the masses of air that move north onto the Asian continent. Warm air from the seas to the south is forced up by the high mountain wall. As it rises, it grows colder and loses its moisture. The moisture falls on the southern side of the mountain ranges. This creates the second of the region's greats, the great rivers.

Great river systems   High in the eastern Himalayas, the Brahmaputra (bräm ə pü' trə) River carves a slow and winding route to the sea. Follow the Brahmaputra's route on the map on page 371. It is 1,800 miles (2,897 km) long.

In Bangladesh the Brahmaputra joins another great river, the Ganges (gan' jēz), which has followed a route almost as long in its journey from north-central India. Most of Bangladesh is made up of the delta land of these two rivers.

The other great river of South Asia, the Indus, also begins in the Himalayas. It flows southwest into the Arabian Sea. Locate the Indus on the map on page 371. Through what countries does it flow?

The Himalaya Mountains form an awesome background for this school in Nepal.

Much of Pakistan is dry, but the Indus River provides water for irrigation. The Indus River plain joins with the Ganges Plain across northern India, and farther east is joined by the Brahmaputra Plain. About half of the people on the Indian subcontinent live in the densely settled valleys of these three great rivers. The plains of these rivers and their tributaries form the world's largest alluvial plain. Often this area is simply called the Indus-Ganges Plain. It is a wide plain that stretches from Pakistan across northern and eastern India and south through Bangladesh.

The great plateau   South of the Indus-Ganges Plain, the Indian Peninsula rises to a great plateau. The southern part of the plateau is known as the Deccan (dek' ən) Plateau. The western edge or ridge is called the Western Ghats (gots). The somewhat lower ridge on the eastern side

Ask: Which of the "four greats" is not shown in an illustration in this lesson? (Great Plateau)

of the plateau is low mountains and hills known as the Eastern Ghats. Between the Western Ghats and the Arabian Sea and between the Eastern Ghats and the Bay of Bengal are the Indian coastal plains. They are rich farming areas.

Most rivers on the Deccan Plateau flow from west to east. The longest river, the Godavari (gə däv′ ə rē), begins in the Western Ghats and flows across India to the Bay of Bengal. Its wide, fertile delta is one of India's main rice-growing areas. Plateau lands with enough moisture are used to grow rice, cotton, and grains.

The great wind   Each year the people of the Deccan Plateau and the river basins of South Asia wait for a great rainstorm. This storm has high winds that are so strong that they sometimes knock down houses. Rain pours down so heavily and quickly that entire villages are sometimes washed out to sea. The storm lasts for 4 or 5 months. It is a once-a-year super storm that brings water, and therefore life, to the Indian subcontinent.

The storm is brought by the **monsoon** (mon sün′). The monsoon is a seasonal wind. It blows from sea to land from roughly April to October. It blows the opposite direction during the rest of the year. This gives most of South Asia a climate of two seasons, wet and dry.

The dry season is at its worst just before the monsoon arrives. The land is parched. Wells and streams have dried up. Many families have run out of food from the last harvest. Yet new planting cannot begin until the rains come. If the monsoon is late or does not last as long as it should, people can starve.

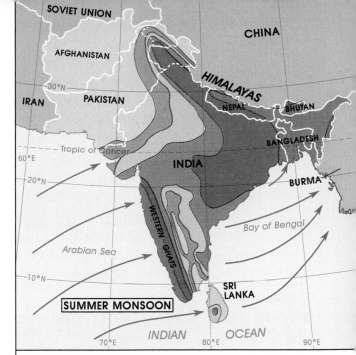

SOUTH ASIAN SUBCONTINENT: Precipitation

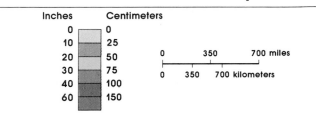

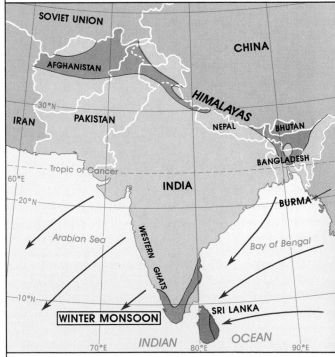

Monsoon winds have a great effect on climate and agricultural output. Winter monsoons are dry, but summer monsoons bring much-needed rain to the subcontinent.

Ask: Which map—top or bottom—shows the dry season in India? (Bottom) How do you know? (Scale showing amounts of precipitation) Refer pupils to the climagraph of Bombay on p. 511. Ask: When are the monsoon rains heaviest? (June and July)

363

Ask pupils to review the lists they made earlier.
Ask: Is there any important information in this
lesson that is not on your list?

The monsoon brings the year's supply of moisture to most of the farmland of South Asia. The monsoon is also important to China, Japan, and the Southeast Asian countries you will read about in the next chapter. In fact, the part of Asia that you are learning about in this unit is sometimes called Monsoon Asia. That should tell you how important the monsoon is to this part of the world.

CHECKUP

1. What is the largest South Asian country?
2. Name South Asia's four greats.
3. What country is mostly made up of the delta land of the Brahmaputra and Ganges rivers?
4. Through what countries does the Indus River flow?
5. Why is the monsoon important to South Asia?

The Many Cultures of South Asia

```
┌─ VOCABULARY ──────────────────────┐
│  Sanskrit          indigo          │
│  linguist          Hindi           │
│  Hinduism          partition       │
│  caste             refugee         │
│  Buddhism                          │
└────────────────────────────────────┘
```

Some very old cultures South Asia is the location of very early human settlement. By 3000 B.C., well-organized and commercial urban people lived in towns and villages in this area. This early civilization, which was centered in the Indus Valley in what is now Pakistan, was a very strong empire by 1500 B.C.

The peoples of the Indus Valley were conquered by a group of invaders who came through mountain passes from the west. The new group destroyed the cit-ies. They occupied the Indus and the Ganges valleys. Called the Aryans (är' ē ənz), this new group brought with them a culture that was the forerunner of modern Indian culture.

Aryan communities were farming villages. The people spoke **Sanskrit** (san' skrit). This language is similar to some of the modern Indian languages. The Aryans wrote their religious songs and scriptures in books. These books, called the *Vedas* (vā' dəz), are sacred to most Indians today.

Other groups entered the Indian subcontinent at later times. Among the most famous were the Greeks. They were led by Alexander the Great. The Greeks occupied the Ganges Valley in 326 B.C.

Isolated villages Most people on the Indian subcontinent were subsistence farmers who lived in villages. Most villages had little contact with each other. Without modern transportation, travel from one village to another was difficult and took a long time.

Because villages were isolated from each other, they developed different languages. Often the languages belonged to the same language family, but had changed so much that everyday conversation was difficult between people of different areas. Language experts, called **linguists**, have counted hundreds of different languages in South Asia.

Early religious conflicts Moslem conquerors eventually entered the Indian subcontinent. They had a different religion from the one developed by the Aryans. It was Islam, the great religion

364

The ruins of Mohenjo-Daro, an ancient city in the Indus Valley, are proof that a great civilization once flourished here. (27°N/68°E; map, p. 371)

Mohenjo-Daro had two-story brick houses and irrigation and sewage systems. Archeologists have found pottery, tools, and toys in the ruins. The ruin in the center background is the citadel.

of the Middle East that you learned about earlier. According to Islamic beliefs, there was only one god. All people under that god were equal.

The Indians also had strong beliefs. By the time the Moslems conquered them, most followed the Hindu (hin′ dü) religion, which grew from the *Vedas*. In **Hinduism** there are many gods, some more important than others. People are not equal in Hinduism. Each person's importance or role in life is set at his or her birth.

When a person's place, or class, is set at birth, it is called **caste** (kast). Caste cannot change over a lifetime. Hindus also believe that each person has more than one life. After each death a person can be reborn in another caste. Whether the caste is higher or lower depends on how well the person has behaved in the previous life.

These beliefs were quite different from Moslem beliefs. The Hindu and Moslem cultures, or ways of everyday life, were very different. Some Moslem rulers allowed Hindus to keep their religion. Others tried to force them to worship Allah, the god of Islam, and to follow the practices of Moslem culture. Finally, one very strong Moslem dynasty joined the Hindu and Moslem cultures together. This was the Mogul Empire. It lasted from 1524 to 1858.

The island of Sri Lanka is home to still another ancient religion. **Buddhism** (büd′ iz əm) had begun in India in the sixth century B.C. Buddhism teaches that

365

Display photographs of buddhas from many Asian countries. Have pupils note cultural and ethnic differences.

selfishness is the cause of all suffering. It did not last as a major religion in India. However, followers of Buddha, the founder of Buddhism, took the religion to other parts of Asia, where it is important today.

Enter the British   By 1600 the Mogul Empire ruled most of the Indian subcontinent. It was a prosperous trading empire. It both exported raw materials and crafted products. It was the empire the British East India Company dealt with when it established a trading post in India in 1612. The Moguls produced many items that the British wanted: silk, spices, cotton, and **indigo.** Indigo is a plant that produces a dark blue dye.

Indigo was very important to the British. The blue dye was needed for uniforms.

For some time the British and Moguls traded peacefully. By the early 1700s the Mogul Empire had weakened. Most of India was divided into small kingdoms, which were often at war with each other. Gradually the British East India Company, and later the British government, took over ruling the subcontinent. This part of Asia had become a British colony. India was the largest and richest of the British colonies.

This would be a good time for those pupils who chose to read *Kim* to make their reports.

The British influence   The British made some important changes in India. The most important things the British did were build roads, railroads, and large ports and establish English as a common language among the educated minority.

This Buddhist shrine is in Sri Lanka. The 22-foot (6.7-km) statue of Buddha was carved in the twelfth century from the stone surrounding it.

Arrange a debate: *Resolved,* That British colonial rule was a benefit to the Indians because it provided them with a common language.

By 1940, India had the largest rail system in Asia. The British also had built new roads, many of them connecting to the railroads. The roads and railroads led from farming and mining areas to ports. Three of these ports are the giant cities of Bombay, Madras, and Calcutta. These ports were collection points for raw materials that were sent to Great Britain for manufacture.

The British allowed few industries on the Indian subcontinent. They wanted most of the people to keep working as farmers. Indians had little opportunity to learn industrial skills. Indian people that could afford industrial products had to buy imports from Great Britain.

British rule had a great impact on the Indian subcontinent. The roads and railroads were helpful to later development. Cities without factories are still a major problem today. The English language for educated people is a mixed blessing. It lets the leaders communicate more easily with other world leaders. However, **Hindi** is India's official language. The problem is that only one third of the people speak it. It is difficult for India to develop a common language.

The partition   British colonial rule ended in 1947. Division of the former colony into India and Pakistan was called the **partition.** *Partition* means "division into parts." The largest part, the huge triangle of the Indian Peninsula, became India. Most people in India are Hindus. Many Moslems lived in two areas east and west of India. This became Pakistan.

At the time of independence in 1947, Hindus and Moslems were fighting each

Mohandas Gandhi: Great Teacher

SOME SAY that the difference between a good teacher and a great teacher is that a great teacher teaches how to live and lives a life worth teaching about. Mohandas Gandhi was such a teacher. His life changed the lives of others. His teachings brought about India's independence. He had such influence that people began to call him Mahatma, a title that means "great soul."

Mr. Gandhi was born in 1869, when India was still a British colony. He was a Hindu, the child of a middle-caste family. He spoke English as well as Hindi. When he was a young man, Mr. Gandhi went to London, England, and became a lawyer. Gandhi devoted his life to fighting injustice. Gandhi's methods of fighting did not involve violence. He felt that violence was a sign of weakness.

Gandhi led the Indian people in a nonviolent revolution that resulted in independence from British rule. As part of that revolution, Indians simply refused to obey unjust laws. In addition, millions of Indian people refused to buy British products or to work in British-owned factories.

By refusing to take up weapons, Gandhi's followers kept their pride. They convinced the world that it was the British who were in the wrong. Mr. Gandhi lived to see India become an independent nation in 1947. When he died in 1948, he was revered as a great teacher by people throughout the world.

Bowhani Junction by John Masters is good adult fiction about the independence period.

Encourage pupils to see the film *Gandhi* if they have a chance to do so.

other. There were many terrible riots throughout the land. Many Moslems living in India fled to the new country of Pakistan. They were **refugees**. A refugee is someone who flees for safety in a time of persecution, war, or disaster. Many Hindus who were living in the places that were to become part of Pakistan fled to India as refugees.

Some 15 million people moved from one country to the other. Some went willingly; others were forced to move. In their new countries they had neither land nor jobs. Many died after they arrived. Many others were killed before they could leave. About a million people were killed at the time of partition.

Pakistan was really like two separate countries. East Pakistan and West Pakistan were divided by 1,500 miles (2,410 km) of India. The people were also divided by culture and traditions. The only thing they had in common was their religion. East Pakistan had about 56 percent of the nation's population. West Pakistan, however, controlled the government, the economy, and the army. There was much unrest between the two parts of Pakistan. In 1972, after a civil war, East Pakistan became the independent nation of Bangladesh. Both Pakistan (formerly West Pakistan) and Bangladesh are still largely Moslem today.

CHECKUP

1. Who were the Aryans?
2. What religion are most people in India today?
3. What religion are most people in Sri Lanka today?
4. Name at least two ways the British influenced India.
5. What was the partition?

The Subcontinent After Independence

A strong nation with many resources
India today is a strong nation. It has many good resources. There are large reserves of iron ore and coal. India makes most of its own steel. It also has important sources of other industrial minerals such as manganese, chromium, and bauxite. It has enough of many of these minerals to export them to other countries.

The rivers of India are good sources of hydroelectric power. New dams have been built since independence. There is a need for many more. Recent discoveries of petroleum and natural gas deposits will provide new energy sources.

The steel industry in India has developed with the help of Great Britain, the Soviet Union, and West Germany, which have built mills such as this one.

Mechanized equipment is not useful on Indian farms, whose average size is 5 acres (2 ha).

One of India's richest resources is the land. At least half of the country's land is arable, especially with irrigation. Farmers on the plateau grow rice, cotton, peanuts, and grains such as wheat, corn, and millet. On river lands they grow **jute** and sugarcane. Jute is used to make burlap and twine. The coastal areas are important for rice and also for rubber, tea, and coconuts.

Although some crops, such as jute and tea, are exported, most Indian crops are used in India. India produces much of its own food now, partly because of a change in farming called the **Green Revolution.** During the 1960s, agricultural scientists discovered new types of wheat and rice that would produce twice as much grain from a planted field. The seeds cost more money, and the fields must be irrigated and fertilized, but farmers can now produce larger amounts of grain than before the Green Revolution.

Continuing problems   There are twice as many people in India today as there were in 1947. Every year the population grows by nearly 15 million. Even with the greater food production of the Green Revolution, more food is needed to feed this growing population.

A large number of people in India are very poor. Some work as sharecroppers for wealthy landowners. Others crowd into the cities, looking for work. Many people live in small shacks made of cardboard or scrap materials. India's cities have millions of people with no homes at all; they sleep on the streets at night.

Unemployment is another of India's serious problems. The country is developing industries as fast as it can. There are several important industrial centers. Jamshedpur (jäm′ shed pür), near Calcutta, is the center for steel production and other heavy industry.

Other important industrial centers process food and textiles. Still others produce automobiles, petrochemicals, and electrical goods. Three of the largest industrial areas are Bombay and nearby Poona, Ahmadabad (äm′ əd ə bäd), and the Madras-Bangalore district. Many people work in government offices in the capital city of New Delhi. There are factories here, too.

Begin a class discussion by asking, Why was the development of new types of rice and wheat called a revolution?

Mother Teresa of Calcutta, a Yugoslavian-born nun, won the Nobel Peace Prize for her work among the poor of India.

Refer pupils to the tables on pp. 332–333 and ask them to note the population density figures for India and Pakistan.

Not all of India's manufactured goods are made in large factories. There is a problem with modern factories. They often do not employ many people, because modern machinery can almost run itself. Many Indians work in **cottage industries.** These are industries in which work is done in the workers' homes. The weaving of fine fabrics such as silk is a cottage industry. The making of jewelry and the making of leather goods are, too.

The people of India still need education. The growing population makes it difficult to provide enough new schools. Half of India's population is under 15 years of age. Many have never had the chance to attend school.

The new countries Bangladesh is one of the world's poorest nations. It has rich farmland that can produce three crops of rice a year. Export crops such as tea and jute are grown. But the country has never been able to repair the damage from earlier wars. There is no modern transportation system. Most Bengalees live in isolated farming villages. Bangladesh is very densely populated. There are 1,736 people per square mile (670 people per sq km).

The rivers that create the rich farmland in Bangladesh are also dangerous. Floods are a frequent disaster. They are caused by typhoonlike storms. These storms also frequently cause tidal waves to sweep in from the Bay of Bengal over the low coastland. One flood and tidal wave, in 1970, killed over 200,000 people.

Pakistan's problem with nature is just the opposite of that of Bangladesh. Much of Pakistan is dry and barren. Farming is centered in the area of the Indus River, which is a source of irrigation. The main crop is wheat. Some livestock, mainly sheep and goats, is raised in the drier parts of the country.

Natural gas is an important resource. The country also has deposits of petro-

Over 20 million workers in India are employed in cottage industries.

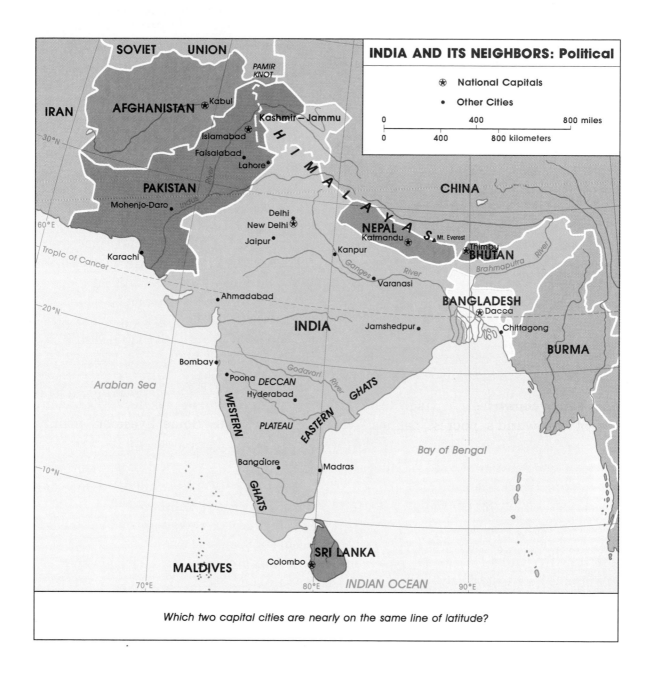

INDIA AND ITS NEIGHBORS: Political

⊛ National Capitals

• Other Cities

Which two capital cities are nearly on the same line of latitude?

leum, coal, and iron ore. The leading industry is the manufacture of cotton cloth. As in India, there is also an important cottage industry in handicrafts. These crafts include embroidery, pottery, and brassware.

Only about 25 percent of the people live in urban areas. Islamabad, the capital, has a population of about 201,000.

The largest city, with a population of nearly 4 million, is Karachi (kə räch′ ē).

CHECKUP

1. What was the Green Revolution?
2. Near what city is India's major steelmaking center?
3. What is a cottage industry?
4. What is a great natural danger in Bangladesh?

Have pupils each make up five short-answer questions based on this chapter. Collect and edit the questions and use them for an Information Bee.

KEY FACTS

1. South Asia is a subcontinent separated from the rest of Asia by high mountain ranges.
2. South Asia has rich alluvial plains between the mountains to the north and the southern plateau area.
3. The Indus Valley is the location of one of the world's oldest human settlements.
4. There is a long history of serious conflict between Moslems and Hindus.
5. Buddhism is another important religion in South Asia.
6. Hundreds of languages are spoken on the South Asian subcontinent.
7. The effects of British colonial policies can still be seen in South Asia today.
8. India has many good resources, including coal and iron ore.
9. The Green Revolution has helped many Indian farmers produce more food.
10. A rapidly growing population is a problem in South Asia.

VOCABULARY QUIZ

Welcome to the decoding room of Project U-speak. We are trying to unscramble words of the U-speakers. They jumble the letters in their words so that all their words begin with the letter U. The sentences below have all been unscrambled, except for one word in each. Your task, should you choose to accept it, is to unscramble the last word in each sentence so that the sentence is correct.

1. INDIA'S MAIN RELIGION IS USHIMIND. **Hinduism**
2. SRI LANKA'S MAIN RELIGION IS UBSHMIDD. **Buddhism**
3. A PLACE WITH MANY PEOPLE IS UPUPLOOS. **populous**
4. MUCH OF INDIA'S LANDSCAPE IS A GREAT UTALAPE. **plateau**
5. INDIA'S FARMLANDS PRODUCED MORE CROPS AFTER THE GREEN UTLIVOOREN. **Revolution**
6. A PLANT WITII LEAVES USED FOR TWINE AND BURLAP IS UJET. **jute**
7. A PORTION OF A LARGE CONTINENT SET OFF FROM THE REST IS A UNCOTSTIBENN. **subcontinent**
8. A LANGUAGE EXPERT IS A USTILING. **linguist**
9. MANUFACTURING THAT WORKERS DO IN THEIR HOMES IS A COTTAGE UNDRYIST. **industry**
10. A PERSON WHO FLEES FOR SAFETY IS A UGEFREE. **refugee**

REVIEW QUESTIONS

1. What are the seven nations in South Asia?
2. Why are the Ganges, Brahmaputra, and Indus important to South Asia?
3. What effect do storms have on the land and people of South Asia?
4. What three religions are important in South Asia?
5. Why did so many languages develop in South Asia? What effect has this had on the region?
6. What was the partition? Why did it happen? What are the names of the countries today that were involved in the partition?

ACTIVITY

Pretend you have a new pen pal your age in India. Write a letter telling about yourself. Tell about the things in your country that are similar to the things you learned about India in this chapter. Explain why you cannot describe what caste you are.

22/SKILLS DEVELOPMENT

UNDERSTANDING A POINT OF VIEW: PARAPHRASING

STATING A POINT OF VIEW

Mohandas Gandhi was a great thinker and a great teacher. He led the successful movement for Indian independence from Great Britain. Gandhi's teachings spread far beyond India. Among the people he influenced was Martin Luther King, Jr.

The passages below are taken from Gandhi's journals and letters. Use a dictionary if there are words you do not know.

SKILLS PRACTICE

Each quotation is followed by two statements. One of the statements is a correct paraphrase of Gandhi's words. A paraphrase is an expression of someone else's ideas in other words that shows an understanding of what was read or heard. For example, Gandhi wrote, "Nonviolence is the first article of my faith." If you were making a report about Gandhi, you might say, "Gandhi did not believe in violence."

By choosing the correct statement or paraphrase below each quotation, you will show that you understand Gandhi's words. Write the letters of your choices on a sheet of paper.

a 1. "We want freedom for our country, but not at the expense or exploitation of others, not so as to degrade other countries."
   a. We do not want to hurt others in our search for freedom.
   b. As we seek our freedom, we will find it necessary to hurt the countries that have held us back.

b 2. "If there were no greed, there would be no occasion for armaments."
   a. People are greedy for armaments.
   b. Greed has resulted in warfare.

a 3. "What appears to be truth to the one may appear to be error to the other."
   a. People do not always agree.
   b. There is a right and a wrong in every situation.

b 4. "India has to flourish in her own climate and scenery and her own literature, even though all three may be inferior to the English climate, scenery, and literature. We and our children must build on our own heritage. If we borrow another, we impoverish our own."
   a. India's climate, scenery, and literature are better than England's.
   b. Each country should appreciate and develop its own climate, scenery, and literature.

b 5. "I believe in the fundamental truth of all great religions of the world. . . . And I believe that, if only we could all of us read the scriptures of the different faiths from the standpoint of the followers of those faiths, we should find that they were at the bottom all one and were all helpful to one another."
   a. Study and appreciation of other religions would be harmful to one's own faith.
   b. Study of other religions would lead one to appreciate them.

b 6. "No matter how insignificant the thing you have to do, do it as well as you can, give it as much of your care and attention as you would give to the thing you regard as most important. For it will be by those small things that you shall be judged."
   a. You should save your attention for things that really matter and do a half-way job on small tasks.
   b. You should try to do your best in everything that you do.

373

A Complicated Physical Setting

> VOCABULARY
> **land bridge**

Landforms Southeast Asia is made up of peninsulas and islands. The peninsulas are arms of the mainland of Asia. The islands stretch south and east of the mainland.

In the northernmost part of Southeast Asia are the Himalayas. In northern Burma and southern China, the Yangtze, Mekong (mā kông′), Salween (sal′ wēn), and Irrawaddy (ir ə wäd′ ē) rivers run side by side in four narrow valleys through the mountains. Both the mountains and the valleys here are far above sea level.

Farther south the mountains fan out and become lower. The valleys between them are wide lowlands. The lower parts of the Irrawaddy and Mekong rivers flow through large alluvial plains that become low-lying deltas near the sea. The fanning out of the mountain ranges has made room for one other river basin, that of the Chao Phraya (chaủ prī′ ə), in Thailand (tī′ land). The large deltas of these rivers make up the major lowland areas of the peninsulas.

Most of the islands are mountainous. Flat land is rare on the islands of Southeast Asia, except Sumatra and Borneo. Much of that land is marshy. There are two areas of active volcanoes. One of these stretches through Sumatra, Java, and the smaller islands east of Java. The other goes from the northern tip of the Celebes (sel′ ə bēz) Islands through the Philippines to Taiwan. Find these islands on the map on page 329.

Volcanic eruptions and intense earthquakes happen often in this part of the world. The most violent eruption of a volcano in recent times took place in August 1883. This was on the island of Krakatau (krak ə tau′), between Sumatra and Java. The volcanic peak of the mountain blew up and fell in on itself, destroying most of the island. Only part of the island was left above water. People 3,000 miles (4,800 km) away claimed that they heard the sound of the volcano blowing up. The collapse of the volcanic cone and the island caused a huge tidal wave. Sea waves of almost 130 feet (40 m) were reported. The tidal wave killed thousands of people along the coasts of Sumatra and Java. Thirty-six thousand people drowned when it washed ashore. The eruption was even felt as far away as England. The ash thrown into the air when the volcano blew up darkened the skies and colored sunsets around the world for the next 2 years.

The fertile soil on the sides of mountains in Indonesia would not be available to farmers if they did not build terraces. These terraced hillsides grow rice.

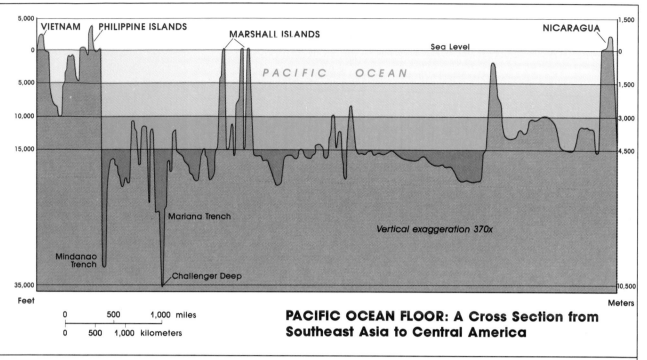

VIETNAM PHILIPPINE ISLANDS MARSHALL ISLANDS Sea Level NICARAGUA

PACIFIC OCEAN

Mariana Trench

Vertical exaggeration 370x

Mindanao Trench

Challenger Deep

Feet

0   500   1,000 miles

0   500   1,000 kilometers

PACIFIC OCEAN FLOOR: A Cross Section from Southeast Asia to Central America

Meters

This map shows two of the deepest underseas areas—the Mindanao Trench and the Mariana Trench. Challenger Deep, the deepest spot on earth, is at the bottom of the Mariana Trench. About how many feet below sea level is Challenger Deep? 35,000 feet (10,500 m) Refer pupils to p. 23 to review profile maps.

Borneo, Java, and Sumatra are connected to the mainland of Southeast Asia by very shallow seas. Nowhere are these seas more than 600 feet (200 m) deep. In fact, these islands and the Philippines were connected to the mainland by **land bridges** until 7,000 years ago. There are very deep seas, however, around the outer edges of the islands. The Mindanao (min də nä′ ō) Trench is a long, narrow undersea canyon just 50 miles (80 km) off the east coast of the Philippine Islands. It is over 30,000 feet (9,144 m) below sea level. The deepest spot on earth is 900 miles (1,500 km) farther east, near Guam.

Climate The climate of mainland Southeast Asia is monsoonal, like India's. The winter months are very dry, but much

Review the rain shadow diagram on p. 99.
rain falls during the summer. In many places there is more than 20 inches (51 cm) of rain in July and August. The western slopes of the mountains get the most rainfall. Some parts of the interior are much drier. They are in the rain shadow of the mountains.

The graphs on page 377 show the precipitation for two places in Burma. Moulmein is located directly on the coast. Mandalay is in the interior. Could you have guessed their location just from reading the graphs?

Most of Southeast Asia is south of the Tropic of Cancer. Therefore the winters are quite warm. The warmest part of the year is just before the monsoon rains begin in the spring. Once the rains start, there is so much cloudiness that July and

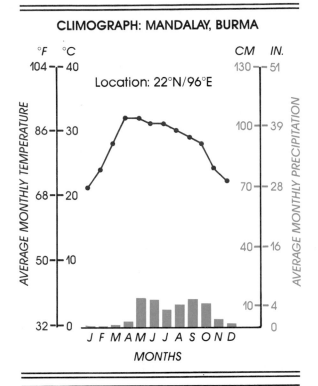

CLIMOGRAPH: MANDALAY, BURMA

Location: 22°N/96°E

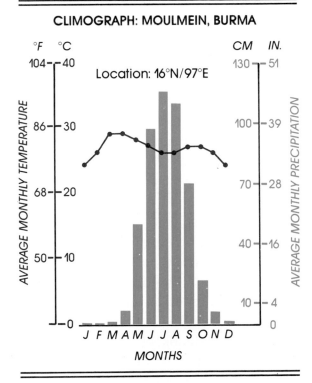

CLIMOGRAPH: MOULMEIN, BURMA

Location: 16°N/97°E

Are the months in which the most rain falls the same in Moulmein and Mandalay? Which place, on the average, is warmer throughout the year?

August are cooler than the spring months.

The Malay Peninsula and the islands of Indonesia (in də nē′ zhə) and the Philippines have a somewhat different climate than the mainland. There is no dry period. There is plenty of rain every month. Temperatures do not change much from day to day or from month to month.

CHECKUP

1. What are the major landforms in Southeast Asia?
2. Where are the seas deepest in this region? Where are they very shallow?
3. What is the rainy season on the mainland of Southeast Asia? Where is it wettest?

Many Peoples and Foreign Influences

┌─ VOCABULARY ─────────────
Mongoloid racial group
└──────────────────────────

The early people   Southeast Asia has been both a homeland and a passage for many groups moving south from the Asian mainland. Long ago the ancestors of the native Australians traveled through Southeast Asia on their way to Australia.

Other groups came much later, moving into Southeast Asia about 2,000 years ago. They settled mainly in the lowlands. Almost all of them belonged to the **Mongoloid racial group**. This group includes most of the people of Southeast Asia, as well as the Chinese, the Japanese, the Koreans, and the Mongolians. Most of the early lowland settlers of Southeast Asia were pushed into the uplands by later invaders. This has had an effect on the history of this part of the world.

Have pupils make a large bar graph for display, illustrating the rates of population growth in each country in Southeast Asia between 1960 and 1980.

377

Influence of other cultures Many important civilizations developed in Southeast Asia. All of them were affected by the powerful cultures of India and China. The Indians were important early traders. India contributed much in the field of art and architecture. The most important Indian contribution was religion. Hinduism, the religion of northern India, spread into what is today Burma, Thailand, Malaysia, and Indonesia. It played an important part in the life of the peoples of the early kingdoms of Southeast Asia. Buddhism later replaced Hinduism in most of Southeast Asia. It also spread to China and Japan.

Chinese influence in Southeast Asia has been even greater. Almost every country now has a large group of Chinese living within its borders. In most countries the Chinese have remained a separate group, keeping their own customs.

Today there are about 20 million Chinese in Southeast Asia. This is by far the largest group of Chinese living outside of China. This group makes up five percent of the total population of Southeast Asia. Thailand, Malaysia, Singapore, Indonesia, and Vietnam each have more than a million Chinese. They are a very important part of the population in these countries. They do much of the retail and wholesale trade. The Chinese are often viewed by the rest of the population as foreigners who profit from the work of the native people.

Another important foreign influence was the Islamic religion, which arrived in the fourteenth century. Islam did not win many converts on the mainland, but it rapidly became the leading religion of the Malay Peninsula and Indonesia. It spread eastward all the way to the southwestern part of the Philippine Islands. With Islam came the mosque and the architecture developed by Moslems in the Middle East.

Have pupils take notes on European and American colonizers, indicating the areas each group colonized.

European and American colonizers Europeans came to Asia because it was a source of many kinds of luxury goods. In Southeast Asia the Europeans were looking mostly for spices—pepper, cloves, nutmeg, and ginger. The Portuguese came first, but were soon driven out by Dutch and English traders. The English eventually controlled Burma and the Malay Peninsula. They also had small colonies on northern Borneo. The Dutch established themselves on most of the islands of Indonesia. The Spanish appeared in Southeast Asia almost as early as the Portuguese. They controlled the Philippine Islands for 400 years.

These ruins of a vast city in what is now Kampuchea are part of an empire that existed over 1,000 years ago.

Temples, monuments, and palaces were all part of the vast city of Angkor, part of the Kymer empire.

Have pupils use an almanac to look up each of the countries of Southeast Asia. Have them note the year of independence and the present form of government of each country, such as Communist, non-Communist, monarchy, federation, or republic.

France and the United States came late as colonial powers. The French began to occupy coastal Vietnam in the middle of the nineteenth century. Later Laos (laùs) and Kampuchea (formerly Cambodia) also came under French control. The United States took over the Philippines in 1898. Only Thailand was not a European or American colony.

Many movements for independence started in the early 1900s. In each colony there were usually a number of groups seeking independence. Sometimes all they could agree on was that colonial power had to go. <u>After World War II all the Southeast Asian countries became independent.</u> The people welcomed independence, but there were problems. The leading political party and important minority groups within a country often could not agree on a form of government or how the country should be run. Sometimes this conflict ended in a divided country.

President Harry Truman presents a pen to General Carlos Romulo after signing the bill that granted independence to the Philippines.

Communism in Southeast Asia

Vietnam was one of these divided countries. It had been part of the French colony of Indochina. After independence, Vietnam was divided into a Communist country (North Vietnam) and a non-Communist country (South Vietnam). This was supposed to be a temporary situation until elections could be held and a permanent government chosen.

The United States wanted to stop the spread of communism in Southeast Asia and so supported non-Communist governments there. In the late 1950s the United States started to send military advisers to help the South Vietnamese government.

By the middle of the 1960s the United States government was fully involved in a war to stop the North Vietnamese from taking over South Vietnam. The war between the two Vietnams went on even after the last American troops left in 1973. Today there is one Vietnam, and it has a Communist government.

CHECKUP

1. When did the Mongoloid peoples begin to move into Southeast Asia?
2. Why do many groups live in upland areas now?
3. What cultures have influenced Southeast Asia?
4. Name two countries that have large Chinese populations.
5. Who were the main colonial powers in the region?

379

The Countries of Southeast Asia Today

VOCABULARY

paddy   constitutional
trade deficit   monarchy
interest

Ten countries with growing problems
The southeastern corner of Asia is a troubled region. Wars, famine, and forced emigration have affected several countries of Southeast Asia in the past decades. Almost every country has economic problems and a fast-growing population.

Farming and food supply in Southeast Asia   Rice is the main food of all of the countries. Two kinds of rice are grown — wet-field rice and dry rice. Wet-field rice is grown mostly in flat lowlands. The young rice shoots are started in seedbeds. They must be transplanted to fields with standing water. These fields are called **paddies.** In most hilly areas, however, dry rice is grown. It grows like wheat or other cereals. But the yield from dry rice is much lower than that from wet rice. Because of this, most of the food in Southeast Asia comes from wet rice farming, and most of the lowlands are covered with rice paddies.

The farmers who grow wet rice also have small fruit and vegetable gardens around their houses. Often they have small ponds in which they raise fish. Pigs and chickens move freely around and under the houses. Many farmhouses are built on raised platforms as protection against floods. Raised houses also allow as much cool air as possible to circulate.

In the uplands of Southeast Asia, root crops and other crops such as dry rice and corn are grown on small patches of land. After a few years, as the yields begin to go down, the fields are abandoned. New ones are cleared in the brush or forest. This system does not produce much food, but there is enough as long as the population does not increase very much. As soon as the farm population goes up, however, there is less land for farmers to turn to. The farmers must then stay on the same plots longer. As a result, they

In Indonesia, rice is spread on mats in the sun to be dried before it is threshed.

GROWING WET-FIELD RICE

1. Rice seedlings, which were started in seedbeds, are planted in the mud of a paddy.

2. Several inches of water in the paddy supplies the constant moisture the rice needs and keeps down the growth of weeds.

3. The water is drained from the paddy just before harvest begins.

4. The grain has turned from green to gold, and the heads of the plants are heavy with rice. Most harvesting is done by hand with simple tools.

5. Threshing, or the separation of the rice from the stalk, can be done by machine or by beating the stalks against screens.

Nearly half the people in the world eat rice as their main food.

get smaller yields. The only new land available is on very steep slopes. These new clearings produce less food and create serious soil erosion.

In recent years, Southeast Asia has had problems growing enough food for its population. So much rice used to be grown in the lowlands that some of it could be exported. Now these countries have to import rice to feed themselves. Each country has tried to increase food production. New crops have been introduced. The dry lowlands of the interiors of Burma and Thailand are being irrigated. But these improvements will not solve the problem, because the population is growing very fast. In 1950 the population of Southeast Asia was 160 million. In 1980 it was 370 million! Farmers would have to grow 16 times more food in the next 100 years to keep up with the present rate of population growth.

Review definitions of *import* and *export* in the Glossary.

Economic problems Southeast Asia has serious economic problems because it imports more than it exports. This is called a **trade deficit.** Factories and industry came with independence. Most of the new industry produces textiles, clothes, and shoes. Southeast Asia also exports rubber, timber, and palm oil.

Most of the Southeast Asian countries have trade deficits because they must import food, manufactured products, and oil. The cost of their imports is much higher than what they get for their exports. All the countries have had to borrow money. Their debts are very large.

Indonesia: a growing giant Indonesia is a nation of islands. Find it on the map on page 331. Indonesia is one of the most populated countries in the world, and it is growing fast. In the last 50 years, it has grown from 60 million to 155 million people. Only 4 nations have more people.

Java is the most important Indonesian island. Almost 100 million people live there. Jakarta (jə kärt′ ə), the capital, has more than 4.5 million inhabitants. The two other cities in Indonesia with more than a million people are also on Java. But most people on Java are crowded onto the farmland. Every acre of the rich volcanic soil has to feed an average of five people. Compared to Java, the rest of Indonesia is nearly empty.

The population of Jakarta is more than ten times greater than it was 40 years ago. (6°S/106°E; map, p. 383)

Jakarta's population was 600,000 in 1945.

Almost everyone in Indonesia speaks a Malay language similar to the languages of Malaysia and the Philippines. Almost all Indonesians practice the Islamic faith. There are more Moslems in Indonesia than in any other country in the world. But even with these similarities, people of each major island think of themselves as a separate ethnic group. Many of them resent the people who live on Java. The Javanese dominate the economic and political life of the country.

An important mineral resource in Indonesia is tin. Rubber is a valuable export. But Indonesia's major natural resource is oil. Eighty percent of Indonesia's export income comes from oil.

Despite its resources, Indonesia does not have enough money to buy the food and other supplies it needs. Why is that? Indonesia borrowed money to modernize its industry and improve its agriculture. Now it must pay back these loans and the **interest** on the loans. Interest is the amount of money that a bank or an individual charges for lending money. Indonesia must use much of the money it gets from oil exports to pay the yearly interest on the money it borrowed.

Some of Indonesia's money is used to buy rice. At one time, Indonesia exported rice. But farm production has not kept up with the rapid increase in population. If farming expanded into places outside of Java, Indonesia could produce much more food. Why hasn't it? Because wet rice, which is the mainstay of the Indonesian diet, cannot grow in these places. Most of the islands of Indonesia are too

mountainous to grow wet rice. Many of the lowlands are tropical swamps, which could only be turned into farmland at tremendous cost. It is cheaper for Indonesia to buy rice with the money it gets from selling oil.

Indonesia's Malay neighbors: Malaysia and the Philippines Malaysia (mə lā′ zhə) is a country divided in many ways. As you can see on the map on this page, the country is divided into large parts by the South China Sea. One of these is the southern part of the Malay Peninsula. The other is the northern part of the island of Borneo. Both parts are made up of

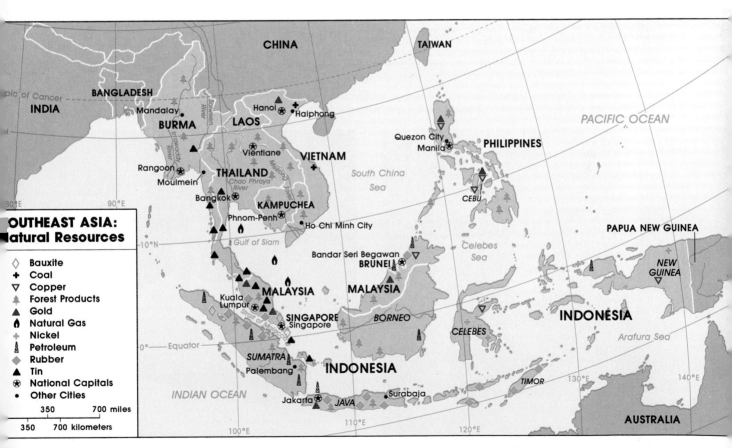

SOUTHEAST ASIA: Natural Resources

◇ Bauxite
+ Coal
▽ Copper
🌲 Forest Products
▲ Gold
◐ Natural Gas
⊹ Nickel
🛢 Petroleum
◆ Rubber
▲ Tin
⊛ National Capitals
• Other Cities

350   700 miles
350   700 kilometers

Teak, mahogany, and other tropical hardwoods are important forest products in this part of the world. In what countries are they found?
Burma, Thailand, Indonesia, Vietnam, Philippines

Synthetic rubber was invented in Germany during World War I. The making of synthetic rubber developed into a giant industry in the United States during World War II, when the Japanese conquest in Southeast Asia cut off nine tenths of the natural rubber supply.

smaller states. Malaysia has a federal government like the United States, but its government is a **constitutional monarchy.** In such a government the monarch serves as head of state and has mostly ceremonial duties. Nine of the states of Malaysia are also ruled by a king. The national king is one of these nine rulers. He is elected for a 5-year term by his fellow rulers.

About half the people in Malaysia are Moslems. A third of the people are Chinese Buddhists. There are also many people who came from India when Malaysia was part of the British Empire.

Malaysia is rich in natural resources. About a third of the world's natural rubber and a third of the world's tin come from the Malay Peninsula. Palm oil is another important export from this region.

The northern Borneo area is an important producer of oil.

Indonesia has another Malay neighbor—Brunei (brü′ nī). This tiny nation in northern Borneo has only 200,000 people. It has rich oil fields and exports oil. Brunei also exports rubber. The country became independent in 1984.

To the north and east of Indonesia is another group of islands—the Philippines. The people of the Philippines are related in both language and ethnic background to the people of Malaysia and Indonesia. However, the Philippine Islands were conquered by Spain more than 400 years ago. Since that time, Roman Catholicism has been the major religion of the country. Only a few people are still Moslems. Today these people are known as Moros.

Latex oozes from a cut in a hevea tree. After treatment, rubber separates from the latex and is fed through rollers. The sheets of crude rubber are hung out to dry.

Political and economic problems have bothered the Philippines since it became independent in 1946. Rapid population growth has caused many of these problems. The population jumped from 19 million to 53 million in the last 30 years. But the resources of the Philippines have not grown with its population. Most exports are farm products, such as sugar, coconuts, and pineapples. These exports do not pay for rice and oil, which are imported. Like Indonesia, the Philippines has a large debt.

There are many political problems, too. The Moros want independence. Many people do not own the land they farm. They want the government to break up some of the large estates into small farms. Many people object to the government because they do not believe it is run democratically.

Singapore: a city-state   Off the southern tip of the Malay Peninsula is an island. This is the city-state of Singapore. Singapore overlooks the Strait of Malacca (mə lak′ ə), one of the most important waterways in the world. The strait connects the Indian Ocean to the China Sea and to the Pacific Ocean, beyond the sea.

Singapore was founded by the British in 1819. It has grown to be an important metropolis of 2.5 million people. For a short time it was part of Malaysia, but it is now an independent country. Three quarters of the people in Singapore are Chinese. Less than 15 percent are Malay.

Singapore has a high standard of living, even though it has no mineral or agricultural resources. It is an important port and industrial and trading center.

The city of Singapore, combining the old and the new, is built around a harbor. It is the busiest port in Southeast Asia. (1°N/104°E; map, p. 383)
Ninety percent of the population of the country of Singapore lives in the city of Singapore.

The countries of the mainland: Burma, Thailand, Vietnam and its neighbors
These countries share a common religion, Buddhism. Their languages are all distantly related to Chinese. All of the countries have minority groups.

However, the countries have very different histories. Burma was strongly influenced by the civilization of India. It was a British colony until 1948. Vietnam was strongly affected by the Chinese civilization. It was a French colony, along with its neighbors Laos and Kampuchea. Thailand has shared ideas with both India and China. It was never a colony of a European country.

The lowlands of Burma are the most important part of the country. The capital city of Rangoon is in the lowlands. Minority groups, who often fight the central government, live in the uplands.

Since independence, Burma has had a Socialist government that has tried to be independent of the West and of Communist countries. Burma produces oil, rubber, and teakwood. Most of Burma's trade is for rice to feed its population.

Thailand is a prosperous country with a number of mineral and agricultural resources. It is able to grow enough of a surplus of rice and other foodstuffs to export them. It also exports rubber and teak. And it is the second largest producer of tin in the world. Its major economic problem is the high price it has to pay for imported oil.

Thailand has a large Chinese minority. But the Chinese have become part of Thai society. Many Chinese have married into Thai families.

Vietnam is like its neighbors in many ways. Its lowland areas are occupied by

Many men and women in the rural areas of Thailand continue to wear traditional clothing. The panung is a piece of cotton or silk wrapped around the body.

people who grow rice for their food. These lowlanders dominate the economy and the government of the country. Minority groups live in the uplands. As in Burma and Thailand, many of the upland people once lived in the lowlands but were pushed out by the more powerful groups. In all these countries the upland groups oppose the government because it is run by lowland people.

The Vietnam War was very costly to the land and people. The Vietnamese must import food and oil. The country is rebuilding its two large cities—Hanoi, in the north, and Ho Chi Minh City (formerly Saigon), in the south.

Laos and Kampuchea are satellite states of Vietnam. As you learned earlier, a satellite state is a country that is influenced and largely controlled by another country. Laos is a relatively poor country and is remote from the rest of the world. Kampuchea has suffered terribly during the last few years. During the Vietnam War a Communist group took over Kampuchea. A million people (a fifth of the total population) were killed or died for lack of food. In 1979 the Vietnamese took over Kampuchea and allowed food and medical relief to reach the people. It will take Kampuchea a long time to recover.

CHECKUP

1. What are the two main kinds of rice grown in Southeast Asia?
2. What is the name of the most densely populated island of Indonesia?
3. What is the political organization of Malaysia?
4. What European nation made a colony of the Philippines?
5. What are the countries of the mainland?

23/CHAPTER REVIEW

KEY FACTS

1. The peninsulas and islands of Southeast Asia are largely mountainous; the deltas of the main rivers on the mainland form the major lowlands.

2. Most new groups that entered the region settled in the lowlands and pushed older groups into the upland areas.

3. Many ideas about religion and architecture were imported from India.

4. The 20 million Chinese in Southeast Asia are mainly merchants and form a separate ethnic group in most countries.

5. Europeans came to the region 400 years ago in search of luxury goods, especially spices.

6. All the countries of Southeast Asia have become independent since World War II; most of them have serious minority problems.

7. Wet rice is grown in most of the lowlands of Southeast Asia, and shifting agriculture is the main type of farming in the uplands.

8. Almost all the countries of Southeast Asia have a fast-growing population and an economy that is not keeping pace.

VOCABULARY QUIZ

From the list of words, select the word that best completes each statement below. Write your answers on a sheet of paper.

a. land bridge
b. rain shadow
c. Mongoloid racial group
d. Hinduism
e. Buddhism
f. satellite state
g. trade deficit
h. paddy

1. The very shallow seas between the mainland and the islands of Borneo, Java, and Sumatra reveal where a _a_ used to exist.

2. The Malays were among the first people of the _c_ to move into Southeast Asia.

3. The need to import food and oil has caused these countries to have a _g_ .

4. One type of rice is grown in a flooded field called a _h_ .

5. The main religion of mainland Southeast Asia is _e_ , which is also the religion of China.

REVIEW QUESTIONS

1. What helped form the major lowlands on the mainland of Southeast Asia?

2. What happened to Hinduism in Southeast Asia?

3. Who were the main colonial powers? What areas did they control?

4. What are the main differences between the people of the lowland and upland areas in the countries of Southeast Asia?

5. How do most of the Chinese earn their living in Southeast Asia?

6. Describe the most important kind of farming that is practiced today in Southeast Asia.

7. What are the main exports of the region?

ACTIVITIES

1. Find the mouths of the Salween and Mekong rivers on the map on page 383. How far apart are they? Trace each river toward its source. Where do the rivers come within 100 miles (161 km) of each other?

2. Write a report on one of the following people: Sukarno, Ho Chi Minh, U Nu, Stamford Raffles, Emilio Aguinaldo, Carlos Romulo.

3. Draw a diagram explaining what causes volcanic eruptions or write a report describing the eruptions of other volcanoes, such as Mount Vesuvius or Mount Pelée.

MAKING A SPECIAL INTEREST MAP

PEOPLE AND THE FOOD SUPPLY

People need about 2,500 calories of food each day in order to stay healthy and to do an average amount of work. Men usually need more calories than women, and adults need more than children, but the average in most countries is about 2,500.

Some countries of the world produce or import enough food to allow their citizens much more than 2,500 calories a day. But other countries have such a small supply of food that many of their citizens are hungry or starving.

Look at the list of countries below. The figure next to each country tells what percent of the needed calories are actually available to each person in that country. A figure of 100% means that 2,500 calories are available to each person each day. A figure of 90% means that only 2,250 calories are available to each person who needs 2,500 calories. A figure of 110% means that 2,750 calories are available to each person who needs 2,500 calories. It is obvious that people in a place with a figure much below 90% are not getting enough to eat and that people in a place with a figure above 110% can usually get more than enough calories.

SKILLS PRACTICE

Using the figures in the table, make a map of Southeast Asia that shows the calorie supply in each country. On an outline map of the region, locate and label the countries of Southeast Asia. Then color each country to show its calorie supply as a percent of its calorie need. You will use the following colors for each category:

less than 90%	= purple
91–100%	= red
101–110%	= orange
more than 110%	= yellow

After coloring your map, answer the following questions on a sheet of paper.

1. What patterns do you see on your map? What region has the most severe shortage of calories? What region has an average calorie supply? What region has a large surplus of calories?

2. How might you explain the pattern in the Laos-Kampuchea-Vietnam region?

3. Why do you suppose Singapore has such a surplus of available calories? Is Singapore a farming country? Who lives in Singapore? How is the country able to get so much food?

4. Use a recent almanac to look up the rates of population growth in each country of Southeast Asia. Make a list of these rates. Which countries are growing fastest? Think about their food supply now. Which countries will have severe food supply problems if their present growth rate continues?

You may wish to reserve questions 2 to 4 for your more able pupils.

PER CAPITA CALORIE SUPPLY AS A PERCENT OF CALORIE NEED

Burma	106%	Philippines	97%
Indonesia	105%	Singapore	134%
Kampuchea	78%	Thailand	105%
Laos	94%	Vietnam	83%
Malaysia	117%		
For comparison only:			
China	105%	Japan	126%
India	91%	United States	135%

8/UNIT REVIEW

Answer Key in back of book.

READING THE TEXT

Turn to page 340 and read the section "A nation develops." On a sheet of paper, write the answers to these questions.

1. What event that affected Chinese history happened in 221 B.C.?

2. During which dynasty did China's population reach 100 million?

3. Which Chinese religion was based on the idea that people should live in harmony with nature?

4. In which religion was respect for the past important?

5. Which of these religions influenced the government of China?

READING A MAP

Turn to the map on page 357, which shows population density in Japan. On a sheet of paper, write the answers to these questions.

1. How many cities in Japan have a population of 1 million or more?

2. What is the population density per square mile in and around Tokyo?

3. Which major Japanese island has a population density of under 100 people per square kilometer?

4. Look at the city index below the map. Are most of the cities listed in the index on the east or the west coast of Japan?

5. What are the grid coordinates on this map for the capital city of Japan?

READING PICTURES

Pictures give information just as written words do. Below is a list of page numbers. On each page is a picture that falls into one of the following information categories: Industry (I), Agriculture (A), Religion (R), and History/Culture (H/C). Study each picture. On a sheet of paper, write the letter of the category that identifies the subject of the picture.

1. p. 361 R	6. p. 335 H/C	11. p. 341 H/C
2. p. 380 A	7. p. 355 I	12. p. 369 A
3. p. 379 H/C	8. p. 365 H/C	13. p. 338 I
4. p. 385 I	9. p. 352 R	14. p. 343 A
5. p. 366 R	10. p. 384 I	15. p. 370 I

READING A TABLE

Turn to the tables on pages 332–333. Use the tables about the countries of Asia to find out whether the statements below are true or false. On a sheet of paper, write T if the statement is true and F if it is false.

1. The population density is greater in Bangladesh than it is in China. T

2. Japan is bigger in area than Indonesia. F

3. The country with the largest population also has the largest area. T

4. The greater part of India's population lives in nonurban areas. T

5. Singapore is the smallest country in area in South and East Asia. F

OCEANIA AND AUSTRALIA

After pupils have read the text on pp. 390–391, have them study the map of Oceania and Australia on pp. 392–393. Ask pupils to identify the terms *Australia, Polynesia, Micronesia,* and *Melanesia* from their text reading and locate these four parts of Oceania on the map. Discuss the importance of the International Date Line. Have pupils locate Pago Pago, American Samoa (14°S/171°W), and Suva, Fiji (18°S/178°E). Be sure pupils understand why it is Sunday in Pago Pago and Monday in Suva. Select other places on the map and ask which day of the week it would be. You will want to use different days of the week.

The World's Largest Ocean

Oceans and seas cover about 70 percent of the earth's surface. The Pacific Ocean with its marginal, or bordering, seas makes up half of the earth's watery cover. The Pacific is nearly twice as large as the Atlantic Ocean.

The Pacific is the deepest of the world's oceans. A depth of over 36,000 feet (10,973 m) has been measured east of the Mariana Islands. That is almost 7 miles (11 km) deep! If Mount Everest, the tallest of mountains, were placed at the bottom of the Pacific Ocean at that place, its highest peak would still be more than a mile below the surface.

The name *Pacific* means "peaceful" or "calm." Ferdinand Magellan, the first European to sail across the great ocean, in 1520, gave the Pacific its name. When he first saw the open sea after a storm-tossed voyage around the tip of South America, the ocean appeared peaceful and calm.

But do not let the name mislead you. The Pacific Ocean is not always peaceful. During certain seasons, tropical storms called typhoons sweep over the Pacific and its islands. Typhoons are similar to the Atlantic storms called hurricanes.

Naming Oceania

Scattered across the Pacific Ocean are thousands of islands. They range in size from Australia, the world's smallest continent, to tiny islands, or islets, so small that no one has ever lived on them. Most of the islets are far too small to be shown on the map.

Some of the islands in the Pacific, such as Japan, Indonesia, and the Philippines, are so close to Asia that they are usually considered part of that continent. On the other hand, Australia and other Pacific Islands differ so greatly from Asia that they are considered a separate region of

Geographers estimate that there are from 20,000 to more than 30,000 islands in the Pacific.

To get an idea of the great size of Oceania, consider this. The distance from Perth, in Western Australia, to Honolulu, in Hawaii, is greater than the world. Years ago a European geographer thought that he needed a single name for this region, even though it consisted of widely scattered islands. He decided that since the region was located "in the Great Ocean—that which of all other is THE OCEAN," he would call it Oceania.

Oceania is larger than any of the continents. Because Oceania is so vast, another European geographer divided it into four parts: Australia, Polynesia, Micronesia, and Melanesia. *Australia* means "southern land" in Latin. The other three names come from Greek. *Polynesia* means "many islands." *Micronesia* means "small islands"; and *Melanesia*, "black islands," so-called because of the dark-skinned people who live there. All of these parts of Oceania are shown on the map on pages 392–393. Can you find them?

Where the Day Begins

Oceania is the part of the world where the calendar changes. The International Date Line passes from north to south through Oceania. It follows the 180th meridian for most of the way. As explained on page 43, the day begins at the International Date Line. When it is Sunday in Pago Pago, American Samoa, east of the line, it is Monday in Suva, the capital of Fiji, west of the line. Travelers going west across the line set their calendars ahead one day. Travelers going east set their calendars back one day.

Pago Pago is the capital of American Samoa, a United States territory. (14°S/171°W; map pp. 392–393)

that between Paris and Peking. Have pupils measure the distance between Perth and Honolulu and between Paris and Peking on a globe.

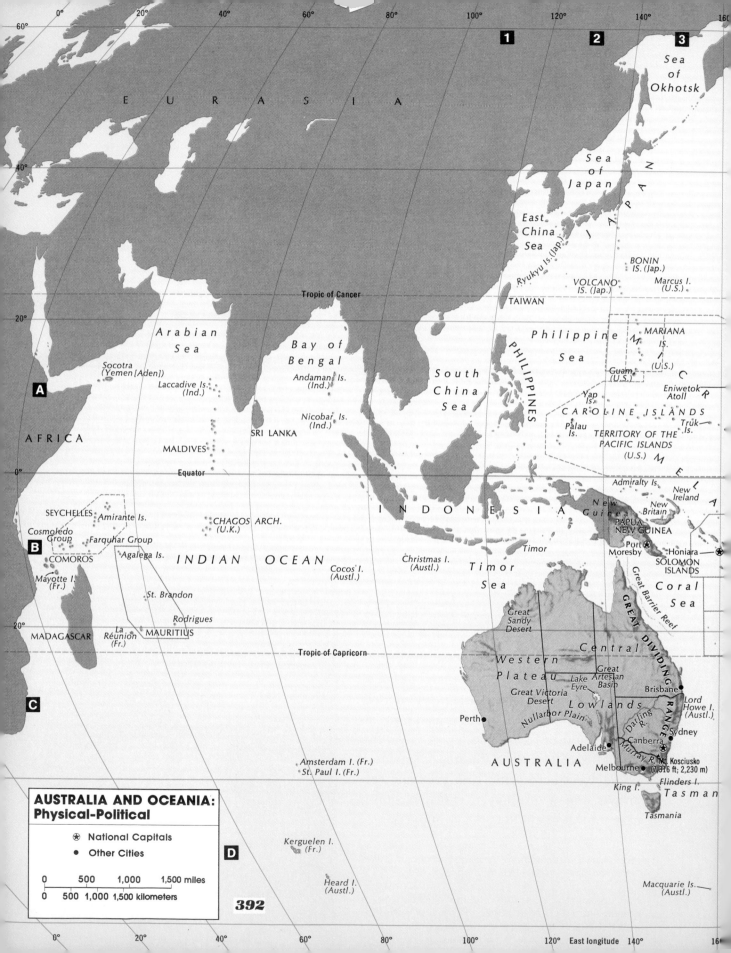

60° 0° **20°** 40° 60° 80° 100° 120° 140° 160°

1 **2** **3**

E U R A S I A

40°

Sea
of
Okhotsk

Sea
of
Japan

East
China
Sea

BONIN
IS. (Jap.)

Marcus I.
(U.S.)

VOLCANO
IS. (Jap.)

RYUKYU IS. (Jap.)

20° Tropic of Cancer

TAIWAN

MARIANA
IS.
(U.S.)

Arabian
Sea

Bay of
Bengal

South
China
Sea

Philippine
Sea

A Socotra
(Yemen [Aden])

Laccadive Is.
(Ind.)

Andaman Is.
(Ind.)

Yap
Is.

Eniwetok
Atoll

CAROLINE ISLANDS

Guam
(U.S.)

AFRICA

Nicobar Is.
(Ind.)

SRI LANKA

MALDIVES

Palau
Is.

Truk
Is.

TERRITORY OF THE
PACIFIC ISLANDS
(U.S.)

0° Equator

I N D O N E S I A

Admiralty Is.

New
Ireland

SEYCHELLES

Amirante Is.

CHAGOS ARCH.
(U.K.)

New
Guinea

New
Britain

B Cosmoledo
Group

Farquhar Group

PAPUA
NEW GUINEA

COMOROS

Agalega Is.

I N D I A N   O C E A N

Christmas I.
(Austl.)

Timor

Port
Moresby

Honiara

Mayotte I.
(Fr.)

Cocos I.
(Austl.)

Timor
Sea

SOLOMON
ISLANDS

St. Brandon

Coral
Sea

Rodrigues

Great
Sandy
Desert

GREAT BARRIER REEF

20° Tropic of Capricorn

MADAGASCAR

La
Réunion
(Fr.)

MAURITIUS

Central

GREAT DIVIDING RANGE

Western
Plateau

Great
Artesian
Basin

Brisbane

Lord
Howe I.
(Austl.)

C Lake
Eyre

Great Victoria
Desert

Lowlands

Darling R.

Sydney

Perth

Nullarbor Plain

Canberra

Adelaide

Murray R.

Mt. Kosciusko
(7,316 ft; 2,230 m)

Amsterdam I. (Fr.)
St. Paul I. (Fr.)

A U S T R A L I A

Melbourne

Flinders I.

King I.

Tasman

Tasmania

AUSTRALIA AND OCEANIA:
Physical-Political

✹ National Capitals
• Other Cities

D Kerguelen I.
(Fr.)

0   500   1,000   1,500 miles

0   500 1,000 1,500 kilometers

Heard I.
(Austl.)

Macquarie Is.
(Austl.)

392

0° **20°** 40° 60° 80° 100° 120° **East longitude** 140° 160°

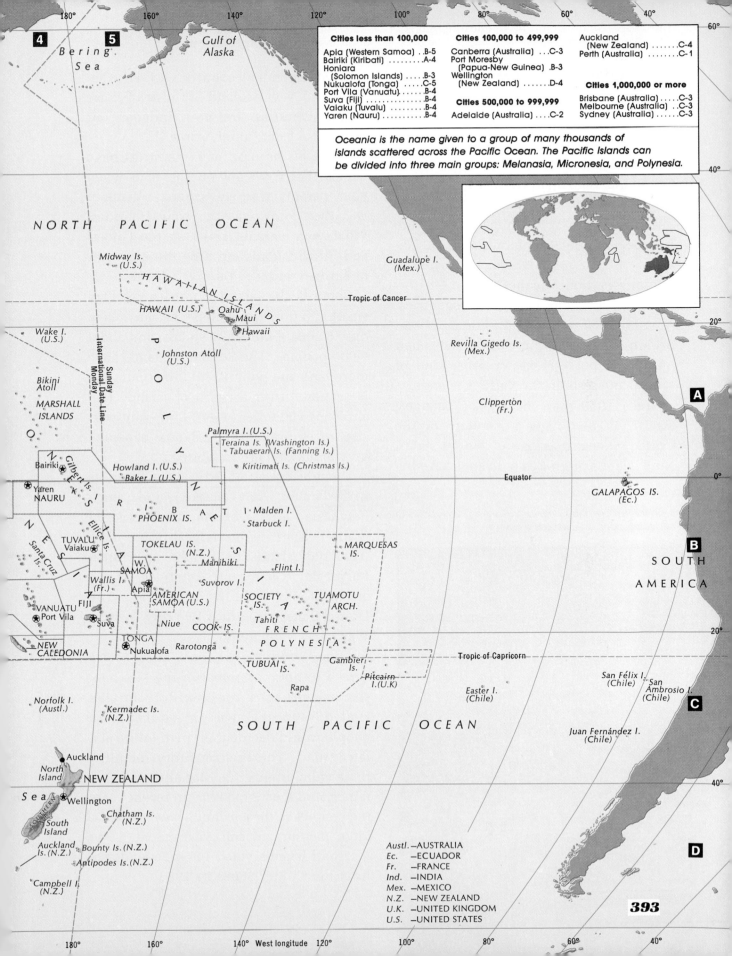

4 **5**

Bering Sea

Gulf of Alaska

Oceania is the name given to a group of many thousands of islands scattered across the Pacific Ocean. The Pacific Islands can be divided into three main groups: Melanesia, Micronesia, and Polynesia.

NORTH PACIFIC OCEAN

Midway Is. (U.S.)

Guadalupe I. (Mex.)

HAWAIIAN ISLANDS

HAWAII (U.S.) Oahu Maui Hawaii

Tropic of Cancer

Wake I. (U.S.)

Revilla Gigedo Is. (Mex.)

Johnston Atoll (U.S.)

International Date Line
Sunday
Monday

Bikini Atoll

Clipperton (Fr.)

MARSHALL ISLANDS

A

Palmyra I. (U.S.)
Teraina Is. (Washington Is.)
Tabuaeran Is. (Fanning Is.)

Bairiki
Gilbert Is.
Howland I. (U.S.)
Baker I. (U.S.)
Kiritimati Is. (Christmas Is.)

Equator

GALAPAGOS IS. (Ec.)

0°

Yaren
NAURU

Malden I.
PHOENIX IS.
Starbuck I.

B

SOUTH

TUVALU
Vaiaku
Ellice Is.

TOKELAU IS. (N.Z.)
Manihiki

MARQUESAS IS.

AMERICA

Santa Cruz Is.

W. SAMOA
Wallis I. (Fr.)
Apia
AMERICAN SAMOA (U.S.)
Suvorov I.

Flint I.

SOCIETY IS.
Tahiti

TUAMOTU ARCH.

VANUATU
Port Vila
FIJI
Suva

Niue
COOK IS.
FRENCH

NEW CALEDONIA
TONGA
Nukualofa
Rarotonga

POLYNESIA

Tropic of Capricorn

20°

TUBUAI IS.
Gambier Is.
Pitcairn I. (U.K)

San Félix I. (Chile)
San Ambrosio I. (Chile)

Norfolk I. (Austl.)

Rapa

Easter I. (Chile)

C

Kermadec Is. (N.Z.)

SOUTH PACIFIC OCEAN

Juan Fernández I. (Chile)

Auckland
North Island
NEW ZEALAND

Sea

Wellington
Chatham Is. (N.Z.)

SOUTHERN
South Island

D

Auckland Is. (N.Z.)
Bounty Is. (N.Z.)
Antipodes Is. (N.Z.)

Campbell I. (N.Z.)

Austl. —AUSTRALIA
Ec. —ECUADOR
Fr. —FRANCE
Ind. —INDIA
Mex. —MEXICO
N.Z. —NEW ZEALAND
U.K. —UNITED KINGDOM
U.S. —UNITED STATES

393

180°   160°   140°   West longitude   120°   100°   80°   60°   40°

Independent Countries and Outside Interests

The political map of Oceania has changed a great deal since 1959. Before that date there were only two independent countries, Australia and New Zealand. Both were then and still are members of the Commonwealth of Nations. All the other islands of Polynesia, Micronesia, and Melanesia were territories or possessions of outside countries. Australia, New Zealand, France, Great Britain, Chile, and the United States had territories, possessions, or some kind of special interests in the various islands.

Since 1959 there have been changes. Hawaii is no longer a territory of the United States; it is one of the 50 states. Nine islands or groups of islands have become independent countries. Like Australia and New Zealand, all nine of these island countries are now independent members of the Commonwealth.

Three of the nine new countries have names that were not on the map when your parents were in school. Vanuatu was then known as the New Hebrides. What your parents knew as the Gilbert and Ellice Islands are now the countries of Kiribati and Tuvalu.

Some of the island countries are very small. Nauru, the smallest, has an area of only 8 square miles (21 sq km) and about 9,000 people. The Solomon Islands have more land and people, but the population is scattered over a chain of islands that stretches 900 miles (1,448 km). Fiji consists of more than 800 islands, of which only about 100 are inhabited.

Outside countries still have interests in the Pacific. New Caledonia and French Polynesia are overseas territories of France. Tahiti is the largest of the more than 100 islands that make up French Polynesia. Guam and American Samoa are territories of the United States. The United States also holds two tiny islands, Wake and Midway.

After World War II the United States agreed to hold a number of the Micronesian islands as a trust territory for the United Nations. It was agreed that these people would decide their own future at a later time. The trust territory included three main groups: the Marianas, the Carolines, and the Marshalls. In recent years the peoples of these islands have gained a large measure of self-government. The Marshall Islands voted for independence from the United States in 1983.

Each year many thousands of live sheep are loaded at Australian ports for overseas export.

AUSTRALIA AND OCEANIA

COUNTRY	FLAG	TOTAL AREA	POPULATION and POPULATION DENSITY	CAPITAL CITY and POPULATION	WHERE PEOPLE LIVE
Australia		2,966,139 sq mi (7,682,000 sq km)	15,300,000 5 per sq mi (2 per sq km)	Canberra 245,500	
Fiji		7,055 sq mi (18,272 sq km)	700,000 99 per sq mi (38 per sq km)	Suva 63,500	
Kiribati		344 sq mi (861 sq km)	60,000 174 per sq mi (70 per sq km)	Bairiki 2,000	
Marshall Islands	In 1983 the Marshall Islands voted for independence from the United States, except in defense matters. There is no flag.	70 sq mi (181 sq km)	33,000 471 per sq mi (182 per sq km)	Majuro N.A.	
Nauru		8 sq mi (21 sq km)	8,000 1,000 per sq mi (381 per sq km)	Yaren N.A.	
New Zealand		103,747 sq mi (268,704 sq km)	3,200,000 31 per sq mi (12 per sq km)	Wellington 136,000	
Papua New Guinea		178,260 sq mi (461,691 sq km)	3,100,000 17 per sq mi (7 per sq km)	Port Moresby 123,000	
Solomon Islands		10,983 sq mi (28,446 sq km)	300,000 27 per sq mi (11 per sq km)	Honiara 15,000	
Tonga		270 sq mi (699 sq km)	100,000 370 per sq mi (143 per sq km)	Nukualofa 20,000	
Tuvalu		10 sq mi (25 sq km)	7,000 700 per sq mi (280 per sq km)	Vaiaku N.A.	
Vanuatu		5,699 sq mi (14,763 sq km)	100,000 18 per sq mi (7 per sq km)	Port Vila 3,000	
Western Samoa		1,097 sq mi (2,842 sq km)	200,000 182 per sq mi (70 per sq km)	Apia 32,000	

Urban ▮ Nonurban ▯ Not Available – ▧   **395**

On the map on pp. 392–393, have pupils locate the 11 independent countries in the region. Be sure pupils note the status of the Marshall Islands.

CHAPTER

24 The Pacific Islands

Sea, Land, and Climate

> VOCABULARY
>
> submerged   reef
> continental   atoll
>   island
> volcanic island   circumference

Mountains under the sea   There are mountains and canyons on the ocean floor. The mountains are higher and the canyons are deeper than those on land. Some of the ocean's mountains are completely **submerged**, that is, they are under water. But in some places the tops of mountains rise above the surface of the water and form islands. A number of the islands in the Pacific are the rugged tops of mountains that rise from the ocean floor.

Continental and volcanic islands New Guinea, the largest of the Pacific Islands, is one of the mountainous ones. Its tallest peaks are higher than any in the United States excluding Alaska. Many geographers believe that New Guinea was once joined to the continent of Asia. For this reason, New Guinea is called a **continental island**. Find New Guinea on the map on pages 392–393.

As you read in Chapter 7, there are volcanoes on the floor of the ocean. Some volcanoes remain submerged. Others have piled lava high above the surface of the water and formed **volcanic islands**, such as Hawaii, Samoa, and Tahiti. Some of these islands have steep, rocky peaks that rise sharply from the sea. Mauna Loa (mou nə lō′ ə), in Hawaii, towers 13,680 feet (4,169 m) above sea level. Some of the island volcanoes are still active and erupt from time to time.

Islands built by living creatures   A third group of Pacific Islands was built, at least in part, by living creatures called coral polyps. Polyps are tiny sea animals with hard, outer skeletons, somewhat like hard cups, into which their bodies fit. Coral polyps live in colonies made up of masses of individuals fastened together in rocklike formations. When billions of these tiny creatures mass together over a long period of time, they form rocklike ridges or mounds in the water. These are called **reefs.** Sometimes shifts in the ocean floor push the reefs above the surface, and islands are formed. Since these islands are made up of the skeletons of countless coral polyps, they are called coral islands.

Coral polyps live only in warm, shallow seawater. They form reefs near the shore or in other places where the water is shallow enough for the sun's rays to reach the ocean floor. The drawing

Before reading the lesson, pupils might preview the Checkup questions on p. 399 and use a dictionary to write down the meanings of the Vocabulary words.

The Society Islands in French Polynesia, shown above, are volcanic in origin.   In Hawaii some volcanoes are still active, as you can see from the picture below.

Have pupils look at the map on pp. 472–473.   Ask: What is the name of the line of latitude that crosses French Polynesia?   (Tropic of Capricorn, 23½° south of Equator)   That crosses the Hawaiian Islands?   (Tropic of Cancer, 23½° north of Equator)

An atoll may be horseshoe shaped, elliptical, or circular. An opening called a channel usually joins the lagoon to the open sea.

A CORAL ATOLL

Lagoon

Channel

An atoll is a circular coral island enclosing or partly enclosing a lagoon. Most atolls are in the Pacific Ocean.

above shows how polyps built up a reef on the edges of an island first formed by a volcano. After a long time the earth shifted, and the center of the island began to sink. As it did so, a shallow body of water, called a lagoon, formed inside the reef. In time the center of the island sank from sight, leaving nothing above the surface of the water but an island made from the skeletons of polyps. Such an island is called an **atoll**. Christmas Island is the largest atoll in the Pacific. Its **circumference**, or distance around, is about 100 miles (160 km).

Climate of the South Sea Isles   Poets and songwriters sometimes call the Pacific Islands the South Sea Isles. *Isle* is a poetic word for "island." The name South Sea Isles calls to mind lands of endless summer, warmed by the sun and cooled by gentle breezes.

There is good reason for this poetic view. The Pacific Islands lie in the tropics. The climate is warm, and regular

ocean winds moderate the heat, particularly on the smaller islands. Indeed, there is little difference in temperature from one month to another, as you can see on the line graph below. The graph shows the average high and low temperatures for each month at Apia, the capital of Western Samoa. Compare Apia's monthly averages with those of Melbourne, Australia. Melbourne is located outside the tropics. Apia has scarcely any seasonal temperature changes. In Melbourne there is a marked difference between summer and winter temperatures. Note that because Australia is south of the Equator, the seasons there are the opposite of those in the Northern Hemisphere. January and February are summer months; July and August are winter months.

This line graph gives two sets of facts about the cities of Apia and Melbourne. It shows the usual high and the usual low temperatures for each month of the year.

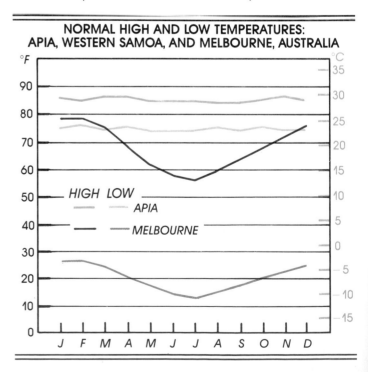

NORMAL HIGH AND LOW TEMPERATURES: APIA, WESTERN SAMOA, AND MELBOURNE, AUSTRALIA

HIGH LOW
APIA
MELBOURNE

Ask: What is the difference between the highest normal temperature and the lowest normal temperature in Apia? (Approximately 12°F, or 7°C) In Melbourne? (Approximately 36°F, or 20°C)

The main seasons in the tropical Pacific Islands are not winter and summer, but wet and dry. The wet season in Melanesia and Polynesia falls between December and March. In Micronesia the wet season comes between May and December.

The South Sea Isles have storms and much rain as well as sunshine and gentle breezes. Apia has an average of 19 to 22 rainy days a month during the wet season. Even during the dry months there is an average of 7 to 14 rainy days a month in Apia. The total yearly rainfall varies from island to island. Some areas, such as western Melanesia, may get at least 150 inches (381 cm) of rainfall a year.

CHECKUP

1. What are continental islands?
2. How are volcanic islands formed? Coral islands?
3. What is a reef? An atoll?
4. What are the main seasons in the tropical Pacific Islands?

People in the Pacific Islands

> VOCABULARY
> catamaran   trust territory
> outrigger   administer
> navigation

The first to come   The Pacific Islands were the last part of the world to be settled. The ancestors of the island people probably came from Asia by way of Indonesia. New Guinea was probably the first island to be inhabited. In the course of many centuries, people moved from island to island until they had spread over the vast Pacific Ocean. This migration took thousands of years. People may have lived in New Guinea 30,000 years

These huge stone statues were built by the early people who came to Easter Island. (27°S/109°W; map, p. 393)

ago. But they probably did not reach Hawaii or New Zealand until A.D. 500— about 1,500 years ago.

We do not know as much as we would like about the early migrations in the Pacific. The early people had no system of writing, so they left no written records or histories. There are few remains because the early people of the Pacific did not build large temples or stone monuments like those of the Egyptians. Nor did they build roads as the ancient Romans did. Yet scholars have learned quite a lot about them. Scholars know that the ancestors of the Pacific Island people used tools skillfully and made good use of the materials they had, such as tree bark and stone. These people understood agriculture, and wherever they went, they took plants and animals with them. The people who reached the widely separated islands of the world's largest ocean had certainly mastered the arts of boatbuilding and sailing. They had no need to build roads. The sea was the highway that led from island to island.

Mystery surrounds the statues of Easter Island. Pupils might use the library to research the physical characteristics of the statues and some of the theories concerning their original purpose and method of erection. Class discussion might follow.   **399**

Outrigger canoes have been used by the peoples of the Pacific Islands for thousands of years. The double-hulled catamarans were developed from the outriggers. Modern engine-driven catamarans are used mostly for recreational purposes. Some pupils might enjoy making a model of an outrigger or a catamaran.

"**Vikings of the Sunrise**" When Europeans first reached the Pacific Island region, or Oceania, the island people sailed the ocean highway in double canoes like those shown in the drawing below. They fastened two canoes together to make one boat that would not tip over easily on rough seas. These double canoes are sometimes called **catamarans**. The islanders also had smaller canoes with **outriggers**. An outrigger is a float attached to the side of a canoe to keep it from tipping.

The large canoes were from 80 to 100 feet (24 to 31 m) long, and they could carry 80 or more persons. Builders sometimes fastened planks on the framework between the two canoes to serve as a deck.

On this deck they built a shelter made of mats. A bed of sand on the deck served as a fireplace for cooking.

The islanders had no metal. They built their canoes with tools fashioned from stone, shells, and cords made from the fibers of plants. They shaped timbers from the trunks of trees, using only their stone axes and adzes. Since they had no nails or screws, they bound the timbers together with ropes of plant fibers. They caulked, or sealed, the cracks with a mixture of coconut husks and gum made from breadfruit. Later in this chapter you will read more about the remarkable breadfruit. The islanders wove sails and mats used in making houses from the long leaves of certain kinds of palm trees.

The people of Oceania built large double canoes that carried them to islands scattered throughout the Pacific Ocean.

This twin-hulled sailing canoe of Hawaii is very much like the early double canoe, shown on the facing page. Today Pacific Islanders continue to sail the ocean highway.

The canoes carried people to islands scattered from Hawaii, in the north, to New Zealand, in the south. Some people even reached Easter Island, which is separated from the nearest inhabited island by more than 1,000 miles (1,600 km). Easter Island is 2,300 miles (3,700 km) off the coast of South America.

The islanders sailed these great distances without the help of a compass. They found directions by the position of the sun during the day and the stars at night. When clouds covered the sky, they observed the direction of the wind and the waves to find their way.

Modern scholars do not all agree about the islanders' skill in **navigation**, the science of steering a course. Some schol-

ars believe that the islanders could steer by sun, stars, wind, and waves only where the islands were close together. These scholars think that the longer journeys were accidents, the result of being blown off course or getting lost. But other scholars believe that accidents cannot explain migrations to such places as Hawaii, New Zealand, and Easter Island. Peter Buck, a scholar descended from the early inhabitants of New Zealand, believed that his ancestors were among the most skillful navigators in history. He compared them favorably with the European Vikings, who sailed across the Atlantic to North America long before Columbus. Buck liked to call his ancestors "Vikings of the Sunrise" since they sailed east rather than west.

Whether they sailed by accident or with intent, the people of the Pacific did reach widely separated islands. We may not be sure about their navigating skills, but we do know that the large double canoes that they built carried them great distances.

Europeans discover the Pacific Islands
Ferdinand Magellan crossed the Pacific in the winter of 1520–1521, but he missed almost all of the islands until he reached the Marianas. The crews of Magellan's ships almost died for lack of food. If you look at the map on page 393, you will see how unlucky Magellan was. There are many islands between the tip of South America and the Marianas where Magellan could have found food and fresh water. But European sailors then had no way of knowing that the islands were there.

Other Spanish explorers came to the Pacific after Magellan. They discovered some of the islands he had missed. The Dutch, who had a trading colony in Indonesia, followed the Spanish. Still later, French and English explorers searched the Pacific and filled in the map with their discoveries. Perhaps the greatest of the explorers of the Pacific was the English sea captain James Cook. Captain Cook made three voyages to the Pacific between 1769 and 1779. You will read more about him in Chapter 25.

When we say that Europeans discovered islands in the Pacific, we mean that Europeans learned about them for the first time. The "Vikings of the Sunrise" already knew about these islands. They reached them long before Captain Cook and other Europeans "discovered" them.

This is a map drawn by Captain James Cook in 1772. The solid yellow line shows the route he intended to follow on his second voyage around the world.

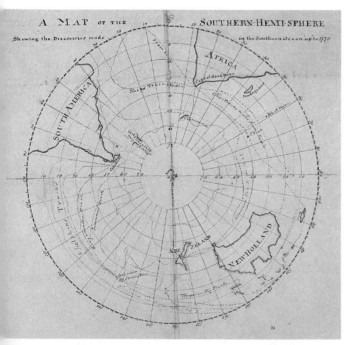

Yet the Europeans did do something that the islanders did not do. European navigators and explorers were the first to map the vast Pacific Ocean.

You can see traces of what these Europeans did in the names of places on a modern map. Europeans named a number of islands after places in Europe, and some of the names have remained. A Dutch navigator named New Zealand after a province of the Netherlands. The British named New Britain and New Caledonia—Caledonia being an old name for Scotland. The name of Norfolk Island came from a county in England. A Spanish explorer gave New Guinea its name to distinguish it from Guinea on the west coast of Africa. African Guinea was a land known earlier to European traders. Some islands, such as the Cook Islands, bear the name of their discoverer. Captain Cook named the Society Islands after the Royal Society of London, which supported his voyages. Spanish explorers gave the names of Spanish rulers to the Marianas and the Carolines. The names of two islands simply indicate the days when Europeans arrived. A Dutch admiral reached Easter Island on Easter Sunday in 1722. Captain Cook discovered Christmas Island on Christmas Eve in 1777.

Outsiders come to trade and teach
Once Europeans learned about the Pacific Islands, they came seeking riches. The Spaniards who followed Magellan hoped to find gold as they had in the Americas. That was the reason why the Spanish discoverer of the Solomon Islands named them after the rich king mentioned in the

On the map on pp. 392–393, have pupils find the places mentioned above that were named by European explorers.

While missionaries brought improvements to the islands, they also in some cases deprived the island peoples of their own traditions and customs. The positive and negative aspects of the missionaries' influence on the peoples of the Pacific might be the basis for a class discussion.

Bible. He hoped the Solomons would make him rich, too.

The gold seekers were disappointed, but later traders found that the islands had other valuable products, such as pearls, colored coral for jewelry, and sandalwood. Sandalwood is a pleasant-smelling wood that keeps its odor for many years. People in Europe, Asia, and the Americas wanted sandalwood for making furniture, ornamental boxes, fans, and various other wood products.

The island people, in turn, wanted a variety of manufactured goods from the outside world. Tribal chiefs particularly wanted guns because they had learned that a chief who had guns could conquer other tribes and rule. Many islanders wanted cloth, cooking pots, and glass beads. They especially valued steel knives, axes, and other hardware. They had discovered that metal tools were bet-ter than the stone ones of their ancestors.

The Pacific Islands became stopping places for sailing ships making the long voyage across the wide ocean. European and American whaling ships hunting in the Pacific stopped at the islands for fresh supplies and refreshment for sea-weary crews. To make their voyages more profitable, whalers carried on trade with the islanders.

Outsiders not only brought trading goods to the islands, they also brought a religion. Missionaries from Europe and America came to teach the Christian religion to the island people. Missionaries printed the Bible and other books in the island languages and taught people to read. The missionaries also tried to introduce the ways of their home countries. Many islanders adopted the religion of the missionaries. Christianity became the major religion in the islands.

Many kinds of whales are now endangered species. The International Whaling Commission tries to protect whales from overhunting. The United States officially ended American whaling in 1971.

Whales were hunted for their meat and for oil, which was used for fuel and for cooking.

Captain James Cook: Navigator and Explorer

TWO HUNDRED YEARS ago the English thought Captain James Cook was "the ablest navigator this or any other country has produced." During his three expeditions to the Pacific, Cook had explored the world's largest ocean from the Antarctic to the Arctic. Perhaps no other person had done so much to fill in blank spaces on the world's map.

People also admired Captain Cook for his modest manner. He carefully avoided exaggerations in his accounts of what he had seen and done. Unlike most officers in the Royal Navy at that time, Captain Cook was not a "gentleman by birth." He had risen from the rank of common seaman because of his knowledge of navigation and his ability to manage sailors.

Captain Cook paid careful attention to details, such as the diet of his crew. He knew that scurvy, a disease common on long sea voyages, could be prevented by eating fresh fruits and vegetables. But how could a ship at sea for weeks keep fresh food aboard? Cook laid in a large supply of sauerkraut as a substitute for fresh vegetables. When the sauerkraut was first served, the sailors refused to eat it. So Cook had sauerkraut served at the officers' table. As he expected, when the sailors saw that the officers got the new dish, they decided it must be the "finest stuff in the world." The sailors began to eat so much sauerkraut that Cook had to ration it.

Outsiders come to settle and rule

After the 1850s, Europeans and Americans came to the Pacific Islands, seeking land. They wanted land on which to grow sugarcane and coconuts because sugar and coconuts could be sold abroad. The sugar and coconut plantations needed workers, but the islanders were not accustomed to working for others. They had always grown and gathered only what they used. So the planters brought people from Asia to work on their plantations. The workers brought to the Fiji Islands came from India. Today half of the Fiji people are descendants of the Indians brought to work on the plantations.

All sorts of other people also came to the islands after the 1850s. These people included sailors who had deserted their ships, fugitives from the law, and drifters seeking out-of-the-way places. The islands became a kind of frontier society without real government. The tribal chiefs could do little to control the odd collection of outsiders who had come to the islands. The missionaries, planters, and traders wanted law and order, so they asked their home governments to take over the islands. A number of the countries were willing to do so, for this was a time when nations were building empires. Many of these nations were acquiring colonies in Africa and Asia, and so they divided up the Pacific Islands. Britain, France, Germany, and the United States took over territory in the Pacific Ocean. Germany lost its holdings after World War I. Australia, New Zealand, and Japan took over the German islands in the Pacific.

The text calls the islands a "frontier society." A committee of pupils might use library resources to research life on the American frontier. Suggest that they consider how government and law and order were affected by life on the American frontier.

By the middle of 1942, Japan had acquired a large number of islands in the Pacific, from the Gilberts to the Solomons. The United States and its European allies succeeded in winning back these islands through a series of hard-fought battles. In 1945, Japan surrendered its Pacific empire.

World War II and afterwards   Although World War II was a conflict between nations in Europe, Asia, and America, some of the bitterest battles of the war were fought in the Pacific Islands. War between Japan and the United States began on December 7, 1941, with a Japanese attack on Hawaii. Six months later the American and Japanese forces fought a big air-and-sea battle over tiny Midway Island. During the years that followed, heavy fighting took place in the Solomon Islands and on New Britain, New Guinea, and Guam.

Thousands of Americans went to the Pacific Islands during the war. The islanders learned a lot about the outside world from the Americans. The Americans, in turn, learned a lot more about the Pacific Islands.

Television sets and thatch-roofed houses are part of life in American Samoa. (14°S/170°W; map, p. 393)

After the war the Micronesian islands that Japan had held became a **trust territory** of the United Nations. As a trust territory the islands belong to no outside country. The United States **administered**, or managed, the islands until it was possible for the people to decide their own future. In recent years the people of the trust islands have become largely self-governing. Indeed, most of the islands have gained some self-government. As you read in the Unit Introduction, there are now nine independent countries in the Pacific Islands.

CHECKUP

1. What skills did the peoples of the Pacific Islands have?
2. What does it mean to say that Europeans "discovered" the Pacific Islands?
3. What traces of European exploration of the Pacific are found on modern maps?
4. Why did Europeans and Americans go to the Pacific Islands?
5. What outside countries acquired territory in the Pacific Islands?

How People Make A Living

```
┌─VOCABULARY────────────────────┐
│  frond              taro       │
│  plantain           copra      │
└───────────────────────────────┘
```

Before the Europeans came   There were few edible plants and almost no animals on the isolated Pacific Islands before people reached them. The first arrivals would have found little to eat except fish, a few berries, some ferns, vines, seaweed, and the fruits of certain palm trees. Almost all of the food plants and the animals now found on the islands were brought there by human beings.

Have pupils write a paragraph about island agriculture, using the Vocabulary words above.

405

The ancestors of the islanders spread plants and animals from Asia throughout the Pacific. Until the coming of the Europeans, the islanders lived by gathering and growing their food and whatever else they used. They fished; they kept pigs and small dogs. They made cloth from the inner bark of the paper mulberry tree. They used wood from palm trees to build canoes and houses. In the warm climate, they did not need much clothing or large houses. When people gather and produce just enough for their own use, they have a subsistence economy.

Two trees, the breadfruit and the coconut palm, provided much of the food and materials that the islanders needed. Breadfruit can be baked, roasted, or dried into flour. It is usually eaten with various other foods. That is the reason it is called breadfruit. Breadfruit trees bear throughout the year, and a single full-grown tree produces enough to feed a family. The trees also provide useful timber, and breadfruit juice is made into glue and caulking for canoes.

The coconut tree was and still is another major source of food on the islands. A coconut can be eaten either green or ripe. The inside of a green coconut is called spoon coconut because it is soft and jellylike. The inside of a ripe coconut contains a sweet, watery juice that people drink. The ripe nutmeat is used in many ways. Island cooks squeeze the fresh nut to get coconut milk and cream. They use the milk in preparing other foods, much as we use cow's milk.

The coconut palm provided more than food. People used its wood for canoes and houses. They thatched their roofs

The breadfruit tree grows about 40 feet (12 m) high. Its oval fruit is one of the most important foods of the Pacific Island region.

with the **fronds,** or leaves. They made brooms from the fronds and rope from the fibers of the coconut husks. The islanders did not make pottery, so they used the coconut shells for bowls. They also grew gourds for containers.

The island people had bananas and a similar fruit called **plantain.** They grew yams and **taro,** a starchy root. Taro is pounded to make a paste, which Hawaiians call poi.

Commercial economy European traders and planters brought a commercial economy to the islands. In a commercial economy, goods are made for sale. For example, islanders no longer simply gather coconuts for their own use as they did in a subsistence economy.

Pupils might make a bulletin-board display showing the possible uses of the breadfruit tree. In addition to the uses mentioned above, the inner bark of the breadfruit can be made into cloth. Its wood can be used for furniture and boats.

Instead they gather nuts for sale to an exporter, or they work on a large coconut plantation. On a plantation, which is often owned by a large business, production is far more organized than it was under the old subsistence economy. Trees are planted in rows and harvested on a regular schedule. As trees get old and bear fewer nuts, new trees are planted. Cattle may graze between the rows of trees. They keep the grass short and make it easier to harvest ripe nuts as they fall. Keeping cattle also gives a plantation another money-making product to sell.

Most coconut for export is dried. Dried coconut is called **copra.** It is eaten in foods, and it is pressed for coconut oil. The oil has many uses ranging from margarine and shortening to brake fluid. Coconut oil is also used to make soap, shampoo, and detergent. Even after the oil is pressed, the remains of the copra are fed to cattle and other livestock.

The people on the islands still grow bananas for their own use, but they also ship them abroad along with pineapples and some citrus fruit. Some of the islands grow sugarcane and coffee for export. Papua New Guinea grows tea and cacao as well as coffee. French Polynesia and Tonga produce vanilla beans from which the popular flavoring is made.

The tropical forests on the larger islands provide enough timber for sale abroad. Western Samoa exports timber, and Papua New Guinea sells both timber and finished lumber.

Fishing remains an important source of food almost everywhere in the islands. Canneries in some places, including Vanuatu, process fish for shipping abroad.

Here copra is drying in the sun. The metal roof of the drying rack rolls on rails to cover the copra during tropical rains. When dried and pressed, copra provides about 60 percent of its weight in oil.

Moana of Western Samoa

Moana lives in a small village set amid swaying palms on the beautiful island of Upolu in Western Samoa. Her home is a thatch-roofed house with blinds that serve to keep out rain. When the blinds are raised, the house becomes an airy pavilion open on all sides to the ocean breeze. Moana can see the ocean from her village, but she does not spend her days playing on the beach. She is far too busy taking care of her eight younger brothers and sisters. She also helps her mother and aunt with many other tasks, such as preparing meals. It is a great deal of work to prepare food, even on an island with plenty of coconuts, bananas, and breadfruit. Moana squeezes milk from coconuts, cleans chickens, or bakes fish and breadfruit wrapped in banana leaves.

Then there is always the laundry to do. The family is a large one, and it is hard work washing clothing by hand in cold water at the village's only water tap. Moana's aunt makes much of the family's clothing, and Moana often helps her because it takes two people to operate their old-fashioned sewing machine. Moana turns the wheel while her aunt feeds the cloth under the needle.

Sometimes when Moana has a little time to herself, she wonders about what she should do when she gets older. Should she remain in the village as her mother and aunt have done? Or should she go to New Zealand and get a job as her older friend, Malu, did? Malu came home last year on a visit and told Moana how much money she was making. It sounded like a lot, but, as Malu said, it takes a lot to live in New Zealand. Moana has a cousin in Auckland, New Zealand, and she could live with her. That would be better than living in one of the crowded boardinghouses she has heard about. But New Zealand seems so far away. Moana likes her village home, and she really does not mind taking care of her brothers and sisters. Yet life in Auckland does sound exciting. Moana is not sure just what she wants to do.

Mining The early Spanish explorers failed to find gold in the Pacific Islands. But today, gold is mined in Fiji and Papua New Guinea, which also has copper and silver. Both New Caledonia and the Solomon Islands have deposits of nickel. Vanuatu has manganese, a metal used in making steel.

Mining is almost the only industry of tiny Nauru (nä ü´rü). The central part of the island has a large deposit of phosphate. The mining and export of phosphate has made Nauru a rich country. But it is not clear what will happen when the phosphate deposit is worked out. Nauru has almost no other resources. You will read more about this in Chapter 26.

The effects of isolation The isolated location of the Pacific Islands has been both an advantage and a disadvantage. It is an advantage in that it attracts tourists from other lands who want to get away from everything. People come to lie on

408 A large copper mine in Papua New Guinea is also among the world's largest gold producers. The mine is located on the island of Bougainville.

Beautiful beaches, such as this one in Hawaii, lure tourists to the Pacific Islands.

the beaches, ride the surf, and dream in the shade of the palm trees. <u>Tourism is a major industry on a number of the islands and creates jobs for many islanders.</u>

Another advantage of the islands' location is that they serve as a stopping place in the middle of a wide ocean. Airplanes flying the Pacific stop at Guam's international airport. The United States has a military base on Guam. The economy of the island depends largely on the airport, the military base, and tourism.

The isolation of the islands has had some disadvantages, too. Because the islands are so separated from the rest of the world, other countries have used them as testing sites for nuclear bombs. In 1946 the United States moved 200 people off the island of Bikini in the Marshall Islands so that it could test bombs there. From 1946 to 1958 the United States exploded 23 bombs on Bikini. People were allowed to return to their homes in the early 1970s. But they

had to leave in 1978 because new tests showed that the site might still endanger their health. The French used Mururoa Atoll in French Polynesia to test their bombs. They exploded bombs in the atmosphere until 1975. Since then, explosions have been underground.

The isolated location of the Pacific Islands has affected the islanders in strangely different ways. Because they were isolated, the islanders used stone tools and weapons long after the rest of the world used metal. Yet, because they were isolated, the islanders lived where outside countries wanted to test their modern, nuclear weapons.

CHECKUP

1. How did people on the Pacific Islands make a living before the coming of the Europeans?
2. How did European traders and planters affect the economy of the Pacific Islands?
3. What are some of the exports from the Pacific Islands?
4. What are some advantages of the location of the Pacific Islands? Some disadvantages?

Ask pupils to make a list of jobs associated with the services required by tourists. These might include jobs in hotels, restaurants, shops. Volunteers might select certain jobs and tell the class why they would like to have the jobs they chose.

KEY FACTS

1. The three kinds of islands in the Pacific are continental islands, volcanic islands, and coral islands.

2. The Pacific Islands have a tropical climate.

3. The ancestors of the Pacific Island people came from Asia. They reached the islands long before the Europeans.

4. After the 1850s, outside nations took control of the Pacific Islands. Today, however, most of the islands are either independent or largely self-governing.

5. Important island crops include breadfruit, coconuts, bananas, plantains, yams, taro, sweet potatoes, sugar, coffee, and vanilla.

6. Gold, copper, manganese, and phosphate are mined in the Pacific Islands.

VOCABULARY QUIZ

Read the following statements. Decide which are true and which are false. Write your answers (**T** or **F**) on a sheet of paper.

T **1.** Submerged mountains are below the ocean's surface.

T **2.** Coral polyps sometimes build reefs on the edges of volcanic islands.

F **3.** The circumference of an island is an enclosed body of water on an atoll.

F **4.** Navigation is the art of building canoes.

T **5.** The migrations of the island people show that their catamarans could sail for long distances.

F **6.** Outriggers were traders from Europe.

T **7.** The United States agreed to administer trust territories for the United Nations.

F **8.** Dried plantain is called copra.

F **9.** Fronds are small isles.

T **10.** Taro is a starchy root used for food.

REVIEW QUESTIONS

1. How were the different kinds of islands in the Pacific formed?

2. How do seasons in the Pacific Islands differ from seasons in places outside the tropics?

3. Why have the ancestors of some Pacific Island people been called "Vikings of the Sunrise"? Describe some of the things these early islanders were able to do.

4. Did Europeans discover the Pacific Islands? What were they the first to do?

5. Why did Europeans and Americans go to the Pacific Islands? What were some of the effects of their presence?

6. What is the difference between a subsistence and a commercial economy? Which did the islanders have before the arrival of outsiders? Which economy do the islanders have today?

7. What are some ways that the location of the Pacific Islands has affected them?

ACTIVITIES

1. Make a graph showing average monthly high and low temperatures in the place where you live or for a city in your region. You may have to look in an almanac for this information.

2. Make paper flags for each of the Pacific Island countries shown in the Table of Countries, page 395. The five stars shown on three of the flags stand for the Southern Cross. Write a short report on the Southern Cross. One country's flag shows that it is located south of the Equator. Can you guess which flag this is?

3. Using the picture on page 400 or a picture from another source, make a model of a Pacific Island canoe.

READING FOR UNDERSTANDING

USING CONTEXT CLUES

In 1835, Charles Darwin, an English naturalist, visited the island of Tahiti. The following selection is from Darwin's account of his visit. Some of the words in the selection have been underlined. You may be able to figure out what these words mean by the way that they are used. The first exercise may help you. It lists each of the underlined words and three other words, one of which has the same meaning as the underlined word.

A VISIT TO TAHITI IN 1835

As soon as we anchored, we were surrounded by canoes. This was our Sunday, but the Monday of Tahiti: if the case had been reversed, we should not have received a single visit; for the injunction not to launch a canoe on the Sabbath is rigidly obeyed.

I was pleased with nothing so much as the inhabitants. There is a mildness in the expressions of their countenances which at once banishes the idea of a savage; and an intelligence which shows that they are advancing in civilization. Nearly all of the natives understand a little English—that is, they know the names of common things; and by the aid of this together with signs, a lame sort of conversation could be carried on. In returning in the evening to the boat we stopped to witness a very pretty scene. Numbers of children were playing on the beach, and had lighted bonfires which illuminated the placid sea; others, in circles, were singing Tahitian verses. We seated ourselves on the sand, and joined their party. The songs were impromptu, and I believe related to our arrival: one little girl sang a line, which the rest took up in parts, forming a very pretty chorus. The whole scene made us unequivocally aware that we were seated on the shores of an island in the far-famed South Seas.

SKILLS PRACTICE: PART I

On a sheet of paper write the letter of the meaning of each word *as it is used in the selection above.*

Example:

reversed: (a) the other way (b) the same (c) backward. The correct answer is **a**.

c **1.** injunction: (a) turning point (b) crossroad (c) command

a **2.** rigidly: (a) strictly (b) seldom (c) usually

b **3.** countenances: (a) wishes (b) faces (c) weapons

a **4.** banishes: (a) gets rid of (b) shows (c) proves

a **5.** lame: (a) poor (b) unusual (c) rich

c **6.** witness: (a) hear about (b) dream of (c) see

c **7.** illuminated: (a) pictured (b) announced (c) lighted

b **8.** placid: (a) deep (b) peaceful (c) salty

a **9.** impromptu: (a) unrehearsed (b) written (c) ancient

c **10.** unequivocally: (a) doubtfully (b) jokingly (c) clearly

SKILLS PRACTICE: PART II

Which of the following statements are true and which are false? Write your answers (**T** or **F**) on a sheet of paper.

T **1.** Darwin's ship had crossed the International Date Line.

T **2.** The Tahitians did not greet ships on Sunday.

T **3.** Darwin liked the people of Tahiti.

F **4.** The Tahitians had a fierce look.

F **5.** The Tahitians knew no English.

F **6.** In the evening when Darwin returned to the boat, the sea had grown rough and stormy.

F **7.** Darwin taught the Tahitian children the songs they sang.

Australia—An Island Continent

-VOCABULARY-
platypus	species
marsupial	extinct

A small continent but a large country
Australia is another part of Oceania. Like the other lands of the region, it is an island. But, unlike the others, it is also a continent. Australia is a country as well —a rather large country. Among the continents it is the smallest. But among the world's countries it is the sixth largest.

Australia is a compact continent, as a comparison of its coast with the much indented coasts of Europe or Asia shows. The western half of Australia is a plateau, much of it rocky and very dry. Two of the world's large deserts, the Great Sandy and the Great Victoria, are on the plateau. The Great Victoria Desert is nearly as large as Texas.

Australia is the flattest of the continents. Its highest land is a belt called the Great Dividing Range, which stretches along the east coast. The Dividing Range separates the well-watered east coastlands from the rest of the continent. The tallest of Australia's mountains, known as the Australian Alps, form the southern end of the Dividing Range. The tallest peak in these mountains is Mount Kosciusko (kos ē us′ kō). It rises 7,316 feet (2,230 m) above sea level. The island of Tasmania, off the southeast coast, is a continuation of the Dividing Range.

Between the Dividing Range and the Western Plateau lies an area of rolling plains known as the Central Lowlands.

Climate Most of Australia is dry. About one third of the continent is desert and receives an average of less than 10 inches (25 cm) of rainfall a year. Another third is fairly dry, getting less than 20 inches (51 cm) of rainfall a year. Only about one tenth of the country, mostly in the southeast, can be considered well watered. Other areas along the southwest and north coasts receive plenty of rain during part of the year, but have seasonal droughts.

Temperatures in Australia vary from hot to mild. The north coast lies within the tropics and has high temperatures throughout the year. But the hottest part of the continent is the dry interior. There, summer temperatures commonly rise to 100°F (37.7°C) and higher. Australia has no truly cold regions. Snow falls regularly only in the higher mountains. Tasmania, the part of the country farthest from the Equator, has a climate somewhat like that of northern California.

Many small caves are found inside Ayers Rock. Paintings made by Australia's earliest known inhabitants cover the walls.

(Top) Australia's most fertile land lies along the well-watered east coast.   (Bottom) Ayers Rock, a popular tourist attraction, is in the dry Western Plateau region.

Have pupils use the Atlas map on pp. 470–471 to find Australia and to show its location in relation to other continents. Ask: In what direction would a person travel to reach Australia from North America? (Southwest)

The Great Barrier Reef   The largest structure ever built by living creatures was not made by human hands. It was built by countless coral polyps along the northeast coast of Australia. The structure, known as the Great Barrier Reef, is made up of thousands of individual reefs and coral islets. It stretches 1,250 miles (2,000 km) and covers an area larger than the state of Nebraska.

The Great Barrier teems with a wide variety of sea life and birds. In 1979, Australia set aside part of the Great Barrier as a marine park. In doing this, the government hoped to protect this remarkable coral structure and the different creatures that live there.

Wildlife of an isolated continent   People in Europe knew little about Australia 200 years ago, so there was great interest when someone brought the skin of an unusual Australian animal to London. The animal appeared to be about the size of a large rabbit and had soft fur, webbed feet, a tail like a beaver's, and a large, flat bill like that of a duck. Many people thought that someone had made a fake skin as a joke. But such suspicions were wrong. The skin was indeed that of a real animal that lives in and along the rivers of eastern Australia—the duckbill **platypus**. There is something even more unusual about the platypus than its bill. It is a mammal, yet it lays eggs. Australia has two such animals. The echidna (i kid′ nə), or spiny anteater, also hatches its young from eggs.

The platypus and echidna are but two of the animals that surprised Europeans when they first came to Australia. Be-

The Great Barrier Reef of Australia is the world's largest coral reef. Many forms of sea life live among the beautiful coral formations. The calm water between the Great Barrier Reef and the mainland offers a sheltered waterway for ships.

cause Australia had been cut off from the other continents for a long period of time, its birds and animals differed from those known elsewhere. One of the first Europeans to see a kangaroo wrote, "Nothing, certainly, I have seen at all resembles him." To the present day, visitors to Australia are fascinated by the kangaroos. Australia has about 46 kinds of kangaroos. A small variety, the wallaby (wol′ ə bē), is no larger than a small dog, but the larger varieties may stand taller than a grown person. All kangaroos have short front legs and large back ones. They do not run; they hop. A large kangaroo can cover 30 feet (9 m) in a single hop and bound across the ground at speeds of up

414   Geologists believe that 50 million years ago a land bridge connected Australia to the Malay Peninsula. The islands of Indonesia were once the mountain peaks of this bridge. After Australia became an island, it developed its unique forms of plant and animal life.

to 30 miles (48 km) an hour. Kangaroos have been known to clear 10-foot (3-m) high fences with a single hop.

Kangaroos are **marsupials** (mär sü′ pē əls). These animals carry their young in a pouch until their young are fully developed. Australia has more than 100 **species**, or kinds, of marsupials. North America has only one, the opossum; and Europe has none. Koalas (kō ä′ ləs), the small, fuzzy Australian animals that look like teddy bears, are not bears at all. They are tree-dwelling marsupials. So are the gliders, animals with a fold of skin between their legs that they can spread and use to glide through the air. Gliders are also known as flying opossums.

Some of Australia's birds seem as unusual as its animals to people from other continents. It surprises people who think that all swans are white to learn that Australia has black swans. It also has emus (ē′ myüs) and mallee (mal′ ē) fowl. Emus are large birds that can run but not fly. Mallee fowl build mounds of vegetation and sand in which to hatch their

Some of the animals that are native to Australia are (below) the kangaroo, (top right to bottom) the koala, the dingo, the emu, and the platypus.

eggs. The male tends the mound and controls the temperature by covering and uncovering the sand on the mound. Australians call one bird the kookaburra (kŭk′ ə bėr ə), which means "laughing jackass," because its call sounds like loud laughter.

Not all of the Australian animals and birds that existed 200 years ago can be seen today. Some have become **extinct**— that is, they have been killed or have died off. Striped marsupials called Tasmanian wolves or tigers were once common, but they are now extinct. Small, bearlike

Kookaburras do not build nests but live in tree holes.

Australia has about 700 species of native birds. The kookaburra, a member of the kingfisher family, is one of the country's best-known birds.

marsupials, the Tasmanian devils, survive only in remote areas of Tasmania. At one time it was feared that koalas might become extinct because they were hunted for fur. Fortunately, the little animals are now protected by strict laws.

CHECKUP

1. Where are the deserts in Australia? What area receives the most rainfall?
2. What is the Great Dividing Range?
3. What is the Great Barrier Reef?
4. What are some of Australia's unusual animals and birds?

Peoples of Australia

┌─VOCABULARY─────────────
│ Aborigine   botany
│ boomerang
└────────────────────────

The earliest known inhabitants Names on the map tell of two peoples who have lived in Australia. Many of the names are English. The states of Queensland and Victoria were named after Queen Victoria of England. The cities of Melbourne, Sydney, and Brisbane were named for English political leaders. New South Wales got its name from Wales, in Great Britain. But not all the names on the map are English. There are also places called Wollongong, Toowoomba, Whyalla, and Wagga Wagga. Find these names on the map on page 488. These names come from the language of people who lived on the continent long before the English even knew about it. The English called these people the **Aborigines** (ab ə rij′ ə nēz). The word *aborigines* is used to refer to

After pupils have read this section, have them discuss the term *aborigine*. Ask: Who might be called the earliest known inhabitants of the United States?

Ask: In what kind of land would the boomerang be most useful? (In open country
with few trees and shrubs)

the earliest known inhabitants of a place. When the word is spelled with a capital *A*, it usually refers to the earliest inhabitants of Australia.

The Aborigines have lived in Australia for thousands of years—no one knows for sure just how long. Their ancestors probably came from Asia over a land bridge that no longer exists. Before the English came, the Aborigines hunted and gathered their food and other materials that they used. They did not plant crops or keep livestock. It is thought that the only animal their ancestors brought to Australia was a species of dog known as the dingo. The Aborigines made tools and weapons from stone, bone, and wood. They speared fish with bone-tipped spears and hunted with a throwing stick called a **boomerang.** A boomerang is shaped in such a way that when skillfully thrown, it comes back to the thrower.

The Aborigines knew a great deal about how to live on the land without growing crops. They knew how to find and prepare edible roots. They gathered certain grass seeds, pressed them into small flat cakes, and baked them in hot ashes. They knew which animals were good to eat and where to find bird eggs. They wore little clothing except for a few animal skins. They could make a fire by whirling a stick in a piece of dry wood.

The Aborigines built no permanent buildings or villages because they were always on the move in an endless search for food. There were probably only 300,000 Aborigines on the continent 200 years ago. The land could not have supported a large population because the people depended on gathering and hunt-

This Aborigine rice farmer is a descendant of the first known inhabitants of Australia.

ing. Today some of the Aborigines live in tribes on lands set aside for them. A number work on ranches and farms, but nearly half of the Aborigines now live in or on the outskirts of towns and cities.

Europeans find Australia   The very first Europeans to reach Australia saw very little of the land or the Aborigines. The crew of a Dutch ship sighted the Cape York Peninsula in 1605, but they did not land. Later a Dutch ship landed on the west coast, but the captain did little more than post a metal plate to show that he had been there. The Dutch called this land New Holland. Several of their ships sailed along parts of the coast, but they never reached the fertile southeast. In 1642 the Dutch explorer Abel Tasman landed on the island later named after him. Tasman reported hearing "certain human sounds" in the deep forest, but he did not catch sight of the people who made them.

Today, although more and more Aborigines live in cities, most live in the rural areas of Queensland, New South Wales, Western Australia, and the Northern Territory. Have pupils locate these areas on the map on p. 419.

William Dampier, an English pirate turned explorer, gave the English their first written account of Australia. Dampier landed on the northwest coast in 1686, and neither the land nor its people impressed him favorably. Of the Aborigines he wrote, "The inhabitants of this country are the miserablest people in the world."

Captain James Cook, who discovered the southeast coast in 1770, saw a very different part of the continent. He gave a very different account of both the land and the people. Cook landed near present-day Sydney at a place he called Botany Bay. He gave it that name because of the many plants that grew there. **Botany** is the study of plants.

Joseph Banks, a scientist aboard Cook's ship, thought that the land could support a large population. After his return to England, Banks wrote of what he had seen in Australia: "The grass was long and luxuriant, and there were eatable vegetables, particularly some sort of spinach. The country was well supplied with water. There was an abundance of timber."

Cook's view of the Aborigines, whom he called natives, differed from that of Dampier. Cook wrote in a report to the government: "From what I have seen of the natives of New Holland they may appear to some to be the most wretched people of earth; but in reality they are far more happier than we Europeans. . . . The earth and sea of their own accord furnished them with all things necessary for life."

Britain claims Australia   Captain Cook claimed the coast he explored for Great Britain. He named this part of the land New South Wales. Other British navigators later explored the rest of the coast and claimed the whole continent for Britain. One of these navigators suggested that the land be called Australia.

The British claimed Australia "by right of discovery," that is, by having been the first Europeans to explore it. In doing this, the British acted as other European countries had acted in the Americas since the time of Columbus. The British thought Australia was virtually an empty land, without farms, cities, or even villages. They knew that if the land was farmed, it would support far more people. No one asked the Aborigines if they wanted strange people to claim the land. It is doubtful whether the Aborigines thought the land empty. Indeed, it is doubtful whether it could have supported a much larger number of people who depended on gathering wild grass seeds and on hunting with boomerangs.

This painting shows Captain Cook supervising the raising of the British flag in New South Wales, Australia. Cook claimed New South Wales for the British.

As the text below indicates, there are several parallels between the exploration and settlement of Australia and that of the United States. Some pupils might research these parallels and write a short report that could be read to the class and discussed.

The coming of the settlers The reports of Cook and Banks encouraged the British to send settlers to New South Wales. The government decided that the faraway land would be a good place to send some convicts from the prisons. The convicts could be made to work the land, and it seemed unlikely that many would find their way home from halfway around the world. The first group of convicts, 570 men and 160 women, arrived in New South Wales in 1788. They were accompanied by 250 free persons. The convicts at first worked on government land. However, as they completed their terms, they could take up farms of their own. The British government sent about 160,000 convicts to Australia before stopping the practice in 1868.

Many free people also went to Australia. They went for the same reason that other Europeans went to America. They wanted land of their own. The settlers brought seeds and animals previously unknown in Australia. They changed the look of the land by clearing forest and bushland and planting fields of wheat, barley, and oats. They pastured sheep and cattle on grassy plains where only kangaroos had once fed.

As the number of settlers increased, the British established other colonies along the coast and on the island of Tasmania. Each of the colonies was separate, much like the 13 colonies the British established in North America. Each colony had its own government. In time the settlers gained control of these governments. In 1901 the colonies united to form the Commonwealth of Australia. A federal government somewhat like that

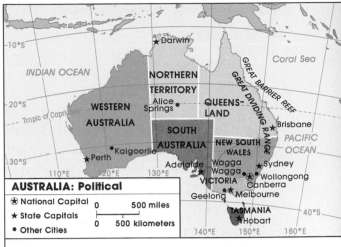

AUSTRALIA: Political

⊛ National Capital
★ State Capitals
• Other Cities

0   500 miles
0   500 kilometers

Australia is the only continent on which all people are under the same government.

of the United States was set up. Each of the former colonies became a state. There are six Australian states: New South Wales, Victoria, South Australia, Queensland, Western Australia, and Tasmania. Northern Territory is not yet a state, but it has limited self-government.

The Commonwealth of Australia has kept certain ties with Great Britain. It is a member of that other commonwealth, the Commonwealth of Nations. The queen of the United Kingdom is also queen of Australia. The Australian flag carries the Union Jack in the upper left corner. The Union Jack is the British flag. The five smaller stars on the Australian flag stand for the Southern Cross, a reminder that this country lies in the Southern Hemisphere.

CHECKUP

1. How did the Aborigines live 200 years ago?
2. Who were some early explorers of Australia?
3. Why did Europeans go to Australia?
4. What kind of government does Australia have?

Australia's coat of arms is particularly interesting, featuring a kangaroo and an emu among the blossoms of a wattle tree.

419

In the 1860s, Australia suffered from a massive infestation of rabbits. Rabbits destroyed crops, ate the pastures, damaged trees, and so forth. How this situation came about and how the problem was solved is an interesting story, which some pupils might want to research.

Australia's Economy and Cities

VOCABULARY
mutton

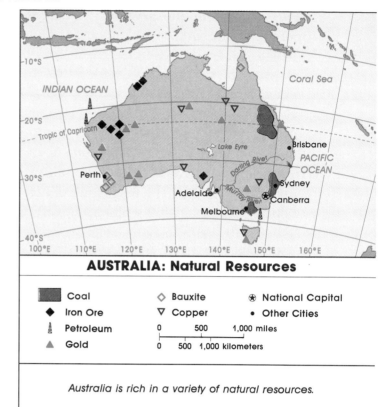

AUSTRALIA: Natural Resources

▪ Coal	◇ Bauxite	✳ National Capital
◆ Iron Ore	▽ Copper	• Other Cities
Petroleum		
▲ Gold	0 500 1,000 miles	
	0 500 1,000 kilometers	

Australia is rich in a variety of natural resources.

Using the grasslands Joseph Banks predicted that sheep would "thrive and increase" in Australia. The grass was "long and luxuriant" and "there were no beasts of prey." It was an accurate prediction. The early settlers found that sheep raising was the most profitable way to make use of the land, partly for the reasons Banks gave. The absence of wolves and bears made the open plains safe for sheep. The country had much grassland, although the grass was not everywhere so thick as Banks thought. Even so, the settlers found that they could raise sheep on the interior plains which were too dry for crops. Wool was the country's first cash crop because the settlers could ship it to Europe even in the days of sailing ships.

Sheep raising is still important to the economy. Australia leads the world in the production of wool. The continent, which has far less than 1 percent of the world's people, has 14 percent of the world's sheep. These sheep supply more than one third of the wool used for clothing in the world. Australia also exports **mutton**, the meat of sheep. In recent years Australia has been exporting live animals to the Middle East.

Although sheep outnumber cattle, Australian livestock raisers in the grasslands also produce beef for export. Dairy cattle need better feed, so they are raised in areas of greater rainfall.

Raising crops Although only a small part of Australia's usable land is suitable for crops, it is an important agricultural country. Wheat is grown in the southeast and southwest, and Australia ranks among the world's top ten producers of wheat. Barley, oats, soybeans, and sunflowers are also grown.

Since part of Australia lies within the tropics, it produces such crops as sugarcane, bananas, and pineapples. Citrus fruits are grown in irrigated areas of New South Wales and Victoria. Grapes, pears, and apples grow in the cooler southeast and on Tasmania. Apples are the country's most important fresh fruit crop.

Only a small part of the population lives on farms today, and the number has decreased in recent years. Yet farm produc-

Ask: Where, do you think, are most dairy products produced in Australia? (In the southeast, especially in Victoria) Remind pupils of what they have learned about Australia's climate, particularly its rainfall.

After pupils have read pp. 420–421, have them make a list of Australia's crops and products. For each item, see if pupils can name a state in the United States that produces that item. Also see if they can name another country that produces each item.

tion has generally increased. Today fewer people can grow more food because of the use of machines and chemicals.

Minerals   The discovery of gold in 1851 set off a gold rush to Australia somewhat like that of 1849 in California. In fact, some of the California forty-niners traveled on to Australia to try their luck. In the 1890s much larger gold deposits were discovered at Kalgoorlie, in Western Australia. Australia still ranks among the world's top ten gold producers, but gold is by no means its only mineral resource. The continent has very large iron deposits in the west, and it leads the world in the export of iron ore. Steel mills in Japan and South Korea depend on Australian mines for iron ore.

Australia also leads the world in mining bauxite. It ranks among the important

Industry in Australia is supported by the rich supply of minerals found on the continent. Iron ore and coal are essential to the nation's thriving steel industry.

producers of lead, zinc, and nickel. It has substantial amounts of coal, manganese, silver, tin, and uranium.

Like the people of the United States, Australians depend largely upon automobiles for transportation. Automobiles use oil, and Australian oil fields produce only about two thirds of what the country needs. The rest is imported.

Manufacturing   Over one fifth of the workers in Australia are employed in manufacturing. Many work in food processing plants, where they pack, can, and freeze the products that come from the farms. Much of the processed food goes to Japan and other parts of East Asia.

Smelters and steel mills use ore and coal from the mines. Factories produce a variety of metal goods and machines ranging from lawn mowers to automobiles.

Today Australia is among the leading producers of many minerals, including iron ore, which is being mined in this photograph.

Statistics on production in Australia over a number of years can be obtained from the United Nations Statistical Yearbook. Pupils might choose a product such as wheat, wool, or iron ore and construct a line graph showing production over a period of years. **421**

Cities—where most Australians live

Nearly nine out of ten Australians live in towns and cities, mostly along the southeast coast. More than half of the people live in the four largest metropolitan areas: Sydney, Melbourne, Brisbane, and Adelaide.

Sydney, the oldest and largest city grew around a magnificent harbor. It has become one of the most important ports and business centers in the southwestern Pacific. Sydney has a climate somewhat like that of southern California. Sydney's climate, fine harbor, and beaches make it an enjoyable city for people who like swimming, surfing, and sailing.

Melbourne, the second largest city, is on the south coast. It is both a manufacturing center and an important port. Melbourne and Sydney are longtime rivals. When the federal government was created, neither city wanted the other to become the permanent capital. So a new capital city was built at Canberra, halfway between Melbourne and Sydney. Canberra is located in the Capital Territory. This territory is not part of any state, somewhat like the District of Columbia in the United States.

Perth, on the southwest coast, receives enough rain for farming. Miles of sparsely populated scrubland and desert separate Perth from Adelaide, its nearest neighbor to the east.

Darwin, the principal city on the tropical north coast, is also isolated. No railroad connects Darwin with the rest of the country. Hobart, the capital of Tasmania, is Australia's southernmost city.

There is a great difference between the continent that Captain Cook saw and

Downtown Sydney, with its many high-rise buildings, borders on Sydney Harbor. The low white building on the right is the Opera House, a famous landmark in Sydney. (34°S/151°E; map, p. 419)

Australia today. The Aborigines hunted and gathered food on land where people now keep livestock and raise crops. The Aborigines fashioned tools from stone and had no use for the iron from which people now make steel. Large cities are now spread over a continent where there had never before been a permanent village. All these changes came about because of the way in which people have used the land's resources. The land did not change; it was changed. You will read more about people's use of resources in Chapter 26.

CHECKUP

1. What use have Australians made of the grasslands?
2. Why is Australia able to produce a wide variety of crops?
3. What minerals are mined in Australia?
4. What are the four largest Australian cities and in what parts of the country are they located? What city is the capital?

Have pupils study a road map of Australia. Show how the routes of major highways relate to land elevations, locations of cities, and physical features. A road map is available from the Australian Information Service, 636 Fifth Avenue, 4th Floor, New York, NY 10020.

New Zealand

> **VOCABULARY**
>
> emblem   annex
>
> Maori

The mountainous islands New Zealand and Australia are neighbors—but not close neighbors. The distance from Sydney to Wellington, the capital of New Zealand, is about the same as that from New York to Dallas. Fiji is about as close to New Zealand as Australia.

Even though we often think of New Zealand and Australia together, the lands are very different. Australia is mostly flat; New Zealand is mountainous. Australia has large deserts; New Zealand has none. A large part of Australia is in the tropics; all of New Zealand lies south of the 34th parallel. Wellington is farther from the Equator than New York.

New Zealand is made up of two main islands. They are North Island and South Island. A rugged range stretches the length of South Island from north to south. Sixteen peaks of over 10,000 feet (3,048 m)

tower majestically in this range. These mountains are called the Southern Alps.

North Island is also a hilly and mountainous land, but it is not so rugged as South Island. The center of North Island is a plateau on which an ancient, water-filled volcano crater forms New Zealand's largest lake. There are still some active volcanoes on North Island. There are also many geysers and hot springs.

New Zealand has neither a hot nor a cold climate. Average summer and winter temperatures in Wellington are about the same as those in San Francisco. Snow is common in the Southern Alps, but not elsewhere. The mountain ranges greatly affect rainfall, particularly on South Island. The western side of the range is the wet side. Rainfall there may average from 60 to more than 100 inches (152 to 254 cm) a year. The east side of the island gets less rain. Many areas average less than 30 inches (76 cm) a year, and they sometimes have summer droughts. Average rainfall does not vary so much on North Island, but all areas there usually receive abundant moisture.

New Zealand is noted for its fine scenery.

No place in New Zealand is far from the coast or out of sight of hills.

Land of the moa and the kiwi   At one time the largest creatures in New Zealand were flightless birds. There were no large animals or people to disturb these birds, which lived on the ground. The largest bird of all, the giant moa (mō′ ə), looked like an ostrich and stood 10 feet (3 m) tall. Not all of the moa birds were as tall as the giant kind. The smallest moa was about the size of a turkey.

There are no moa birds of any kind today. The giant moa was extinct even before Europeans reached the islands. The last of the smaller moas probably died out more than 150 years ago. All that is left of these creatures are bones buried in swamps and other places. No one knows for sure what happened to the moas. It is thought that the first people and their dogs killed them.

One flightless bird, the kiwi (kē′ wē), has survived and become New Zealand's **emblem,** or symbol. It appears on coins, bills, and postage stamps. A kiwi is about the size of a chicken and lays an egg that weighs about 1 pound (.45 kg). Kiwis are hard to see because they live in the bush, sleep by day, and feed at night. Because kiwis are the national emblem, strict laws protect them today.

Maoris—the first people   New Zealand's first human inhabitants probably reached the islands about a thousand years ago. They came from some of the other Pacific Islands and were of Polynesian background. They probably came in double canoes like those described in Chapter 24. The descendants of the first arrivals call themselves **Maoris** (mä′ ō rēz). The name means "natives of this land."

They were indeed natives of the land by the time the first Europeans arrived. The Maoris called New Zealand "Land of the Long White Cloud." Perhaps they called it that because of the clouds that covered its mountains.

The Maoris fished, hunted, and tilled the soil with digging sticks and small wooden spades. They grew root crops from the Pacific Islands, such as yams, taro, and sweet potatoes. But New Zealand was too cool for such tropical trees as banana, coconut, and breadfruit trees. The Maoris built houses and lived in villages sometimes surrounded by stockades of logs. They put up the stockades for protection, because they were divided into tribes that sometimes warred with each other. The Maoris wove beautiful mats and fashioned gorgeous robes from colorful bird feathers. They decorated their weapons, their houses, and themselves. They put tattoos on their faces and bodies.

One out of every 12 New Zealanders is a Maori. The Maoris play important roles in the life of the nation.

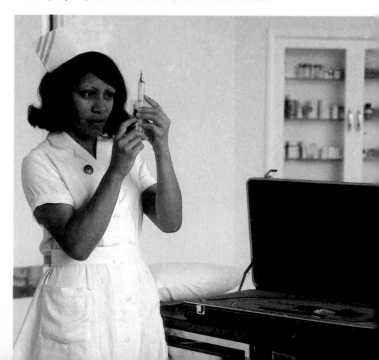

The earliest Maoris were called *moa hunters* because the moa birds were the main target of their hunts.

The arrival of Europeans   Abel Tasman, the Dutch navigator who discovered Tasmania, was the first European to see New Zealand. Tasman saw nothing of the country except the coast. In his report to the Dutch trading company, however, he said New Zealand was "a beautiful land." He added that he had "found no treasures or matters of great profit." Since the trading company was more interested in profits than beauty, they did not follow up Tasman's discovery. New Zealand and the Maoris were left undisturbed until Captain James Cook arrived.

Cook came in 1769, and his account gave Europeans their first ideas about the country. He felt sure that the Maoris and the Pacific Islanders must have had the same ancestors because they spoke similar languages and lived in much the same way. Cook was favorably impressed by the Maoris. He wrote that "the natives of the country are a well made active people. They seem to enjoy a good state of health and many of them live to a good old age." There were some unfortunate clashes between the Maoris and Cook's crew. Yet Cook declared that the Maoris were "as modest and reserved in their behavior as the most polite nations of Europe."

Cook reported that New Zealand was a fertile land with ample room for hardworking settlers. If people would come from England, "they would very soon be supplied not only with necessaries but many of the luxuries of life."

Settlers were slow to take Cook's advice, but other people came. Traders came to exchange guns and tools for sealskins and timber. The Maoris wanted guns because they quickly learned the ad-

Detailed woodcarving was a skill of the early Maoris. The tradition continues among the Maoris of today.

vantage of having them in wars. Whaling ships stopped, as they did elsewhere in the Pacific Islands, both to refresh their crews and to trade. Missionaries came to teach the Maoris about Christianity.

Britain **annexed,** or added, New Zealand to its empire in 1840. After that, settlers came in increasing numbers. They began to change the islands in the same ways that other settlers were changing Australia. When the settlers first arrived, dense forests covered over half the land. The settlers changed forests into pastures. They cut timber, and they cleared vast areas by wasteful burning. The Maoris grew alarmed at what was happening. War broke out, and in the end the Maoris lost.

As the number of settlers grew, New Zealand gained self-government. In 1907 it became an independent country. However, like Australia, New Zealand has kept ties with the United Kingdom. The queen of the United Kingdom is also queen of New Zealand. New Zealand belongs to the Commonwealth of Nations as Australia does.

As New Zealand changed, so did many of the Maoris. They went to school, learned English, and adopted a new way of life. Some took part in politics and were elected to New Zealand's Parliament. Maoris today make up more than 8 percent of the country's population. At one time most Maoris lived on the land. Today more than half of them live in towns and cities. Auckland, the largest city, has many Maoris.

Many Polynesian people from other Pacific Islands have also moved to New Zealand in recent years. Most of these immigrants have gone to the cities. Because of Auckland's large Maori and Polynesian immigrant population, it has been called the largest Polynesian city in the world.

New Zealand's economy   The burning of much forestland was wasteful, but the pastures became the basis of New Zealand's economy. Wool was the settlers' first cash crop, and wool remains a major export today. New Zealand is second only to Australia as an exporter of wool. New Zealand also exports a great deal of mutton, beef, and, above all, dairy products. The country's green pastures are well suited to dairy cattle, and its dairy industry is one of the world's most efficient. New Zealand ships butter and cheese to many lands overseas.

New Zealand grows some fruits, such as apples, for export. It is also the chief source of a fruit called the kiwi. The name was given to the fruit supposedly because it is shaped like the body of the flightless bird. You can see this kind of kiwi at the supermarket.

Today more New Zealanders work in industry than on sheep, dairy, or fruit farms. They make metalware, plastics, textiles, and machinery. But processing the food that comes from the farms con-

Pupils might make comparisons between Australia and New Zealand under headings such as *First people, Climate* and *Farming.*
As in Australia, sheep in New Zealand are raised for wool and meat.

Auckland, shown in the distance, in New Zealand's largest city and chief port. It has fine libraries, parks, an art gallery, and a university. (37°S/175°E; map, p. 393)

tinues to be one of the country's most important industries.

More than eight out of ten New Zealanders today live in urban areas. The majority live on North Island. The country's two largest cities, Auckland and Wellington, the capital, are on North Island. Christchurch is the principal city on South Island. The name of this city is a reminder that most of the early settlers came from England. Christchurch was named for a college in Oxford University, in England.

CHECKUP

1. What are some differences between New Zealand and Australia?
2. Describe the two main islands of New Zealand.
3. Who are the Maoris?
4. In what ways did the settlers change New Zealand? How did this affect its economy?
5. What are the three largest cities of New Zealand? Which is the capital?

Pupils might look up the verb *calve* in the dictionary, noting the relationship between its two major definitions.

Antarctica

┌─VOCABULARY──────────────┐
calving
└──────────────────────────┘

The frozen continent   Antarctica is the fifth largest continent. It is bigger than either Europe or Australia. It is an island continent with coasts on the Pacific, Atlantic, and Indian oceans.

The name of this continent indicates its location on the globe. *Antarctica* means "opposite the Arctic." The earth's North Pole is in the Arctic, its South Pole in Antarctica. The poles are at opposite ends of the earth's axis. Both the Arctic and Antarctica have dark winters, when the sun never rises, and bright summers, when the sun never sets. But winter and summer come at opposite times. When it is winter in the Arctic, it is summer in Antarctica.

A sheet of ice covers most of Antarctica. In most places the ice is more than 1 mile (1.6 km) thick. The continent has high, rocky mountains, but only the peaks stick out above the ice sheet. There are also a few dry valleys, sometimes called oases, that are bare of ice. Glaciers are the rivers of Antarctica. Glaciers are streams of ice that move slowly to the sea. There, large pieces of ice break off and form icebergs. The breaking off of these huge pieces of ice is called **calving.**

Climate   Ice-covered Antarctica has the coldest climate in the world. August, coming at the end of the long winter night, is the coldest month of the year. The coldest temperature ever recorded on earth was measured during July in Antarctica. The thermometer dropped to

In some places, Antarctica's ice sheet stretches well beyond the land, forming huge cliffs that rise out of the ocean.   **427**

The Adélie penguins, the most common type in Antarctica, weigh about 15 pounds (7 kg).

−129°F (−90°C). Summer temperatures rise well above freezing, particularly in the coastal region. A high of 58°F (15°C) has been recorded during the summer on the Antarctic Peninsula, which sticks out toward the tip of South America.

Although Antarctica is a frozen, ice-covered continent, it does not receive a great deal of snow. In fact, it is sometimes called the "white desert." The yearly snowfall in the center of the continent equals less than 3 inches (7.6 cm) of rainfall. The thick ice sheet builds up because the snow does not melt.

Plants, animals, and minerals   There is life on the frozen continent, but one sometimes has to look closely to see it. Tiny lichens and certain mosses grow on exposed rock. During short periods of the sunny Antarctic summers, very small insects, including mites, live in these plants. The only animals within the Antarctic Circle are those that live in the sea, such as whales, dolphins, and seals. Many kinds of seabirds can be seen in Antarctica during the summer months. The penguin is certainly the best known of the Antarctic birds. The largest of the penguins, the emperor penguin, remains in Antarctica throughout the year. A full-grown emperor penguin stands nearly 4 feet (1.2 m) tall and may weigh from 55 to 100 pounds (25 to 45 kg).

Antarctica is known to have coal, and it is thought that other minerals lie beneath the ice sheet. At present there is no practical way to make use of these resources. Compared to other continents, Antarctica has few natural resources.

Oil, gas, uranium, copper, chromium, iron, and other minerals may lie beneath Antarctica. Pupils might discuss the possibility of someday being able to mine this area for minerals that may have been depleted elsewhere. Encourage ideas on how this might be accomplished.

The polar ice sheets are slowly getting smaller. The effect of such changes will not be noticeable in our lifetime. But if the change continues for thousands of years, the climate of the polar regions and possibly other areas of the earth will also change.

People on the frozen continent For thousands of years, Antarctica was a continent without people. People did not even know for certain that such a continent existed. Captain Cook tried to find out what lay at the South Pole. He sailed south until his ship could go no farther through the ice pack. Cook thought that the ice pack probably "extended quite to the Pole or perhaps joins to some land." Cook doubted whether it was possible to find out, as it seemed impossible to go farther south. The man who explored the Pacific Islands, Australia, and New Zealand never saw this other continent.

In 1820 others did see the coast of Antarctica, but it was nearly a century before anyone explored the continent.

After 1900, explorers from several countries went to Antarctica, and there developed a race to the Pole. In December 1911, Roald Amundsen and a team of Norwegians traveling on skis and sleds finally made it to the South Pole. A month later a British expedition led by Robert Scott reached the Pole only to find that Amundsen had arrived there first.

Although the South Pole had been reached, much of the large continent remained unexplored. Admiral Richard E. Byrd, an American naval officer, established a base for exploration called Little America in 1929. Byrd's expedition used airplanes as well as dog sleds and was able to explore large areas no one had ever seen.

Researchers in Antarctica travel on sledges pulled by dogs called huskies.

Pupils might use library resources to research one of the Antarctic explorers for a written report. Some explorers to research are James Cook, John Davys, James Weddell, James Clark Ross, Adrien de Gerlache, Robert Scott, and Richard E. Byrd. **429**

Argentina established this permanent scientific observation station in Antarctica.

Explorers filled in the blank space on the map by giving names to the mountains and to other parts of the ice-covered continent. The Norwegians used their queen's name for Queen Maud Land, and the British put Queen Victoria's name on yet another part of the world with Victoria Land. An early French explorer named Adélie Coast after his wife, and Byrd followed his example in naming Marie Byrd Land. Byrd named the Rockefeller Plateau and the Ford Ranges after two men who had backed his expedition. Perhaps the strangest name of all in Antarctica is Executive Committee Range.

A base for scientific observation As Antarctica was explored, different countries claimed parts of the continent. Sometimes two or more countries claimed the same areas. There was no possibility of settlers coming to live on these claims, and carving up the continent threatened scientific investigations. The best use for Antarctica at present is probably as a base for scientific observation. The frozen continent offers an unusual place from which to study weather, the earth, and wildlife. One scientist has described the land as "a fresh book of natural history." Fortunately, 12 countries agreed in 1959 to permit "freedom of scientific investigation" throughout Antarctica without regard to national claims. They also agreed not to use the continent for military purposes. This meant that they would not test nuclear weapons there. Later four other nations signed the agreement, called the Antarctic Treaty.

Various countries maintain scientific observation stations in Antarctica. Tourists even go to Antarctica now. Antarctica is no longer a continent without people, but it remains a continent without inhabitants.

CHECKUP

1. Why is Antarctica called a "white desert"?
2. What kinds of life are found in Antarctica?
3. What is the best use for Antarctica today?

Have pupils imagine that they have become Antarctica's first permanent inhabitants. Have them write a series of diary entries recording information about weather, wildlife, housing, food, newly discovered natural resources, recreation, pleasures, and dissatisfactions.

KEY FACTS

1. Australia is a flat and mostly dry continent except for the southeast and some coastal areas, where most people live.
2. The Aborigines lived by hunting and gathering.
3. Australia leads the world in the production of wool and bauxite and in the export of iron ore.
4. New Zealand, a mountainous and well-watered land, was first inhabited by the Maoris, who came from the Pacific Islands.
5. Farms are important to New Zealand's economy, but the majority of New Zealanders work in industry and live in towns and cities.
6. A thick sheet of ice covers most of Antarctica, the fifth largest continent.
7. An international agreement permits the free use of Antarctica for scientific investigation.

VOCABULARY QUIZ

On a sheet of paper write each word from the list below and its definition.

a. marsupial
b. species
c. extinct
d. Aborigine
e. boomerang
f. botany
g. mutton
h. emblem
i. annex
j. calving

d 1. Early inhabitant of Australia
c 2. No longer existing
b 3. Groups of plants or animals that are alike
j 4. Breaking off of pieces of ice, which form icebergs
a 5. An animal that carries its young in a pouch
h 6. A symbol or sign
e 7. A throwing stick used as a weapon
f 8. The study of plants
g 9. The meat of sheep
i 10. To join or add to a larger or more important thing

REVIEW QUESTIONS

1. What kinds of climate does Australia have?
2. What are the differences between the ways the Aborigines made use of the continent of Australia and the ways the settlers from Europe made use of it?
3. What ties do Australia and New Zealand have with the United Kingdom?
4. How did the Maoris and the Aborigines differ?
5. How did Captain Cook's report on Australia and New Zealand affect those lands?
6. What are some of Australia's important exports? What are New Zealand's important exports?
7. What would you see if you flew over Antarctica?
8. What is the Antarctic Treaty?

ACTIVITIES

1. Make a travel poster advertising trips to Australia and New Zealand. Emphasize things that you think people would most want to see. For additional information you may want to consult an encyclopedia or other source.
2. Plan a television documentary program on either Australia or New Zealand. Make a list of at least six topics you would like the program to cover. For each topic write directions for a camera crew, indicating scenes that they should shoot. Describe how you would open the program. Write the script for the announcer's opening and closing statements.

25/SKILLS DEVELOPMENT

USING POLITICAL AND PHYSICAL MAPS

PLACE GEOGRAPHY ON POLITICAL AND PHYSICAL MAPS

Each of the following exercises gives the maps you will need to find the information to complete the exercise. Write your answers on a sheet of paper.

SKILLS PRACTICE: Part I

Use the map of Australia on page 419 to find each of the places listed below. Write the state or territory in which each place is located.

1. Melbourne
2. Alice Springs
3. Darwin
4. Perth
5. Hobart
6. Adelaide
7. Sydney
8. Brisbane

SKILLS PRACTICE: Part II

Use the maps on pages 392–393 and page 419 to answer these questions.
1. Between what two oceans does Australia lie?
2. On which coast is the Great Barrier Reef?
3. What are the names of two rivers in Australia? Two deserts?
4. Which territory and states are partly within the tropics?
5. What is the national capital of Australia?

SKILLS PRACTICE: Part III

Use the map of Australia and Oceania on pages 392–393 to find the answer to each of the following questions.
1. Which Pacific Island country is Australia's nearest neighbor? (a) Tonga (b) Papua New Guinea (c) Western Samoa
2. Which of the following islands lies farthest east? (a) Hawaii (b) Solomon Islands (c) Easter Island
3. Which of the following is located north of the Equator? (a) Hawaii (b) Vanuatu (c) Nauru
4. Which of the following is nearest to Papua New Guinea? (a) Solomon Islands (b) Fiji (c) French Polynesia

Use the same map to answer this question.
5. When it is noon on Sunday in Hawaii, what day is it in each of the following island countries?

a. Tahiti
b. Solomon Islands
c. Fiji
d. Nauru
e. Vanuatu
f. American Samoa
g. French Polynesia
h. New Zealand

COMPARING MAPS FOR INFORMATION

To answer the questions below, you will have to compare information from two maps. The page on which each map appears is shown in parentheses after the placename(s).

SKILLS PRACTICE: Part IV

Which city in each pair of cities below is located nearer the Equator?
1. Wellington, New Zealand (p. 488), or Washington, D.C. (p. 477)
2. Melbourne, Australia (p. 488), or Omaha, Nebraska (p. 477)
3. Darwin, Australia (p. 488), or Panama, Panama (p. 477)
4. Honolulu, Hawaii (p. 393), or Rangoon, Burma (p. 331)
5. Brisbane, Australia (p. 392), or Cape Town, South Africa (p. 287)

9/UNIT REVIEW

Answer Key in back of book.

READING THE TEXT

Turn to page 430 and read the section "A base for scientific observation." On a sheet of paper, write the answers to these questions.

1. What happened as Antarctica was explored?

2. What is the present best use of Antarctica?

3. In what year was an agreement signed to allow freedom of scientific investigation throughout the continent? How many countries have signed the agreement?

4. What else did these countries agree to?

5. Why has Antarctica been described as "a fresh book of natural history"?

READING A MAP

Turn to the map on pages 392–393 and study it carefully. On a sheet of paper, write the answers to the following questions.

1. How many cities shown on the map have a population of 1 million or more? In what country are they?

2. What line of longitude does the International Date Line follow for most of its length?

3. If it is Sunday, March 11, in Apia, what is the day and date in Wellington?

4. Are all the United States territories in the Pacific area located east of the International Date Line?

5. In what sea is the Great Barrier Reef?

READING A PICTURE

Study the picture on page 403. On a sheet of paper, write the answers to the following questions.

1. What is happening in the lower left-hand corner of the picture?

2. What is the function of the man standing in the front of the boat?

3. What does the man facing the rowers do?

4. What is the approximate size of the whale in comparison to the size of the rowboats?

5. What is the source of power for the ships in the background?

READING A GRAPH

Turn to page 398 and examine the graph that shows temperature fluctuations for two cities. On a sheet of paper, write the answers to the following questions.

1. What is the temperature range in degrees Fahrenheit in Apia?

2. During which months is the temperature the highest in Melbourne?

3. Which are the winter months in Melbourne?

4. Which city has an average annual temperature of about 27°C?

5. In which city would sweaters and light overcoats be part of a person's wardrobe?

UNIT
10

TAKING A WORLD VIEW

Captain McCandless is wearing a Manned Maneuvering Unit, or MMU. It is a nitrogen-propelled, hand-controlled device that is 50 inches (127 cm) high and 30 inches (76 cm) deep and consists of 24 tiny jet thrusters. Hand controls are located at the ends of the armrests, which extend from the pack. In the near future, astronauts wearing MMUs will be able to build space stations.

Two Ways to View the World

Walking is the oldest way to travel; orbiting the earth in a space shuttle is the newest. Both forms of travel offer views of the earth's surface, but the views are very different. Pedestrians, as walkers are called, see the world at close range. They can see pebbles in a brook, the different kinds of plants that grow in the soil, and the many creatures that live on the earth. Astronauts in a space shuttle view the world from a distance. They can see the delta of a large river, the coastline of a continent, or the shape of a whole island set in the ocean.

In some ways, pedestrians see more than astronauts, but, in other ways, astronauts see more than pedestrians. Each has a different perspective, or point of view, and each perspective has its uses. An astronaut cannot look for lost coins, and a pedestrian cannot observe the shape of the Red Sea. But each should understand the limits of their perspective. The pedestrian should know that the brook is but one tiny feature of the earth's surface, and the astronaut should realize that distance obscures, or hides from view, most surface features.

In earlier units you have viewed the world from regional perspectives. Each unit has described one part of the world so that you might take a close look at that region—a sort of pedestrian view. But we must also view the world from different perspectives in order to understand it. The picture on the facing page shows the perspective of this final unit; it takes a world view.

On February 7, 1984, Captain Bruce McCandless stepped away from the space shuttle Challenger *and became the first human to walk in space completely free of a spacecraft.*

Ask pupils to think about all the places they have studied this year and to tell which place they would most like to visit. Have each pupil then plan an imaginary trip to the place selected. Planning should include a review of appropriate parts of the textbook.

Different Regions with Some Common Concerns

By studying different regions and nations, you have learned that the world has much diversity, that is, many differences. Not only do lands and climate differ, but peoples at different times have made use of the same land in different ways. Understanding diversity makes the world even more interesting. And the world will, no doubt, retain much of its diversity in the future. Yet changes have occurred because of what writers sometimes call "the shrinking world."

This term does not mean, of course, that the distance around the earth has shrunk. The shrinking world refers to the shortening of travel time.

Three hundred years ago the speed of travel was very slow—that of a sailing ship by sea and of a horse on land. Even at the beginning of this century, it took 6 weeks or more to reach India from the United States by steamship. A hundred years earlier a sailing ship might have taken as many months. Now we can get to India is less than 20 hours. Columbus took 70 days to cross the Atlantic. Now the trip is a short plane flight.

Before the airplane, it took about 7 days to travel to Honolulu from Washington, D.C. According to the map below, what is the flying time, in hours, between these cities? 11 hours

THE SHRINKING WORLD
Numbers in parentheses show flying time, in hours, from Washington, D.C.

The cities shown on this map are the 25 largest cities in the world, based on population figures from the most current world source for such data—*Calendario Atlante de Agostini*, 1983 edition.

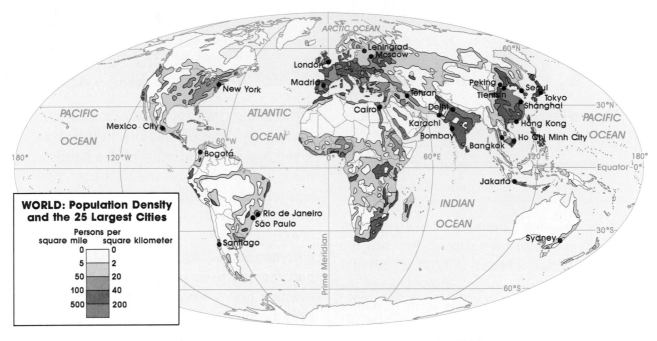

The population density map shows that people are not evenly spread over the earth. Which of the 25 largest cities in the world is located in the United States? New York City

Ask pupils to point out areas of high and low population density.

As a result of the shortening of travel time, contacts between regions have greatly increased. Both people and goods move with greater ease from one land to another. As people have more to do with each other, they become more concerned about some of the same things.

The world map on this page relates to one common concern—namely, where will a growing world population live? The map does not show the location of separate nations. It shows the location of the human race—the whole human race. Land covers only the smaller part of the earth's surface, and most people live on only a part of the land surface. Much of the world is sparsely settled because it is too cold or too dry to support many people. As the number of people increases, people move. They move not only within regions, they move from one region to another. Since there are many

places where people cannot live, they move into lands where other people already live. Crowding in one place produces crowding in others. For this reason, population growth has become a world concern, not just a concern of the most crowded countries.

Resources, like people, are also spread unevenly over the earth. The minerals and fuels wanted in one region are found in another. The largest amounts of productive soil are not located in the lands that have the most people to feed. Because people must use resources to live, access to the ones they need—or want—is a concern of people all over the world.

Chapter 26 in this unit treats two important world concerns: the number of people and the use of resources. Chapter 27 describes why and how people of different regions have found ways to work together.

Population Growth

┌─ VOCABULARY ─────────────────────┐
growth rate   typhoid
cholera   commuter
└──────────────────────────────────┘

How a tiny country became rich
When an English sea captain first saw the Pacific island of Nauru in 1789, he called it Pleasant Island. It was a good name for the coral island. The low cliffs formed a backdrop for the palms along the beach. The people of Nauru probably numbered about 1,000 in 1789. Like other Pacific Islanders they lived by fishing, growing a few roots, and harvesting coconuts and bananas. They made little use of the rocky plateau that covered four fifths of their island. Nothing much grew among the rocks except a few coconut palms.

In 1900 a New Zealander discovered that Nauru's rocky plateau consisted of high-grade phosphate. It is very valuable for fertilizer. A few years later a foreign company began to mine the phosphate rock and ship it abroad. The mining of this tiny island with an area of only 8 square miles (21 km) has continued to the present day. Over the years millions of tons of the island's rocky center have been dug up and exported. Locate Nauru on the map on pages 392–393.

After Nauru became independent in 1968, income from the export of phosphate made it a rich country. Nauruans have never done much work in the mine. Foreign workers do most of the hand labor. Today most Nauruans have other jobs with the mining company or work for the government. They no longer fish —except for fun. They do not depend on coconuts and bananas for food. They import most of their food, along with automobiles, motor scooters, radios, and other manufactured goods. During times of drought they even import water from Australia or Japan. Nauruans pay no taxes, but the government provides free medical and dental care, education, bus transportation, and even copies of the island's only newspaper. The export of phosphate pays for all of this. Nauruans live by the sale of one important resource—the island itself.

The number of people on Nauru has grown with its wealth. Its population in 1900 was probably not much larger than it was in 1789. Today about 8,000 people live on Nauru. This is seven or eight times the number of people that were there when the English captain first sighted Pleasant Island.

A time of great growth The history of Nauru is unusual. Yet in at least one way, it is like that of the rest of the world. Both Nauru and the world as a whole have had

High-grade phosphate, mined on the Pacific island of Nauru, is made into fertilizer at this island processing plant.

Information on the population of your community or county at the last census and at earlier censuses is available at your library, courthouse, or city hall. Pupils can use the records to figure the percentage of growth or loss of population for several decades. Discuss possible reasons for change.

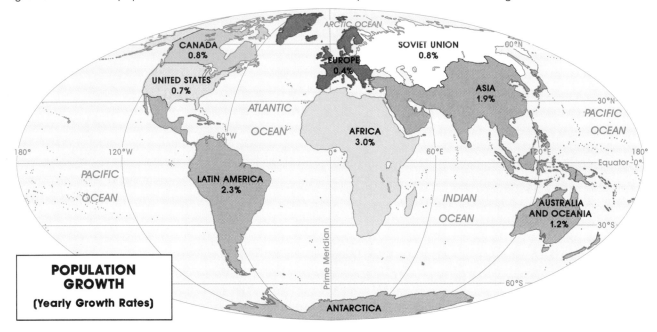

POPULATION GROWTH
(Yearly Growth Rates)

Which area of the world has the largest yearly growth in population? Africa

large increases in population. Such rapid growth has been unusual in history, as the graph on page 33 shows. Before 1600 the world's population grew slowly. But note what happened after 1600. Not only did the population grow, but it grew at an increasingly rapid rate. It took 600 years, between 1000 and 1600, for the world's population to double, but it doubled again in less than 50 years after 1940.

The population **growth rate** of a place is figured by comparing the average number of deaths and births for every 1,000 persons in the place. In order to be more accurate, the rates are often stated in decimal fractions. For example, in 1980 in the United States, there were 16.2 births and 8.9 deaths for every 1,000 people. Since there were 7.3 more births than deaths, the growth rate was 7.3 per 1,000. To state the growth rate another way, for every 1,000 people at the beginning

of the year, there were 1,007.3 at the end of the year.

For the world as a whole, the growth rate before 1600 was less than 1. By 1900 it was 5.4, and by 1981 it had jumped to 18. Never before in the world's history had population multiplied so rapidly, and the great growth continues. In the year of 1981 alone, the world gained 93 million more inhabitants. This is more people than live in the six most populated states of the United States.

The growth rate varies from one place to another. Europe had a growth rate of 5 in 1982 as compared with a rate of 29 in Africa. The number of births and deaths nearly balance each other in some European countries, such as Denmark and East Germany. However, Kenya, in Africa, had a growth rate of more than 38 in 1980. Mexico had a high growth rate of more than 35 the same year.

440 Some countries have national programs aimed at reducing the population growth. China, for example, which has one fifth of the world's population, discourages families from having more than one child.

Why population grew rapidly   The great jump in the rate of population growth happened partly because people have learned to control and even prevent certain diseases.   Finding ways to make water and milk safe to drink has checked the spread of such diseases as **cholera** (kol′ ər ə) and **typhoid** (tī′ foid).   These diseases once took many lives.   Vaccination has protected people from smallpox and other diseases.   Learning how flies and mosquitoes spread sickness has caused people to clean up places where these insects could breed.

Because of sanitation and better health care, more babies lived through their first year.   At one time a large number of babies died before their first birthday.   In 1900 in the United States, the first year death rate for babies was 162.4 per 1,000.   More than 1 out of every 6 babies born at that time died within the first year.   In 1982 the first year death rate was 11.2 per 1,000, or 1 out of 89.   Some countries, such as Sweden and Japan, have even lower infant death rates.   Some poor countries, however, still have very high infant death rates.

In Guatemala, children receive an oral polio vaccine. It protects them against polio, a crippling disease.

A scientist conducts experiments in plant breeding.   The goal is to produce stronger, healthier food plants.

A growth in the world's food supply also helped make possible the great jump in population.   Before 1900, new croplands in the Americas and Australia provided more food.   In recent years the use of fertilizers, insecticides, better seeds, and more irrigation has increased world food production.

The growing city population   Most of the world's people lived in rural areas before 1800.   Fewer than three percent lived in cities.   Today well over one third of the world's people live in cities.   City dwellers form the majority in Europe, the Americas, and Australia.   A majority is the larger number or greater part.   In Africa and Asia more people live in rural areas than in cities, but there are very large cities on both continents.

Few United States cities have grown as rapidly as Los Angeles. (34°N/118°W; map, p. 68)

Pupils might talk to an older person about the changes in farm and city life and make a report on the interview.

People have moved to cities partly because there is no longer room for them to make a living on the land. As more babies and children survived, only some of them could remain on the family farms. The others had to move to the cities to take jobs in workshops and factories. The use of machines and chemicals in farming has further reduced the need for people to work on the land. The average size of farms in the United States has increased, since fewer farmers are able to till more land. In 1880 the average American farm was 134 acres (54 ha), but by 1982 it was 433 acres (173 ha).

The shapes of the growing cities have depended partly on how people travel to work. Before 1850, large cities were densely populated because most people had to live within walking distance of the place where they worked. The development of trolley lines and railroads made it possible for people to live farther from their work. Cities spread over the land, and for a time their shapes usually followed the tracks. Suburbs grew around stations on the rail lines, leaving open country in between. The coming of the automobile changed this pattern of growth. People could live anywhere near enough to drive to work. The open spaces between the railroad suburbs filled in as **commuters** drove to the stations. A commuter is someone who travels regularly to and from work by train, bus, automobile, or some other means of transportation.

Areas near the central part of the cities, which had remained open because they were not served by rail lines, now filled in. Wherever the automobile came into common use, cities began a spread that became a sprawl.

CHECKUP

1. How did Nauru become a rich country?
2. What happened to the world's population after 1600?
3. How do you figure population growth rate?
4. Why did the world's population increase so rapidly?
5. Why did cities grow? What affected the shape in which they grew?

Have pupils discuss the advantages and disadvantages of the spread of cities into the countryside of the United States.

The Use of Resources

┌─ VOCABULARY ─────────────────┐
kerosene   toxic
└──────────────────────────────┘

What makes a resource useful? A natural resource is a form of wealth supplied by nature. Whether a particular thing is considered a form of wealth depends on whether people can make use of it. So people in different times and places may have different ideas about whether something supplied by nature is or is not a natural resource. Before 1900 the people of Nauru had very little use for the rocky plateau on their little island. They had no use for the rocks except to make sinkers for their fishing lines. They thought it very strange that outsiders went to so much trouble to dig the rocky dirt on their island. For the people of Nauru in 1900, the rock was not a form of wealth. Today they well understand that phosphate rock is Nauru's greatest wealth, their most valuable natural resource.

People can live only by making use of the earth's natural resources. Resources include not only minerals, soil, water, forests, and wildlife, but also air and the energy of the sun when people know how to make use of them. For the Australian Aborigines, wildlife was the continent's greatest resource. For the European settlers, Australia's soil and minerals were the most important forms of wealth supplied by nature. <u>Knowledge of how to use a resource gives it worth.</u>

Some resources can be used up The people of Nauru have lived well in recent years by selling their major natural resource. Unfortunately, the supply of phosphate rock on the tiny island is limited. The supply will be used up in the near future. Someday the last scoop of rock will be loaded on board ship, and the mine will be closed. What will happen then? Some islanders are reported to reply with an old saying: "Tomorrow will take care of itself." Fortunately,

Too often people mistreat the world's natural resources. Hunters kill thousands of elephants, chiefly for their ivory tusks. The supply of bauxite and other minerals is not endless. We must not waste them.

When Edwin Drake struck oil in 1859 in Oil Creek at Titusville, Pennsylvania, he only drilled through 70 feet (24 m) of rock. Today oil prospectors drill over 25,000 feet (7,620 m) into the earth's crust. This is about 5 miles (8 km).

other Nauruans think that they had better plan today to take care of themselves tomorrow.

The government of Nauru has invested part of the profits from the phosphate abroad. Nauru owns the tallest building in Melbourne, Australia, as well as hotels and other buildings on different Pacific islands. The government hopes that in the future Nauruans will be able to live on the income from foreign investments. Perhaps they will be able to. In any case, they will not be able to depend on phosphate mining much longer.

The Nauruans are not the only people to face the problem of what to do when they have used up a limited resource. The people of the whole world face this problem as they use up more and more of the earth's limited resources.

The world has used a great deal of oil. Most of the oil has been consumed since

1859, when the first well was drilled in Pennsylvania. Before that time, people had made little use of the black substance that seeped from rocks, even though they had known about it for thousands of years. The ancient Romans knew about petroleum, a word that means "rock oil." It was not until chemists discovered a way to get **kerosene** from rock oil that people came to consider oil valuable. Kerosene is a thin oil made from petroleum. It is used in lamps and stoves, to run farm machines, and as a fuel for jet planes.

As oil became valuable, more wells were drilled in Pennsylvania. For a time the state was the world's leading source of petroleum. For about 20 years, more and more oil was pumped from the Pennsylvania oil fields. Then some of the wells dried up. Production declined, and today the onetime world leader produces very little oil.

Oil and natural gas are two of the earth's most important natural resources.

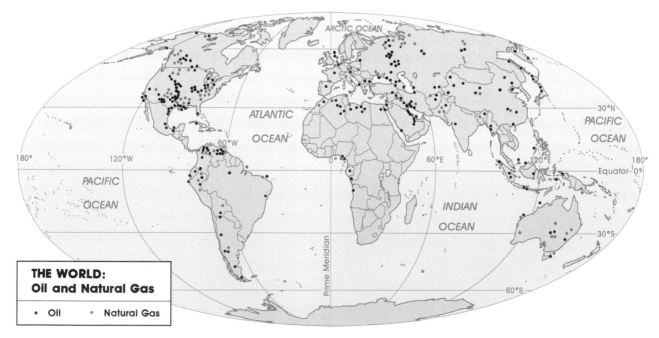

THE WORLD:
Oil and Natural Gas

• Oil   • Natural Gas

444   The Prudhoe Bay oil field is the largest in North America. The building of the Trans-Alaska Pipeline was an engineering feat and the subject of much controversy. Pupils might report on its construction and on environmentalists' objections. Class discussion could follow.

Although the oil in some fields was used up, engineers discovered others. They drilled for oil on every continent and even under the sea along the coasts. Oil was sometimes called "black gold," because chemists found so many uses for it. Oil is more than a major source of energy. It is also a raw material for making plastics, cloth, medicines, and thousands of other products. "Black gold" is one of the most valuable natural resources.

People have not used up all of the world's oil, but they have used much of the oil that is easiest to get from the earth. It now costs more to find oil, because wells must be drilled deeper and often in hard-to-reach places. No one knows for sure how much oil remains in the ground. However, we do know that there is less than there once was.

What will happen as the world keeps using more oil? Some people give the same answer as those Nauruans who say, "Tomorrow will take care of itself." Others believe that we should carefully conserve the oil we still have and that we should develop other resources to take the place of oil. The world's oil problem is not as bad as Nauru's phosphate problem, but it is the same kind of problem.

Soil—valuable dirt There is a saying: "There is no such thing as a free lunch." It means that we must always pay in some way for whatever we get. The saying applies to our use of soil, another very valuable resource. Soil is the top layer of the earth, in which plants grow. Without soil neither human beings nor animals could exist. Every time a crop is raised and

Rachel Carson: Biologist and Author

IN THE SUMMER OF 1919 a 12-year-old girl named Rachel Carson excitedly read a story entitled "A Famous Sea Fight." It excited her because she was its author. Years later Rachel Carson wrote many magazine articles and several books, but she doubted if their publication had ever excited her as much as seeing her first words in print.

Rachel Carson was interested in the outdoors as well as writing. She liked to learn about all sorts of living things. When Carson went to college, she studied biology — the science of living things. Later she took a job as a biologist for the U.S. Fish and Wildlife Service. She never lost her love of the outdoors.

While working as a government biologist, Rachel Carson became concerned with the widespread use of DDT and other powerful new pesticides. She became convinced that spraying pesticides to kill mosquitoes, elm beetles, and fire ants also destroyed many beneficial insects and fish, birds, and other wildlife. In 1962, Rachel Carson published a book, Silent Spring, in which she summed up what she had learned about the widespread use of pesticides. She described how the careless use of poisons had produced "silent springs" by killing off so many songbirds. But Silent Spring was more than a book about pesticides and birds. It was a plea for a more thoughtful relationship between people and nature.

harvested, something is taken out of the soil. If something is always taken from the soil and nothing is put back, the soil becomes poorer and produces increasingly poorer crops. In time the soil may become so worn out that it is no longer worth planting. When that happens, we have paid for our "free lunch" with the soil itself.

To preserve soil, something must be put into it. This can be done by fertilizing with decaying organic material or with artificial fertilizers. Soil can also be restored by planting clover or alfalfa. These plants restore elements that other crops take out.

Much valuable soil is lost through erosion, a word that means "eaten away." Both water and wind can eat away the soil. Heavy rains and floods wash soil into streams and rivers. A muddy stream shows that a resource is being lost. High winds blow top soil away, particularly from plowed fields, where the grass cover has been removed.

Erosion can be controlled by certain planting and plowing methods. Contour plowing prevents erosion.

Much valuable soil is lost through erosion. Both water and wind can eat away the soil.

In view of the importance of soil, it is curious that people sometimes say that something nearly worthless is "as cheap as dirt." The comparison is not a good one, for it suggests that dirt—another word for "soil"—is very common and of little value. In fact, a country is fortunate if it has much arable soil. Soil that can be cultivated is not evenly distributed over the earth's land surface. Most of the earth has neither the soil nor the climate to grow crops. The United States is fortunate to have such a large part of the earth's fertile soil. Soil is probably America's greatest natural resource—particularly in a world with such a rapidly growing population.

Many Americans seem not to have understood or appreciated their country's good fortune. Perhaps that is why they have too often used it as if it were "dirt cheap." In earlier times they did little to restore soil. They wore it out and then moved west. They were also slow to take steps to protect soil from erosion. More recently, Americans have covered many square miles of good cropland with sprawling cities. They have buried huge amounts of their nation's great resource under parking lots.

Pollution and two essential resources

Not all natural resources are necessary for life. People can live without coal, oil, or metals. The Australian Aborigines did so for thousands of years. But no people could live without two essential resources, water and air.

In spite of their importance, people have often used water and air carelessly. They waste these resources, not by destroying them, but by polluting them, or making them dirty. Cities empty wastes into streams, rivers, and lakes from which other cities draw water. It was a long time before laws required cities to have sewage treatment plants. Some industries dump **toxic**, or poisonous, wastes into streams, rivers, and lakes. In recent years, laws and regulations have been made to control this kind of pollution.

People have put waste into the air ever since they started making fires. Air pollution, however, did not become a serious problem until people started living in cities. Now many of the world's people live in cities, and pollution of the air has grown with the cities. Thousands of chimneys and smokestacks pour soot and gas into the air that people must breathe. The exhaust from automobiles and trucks

Smoke and gases from factories such as this sugar refinery combine with the fumes of automobiles to produce air pollution. This is a threat to health all over the world.

If oil spills such as the one above are not cleaned up, they can hurt people, beaches, plants, and wildlife. A spill may result from a problem with an offshore oil well or from an oil tanker that has been broken up by a storm.

adds to the pollution, which makes the air not only unpleasant but also harmful to people's health. As pollution has grown worse, governments have tried to control both the amount and kinds of waste put into the air. Laws and regulations have not done away with all pollution, but they have limited it somewhat.

Pollution of the air also pollutes water. Gases from automobiles, homes, factories, and electric power plants form acids in the air. These acids fall back to the earth in rain. Acid rain harms plants and kills fish in lakes far away from the sources of air pollution. The harm done by acid rain has made people in rural areas as well as city dwellers realize that we can spoil our most important resources.

CHECKUP

1. What makes a particular resource valuable?
2. What can be done to preserve soil?
3. What are some forms of water pollution? Air pollution?

Looking to the Future

┌─ VOCABULARY ──────────────────┐
forecast   assumption
projection
└───────────────────────────────┘

The problem of forecasts and projections   The graph of world population growth on page 33 tells about the past. It does not tell how many people there will be in the future. Yet we can use this graph to show our **forecast,** or statement of what is coming. Suppose you extend, or project, the growth line on the graph to the year 2000. How sharply should the line rise on the **projection?**

Since you have no sure way of knowing how fast the world's population will grow, you must make an **assumption** about future growth rates. An assumption is a statement that is supposed to be true but has not been proved true. Should you assume that population in the next 100 years will keep on growing at the same rate as in the past 100 years? Or should you assume that the growth rate will level off and the birthrate and death rate will balance each other? The accuracy of the projection depends on the accuracy of your assumptions. There is no way to prove an assumption about the future until the future has become history. Yet it is probably worthwhile as we face the future to think as best we can about what may happen in the future.

A crowded world   It seems unlikely that the world's population will keep on growing at the same rate as it has in the past. Indeed, if the population of the world continued to double every 40 or 50 years after the year 2000, the earth would soon have standing room only. Even if the rate of increase does drop sometime in the future, the world will still have far more people than ever before in its history. It will be a more crowded world than people have ever known.

Most of the future population will probably live in cities, as do people in much of the world today. Getting and keeping clean water and air will likely remain problems in the future. Will cities continue to sprawl over the countryside?

People may wish them to, but people may not be able to give up much cropland in the future.

Search for new ways to use resources

As supplies of resources have been used, people have discovered new ones or new ways to use old ones. In all likelihood, people living in the crowded world of the future will give much attention to the search for new ways to use resources.

Such a forecast is based on what has happened in recent years. The rising costs of oil and coal encouraged the search for other sources of energy. Sometimes the new sources have made new problems. The development of nuclear power plants brought a new pollution problem—how to get rid of nuclear waste.

The problem of nuclear waste encouraged experiments with other sources of energy. One such experiment used the waste from livestock feedlots to make gas to take the place of natural gas. A number of experiments tried "to harvest the wind" by using windmills to make electric

THE WORLD'S TWENTY-FIVE LARGEST CITIES		
City	Population	Rank
Shanghai, China	11,859,748	1
Peking (Beijing), China	9,230,687	2
Mexico City, Mexico	8,988,230	3
Tokyo, Japan	8,646,520	4
Seoul, South Korea	8,366,756	5
Moscow, U.S.S.R.	7,831,000	6
Tientsin (Tianjin), China	7,764,000	7
New York City, U.S.A.	7,071,639	8
Cairo, Egypt	6,818,318	9
London, England	6,696,008	10
Bombay, India	5,970,575	11
São Paulo, Brazil	5,924,615	12
Karachi, Pakistan	5,103,000	13
Bangkok, Thailand	4,870,000	14
Jakarta, Indonesia	4,576,009	15
Tehran, Iran	4,498,159	16
Bogotá, Colombia	4,293,913	17
Rio de Janeiro, Brazil	4,251,918	18
Leningrad, U.S.S.R.	4,073,000	19
Hong Kong	3,948,179	20
Santiago, Chile	3,448,700	21
Ho Chi Minh City, Vietnam	3,419,978	22
Delhi, India	3,287,782	23
Sydney, Australia	3,231,700	24
Madrid, Spain	3,158,818	25

These windmills, located east of San Francisco in the Altamont Pass, drive generators to produce electricity.

The United States is the world's biggest user of oil. We have only about 5 percent of the world's population, but we use about 30 percent of the world's oil production. **449**

power. There have been a number of efforts to make greater use of the sun's energy. People have realized that solar energy is a natural resource that can be used more than it has been in the past. Solar water heaters have become common. Various kinds of solar-heated houses have been built, especially in places that have a lot of sunshine. Scientists have made solar cells that change sunlight into a reliable source of electricity for many years. The cells are used on space satellites and even in small calculators.

Efforts to find new ways to use resources will have to become even more common in the future. Otherwise the world will become poorer in both energy and materials.

What kinds of jobs will there be? The development of new ways to use resources should create new kinds of jobs. The drilling of the first oil well started an industry that employed thousands of workers. Many of the jobs that people have today did not exist 50 years ago. Many of these jobs came into being because of space-age technology. On the other hand, the jobs of many skilled craftworkers, such as harness makers, hardly exist today.

Recent history gives some ideas about the kinds of jobs people will have in the future. For example, the number of farmers has been decreasing. It seems unlikely that there will be a great many farmers in the future. A few people will probably continue to feed many.

Special metal plates called collectors provide solar energy to heat this house. Each collector absorbs heat from sunlight, which is changed into a usable form of energy.

A robot is a mechanical device that operates automatically. Above, you see a robot serving as a guide dog for a blind person and another robot shearing a sheep.

In the past many people worked in factories, assembly plants, and steel mills. Today electronically controlled robots are taking the place of many workers. Automatic robot welding machines replace human welders in automobile plants. Even the factories that make automatic machines use robots to make robots. It seems likely that the use of robots and automatic machines in factories will increase. Many jobs of the future will be for people who know how to design and operate such factories.

Computers are replacing certain types of office workers. However, computers create jobs for others. Offices need fewer filing clerks, but they need more computer operators. Just how many new jobs the computer industry will create is not clear. There may not, for example, be as great a need for workers to repair computers as some people have expected. Computers of the future will be able to tell users what needs to be replaced when the machines do not function properly.

In the future many people will work in the service industries, which provide everything from health care to food and entertainment. Other workers will have jobs taking care of people, including both children and the aged. Largely automated factories may produce more goods in the future, but it is also thought that there will still be a need for many people to sell and service the goods that robots make.

Forecasts and projections about the future can be neither sure nor complete. We cannot be sure that present trends will continue. Even more important, we cannot know what unexpected things may happen. It is well to think about the future, but it is wise to remember that our assumptions may limit us.

CHECKUP

1. What is a population projection?
2. What are some sources of energy that may take the place of coal and oil?
3. Why may there be fewer jobs in factories in the future?

Pupils will undoubtedly have had their own experiences with computers. Some idea of the enormous influence computers are having on our society may be gained by having pupils tell how they or their families have used computers or have been in some way affected by them.

KEY FACTS

1. The world's population has grown at a rapid rate since 1700 because of improved sanitation, health care, and an increased food supply.

2. Before 1800 most of the world's people lived in rural areas. Today well over one third of the world's people live in cities.

3. The value of a natural resource depends upon the use people can make of it.

4. Some resources can be used up, some can be lost through neglect, and others can be spoiled by pollution.

5. It seems probable that in the future people will find both new ways to use resources and new kinds of jobs.

VOCABULARY QUIZ

On a sheet of paper write the five statements below. Choose a word or words from the list to correctly fill in the blanks in the statements.

a. majority   e. commuter
b. growth rate   f. toxic
c. assumption   g. cholera
d. typhoid   h. projection

1. The difference between the average number of births and deaths for every 1,000 persons is the growth rate .

2. At one time, __typhoid__ and __cholera__ took many lives.

3. An extension of the growth line on a population graph to a year in the future is a projection .

4. An assumption is a statement that is supposed to be true but has not been proved true.

5. Streams, rivers, and lakes have been polluted by __toxic__ wastes.

REVIEW QUESTIONS

1. In what two ways is the story of Nauru like that of the rest of the world?

2. In 1980, France had a birthrate of 14.8 per 1,000 and a death rate of 10.1 per 1,000. What was the growth rate?

3. What were the reasons for the rapid growth in the world's population?

4. How many of the world's people live in cities? On which continents are city dwellers a majority? A minority?

5. What are natural resources? Name some of the main ones.

6. Give examples of the careless use of soil, water, and air.

7. What forecasts are made in this chapter concerning (a) population, (b) resources, (c) jobs?

ACTIVITIES

1. Make a population graph similar to that on page 33 showing the growth of the population of the United States from 1790 to the present. Use an almanac or other reference book for census figures.

2. Make a poster advertising the natural resources of your area and the ways they are used.

3. Prepare a report about an occupation that you would like to have one day. In your report tell why you think there will still be such an occupation in the future. Describe what you would have to do to prepare for the occupation you have chosen.

4. Choose two cities listed in the table on page 449. For 2 weeks, look in the newspaper and news magazines for articles about the two cities. Then compare the two sets of articles. What likenesses between the two cities do the articles show? Differences?

26/SKILLS DEVELOPMENT

MAKING OUTLINES

THE USEFULNESS OF OUTLINES

An outline is one way to make notes on what you read. Making an outline is a good way to fix material in your mind. An outline also provides a quick way to review. You will find it helpful to prepare an outline for either an oral or a written report.

In making an outline, you list ideas in order of importance. One pattern for an outline follows.

I. Main topic
  A. Subtopic
    1.
    2.   Points to develop
      a.   subtopics
      b.

The number of main topics, subtopics, and development points will vary according to the material being outlined.

SKILLS PRACTICE

Chapter 26 is easily divided into three main topics. You can see these topics in the outline in the second column.

1. Topic I has been completely worked out as an example. Compare this part of the outline with the material covered on pages 438–442.
2. Topic II has subtopics but no development points. Complete this part of the outline on a sheet of paper by filling in points that develop the subtopics. You will find this information in the paragraphs in Chapter 26 that follow each subtopic. Ask yourself, "What is the main fact or idea of this paragraph?"
3. Topic III has not been worked out. Add both subtopics and points to develop them. Make sure that the points under a subtopic relate to and develop that subtopic.

OUTLINE OF CHAPTER 26
People and Resources

I. Population Growth
  A. How a tiny country became rich
    1. Before 1900, Nauru was like other Pacific islands.
    2. The discovery of phosphate provided new wealth.
    3. The population increased rapidly.
  B. A time of great growth
    1. The world's population increased rapidly after 1700.
    2. A place's growth rate is the difference between the average number of deaths and births per 1,000 persons.
  C. Why population grew rapidly
    1. Some diseases were controlled and prevented.
    2. The world's food supply increased.
      a. New croplands were cultivated.
      b. Agricultural methods were improved.
  D. The growing city population
    1. Over one third of the world's people live in cities.
    2. Why have the cities grown?
      a. There was no longer room for some people to make a living on the land.
      b. Fewer people can now till more land.
    3. Commuter travel has shaped cities.
II. The Use of Resources
  A. What makes a resource useful?
  B. Some resources can be used up
  C. Soil—valuable dirt
  D. Pollution and two essential resources
III. Looking to the Future

CHAPTER

27 An Interdependent World

International Trade

VOCABULARY

interdependent   logotype

surplus   multinational

quota

The interdependence of independent nations   After World War II, 51 countries of the world formed the United Nations. The member nations of the UN agreed to work together for world peace, but they also declared that each nation remained independent. Yet the independent nations of the world are, in fact, **interdependent**. In other words, they depend on each other in many ways.

The interdependence of nations is by no means new. Nations have long depended on trade with other nations for goods they needed or wanted but did not produce. In the time of Columbus, Europeans sailed to Asia in order to buy spices that they could not grow at home. Since then, international trade has grown greatly.

Fifty or sixty years ago, geography books sometimes pointed out that the usual American breakfast depended upon trade with distant countries. Coffee came from Central or South America, cocoa from West Africa, tea from South Asia, and bananas from Central America.

Today we still depend on those places for coffee, cocoa, tea, and bananas, but they are only a few of the foods we get from other lands. A trip to the supermarket will show you how much we now depend on other countries. You can find canned meat from Argentina and Brazil and sardines from Norway, Spain, and Scotland. During the winter months many of our fresh vegetables come from Mexico. Bananas still come from Central America, but supermarkets may also have Granny Smith apples from New Zealand or grapes from Chile. If you have a taste for some less common fruits, you may buy kumquats from Australia or South Africa, kiwis from New Zealand, or ugli fruit from Jamaica. If you buy nuts, the cashews will probably have come from India, and the Brazil nuts will, of course, have come from Brazil. It is the only country that grows that kind of nut.

Americans use not only food from other countries but many other things as well. Children play with toys from Germany, Norway, Taiwan, and a number of other places. An American may wear a shirt made in South Korea, a sweater of Australian wool made in Hong Kong, and shoes manufactured in Italy or Spain. Many Americans drive automobiles made in Japan. The stereos and television sets in many homes are also made in Japan.

Flags of many countries fly at the United Nations headquarters in New York City. (41°N/74°W; map, p. 68)

Ask each pupil to make a list of ten imported items that he or she has eaten, worn, or used in some way. Ask pupils if they can think of a reason why each item was imported. Some pupils might use a visit to a store to make a longer list of imported items and their countries of origin.

Florists sell flowers grown in Israel, and hardware stores have tools made in Taiwan. In your kitchen you may slice a carrot grown in Mexico with a German knife and cook it in a pot made in France or Sweden.

What the United States sells While the United States depends on other countries for many goods, other countries, in turn, depend on the United States. They get their airplanes, farm machinery, office machines, and computers from the United States. Countries that sell oil to the United States use American oil-drilling and pipeline equipment to get and transport the oil.

The United States also supplies large amounts of food to the world. Because of its fertile soil and advanced farming methods, the United States raises more corn, wheat, and soybeans than Americans can use. This **surplus** makes up an important part of America's exports.

A growing number of the world's people have come to depend on imported food. Much of the food comes from the United States. Parts of Asia, Africa, and Latin America—lands that once raised most of their own basic foods—now depend, at least in part, on imports. The rapid growth of population is one important reason for this growing dependence. For example, Nigeria, the largest African country, at one time not only fed itself but exported food. Now Nigeria depends partly on imports to feed its people. The reason for the change is easy to understand. Nigeria's population jumped from 30 million in 1950 to over 84 million in 1983. During the 1970s, Nigeria enjoyed

A container ship leaves San Francisco Bay, bound for ports across the Pacific Ocean.

an oil boom. Not only did Nigeria have oil to sell, but the price of oil also rose rapidly. Part of the oil profits went to pay for food for the growing population. Thousands of Nigerians left the land and flocked to the cities, seeking jobs. Many developed a taste for imported foods. As a result the country not only had more people, it also had people who ate fewer yams grown at home and more chicken imported from the United States.

People in other countries have also come to prefer Western-style foods, particularly meat. One writer calls the change in eating habits "the hamburger revolution." America's favorite meat sandwich has become popular in cities from Tokyo and Taipei to Mexico City.

An interesting exercise might be to compare the percentages of people who are employed in industry in various countries. A reliable almanac will provide this information.

The demand for more meat has produced a demand for more cattle and for more cattle feed. In 1981 and 1982 the United States exported one fourth of its corn crop and one half of its soybeans.

Why nations buy certain products It is easy to understand why nations import goods they cannot produce. If Americans want to eat bananas, bananas must be imported from the countries where they are grown. But why are clothing, toys, and automobiles imported if they are also made in America? There are two answers: quality and price.

A country that specializes in making a certain product may turn out goods of such quality that buyers abroad prefer them to goods made in their own countries. Swedish toy makers design and make wooden toys that are sold in American stores. The Swiss have long specialized in making watches and scientific instruments, which they export to coun-

tries that make these products, too. American companies specialize in making office machines and computers, which they export to other countries.

Lower prices, however, probably have more to do with the success of imports. Americans buy clothing made in Asia or Latin America largely because it is cheaper. Workers in Hong Kong, Taiwan, and South Korea are paid less than those in the United States. As a result the shirts, blouses, sweaters, and dresses they make are cheaper than those made in America. The cost of labor is figured in the price of the item.

Sometimes a country is able to make goods more cheaply because it has newer and more efficient factories and plants. In general the country with the most recently built steel mills can produce the cheapest steel. In the 1970s the American steel industry, an old industry, lost business to countries with new steel plants.

This is the market at Alkmaar, the Netherlands, world famous for its cheeses.

The first definitely protective tariff was not adopted until 1816. A lively discussion can be structured around the pros and cons of protecting American industry by such restrictions.

Restricting trade to protect home industries When importing goods makes them cheaper, buyers will be helped. However, others may be hurt. Americans who buy cheaper shirts made abroad have more money in their pockets. But if many imported shirts are sold, American shirt factories will have to shut down. American shirt buyers will get bargains, but American shirt makers will lose their jobs.

People whose businesses and jobs are threatened by imports sometimes seek help from their government. They want protection from foreign goods in the form of **quotas** or protective tariffs. By setting a quota, a country limits the amount of goods that may be imported. A protective tariff is a tax on imported goods that is high enough to make them at least as expensive as goods made at home.

Quotas and tariffs may protect home industries, but they have other effects, too. Buyers who have to pay more for shirts have less money to buy jeans or other goods made at home. Stores do less business. Restrictions on imports from other countries usually affect a country's own exports. If Taiwan and Japan sell fewer shirts and automobiles to the United States, they will have less money to buy American farm products. In the long run international trade makes it possible for more people to have more goods. But people put out of work by imported goods may point out that in the short run international trade cost them their jobs. This is one of the problems of an interdependent world.

Doing business in many nations The symbols of businesses that often appear on products and in advertisements are called **logotypes**, or logos. Some logos are at least as well-known as national flags. An American traveling abroad will see the familiar logo of an oil company on ships at sea and at service stations and on storage tanks in foreign countries. Magazines published in Italy, India, Spain, and

These familiar logotypes greet Americans wherever they travel in the world.

This bank does business with many nations, as shown by the board in the trading room.

a number of other countries contain advertisements for brand names well-known in the United States or Britain.

Products bearing American or British brand names in Europe, Asia, and Latin America are not necessarily imports. Many corporations are **multinational.** A multinational corporation has plants or businesses in more than two countries. The logos of American automobile makers appear on cars made in Europe, Asia, and Latin America. A number of American corporations operate plants or businesses in other countries, and a number of corporations from other countries operate plants or businesses in the United States. National boundaries do not limit the business of multinational corporations.

Computers, satellites, and "offshore offices" The development of computers and communication satellites has made it possible for a business in one country to have office work done in another. Many companies in Japan, Australia, and the United States have part of their office work force in India, Taiwan, the Philippines, or the Caribbean countries. Workers in these "offshore offices" put information on computer tapes to be returned to the home offices.

New ways of sending and storing information have changed the ways that businesses operate. If satellite communication becomes less costly, "offshore offices" may become even more common. Banks and insurance companies may become still more multinational. National boundaries in the future may do even less to limit the ways the world does business.

CHECKUP

1. What are some products the United States imports? What are some of its exports?
2. How may specialization affect a country's products?
3. Why are some countries able to make goods more cheaply than others?
4. How may tariffs be used to protect home industries?
5. What is a multinational corporation?

After pupils have read "Doing business in many nations," ask them to name some corporations that operate in more than one country. (Coca Cola, Exxon, McDonald's and so on) **459**

The sea bottom has become important because of the oil, manganese, and other mineral resources found there. Many nations have signed a treaty that sets rules for developing these resources. This treaty has not been ratified by the United States. Ask: Who do you think should control undersea resources?

Why and How Nations Work Together

Rules of the sea In order to trade with each other, nations must have some common rules or understandings. Some of the rules are very old. When traders began to sail the seas, they developed customs and laws governing the way they sailed and did business. More than 2,000 years ago, the Greeks and the Romans had such rules. They called the rules the law of the sea. Nations today still observe a set of laws, now called **maritime** law, for ships on the **high seas**. The high seas are the oceans and saltwater seas beyond the strip of territorial waters along a country's coast. Many countries, including the United States, now extend their control over surface waters to 200 miles from their coasts. Under maritime law the high seas belong to no country. All ships are free to sail the high seas. Each country is responsible for keeping law and order on ships flying its flag. All ships follow certain common safety rules in order to avoid accidents at sea. If an accident takes place, maritime law has rules for fixing responsibility. Rules of the sea are as necessary as rules of the road.

Nations have sometimes ignored maritime law. In times of war some countries have denied freedom of the high seas not only to enemy ships but to those of other countries trading with an enemy. But in times of peace, nations generally observe these international laws simply because the laws are so useful. Maritime law is necessary if countries use the seas for trade.

Airspace and outer space When people traveled on land and sea only, there was little question about who owned airspace. For the most part, people followed an old rule—whoever owns the land, owns what is above it. Once people began to fly balloons and airplanes, the old rule no longer served. Questions arose about the right to fly over land. Some people thought there should be freedom of the air just as there was freedom of the high seas. But nations refused to accept this rule, partly because of the danger of bombing from the air. Instead it was agreed that the airspace over a country is part of that country, although the air does not belong to individual people. Airplanes from one country must have permission to fly into another coun-

Kai Tak Airport in Hong Kong serves airliners from many countries. Hong Kong is a major trade center in South China. (22°N/114°E; map, p. 331)

On April 12, 1981, the United States launched the first space shuttle, Columbia. It was designed to be launched like a rocket and to fly like an airplane. On a later shuttle flight in 1983, Sally Ride became America's first woman astronaut to fly in space.

try's airspace. Airplanes from all countries may fly over the oceans because no country can claim the high seas.

Even though each country governs its own airspace, the great number of international flights makes it necessary for pilots to follow the same flight rules. For this reason the nations set up the International Civil Aviation Organization. It recommends standard rules.

Sometimes national control of airspace has resulted in tragedy. On September 1, 1983, a Korean airliner flying from Anchorage, Alaska, to Seoul, South Korea, strayed into Soviet airspace. A Soviet fighter plane shot it down. All 269 people on board the Korean plane were killed. The shooting down of a civilian passenger plane shocked people throughout the world. However, the Soviet government insisted that its plane was only defending Soviet airspace.

The launching of space satellites that orbit the earth raised an important new question, How far up does a nation's airspace go? Could one nation refuse to allow the satellites of another nation to pass over its territory? The nations realized that the old rule about airspace could not apply to outer space. In 1963 it was agreed that no nation could claim outer space. Any nation could send satellites into space for exploration or other peaceful purposes. According to the 1963 agreement, nations would not explode a nuclear device in space or use space for other military purposes.

There are still some problems with the international law of outer space. Where does a country's airspace end, and outer space begin? The world has not as yet worked out an exact definition of outer space. Outer space is generally taken to be the area beyond the earth's atmosphere in which an unpowered satellite may remain in orbit. This means that the limit of a country's airspace is somewhere between 70 to 100 miles (113 to 161 km) above its surface. It has also proved difficult to distinguish clearly between peaceful and military uses of space. A number of experiments in space could have military uses.

Nations work together to send messages
For more than a hundred years, nations have depended on each other to deliver mail. Before 1875 there was no general system for sending letters from one country to another. Each country made separate agreements with other countries. Each letter needed special handling because postage had to be paid to each country through which the letter passed, and rates differed from one country to another.

To make the sending of mail easier, a group of countries formed the Universal Postal Union in 1874. Each member of the union agreed to forward and deliver foreign letters by the most rapid means used for its own mail. Most nations of the world now belong to the union. It sets postal standards, such as rates and sizes of letters. Because nations work together through the postal union, you can send a letter with an American stamp on it to almost any place in the world.

Every new means of communication has brought a new need for nations to work together. A year before the completion of the first successful Atlantic cable in 1866, a group of countries created the International Telegraph Union. The union drew up rules for sending international messages. Later the nations created a similar body for international telephone service. Today the Interna-

After several failed attempts, the Atlantic telegraph cable was successfully laid on the ocean floor in 1866. The inset shows the Great Eastern paying out the Atlantic cable.

Ground stations use large antennae to send and receive signals to and from orbiting satellites.

tional Telecommunication Union helps nations solve problems in international radio, telephone, telegraph, and satellite communications. Because it costs a great deal to put a communications satellite in orbit, nations share their use. The United States shares the use of its satellites with certain other nations. They work together in using this truly global means of communication.

Working together in the United Nations
The United Nations is the largest of the international organizations. When the UN was created in 1945, it had 51 member nations. Today there are more than three times that number.

The UN has two governing bodies, the General Assembly and the Security Council. Every member nation has a seat and a vote in the General Assembly. Only 15 nations are members of the Security

The 123,000 people of Vanuatu are represented by one vote in the U.N. General Assembly. So are China's 1 billion people.

Council. The five permanent Council members are China, France, the Soviet Union, the United Kingdom, and the United States. The General Assembly elects ten other Security Council members. Each of the permanent members has **veto** power. This means that the Security Council can take no action that has been vetoed, or voted down, by any of the permanent members. When the UN was formed, it was hoped that the member nations would act together to maintain peace. Such has not been the case.

The first purpose of the United Nations is to help keep peace in the world. Those who wrote the Charter of the United Nations expressed the hope that the organization would save the world from the "scourge of war." It has not done so. However, the UN has become a center

Throughout its history, the United Nations has often been called upon to prevent a dangerous situation from turning into a war.

463

Write to United Nations Publications, Room A-3315, United Nations, New York, NY 10017, for a list of all UN publications. Pupils might select material of interest and send for several publications to share with the class.

THE UNITED NATIONS AND ITS AGENCIES

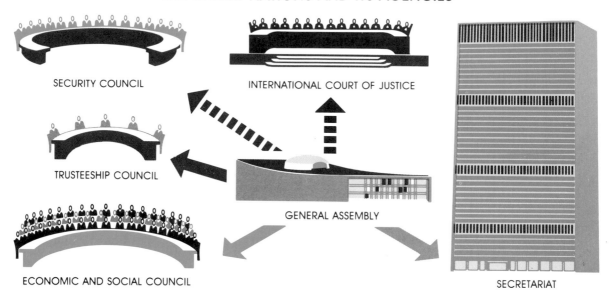

SECURITY COUNCIL

INTERNATIONAL COURT OF JUSTICE

TRUSTEESHIP COUNCIL

GENERAL ASSEMBLY

ECONOMIC AND SOCIAL COUNCIL

SECRETARIAT

The United Nations works through dozens of different agencies. The five main ones are shown in relation to the central body, the General Assembly. Solid arrows point to agencies over which the Assembly has direct responsibility and control. The Security Council, while working with the General Assembly, is not governed by it. The 15 judges on the International Court of Justice are elected but not controlled by the General Assembly and the Security Council. The Economic and Social Council supervises the work of a number of the United Nations' specialized agencies.

where nations meet to talk over their problems and try to find solutions. Special agencies of the UN, such as the Universal Postal Union and the International Telecommunication Union, give nations a means for working together for a better world.

The UN has a number of other special agencies. One provides for refugees, people driven from their homes by war or revolution. Another agency raises funds to help children in the less-developed countries. The World Health Organization works to better the health of all peoples, but especially those in the developing countries. The International Monetary Fund helps nations manage their credit and money systems. It is also through these different agencies that nations work together within the UN. There is more to the UN than the General Assembly and the Security Council.

Other groups through which nations act
Countries that belong to the United Nations may also belong to a regional organization. The members of these groups are located in a certain region, or part of the world. A regional organization may have some of the same purposes as the UN. For example, the Organization of American States (OAS), like the UN, aims to keep peace and provide for the peaceful settlement of disputes. The OAS includes most of the countries in North and South America.

The European Economic Community (EEC), sometimes called the Common

Belgium, Canada, Denmark, France, Greece, Iceland, Italy, Luxembourg, Netherlands, Norway, Portugal, Spain, Turkey, Great Britain, the United States, and West Germany are the members of NATO. Have pupils find these countries on the map on pp. 470–471.

Market, is made up of ten European countries. The organization was set up to help make trade easier between the member nations. You learned about the Common Market in Chapter 10.

Countries in other parts of the world have also formed regional groups, although none are so closely knit as the European Economic Community. African countries have the Organization of African Unity (OAU). There is an Association of Southeast Asian Nations (ASEAN) and an Arab League made up of countries in the Middle East and North Africa.

Alliances—acting together for defense

Some international organizations are set up to help nations defend themselves. For centuries, countries have made **alliances**, agreements in which nations promise to act together in the event of war. When the United Nations was formed, it was hoped that it would take the place of alliances. If the UN could settle disputes and keep peace, nations could depend on it for security. Unfortunately the UN has had limited success in keeping peace, and nations have been unwilling to depend on only the UN for security. Instead, nations have come to rely on alliances for defense.

The United States, Canada, and a group of Western European countries formed the North Atlantic Treaty Organization, often called NATO. The members of NATO agreed that an armed attack against one or more of them in Europe or North America would be considered an attack against all. The Soviet Union organized an alliance of Communist countries in Eastern Europe called the Warsaw Pact. In both alliances members depend on each other for defense.

There are many kinds of flags besides national ones. Some flags stand for international organizations, such as the UN. Other flags stand for regional groups, such as NATO.

FLAGS OF WORLD ORGANIZATIONS

The United Nations

Organization of American States (OAS)

Organization of African Unity (OAU)

Arab League

Olympic Games

North Atlantic Treaty Organization (NATO)

The 1984 Winter Olympic Games opened with colorful ceremony at Sarajevo (sar′ ə ye vō),
Yugoslavia. (44°N/18°E; map, p. 487)

International games: the Olympics
Alliances are as old as the ancient Greek cities. The Greek cities were much like modern nations. Each city made its own laws, governed itself, defended itself, made alliances, and sometimes fought wars.

Every 4 years, athletes from the Greek cities journeyed to Olympia. They came to take part in games held to honor their gods. All wars stopped during the season of the Olympic Games so that athletes and spectators could travel to Olympia.

About a hundred years ago, a French scholar, Pierre de Coubertin, proposed that modern nations revive the Olympic Games. He believed that the games "would constitute the highest of international activities." He insisted that if athletes from different nations came together, "the cause of peace will have received a new and powerful support."

Coubertin convinced a group of leaders from different nations to hold the first modern Olympic Games at Athens in 1896. Since then the Olympic Games have been held in 15 different countries on 4 continents. The games have not made the world more peaceful. Modern nations, unlike the Greek cities, do not stop fighting during the games. Instead the games were suspended once during World War I and twice during World War II. Yet the Olympic Games have become a truly international activity. An international committee controls the games, and athletes from many nations take part. The Olympic Games are yet another way in which the people of independent nations act together in an interdependent world.

CHECKUP

1. What rules have nations followed concerning claims to the high seas, airspace, and outer space?
2. What is the difference between the governing bodies of the United Nations?
3. What are regional organizations?
4. What is NATO? What is the Warsaw Pact?

Pupils might use library resources to report on aspects of the Olympics (types of competition, summer and winter games, separate men's and women's events, leading medal-winning nations, records). Reports could be read to the class.

27/CHAPTER REVIEW

KEY FACTS

1. Nations depend on trade for goods they need or want but do not produce.

2. Nations may import goods they can produce because of the high quality or low price of the imports.

3. Quotas and protective tariffs are used to restrict imports.

4. National boundaries do not limit the business of multinational corporations.

5. Nations follow various rules in using the high seas, airspace, and outer space.

6. International bodies, such as the United Nations and its agencies, provide ways for nations to work together.

VOCABULARY QUIZ

Read the following statements. Decide which are true and which are false. Write your answer (**T** or **F**) on a sheet of paper.

F **1.** Maritime law governs a nation's airspace.

T **2.** A logotype identifies a company's products and property.

T **3.** A veto by a permanent member of the UN Security Council means that an action has been voted down.

F **4.** A country that produces less of a product than it uses has a surplus.

T **5.** A quota is a limit on the amount of a product that may be imported.

T **6.** Multinational corporations own and operate businesses in different countries.

T **7.** The North Atlantic Treaty Organization is an alliance of nations.

F **8.** Refugees are people who will not leave their homeland.

F **9.** The high seas are north of the Arctic Circle.

F **10.** Interdependent nations need nothing from other nations.

REVIEW QUESTIONS

1. Why is it said that independent countries depend on each other for many of their goods?

2. Why do nations buy goods or services that they can produce?

3. Why do nations restrict trade? What methods do they use? What are the results?

4. How do companies do business in more than one country?

5. Why have nations accepted common rules for the use of the high seas, airspace, and outer space? What are some of these rules?

6. Why did nations agree to form the Universal Postal Union?

7. How does the veto power in the United Nations Security Council work?

8. What are some of the things that nations do through the special agencies of the UN?

9. Why are the Olympic Games called an international activity?

ACTIVITIES

1. Make a list of things in your home that were either grown or made in another country.

2. Draw a cartoon showing that the United States both buys goods from and sells goods to other countries.

3. Make a poster for a United Nations Day.

4. Write a report on one of the following special agencies of the United Nations: International Labor Organization (ILO); Food and Agriculture Organization (FAO); UN Educational, Scientific, and Cultural Organization (UNESCO); World Health Organization (WHO); International Monetary Fund (IMF); International Telecommunication Union (ITU); World Meteorological Organization (WMO); International Bank for Reconstruction Development (World Bank).

READING A MILEAGE CHART

HOW TO READ A MILEAGE CHART

A mileage chart presents information about distances in a compact, easy-to-read form. The chart below shows airline distances between nine world cities. Suppose you want to find the distance between New York and Los Angeles. Find *New York* on the left side of the chart. Put your finger on *New York*. Now find *Los Angeles* at the top of the chart. Put a finger of your other hand on *Los Angeles*. Move both fingers, one across and one down, until they meet. They should meet at 2,451. That is about the number of air miles between New York and Los Angeles.

SKILLS PRACTICE: Part I

On a sheet of paper, write the distance between each of the following pairs of cities.
1. Bombay and Melbourne **6,097**
2. New York and Paris **3,622**
3. Tokyo and New York **6,735**
4. Honolulu and Paris **7,434**
5. Los Angeles and Rio de Janeiro **6,296**

SKILLS PRACTICE: Part II

Using information from the chart, decide if the following statements are true or false. Write your answers on a sheet of paper.

T 1. A trip from Honolulu to Los Angeles is shorter than a trip from Honolulu to Apia.

T 2. A trip from Apia to Melbourne is shorter than a trip from Apia to Los Angeles.

F 3. A New York to Paris trip is longer than one from New York to Rio de Janeiro.

T 4. There is less than 100 miles difference between a flight from Melbourne to New York and a flight from Melbourne to Paris.

F 5. A flight from Tokyo to Honolulu is longer than one from Tokyo to Bombay.

SKILLS PRACTICE: Part III

Make a chart showing either airline or highway distances between at least six cities in the United States. Use an almanac, highway atlas, or other reference source for information about the distances.

AIR MILEAGE CHART	Apia, Western Samoa	Bombay, India	Honolulu, U.S.A.	Los Angeles, U.S.A.	Melbourne, Australia	New York, U.S.A.	Paris, France	Rio de Janeiro, Brazil	Tokyo, Japan
Apia, Western Samoa		8154	2604	4828	3113	7242	9990	8120	4656
Bombay, India	8154		8020	8701	6097	7794	4359	8257	4188
Honolulu, U.S.A.	2604	8020		2557	5513	4959	7434	8190	3850
Los Angeles, U.S.A.	4828	8701	2557		7931	2451	5601	6296	5470
Melbourne, Australia	3113	6097	5513	7931		10,355	10,396	8186	5089
New York, U.S.A.	7242	7794	4959	2451	10,355		3622	4820	6735
Paris, France	9990	4359	7434	5601	10,396	3622		5703	6033
Rio de Janeiro, Brazil	8120	8257	8190	6296	8186	4820	5703		11,535
Tokyo, Japan	4656	4188	3850	5470	5089	6735	6033	11,535	

10/UNIT REVIEW

Answer Key in back of book.

READING THE TEXT

Turn to page 438 and read the section "How a tiny country became rich." On a sheet of paper, answer the following questions.

1. Why was Pleasant Island a good name for Nauru in 1789?

2. What was the population of Nauru in 1789 and how did the people make a living?

3. What is one use for phosphate?

4. What is the population of Nauru today and how do the people make a living?

5. Is Pleasant Island still a good name for Nauru today?

READING A MAP

Turn to the map on page 444. It shows oil and natural gas deposits throughout the world. Study the map to decide which statements below are true and which are false. On a sheet of paper, write **T** if the statement is true and **F** if the statement is false.

1. All the inhabited continents have oil and natural gas deposits. T

2. There are no offshore oil deposits. F

3. Most of the oil and natural gas in Africa is found on the east coast. F

4. North America has many oil and natural gas deposits. T

5. There is no natural gas in Australia. F

READING PICTURES

Look at the pictures in Chapters 26 and 27. Then, on a sheet of paper, write the page numbers of the pictures that fit the descriptions below. Be prepared to explain why you made the choices you did.

1. Find three pictures that show poor use of resources.

2. Find a picture that shows "doing business in many nations."

3. Find two pictures that show international cooperation.

4. Find a picture that shows an energy source.

5. Find a picture that shows how technology can affect the future.

READING A TABLE

Study the table on page 449. It lists the world's 25 largest cities. On a sheet of paper, write the answers to these questions.

1. How many of the cities on the list are in Asia?

2. How many European cities are on the list?

3. Which United States city is on the list? What is its rank?

4. How many cities on the list are in the Western Hemisphere?

5. What is the population of the world's largest city?

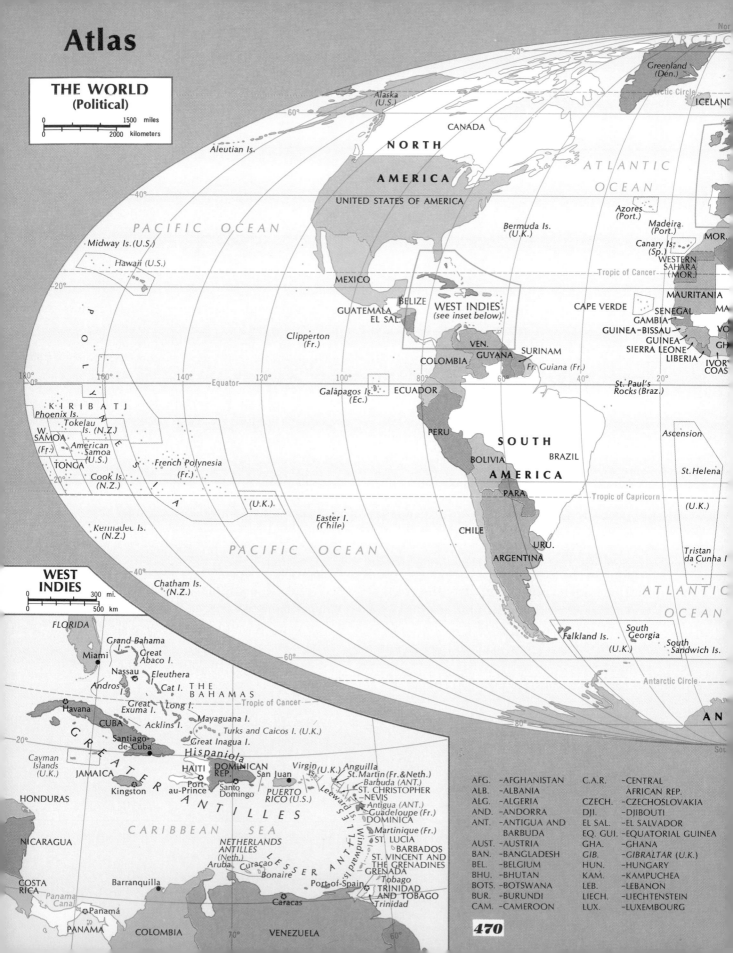

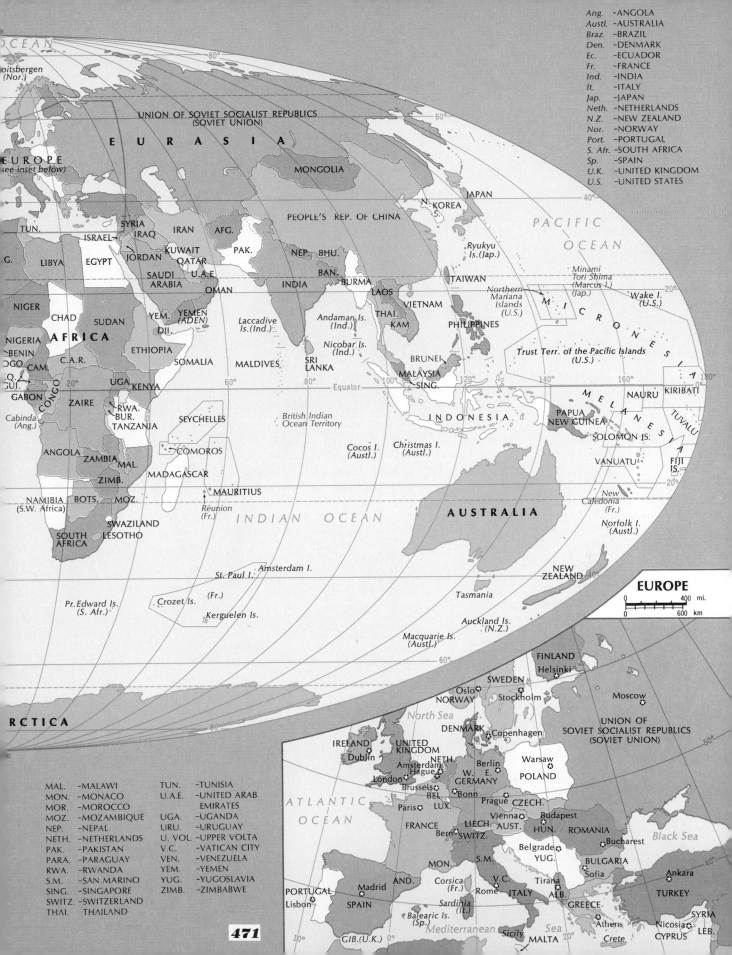

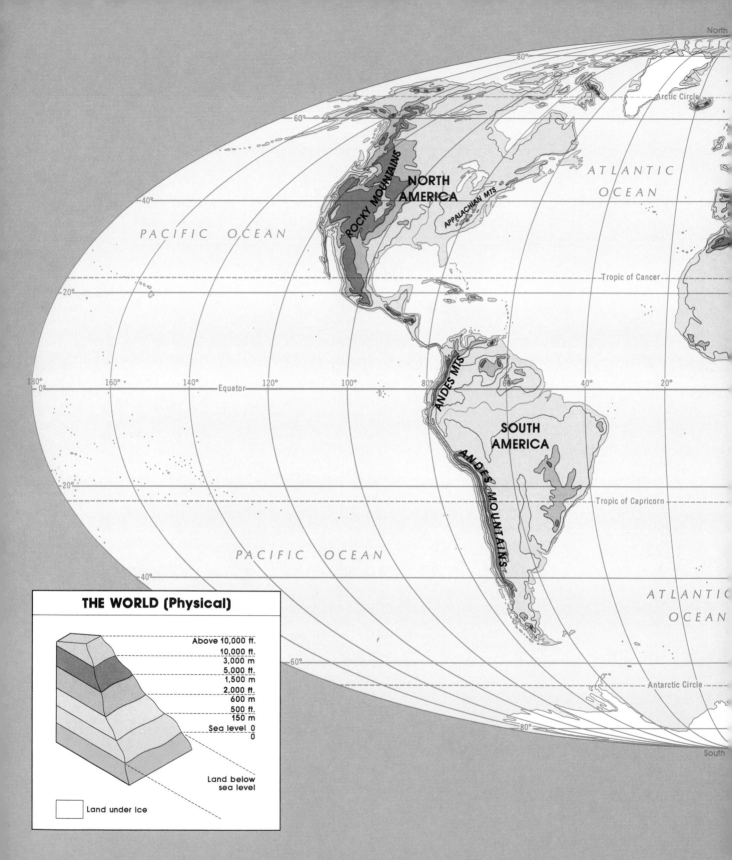

ARCTIC

North

Arctic Circle

ATLANTIC
OCEAN

NORTH
AMERICA

ROCKY MOUNTAINS

APPALACHIAN MTS

PACIFIC OCEAN

Tropic of Cancer

ANDES MTS

SOUTH
AMERICA

ANDES MOUNTAINS

Equator

PACIFIC OCEAN

Tropic of Capricorn

ATLANTIC
OCEAN

Antarctic Circle

South

THE WORLD (Physical)

Above 10,000 ft.
10,000 ft.
3,000 m
5,000 ft.
1,500 m
2,000 ft.
600 m
500 ft.
150 m
Sea level 0
0

Land below
sea level

Land under ice

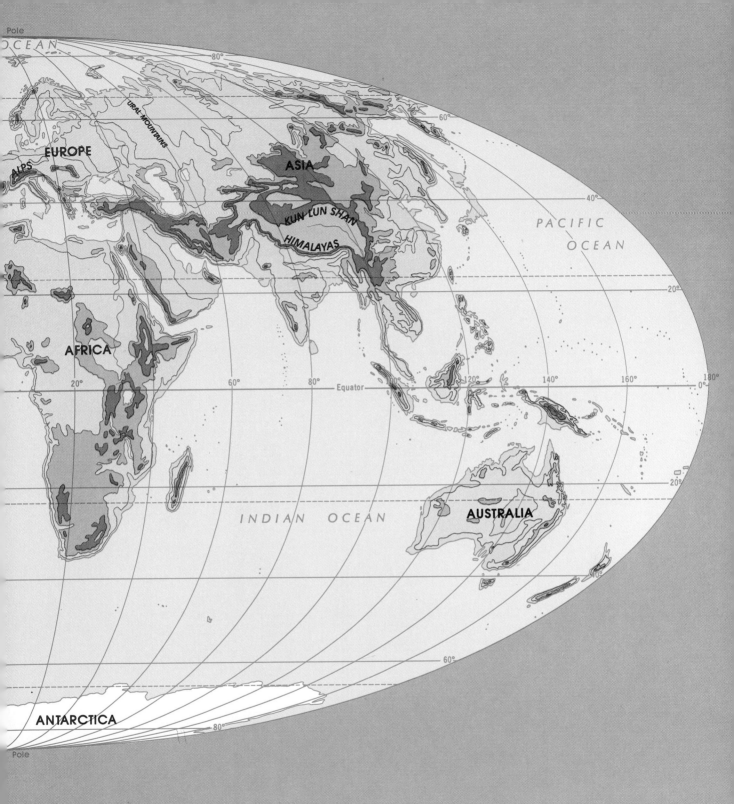

Pole

OCEAN

80°

URAL MOUNTAINS

60°

EUROPE

ALPS

ASIA

40°

KUN LUN SHAN

PACIFIC

HIMALAYAS

OCEAN

20°

AFRICA

20°

60°   80°   Equator   100°   120°   140°   160°   180°
0°

INDIAN OCEAN

AUSTRALIA

20°

60°

ANTARCTICA

80°

Pole

CANADA

90° 85° 80° 75° 70° 65°

45°

Quebec
St. Lawrence R.
Bay of Fundy
MAINE

Lake Superior
Duluth

MINNE-
SOTA

St. Paul
Minnea-
polis

Ottawa
Montreal

ADIRONDACK
MTS.
VT.
Montpelier
N.H.
Concord
Manchester
Augusta
Portland

WISCONSIN
Green
Bay
Milwaukee
Madison

MICHIGAN

Lake Huron

Toronto
L. Ontario
Rochester
Buffalo
Syracuse
NEW YORK
Albany
Hudson R.
MASS.
Springfield
Boston
C. Cod
Providence
Hartford
R.I.
CONN.
40°

Flint
Grand
Rapids

Lake Michigan

Lansing
Detroit
Dearborn

Lake Erie
Erie

Cleveland
PENNSYLVANIA
Jersey City
Newark
New York
Bridgeport
Long Island

IOWA
Waterloo
Rockford
Racine
Chicago
Gary
Hammond
South
Bend
Toledo
Fort
Wayne
Akron
Youngstown
Canton
Pittsburgh
Harrisburg
ALLEGHENY MTS.
Philadelphia
Trenton
NEW JERSEY
Atlantic City

Davenport
Des
Moines

Illinois R.

Peoria
Springfield
INDIANA
Indianapolis
OHIO
Dayton
Columbus
Ohio R.
W.VA.
Washington
D.C.
Baltimore
MD. Dover
Annapolis
C. May
DELAWARE

Missouri
Kansas City
Kansas City
Jefferson
City
St. Louis
MISSOURI
Springfield

Wabash R.

Cincinnati
Louisville
Frankfort
Hunting-
ton
Lexington
Evansville
KENTUCKY
Charleston
VIRGINIA
Richmond
C. Charles
Chesapeake Bay
35°

APPALACHIAN MOUNTAINS
BLUE RIDGE

Roanoke
Newport News
Norfolk
Portsmouth

Ozark
Plateau
Cumberland R.
Nashville
TENNESSEE
Knoxville
Mt. Mitchell
6,684 ft.
Charlotte
Winston-Salem
Greensboro
NORTH
CAROLINA
Raleigh
C. Hatteras

Fort
Smith
ARKANSAS
Little
Rock
Memphis
Huntsville
Tennessee R.
Chattanooga

SOUTH
CAROLINA
Columbia
C. Fear

UNITED STATES
OF AMERICA
(Physical-Political)

Atlanta
Birmingham
GEORGIA
Macon
Charleston
30°

CONN. —CONNECTICUT
D.C. —DISTRICT
OF COLUMBIA
MASS. —MASSACHUSETTS
MD. —MARYLAND
N.H. —NEW HAMPSHIRE
R.I. —RHODE ISLAND
VT. —VERMONT
W.VA. —WEST VIRGINIA

C. —Cape
Mt. —Mountain
Pen. —Peninsula
Pk. —Peak

International boundaries
State boundaries
National capitals
State capitals
Other cities

Elevations
Feet   Meters
10,000   3,000
5,000   1,500
2,000   600
1,000   300
0   0

Miles
0   300
Kilometers
0   500

Shreveport
MISSISSIPPI
Jackson
ALABAMA
Montgomery
Columbus
Savannah

Coastal Plain
Mississippi R.
Alabama R.

LOUISIANA
Baton Rouge
Mobile
Pensacola
Tallahassee
Jacksonville
ATLANTIC
OCEAN

Beaumont
New Orleans
C. San Blas
25°

Mississippi
Delta
FLORIDA
C. Canaveral

GULF OF MEXICO
Tampa
St. Petersburg
C. Sable

Fort Lauderdale
Miami
Nassau
BAHAMAS

Florida Keys
Straits of Florida
Tropic of Cancer
Havana
CUBA

85° 80° 75°

475

160° 155°
Kauai
Niihau
HAWAII
Oahu
Molokai
Honolulu
Lanai
Maui
Kahoolawe
20°
160°
Same scale
as main map
Hawaii
Hilo

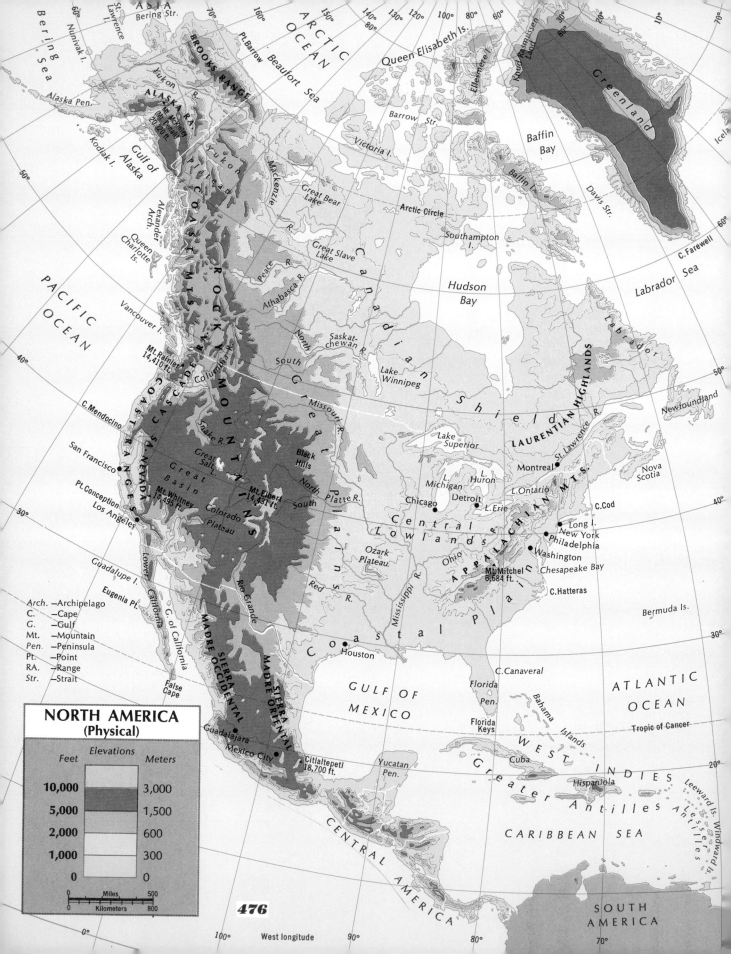

NORTH AMERICA
(Physical)

Feet	Elevations	Meters
10,000		**3,000**
5,000		**1,500**
2,000		**600**
1,000		**300**
0		**0**

Arch. —Archipelago
C. —Cape
G. —Gulf
Mt. —Mountain
Pen. —Peninsula
Pt. —Point
RA. —Range
Str. —Strait

Miles 500
Kilometers 800

476

ASIA
Bering Str.

ARCTIC OCEAN

Queen Elisabeth Is.
Knud Rasmussen Land
Greenland

Bering Sea
Nunivak I.
St. Lawrence I.
Pt. Barrow
Beaufort Sea
Ellesmere I.
Icela

Alaska Pen.
Kodiak I.
BROOKS RANGE
ALASKA RA.
Mt. McKinley Denali 20,320 ft.
Yukon R.
Barrow Str.
Baffin Bay
Baffin Is.
Davis Str.
C. Farewell

Gulf of Alaska
Yukon Plateau
Victoria I.
Southampton I.
Labrador Sea

PACIFIC OCEAN
Alexander Arch.
Queen Charlotte Is.
Vancouver I.
COAST MTS.
Great Bear Lake
Mackenzie R.
Arctic Circle
Hudson Bay
Labrador
Newfoundland

ROCKY MOUNTAINS
Peace R.
Great Slave Lake
Canadian Shield
LAURENTIAN HIGHLANDS

C. Mendocino
Mt. Rainier 14,410 ft.
CASCADE RANGE
Columbia R.
Athabasca R.
Saskatchewan R.
St. Lawrence R.
Montreal
Nova Scotia

San Francisco
COAST RANGES
SIERRA NEVADA
Snake R.
Great Salt L.
North
South
Lake Winnipeg
Lake Superior
L. Michigan
L. Huron
L. Ontario
C. Cod

Pt. Conception
Los Angeles
Great Basin
Mt. Elbert 14,431 ft.
Black Hills
Missouri R.
Chicago
Detroit
L. Erie
Long I.
New York
Philadelphia

Mt. Whitney 14,495 ft.
Mt. Elbert 14,431 ft.
Colorado Plateau
North Platte R.
South
Great Plains
Central Lowlands
APPALACHIAN MTS.
Washington
Chesapeake Bay

Guadalupe I.
Eugenia Pt.
Lower California
G. of California
Red R.
Ozark Plateau
Ohio R.
Mt. Mitchell 6,684 ft.
C. Hatteras

Rio Grande
Mississippi R.
Coastal Plain
Bermuda Is.

False Cape
SIERRA MADRE OCCIDENTAL
SIERRA MADRE ORIENTAL
Houston
GULF OF MEXICO
C. Canaveral
Florida Pen.
ATLANTIC OCEAN

Guadalajara
Mexico City
Citlaltepetl 18,700 ft.
Yucatan Pen.
Florida Keys
Bahama Islands
WEST INDIES
Tropic of Cancer

Cuba
Greater Antilles
Leeward Is.
Lesser Antilles

CENTRAL AMERICA
Hispaniola
CARIBBEAN SEA
Windward Is.

West longitude
SOUTH AMERICA

ASIA

ARCTIC OCEAN

Barrow

Alaska (U.S.)

Fairbanks

Anchorage

Dawson

Juneau

Gulf of Alaska

Beaufort Sea

Arctic Circle

Port Radium

Great Bear Lake

Great Slave Lake

Thule

GREENLAND (Den.)

Pond Inlet

Baffin Bay

ICELAND

Godthaab

PACIFIC OCEAN

Victoria
Vancouver
Seattle
Portland
Spokane

Edmonton

Calgary

Regina

Lake Winnipeg

Winnipeg

Churchill

Hudson Bay

C A N A D A

Labrador Sea

Goose Bay

Seven Islands

Gander
St.John's

San Francisco

Salt Lake City

Great Salt L.

Los Angeles

San Diego

Phoenix

Guadalupe I. (Mex.)

Denver

Colorado

Minneapolis St.Paul
Milwaukee
Omaha
Chicago
Kansas City
St.Louis
Cincinnati

U N I T E D   S T A T E S   O F   A M E R I C A

Missouri R.

Detroit
Cleveland
Pittsburgh

Great Lakes

Quebec
Montreal
Ottawa
Toronto
Buffalo
Boston

New York
Philadelphia
Washington Baltimore

Halifax

Norfolk

Ohio

El Paso

Dallas

Arkansas R.

Memphis

Atlanta

Mississippi

San Antonio

Houston

New Orleans

Monterrey

Rio Grande

G. of California

Tropic of Cancer

MEXICO

Guadalajara

Mexico City

Orizaba

GULF OF MEXICO

Miami

Grand Bahama I.
Great Abaco I.
Nassau Eleuthera I.
Andros Cat I.
I. Long I.
Gr. Exuma I. Mayaguana I.
Acklins I.

THE BAHAMAS

Bermuda Is. (U.K.)

ATLANTIC OCEAN

Havana

Cayman Islands (U.K.)

CUBA

Santiago-de-Cuba

Gr.Inagua I.

HAITI
Port-au-Prince

JAMAICA Kingston

PUERTO RICO (U.S.)
Virgin Is. (U.S.&U.K.)

DOMINICAN REPUBLIC
Santo Domingo
ANTIGUA AND BARBUDA
ST. CHRISTOPHER-NEVIS
Guadeloupe (Fr.)
DOMINICA
Martinique (Fr.)
ST. LUCIA
ST. VINCENT AND THE GRENADINES
GRENADA

Neth. Antilles (Neth.)

CARIBBEAN SEA

Belmopan

BELIZE

GUATEMALA
Guatemala

HONDURAS
Tegucigalpa

San Salvador
EL SALVADOR

NICARAGUA

Managua

San José

COSTA RICA

Panama Canal

Panamá

PANAMA

TRINIDAD AND TOBAGO

SOUTH AMERICA

Den. —DENMARK
Fr. —FRANCE
Neth. —NETHERLANDS
Mex. —MEXICO
U.K. —UNITED KINGDOM
U.S. —UNITED STATES

NORTH AMERICA
(Political)

— International boundaries
⊛ National capitals
• Other cities

0   500 miles
0   800 kilometers

West longitude

477

CARIBBEAN SEA

Guajira Pen.

Margarita I.

Tobago

Trinidad

Caracas

Orinoco R. Delta

G. of Panama

Maracaibo

L.

Orinoco R.

Devils I.

C. Orange

Arch. —Archipelago
C. —Cape
G. —Gulf
Mt. —Mountain
Pen. —Peninsula
Pt. —Point

Malpelo I.

Mt. Tolima 19,049 ft.

Bogotá

Cauca R.

Magdalena R.

Meta R.

Llanos

GUIANA HIGHLANDS

Angel Falls

Caqueta R.

Orinoco R.

Río Negro

A M A Z O N

Amazon R. Delta

Marajó I.

Equator

Mt. Chimborazo 20,561 ft.

Gulf of Guayaquil

Japura

Amazon R.

Tapajóz R.

Xingu R.

Tocantins R.

C. São Roq.

Marañón R.

Aguja Pt.

B A S I N

Juruá

R.

Purus

R.

Madeira

Araguaia R.

Tocantins R.

Parnaíba

São Francisco R.

Mt. Huascarán 22,205 ft.

Ucayali R.

Beni R.

Mamoré R.

Mato Grosso Plateau

Brasília

B R A Z I L I A N

H I G H L A N D S

Lima

A N D E S

Mt. Ancohuma 21,490 ft.

Lake Titicaca

L. Poopó

Pilcomayo R.

Gran Chaco

Paraguay R.

Paraná R.

Mt. Bandeira 9,452 ft.

São Paulo

C. Frio

Rio de Janeiro

Tropic of Capricorn

PACIFIC OCEAN

M O U N T A I N S

Salado R.

ATLANTIC OCEAN

San Felix I. San Ambrosio I.

Mt. Aconcagua 22,834 ft.

Santiago

P a m p a s

Salado R.

Paraná R.

Uruguay R.

Juan Fernández Is.

Buenos Aires

Montevideo

Río de la Plata

Colorado R.

Blanca Bay

SOUTH AMERICA
(Physical)

Chiloé I.

P a t a g o n i a

San Matías Gulf
Valdés Pen.

Elevations

Feet

Meters

Chonos Arch.

Taitao Pen.

Gulf of San Jorge

C. Tres Puntas

Feet		Meters
10,000		3,000
5,000		1,500
2,000		600
1,000		300
0		0

Grande Bay

Strait of Magellan

Strait of Magellan

Falkland Is. (U.K.)
(Malvinas Is.)

Miles
0   500

Kilometers
0   800

478

Tierra del Fuego

Cape Horn

West longitude

SOUTH AMERICA
(Political)

─────── International boundaries
✪ National capitals
● Other cities

Col. —COLOMBIA
Fr. —FRANCE
U.K. —UNITED KINGDOM

0 ———— 500 miles
0 ———— 800 kilometers

479

Barranquilla
Cartagena
Maracaibo
Valencia
Caracas
Barquisimeto
Cúcuta
San Cristóbal
Bucaramanga
Medellín
Bogotá
Malpelo I. (Col.)
Cali
COLOMBIA
VENEZUELA
Orinoco R.
Port-of-Spain
TRINIDAD AND TOBAGO
Georgetown
GUYANA
Paramaribo
Cayenne
SURINAM
Fr. Guiana (Fr.)

Quito
ECUADOR
Guayaquil
Iquitos
Amazon R.
Manaus
Belém
São Luís
Fortaleza

Trujillo
PERU
Callao
Lima
Cuzco
Arequipa
Lake Titicaca
La Paz
BOLIVIA
Sucre
Recife
Maceió
BRAZIL
Salvador
Brasília (Federal District)
Belo Horizonte

PACIFIC OCEAN
Chuquicamata
Antofagasta
San Felix I. (Chile)
San Ambrosio I. (Chile)
PARAGUAY
Asunción
Tucumán
Rio de Janeiro
São Paulo
Niterói
Santos
Curitiba
Tropic of Capricorn

CHILE
Córdoba
Santa Fe
Paraná
Rosario
Valparaiso
Santiago
Juan Fernández Is. (Chile)
Concepción
ARGENTINA
Buenos Aires
La Plata
URUGUAY
Montevideo
Paraná R.
Pôrto Alegre
Rio de la Plata
Mar del Plata
Bahía Blanca

ATLANTIC OCEAN

Strait of Magellan
Punta Arenas
Falkland Is. (U.K.) (Malvinas Is.)

Equator
Tropic of Capricorn
West longitude

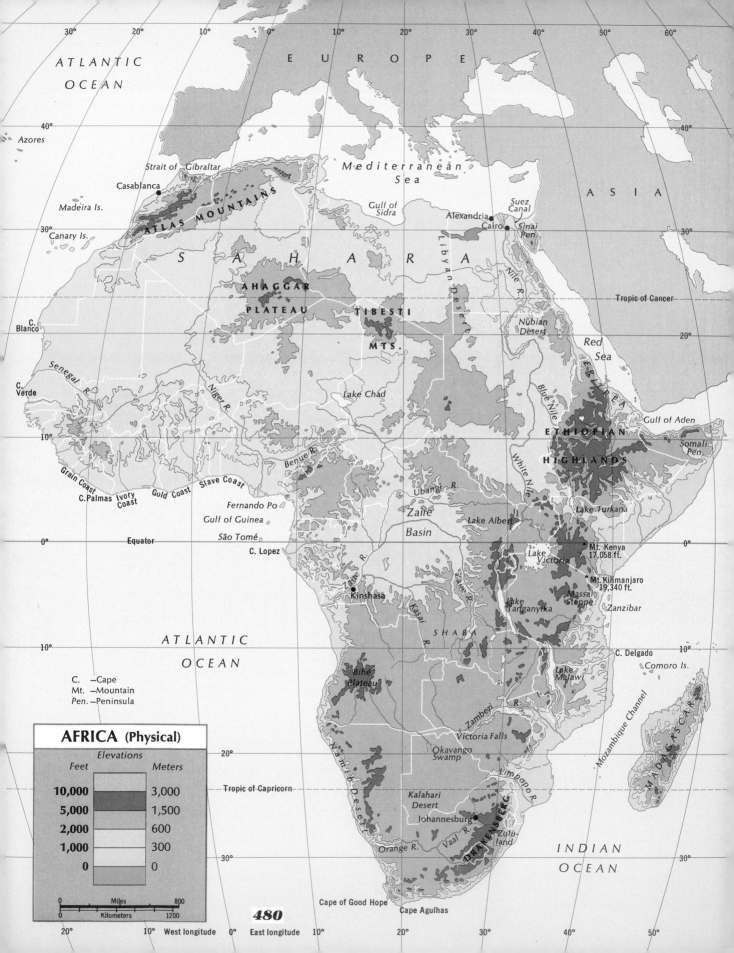

ATLANTIC
OCEAN

E U R O P E

A S I A

Azores

Strait of Gibraltar
Casablanca

Madeira Is.

Canary Is.

Mediterranean
Sea

Gulf of
Sidra

Alexandria
Cairo

Suez
Canal

Sinai
Pen.

ATLAS MOUNTAINS

S A H A R A

AHAGGAR

PLATEAU

TIBESTI

MTS.

Libyan Desert

Nile R.

Tropic of Cancer

Nubian
Desert

Red
Sea

C.
Blanco

C.
Verde

Senegal R.

Niger R.

Lake Chad

Blue Nile

E R I T R E A

Gulf of Aden

Somali
Pen.

ETHIOPIAN

HIGHLANDS

Grain Coast

C. Palmas

Ivory
Coast

Gold Coast

Slave Coast

Benue R.

Fernando Po

Gulf of Guinea

São Tomé

Ubangi R.

Zaire

Basin

Lake Albert

White Nile

Lake Turkana

Mt. Kenya
17,058 ft.

Equator

C. Lopez

Zaire R.

Kinshasa

Kasai R.

Lake
Victoria

Massai
Steppe

Mt. Kilimanjaro
19,340 ft.

Zanzibar

Lake
Tanganyika

SHABA

C. Delgado

Comoro Is.

ATLANTIC

OCEAN

C. —Cape
Mt. —Mountain
Pen. —Peninsula

Bihé
Plateau

Lake
Malawi

MADAGASCAR

Mozambique Channel

Namib Desert

Zambezi

R.

Victoria Falls

Okavango
Swamp

Limpopo R.

AFRICA (Physical)

Elevations

Feet   Meters

Tropic of Capricorn

Kalahari
Desert

Johannesburg

10,000	3,000
5,000	1,500
2,000	600
1,000	300
0	0

Vaal R.

Orange R.

DRAKENSBERG

Zulu-
land

INDIAN

OCEAN

Miles   800

Kilometers   1200

480

Cape of Good Hope

Cape Agulhas

West longitude   East longitude

ATLANTIC OCEAN

EUROPE

Mediterranean Sea

ASIA

Algiers
Tunis
Tangier
Rabat
Casablanca
Oran
TUNISIA
Tripoli
Benghazi
Alexandria
Cairo

MOROCCO
Marrakesh
Madeira Is.
(Port.)
Canary Is.
(Sp.)
El Aaiún

ALGERIA

LIBYA

EGYPT

WESTERN SAHARA (MOROCCO)

Tropic of Cancer

MAURITANIA
Nouakchott

MALI
Tombouctou

NIGER

CHAD

Port Sudan
Red Sea

Khartoum
Asmara

Dakar
SEN.
4 Banjul
5
Bissau GUINEA
Conakry
0 Freetown

Bamako
Niamey
U.VOL.
Ouagadougou
BENIN

Lake Chad

N'Djamena

SUDAN

Djibouti 2 *Gulf of Aden*
Addis Ababa

SOMALIA

NIGERIA

CENTRAL AFRICAN REPUBLIC

Bangui

ETHIOPIA

Mogadishu

IVORY COAST
GHANA 10
Accra Porto Novo
Lomé Lagos
LIB.
Monrovia
Abidjan
Malabo
3
SÃO TOMÉ - PRÍNCIPE
São Tomé

CAMEROON
Yaoundé
Libreville
GABON
CONGO

Brazzaville
Kinshasa
Cabinda (Angola)

ZAIRE

UGA.
Kampala
7 Kigali
1 Bujumbura

KENYA
Nairobi
Lake Victoria

Mombasa

TANZANIA
Zanzibar
Dar es Salaam

ATLANTIC OCEAN

Luanda

ANGOLA

ZAMBIA
Lusaka

MAL.
Lilongwe
Zambezi R.

COMOROS
Moroni

Mayotte I. (Fr.)

MADAGASCAR
Antananarivo

Harare
ZIMBABWE

MOZAMBIQUE

NAMIBIA (S.W. AFRICA)

Tropic of Capricorn
Walvis Bay (S. Afr.)
Windhoek

BOTSWANA

Gaborone
Johannesburg

Pretoria
Maputo
Mbabane 9
Maseru 6

SOUTH AFRICA

Durban

Umtata

Cape Town
Port Elizabeth

INDIAN OCEAN

481

1—BURUNDI
2—DJIBOUTI
3—EQUATORIAL GUINEA
4—GAMBIA
5—GUINEA–BISSAU
6—LESOTHO
7—RWANDA
8—SIERRA LEONE
9—SWAZILAND
10—TOGO

LIB.   —LIBERIA
MAL.   —MALAWI
SEN.   —SENEGAL
UGA.   —UGANDA
U. VOL. —UPPER VOLTA

Fr.   —FRANCE
Port. —PORTUGAL
S.Afr. —SOUTH AFRICA
Sp.   —SPAIN

AFRICA (Political)

⎯⎯⎯ International boundaries
✜ National capitals
● Other cities

0   800 mi.
0   1200 km

West longitude   East longitude

EURASIA (Physical)

Elevations

Feet	Meters
10,000	3,000
5,000	1,500
2,000	600
1,000	300
0	0

Miles 0 — 800
Kilometers 0 — 1200

Mt. —Mountain
Pen. —Peninsula
RA. —Range
Str. —Strait

Laptev Sea
Pen.
New Siberian Is.
CHERSKI RA.
KOLYMA RANGE
CENTRAL RA.
Bering Sea
Aleutian Is.
International Date Line
Sunday
Monday
Tropic of Cancer

Central Siberian Plateau
SIBERIA
VERKHOYANSK RA.
Lena R.
Lower Tunguska R.
Angara R.
Yenisey R.
SAYAN MTS.
Lake Baykal
Shilka R.
Aldan R.
Amur R.
Sea of Okhotsk
Kamchatka Peninsula
Sakhalin
Kuril Islands
Hokkaido
Honshu
Sea of Japan
Tokyo
Kyoto
Fujiyama 12,388 ft.
Shikoku
Kyushu

Mongolian Plateau
The Gobi
GREAT KHINGAN MTS.
Manchuria Plain
Harbin
Shenyang
Dairen
Peking
Tientsin
Hwang Ho (Yellow R.)
Great Wall
North China Plain
Yellow Sea
Korea Strait
NAN SHAN
SHAN of et
Chungking
Yangtze R.
Shanghai
East China Sea
Okinawa
Ryukyu Islands
BOHEA HILLS
Taiwan
Canton
Si R.
Hong Kong
Luzon Strait

YAS
Brahmaputra R.
Salween R.
Calcutta
Irrawaddy R.
Bay of Bengal
Andaman Is.
Andaman Sea
Nicobar Is.
Str. of Malacca
Mekong R.
INDOCHINA PENINSULA
Gulf of Siam
Ho Chi Minh City
Malay Pen.
Sumatra
Mentawai Is.
Bangka
Natuna Is.
Borneo
SUNDA ISLANDS
Jakarta
Java
Java Sea
Bali
Lombok
Sumbawa
Flores
Sumba
Timor

Hainan
South China Sea
Philippine Islands
Luzon
Manila
Mindoro
Panay
Palawan
Negros
Samar
Mindanao
Celebes Sea
Celebes
Buru
Ceram
MOLUCCAS
Halmahera
Aru Is.
SNOW MTS.
New Guinea
Arafura Sea
AUSTRALIA
Coral Sea

Philippine Sea
PACIFIC OCEAN
Equator
Admiralty Is.
New Ireland
New Britain

483

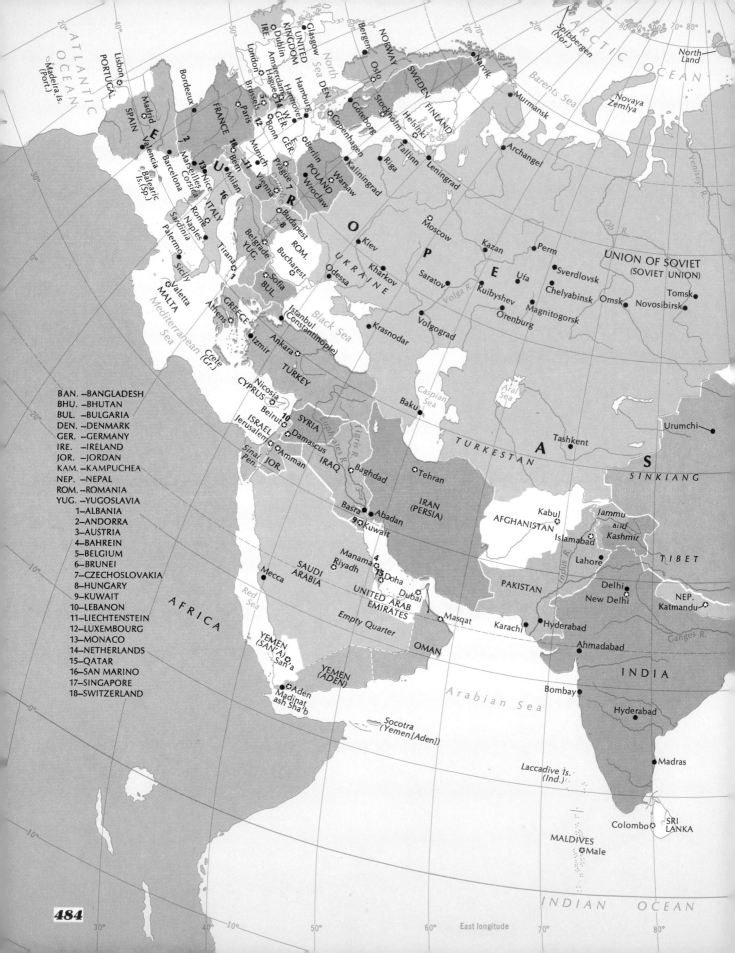

ATLANTIC OCEAN

Madeira Is. (Port.)

PORTUGAL
Lisbon

SPAIN
Madrid
Valencia
Balearic Is.(Sp.)
Barcelona

Bordeaux

FRANCE
Paris
Marseilles
13 Nice
Corsica
Sardinia

UNITED KINGDOM
Glasgow
IRE.
Dublin
London
Amsterdam
Brussels
Hamburg
Hannover
GER.
GER.
Bonn
Berlin
Munich
Vienna
Prague 7
Wrocław

NORWAY
Bergen
Oslo
Göteborg
Copenhagen
DEN.
Stockholm
Helsinki
SWEDEN
Narvik

FINLAND
Murmansk

Novaya Zemlya

ARCTIC OCEAN
Spitsbergen (Nor.)
North Land

Barents Sea

Tallinn
Riga
Kaliningrad
Leningrad
Archangel

POLAND
Warsaw

Moscow
Kiev
Kharkov
Odessa

UKRAINE

Kazan
Saratov
Kuibyshev

Perm
Ufa
Sverdlovsk
Chelyabinsk
Magnitogorsk
Orenburg

UNION OF SOVIET
(SOVIET UNION)

Omsk
Novosibirsk
Tomsk

EUROPE

ITALY
Milan
Rome
Naples
Palermo
Sicily

Bern 11
16
3

Budapest
8
ROM.
Bucharest

YUG.
Belgrade
Tirana
1

Sofia
BUL.

GREECE
Athens
Crete (Gr.)
Izmir

Istanbul (Constantinople)
Ankara
TURKEY

Black Sea

Krasnodar
Volgograd

ASIA

Baku
Caspian Sea
Aral Sea

TURKESTAN
Tashkent

SINKIANG
Urumchi

Volga R.

MALTA
Valetta

Mediterranean Sea

CYPRUS
Nicosia

SYRIA
Beirut 10
Damascus
ISRAEL
Jerusalem
Amman
JOR.
Sinai Pen.

IRAQ
Baghdad
Basra
Abadan

Euphrates R.
Tigris R.

Tehran

IRAN (PERSIA)

Kabul
AFGHANISTAN
Islamabad

Jammu and Kashmir

TIBET

BAN. —BANGLADESH
BHU. —BHUTAN
BUL. —BULGARIA
DEN. —DENMARK
GER. —GERMANY
IRE. —IRELAND
JOR. —JORDAN
KAM. —KAMPUCHEA
NEP. —NEPAL
ROM. —ROMANIA
YUG. —YUGOSLAVIA
  1—ALBANIA
  2—ANDORRA
  3—AUSTRIA
  4—BAHREIN
  5—BELGIUM
  6—BRUNEI
  7—CZECHOSLOVAKIA
  8—HUNGARY
  9—KUWAIT
 10—LEBANON
 11—LIECHTENSTEIN
 12—LUXEMBOURG
 13—MONACO
 14—NETHERLANDS
 15—QATAR
 16—SAN MARINO
 17—SINGAPORE
 18—SWITZERLAND

9 Kuwait

Manama
Riyadh
4
15 Doha
Dubai

SAUDI ARABIA
Mecca

UNITED ARAB EMIRATES

Empty Quarter

OMAN
Masqat

PAKISTAN
Lahore
Karachi

Indus R.

Delhi
New Delhi
NEP.
Katmandu

Hyderabad
Ahmadabad

Ganges R.

INDIA

AFRICA

Red Sea

YEMEN (SAN'A)
San'a

YEMEN (ADEN)
Aden
Madinat ash Sha'b

Socotra (Yemen [Aden])

Arabian Sea
Bombay
Hyderabad

Laccadive Is. (Ind.)

Madras

MALDIVES
Male

Colombo
SRI LANKA

INDIAN OCEAN

East longitude

484

EURASIA (Political)

Gr.	—GREECE
Ind.	—INDIA
Jap.	—JAPAN
Nor.	—NORWAY
Port.	—PORTUGAL
Sp.	—SPAIN
U.K.	—UNITED KINGDOM
U.S.	—UNITED STATES
U.S.S.R.	—SOVIET UNION

International boundaries
Indefinite or temporary boundaries
⊛ National capitals
● Other cities

0   800 mi.
0   1200 km

485

EUROPE (Physical)

Elevations

Meters				
3,000	1,500	500	200	0

Feet				
10,000	**5,000**	**1,650**	**650**	**0**

Miles

Kilometers

ASIA

ARCTIC OCEAN

Barents Sea

Caspian Sea

CAUCASUS MOUNTAINS
Mt. Elbrus
(18,480 ft.; 5,640 m)
Baku

UNION OF SOVIET SOCIALIST REPUBLICS (SOVIET UNION)

Ural R.

Kuibyshev

Saratov

Volga R.

Vologda

Don R.

Rostov

Donetsk

Dnepropetrovsk

Zaporozhye

Gorki

Moscow

Voronezh

Kharkov

Kiev

Dnieper R.

Odessa

Crimea

Black Sea

CYPRUS
Nicosia

Rhodes (Gr.)

Aegean Sea

Leningrad

FINLAND

Helsinki

Riga

Minsk

European Plain

North European Plain

Vistula R.

Warsaw

Łódź

POLAND

Pripet R.

Oder R.

Elbe R.

CARPATHIAN MTS.

Budapest

Danube

Hungarian Plain

HUNGARY

ROMANIA

Bucharest

Sofia

BULGARIA

Rhodope MTS.

Mt. Olympus
(9,570 ft.; 2,920 m)

GREECE

Athens

Crete (Gr.)

Barents Sea

Gulf of Bothnia

SWEDEN

Stockholm

NORWAY

Oslo

DENMARK

Copenhagen

Baltic Sea

North Sea

Hamburg

Berlin

EAST GERMANY

WEST GERMANY

Cologne

Amsterdam

NETHERLANDS

BELGIUM

Ghent

LUXEMBOURG

Paris

Rhine R.

CZECHOSLOVAKIA

Prague

Munich

Vienna

AUSTRIA

LIECHTENSTEIN

SWITZ.

ALPS

DINARIC ALPS

YUGOSLAVIA

Belgrade

Adriatic Sea

ALBANIA

Tirane

Zurich

Matterhorn
(14,690 ft.; 4,480 m)
Mt. Blanc
(15,770 ft.; 4,810 m)

Milan

Monte Como
(9,560 ft.; 2,910 m)

Lombardy

APENNINES

San Marino

VATICAN CITY

Rome

ITALY

MONACO

Corsica (Fr.)

Sardinia (It.)

Naples

Mt. Vesuvius
(4,190 ft.; 1,290 m)

Sicily (It.)

MALTA

Mediterranean Sea

Norwegian Sea

Faeroe Is. (Den.)

Shetland Is. (U.K.)

Orkney Is. (U.K.)

Outer Hebrides (U.K.)

Glasgow

UNITED KINGDOM

Birmingham

London

English Channel

IRELAND

Dublin

ICELAND

Reykjavik

ATLANTIC OCEAN

Bay of Biscay

FRANCE

Marseilles

PYRENEES
Pico de Aneto
(11,170 ft.; 3,400 m)

ANDORRA

Barcelona

Balearic Is. (Sp.)

SPAIN

Madrid

Meseta

Gibraltar (U.K.)

PORTUGAL

Lisbon

AFRICA

West Longitude

East Longitude

486

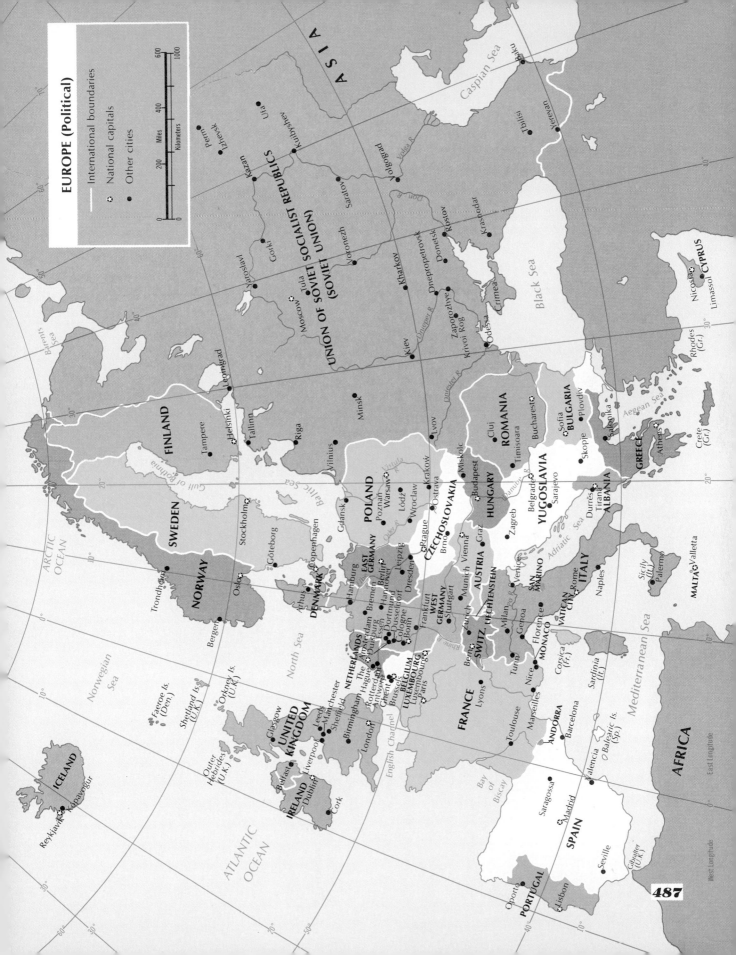

EUROPE (Political)

International boundaries
☆ National capitals
• Other cities

Miles / Kilometers scale: 0 200 400 600 / 0 1000

ASIA

Caspian Sea
Baku
Yerevan
Tbilisi
Krasnodar
Rostov
Donetsk
Crimea
Odessa
Black Sea

Barents Sea

Perm
Izhevsk
Ufa
Kazan
Kubyshev
Saratov
Volgograd
Voronezh
Gorki
Yaroslavl
Tula
Moscow
UNION OF SOVIET SOCIALIST REPUBLICS (SOVIET UNION)
Kharkov
Dnepropetrovsk
Zaporozhye
Krivoi Rog
Kiev
Minsk
Lvov
Volga R.
Don R.
Dnieper R.

NICOSIA CYPRUS
Limassol
Rhodes (Gr.)
Aegean Sea
Salonika
Plovdiv
Crete (Gr.)
Athens
GREECE

FINLAND
Tampere
Helsinki
Tallinn
Riga
Vilnius
Leningrad

SWEDEN
NORWAY
Trondheim
Oslo
Bergen
Göteborg
Stockholm
Gulf of Bothnia
Baltic Sea

ARCTIC OCEAN

DENMARK
Copenhagen
Århus
Gdansk
Poznań
POLAND
Warsaw
Łódź
Wrocław
Kraków
Oder R.
Vistula R.

EAST GERMANY
Hamburg
Bremen
Berlin
Hannover
Leipzig
Dresden
WEST GERMANY
Dortmund
Essen
Düsseldorf
Cologne
Bonn
Frankfurt
Stuttgart
Munich
Rhine R.

CZECHOSLOVAKIA
Prague
Brno
Ostrava
Bratislava

HUNGARY
Budapest
Miskolc

ROMANIA
Cluj
Timişoara
Bucharest

BULGARIA
Sofia

YUGOSLAVIA
Zagreb
Belgrade
Sarajevo
Skopje
Danube R.

AUSTRIA
Vienna
Graz
LIECHTENSTEIN
SWITZ.
Zürich
Bern
Geneva
Turin
Milan
Genoa
Venice
Florence
SAN MARINO
ITALY
Rome
VATICAN CITY
Naples
MONACO
Nice
Marseilles
Corsica (Fr.)
Sardinia (It.)
Sicily (It.)
Palermo
MALTA Valletta
ALBANIA
Tirana
Durrës
Adriatic Sea

NETHERLANDS
Amsterdam
The Hague
Rotterdam
Duisburg
Ghent
Antwerp
BELGIUM
Brussels
LUXEMBOURG
Luxembourg
Paris
FRANCE
Lyons
Toulouse
Bordeaux
Bay of Biscay

ICELAND
Reykjavik
Kópavogur

Faeroe Is. (Den.)
Shetland Is. (U.K.)
Orkney Is. (U.K.)
Outer Hebrides (U.K.)

UNITED KINGDOM
Glasgow
Belfast
IRELAND
Dublin
Cork
Liverpool
Manchester
Leeds
Sheffield
Birmingham
London
English Channel
North Sea
Norwegian Sea

ANDORRA
Barcelona
Valencia
Balearic Is. (Sp.)
SPAIN
Madrid
Saragossa
Seville
Gibraltar (U.K.)
PORTUGAL
Oporto
Lisbon

Mediterranean Sea
AFRICA
West Longitude
East Longitude

ATLANTIC OCEAN

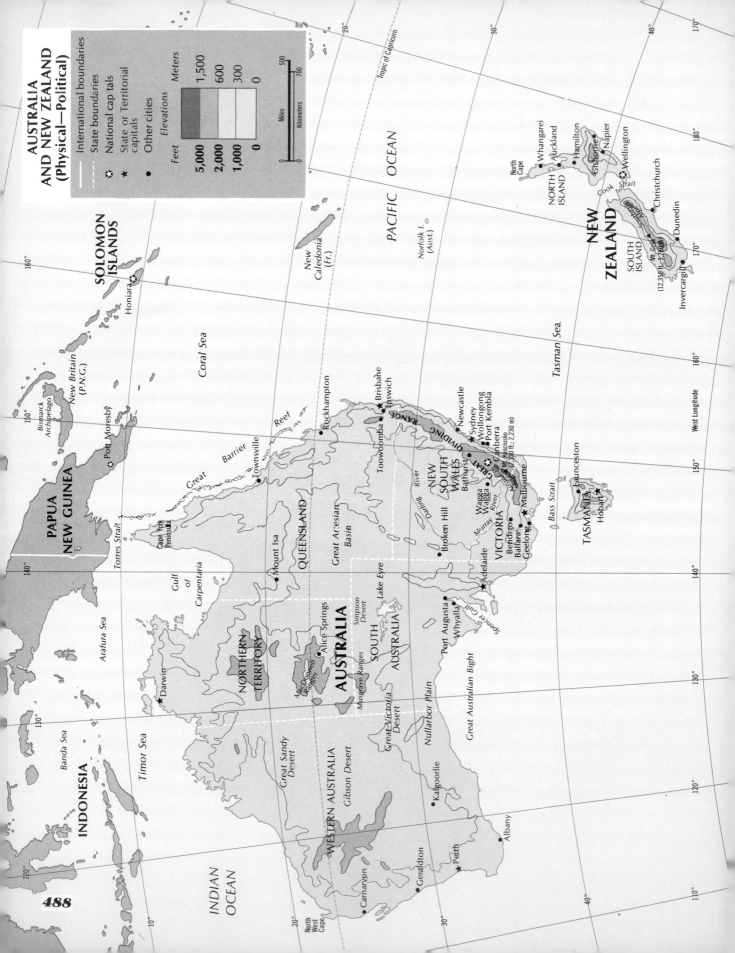

AUSTRALIA AND NEW ZEALAND (Physical—Political)

International boundaries
State boundaries
National capitals
★ State or Territorial capitals
• Other cities

Elevations

Feet		Meters
5,000		1,500
2,000		600
1,000		300
0		0

Miles
Kilometers

INDONESIA

Banda Sea

Timor Sea

Arafura Sea

Bismarck Archipelago

New Britain (P.N.G.)

PAPUA NEW GUINEA

Port Moresby

SOLOMON ISLANDS

Honiara

Coral Sea

New Caledonia (Fr.)

PACIFIC OCEAN

Norfolk I. (Aust.)

Torres Strait

Cape York Peninsula

Gulf of Carpentaria

Darwin

NORTHERN TERRITORY

Alice Springs

MacDonnell Ranges

Musgrave Ranges

Simpson Desert

Great Sandy Desert

Gibson Desert

Great Victoria Desert

WESTERN AUSTRALIA

Carnarvon

North West Cape

Geraldton

Kalgoorlie

Perth

Albany

Nullarbor Plain

Great Australian Bight

SOUTH AUSTRALIA

AUSTRALIA

Lake Eyre

Port Augusta

Whyalla

Spencer Gulf

Adelaide

Great Artesian Basin

QUEENSLAND

Mount Isa

Townsville

Great Barrier Reef

Rockhampton

Toowoomba

Brisbane
Ipswich

Darling River

Broken Hill

NEW SOUTH WALES

Bathurst

Newcastle
Sydney
Wollongong
Port Kembla

GREAT DIVIDING RANGE

Canberra

Wagga Wagga

Murray River

VICTORIA

Bendigo
Ballarat
Geelong
Melbourne

Mt. Kosciusko (7,330 ft.; 2,230 m)

Bass Strait

TASMANIA

Launceston

Hobart

Tasman Sea

INDIAN OCEAN

NEW ZEALAND

North Cape

Whangarei
Auckland
Hamilton
Gisborne
Napier

NORTH ISLAND

Wellington

Cook Strait

SOUTH ISLAND

Southern Alps

Christchurch

Mt. Cook (12,350 ft.; 3,760 m)

Dunedin

Invercargill

Tropic of Capricorn

West Longitude

GAZETTEER

The Gazetteer is a geographical dictionary. It shows latitude and longitude for cities and certain other places. Latitude and longitude are shown in this form: 9°N/39°E. This means "9 degrees north latitude and 39 degrees east longitude." The page reference tells where each entry may be found on a map.

Key to Pronunciation

a	hat, cap							
ā	age, face	i	it, pin	ou	house, out	zh	measure, seizure	
ã	care, air	ī	ice, five	sh	she, rush	ə	represents:	
ä	father, far	ng	long, bring	th	thin, both		a	in about
ch	child, much	o	hot, rock	ŦH	then, smooth		e	in taken
e	let, best	ō	open, go	u	cup, butter		i	in pencil
ē	equal, see	ô	order, all	u̇	full, put		o	in lemon
ėr	term, learn	oi	oil, voice	ü	rule, move		u	in circus

This Key to Pronunciation is from *Scott, Foresman Intermediate Dictionary*, by E. L. Thorndike and Clarence L. Barnhart. Copyright © 1983, by Scott, Foresman and Company. Reprinted by permission.

Accra (ə' krä). Capital of and most populated city in Ghana. Port city located on Atlantic Ocean. (6°N/0° long.) p. 287.

Addis Ababa (ad ə sab' ə bə). Capital of and most populated city in Ethiopia. Located at an elevation of 7,900 ft (2,408 m). (9°N/39°E) p. 287.

Adelaide (ad' əl ād). Capital of the Australian state of South Australia. Located near a gulf of the Indian Ocean. (35°S/139°E) p. 419.

Aden (äd' ən). Capital of Yemen (Aden). Located on the Gulf of Aden. (13°N/45°E) p. 251.

Adriatic Sea (ā drē at' ik sē). An arm of the Mediterranean Sea located between Italy and the Balkan Peninsula. p. 145.

Aegean Sea (i jē' ən sē). Part of the Mediterranean Sea located between the eastern coast of Greece and the western coast of Turkey. Bounded on the north by Greek mainland and on the south by Crete. p. 145.

Alexandria (al ig zan' drē ə). Second most populated city in Egypt. Located in the Nile Delta. (31°N/30°E) p. 251.

Algiers (al jirz'). Capital of Algeria. Located on the Mediterranean Sea. (37°N/3°E) p. 251.

Alps (alps). Mountain system extending in an arc from the Mediterranean coast between Italy and France through Switzerland and Austria and into the northwest coast of Yugoslavia. The highest peak is Mont Blanc, with an elevation of 15,771 ft (4,807 m). p. 143.

Amazon River (am' ə zän riv' ər). Second longest river in the world. Tributaries rise in the Andes Mountains and Guiana Highlands. Flows into the Atlantic Ocean near Belém, Brazil. p. 89.

Amman (a män'). Capital of Jordan. (32°N/36°E) p. 251.

Amsterdam (am' stər dam). Capital of the Netherlands. Connected to the North Sea by canal. (52°N/5°E) p. 145.

Anatolia (an ə tō' lē ə). Peninsula on which Asian Turkey is located. This peninsula lies between the Black and Mediterranean seas. p. 482.

Andes Mountains (an' dēz mount' ənz). High mountains that stretch north to south along the western side of South America. Highest peak, with an elevation of 22,840 ft (6,690 m), is Mt. Aconcagua. p. 89.

Ankara (ang' kə rə). Capital of Turkey. (41°N/33°E) p. 211.

Antwerp (ant' wərp). Chief port of Belgium. Located on the Schelde River about 50 miles (80 km) from the North Sea. (51°N/4°E) p. 170.

Apennines (ap' ə nīnz). Mountains in Italy. They extend from northwest Italy near Genoa to the southern tip of the Italian Peninsula. Its highest peak is Monte Corno, with an elevation of 9,560 ft (2,914 m). p. 143.

Appalachian Mountains (ap ə lā' chən mount' ənz). Chain of mountains stretching from Canada to Alabama. The highest peak is Mt. Mitchell at 6,684 ft (2,037 m). p. 53.

Arabian Peninsula (ə rā' bē ən pə nin' sə lə). Large peninsula located east of the Red Sea. p. 249.

Arabian Sea (ə rā' bē ən sē). Part of the Indian Ocean located between India and the Arabian Peninsula. p. 251.

489

Arctic Ocean (ärk' tic ō' shən). Large body of water north of the Arctic Circle. p. 55

Asunción (ə sün sē ōn'). Capital of Paraguay. Located on Paraguay River. (25°S/58°W) p. 91.

Aswān (a swän'). City on the Nile River. Site of Aswan High Dam. (24°N/33°E) p. 260.

Atacama Desert (ät ə käm' ə dez' ərt). Dry area in Chile. Major source of nitrates. p. 127.

Athens (ath' ənz). City-state in ancient Greece. Today, the capital of and largest city in modern Greece. (38°N/24°E) p. 145.

Atlantic Ocean (ət lant' ik ō' shən). Large body of water separating North and South America from Europe and Africa. p. 44.

Atlas Mountains (at' ləs mount' ənz). Located in Morocco, Algeria, and Tunisia, along northern edge of the Sahara. The highest peak is Toubkal, with an elevation of 13,671 ft (4,167 m). p. 249.

Baghdad (bag' dad). National capital of and most populated city in present-day Iraq. Located on the Tigris River. (33°N/44°E) p. 251.

Baku (bä kü'). Large city in the Soviet Union. Located on a peninsula in the Caspian Sea. Center of rich oil field. (40°N/50°E) p. 211.

Balkan Mountains (bôl' kən mount' ənz). Range of mountains stretching east-west across Bulgaria. Highest point is Botev Peak, with an elevation of 7,793 ft (2,375 m). p. 209.

Balkan Peninsula (bôl' kən pə nin' sə lə). Peninsula in southeast Europe between the Adriatic and Ionian seas on the west and the Aegean and Black seas on the east. Usually thought to consist of Greece, Albania, Bulgaria, Romania, and European Turkey. p. 482.

Baltic Sea (bôl' tik sē). Part of the Atlantic Ocean, south and southwest of Sweden. p. 145.

Bangkok (bang' käk). Capital of and most populated city in Thailand. Located on the Chao Phraya (river). (14°N/101°E) p. 331

Barcelona (bär sə lō' nə). Large important port city in northeast Spain, on the Mediterranean Sea. (41°N/2°E) p. 197.

Barents Sea (bar' əns sē). Part of the Arctic Ocean north of Norway and European U.S.S.R. p. 145.

Bay of Bengal (bā əv ben gôl'). Part of the Indian Ocean between the east coast of India and the Malay Peninsula. p. 331.

Beaufort Sea (bō' fərt sē). Part of the Arctic Ocean northeast of Alaska. p. 55.

Beirut (bā rüt'). Capital of Lebanon. Located on the eastern shore of the Mediterranean Sea. (34°N/36°E) p. 251.

Belgrade (bel' grād). Capital of Yugoslavia. Located where the Sava River joins the Danube River. (45°N/21°E) p. 211.

Benghazi (ben gäz' ē). Port city in Libya. (32°N/20°E) p. 251.

Bering Sea (bir' ing sē). Part of the North Pacific Ocean bounded on the east by mainland of Alaska and on the south and southeast by the Aleutian Islands. p. 55.

Bering Strait (bir' ing strāt). Narrow body of water connecting the Arctic Ocean and Bering Sea. Separates Asia from North America. p. 476.

Berlin (bər lin'). Formerly the capital of Germany. Today a divided city located in East Germany. East Berlin is the capital of East Germany. West Berlin, although surrounded by East Germany, is a part of West Germany. (53°N/13°E) p. 211.

Bern (bərn). Capital of Switzerland. (47°N/7°E) p. 145.

Birmingham (bər' ming ham). The second most populated city in the United Kingdom. (53°N/2°W) p. 145.

Black Sea (blak sē). Large sea located on the southern divide between Europe and Asia. p. 211.

Bogotá (bō gə tô'). Capital of Colombia. Located in the Andes Mountains. (5°N/74°W) p. 91.

Bordeaux (bôr dō'). Large city in France, located on the Garonne River. (45°N/1°W) p. 170.

Bosporus (bäs' pə rəs). Narrow body of water separating European Turkey from Asian Turkey. Connects the Black Sea and the Sea of Marmara. p. 273.

Brahmaputra River (bräm ə pü' trə riv' ər). Rises in southwestern Tibet. Joins the Ganges River near Dacca, India, before flowing into the Bay of Bengal. In China this river is called the Tsangpo. p. 331.

Brasília (brə zil' yə). Capital of Brazil. (16°S/48°W) p. 91.

Brazilian Highlands (brə zil' yən hi' ləndz). Highland area located in southeast Brazil. p. 89.

Brisbane (briz' bən). Capital of the Australian state of Queensland. Port city located on the east coast of Australia. (28°S/153°E) p. 419.

Bucharest (bü' kə rest). Capital of Romania. Located on a tributary of the Danube River. (44°N/26°E) p. 211.

Budapest (büd' ə pest). Capital of Hungary. Located on both sides of the Danube River. (48°N/19°E) p. 211.

490

Buenos Aires (bwā nə sar′ ēz). Capital of and most populated city in Argentina. Located on the Río de la Plata. (35°S/58°W) p. 91.

Cabinda (kə bin′ də). Part of Angola separated from the rest of the country by part of Zaire. p. 287.

Cairo (kī′ rō). Capital of Egypt. Most populated city in Africa. Located on the east side of the Nile River. (30°N/31°E) p. 251.

Calgary (kal′ gə rē). City in Alberta, Canada. (51°N/114°W) p. 83.

Canadian Shield (kə nād′ e ən shēld). Upland region extending in a horseshoe shape from the Labrador coast to the Arctic Ocean west of Victoria Island. p. 74.

Canberra (kan′ ber ə). Capital of Australia. Located in southeastern Australia. (35°S/149°E) p. 419.

Canton (kan′ tän) Chief port of south China. Located in the delta of the Hsi River. (23°N/113°E) p. 331.

Cape Agulhas (kāp ə gəl′ əs). Southernmost point of Africa. It is located at 20°E longitude, which serves as the dividing line between the Indian and Atlantic oceans. (35°S/20°E) p. 283.

Cape of Good Hope (kāp əv gůd hōp). Located on southwest coast of South Africa. (34°S/19°E) p. 283.

Cape Town (kāp′ toun). Seaport city on southwest coast of South Africa. (34°S/18°E) p. 287.

Caracas (kə rak′ əs). Capital of and most populated city in Venezuela. (11°N/67°W) p. 91.

Caribbean Sea (kar ə bē′ ən sē). Part of the Atlantic Ocean bounded by South America on the south, Central America on the west, and Cuba, Puerto Rico, and other islands on the north and east. p. 89.

Carpathian Mountains (kär pā′ thē ən mount′ ənz). They stretch from the Alps in the west to the Balkans in the east. Highest peak is Gerlachouka Peak, with an elevation of 8,711 ft (2,655 m). p. 209.

Caspian Sea (kas′ pē ən sē). Largest totally inland body of water in the world. Except for its southern shore, which borders Iran, the Caspian is completely within the Soviet Union. p. 209.

Caucasus Mountains (kô′ kə səs mount′ ənz). Very high mountains in the Soviet Union. They form part of the southern divide between Europe and Asia. Highest peak is Mt. Elbrus, with an elevation of 18,481 ft (5,633 m). p. 209.

Cayenne (kī en′). Capital of French Guiana. (5°N/52°W) p. 91.

Central America (sen′ trəl ə mer′ ə kə). Made up of Guatemala, El Salvador, Honduras, Nicaragua, Costa Rica, Panama, and Belize. p. 119.

Chaco (chäk′ ō). Plains of the Paraná and Paraguay rivers. p. 89.

Charlottetown (shär′ lət toun). Capital of Prince Edward Island, Canada. (46°N/63°W) p. 83.

Chicago (shə käg′ ō). One of six cities in the United States with a population of more than 1,000,000. Located in Illinois, on the southern tip of Lake Michigan. (42°N/88°W) p. 68.

Christchurch (krīs′ chərch). City in New Zealand. Located on South Island. (44°S/173°E) p. 488.

Coast Ranges (kōst rānj′ əz). Mountains along the Pacific coast of North America. They stretch from Alaska to California. p. 476.

Copenhagen (kō pən hā′ gən). Capital of and largest city in Denmark. An important port. (56°N/13°E) p. 145.

Córdoba (kôrd′ ə bə). Large city in Argentina. (31°S/64°W) p. 91.

Crete (krēt). Largest island in Greece. Located in the Mediterranean Sea. p. 145.

Damascus (də mas′ kəs). Capital of Syria. (34°N/36°E) p. 251.

Danube River (dan′ yüb riv′ ər). Second longest river in Europe. It begins in the Alps and flows into the Black Sea in Romania. The Danube passes through or borders eight European countries. Three capitals are located on it. p. 211.

Dardanelles (därd ən elz′). Narrow strait in Turkey connecting the Sea of Marmara and the Aegean Sea. p. 273.

Darwin (där′ wən). Capital of Northern Territory, Australia. Port city on the Timor Sea. (12°S/131°E) p. 419.

Dead Sea (ded sē). Salt lake located on the border between Israel and Jordan. (32°N/36°E) p. 276.

Delhi (del′ ē). City in India. Located on the Jumna River. (29°N/77°E) p. 331.

Detroit (di troit′). One of six cities in the United States with a population of more than 1,000,000. Located on the Detroit River, in Michigan, near Lake Erie. (42°N/83°W) p. 68.

Djibouti (jə büt′ ē). Capital of the country of Djibouti. Located on the Gulf of Aden. (12°N/43°E) p. 287.

Dnieper River (nē′ pər riv′ ər). Located in the Soviet Union. It rises in Valdai Hills and flows into Black Sea. p. 211.

Don River (dän riv′ ər). Located in the Soviet Union. Rises south of Moscow and flows into the Sea of Azov, which is part of the Black Sea. Connected by canal to Volga River. p. 211.

Dresden (drez′ dən). Industrial city in East Germany. Located on the Elbe River. (51°N/14°E) p. 211.

East Berlin (ēst bər lin′). Capital of East Germany. Communist part of the divided city of Berlin. (53°N/13°E) p. 211.

Eastern Ghats (ē′ stərn gôts). Mountains located along eastern coast of India. Highest peak is Dodabetta, at an elevation of 8,640 ft (2,633 m). p. 371.

Edmonton (ed′ mən tən). Capital of Alberta, Canada. Located on the North Saskatchewan River. (54°N/113°W) p. 83.

Elbe River (el′ bə riv′ ər). Rises in northwest Czechoslovakia and flows through Czechoslovakia, East Germany, and West Germany into the North Sea. p. 209.

Elburz Mountains (el bůrz′ mount′ ənz). Located in northern Iran. They separate the Iranian Plateau from the Caspian Sea. Highest peak is Mount Damāvand, with an elevation of 18,834 ft (5,571 m). p. 249.

Euphrates River (yů frāt′ ēz riv′ ər). Rises in mountains in eastern Turkey and flows through Syria into Iraq where it joins with the Tigris River near Al Qurna to form the Shatt-al-Arab, which flows into the Persian Gulf. p. 249.

Falkland Islands (fô′ klənd ī′ ləndz). Located in the South Atlantic Ocean, east of the southern tip of South America. p. 91.

Florence (flôr′ əns). City in Italy located on the Arno River at the base of the Apennines. (44°N/11°E) p. 201.

Fortaleza (fôrt əl ā′ zə). Port city in northeast Brazil. (4°S/39°W) p. 91.

Fraser River (frā′ zər riv′ ər). Rises in Canadian Rockies and flows into Pacific Ocean near Vancouver, British Columbia, p. 79.

Fredericton (fred′ ə rik tən). Capital of New Brunswick, Canada. (46°N/67°W) p. 83.

Ganges River (gan′ jēz riv′ ər). Sacred river of India. Rises in the Himalayas. Joined by the Brahmaputra near Dacca before flowing into the Bay of Bengal. p. 331.

Gdańsk (gə dänsk′). City in Poland. Located on Baltic Sea. Formerly called Danzig. (54°N/19°E) p. 218.

Georgetown (jôrj′ toun). Capital and chief port of Guyana. (7°N/58°W) p. 91.

Gobi Desert (gō′ bē dez′ ərt). Dry area located in Mongolia. p. 329.

Gold Coast (gōld kōst). Located along Gulf of Guinea between Ivory Coast and Slave Coast. Named for large amounts of gold once mined in the area. p. 480.

Grand Banks (grand banks). Rich fishing area in Atlantic Ocean south of Newfoundland. p. 79.

Great Barrier Reef (grāt bar′ ē ər rēf). World's largest deposit of coral. Located in the Coral Sea off the northeast coast of Australia. p. 419.

Great Dividing Range (grāt də vīd′ ing rānj). Mountain area of Australia. Extends from north to south near most of the east coast. Highest peak is Mt. Kosciusko, at 7,305 ft (2,226 m). p. 419.

Greater Antilles (grāt′ ər an til′ ēz). Group of islands in the West Indies. They include the islands of Cuba, Jamaica, Puerto Rico, and Hispaniola. p. 470.

Great Lakes (grāt lāks). Five large lakes located in North America mostly along the border between Canada and the United States. pp. 474–475.

Great Slave Lake (grāt slāv lāk). The deepest lake in the Western Hemisphere. It is 2,015 ft (614 m) deep. It is in the Northwest Territories, Canada. (62°N/114°W) p. 83.

Greenland (grēn′ lənd). Large island belonging to Denmark, off the coast of northeast North America. Excluding the continent of Australia, it is the largest island in the world. p. 476.

Guadalajara (gwäd ə lə här′ ə). Second most populated city in Mexico. (21°N/103°W) p. 103.

Guiana Highlands (gē an′ə hī ləndz). Located in northern South America from Venezuela through French Guiana. p. 89.

Gulf of Aden (gəlf əv äd′ ən). Part of the Arabian Sea located between Africa's Somalia Peninsula and the Arabian Peninsula. p. 251.

Gulf of Mexico (gəlf əv mek′ si kō). Body of water surrounded by the United States, Mexico, and Cuba. p. 477.

Gulf of Oman (gəlf əv ō′ män). Part of the Indian Ocean located between the Arabian Peninsula and southeast Iran. p. 251.

Halifax (hal′ ə faks). Capital of Nova Scotia, Canada. Located on the Atlantic Ocean. (45°N/64°W) p. 83.

Hamburg (ham′ bərg). Busy port city on the Elbe River in West Germany. (54°N/10°E) p. 145.

Hamilton (ham′ əl tən). Industrial city in Ontario, Canada. (43°N/80°W) p. 83.

Hanoi (ha noi′). Capital of Vietnam. Located on the Red River. (21°N/106°E) p. 331.

Havana (hə van′ ə). Capital of Cuba and the most populated city in the West Indies. (23°N/82°W) p. 91.

Himalayas (him ə lā′ əz). The world's highest mountain system. Located in central Asia. Mt. Everest, at 29,028 ft (8,848 m), the highest peak in the world, is located in the Himalayas. p. 329.

Hindu Kush (hin dü kush′). Very high mountain range located mostly in Afghanistan. Highest point is Wu-lu-k′o-mu-shih with an elevation of 25,348 ft (7,726 m). p. 329.

Hiroshima (hir ə shē′ mə). Industrial city in Japan. On August 6, 1945, the city was destroyed by an atomic bomb. This was the first time an atomic bomb was ever used in warfare. (34°N/132°E) p. 357.

Hispaniola (his pən yō′ lə). Second largest island in the West Indies. pp. 470–471.

Hobart (hō′ bärt). Capital of the Australian state of Tasmania. (43°S/147°E) p. 419.

Ho Chi Minh City (hō chē min sit′ ē). City formerly called Saigon. Name was changed in 1975 following the Communist takeover of South Vietnam. (11°N/107°E) p. 331.

Hokkaidō (hä kīd′ ō). Northernmost of the four main islands of Japan. p. 329.

Hong Kong (häng′ käng). British Colony in southeast China. (22°N/114°E) p. 331.

Honshū (hän′ shü). Largest of Japan's four major islands. p. 329.

Hudson Bay (həd′ sən bā). Large body of water in Canada. Connected with Atlantic by Hudson Strait. p. 55.

Hungarian Plain (həng ger′ ē ən plān). Located mostly in Hungary. The Danube River crosses this plain. p. 216.

Hwang Ho (hwäng′ hō). Chinese river that starts in the mountains of Tibet and flows into the Yellow Sea. p. 331.

Iberian Peninsula (ī bir′ ē ən pə nin′ sə lə). European peninsula southwest of Pyrenees. Spain and Portugal are on this peninsula. p. 143.

Indian Ocean (in′ dē ən ō′ shən). Large body of water between Africa and Australia. p. 44.

Indus River (in′ dəs riv′ ər). Rises in Tibet and flows into the Arabian Sea in Pakistan near its border with India. p. 331.

Irkutsk (ir kütsk′). City in Siberia. Located near Lake Baikal and the Lena River. (52°N/104°E) p. 211.

Iron Gate (ī′ ərn gāt). Pass or gap between Carpathian and Balkan mountains through which the Danube River flows. (45°N/23°E) p. 216.

Istanbul (is təm bül′). Turkish name for city of Constantinople. Most populated city in Turkey. Located on both sides of the Bosporus. Part of the city is in Europe and part is in Asia. (41°N/29°E p. 273.

Isthmus of Suez (is′ məs əv sü ez′). Narrow piece of land that separates the Red and Mediterranean seas. p.

Ivory Coast (īv′ rē kōst). Coast region of western Africa, along the Gulf of Guinea between the Gold Coast and the Grain Coast. p. 480.

Jakarta (jə kärt′ ə). Capital of Indonesia. One of the world's most populated cities. Located on the northwest coast of Java. (6°S/107°E) p. 331.

Java (jäv′ ə). Island that is part of Indonesia. Located between the Java Sea and the Indian Ocean. p. 329.

Jerusalem (jə rü′ sə ləm). Capital of Israel. Holy city for Jews, Christians, and Moslems. (32°N/35°E) p. 251.

Johannesburg (jō han′ əs bərg). Most populated city in South Africa. (26°S/28°E) p. 287.

Jordan River (jôrd′ ən riv′ ər). Rises in Syria and flows south through the Sea of Galilee and into the Dead Sea. p. 276.

Jura Mountains (jùr′ ə mount′ ənz). Mountains along the border between France and Switzerland. p. 171.

Jutland Peninsula (jət′ lənd pə nin′ sə lə). Peninsula located between the North and Baltic seas. Denmark and part of West Germany are located on it. p. 143.

Kabul (käb′ əl). Capital of and most populated city in Afghanistan. (35°N/69°E) p. 331.

Kalahari Desert (kal ə här′ ē dez′ ərt). Dry plateau region located in Botswana, South Africa, and Namibia. p. 283.

Kiev (kē′ ef). One of the oldest cities in Soviet Union. Today a large city located on the Dnieper River. (50°N/31°E) p. 211.

Kingston (king′ stən). Capital and chief seaport of Jamaica. (18°N/77°W) p. 91.

Kinshasa (kin shäs′ ə). City in Zaire. Located on the Congo River. Formerly known as Leopold-ville. (4°S/15°E) p. 287.

Kyūshū (kē ü′ shü). Most southern of the four main islands of Japan. p. 329.

Lagos (lā′ gäs). Capital of and most populated city in Nigeria. Located on Gulf of Guinea. (6°N/3°E) p. 287.

Lake Baikal (lāk bī kôl′) **or Baykal.** The world's deepest lake. It is 5,712 ft (1,741 m) deep. Located in Soviet Union. p. 211.

Lake Chad (lāk chad). Located on borders be-tween Niger, Chad, Nigeria, and Cameroon. Size of this lake varies depending on season. p. 283.

Lake Malawi (lāk mə lä′ wē). Located between Malawi, Tanzania, and Mozambique. Formerly known as Lake Nyasa. p. 283.

Lake Victoria (lāk vik tōr′ ē ə). One of the largest bodies of fresh water in the world. Located in eastern Africa, Kenya, Uganda, and Tanzania all have coastlines on this lake. p. 283.

La Paz (lə paz′). Most populated city in Bolivia. The third highest city in the world. Its elevation is 11,736 ft (3,577 m). (17°S/68°W) p. 91.

Laurentian Highlands (lô ren′ chən hi′ ləndz). Highland area in Quebec province, Canada, north of St. Lawrence River. Also called Laurentide Hills. p. 53.

Leipzig (līp′ sig). Industrial city in East Germany. (51°N/12°E) p. 211.

Lena River (lē′ nə riv′ ər). Rises near Lake Baikal and flows north into the Arctic Ocean. p. 211.

Leningrad (len′ ən grad). Second most populated city in the Soviet Union. Located on the Gulf of Finland. Once called St. Petersburg. Formerly the capital of the Russian empire. (60°N/30°E) p. 211.

Lesser Antilles (les′ ər an til′ ēz). Group of islands in the West Indies. Included in this island group are Virgin Is., Leeward Is., and Windward Is. p. 470.

Lhasa (läs′ ə). Major city in Tibet. It is the second highest city in the world. Its elevation is 12,002 ft (3,658 m). (30°N/91°E) p. 485.

Lima (lē′ mə). Capital of and most populated city in Peru. (12°S/77°W) p. 91.

Lisbon (liz′ bən). Capital of Portugal. Mainland Europe's westernmost port city. (39°N/9°W) p. 145.

Llanos (lan′ ōz). Large plain in northern South America. Drained by the Orinoco River. p. 143.

London (lən′ dən). Capital and most populated city in the United Kingdom. Located along the Thames River. (52°N/0° long) p. 145.

Los Angeles (lô san′ jə ləs). City in southern Cali-fornia on the Pacific Ocean. One of six cities in the United States with a population of more than 1,000,000. (34°N/118°W) p. 68.

Macao (mə kaù′). Portuguese colony located in southern China on the South China Sea. (22°N/113°E) p. 329.

Macdonnell Range (mək dän′ əl rānj). Mountains in central Australia. Highest peak is Mt. Ziel, with an elevation of 4,953 ft (1,510 m). p. 488.

Madagascar (mad ə gas′ kər). Island located in the Indian Ocean off the southeast coast of Africa. Excluding Australia it is the world's fourth largest island. The nation of Madagascar is on this is-land. p. 283.

Madrid (mə drid′). National capital of Spain. Sec-ond most populated city in Europe. (40°N/4°W) p. 145.

Malay Peninsula (mə lā′ pə nin′ sə lə). Located in southeast Asia. Parts of Malaysia and Thailand are on this peninsula. pp. 482–483.

Manaus (mə nous′). City in rain forest of Brazil. Located on the Negro River, a branch of the Ama-zon River. (3°S/60°W) p. 91.

Manchuria (man chùr′ ē ə). Part of China located in northeast China. p. 485.

Manila (mə nil′ ə). Capital of and most populated city in the Philippines. Located on Manila Bay on the island of Luzon. (15°N/121°E) p. 331.

Mecca (mek′ ə). Birthplace of Mohammed. Holy city for Moslems. Located in Saudi Arabia. (21°N/40°E) p. 270.

Medina (mə dē′ nə). City in Saudi Arabia. Mo-hammed's trip from Mecca to Medina in 622 is called the Hegira. (24°N/40°E). p. 270.

Mediterranean Sea (med ə tə rān′ nē ən sē). Large body of water surrounded by Europe, Africa, and Asia. It is the largest sea in the world. p. 143.

Mekong River (mā′ kông riv′ ər). River in South-east Asia. Rises in Tibet. Forms most of the boundary between Thailand and Laos. Flows into the South China Sea in southern Vietnam. p. 329.

Melbourne (mel′ bərn). Capital of the Australian state of Victoria. Located near the coast in south-eastern Australia. (38°S/145°E) p. 419.

Meuse River (myüz riv′ ər). Rises in northeast France and flows north through Belgium and the Netherlands into the North Sea. In the Nether-lands it forms a common delta with the Rhine River. p. 171.

Mexico City (mek′ si kō sit′ ē). Capital of Mexico. The most populated city in North America. (19°N/99°W) p. 91.

Milan (mə lan′). Industrial city in northern Italy. Second most populated city in Italy. (45°N/9°E) p. 145.

Mississippi River (mis ə sip′ ē riv′ ər). Second longest river system in the United States. Rises in northern Minnesota and flows into the Gulf of Mexico near New Orleans, Louisiana. pp. 474–475.

Missouri River (mə zùr′ ē riv′ ər). Longest river system in the United States. Rises in western Montana and flows into Mississippi River near St. Louis, Missouri. pp. 474–475.

Mombasa (mäm bäs′ ə). Seaport city on east coast of Kenya. (4°S/40°E) p. 295.

Mont Blanc (mōn blän′). Located in the French Alps, near the border with Italy. The highest peak in the Alps. Its elevation is 15,771 ft (4,807 m). p. 143.

Monterrey (mänt ə rā′). Industrial city in Mexico. (26°N/100°W) p. 103.

Montevideo (mänt ə və dā′ ō). Capital of and most populated city in Uruguay. Located on the Rio de la Plata. (35°S/56°W) p. 91.

Montreal (män trē ôl′). Most populated city in Canada. Located on Montreal Island in the St. Lawrence River. (46°N/74°W) p. 83.

Moscow (mäs′ kaù). Capital of the Soviet Union. The most populated city in Europe. (56°N/38°E) p. 211.

Mount Damavand (mount dam′ ə vand). Highest peak in Iran. Located in Elburz Mountains. Its elevation is 18,834 ft (5,571 m). (36°N/52°E) p. 249.

Mount Everest (mount ev′ rəst). Highest peak in the world. Located in the Himalayas at an elevation of 29,028 ft (8,848 m). (28°N/87°E) p. 329.

Mount Kenya (mount ken′ yə). Located in central Kenya. Second highest point in Africa, with an elevation of 17,058 ft (5,199 m). (0° lat./37°E) p. 283.

Mount Kilimanjaro (mount kil ə mən jär′ ō). Highest mountain peak in Africa. Its elevation is 19,340 ft (5,895 m). Located in northeast Tanzania near the Kenyan border. (3°S/37°E) p. 283.

Mount Kosciusko (mount käz ē əs′ kō). Highest peak in the Australian Alps. Located in southeast Australia. Its elevation is 7,305 ft (2,226 m). (36°S/148°E) p. 392.

Murray River (mər′ ē riv′ ər). Most important river in Australia. Rises in the Great Dividing Range. Flows into the Indian Ocean near Adelaide. p. 392.

Nairobi (nī rō′ bē). Capital of and most populated city in Kenya. (1°S/37°E). p. 287.

Namib Desert (näm′ ib dez′ ərt). Dry area along coast of Namibia. p. 283.

Naples (nā′ pəlz). Important port city in Italy. Located on part of the Mediterranean Sea called the Tyrrhenian Sea. (40°N/15°E) p. 145.

New Delhi (nü del′ ē). Capital of India. Located on the Jumna River. (29°N/77°E) p. 331.

New York City (nü yôrk sit′ ē). Most populated city in the United States. Located at mouth of the Hudson River in the state of New York. (41°N/74°W) p. 68.

Nice (nēs). Resort city on Mediterranean coast of France. (44°N/7°E) p. 487.

Niger River (nī′ jər riv′ ər). Rises in Guinea near Sierra Leone border. Flows into Gulf of Guinea in Nigeria. p. 287.

Nile River (nīl riv′ ər). The longest river in the world. Flows into the Mediterranean Sea at Alexandria, Egypt. p. 249.

North China Plain (nôrᴛʜ chī′ nə plān). Large plain located in eastern China. p. 329.

North European Plain (nôrᴛʜ yùrə p ē′ ən plān). Large area of flat land stretching from southwestern France through Belgium, the Netherlands, the Germanies, and Poland into the Soviet Union. The southeastern part of the United Kingdom is also part of this plain. p. 143.

North Island (nôrᴛʜ ī′ lənd). Northernmost of the two major islands of New Zealand. pp. 392–393.

North Sea (nôrᴛʜ sē). Part of the Atlantic Ocean between Great Britain and the European continent. p. 143.

Ob River (äb riv′ ər). Rises in the Altai Mountains and flows north into the Arctic Ocean. Located in the Soviet Union. p. 209.

Oder River (ōd ər riv′ ər). Rises in Czechoslovakia and flows north through Poland. Near Frankfurt, East Germany, it is joined by the Neisse River. It then flows north to the Baltic Sea, forming the boundary between Poland and East Germany. p. 209.

Ohio River (ō hi' ō riv' ər). Formed at Pittsburgh, Pennsylvania by the joining of the Allegheny and Monongahela rivers. Flows into the Mississippi River at Cairo, Illinois. Forms part of the boundary of five states. p. 474–475.

Orange River (ôr' inj riv' ər). Longest river in South Africa. Part of it forms the boundary between South Africa and Namibia. Flows into the Atlantic Ocean at Alexander Bay. p. 283.

Orinoco River (ôr ə nō' kō riv' ər). Located in Venezuela. Rises in the Guiana Highlands and flows into the Atlantic Ocean near Trinidad and Tobago. p. 89.

Osaka (ō säk' ə). Second most populated city in Japan. Major seaport located on Osaka Bay on Honshū Island. (35°N/136°E) p. 331.

Oslo (äz' lō). National capital of Norway. Located on Oslo Fjord. (60°N/11°E) p. 145.

Ottawa (ät' ə wə). Capital of Canada. (45°N/76°W) p. 83.

Pacific Ocean (pə sif' ik ō' shən). Large body of water stretching from the Arctic Circle to Antarctica and from the western coast of North America to the eastern coast of Asia. p. 44.

Pampas (pam' pəz). Fertile agricultural plains area in Argentina and Uruguay. p. 89.

Paraguay River (par' ə gwī riv' ər). Rises in Brazil and flows into the Paraná River at the southwest corner of Paraguay. p. 89.

Paramaribo (par ə mar' ə bō). Seaport city and capital of Surinam. (6°N/55°W) p. 91.

Paraná River (par ə na' riv' ər). Formed in Brazil; flows into the Río de la Plata. p. 89.

Paris (par' əs). National capital and most populated city of France. Located on the Seine River. (49°N/2°E) p. 145.

Patagonia (pat ə gō' nyə). Barren plains area in southern Argentina. p. 89.

Peking (pē king'). Capital of China. Fourth most populated city in the world. (40°N/116°E) p. 331.

Persia (pər' zhə). Ancient kingdom in the area that today is called Iran. pp. 484–485.

Persian Gulf (pər' zhən gəlf). Arm of the Arabian Sea. Separates Iran and Saudi Arabia. Connected with the Gulf of Oman and Arabian Sea by the Strait of Hormuz. p. 251.

Perth (pərтн). Capital of the Australian state of Western Australia. Located on the west coast of Australia. (32°S/116°E) p. 419.

Philadelphia (fil ə del' fyə). City at the point where Delaware and Schuylkill rivers join. One of six cities in the United States with a population of more than 1,000,000. (40°N/75°W) p. 68.

Pik Kommunizma (pēk' kə mü nēz' mə). Highest point in Soviet Union. Located in the Pamirs. It has an elevation of 24,590 ft (7,495 m). Formerly called Stalin Peak. (39°N/72°E) p. 209.

Ploiesti (plô yesht' ē). City in Romania. Located in a large oil field. (45°N/26°E) p. 218.

Polynesia (päl ə nē' zhə). Large group of small islands in central and southeast Pacific Ocean. pp. 392— 393.

Po River (pō riv' ər). Longest river in Italy. Starts in Alps and flows into the Adriatic Sea south of Venice. p. 143.

Port-au-Prince (pōrt ō prins'). Capital of and chief seaport in Haiti. (19°N/72°W) p. 91.

Pôrto Alegre (pōrt' ü ə leg' rə). Seaport city in southern Brazil on an inlet of the Pacific Ocean. (30°S/51°W) p. 91.

Prague (präg). Capital of Czechoslovakia. Located on the Vltava River. (50°N/14°E) p. 211.

Pretoria (pri tōr' ē ə). Capital of South Africa. Located on tributary of Limpopo River. (26°S/28°E) p. 287.

Pyrenees (pir' ə nēz). Mountains along border between France and Spain. Highest peak is Pico de Aneto, 11,168 ft (3,404 m). p. 143.

Quebec (kwi bek'). City in Canada, on the north side of the St. Lawrence River. It was founded in 1608 by Samuel de Champlain. Today it is the capital of the province of Quebec. (52°N/72°W) p. 83.

Quito (kē' tō). Capital of and most populated city in Ecuador. (0° lat./79°W) p. 91.

Rangoon (ran gün'). Capital of and most populated city in Burma. Located on the Rangoon River. (17°N/96°E) p. 331.

Recife (rə sē' fə). Seaport city located on the Atlantic coast on the eastern bulge of Brazil. (8°S/35°W) p. 91.

Red Sea (red sē). Large sea separating part of eastern Africa from Asia. p. 251.

Rhine River (rīn riv' ər). Starts in the Alps in Switzerland. Flows north into the North Sea in the Netherlands. p. 143.

Rhodes (rōdz). Greek island in the southeast Aegean Sea. p. 203.

Rhone River (rōn riv' ər). Starts from a glacier in the Alps in Switzerland and flows through France and into the Mediterranean Sea near Marseilles, France. p. 143.

Rio de Janeiro (rē' ō dā zhə nēr' ō). The second most populated city in South America. Major port of Brazil. Located on the Atlantic coast. (23°S/43°W) p. 91.

Río de la Plata (rē ō del ə plät' ə). Body of water at the point where the Paraná and Uruguay rivers flow into the Atlantic Ocean. p. 89.

Rio Grande (rē ō grand'). Rises in the Rocky Mountains in Colorado. It empties into the Gulf of Mexico near Brownsville, Texas. It forms the boundary between Texas and Mexico. p. 53.

Riyadh (rē yäd'). Capital of Saudi Arabia. (25°N/47°E) p. 251.

Rocky Mountains (räk' ē mount' ənz). Longest mountain chain in the United States. Stretches from Alaska to Mexico. Highest peak is Mt. Elbert, with an elevation of 14,433 ft (4,399 m). p. 53.

Rome (rōm). Capital and most populated city in Italy. Located on the Tiber River. Most important city in the Roman Empire. (42°N/13°E) p. 145.

Rosario (rō zär' ē ō). City in Argentina. Located on the Paraná River. (33°S/61°W) p. 91.

Sahara (sə har' ə). The largest desert in the world. Located in North Africa. p. 249.

St. John's (sānt jänz). Capital of Newfoundland, Canada. Located on southeast coast of Newfoundland Island. (48°N/53°W) p. 83.

St. Lawrence River (sānt lôr' əns riv' ər). Forms part of the boundary between Canada and the United States. Flows northeast from Lake Ontario to the Atlantic Ocean at the Gulf of St. Lawrence. p. 53.

Salvador (sal' və dôr). Seaport city on east coast of Brazil. (13°S/39°W) p. 91.

San'a (sä na'). Capital of Yemen (San'a). Located on a plateau at an elevation of 7,750 ft (2,362 m). (15°N/44°E) p. 251.

San Juan (san hwän'). Capital of and most populated city in Puerto Rico. (18°N/66°W) pp. 470–471.

Santiago (sant ē äg ō). Capital of and most populated city in Chile. (33°S/71°W) p. 91.

Santo Domingo (sant əd ə min' gō). Capital of and chief seaport of the Dominican Republic. (18°N/70°W) p. 91.

São Paulo (sou pou' lü). The most populated city in South America. Located in Brazil. (24°S/47°W) p. 91.

Sarajevo (sär ə ye vô). City in Yugoslavia. Site of 1984 Winter Olympics. (44°N/18°E) p. 487.

Scandinavia (skan də nā' vē ə). Consists of the countries of Norway, Sweden, Denmark, Finland, and Iceland. p. 145.

Sea of Marmara (sē əv mär' mə rä). Body of water between European Turkey and Asian Turkey. Connects the Bosporus and the Dardanelles. (41°N/28°E) p. 273.

Senegal River (sen i gôl' riv' ər). Rises in Guinea. Flows into the Atlantic Ocean at Saint-Louis, Senegal. Forms boundary between Senegal and Mauritania. p. 283.

Seoul (sōl). Capital of South Korea. One of the world's most populated cities. (37°N/127°E) p. 331.

Shanghai (shang hī'). The world's most populated city. Located on the delta of the Yangtze River in China on the East China Sea. (32°N/122°E) p. 331.

Shikoku (shi kō' kü). Smallest of the four main islands of Japan. p. 329.

Siberia (sī bir' ē ə). Part of the Soviet Union covering much of the area between the Ural Mountains and the Pacific Ocean. p. 209.

Sicily (sis' ə lē). Largest island in the Mediterranean Sea. Part of Italy. p. 145.

Sierra Madre Occidental (sē er' ə mäd' rē äk sə den täl'). North-south mountain range in western Mexico. p. 89.

Sierra Madre Oriental (sē er' ə mäd' rē ōr ē en täl'). North-south mountain range in eastern Mexico. p. 89.

Sierra Nevada (sē er' ə nə vad' ə). High mountain range located mostly in eastern California. Mount Whitney, with an elevation of 14,494 ft (4,418 m), is located in this range. It is the highest peak in the United States outside of Alaska. p. 53.

Silesia (sī lē' zhə). Located in Poland and Czechoslovakia. An important European coalfield. p. 218.

Sinai Peninsula (sī' nī pə nin' sə lə). Peninsula in eastern Egypt separated from Egypt by the Suez Canal. p. 482.

Singapore (sing' ə pōr). City on the island of Singapore. Also the capital of the nation of Singapore. One of the world's busiest ports. Located on Singapore Strait. (1°N/104°E) p. 331.

Sofia (sō' fē ə). Capital of Bulgaria. (43°N/23°E) p. 211.

Southern Alps (səŦH′ ərn alps). Mountain range on South Island in New Zealand. Highest peak is Mt. Cook, with an elevation of 12,349 ft (3,764 m). pp. 392–393.

South Island (souŦH ī′ lənd). Largest of New Zealand's islands. pp. 392–393.

Stonehenge (stōn′ henj). Remains of prehistoric structure near Salisbury, England. The original structure was built about 4,000 years ago. (51°N/ 2°W) p. 150.

Strait of Gibraltar (strāt əv jə brôl′ tər). Narrow neck of water separating the Iberian Peninsula from North Africa. It connects the Mediterranean Sea with the Atlantic Ocean. (36°N/6°W) p. 145.

Strait of Hormuz (strāt əv hôr′ məz). Narrow body of water connecting the Persian Gulf and the Gulf of Oman. (27°N/56°E) p. 251.

Strait of Malacca (strāt əv mə′ lak ə). Narrow channel of water between the Malay Peninsula and the island of Sumatra. p. 331.

Sucre (sü′ krā). Capital of Bolivia. Located in the Andes Mountains. (19°S/65°W) p. 91.

Sudbury (səd′ ber ē). Nickel-mining town in Ontario, Canada. World's largest supply of nickel is in the area. (47°N/81°W) p. 79.

Suez Canal (sü ez′ kə nal′). Waterway that joins Red and Mediterranean seas. Construction started in 1854 and completed in 1869. (30°N/ 33°E) p. 251.

Sumatra (sú mä′ trə). Large island in Indonesia. p. 329.

Sunda Islands (sən′ də ī lənz). Group of islands in Southeast Asia. They include Sumatra, Java, Borneo, Celebes, Bali, and Timor. p. 329.

Sydney (sid′ nē). Capital of the Australian state of New South Wales. Most populated city in Australia. Port city located on Tasman Sea, which is part of the Pacific Ocean. (34°S/151°E) p. 419.

Taipei (tī pā′). Capital of and most populated city in Taiwan. (25°N/122°E). p. 331.

Tasmania (taz mā′ nē ə). Island off the coast of Australia. Also one of Australia's states. p. 419.

Tehran (tā ə ran′). Capital of Iran. Located at base of Elburz Mountains. (36°N/51°E) p. 251.

Thames River (temz riv′ ər). River in Great Britain on which London is located. p. 143.

Tiber River (tī′ bər riv′ ər). River in Italy. It rises in the Apennines and flows through Rome to the Mediterranean Sea. p. 201.

Tibet (tə bet′). High mountainous area in China near border with India and Nepal. pp. 484–485.

Tigris River (tī′ grəs riv′ ər). Rises in Turkey and flows into Iraq, where it joins with the Euphrates River near Al Qurna to form the Shatt-al-Arab, which flows into the Persian Gulf. p. 251.

Tirana (ti rän′ ə). Capital of Albania. (41°N/20°E) p. 211.

Tokyo (tō′ kē ō). Capital of Japan. Located on the island of Honshū on Tokyo Bay. Second most populated city in the world. (36°N/140°E) p. 331.

Toronto (tə ränt′ ō). Capital of Ontario, Canada. Located on northeast end of Lake Ontario. (44°N/ 79°W) p. 83.

Tripoli (trip′ ə lē). Capital of Libya. Port city on the Mediterranean Sea. (33°N/13°E) p. 251.

Tunis (tü′ nəs). Capital of Tunisia. Seaport located on the Mediterranean Sea. (37°N/10°E) p. 251.

Ukraine (yü krān′). Part of the Soviet Union. Wheat grows well in the rich black soil of the area. p. 236.

Ulan Bator (ü′ län bä′ tôr). Capital of Mongolia. (48°N/107°E) p. 337.

Ural Mountains (yūr′ əl mount′ ənz). Located in the Soviet Union. They form the east-west divide between Asia and Europe. p. 209.

Vancouver (van kü′ vər). City in British Columbia, Canada. Located on an inlet of the Pacific Ocean. Canada's most important Pacific seaport. (49°N/ 123°W) p. 83.

Victoria (vik tōr′ ē ə). Capital of British Columbia, Canada. Located on Vancouver Island. (48°N/ 123°W) p. 83.

Vienna (vē en′ ə). Capital of and largest city in Austria. Located on the Danube River. (48°N/ 16°E) p. 145.

Vistula River (vis′ chə lə riv′ ər). Longest river in Poland. Rises in Carpathians and flows into the Baltic Sea near Gdańsk. p. 211.

Vladivostok (vlad ə və stäk′). City in the Soviet Union. Eastern end of the Trans-Siberian Railroad. Located on the Sea of Japan. (43°N/132°E) p. 211.

Volga River (väl′ gə riv′ ər). Longest river in Europe. Rises in the Valdai Hills. Flows into Caspian Sea at Astrakhan. p. 211.

Wales (wālz). One of the four major political divisions of the United Kingdom. p. 150.

Warsaw (wôr′ sô). Capital of Poland. Located on the Vistula River. (52°N/21°E) p. 211.

Washington, D.C. (wôsh′ ing tən). Capital of the United States. Located on the Potomac River (39°N/77°W) p. 68.

Wellington (wel′ ing tən). Capital of New Zealand. Located on North Island and Cook Strait. (41°S/175°E) p. 392.

West Berlin (west bər lin′). West German city located in East Germany. Part of divided city of Berlin. (53°N/13°E) p. 145.

Western Ghats (wes′ tərn gôts). Mountains located along western coast of India. Highest peak is Anai Mudi at an elevation of 8,841 ft (2,695 m). p. 371.

West Indies (west in′ dēz). Group of islands stretching about 2,500 mi (4,023 km) from near Florida to near Venezuela. pp. 470–471.

Whitehorse (hwīt′ hôrs). Capital of Yukon Territory, Canada. (61°N/135°W) p. 83.

Winnipeg (win′ ə peg). Capital of Manitoba, Canada. Located on the Red River. (50°N/97°W) p. 83.

Yangtze River (yang′ sē riv′ ər). One of the world′s longest rivers. Rises in Tibet. Flows into East China Sea near Shanghai, China. p. 331.

Yellowknife (yel′ ə nīf). Capital of Northwest Territories, Canada. Located on Great Slave Lake at the mouth of Yellowknife River. (62°N/114°W) p. 83.

Yenisei River (yen ə sā′ riv′ ər). Located in the Soviet Union. One of the world′s longest rivers. Rises in the Sayan Mountains. Flows into Kara Sea, which is part of Arctic Ocean. p. 209.

Yucatán Peninsula (yü kə tan′ pə nin′ sə lə). Located in Central America. Separates the Gulf of Mexico and the Caribbean Sea. p. 476.

Yukon River (yü′ kän riv′ ər). The third longest river in North America. Formed in Yukon Territory, Canada, and flows into the Bering Sea. p. 83.

Zagros Mountains (zag′ rəs mount′ ənz). Mountains that stretch from northwest Iran to near southern end of Persian Gulf. Highest peak is Zardeh Kuh. Its elevation is 14,921 ft (4,548 m). p. 249.

Zaire River (zə ir′ə riv′ ər). One of the world′s longest rivers. Rises in southeast Zaire as the Lualaba River. Flows into Atlantic Ocean at Matadi, Zaire. p. 283.

Zambezi River (zam bē′ zē riv′ ər). Rises in Angola. Flows into the Indian Ocean in Mozambique. Forms boundary between Angola and Zimbabwe. p. 283.

Zanzibar (zan′ zə bär). Island belonging to Tanzania. Located in the Indian Ocean off the coast of Tanzania. Also the name of the chief city on the island. (6°S/39°E) p. 287.

Zurich (zür′ ik). City on the Swiss Plateau in Switzerland. (47°N/9°E) p. 185.

GLOSSARY

Aborigine (ab ə rij′ ə nē). The earliest known inhabitant of Australia. p. 417.

acid rain (as′ id rān). Rain or snow that has a high amount of certain acids due to air pollution. p. 66.

administer (ad min′ ə stər). To manage or direct the affairs of. p. 405.

adobe (ə dō′ bē). A building material made of sun-dried mud and straw. p. 103.

alliance (ə lī′ əns). An agreement by persons, groups, or nations to act together for some special purpose or benefit. p. 465.

alloy (al′ oi). A mixture of two or more metals. p. 78.

alluvial (ə lü′ vē əl). Consisting of material such as clay, silt, sand, or gravel that has been gradually deposited by flowing water. Some of the most fertile land in the world is made up of alluvial soils deposited in the deltas of the great rivers. p. 340.

altiplano (äl ti plä′ nō). A plateau of flat or rolling land in the Andes. p. 124.

altitude (al tə′ tüd). Height above sea level. Altitude is usually measured in feet or meters. p. 4.

annex (ə neks′). To join or add to a larger or more important thing. p. 425.

Antarctic Circle (ant ärk′ tik sėr′ kəl). A line of latitude that circles the earth at 66 1/2°S. p. 41.

apartheid (ä pärt′ hāt). The forced separation, by law, of whites and nonwhites in South Africa. p. 311.

Arabize (ar′ ə bīz). To cause to adopt Arab ways. p. 257.

arable (ar′ ə bəl). Suitable for growing crops. p. 106.

Arawak (ä′ rä wäk). Indians of the Caribbean region who were good farmers. p. 113.

archipelago (är kə pel′ ə gō). A group of islands. p. 203.

Arctic Circle (ärk′ tik sėr′ kəl). A line of latitude that circles the earth at 66 1/2° north latitude. p. 40.

artisan (är′ tə zən). A craftworker; a person skilled in some industry or trade. p. 319.

asbestos (as bes′ təs). A mineral that does not burn or conduct heat; also, fireproof products made from the mineral. p. 79.

assumption (ə sump′ shən). A statement that is assumed or supposed to be true, but has not been proved true. p. 448.

atoll (at′ ol). A ring-shaped coral island enclosing or partly enclosing a lagoon. p. 398.

axis (ak′ sis). An imaginary line that goes through the earth from the North Pole to the South Pole. p. 38.

Bantu (ban′ tü). A family of African languages. p. 300.

barbarian (bär bār′ ē ən). A person crude in dress and habits; a person who is not civilized. p. 342.

bar graph (bär graf). A kind of graph that uses bars to show information. p. 33.

basin (bā′ sən). A low area almost entirely surrounded by higher land. p. 170.

bauxite (bôk′ sīt). An ore used in making aluminum. p. 64.

Bedouin (bed′ u̇ in). Wandering Arab herders. p. 257.

Berber (bėr′ bər). A person from Morocco whose ancestors lived in northwest Africa before the Arabs conquered it. The Berbers managed to keep many of their old ways. p. 257.

Berlin wall (bər lin′ wôl). A concrete wall that divides the city of Berlin into East Berlin and West Berlin. p. 216.

black nationalism (blak nash′ə nə liz əm). The idea that black Africans ought to control their own nations. p. 308.

Boers (bôrz). Early Dutch settlers in South Africa; Dutch word for "farmers." p. 308.

500

boomerang (bü′ mə rang). A bent throwing stick that can be thrown in such a way that it comes back to the thrower. The Aborigines hunted with a boomerang. p. 417.

botany (bot′ ə nē). The study of plants. p. 418.

Buddhism (bùd′ iz əm). A religion founded by Siddhartha Gautama in India in the sixth century B.C. p. 365.

bureaucrat (byùr′ ə krat). A person in charge of a government department or bureau. p. 300.

cacao (kə kā′ ō). The seeds from which cocoa and chocolate are made; the tree that bears these seeds. p. 133.

calving (kav ing). The breaking off of pieces of ice, which form icebergs. p. 427.

canal (kə′ nal). A waterway created by people rather than by nature. p. 121.

canton (kan′ tən). A small territorial division of a country, which functions as a separate political unit. A canton corresponds to a state in the United States. Switzerland is divided into cantons. p. 189.

canyon (kan′ yən). A deep valley with steep sides, usually with a stream or river running through it. p. 6.

cape (kāp). A piece of land extending into the water. A cape is smaller than a peninsula. p. 8.

capital (kap′ ə təl). Money used to develop a country's economy. p. 132.

capitalism (kap′ ə tə liz əm). An economic system in which people or groups of people own land, factories, and other means of production. They compete with one another to produce goods and services for profit. p. 182.

caravan (kar′ ə van). A group of people traveling together, usually on animals or in vehicles. p. 256.

Carib (kar′ ib). Indians of the Caribbean region who were once warlike. p. 113.

cartographer (kär tog′ rə fər). A person who makes maps. p. 12.

caste (kast). A system that separates people into groups, or classes, based on birth. p. 365.

catamaran (katə mə ran′). Two canoes fastened together to make one boat. Sometimes planks fastened on the framework serve as a deck. p. 400.

census (sen′ səs). A government count of the number of people in a country. The United States has a census every 10 years. p. 31.

chernozem (cher′ nə zem). The fertile black soils of the steppes. p. 232.

cholera (kol′ ər ə). An intestinal disease of humans and animals that may result in death. Strict sanitary measures are necessary to prevent cholera. p. 441.

circumference (sər kum′ fər əns). The distance around. p. 398.

civilization (siv ə lə zā′ shən). A stage of cultural development marked by the presence of cities, trade, government, art, writing, and science. p. 100.

climate (klī′ mit). The pattern of weather that a place has over a period of years. Temperature and precipitation are two important parts of climate. p. 34.

climograph (klī′ mō graf). A graph that shows both the average temperature and the average precipitation for a certain place over a period of time. p. 45.

clove (klōv). A spice made from the dried flower buds of a tropical evergreen tree. p. 297.

cobalt (kō′ bôlt). A hard, shiny, silver-white, magnetic metal that occurs only in combination with other metals, such as iron and nickel. Cobalt is used in steel for hardness. p. 294.

collective (kə lek′ tiv). A farm that a group of people operates together to produce and to share the products. p. 218.

colony (kol′ə nē). A place that is settled at a distance from the country that governs it. p. 114.

combine (kom′ bīn). A farm machine that cuts wheat and separates the grain from the stalks. p. 28.

commerce (kom′ ərs). The buying and selling of goods. p. 318.

commercial agriculture (kə mėr′ shəl ag′ rə kul chər). Growing crops for sale. p. 105.

commonwealth (kom′ ən welth). An association of countries that were once part of the British Empire. p. 84.

commune (kom′ yün). A community, often rural, in which labor, decision-making, and profits are shared. p. 343.

commuter (kə myü′ tər). Someone who travels regularly to and from work by train, bus, automobile, or some other means of transportation. p. 442.

compass rose (kum′ pəs rōz). A small drawing on a map, used to show direction. p. 14.

compulsory education (kəm pul′ sər ē ej ù kā′ shən). Education that is required by a government. p. 354.

Confucianism (kən fyü′ shə niz əm). A religion based on the teachings of the philosopher Confucius. Confucianism teaches respect for the past and one's ancestors and stresses the importance of having only superior people rule a well-ordered society. p. 341.

coniferous (kə nif′ ər əs). Having cones. Almost all coniferous trees have needles and are also called evergreen trees. p. 48.

conquistadores (kon kwis′ tə dôrz). Spanish soldiers of the sixteenth century. p. 100.

conservative (kən sėr′ və tiv). Wanting to keep things as they are or as they were in the past; being opposed to sudden change. p. 271.

constitutional monarchy (kon stə tü′ shə nəl mon′ ər kē). A government in which the monarch or ruler serves as head of state and has only those powers given to the ruler by the constitution and laws of the nation. p. 384.

consumer goods (kən sü′ mər gúdz). Things that are grown or made by producers and are used by people. p. 239.

contiguous (kən tig′ yü əs). Touching or adjoining. p. 42.

continent (kon′ tə nənt). A very large body of land. There are seven continents: Asia, Africa, North America, South America, Europe, Australia, and Antarctica. p. 6.

continental island (kon tə nen′ təl ī′ lənd). An island that is part of a continent, usually separated from it by a stretch of water. p. 396.

conuco system (kō nü′ kō sis′ təm). The method of planting crops developed by the Arawak Indians. p. 113.

conveyor (kən vā′ ər). A moving belt that carries things from place to place. p. 56.

cooperative (kō op′ rə tiv). An organization owned and operated by those using their services. p. 164.

copal (kō′ pəl). A tree resin used in varnish. p. 249.

copra (kōp′ rə). Dried coconut meat. Coconut oil is pressed from copra. p. 407.

Copt (kopt). A member of a Christian group in Egypt that resisted adopting Arab ways. Today Egypt has more than one million Copts. p. 257.

coral (kôr′ əl). A hard, chalky, rocklike material consisting of the shells of coral polyps. p. 110.

cottage industry (kot′ ij in′ də strē). An industry where the workers make products in their own homes. Silk weaving, the making of jewelry, and the making of leather goods are sometimes examples of cottage industries. p. 370.

Creole (krē′ ōl). A Haitian language that combines the French and African languages. p. 116.

culture (kul′ chər). The way of life of a people. p. 100.

deciduous (di sij′ ù əs). Losing leaves at the end of a growing season. p. 47.

delta (del′ tə). The land that is formed by mud and sand deposited at the mouth of a river. p. 6.

demilitarized zone (dē mil′ə tə rizd zōn). An area free of military control, where there are no troops or weapons. p. 344.

deplete (di plēt′). Reduce or exhaust the supply of a natural resource. p. 62.

depopulate (dē pop′ yə lāt). To reduce the population of an area. p. 220.

descendant (di sen′ dənt). One who comes from a specific family or ancestor. p. 67.

desert (dez′ ərt). A very dry place, with little rainfall and few plants. p. 46.

developing country (di vel′ əp ing kun′ trē). A country that is not highly industrialized, where wealth is in the hands of only a few, and where there are many poor people. p. 96.

diagram (dī′ ə gram). A special kind of drawing that explains how something works or why something happens. p. 30.

dialect (dī′ ə lekt). A variation of a language, as spoken in a certain region. p. 182.

dike (dīk). A wall or bank built to control or hold back the water of a river or sea. p. 176.

distortion (dis tôr′ shən). A twisting or stretching out of shape. p. 20.

dormant (dôr′ mənt). Inactive. p. 350.

double cropping (dub′ əl krop′ ing). The practice of planting twice a year. p. 336.

drought (drout). A long, dry period with no rain. p. 45.

dry farming (drī fär′ ming). A method of farming in which only certain crops are grown and the moisture in the soil is conserved. p. 256.

dual economy (dü′ əl i kon′ ə mē). An economy in which a few people are very rich and most people are very poor. p. 131.

dynasty (dī′ nə stē). A family of rulers. p. 340.

earthquake (ėrth′ kwāk). A shaking of the earth caused by movement beneath the earth's surface. p. 120.

economic activity (ē kə nom′ ik ak tiv′ ə tē). An activity that has to do with the production and sale of goods and services. p. 59.

economics (ē kə nom′ iks). The study of how goods and services are produced and consumed. p. 45.

ejido (e hē′ dō). A small farm owned and worked by several families or by an entire village. p. 104.

elevation (el ə vā′ shən). The height of something. The elevation of land is its distance above or below sea level, usually measured in feet or meters. p. 22.

emblem (em′ bləm). A symbol or sign. p. 424.

emigrant (em′ə grənt). A person who leaves one country to settle in another. p. 155.

Enclosure Movement (en klō′ zhər müv′ mənt). A change in the use of the land that transformed open fields into areas enclosed by fences or hedges. This change began in the 1300s and continued until the 1800s. p. 155.

equinox (ē′ kwə noks). Either of the two times in the year when the sun's direct rays are over the Equator and day and night are of equal length. p. 41.

era (ir′ ə). A period of years counted from a set point in time. p. 153.

escarpment (es kärp′ mənt). The steep slope, or drop, at the edge of a plateau. p. 304.

ethnic group (eth′ nik grüp). A group of people who share many traits and customs. p. 224.

European Economic Community (yür ə pē′ ən ē kə nom′ ik kə myü′ nə tē). An organization of a group of European countries whose purpose is to make trade easier between them. p. 179.

exploitation (eks ploi tā′ shən). Taking large profits from a country, leaving very little for the people who live there. p. 301.

export (eks′ pôrt). A product sold by one country to another. Also, to send out of the country for sale. p. 96.

extinct (ek stingkt′). No longer existing. p. 416.

fallow (fal′ ō). Not cultivated or planted for a season or more. p. 256.

famine (fam′ ən). A very great shortage of food. p. 157.

fault line (fôlt līn). A break or crack in the earth's crust. p. 266.

federal (fed′ ər əl). Having to do with a form of political organization in which power is distributed between the national government and the governments of the states or provinces. p. 82.

fellahin (fel ə hēn′). A group of crop-raising farmers in North Africa who opposed the Bedouins. p. 257.

fertile (fėr′ təl). The state of soil that is rich in minerals needed by plants for good growth. p. 118.

fertilizer (fėr′ tə lī zər). A material added to soil to help plants grow faster and bigger. p. 107.

figurehead (fig′ yər hed). A leader with no real power. p. 353.

fish farm (fish färm). A pond or bay in which fish are kept and raised to be sold commercially. p. 351.

fjord (fyôrd). A long, narrow, often deep inlet of the sea lying between steep cliffs. p. 6.

Fleming (flem′ ing). One of a group of people inhabiting chiefly the northern part of Belgium. p. 177.

flood plain (flud plān). A plain that borders a river and that has been formed from deposits of mud and sand carried by the river and deposited during floods. p. 339.

fodder (fod′ ər). A coarse feed for livestock. It is often a mixture of hay and cornstalks with their leaves. p. 221.

forecast (fôr′ kast). A statement or prediction about some future happening or condition, usually made as a result of the careful study of available information. p. 448.

frond (frond). The leaf of a coconut palm or a fern. p. 406.

frontier (frun tir′). A place with room for more settlement. p. 124.

geologic history (jē ə loj′ ik his′ tər ē). The history of the formation of the earth's surface. p. 292.

geyser (gī′ zər). A fountain of steam and water that has been heated by hot lava and forced above the ground by volcanic gases. p. 160.

glacier (glā′ shər). A large mass of ice formed from snow on high ground and moving very slowly down a mountainside or along a valley. p. 160.

graphics (graf′ iks). A map, photograph, diagram, table, graph, or time line used to present information. p. 26.

great circle (grāt sėr′ kəl). Any circle on the earth's surface that divides the earth into equal parts. The Equator is a great circle. p. 19.

Green Revolution (grēn rev ə lü′ shən). The growing of more crops on the same amount of land, due to the development of new types of grain by agricultural scientists. p. 369.

grid (grid). A network of lines that forms a pattern of crisscrosses. p. 18.

gross national product (grōs nash′ ə nəl prod′ əkt). The total value of all the goods and services that a country produces. p. 355.

gulf (gulf). A part of an ocean or a sea that extends into the land. p. 7.

habitat (hab′ ə tat). The place where an animal or a plant naturally lives or grows. p. 62.

hacienda (hä sē en′ də). A very large farm. p. 104.

hamlet (ham′ lit). A small village of groupings of houses, barns, and stables that may belong to only two or three families. p. 165.

harbor (här′ bər). A protected body of water, safe for ships. p. 7.

hearsay (hir′ sā). Common talk. p. 353.

heavy industry (hev′ ē in′ də strē). Industry that manufactures products for use by other industries. p. 239.

hegira (hi jī′ rə). Mohammed's flight (journey) from Mecca to Medina in A.D. 622. p. 268.

hemisphere (hem′ ə sfir). Half the earth or the globe. p. 16.

high seas (hī sēz). The oceans and saltwater seas beyond the strip of territorial waters along a country's coast. p. 460.

High Veld (hī velt). The upland grassland area of South Africa. p. 304.

Hindi (hin′ dē). The official language of India. p. 367.

Hinduism (hin′ dù iz əm). One of the world's oldest living religions. Hinduism is practiced by most of the people of India. p. 365.

host country (hōst kun′ trē). A country that receives people who are coming from another country. p. 197.

humidity (hyü mid′ ə tē). The amount of water or dampness in the air. p. 45.

hydroelectric power (hī drō i lek′ trik pou′ ər). Electricity produced from moving water. p. 64.

iceberg (īs′ bėrg). A large piece of ice that has broken off a glacier and floated out to sea. p. 48.

illiteracy (i lit′ ər ə sē). The state of not knowing how to read or write. p. 354.

immigration (im′ ə grā′ shən). The movement of people from one country who come into another country to live. p. 82.

import (im′ pôrt). A product one country buys from another. Also, to bring products into a country. p. 96.

independent nation (in di pen′ dənt nā′ shən). A nation that has its own government. p. 115.

indigo (in′ də gō). A plant that produces a dark blue dye. p. 366.

industrial diamond (in dus′ trē əl dī′ mənd). A diamond used in grinders, drills, and phonograph needles, not used as jewelry. p. 295.

Industrial Revolution (in dus′ trē əl rev ə lü′ shən). The period of great change from an agricultural to an industrial society, brought about by the invention of power-driven machines. p. 155.

industry (in′ də strē). Manufacturing of goods. p. 62.

in-migration (in′ mī grā′ shən). Movement into a region or community. p. 201.

interdependent (in tər di pen′ dənt). Dependent upon each other. p. 454.

interest (in′ tər ist). The amount of money that a bank or an individual charges for lending money. p. 383.

interior (in tir′ ē ər). The part of a region or a country that is away from coasts or borders. p. 161.

internal drainage (in tėr′ nəl drā′ nij). An area in which rivers flow into lakes rather than into oceans. p. 230.

International Date Line (in tər nash′ ə nəl dāt līn). A line running north and south through the Pacific Ocean, mostly along the 180th meridian. The International Date Line marks the place where each new calendar day begins. p. 43.

interpolation (in tėr pə lā′ shən). The process of finding an unknown number between two known numbers in a series. p. 18.

irrigation (ir ə gā′ shən). The watering of crops or other plants by pipes, canals, or ditches. p. 28.

island (ī′ lənd). A body of land completely surrounded by water. p. 7.

isthmus (is′ məs). A narrow strip of land connecting two larger bodies of land. p. 7.

juku (jü′ kü). A separate Japanese school that helps students prepare for examinations. p. 356.

jute (jüt). A plant, raised mostly in the Ganges Delta, from which the fiber for burlap and twine is obtained. p. 369.

kerosene (ker′ ə sēn). A thin oil made from petroleum and used in lamps and stoves, to run farm machines, and as a fuel for jet planes. p. 444.

key (kē). A device on a map that tells what real things and places the symbols on the map stand for. p. 14.

kibbutz (ki büts′). An Israeli community of farmers who work together and share all the property and income. p. 277.

kilometer (kil′ə mē tər). A measure of distance in the metric system. A kilometer (km) is a little more than half a mile. p. 11.

kremlin (krem′ lən). The Russian word meaning "fortress." Today when people speak of the *Kremlin*, they usually mean the Soviet government. p. 234.

kulak (kü läk′). A farmer who owned enough land to make a living from it, considered too wealthy by the Soviet Communists. p. 242.

Kurdistan (kėr′ də stan). A region of about 75,000 square miles (194,000 sq km) that lies in Turkey, Iraq, Iran, and Syria. The Kurds want their large region to be independent. p. 274.

lagoon (lə gün′). A large, shallow body of water near a larger body of water. p. 322.

lake (lāk). A body of water completely surrounded by land. p. 8.

land bridge (land brij). A narrow strip of land that connects two larger pieces of land. p. 376.

landlocked (land′ lokt). Not having a seacoast. p. 136.

land reform (land rē fôrm). A change in the way land is owned. p. 104.

latifundia (lat ə fun′ dē ə). Large farming estates in South America. p. 130.

latitude (lat′ ə tüd). Distance, measured in degrees, north and south of the Equator. Lines of latitude are used to locate places on a map or globe. p. 16.

liberator (lib′ ə rā tər). A leader of a movement for independence. p. 130.

lichen (lī′ kən). A plant that grows on rocks and other surfaces and that has no roots, stems, leaves, or flowers. p. 48.

life expectancy (līf ek spek′ tən sē). Average length of life, or the number of years a person may be expected to live. p. 355.

light industry (līt in′ də strē). Industry that manufactures products for use by consumers. p. 239.

lignite (lig′ nīt). A coal of low quality, called brown coal. p. 214.

line graph (līn graf). A kind of graph that shows information by using lines. A line graph usually shows how changes take place over a period of time. p. 33.

linguist (ling′ gwist). A person who studies the history and form of language. p. 364.

llama (lä′ mə). A woolly animal, bigger than a donkey and smaller than a camel, used for carrying goods. Its wool can be used to make cloth. p. 128.

llanos (lä′ nōz). Plains in Colombia and Venezuela drained by the Orinoco River. *Llanos* is the Spanish word for "plains." p. 133.

lock (lok). An enclosed area on a canal, with gates on both sides, used for raising or lowering ships as they go from one water level to another. p. 74.

loess (lō′ is). Wind-deposited dust, predominantly silts. Many particles are angular in shape, which allows the deposits to stand in steep, or vertical, bluffs. p. 340.

logotype (lôg′ ə tīp). An identifying symbol for a product or a company. p. 458.

longitude (lon′ je tüd). Distance, measured in degrees, east and west of the Prime Meridian. Lines of longitude are imaginary circles that go around the earth and pass through the North Pole and the South Pole. p. 16.

Maghreb (məg′ rəb). A region covering part of Morocco, Tunisia, and Algeria that receives more rain than any other part of North Africa. p. 261.

Malagasy (mal ə gas′ ē). The language of Madagascar, which is a combination of Malay and Indonesian. p. 313.

mangrove (mang′ grōv). A tropical tree whose wood is used for fuel, and whose bark is a source of tannin. Mangroves grow in swamps and along riverbanks. p. 316.

manor (man′ ər). A small farming village surrounded by open fields and pastures, and separated from the next manor by large forests or woodlands. p. 154.

Maori (mä′ ō rē). A descendant of the first inhabitants of New Zealand. p. 424.

maritime (mar′ ə tīm). Of the sea. p. 460.

marsupial (mär sü′ pē əl). An animal, such as the kangaroo, that carries its young in a pouch until the young are fully developed. p. 415.

medieval (mē dē ē′ vəl). Relating to the period from about A.D. 500 to about A.D. 1450, known as the Middle Ages. p. 154.

meridian (mə rid′ ē ən). Line of longitude running in a north-south direction on a map or globe. The number on the line shows how far the line is east or west of the Prime Meridian. p. 16.

mestizo (mes tē′ zō). Person of Spanish and Indian ancestry. p. 102.

metropolitan area (met rə pol′ ə tən ār′ ē ə). An area made up of a large city or several large cities and the surrounding towns, smaller cities, and other communities. p. 67.

migration (mī grā′ shən). The movement of people from one place to another. p. 189.

minifundia (min ē fənd′ ēə). Small farms in South America that were created by breaking up the latifundia. p. 131.

Mongoloid racial group (mong′ gə loid rā′ shəl grüp). A group with common characteristics and that includes most of the people of Southeast Asia, China, Japan, Korea, and Mongolia. p. 377.

Mongols (mong′ gəlz). An Asian people living in Mongolia and parts of China and Siberia. p. 233.

monsoon (mon sün′). Seasonal wind that blows from the land to the water in one season and from the water to the land in the other. p. 363.

montage (mon täzh′). A group of several pictures arranged to give a more complete or well-rounded portrayal of a subject. p. 26.

mountain (moun′ tən). A piece of land that rises steeply from the land around it. p. 8.

multinational (mul ti nash′ ə nəl). Having plants or businesses in more than two nations. p. 459.

mutton (mut′ ən). The meat of sheep. p. 420.

natural resource (nach′ ər əl ri sôrs′). Something that is provided by nature and is useful to people. p. 23.

navigable (nav′ ə gə bəl). Able to be traveled by ships and boats. p. 299.

navigation (nav ə gā′ shən). The science of steering a course, usually in a ship or an aircraft. p. 401.

neutral (nü′ trəl). Standing apart in an argument or fight and not taking sides. p. 188.

nickel (nik′ əl). A hard silver-white metal that is used for coins, as an alloy of steel, and for nickel plating. p. 78.

nitrate (nī′ trāt). A mineral used in fertilizers and explosives. p. 134.

nomad (nō′ mad). A person who wanders from place to place, having no permanent home. p. 257.

nonrenewable resource (non ri nü′ ə bəl ri sôrs′). A resource that cannot be replaced by nature or people. p. 64.

North European Plain (nôrth yur ə pē′ ən plān). An area of low-lying and almost flat land in Europe that stretches to the north and east from southwestern France. This plain goes through France, Belgium, the Netherlands, Germany, Denmark, Poland, Russia, and the southern and eastern parts of the British Isles. p. 160.

nuclear power (nü′ klē ər pou′ ər). Power produced by atomic energy. p. 65.

oasis (ō ā′ sis). A place in a desert that has enough water for plants and trees to grow. p. 256.

oasis agriculture (ō ā′ sis ag′ rə kul chər). Farming in that part of a desert where water is available. p. 256.

ocean (ō′ shən). A very large body of salt water. There are four oceans: the Pacific, Atlantic, Indian, and Arctic. p. 8.

ocean current (ō′ shən kėr′ ənt). A regular movement of the surface water of an ocean or a river, caused mostly by winds and differences of water temperature. p. 43.

OPEC. The Organization of Petroleum Exporting Countries, or OPEC, an international organization that plays a big role in determining the price of oil in the world. OPEC has member countries from Asia, Africa, and South America. p. 270.

out-migration (out mi grā′ shən). Movement from one region into another region. p. 197.

outrigger (out′ rig ər). A float attached to the side of a canoe to keep it from tipping. p. 400.

paddy (pad′ ē). A rice field, particularly a field in which irrigated rice is raised. p. 380.

Palestinian (pal ə stin′ ē ən). A person who lived in the land once known as Palestine. p. 276.

parallel (par′ ə lel). A line of latitude running in an east-west direction on a map or globe. The number on the line shows how far the line is north or south of the Equator. p. 16.

partition (pär tish′ ən). Division into parts. p. 367.

peat (pēt). Plant matter used as a fertilizer or fuel. It is made of partially rotted plants and moss. p. 151.

peninsula (pə nin′ sə lə). A piece of land almost surrounded by water and connected to a larger body of land. p. 8.

per capita income (pər kap′ ə tə in′ kum). The amount of income each person in a country would have if the country's total income were divided equally among all of its people. p. 216.

permafrost (pėr′ mə frôst). Permanently frozen ground, sometimes extending to great depths below the earth's surface in very cold regions. p. 48.

petrochemical (pet rō kem′ ə kəl). A chemical or synthetic material produced from petroleum or natural gas. p. 69.

petroglyph (pet′ rə glif). A rock carving, usually done by people who lived in prehistoric times. p. 38.

philosopher (fə los′ ə fər). A person who searches for truth by reasoning. p. 341.

phosphate (fos′ fāt). A mineral used in making fertilizers and detergents. p. 262.

physical features (fiz′ ə kəl fē′ chərz). The different shapes of land and water on the earth's surface. p. 4.

pictograph (pik′ tə graf). A kind of graph that uses symbols, instead of numbers, to represent fixed amounts of a particular thing. p. 32.

pie graph (pī graf). A kind of graph drawn in the shape of a circle. Sometimes a pie graph is called a circle graph. p. 32.

piedmont (pēd′ mont). The foothills of a mountain range. p. 135.

pitchblende (pich′ blend). The brownish-black mineral that is the chief source of uranium. p. 81.

plain (plān). An almost level area that stretches for miles and miles. p. 9.

plantain (plan′ tən). A kind of large banana. p. 406.

plantation (plan tā′ shən). A large farm that grows one specific crop. p. 116.

plateau (pla tō′). An elevated plain raised sharply above surrounding land at least on one side. p. 9.

platypus (plat′ ə pəs). A small animal that lives in and along the rivers of eastern Australia and Tasmania. The platypus has a large, flat bill like that of a duck; soft fur; webbed feet; and a broad flattened tail. p. 414.

PLO. The Palestine Liberation Organization, an organization established by a group of Palestinians to retake Palestine by force. p. 277.

polder (pōl′ dər). A piece of land reclaimed from the water, usually by building dikes and pumping the water out of the area enclosed by the dikes. p. 176.

political map (pə lit′ ə kəl map). A map that shows the different countries in the world or the different states in a country. p. 20.

population density (pop yə lā′ shən den′ sə tē). The average number of people per given unit of area (such as a square mile or square kilometer) in a state, country, or other area. p. 31.

population exchange (pop yə lā′ shən eks chānj′). The process of one country or area giving up a group of people and receiving or taking another group of people. p. 204.

population growth rate (pop yə lā′ shən grōth rāt). The difference between the average number of births and the average number of deaths per year for every 1,000 persons. p. 440.

populous (pop′ yə ləs). Having a large number of people. p. 355.

prairie (prār′ ē). A mid-latitude region of tall grasses. *Prairie* comes from a French word meaning "meadow." p. 77.

precipitation (pri sip ə tā′ shən). The moisture that falls on the earth's surface in the form of rain, snow, sleet, hail, fog, or mist. p. 34.

profile (prō′ fīl). A special kind of drawing that shows an area of land with the earth cut away to sea level. p. 22.

projection (prə jek′ shən). **1.** The representation on a map of all or part of the earth's grid system. p. 20. **2.** An extension of a line on a graph to a year in the future. p. 448.

protectorate (prə tek′ tər it). An area under the control of another country until that area becomes independent. p. 311.

province (prov′ əns). A division of a country. A Canadian province is similar to a state in the United States. p. 72.

pulp (pulp). A mixture of ground wood and chemicals that is used to make paper. p. 59.

pyrethrum (pī rē′ thrəm). Flowers of this plant are used in making insecticides. p. 297.

Quechua (kech′ wä). The language of the Incas, still spoken today by some South American Indians. p. 130.

quota (kwō′ tə). A limit placed by one nation on the amount of goods that may be imported from other nations. p. 458.

radioactive (rā dē ō ak′ tiv). Giving off harmful rays. p. 78.

rain forest (rān fôr′ ist). A large, very thick forest, usually of broad-leaved trees. p. 46.

rain shadow (rān shad′ ō). An area that does not get much rain, because it is on the protected side of a mountain. p. 99.

raw material (rô mə tir′ ē əl). Substances in their natural state that are used to make manufactured or finished products. p. 191.

reconquest (rē kon′ kwest). A time of regaining or conquering again. p. 199.

reef (rēf). A narrow ridge of coral, rocks, or sand at or near the surface of the water. p. 396.

refinery (ri fī′ nər ē). A factory where raw material, such as sugar or oil, is changed or purified. p. 105.

refugee (ref yə jē′). Someone who flees for safety in a time of persecution, war, or disaster. p. 368.

region (rē′ jən). An area of land whose parts have one or more common characteristics. p. 45.

regional specialization (rē′ jə nəl spesh ə lə zā′ shən). An economic activity that is the specialty of a particular region. p. 59.

relief map (ri lēf′ map). A map that shows the elevation of land on the earth's surface. p. 22.

renewable resource (ri nü′ ə bəl ri sôrs′). A resource that can be replaced by nature or by people. p. 59.

reserves (ri zėrvz′). A supply of fuel or other things that are available or that have been set aside for future use. p. 80.

reservoir (rez′ ər vwär). A place where water is collected and stored for use. p. 176.

revenue (rev′ ə nü). Income. p. 270.

revolution (rev ə lü′ shən). One complete turn of the earth around the sun. p. 38.

rift valley (rift val′ ē). A canyonlike hollow that was made when the earth's surface pulled apart. p. 266.

river (riv′ ər). A long, narrow body of water that flows through the land. p. 9.

rotation (rō tā′ shən). One complete turn of the earth on its axis. The earth takes 24 hours to complete one rotation. p. 42.

Sahel (sə hel′). A semidesert area in Africa that lies south of the Sahara and that has severe droughts. p. 316.

Sanskrit (san′ skrit). The ancient language of India that was used to write the religious songs and scriptures of the *Vedas,* sacred books to most Indians today. Sanskrit is similar to some of the modern Indian languages. p. 364.

satellite (sat′ə līt). **1.** An artificial object launched by rocket into an orbit around the earth or other planet. p. 29. **2.** A country that claims to be independent but is actually controlled by another country. p. 218.

saturate (sach′ə rāt). To fill completely. p. 80.

savanna (sə van′ ə). A treeless grassland, or a grassland with scattered trees and bushes, especially in tropical lands that have seasonal rains. p. 46.

scale (skāl). The relationship between distance on a map and distance on the earth. Also, the line, drawn on maps, that shows this relationship. p. 11.

Scandinavian Shield (skan də nā′ vē ən shēld). The oldest landform region of Scandinavia, a flat land of hard rocks and thin soils. It covers most of Sweden and all of Finland. p. 159.

sea (sē). A large body of salt water, smaller than an ocean. p. 8.

secede (si sēd′). To withdraw formally from an organization or nation. p. 236.

self-sufficient (self sə fish′ ənt). Able to produce needed goods, not having to import necessities. p. 338.

separatist (sep′ ə rə tist). A person who wants political independence for a part of a country. p. 84.

serf (sėrf). A person who lived and worked on a manor. Serfs could not leave the manor without the permission of the lord of the manor. p. 154.

Shiite (shē′ īt). A branch of the Islamic religion. About one fifth of the world's Moslems are Shiite Moslems. Most people in present-day Iran and Iraq are Shiites, followers of the Shiite faith. p. 268.

shogun (shō′ gun). A military ruler of early Japan. p. 353.

silt (silt). Very fine pieces of soil and ground stone carried by moving water or wind. p. 339.

sisal (sis′ əl). A fiber used in making rope and twine. p. 313.

slash-and-burn farming (slash′ ən bėrn′ fär′ ming). A system of farming in which farmers cut, or slash, tree branches and other plant growth and let the vegetation dry so that it will burn. Then they burn the dried vegetation, clearing the ground and enriching the soil at the same time. After this, they plant crops. p. 321.

smelting (smel′ ting). The process of separating a metal from other materials in its ore. p. 62.

socialism (sō′ shə liz əm). A system of government ownership of land and industry. p. 235.

social reform (sō′ shəl ri fôrm′). A change intended for the good of the people. p. 354.

Solidarity (sol ə dar′ ə tē). A Polish labor organization that was independent of the Communist government of Poland. p. 218.

solstice (sol′ stis). Either of the two times in the year when the sun's most direct rays are as far north or south of the Equator as they will ever be. p. 40.

spawn (spôn). To produce or deposit eggs, referring to fish and other animals growing or living in water. p. 62.

species (spē' shēz). Groups of plants or animals that are alike. p. 415.

steppe (step). One of the belts of grassland in Europe and Asia, somewhat like the prairie of North America. There are also steppes in Africa. p. 46.

strait (strāt). A narrow waterway that connects two larger bodies of water. p. 9.

subcontinent (sub kon' tə nənt). A landmass of great size, but smaller than the continents. p. 360.

submerged (səb mėrjd'). Covered with water. p. 396.

subsistence farmer (səb sis' təns fär' mər). A farmer with only enough land to grow crops for family use. p. 105.

sugarcane (shȯg' ər kān). Plant with a tall stalk that is used to make sugar. p. 105.

Sunni (sȯn' ē). A branch of the Islamic religion. Most Moslems are Sunni Moslems. p. 268.

surplus (sėr' pləs). The amount over and above what is needed or used. p. 456.

sustained yield (sə stānd' yēld). A steady amount of a crop produced each year, often helped by controlled harvesting. p. 59.

Swahili (swä hē' lē). A language of eastern and central Africa. Swahili has many Arabic, Persian, and Indian words. p. 296.

symbol (sim' bəl). Something that stands for, or suggests, something else. p. 14.

table (tā' bəl). A list of facts arranged in columns and rows to show some relationship. p. 31.

tableland (tā' bəl land). A plateau. p. 334.

taiga (tī' gə). The great coniferous forest region of the northern and western Soviet Union. p. 231.

tannin (tan' ən). A plant extract used to tan leather. p. 136.

Taoism (tou' iz əm). A religion based on the teachings of the philosopher Lao-Tzu. Taoism urges people to live in harmony with nature. p. 341.

tariff (tar' if). A tax on imports or, in some countries, on exports. p. 179.

taro (tä' rō). A starchy root grown in the Pacific Islands. Taro is pounded to make a food paste, which Hawaiians call poi. p. 406.

tar sands (tär sandz). Beds of sand saturated with thick, sticky oil. p. 80.

technology (tek nol' ə jē). The knowledge and skill people use to make things. p. 172.

temperate (tem' pər it). Not extreme. A temperate climate is neither extremely hot or cold nor extremely wet or dry. p. 41.

temperature (tem' pər ə chər). The amount of heat or cold as measured on a given scale, such as the Fahrenheit scale or the Celsius scale. p. 34.

temporary migration (tem' pə rer ē mī grā' shən). The moving from one place to settle for a limited time in another place. p. 197.

terrace (ter' is). Flat shelves of land, arranged like wide steps on a mountainside. p. 128.

textile mill (teks' təl mil). A factory where fibers and yarns are turned into cloth. p. 105.

time line (tīm līn). A special scale drawing that tells when events took place and shows the length of time between events. p. 35.

tourism (tu̇r' iz əm). The industry that serves people who travel for pleasure. p. 173.

tourist (tu̇r' ist). Someone who travels to a place on vacation. p. 107.

toxic (tok' sik). Poisonous. p. 447.

trade deficit (trād def' ə sit). An unfavorable balance of trade that results when a nation imports more than it exports. p. 382.

tradition (trə dish' ən). The way in which people have done things for years and years. p. 29.

tributary (trib' yə ter ē). A stream or river that flows into a larger body of water. p. 124.

Tropic of Cancer (trop' ik ov kan' sər). A line of latitude that circles the earth at 23 1/2° north latitude. p. 40.

Tropic of Capricorn (trop' ik ov kap' rə kôrn). A line of latitude that circles the earth at 23 1/2° south latitude. p. 41.

tropics (trop' iks). The zone between the Tropic of Capricorn and the Tropic of Cancer. p. 126.

trust territory (trust ter' ə tôr ē). A territory, region, or small country administered by another country for the United Nations. p. 405.

tsar (czar) (zär). The title of rulers of the Russian empire. p. 234.

tundra (tun' drə). A rolling plain without trees, found in the Arctic area of the high latitudes. p. 48.

tungsten (tung' stən). A hard, heavy metal that is often mixed with steel to create a material hard enough to use in the making of machine tools. Tungsten is also used to make the filaments in electric light bulbs. p. 198.

typhoid (tī' foid). A serious bacterial disease that results in fever, weakness, and, in severe cases, death. Typhoid is caused by contact with contaminated food or water. Strict sanitary measures are necessary to prevent typhoid. p. 441.

typhoon (tī fün'). A tropical storm occurring in the region of the Philippines or the China Sea, accompanied by strong winds and heavy rain. p. 350.

uranium (yù rā' nē əm). A hard, very heavy radioactive metal found in pitchblende, which is used to produce atomic energy. p. 81.

valley (val' ē). A long, low place between hills or mountains. p. 9.

vegetation (vej ə tā' shən). Plant growth. p. 45.

veterinarian (vet ər ə nār' ē ən). A doctor who treats animals. p. 56.

veto (vē' tō). The right to reject bills passed by a lawmaking body or to refuse to take action on a matter. p. 463.

vineyard (vin' yərd). A place where grapes are grown. p. 170.

volcanic ash (vol kan' ik ash). The result of volcanic eruptions, which adds minerals to the soil and aids fertility. p. 119.

volcanic island (vol kan' ik ī' lənd). An island formed by volcanic eruptions that have piled lava high above the surface of the water. p. 396.

volcano (vol kā' nō). An opening in the earth, usually at the top of a cone-shaped hill or mountain, out of which gases, rock, ashes, and lava may pour from time to time. Also, the hill around such an opening. p. 30.

Walloon (wo lün'). One of a group of people inhabiting chiefly the southern part of Belgium. p. 177.

weather (weŦH' ər). The condition of the air at a certain time, in terms of precipitation, temperature, and other factors. p. 23.

zinc (zingk). A shiny, blueish-white metal that is applied to other metals, such as iron and steel, to prevent them from rusting. p. 78.

Zionists (zī' ə nists). People who wanted to make a Jewish homeland in Palestine. People who support the modern state of Israel. p. 276.

EQUATORIAL: SINGAPORE, SINGAPORE

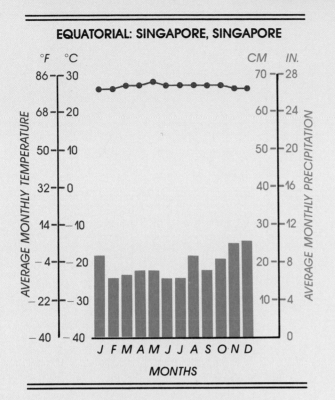

SAVANNA: BOMBAY, INDIA

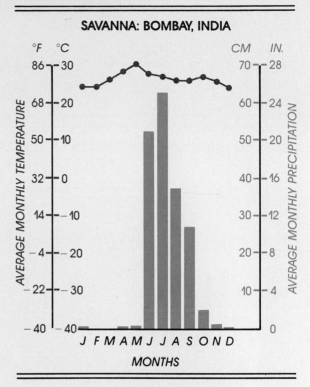

DESERT: CAIRO, EGYPT

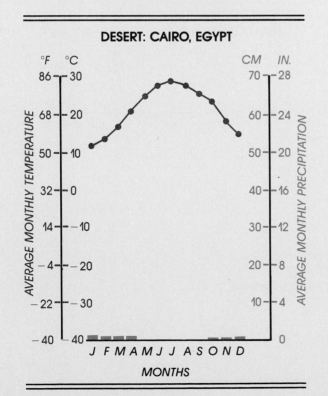

SEMIDESERT: TEHRAN, IRAN

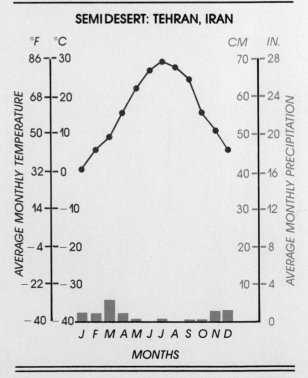

CLIMATE DATA

MEDITERRANEAN: JERUSALEM, ISRAEL

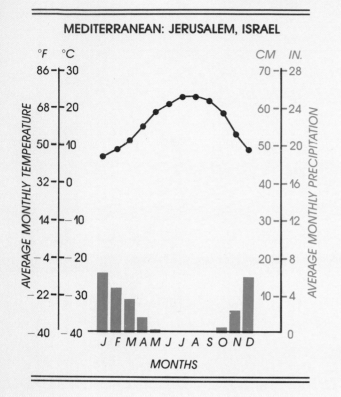

HUMID SUBTROPICAL: TOKYO, JAPAN

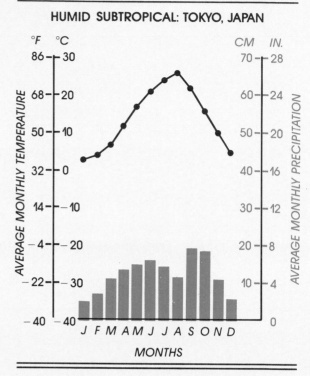

WEST COAST MARINE: VANCOUVER, CANADA

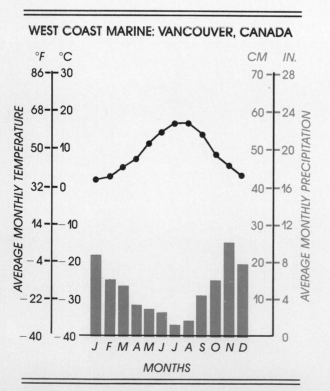

HUMID CONTINENTAL: WARSAW, POLAND

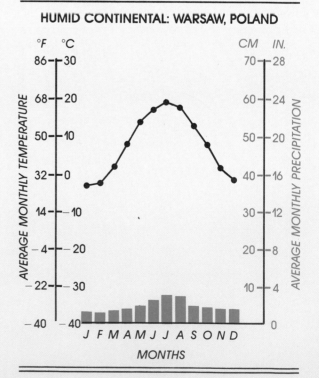

CLIMATE DATA

SUBARCTIC: OKHOTSK, SOVIET UNION

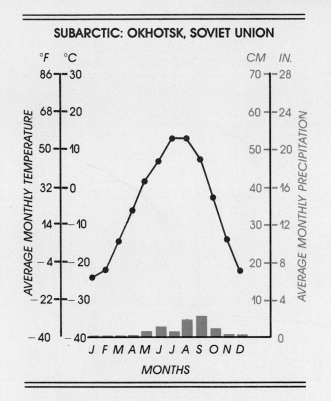

TUNDRA: IVIGTUT, GREENLAND

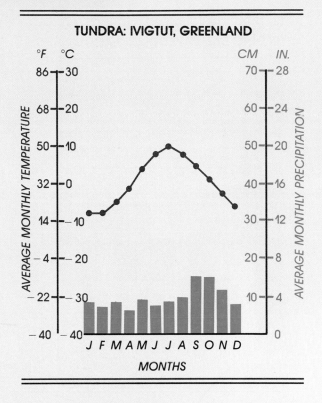

ICECAP: LITTLE AMERICA, ANTARCTICA

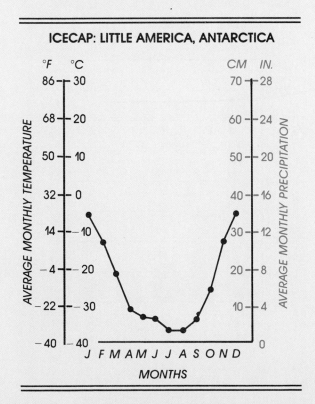

MOUNTAIN: BOGOTÁ, COLOMBIA

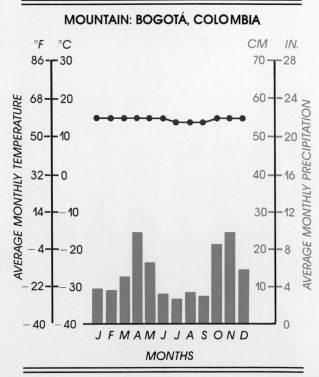

LEADING BARLEY-PRODUCING COUNTRIES

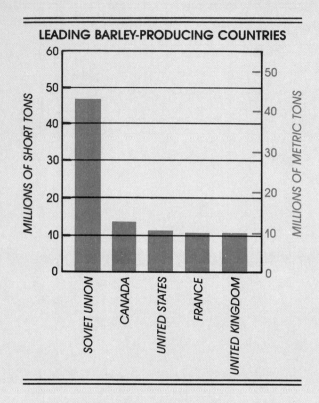

LEADING CACAO (COCOA) BEAN-PRODUCING COUNTRIES

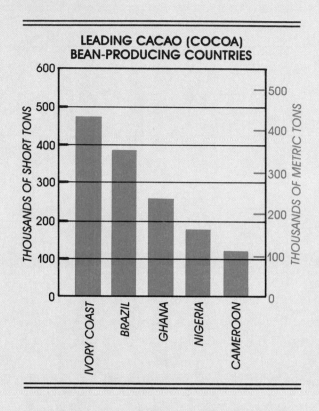

LEADING CATTLE-PRODUCING COUNTRIES

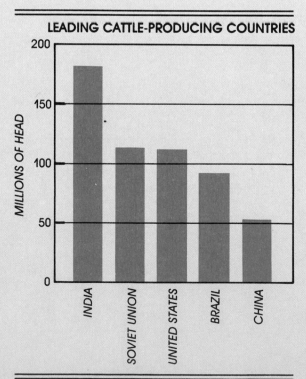

LEADING COFFEE-PRODUCING COUNTRIES

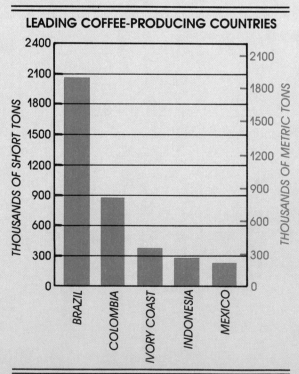

AGRICULTURAL DATA

LEADING CORN-PRODUCING COUNTRIES

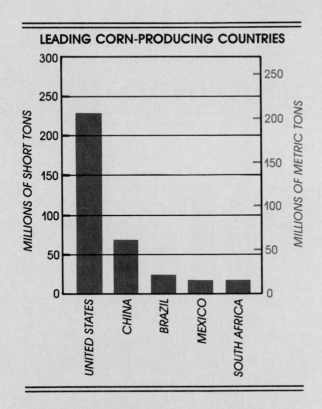

MILLIONS OF SHORT TONS / MILLIONS OF METRIC TONS

UNITED STATES, CHINA, BRAZIL, MEXICO, SOUTH AFRICA

LEADING COTTON-PRODUCING COUNTRIES

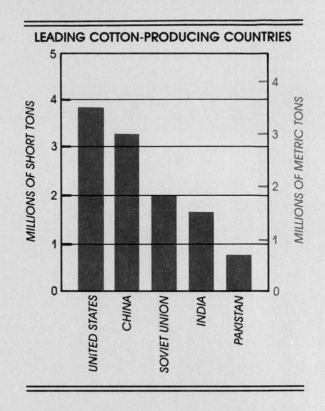

MILLIONS OF SHORT TONS / MILLIONS OF METRIC TONS

UNITED STATES, CHINA, SOVIET UNION, INDIA, PAKISTAN

LEADING FISH-PRODUCING COUNTRIES

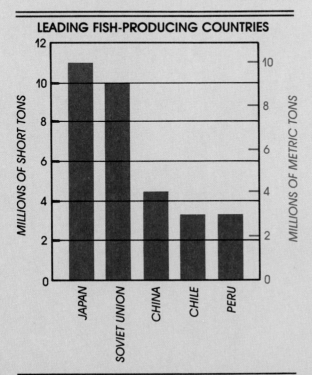

MILLIONS OF SHORT TONS / MILLIONS OF METRIC TONS

JAPAN, SOVIET UNION, CHINA, CHILE, PERU

LEADING POTATO-PRODUCING COUNTRIES

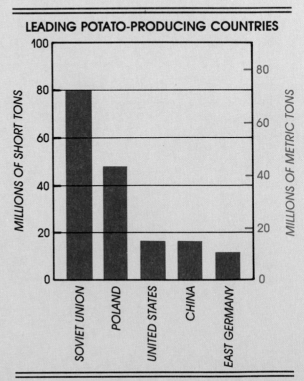

MILLIONS OF SHORT TONS / MILLIONS OF METRIC TONS

SOVIET UNION, POLAND, UNITED STATES, CHINA, EAST GERMANY

AGRICULTURAL DATA

LEADING RICE-PRODUCING COUNTRIES

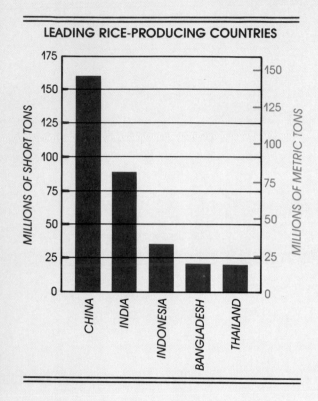

MILLIONS OF SHORT TONS (left axis): 0, 25, 50, 75, 100, 125, 150, 175

MILLIONS OF METRIC TONS (right axis): 0, 25, 50, 75, 100, 125, 150

CHINA, INDIA, INDONESIA, BANGLADESH, THAILAND

LEADING TEA-PRODUCING COUNTRIES

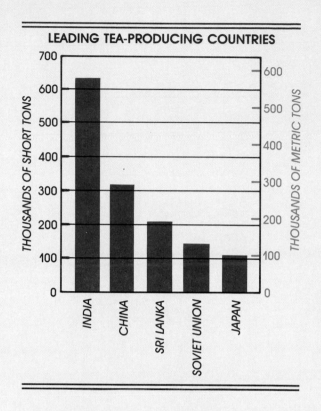

THOUSANDS OF SHORT TONS (left axis): 0, 100, 200, 300, 400, 500, 600, 700

THOUSANDS OF METRIC TONS (right axis): 0, 100, 200, 300, 400, 500, 600

INDIA, CHINA, SRI LANKA, SOVIET UNION, JAPAN

LEADING TOBACCO-PRODUCING COUNTRIES

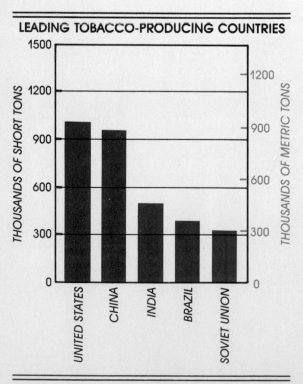

THOUSANDS OF SHORT TONS (left axis): 0, 300, 600, 900, 1200, 1500

THOUSANDS OF METRIC TONS (right axis): 0, 300, 600, 900, 1200

UNITED STATES, CHINA, INDIA, BRAZIL, SOVIET UNION

LEADING WOOL-PRODUCING COUNTRIES

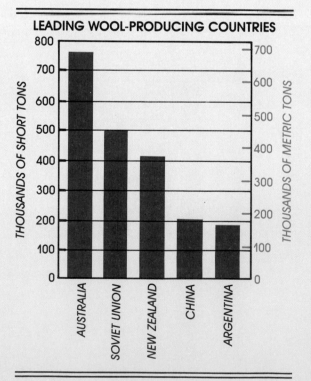

THOUSANDS OF SHORT TONS (left axis): 0, 100, 200, 300, 400, 500, 600, 700, 800

THOUSANDS OF METRIC TONS (right axis): 0, 100, 200, 300, 400, 500, 600, 700

AUSTRALIA, SOVIET UNION, NEW ZEALAND, CHINA, ARGENTINA

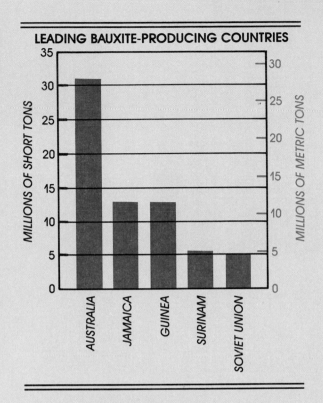

LEADING BAUXITE-PRODUCING COUNTRIES

MILLIONS OF SHORT TONS
MILLIONS OF METRIC TONS

AUSTRALIA, JAMAICA, GUINEA, SURINAM, SOVIET UNION

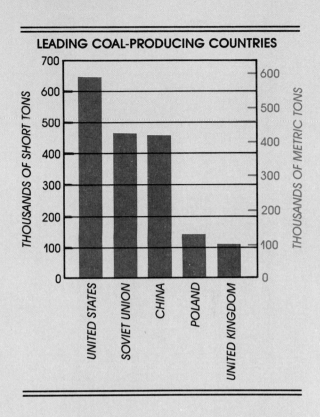

LEADING COAL-PRODUCING COUNTRIES

THOUSANDS OF SHORT TONS
THOUSANDS OF METRIC TONS

UNITED STATES, SOVIET UNION, CHINA, POLAND, UNITED KINGDOM

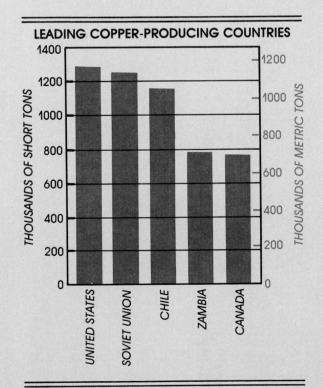

LEADING COPPER-PRODUCING COUNTRIES

THOUSANDS OF SHORT TONS
THOUSANDS OF METRIC TONS

UNITED STATES, SOVIET UNION, CHILE, ZAMBIA, CANADA

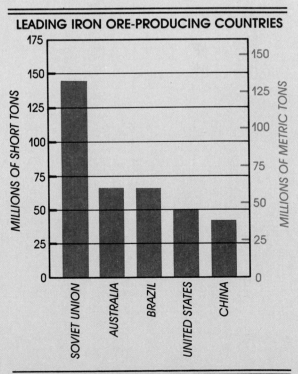

LEADING IRON ORE-PRODUCING COUNTRIES

MILLIONS OF SHORT TONS
MILLIONS OF METRIC TONS

SOVIET UNION, AUSTRALIA, BRAZIL, UNITED STATES, CHINA

LEADING LEAD-PRODUCING COUNTRIES

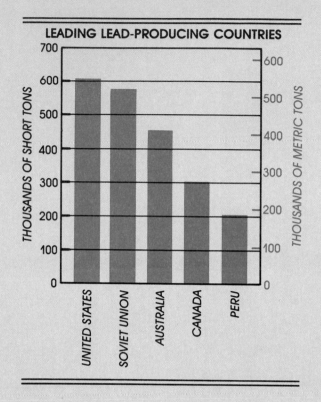

LEADING STEEL-PRODUCING COUNTRIES

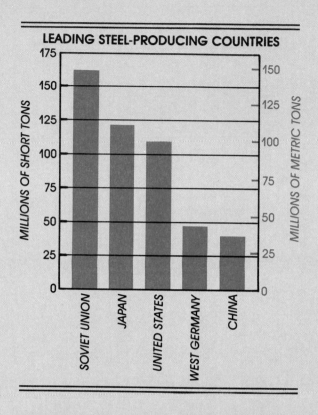

LEADING TIN-PRODUCING COUNTRIES

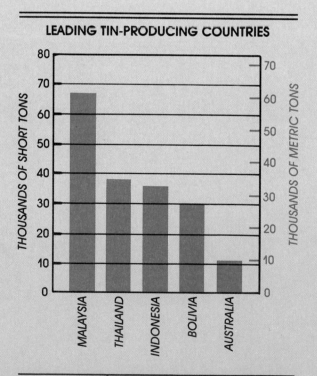

LEADING ZINC-PRODUCING COUNTRIES

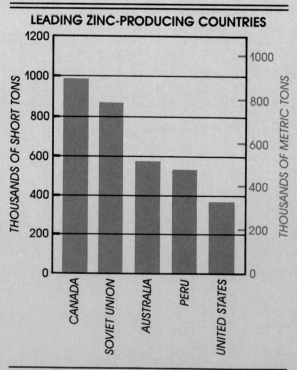

LANDFORM DATA

THE WORLD: LARGEST ISLANDS IN AREA

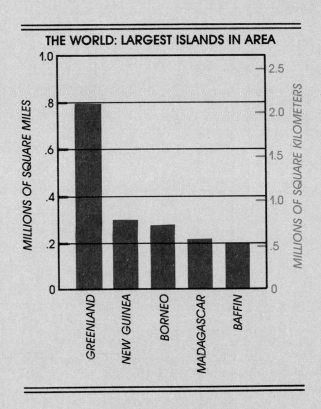

THE WORLD: LARGEST NATURAL LAKES IN AREA

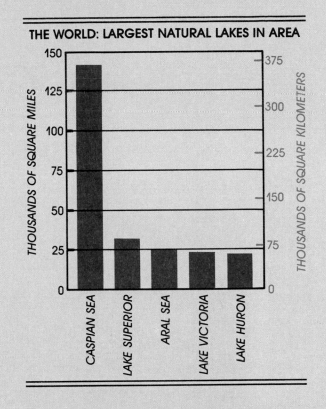

THE WORLD: LONGEST RIVERS

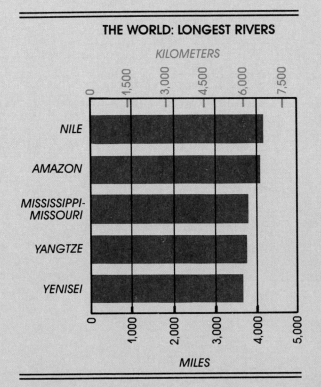

THE WORLD: LARGEST SEAS

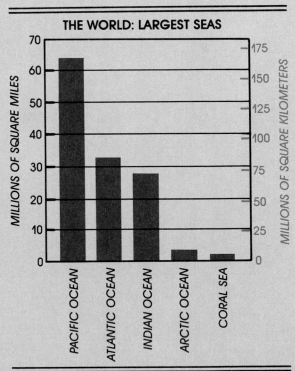

POPULATION DATA

COUNTRIES WITH LARGEST POPULATIONS

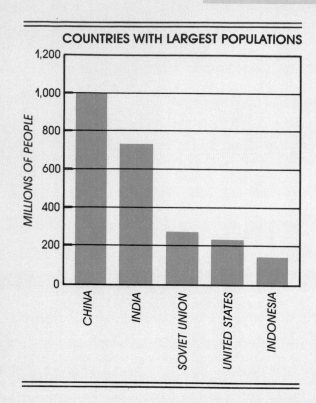

MILLIONS OF PEOPLE

1,200 — 1,000 — 800 — 600 — 400 — 200 — 0

CHINA, INDIA, SOVIET UNION, UNITED STATES, INDONESIA

COUNTRIES WITH HIGHEST PER CAPITA GROSS NATIONAL PRODUCT

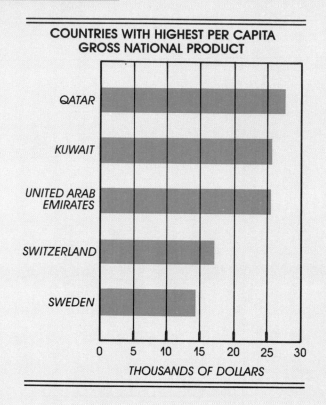

QATAR, KUWAIT, UNITED ARAB EMIRATES, SWITZERLAND, SWEDEN

0   5   10   15   20   25   30

THOUSANDS OF DOLLARS

COUNTRIES WITH LONGEST AND SHORTEST LIFE EXPECTANCIES AT BIRTH

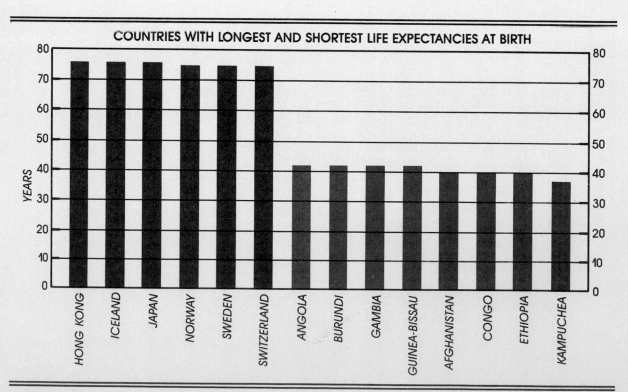

YEARS

80 — 70 — 60 — 50 — 40 — 30 — 20 — 10 — 0

HONG KONG, ICELAND, JAPAN, NORWAY, SWEDEN, SWITZERLAND, ANGOLA, BURUNDI, GAMBIA, GUINEA-BISSAU, AFGHANISTAN, CONGO, ETHIOPIA, KAMPUCHEA

INDEX

Creole language, 116
Crete, 203
Cuba, 110, 116
Culture
    Caribbean, 113
    Central American, 113
    Mexican, 100–101
Cyclades, 203
Cyprus, 204
Cyrillic alphabet, 233
Czechoslovakia, 219–220
Czechs, 219

D

Dairy farming, 60, 74, 171, 426
Damascus, Syria, 272
Dampier, William, 418
Dams, 225
Danube River, 190, 191, 225
Dardanelles, 273
Darwin, Australia, 422
Date palm, 256
Dead Sea, 266
Deccan plateau, 362–363
Deciduous trees, 47
Delta, 6
Demilitarized zone, 344
Denmark, 159, 164
Depletion, 62
Desert climate, 46
Detroit, Michigan, 69
Developing countries, 96, 131
Dialects, 182, 188
Diamonds, 137, 307, 310
Dikes, 176–177
Dinaric Alps, 221, 224
Distortion, of maps, 20
Dnieper River, 230
Dominican Republic, 117
Dominion of Canada, 82
Don River, 230
Doña Marina, 101
Donets Basin, 238, 241
Double cropping, 336
Double Eagle II, 4–5
Drake, Francis, 114
Dresden, East Germany, 216
Drought, 323–324
Dry farming, 256

Dry rice, 380
Dual economy, 131
Dublin, Ireland, 148
Dutch East India Company, 308
Dutch Guiana, 132
Dynasties, 340

E

Earth
    climate regions of, 45–48
    oceans of, 43–44
    seasons of, 38, 40–41
    temperature zones of, 41
    time zones of, 42–43
Earthquakes, 120, 348
East Africa, 296–298
East and Equatorial Africa
    East Africa, 296–298
    Equatorial Africa, 299–301
    land and water in, 292, 294
    resources of, 294–295
East Berlin, East Germany, 214
Easter Island, 401
Eastern Europe, 214–225
Eastern Ghats, 363
Eastern Hemisphere, 17
Eastern Orthodox Church, 203
East Germany, 182, 214–216
Echidna, 414
Economic activity, 59
Ecuador, 133
Education
    in Africa, 298
    in Japan, 354, 356–357
    in Mexico, 107
    in the Soviet Union, 244
Egypt, 254, 259–261
Einstein, Albert, 186
Ejidos, 104
Elbe River, 214
Elburz Mountains, 266
Electricity, 65–66
Elevation, 22
Elizabeth II (Queen of Great Britain), 82

El Salvador, 120
Enclosure Movement, 154–155
Energy resources, 80
England
    in the Caribbean islands, 114, 117
    in the Pacific Islands, 402
    See also British Isles; Great Britain.
English language, 84, 148, 155
Equal-area projection, 20–21
Equator, 16–17, 19, 46–47, 126
Equatorial Africa, 299–301
Equatorial climate, 46
Equinox, 41
Eskimos, 78
    See also Inuit.
Ethiopia, 297
Ethnic groups, 224, 237
Euphrates River, 266, 268
Europe, 6
European Economic Community (EEC), 464–465
European Russia, 228, 231
Europeans, 82, 102, 258, 269, 308, 320, 342, 378, 401, 417–419
Everest, Mount, 360
Exotic animals, 128
Exports, 96, 131, 133–134, 137, 187, 301, 355

F

Factories, 103–104, 107, 241, 309, 355, 369–370, 421
Falkland Islands, 124
Farming
    in Africa, 256, 259–260, 309, 320–321, 323
    in Australia, 420
    in Canada, 74, 77
    in the Caribbean, 113
    in Central America, 120
    in China, 336, 343
    in Eastern Europe, 217–218, 220

in India, 369
in the Mediterranean, 196
in Mexico, 105–106
in the Middle East, 268
in the Pacific Islands, 404, 407
in Southeast Asia, 380–381
in Southern Africa, 309
in the Soviet Union, 242–243
in the United States, 58–61
in Western Europe, 170–171
See also Plantations.
Federal government, 82
Federal Republic of Germany. See West Germany.
Fellahin, 257
Fertilizers, 134
Fiji, 404
Finland, 159, 163, 165
Fish canning, 62
Fish farms, 351
Fishing, 60, 62, 74, 126, 134, 163, 351, 407
Five-year plans, 239, 243
Fjord, 6, 161
Flat map, 20
Flemings, 177–178
Flood plain, 339
Florence, Italy, 200, 201
Florida, 59
Flour mills, 107
Fodder, 221
Food Processing, 426–427
Ford, Henry, 64
Forecast, 448
Forests, 5, 9, 106, 164, 231, 238
Forum, 202
France, 169
    agriculture in, 170–171
    Caribbean colonies of, 116
    economy of, 171–173
    history of, 168
    Paris, 171–172, 174
    rule of Algeria by, 258, 262–263
Frankfurt, 184
Franks, 168, 170
Fraser River, 78

PICTURE INDEX

CREDITS

Unit 1   2: Dan De Wilde for Silver Burdett.

Chapter 1   5: Vanthey/Sygma. 6: t. Glenn Short/Bruce Coleman; m.b. R.N. Mariscal/Bruce Coleman; b. Björn Bölstad/Peter Arnold, Inc. 7: m.t. © Harald Sund; m.b. Lawrence Lowry. 8: t. Lawrence Lowry; m.t. © Harald Sund; m.b. DiMaggio-Kalish/Peter Arnold, Inc.; b. © Harald Sund. 9: t. C. Haagner/Bruce Coleman; m.t. © 1985 Loren McIntyre/Woodfin Camp & Associates; b. Klaus D. Francke/Peter Arnold, Inc. 10: U.S. Department of Agriculture. 12: Courtesy R.R. Donnelley Cartographic Services. 14: Air Photographics Inc. 15: Photo Science, Inc., Gaithersburg, Maryland.

Chapter 2   27: t.l. John Elk/Bruce Coleman; m.l. D.A. Davidson/Tom Stack & Associates; b.l. Eugene Luttenberg/Bruce Coleman; t.r. Yoram Kahana/Peter Arnold, Inc.; m.r. S.J. Chamola/Taurus Photos; b.r. © 1985 Kal Muller/ Woodfin Camp & Associates. 28: t. Don Crawford/Atoz Images; b. Bruno Zehnder/Peter Arnold, Inc. 29: NASA. 30: r. © Krafft-Explorer/Photo Researchers, Inc.

Chapter 3   39: Karl Kernberger/Atoz Images; inset © David Brill. 48: Nancy Simmerman/Atoz Images.

Unit 2   52: Dan De Wilde for Silver Burdett.

Chapter 4   57: t. Jonathan Wright/Bruce Coleman; b. Courtesy Swift Independent Packing Company. 60: l. © Georg Gerster/Photo Researchers, Inc.; r. ©Arthur Tress/Photo Researchers, Inc. 63: Mark Sherman/Bruce Coleman. 66: Brian Parker/Tom Stack & Associates. 67: Keith Gunnar/Bruce Coleman. 69: Phil Degginger/Bruce Coleman.

Chapter 5   73: © Paolo Koch/Photo Researchers, Inc. 77: © Russ Kinne/ Photo Researchers, Inc. 81: © G.R. Roberts/Photo Researchers, Inc. 84: George Hunter.

Unit 3   88: Dan De Wilde for Silver Burdett.

Chapter 6   97: © Victor Englebert/Photo Researchers, Inc. 106: R. Bunge/ Bruce Coleman.

Chapter 7   111: Nicholas DeVore III/Bruce Coleman. 115: S.L. Craig/Bruce Coleman. 116: The Bettmann Archive. 120: K. Kummels/Shostal Associates. 121: The Bettmann Archive.

Chapter 8   125: © F. Gohier/Photo Researchers, Inc. 129: Jacques Jangoux/ Peter Arnold, Inc. 132: © Georg Gerster/Photo Researchers, Inc. 133: Norman O. Tomalin/Bruce Coleman. 135: © Lisl Steiner/Photo Researchers, Inc. 136: Ted Gruen/Bruce Coleman. 138: © Susan McCartney/Photo Researchers, Inc.

Unit 4   142: Dan De Wilde for Silver Burdett.

Chapter 9   149: J. Messerschmidt/Bruce Coleman. 150: Wedigo Fershland/ Bruce Coleman. 151: © 1985 Anthony Howarth/Woodfin Camp & Associates. 153: Art Resource. 154: © Macdonald Educational Limited. 157: Spencer Swanger/Tom Stack & Associates. 158: M. Freeman/Bruce Coleman. 160: F. Erize/Bruce Coleman. 161: J. Messerschmidt/Bruce Coleman. 163: John Brownlie/Bruce Coleman. 164: J. Messerschmidt/Bruce Coleman.

Chapter 10   169: Norman Thompson/Taurus Photos. 173: t. J. Messerschmidt/Bruce Coleman; b. Mel Baughman/Bruce Coleman. 174: R. Thompson/Taurus Photos. 175: D. Forbert/Shostel Associates. 176: Lee Foster/ Bruce Coleman. 178: t. J. Messerschmidt/Bruce Coleman; b. Vance Henry/ Taurus Photos. 179: J.P. Conrardy/Taurus Photos.

Chapter 11   183: E. Streichan/Shostal Associates. 187: E.R. Degginger. 189: J. Messerschmidt/Bruce Coleman. 191: Eric Carle/Shostal Associates.

Chapter 12   195: Steve Vidler/Leo de Wys, Inc. 196: Bob Krist/Leo de Wys, Inc. 200: Jonathan Blair/Black Star. 202: Everett Johnson/Leo de Wys, Inc. 204: Jessica Ehlers/Bruce Coleman.

Unit 5   208: Dan De Wilde for Silver Burdett. 212: © 1983 Rhoda Baer/ Folio.

Chapter 13   215: A. Tessore/Shostal Associates. 216: ©Bernard Wolff/Photo Researchers, Inc. 219: P. Pontoni/Bruce Coleman. 220: C. Niedenthal/ Black Star. 221: © Laszlo Hege/Photo Researchers, Inc. 222: Peter Schmid/ Shostal Associates. 224: © Susan McCartney/Photo Researchers, Inc. 225: © Paolo Koch/Photo Researchers, Inc.

Chapter 14   229: Bernard Silberstein/Shostal Associates. 230: Jonathan Wright/Bruce Coleman. 231: Shostal Associates. 233: Plessner International/The Stock Shop. 234: Tom Tracy/The Stock Shop. 237: © 1985 Juha Jormanainen/Woodfin Camp & Associates. 238: © 1985 Howard Sochurek/Woodfin Camp & Associates. 241: Irving Shapiro/The Stock Shop. 242: Shostal Associates. 243: Kurt Scholz/Shostal Associates. 244: J. Messerschmidt/The Stock Shop.

Unit 6   248: Dan De Wilde for Silver Burdett. 249: b. ©Georg Gerster/Photo Researchers, Inc.

Chapter 15   255: © Kazuyoshi Nomachi/Photo Researchers, Inc. 258: t. Giorgio Ricatto/Shostal Associates; b. L. Garbison/Shostal Associates. 261: © Mario Fantin/Photo Researchers, Inc. 263: Bruno Barbey/Magnum.

Chapter 16   267: © Louis Goldman/Photo Researchers, Inc. 268: Jonathan Wright/Bruce Coleman. 269: © Mehmet Biber/Photo Researchers, Inc. 272: l. © Stephanie Dinkins/Photo Researchers, Inc.; r. Norman O. Tomalin/ Bruce Coleman. 274: © Paolo Koch/Photo Researchers, Inc. 277: © Louis Goldman/Photo Researchers, Inc. 278: Dankwart Von Knobloch/Shostal Associates.

Unit 7   282: Dan De Wilde for Silver Burdett.

Chapter 17   293: M.P. Kahl/Bruce Coleman. 296: © John Moss/Photo Researchers, Inc. 299: © Georg Gerster/Photo Researchers, Inc. 300: Historical Pictures Service, Chicago.

Chapter 18   305: M.P. Kahl/Bruce Coleman. 306: Keith Gunnar/Bruce Coleman. 309: W. Hodge/Peter Arnold, Inc. 310: Dicks Blum/Peter Arnold, Inc. 313: Giorgio Ricatto/Shostal Associates.

Chapter 19   317: Jacques Jangoux/Peter Arnold, Inc.; inset © Georg Gerster/ Photo Researchers, Inc. 319, 322: © Georg Gerster/Photo Researchers, Inc. 324: D. Waugh/Peter Arnold, Inc.

Unit 8   328: Dan De Wilde for Silver Burdett.

Chapter 20   335, 338: Kurt Scholz/Shostal Associates. 340: A. Tessore/ Shostal Associates. 341: © Georg Holton/Photo Researchers, Inc. 342, 343: © Paolo Koch/Photo Researchers, Inc. 345: Harvey Lloyd/Peter Arnold, Inc.

Chapter 21   349: D.&J. Heaton/The Stock Shop. 350: Jerry Cooke for Sports Illustrated, © Time Inc. 351: W.H. Hodge/Peter Arnold, Inc. 352: Earl Luby/Shostal Associates. 353: Historical Pictures Service, Chicago. 354. Brown Brothers. 355: D. Forbest/Shostal Associates.

Chapter 22   361: © Bernard Wolff/Photo Researchers, Inc. 362: © Farrell Grehan/Photo Researchers, Inc. 365: D. Waugh/Peter Arnold, Inc. 366: Robert Frerck/Odyssey Productions. 368: © Brian Brake/Photo Researchers, Inc. 369: Jacques Jangoux/Peter Arnold, Inc. 370: Shostal Associates.

Chapter 23   375: © George Holton/Photo Researchers, Inc. 378: Manley Photo/Shostal Associates. 379: Historical Pictures Service, Chicago. 380: Shostal Associates. 382: Kurt Scholz/Shostal Associates. 384: l. J. David Day/Shostal Associates; r. Carlos Sanuvo/Bruce Coleman. 385: © Georg Gerster/Photo Researchers, Inc. 386: Harry Redl for Silver Burdett.

Unit 9   390: Dan De Wilde for Silver Burdett. 391: William Ferguson. 394: Ken Stepnell/Bruce Coleman.

Chapter 24   397: t. Nicholas DeVore III/Bruce Coleman; b. William Ferguson. 399: Roberto Bunge/Bruce Coleman. 401: Nicholas DeVore III/Bruce Coleman. 402: Reproduced from the original in the Mitchell Library, Sydney, Australia. 403: The Bettmann Archive. 405: © 1985 Thomas Nebbia/ Woodfin Camp & Associates. 406: Norman Myers/Bruce Coleman; inset Robert Dunne/Bruce Coleman. 407: William Ferguson. 409: Robert Western/Atoz Images.

Chapter 25   413: Robert Frerck/Odyssey Productions. 414: t. R. Gordon/Atoz Images; b. Ron & Valerie Taylor/Bruce Coleman. 415: b.l. Jen & Des Bartlett/ Bruce Coleman; t.r. Robert Dunne/Bruce Coleman; t.m. Joseph Van Wormer/ Bruce Coleman; b.m. Eric Crichton/Bruce Coleman; b.r. Robert Frerck/Odyssey Productions. 416: Karen Phillips/Atoz Images. 417: Robert Frerck/Odyssey Productions. 418: Tate Gallery, London. 421, 422: Robert Frerck/Odyssey Productions. 423: Andris Apse/Bruce Coleman. 424: Bill Noel Kleeman/ Tom Stack & Associates. 425: David Moore/Black Star. 426: Andris Apse/ Bruce Coleman; inset Robert Frerck/Odyssey Productions. 427, 428: Guy Mannering/Bruce Coleman. 429, 430: Stella Hardee/Bruce Coleman.

Unit 10   434: Dan De Wilde for Silver Burdett. 435: NASA.

Chapter 26   439: William Ferguson. 441: l. CAG/Atoz Images; r. Robert Frerck/Odyssey Productions. 442: Mark Sherman/Bruce Coleman. 443: l. Carol Hughes/Bruce Coleman; r. C.B. & D.W. Frith/Bruce Coleman. 446: t. Cary Wolinsky/Stock, Boston; b. David Schwimmer/Bruce Coleman. 447: Uniphoto/Bruce Coleman. 448: Tom Myers/Atoz Images. 449: David Madison/Bruce Coleman. 450: Jonathan Wright/Bruce Coleman. 451: l. Bruno Zehnder/Peter Arnold, Inc.; r. Cary Wolinsky/Stock, Boston.

Chapter 27   455: Jonathan Atkin/Kay Reese & Associates. 456: Peter Fronk/ Atoz Images. 457: George Rockwin/Bruce Coleman. 458: Robert Rattner/ Kay Reese & Associates. 459: D. Brewster/Bruce Coleman. 460: Walter Imber/Kay Reese & Associates. 461: NASA. 462: Historical Pictures Service, Chicago; inset Culver Pictures. 463: t. Robert Frerck/Odyssey Productions; b. Michel Laurent/Gamma. 466: Manny Millan for Sports Illustrated, © Time Inc.

3 4 5 6 7 8 9 10—RRD—93 92 91 90 89 88 87 86

TEACHER'S ANSWER KEY

A WORLD VIEW

CONTENTS

ANSWER KEY

ANSWER KEY

Where possible, answers for Activities in Chapter Reviews are provided. Some Activities require individualized responses for which specific answers are not appropriate.

UNIT 1 LEARNING ABOUT THE EARTH

CHAPTER 1 Understanding Maps and Globes

ANSWERS FOR CHECKUP QUESTIONS

PAGE 10

1. Physical features are the different shapes of the earth's land and water.

2. The seven continents are Africa, Antarctica, Asia, Australia, Europe, North America, and South America.

The four oceans of the world are the Pacific Ocean, the Atlantic Ocean, the Indian Ocean, and the Arctic Ocean.

About three fourths of the earth's surface is covered by ocean.

3. An island is a body of land with water all around it. A peninsula is a stretch of land with water nearly all the way around it.

An ocean is larger than a sea.

A gulf is a part of an ocean or sea that pushes inland. A harbor is a protected body of water, often protected by an arm of land lying between the harbor and a larger body of water, such as an ocean or a sea.

A mountain is a piece of land rising steeply from the land around it. A plain is an almost level area.

A river is a long, narrow body of water that flows through the land. A strait is a narrow waterway that connects two larger bodies of water.

4. A canyon is a very deep valley with very steep sides. A fjord is a long, narrow, often deep inlet of the sea lying between steep cliffs. A delta is a low plain built up by mud and sand deposited at the mouth of a river. An isthmus is a narrow strip of land connecting two larger bodies of land. A lake is a body of water with land all around it.

PAGE 19

1. The scale on a map tells us that a certain number of inches on a map stands for a certain number of feet or miles on the earth. Three different ways to show map scale are in words, as a fraction or a ratio, and by a straight line with distances marked off on it.

2. Lines of latitude measure distance north and south of the Equator. Lines of longitude measure distance east and west of the Prime Meridian.

3. The letter N or S must be used after a degree of latitude because it tells whether a place is in the Northern or the Southern Hemisphere. The letter E or W must be used after a degree of longitude because it tells whether a place is in the Eastern or the Western Hemisphere.

PAGE 23

1. The Equator is a great circle because it divides the earth into the Northern Hemisphere and the Southern Hemisphere.

2. The four features of the earth's surface that can be shown correctly together on a globe but not on a flat map are shape, size, direction, and distance.

3. The difference between a political map and a relief map is that a political map uses colors to show countries and their boundaries, and a relief map uses colors to show differences in the elevation, or the height, of the land.

4. The elevation of land is measured from sea level, which is the average level of the oceans.

5. Three examples of special-purpose maps are a road map, a weather map, and a natural resource map.

ANSWERS FOR CHAPTER REVIEW

PAGE 24

Vocabulary Quiz

1. b 2. a 3. b 4. b 5. b 6. a 7. b 8. b 9. b 10. a

Review Questions

1. Answers will vary. Each of the following is a physical feature that is made up of water:

a. fjord—a long, narrow, and deep inlet of the sea between steep cliffs

b. gulf—a part of an ocean or a sea that pushes inland

ANSWER KEY

c. harbor—a protected body of water where ships can safely dock

d. lake—a body of water with land all around it

e. ocean—a very large body of salt water

f. river—a long, narrow body of water that flows through the land

g. strait—a narrow waterway connecting two larger bodies of water

2. Answers will vary. Each of the following is a physical feature that is made up of land:

a. canyon—a deep valley with steep sides

b. continent—a huge body of land on the earth's surface

c. delta—a low plain built up by mud and sand deposited at the mouth of a river

d. island—a body of land with water all around it

e. mountain—a piece of land rising steeply from the land around it

f. peninsula—a stretch of land with water nearly all the way around it

g. plain an almost level area that stretches for miles and miles

h. valley—a long, low place between hills or mountains

3. The 0° line of latitude is called the Equator. This parallel divides the earth into the Northern Hemisphere and the Southern Hemisphere.

4. Lines of latitude and longitude are used to locate places by measuring distances in degrees. The crossing lines of latitude and longitude form boxes. The grid system that is formed by these boxes helps us to locate a place when the latitude and longitude is known.

5. A relief map shows mountains, hills, plains, and plateaus as they would be seen from above. A cross section, or profile, is a side view. It shows how an area of land would look if the earth were cut away to sea level.

Activities
3. **a.** Shanghai—Asia
b. Cairo—Africa
c. Mexico City—North America
d. São Paulo—South America
e. Sydney—Australia
f. Moscow—Europe

ANSWERS FOR SKILLS DEVELOPMENT

PAGE 25
Glossary
1. A glacier is a large mass of ice formed from snow on high ground and moving very slowly down a mountainside or along a valley.

2. Weather is the condition of the air at a certain time, in terms of precipitation, temperature, and other factors. Climate is the pattern of weather that a place has over a period of years.

3. Permafrost is permanently frozen ground, sometimes extending to great depths below the earth's surface in very cold regions.

Gazetteer
1. The latitude of Mexico City is 19°N, and its longitude is 99°W.

2. The highest peak in the Alps is Mont Blanc, with an elevation of 15,771 feet (4,807m).

3. The Danube River starts in the Alps.

Atlas: North America
1. The elevation range of the land around the Great Salt Lake is from 1,500 to 3,000 meters.

2. The Red River flows into the Mississippi River.

3. The large mountain range in the eastern part of the United States is the Appalachians.

Atlas: South America
1. The national capital of Chile is Santiago.

2. The Falkland Islands belong to the United Kingdom.

3. The latitude of Quito, the national capital of Ecuador, is 0°, and its longitude is 78°W.

Skills Practice
1. F 2. F 3. F 4. T 5. F

ANSWERS FOR CHECKUP QUESTIONS

PAGE 30

1. Graphics are maps, photographs, diagrams, tables, graphs, and time lines that are used to present information. Each of these six kinds of graphics will be used in this book.

2. Answers will vary. Two things that can be observed in photographs are similarities and differences—including those between people and between places in the world.

3. A diagram explains how a thing works or why something happens.

PAGE 35

1. A table is a list of facts. The information is arranged in columns and rows to show relationships.

2. A pie graph shows the parts of a whole.

3. A bar graph is a kind of graph that uses bars to show information. The facts on bar graphs are easily compared.

4. The advantage of a line graph is that it is generally the best kind of graph for showing how things change over a period of time.

5. Time lines and maps both have a scale. The purpose of a time line is that it tells when events took place and the length of time between events.

ANSWERS FOR CHAPTER REVIEW

PAGE 36

Vocabulary Quiz

1. e **2.** term not on list **3.** f **4.** d **5.** g **6.** h
7. i **8.** c **9.** b **10.** a **11.** term not on list **12.** j

Review Questions

1. Answers will vary. However, pupils should give an explanation that incorporates the following idea.

Ideas, emotions, and information can sometimes be conveyed more effectively by one picture than by many (even a thousand) words.

Also, a picture so often speaks with such beauty and awesomeness that it would take "a thousand words" to express the emotions and thoughts inspired and created by the picture.

2. When a volcano erupts, the following things happen. Melted rock, called magma, is located in the ground under layers of solid rock. Sometimes there is a channel, also called a conduit, from the earth's surface to the magma. The opening of this channel at the earth's surface is known as a crater. Since the magma is under pressure from the layers of solid rock, the magma sometimes pushes its way upward through the conduit and erupts at a central vent and sometimes at side vents, too. Rocks, steam, and gas may be thrown high into the air. Then hot lava may flow down the sides of the volcano.

3. Population density tells how closely together people live in a certain area of land; it is the average number of people for each square mile (or sq km) of land. To find the population density of the United States, you divide the total number of people who live in the United States by the total land area of the United States.

4. The difference between a line graph and a bar graph is that a line graph shows how things change over time and a bar graph shows comparisons.

5. Climate is the pattern of weather that a place has over a period of time.

6. In 1903 the Wright Brothers invented the airplane.

Activity
Answers will vary.

ANSWERS FOR SKILLS DEVELOPMENT

PAGE 37
Skills Practice

1. The center of the solar system is the sun.

2. There are nine planets in the solar system.

3. Mercury is the planet nearest to the sun.

4. Pluto is the planet farthest from the sun.

5. Mars is the fourth planet from the sun.

6. Pluto and Neptune travel in orbits that cross one another.

7. The Asteroid Belt is between Mars and Jupiter.

8. Venus and Mars are nearest the earth.

9. Earth is the planet in the diagram with a moon.

10. Jupiter is the largest planet.

ANSWER KEY

CHAPTER 3 **World Patterns**

ANSWERS FOR CHECKUP QUESTIONS

PAGE 44

1. The earth revolves around the sun in an oval path called an orbit. At the same time that the earth moves around the sun, the earth is rotating on its axis every 24 hours, causing day and night.

2. A solstice is either of the two times in the year when the sun's most direct rays are as far north or south from the Equator as they will ever be. An equinox is either one of two times in the year when the sun's direct rays are over the Equator.

3. The low latitudes (tropics) are generally warm; the middle latitudes (temperate zones) are changeable; the high latitudes (frigid zones) are cool to cold.

4. The earth's rotation from west to east causes differences in time in the United States. The time on the east coast of the country is 3 hours earlier than the time on the west coast. There are four time zones within the 48 contiguous states.

5. The International Date Line is halfway around the world from the Prime Meridian. The International Date Line follows along much of the 180° meridian and marks the spot where a new calendar day begins.

6. The major ocean currents generally move in a circular pattern. The four major oceans of the world are the Atlantic, Pacific, Indian, and Arctic oceans.

PAGE 48

1. Weather is the condition of the atmosphere in a particular place at a particular time. Climate, on the other hand, is the average condition of the weather over a wide area for a period of years.

2. Natural vegetation includes trees, shrubs, grasses, and mosses that were here long before people appeared on the earth. Farmers have planted the crops they grow.

3. Deciduous trees are broad-leaved trees, which lose their leaves in the fall. Deciduous trees are found in the marine climate region. Coniferous trees produce seeds in cones. They are evergreen, since they do not shed their thin, needlelike leaves all at once. Coniferous trees are found in the subarctic climate.

4. The temperatures are not as extreme as in the subarctic climate. The climate is moderated by the oceans. Precipitation is light. A tundra is a barren land. No trees grow, because the ground below the top layer of soil remains frozen.

ANSWERS FOR CHAPTER REVIEW

PAGE 49

Vocabulary Quiz

1. T **2.** F (An equinox is a time of year when the sun's direct rays are over the Equator.) **3.** F (It takes 365¼ days for the earth to make one revolution.) **4.** F (The Tropic of Cancer is a line of latitude located at 23½° north.) **5.** T **6.** F (Economics is the study of how goods and services are used.) **7.** F (Coniferous trees are the natural vegetation of the subarctic climate.) **8.** F (Humidity is the moisture in the air.) **9.** T **10.** T

Review Questions

1. It is winter in the Southern Hemisphere when the South Pole is inclined away from the sun. At the same time the North Pole is inclined towards the sun, so it is summer in the Northern Hemisphere.

2. *Temperate* is a poor name for the climates of the middle latitudes because few places in this zone are really temperate. It would be better to speak of the middle latitudes as being variable, or changeable, in temperature.

3. There are four time zones in the contiguous states of the United States. The United States, all states and possessions, have eight time zones. There are 24 time zones in the world.

4. Oceans and other large bodies of water moderate, or make less severe, the temperatures on nearby land.

5. Weather is closely related to economics because if the weather is good, more goods and services can be produced and used. If the weather is bad, less goods and services can be produced and used.

6. **(a)** Both the equatorial and savanna climates are found in the low latitudes. The temperatures are high throughout the year in both climates. In the equatorial climate, the rain is heavy all year round; in the savanna, rainfall is heavy for only part of the year and very light for the other part. **(b)** Both the desert and the semidesert regions have variable temperatures throughout the year. The desert region gets so little precipitation that little vegetation grows. In the semidesert region, however, enough rain falls to allow short grass to grow. (c) The west coast marine and humid continental climates are usually found in the same latitude. The marine climate region is usually on the western side of continents where the oceans moderate the climate. On the other hand, the humid continental climate is found in the deep interior of a continent or along a continent's eastern edge. The humid continental climate has colder winters and hotter summers than the west coast marine climate.

7. An iceberg is a large piece of ice floating in the sea.

Activities

1. Answers will vary.

2. World Climate Regions: (see chart)

Region	Latitude	Temperature	Precipitation	Vegetation
Equatorial	low	high	heavy all year	evergreen rain forest
Savanna	low	high	heavy for part of year and very light for the other part	tall grasses
Desert	low to middle	hot in day; cold at night	low	little
Semidesert	low to middle	variable	moderately low	short grasses
Mediterranean	middle (35° N or S of Equator on west side of continent)	hot in summer; cool in winter	summer dry; winter wet	grasses and broad-leaved evergreen scrub and brush
Humid subtropical	middle (35° N or S of Equator on east coast of continent)	hot in summer; cool in winter	year-round, with more in summer	Vegetation varies. For example, Florida has broad-leaved trees; parts of Brazil have grasslands; southeastern Australia has broad-leaved forest.
West coast marine	middle (40° to 60° N or S of Equator on west coast of continent)	warm in summer; cool in winter	year-round, with more in winter	deciduous trees
Humid continental	middle (40° to 60° N or S in interior of continent or on east coast)	variable, with warm to hot summer and cold to very cold winter)	variable	coniferous evergreen trees and broad-leaved deciduous trees
Subarctic	high	short, cool summer; long, cold winter	light	coniferous evergreen trees
Tundra	high	not as extreme as Subarctic	light	mosses, lichens, and other hardy plants
Ice cap	extreme north or south	year-round average temperature below freezing	light	none

ANSWER KEY

ANSWERS FOR SKILLS DEVELOPMENT

PAGE 50

Skills Practice I

1. July is the warmest month in New York. August is the warmest month in San Diego.

2. San Diego is warmer all year-round.

3. The average January temperature in New York is below freezing.

Skills Practice II

1. San Diego has almost no precipitation from June through September.

2. New York averages about 4½ inches (11 cm) of precipitation in August. San Diego averages about 1½ inches (4 cm) of precipitation in February.

ANSWERS FOR UNIT REVIEW

PAGE 51

Reading the Text

1. People use lines of latitude and longitude for telling directions and locating places.

2. Lines of latitude measure distance north and south of the Equator. Lines of longitude measure distance east and west of the Prime Meridian.

3. The Equator divides the earth into the Northern Hemisphere and the Southern Hemisphere.

4. Lines of latitude are also called parallels. Lines of longitude are also called meridians.

5. The Prime Meridian passes through Greenwich, England, so it is sometimes referred to as the Greenwich Meridian.

Reading a Map

1. Okhotsk is located farthest east on the map.

2. You would be going west if you traveled from Warsaw to Vancouver, B.C.

3. You would be going south if you traveled from Ivigtut to Little America.

4. Okhotsk is in the subarctic climate region.

5. Cairo is in the desert climate region.

Reading a Picture

1. F 2. F 3. T 4. T 5. T

Reading a Graph

1. Mt. Everest is the highest mountain in the world.

2. The highest mountain in North America is Mt. McKinley. It is about 20,000 feet (6,100 m) high.

3. Mt. Elbrus is located in the Soviet Union.

4. Mt. Kilimanjaro is lower than Mt. Aconcagua.

5. Mt. Aconcagua is located on the continent of South America.

UNIT 2 THE UNITED STATES AND CANADA

CHAPTER 4 The United States of America

ANSWERS FOR CHECKUP QUESTIONS

PAGE 62

1. Winter wheat is planted in the fall and harvested in the spring or early summer. Spring wheat is planted in the spring, and harvest begins in mid-summer. Winter wheat is grown mainly in Kansas. Spring wheat is grown mainly in North and South Dakota and eastern Montana.

2. Some products associated with particular states are (a) Iowa—wheat and corn, (b) Florida—oranges, (c) Washington—apples and lumber, (d) Wisconsin—dairy cattle, (e) California—fruits, nuts, and vegetables, (f) Texas—beef cattle and wheat.

3. Forests and fish are considered renewable resources because nature can replace the supply that is consumed wisely.

PAGE 66

1. Iron ore and coal are two natural resources important in steelmaking. Minnesota is the principal producer of iron ore in the United States; coal is found widely in Pennsylvania, West Virginia, Kentucky, Wyoming, and Illinois.

2. Aluminum is used to make aircraft parts, pots and pans, chewing gum wrappers, and drink cans. Copper is mainly used in the making of electric wire.

3. Metal ores are called nonrenewable resources because once they are consumed they are gone from the earth and are not replaced by nature.

4. Acid rain is rain that contains so much pollution that it damages plants and fish.

5. Hydroelectric power is relatively nonpolluting, and it uses a renewable resource. Its disadvantages are that it requires special kinds of dam sites and that nearby farmland or wildlife habitats are often flooded.

PAGE 69

1. The population of the United States is about 234 million.

2. Population density refers to the average number of people within a given area, such as a square mile or a square kilometer. The population density around Boston is higher than 500 persons per square mile (higher than 200 per sq km).

3. New York, Chicago, Los Angeles, Philadelphia, Houston, and Detroit each have a population of 1 million or more.

4. A metropolitan area is an area made up of a large city or several large cities and the surrounding towns, cities, and other communities.

5. Houston is a leader in oil refining.

ANSWERS FOR CHAPTER REVIEW

PAGE 70

Vocabulary Quiz

1. g 2. c 3. a 4. j 5. e 6. b 7. f 8. d 9. h 10. i

Review Questions

1. Much of the land of the Great Plains is too dry or too rugged for farming, but it is wet enough to grow grass for cattle grazing.

2. Many farmers cannot afford to buy the expensive wheat combines.

3. A renewable resource is one that can be replaced by natural processes as it is used up. A nonrenewable resource cannot be replaced in this or any other way. Trees are a renewable resource; iron ore is a nonrenewable resource.

4. West Virginia, Kentucky, Pennsylvania, Illinois, and Wyoming are the leading coal-producing states.

5. Nuclear power is produced by atomic energy; hydroelectric power is produced by the energy of running or falling water.

6. The greatest areas of population density are in the metropolitan sections of the northeastern United States. The largest areas of least population density are Alaska and sections of the western United States.

7. New York City is a clothing and publishing center; Chicago is an important port on Lake Michigan.

Activities

1. Answers might include some of the following: Steel products; kitchen appliances, auto parts, bicycle parts, toys, flatware, workshop tools, wire, nails, pipe, paperclips, razor blades, pots and pans,

ANSWER KEY

steel wool, eyeglass frames. Petrochemicals; ammonia, cosmetics, dyes, clothing fibers, ink, insecticides, paint, plastics, plant fertilizers.

2. Use the map on page 68 as a reference.

ANSWERS FOR SKILLS DEVELOPMENT

PAGE 71

Skills Practice I

1. 70° F(21° C) is the highest temperature shown by an isotherm. 52° F(11° C) is the lowest temperature shown by an isotherm.

2. Key West has the warmest average January temperature. Tallahassee and Jacksonville have the coldest average January temperatures.

3. Orlando is warmer on the average than Gainsville.

4. Tallahassee is between 54° F(12° C) and 56° F (13° C).

5. Orlando, Tampa, Daytona Beach, and Fort Pierce have average January temperatures between 60° and 66° F.

Skills Practice II

1. The coldest parts of the world are near the North Pole and South Pole.

2. The hottest parts are near the Equator.

3. The average annual temperature for places in the orange areas on the map is 60°–70° F(16°–21° C).

4. The lowest average temperature for Australia is 50°–60° F(10°–16° C).

5. Answers will vary.

CHAPTER 5 Canada

ANSWERS FOR CHECKUP QUESTIONS

PAGE 78

1. Most of Canada is a wilderness because large parts of it are too cold for most people; crops cannot be grown in many places.

2. The Atlantic Provinces are New Brunswick, Nova Scotia, Prince Edward Island, and Newfoundland. Farming and fishing are two ways that people earn a living in these provinces.

3. The St. Lawrence Seaway is important because it is a water route between the Great Lakes and the Atlantic Ocean.

4. The Canadian Rockies and the Coast Ranges are the two main mountain ranges of western Canada. Four of the major rivers are the Columbia, Yukon, Fraser, and Mackenzie.

PAGE 81

1. The leading minerals produced in Canada include zinc, lead, copper, nickel, asbestos, iron, gold, silver, platinum, and pitchblende.

2. Most of Canada's petroleum is found in Alberta.

3. Tar sands are beds of sand saturated with oil. They may become an important source of oil when cheaper sources have been used up.

4. Canada's chief source of power is its lakes and rivers.

PAGE 84

1. The Inuit (Eskimos) and the Indians are the native peoples of Canada. The Indians lived on the prairies and in the subarctic forest. The Inuit lived on the tundra along the Arctic Coast. Today most of them live in villages and towns.

2. Most Canadians are of European descent.

3. The people who wanted to remain British citizens left the United States after it became independent and went to Canada, which had remained British.

4. Canada has a federal form of government.

5. The British Commonwealth is a voluntary association of countries that were once ruled by Great Britain.

ANSWERS FOR CHAPTER REVIEW

PAGE 85

Vocabulary Quiz

1. g 2. d 3. h 4. e 5. f 6. b 7. j 8. i 9. c 10. a

Review Questions

1. The five regions of Canada are the Atlantic Provinces (New Brunswick, Nova Scotia, Prince Edward Island, and the island part of Newfoundland); the St. Lawrence Valley and Lakes Peninsula (parts of

Quebec and Ontario); the Canadian Shield (most of Newfoundland, Quebec, Ontario, Manitoba, and the Northwest Territories; parts of Saskatchewan and Alberta); the Interior Plains (parts of Manitoba and the Northwest Territories, most of Saskatchewan and Alberta, northeastern tip of British Columbia); and the Cordillera (parts of Alberta and the Northwest Territories, most of British Columbia, and all of the Yukon Territory).

2. The coldness of the north has caused a concentration of Canada's population in the southern part of the country, near the United States border.

3. The Lakes Peninsula is located on Lake Huron, Lake Erie, and Lake Ontario.

4. Canada's longest river is the Mackenzie. It connects the Great Slave Lake to the Arctic Ocean.

5. French is the chief language of the province of Quebec.

Activities
Answers will vary.

ANSWERS FOR SKILLS DEVELOPMENT
PAGE 86
PAGE 86
Skills Practice

1. T	6. T
2. F	7. F
3. T	8. T
4. T	9. F
5. T	10. T

ANSWERS FOR UNIT REVIEW

PAGE 87
Reading the Text
1. Canada is described as a vast country because it is the second largest country in the world and covers most of the northern half of North America.

2. Canada shares boundaries with the United States in the south and the northwest.

3. A Canadian province has its own local government. Canadian territories do not have enough people to have their own government and are run mainly by the national government.

4. Canada and the United States share the same continent. They are similar in size. The chief landforms of Canada continue into the United States. Both nations are divided into smaller political units. People in both countries speak English. Both nations have been settled largely by people from Europe.

5. One outstanding difference between Canada and the United States is that most of Canada is wilderness, while much of the United States has been settled.

Reading a Map
1. More people live in the eastern half of the United States.

2. Denver's population density is 50 to 100 persons per square mile.

3. Boston has the highest population density.

4. Phoenix has the lowest population density of the 25 cities shown on the map.

5. Philadelphia and Los Angeles are both cities with more than a million people, and they both have a population density above 500 persons per square mile.

Reading a Picture
1. Montreal is located on a river.

2. Montreal is built around a mountain.

3. Montreal has a large harbor.

4. Montreal is a center for business, trade, and transportation.

5. Montreal is one of the largest cities in Canada.

Reading Graphs
1. Canada and the Soviet Union are leading producers of both wheat and nickel.

2. Canada produces approximately 210 thousand short tons of nickel.

3. India produces approximately half the wheat that the United States produces.

4. New Caledonia is the third largest producer of nickel in the world.

5. China produces more wheat than India.

ANSWER KEY

UNIT 3 LATIN AMERICA

CHAPTER 6 Mexico: Gateway to Latin America

ANSWERS FOR CHECKUP QUESTIONS

PAGE 99

1. Mexico is the first country south of English-speaking America and is the northernmost country of Latin America. Many people from the United States live in Mexico, and many people from Mexico live in the United States. Also, Mexico is somewhere in between being as wealthy, modern, and industrialized as English-speaking America and as poor and agricultural as most of the other Latin American countries.

2. The Sierra Madre Oriental follows Mexico's east coastline. The Sierra Madre Occidental follows the west coastline.

3. It is called the Great Plateau.

4. The eastern coast gets the most rain because the trade winds that blow onto Mexico from the Caribbean Sea carry moisture that becomes rain as the air rises at the mountains.

PAGE 104

1. The Indian civilizations, which include the Maya and the Aztec, and the Spanish who came as colonizers both made important contributions to Mexican culture.

2. Mexico City, the country's largest city and capital, is on the site of the Aztec city of Tenochtitlán.

3. People build houses from scrap material—boxes, burlap, flattened tin cans—on the outskirts of the cities. Sometimes these dwellings become permanent parts of the cities.

PAGE 107

1. Mexico's commercial farmers grow sugarcane, cotton, and vegetables. They also grow coffee, fruits, and henequen. Cotton and henequen are not eaten.

2. Mexican farmers raise livestock, especially cattle, but also chickens, pigs, hogs, and goats.

3. Iron and coal are used to make steel. Steel is used in automobiles and other heavy machines, bicycles, motors, refrigerators, and pins.

4. Silver, sulfur, and copper are three valuable mineral resources. Two other important resources are lead and zinc. Petroleum is one of Mexico's most important resources. Other valuable resources are forests and beaches.

5. Tourists spend money in the country they visit. They bring income to craftworkers and also to hotel, restaurant, and airport workers.

ANSWERS FOR CHAPTER REVIEW

PAGE 108

Vocabulary Quiz

1. conquistadores
2. imports
3. culture
4. exports
5. adobe
6. rain shadow
7. mestizos
8. refinery
9. ejidos
10. tourists

Review Questions

1. Travel is made difficult by the rugged terrain and the absence of many navigable rivers. When land is mountainous, roads and railroads cannot be built in a straight line between two places but must wind back and forth as they go up and down the mountains so that they are not too steep for travel. Tunnels through mountains make travel distances shorter but are costly to build.

2. A developing country does not have enough wealth to provide schools to educate all the children. Most people in a developing country are poor and do not have decent food, clothing, shelter, and medical care. Developing countries are not highly industrialized. Many people in developing countries work as farmers in the way that their grandparents did.

3. Before land reform, most land was owned as large farms called haciendas. People who worked on the haciendas for the wealthy landowners were not able to earn decent wages. Land reform took land away from the wealthy landowners and let the people who did the farm work keep most of what they produced. Farming villages that owned land after land reform are called ejidos.

4. In subsistence farming, farms are small, and the food grown is needed by the farmers. Families are poor and do not have any extras. In commercial farming there is enough land to grow crops for sale. Farms are larger, and the farmers usually can afford farm machinery and modern conveniences such as indoor plumbing.

5. Sugarcane is grown in the tropical lowlands. It is an important crop because it is used to make sugar, which, in turn, is used in many products. Many people earn their living by growing and harvesting sugarcane, making sugar from the sugarcane, and working in factories that use sugar to make other products, such as candy and soda.

6. The United States imports many fresh vegetables and fruits from Mexico, such as tomatoes and strawberries. It also imports products made from cotton and henequen.

Activities
Answers will vary.

ANSWERS FOR SKILLS DEVELOPMENT

PAGE 109
Skills Practice

1. d 2. i 3. n 4. l 5. j 6. h 7. b 8. a 9. m 10. f 11. e 12. k 13. c 14. g

1. airplane	6. family
2. office	7. civilization
3. map	8. education
4. football	9. petroleum
5. cream	10. soup

CHAPTER 7 Central America and the Caribbean Islands

ANSWERS FOR CHECKUP QUESTIONS

PAGE 112
1. Central America is the isthmus that connects North and South America.

2. Some are volcanoes, usually inactive. Others are coral islands formed from the gradual buildup of shells of the coral polyp.

3. The tierra caliente (warm, tropical), the tierra templada (temperate), and the tierra fría (cool, upland) are three Central American climate zones.

PAGE 115
1. The Mayan civilization began in Guatemala and spread north to Mexico as well as to other countries of Central America.

2. The Arawak were the farming Indians.

3. The Spanish brought Christianity to the region.

4. Spain was not the only country to have colonies in this region. Other colonial powers in the Caribbean included England, France, and the Netherlands. Also, many Africans were brought as slaves.

5. No, most are independent nations.

PAGE 118
1. Cuba is the largest island.

2. Haiti and the Dominican Republic share the same island. Haiti was a colony of France.

3. Bauxite and beaches are two important Jamaican resources.

4. Puerto Rico is a territory of the United States.

5. No, most people in Puerto Rico live in cities and towns.

PAGE 121
1. The highest mountain in Central America is in Guatemala.

2. Volcanic ash adds new minerals to the soil and makes it more fertile.

3. Belize used to be a British colony.

4. Costa Rica has the fewest subsistence farmers.

5. A canal was built in Panama.

ANSWERS FOR CHAPTER REVIEW

PAGE 122
Vocabulary Quiz
1. T 2. T 3. T 4. T 5. T 6. F (Creole is a language spoken in Haiti.) 7. T 8. T 9. F (A colony is a place that is settled at a distance from the country that governs it.) 10. F (A canal to connect the Atlantic and Pacific oceans was built in Panama.)

ANSWER KEY

Review Questions

1. Central America and the Caribbean islands lie between North and South America. This region is very close to Mexico and to English-speaking America. It also is an important transportation route for the world, since ships can travel between the Atlantic Ocean and the Pacific Ocean by going through the Panama Canal.

2. The tierra caliente, the climate in lowland areas, is always warm. When it is wet, as it usually is, bananas are a common crop. Drier areas are suitable for cotton. The tierra templada is the mild climate of the mountain slopes and valleys and of some plateau lands. Coffee is a common cash crop in the tierra templada of Central America. The tierra fría is the cooler climate of the land above 5,500 feet (1670 m), which is used mainly for subsistence crops, such as potatoes and corn.

3. The Arawaks were farmers who used the conuco system of planting several types of crops in one spot. The Caribs were a conquering group that sailed to different islands in large canoes. They also fished and grew cotton, which they wove into sails for their canoes. The Mayan kingdom of Central America included lands that are now part of the modern countries of Guatemala, Honduras, and Mexico.

4. The economies of many of the Caribbean islands benefit from tourism as well as farming. In addition, some have valuable mineral resources such as bauxite (Jamaica, Dominican Republic, Haiti) and nickel (Cuba).

5. The Panama Canal is the one waterway ships can travel from the Atlantic Ocean to the Pacific Ocean without traveling all the way around South America. Ships from all parts of the world use it.

Activities
Answers will vary.

ANSWERS FOR SKILLS DEVELOPMENT

PAGE 123

Skills Practice
Coffee beans are picked by hand.

The berries are dried and cured.

Machines remove the beans from the berries and sort them.

The beans are graded and tested.

The beans are roasted at high heat.

The coffee is ground and packed in tins.

CHAPTER 8 South America

ANSWERS FOR CHECKUP QUESTIONS

PAGE 128

1. South America has 12 countries; French Guiana and the British-controlled Falkland Islands are the colonies.

2. The Andes is the South American mountain range that runs along the west coast.

3. The Amazon is an enormous river, most of which is in Brazil. Titicaca is the world's highest large lake. The altiplano is a plateau high in the Andes.

4. Mineral resources, valuable animals, and fish are important resources.

5. Late December is the warmest time in the middle latitudes of South America.

PAGE 130

1. The Incas redesigned the mountain slopes to make flat terraces, with stone walls to hold the soil in place.

2. Portugal, Great Britain, the Netherlands, and France have had or still have colonies.

3. Simón Bolívar was a liberator who helped to bring about independence from Spain in most of South America by 1824.

PAGE 131

1. Latifundia are large landholdings on which food is grown mostly for export. Minifundia are very small landholdings on which subsistence farming takes place.

2. South America's population is growing rapidly. It doubled between 1955 and today.

3. A dual economy has a few rich people, but most people are very poor. A dual economy lacks a strong middle class.

PAGE 138

1. Petroleum is bringing new capital to these South American countries.

2. Coffee is the leading export of Colombia.

3. Tin is mined in Bolivia, and copper is mined in Chile.

4. Bolivia and Paraguay are landlocked countries.

5. The Pampas are in Argentina.

6. Brasília is a new city located far from the coast. It was a planned city.

ANSWERS FOR CHAPTER REVIEW

PAGE 139
Vocabulary Quiz

1. tributary
2. altiplano
3. liberator
4. llanos
5. cacao
6. tropics
7. landlocked

Review Questions

1. The Andes Mountains and the Amazon River are the geographic features that dominate South America.

2. The Incas were the first colonizers in South America. Their empire extended from present-day Peru to Chile, nearly 3,000 miles (4,825 km).

3. Bauxite—Guyana or Surinam; cacao—Brazil or Ecuador; coffee—Brazil or Colombia; copper—Chile; fish or fish meal—Peru; tannin—Paraguay; tin—Bolivia; wool—Argentina or Uruguay; beef—Argentina, Uruguay, or Brazil.

Activity
Answers will vary.

ANSWERS FOR SKILLS DEVELOPMENT

PAGE 140
Skills Practice
Answers will vary.

ANSWERS FOR UNIT REVIEW

PAGE 141
Reading the Text

1. Many latifundia were divided into smaller farms called minifundia during periods of land reform.

2. South American cities are growing rapidly because many people who are looking for work are moving to the cities from the countryside.

3. Agricultural products and mineral resources are the main exports of South America.

4. A dual economy is one in which there are only a few very rich people and many very poor people.

5. Most developing countries have rapidly growing populations, dual economies, and little industry.

Reading a Map

1. Puerto Rico is directly east of the Dominican Republic and is a territory of the United States.

2. Belize and El Salvador do not have coasts on both the Pacific Ocean and the Caribbean Sea.

3. Aruba is at 70°W.

4. Most of the countries of this region lie between 10°N and 20°N.

5. It is approximately 1,000 miles between Havana, Cuba, and Panamá, Panama.

Reading a Picture

1. Aztecs
2. stones
3. church
4. Spanish
5. tall buildings

Reading a Diagram

1. In the tierra templada the temperature is neither too hot nor too cold.

2. The tierra fría is above 2,100 meters.

3. Guayaquil, in the tierra caliente, is more likely to have a higher annual temperature.

4. The tierra caliente is between 0 and 3,000 feet (0 and 900 m).

5. Temperature tends to go down with increase in elevation.

ANSWER KEY

CHAPTER 9 The British Isles and Scandinavia

ANSWERS FOR CHECKUP QUESTIONS

PAGE 152

1. The Republic of Ireland and the United Kingdom of Great Britain and Northern Ireland are the two governments of the British Isles.

2. London is the capital of the United Kingdom.

3. Highland Britain and Lowland Britain are the two landform regions of the British Isles.

4. The British Isles have higher winter temperatures than most places in the same latitude because west winds bring marine air from the Atlantic Ocean to the British Isles, and in the winter this air blows off of the warm waters of the Gulf Stream.

PAGE 158

1. The Celts contributed many place-names, including that of Britain itself. They also brought farming and ox-drawn plows to the British Isles. The Angles, Saxons, and Jutes set up small farming villages over much of Lowland Britain. They established almost all of the villages in existence today.

2. Sheep raising became more important than farming for two reasons. The first was the developing wool trade with Flanders. The second reason was that, as a result of this growth in trade, sheep raising became more profitable than growing crops.

3. The Industrial Revolution caused many people to move from rural areas. People stopped living on farms and making goods in their homes. Cottage industries gave way to factories. At first many of the factories were located in the country. Soon, however, they moved to the cities. Cities also grew up around factories. There was a general shift of population from Lowland Britain to the edge of Highland Britain. Before the Industrial Revolution most of the people lived in Lowland Britain. After 1850 the population was densest in the coalfields in Highland Britain. London was the exception. It continued to grow and became a huge city, even though it was located in the lowlands of the southeast.

4. The two world wars were very costly to Britain. Much of Britain's accumulated wealth was used up in the two wars. Britain lost many men, particularly in World War I. As a result, Britain was no longer the leading industrial, trading, and financial nation in the world.

5. Northern Ireland is the home of a million Protestants as well as many Catholics.

6. The Irish population declined in the nineteenth century because of the potato famine of the 1840s. Many Irish emigrated from Ireland to the United States and other English-speaking countries.

PAGE 165

1. The Scandinavian Shield covers most of Sweden and all of Finland. The Shield has iron ore, forests, and waterpower.

2. Only a few small glaciers are left in the mountains of Norway. Earlier, glaciers deepened and widened river valleys and carved out troughs below sea level. Later, water filled the troughs. These inlets are called fjords. In Denmark material was left by retreating and melting ice. These deposits have resulted in soils that are good for farming.

3. Four Scandinavian languages and Finnish are the major languages of the region. Icelandic, Norwegian, Swedish, and Danish are the four Scandinavian languages. Swedish, Danish, and Norwegian are very similar.

4. Finland has a democratic government and a high standard of living. It exports high-quality goods. Its people are Lutherans. In these ways, Finland is very much like the other Scandinavian countries. It is unlike the others in that most of the Finns speak Finnish, a language unrelated to the Scandinavian languages. Finland's history is also different.

5. Iceland depends almost entirely on fishing for its livelihood; Norway largely depends on fishing, its merchant marine, and North Sea oil. Sweden is the most industrialized of the Scandinavian countries. Denmark has the most farming.

ANSWERS FOR CHAPTER REVIEW

PAGE 166
Vocabulary Quiz
1. j **2.** i **3.** b **4.** a **5.** g **6.** h **7.** f **8.** d **9.** e
10. c

REVIEW QUESTIONS

1. A marine climate is one in which winters are not very cold and summers are mild. In a marine climate, temperatures are greatly affected by the ocean.

2. People moved to cities, and cities grew up around factories. The population grew rapidly, and the United Kingdom became a nation of industries and factory workers instead of agriculture and farmers. The Industrial Revolution also stimulated trade.

3. When Great Britain gave Ireland its independence, the Protestant North Irish demanded that the northeastern corner of Ireland remain part of the United Kingdom.

4. The major resources are fish in Iceland; fish, oil, natural gas, iron ore, and waterpower used to produce electricity in Norway; iron ore, rivers, and forests in Sweden; good trading location and farmland in Denmark; and forests in Finland.

5. The economies of the Scandinavian countries differ in that the exports of the five countries are based on different natural resources. The five economies are similar in that all five countries have developed export industries that have a reputation for the high quality of their products. In each country the economy supports a very high standard of living.

Activities
1. a. one (Lutheran)

b. one (Roman Catholic)

c. three (Church of England, Presbyterian, Methodist)

d. two (Church of England and Roman Catholic)

2. Answers will vary.

ANSWERS FOR SKILLS DEVELOPMENT

PAGE 167
Skills Practice
1. The first report says a major famine was happening in Ireland.

2. According to the report, 5,000 people did not have food for the next day.

3. The misery in Ireland was caused by crop failure.

4. Oats was the second crop that failed in Ireland at this time.

5. People left Ireland for the United States in search of food and a better life.

6. A hovel is a shed or open-roofed shelter.

7. People crawled to the shore to collect seaweed for food.

8. Answers will vary.

9. Answers will vary.

CHAPTER 10 France and the Low Countries

ANSWERS FOR CHECKUP QUESTIONS

PAGE 174
1. The three groups of people who helped to create modern France were the Celts (or Gauls), the Romans, and the Franks.

2. France has four main kinds of industrial regions. The most important industrial region is Paris and its surrounding area, which employs the most workers and produces the most valuable goods. Northern France and the Central Massif are industrial regions based on coal and iron ore. Textiles are also made in these regions. Southern France has many industries based on new technology, such as the aircraft industry and industries using hydroelectric power. Tourism is a well-developed industry in France, especially on the Mediterranean coast, in the Alps, and in the Loire Valley.

3. Paris is the center of France in every way. It is the capital and political center. It is the largest city in France. It is the hub of the road and rail network. It is the leading industrial region of France. It is also the artistic and intellectual center of the country. It is admired and respected by French-speakers throughout the world.

PAGE 179
1. The deltas formed by the sediment deposited by the Rhine, Meuse, and Schelde rivers make up much of the land above sea level in the Low Countries. The same rivers have also supplied the sand that coastal currents have deposited along the shore. In this way the rivers have helped to form the protective walls of coastal sand dunes. The barge traffic on

ANSWER KEY

these rivers makes Antwerp and Rotterdam two of the leading ports in the world.

2. The Zuider Zee project was aimed at closing off the Zuider Zee, making it a freshwater lake, and creating some large agricultural polders. The Delta project was aimed at closing the gaps at the outer edge of the Rhine Delta that allowed disastrous storms to invade the Netherlands. A third project is still being planned.

3. In the nineteenth century the Walloons were richer than the Flemings and had most of the positions of high rank. The coal mines in the Walloon region made their region very rich. In the nineteenth century the Flemings were poor farmers with large families and were unable to get good jobs. Now the Flemings are richer and they outnumber the Walloons.

4. The Common Market had its beginnings in an economic agreement among the three Benelux countries. The agreement facilitated the production and movement of coal, iron ore, and steel by abolishing tariffs on imports and exports. Now it allows the free movement of goods and workers across the borders of its ten member countries. The main advantage for member countries is the availability of a variety of goods at reasonable prices.

ANSWERS FOR CHAPTER REVIEW

PAGE 180
Vocabulary Quiz
1. c 2. b 3. g 4. e 5. a 6. h 7. j 8. d 9. i 10. f

Review Questions
1. The Germanic invaders who called themselves Franks were the people who gave France its name.

2. Paris is the most important industrial area in France.

3. A polder is a piece of land lying below sea level that has been reclaimed from the sea and enclosed by dikes. Polders have been in existence since before the thirteenth century.

4. Luxembourg's greatest wealth comes from its iron ore deposits. The country also has excellent soils.

5. The Common Market was started by the Netherlands, Belgium, Luxembourg, France, West Germany, and Italy. Denmark, Ireland, the United Kingdom, and Greece joined later.

Activity
Garonne, 385 miles (620 km); Loire, 650 miles (1,050 km); Meuse, 575 (925 km); Rhine, 820 miles (1,320 km); Rhone, 500 miles (800 km); Saône, 232 miles (373 km).

ANSWERS FOR SKILLS DEVELOPMENT

PAGE 181
Skills Practice
1. The population density increased by 107 per square mile between 1820 and 1880.

2. The population of the Netherlands more than doubled during the following periods: 1800–1900; 1860–1920; 1900–1960; 1920–1980.

3. In 1960, the population density of the Netherlands became greater than the 1980 population density of the United Kingdom.

CHAPTER 11 Central Europe

ANSWERS FOR CHECKUP QUESTIONS

PAGE 186
1. The Federal Republic of Germany is commonly called West Germany. The German Democratic Republic is commonly called East Germany.

2. Invisible language boundaries and religious boundaries are some of the invisible lines that divide the people of Germany.

3. Coal is the major resource of the Ruhr. The southwest is growing fast today because it has many jobs to offer people.

PAGE 190
1. Most of the people in Alpine Switzerland live in towns in the valleys of the Rhine and the Rhone.

2. The industries of Switzerland include many kinds of manufacturing, banking, and tourism.

3. German, French, Italian, and Romansh are the four languages of Switzerland.

4. Each canton has its own history, customs, and way of speaking.

PAGE 191

1. Most of Austria's cities and transportation routes are located along the river valleys between the ridges of the Alps.

2. The modern resources of the Austrian Alps are the swift-moving rivers, the minerals, and the scenery.

3. Vienna's excellent position made it a good place for a settlement. It is located on a major north-south route and on the Danube River, which allows easy movement in an east-west direction.

ANSWERS FOR CHAPTER REVIEW

PAGE 192

Vocabulary Quiz
1. c 2. c 3. c 4. a 5. a

Review Questions
1. West Germany has a democratic government, and East Germany has a Communist government.

2. German is the main language of all three countries, but there are regional variations that are strong enough to be called dialects.

3. Manufacturing, banking, and tourism are three important industries in Switzerland. Manufacturing of high-cost products, such as watches, chemicals, and electrical equipment, developed because of the availability of skilled labor. Banking developed largely because of Switzerland's neutrality and economic stability. Tourism developed because of the magnificent natural scenery and the beautiful towns and villages that make up the Swiss landscape.

4. Valleys are located between the two main ridges of the Alps. Most of Austria's settlements and transportation routes are along these valleys.

5. Today, Vienna employs many people in the banking and insurance businesses.

6. They support a high standard of living for the people of the three countries. The Ruhr, the Swiss Plateau, and western Austria are the main industrial areas of the three countries.

Activity
Austria joined the United Nations in 1955; West Germany joined in 1973. Switzerland has never joined because the Swiss feel that such membership would violate their nation's policy of neutrality.

ANSWERS FOR SKILLS DEVELOPMENT

PAGE 193

Skills Practice: Part I
1. Denmark

2. Greece

3. Ireland

4. Norway

5. Netherlands

Skills Practice: Part II
1. Geneva

2. Zurich

3. Bern

Skills Practice: Part III
1. T 2. T 3. F 4. F 5. T

CHAPTER 12 Mediterranean Europe

ANSWERS FOR CHECKUP QUESTIONS

PAGE 197

1. Winter is the rainy season in Mediterranean Europe.

2. Early civilizations in the eastern Mediterranean founded towns and introduced banking, the alphabet, art, and science, among other things, to lands in the western Mediterranean.

3. Mediterranean agriculture depends on irrigation. Tree crops are very important in the Mediterranean. Sheep, goats, donkeys, and mules are more common in the Mediterranean than cattle or horses. Mediterranean settlements are clustered villages, often on hilltops. They are crowded and compact.

4. Many of the people who have temporarily migrated to northern Europe send money back to their families in Mediterranean Europe.

PAGE 199

1. The Meseta is a plateau in central Spain and northern Portugal. It is bordered on the north by the Pyrenees and on the south by the Sierra Nevada.

ANSWER KEY

2. Roman aqueducts, stadiums, walls, and statues can still be seen in Spain. The Spanish people speak a Romance language and practice Roman Catholicism.

3. The Moors introduced schools of science and medicine. They also brought new crops, such as sugarcane, citrus fruits, and rice.

4. Until recently, Spain and Portugal have been less developed than other parts of Western Europe in their industry, government, schooling, public health, and standard of living.

PAGE 202

1. The lowlands of Italy are the Po Valley, Tuscany, Latium, and Campania. The Po Valley is the most important industrial and agricultural part of Italy. Tuscany is the site of historic towns, such as Florence and Pisa. Latium's principal city is Rome, and Campania's principal city is Naples.

2. Millions of people from southern Italy have migrated to other areas because the south is the poorest part of Italy. It has many people and few jobs. It has few cities, little industry, and its agriculture is not very productive. The government has spent billions of dollars on improving agriculture and starting industry in the south.

3. Rome was the capital of one of the most important empires in the world. Today it is still a political capital. Because Vatican City, the center of Roman Catholicism, is on the edge of Rome, Rome could also be called a religious capital.

PAGE 204

1. The most important mineral resource in Greece is bauxite. Greece lacks coal and oil.

2. Constantinople was the center of Greek life after A.D. 330.

3. The Greeks belong to the Eastern, or Greek, Orthodox Church.

4. Modern Greece depends on its merchant fleet and tourism as sources of income.

ANSWERS FOR CHAPTER REVIEW

PAGE 205
Vocabulary Quiz
1. a **2.** d **3.** b **4.** c **5.** e

Review Questions
1. The Meseta is a plateau in the central part of Spain and northern Portugal.

2. Tourism brings in foreign currency to help pay for imports. Out-migration relieves the population pressure, and money sent back to the homeland by the migrants often is an important source of national income for the Mediterranean countries.

3. The Spanish problem areas today are mainly the regions where minorities live. The Basques and the Catalans in particular are not satisfied with the way they are treated by the central government.

4. The poorest and least industrial area of Italy is the south. It is a farming region with only one large city. There are many people in the south and few jobs. It has made the least economic progress of the three regions.

5. The Forum and the Colosseum are two of the most impressive ruins of Rome. The Forum was a meeting area and marketplace for the Romans. The Colosseum was the largest stadium in Rome. Various kinds of games and fights were held there.

6. Modern Greece cannot produce enough food for its population, and the resources for industry are limited. Trade and out-migration are as important to modern Greece as they were to ancient Greece.

Activity
Answers will vary.

ANSWERS FOR SKILLS DEVELOPMENT

PAGE 206
Skills Practice
Answers are provided as annotations on page 206.

ANSWERS FOR UNIT REVIEW

PAGE 207
Reading the Text
1. They are all trading nations, and they all have a very high standard of living.

2. Iceland's economy is dependent on fishing.

3. Norway leads the world in the production of electricity.

4. Sweden has the highest level of industrialization in Scandinavia.

ANSWER KEY

5. Finland's economy is linked to that of the Soviet Union by very close trade connections.

Reading a Map
1. The Pyrenees are the mountains in the extreme south of France. This region of France borders on Spain.

2. The Garonne River flows in the southwestern part of France. It flows in a northwesterly direction.

3. The distance between Paris and Brussels is approximately 180 miles. The distance between Paris and Amsterdam is approximately 280 miles.

4. Both the Netherlands and Luxembourg are primarily North European Plain.

5. Brittany is the extreme western region of France. The Loire River runs through this region.

Reading a Picture
1. Passenger transport and cargo transport are the two uses being made of the river. Automobile transport is the second type of transportation shown in the picture.

2. The lush, green vegetation and the free-flowing river are two examples of a mild climate.

3. The church with its prominent white steeple is evidence of a Christian community in this village.

4. The region has a hilly terrain.

5. Answers will vary. This section of Germany is a tourist center due to its scenery and mild climate.

Reading a Chart
1. Home furnishings are made from the trunk of the olive tree.

2. The bud and the fruit of the olive tree are sources of food for humans.

3. The oil of the olive tree is a source of soap and beauty products.

4. The olive branch is a symbol of peace and victory.

5. The leaves of the olive tree provide food for animals.

ANSWER KEY

CHAPTER 13 Eastern Europe

ANSWERS FOR CHECKUP QUESTIONS

PAGE 218

1. The North European Plain covers most of East Germany and Poland.

2. The East German government first placed barbed wire and lookout towers along the border with West Germany. Then East Germany built a concrete wall, known as the Berlin wall, through the city of Berlin.

PAGE 221

1. The lowlands of Czechoslovakia are in Bohemia and Moravia.

2. Grass is the natural vegetation of the steppes.

3. The region inhabited by the Czechs had mines, industries, and prosperous agriculture. It was also an important part of the Holy Roman Empire. Slovakia remained poor and rural partly because Hungary used it as a food-producing colony and source of cheap labor. The Hungarians did not develop the region.

4. The Magyars were the ancestors of the modern Hungarians.

5. Industrialization began in Hungary after World War II.

PAGE 225

1. The main ethnic groups in Romania are the Romanians, Hungarians, and Germans; Bulgaria is inhabited mainly by Bulgarians.

2. The three regions of Romania are Walachia, the Carpathian Mountains, and Transylvania.

ANSWERS FOR CHAPTER REVIEW

PAGE 226
Vocabulary Quiz
1. g 2. d 3. c 4. a 5. e 6. j 7. i 8. b 9. h
10. f

Review Questions

1. The main resources of the northernmost parts of East Germany and Poland are their seaports.

2. In Hungary today most of the farms are collective farms. Wheat and corn are the major crops.

3. Czechoslovakia exports industrial goods, and food and raw materials are imported. This provides the needed food for the people of Czechoslovakia.

4. Yugoslavia has a different ethnic group in each of its republics.

5. The Communist government of Yugoslavia has always been independent of the Soviet Union.

Activity
Answers will vary.

ANSWERS FOR SKILLS DEVELOPMENT

Skills Practice
Answers will vary.

CHAPTER 14 The Soviet Union

ANSWERS FOR CHECKUP QUESTIONS

PAGE 232

1. European Russia, Western Siberia, Central Siberia, and Soviet Central Asia are the four main lowland regions of the Soviet Union. Mountains are found along the southern border of the Soviet Union.

2. The Caspian Sea is the world's largest inland body of water.

3. The cold seas surrounding the Soviet Union give it a continental climate, with severe winters and not much precipitation.

4. The coldest part of the Soviet Union is in northeastern Siberia. Central Asia is the hottest part of the Soviet Union.

PAGE 237

1. Balkan missionaries converted the Russians to Christianity.

2. *Moskva* means "the bear's den" in Finnic. The settlement of Moskva was the beginning of Moscow.

This is how the use of a bear as a symbol of the Russians originated.

3. A kremlin is a kind of fort. It got its name from the Slavs. Moscow's Kremlin became the center of Russia's government. So when people speak of the Kremlin today, they usually mean the Soviet government.

4. The Communists and their supporters overthrew the Russian government, gaining control of Moscow and making it the capital.

5. There are 15 republics in the U.S.S.R. Each one is the home territory of one of the major ethnic groups in the country.

PAGE 244

1. In the Soviet Union a five-year plan is a kind of blueprint of planned development for the country. It includes a list of tasks to be done, such as building factories, opening up mines, making machines and tools, and so forth. Agriculture and consumer goods have suffered under the five-year plans because most of the country's resources have gone into developing heavy industry.

2. Moscow, the area around the coalfields of the Donets Basin, Leningrad, the southern Ural Mountains, and the area around the Kuznetsk coalfields are the five main industrial regions of the Soviet Union.

3. The kulaks were farmers who owned enough land to make a living from it. They resisted the idea of collective farms. Today there are state-owned farms, collective farms, and small private plots in the Soviet Union.

ANSWERS FOR CHAPTER REVIEW

PAGE 245
Vocabulary Quiz
1. h 2. b 3. d 4. i 5. f 6. a 7. c 8. j 9. e
10. g

Review Questions
1. The Soviet Union's most important industrial area is Moscow. The industrial area that is centered around the Kuznetsk coalfields in Siberia has developed since the 1930s.

2. The development of railroads in the Soviet Union has been slow because less attention has been paid to transportation than to heavy industry. Also, building railroads in faraway places with a severe climate is difficult.

3. On state-owned farms the workers are salaried employees of the state. Collectives are run by all the people who work the land, and the profits are divided. State-owned farms are usually much larger and more specialized than collective farms. The individual plots of land are important because their output is necessary to feed the people of the Soviet Union. These plots of land produce 30% of the food in the country.

4. The government of the Soviet Union considers education to be very important. The government makes the decisions about what subjects are taught and which books are used in the schools.

Activity

Republic	Ethnic Group	Language	Religion
Armenia	Armenian	Armenian	Armenian
Azerbaija	Turkic	Azerbaijan	Muslim
Belorussia	Slav	Belorussian	Russian Orthodox
Estonia	Finno-Ugric	Estonian	Eastern Orthodox
Georgia	Georgian	Georgian	Roman Catholic
Kazakh	Turkic	Kazakh	Muslim
Kirgiz	Turkic	Kirgiz	Muslim
Latvia	Finno-Ugric	Latvian	Lutheran
Lithuania	Finno-Ugric	Lithuanian	Roman Catholic
Moldavia	Moldavian	Moldavian	Eastern Orthodox
Russian Soviet Federative Socialist Republic	Slav	Russian	Russian Orthodox
Tajik	Tajik	Tajik	Muslim
Turkmen	Turkic	Turkmen	Muslim
Ukraine	Slav	Ukranian	Russian Orthodox
Uzbek	Turkic	Uzbek	Muslim

ANSWER KEY

ANSWERS FOR SKILLS DEVELOPMENT

PAGE 246

Skills Practice

1. The width and navigability of the Volga are described. The early history of navigation on the Volga is given. Two words to describe the Volga might be *wide* and *slow-flowing.*

2. Navigation on the Volga today is described.

3. There are four supporting sentences. They give details of present-day problems confronting those who use the Volga for navigation.

ANSWERS FOR UNIT REVIEW

PAGE 247

Reading the Text
1. F 2. T 3. T 4. T 5. T

Reading a Map
1. T 2. T 3. F 4. F 5. F

Reading a Picture
1. F 2. T 3. F 4. T 5. F

Reading a Chart
1. F 2. T 3. F 4. F 5. T

ANSWER KEY

UNIT 6 NORTH AFRICA AND THE MIDDLE EAST

CHAPTER 15 North Africa

ANSWERS FOR CHECKUP QUESTIONS

PAGE 256

1. The Sahara lies in all five North African countries: Egypt, Libya, Tunisia, Algeria, and Morocco.

2. The coast of North Africa has a Mediterranean climate, and winter storms from the sea bring much rain to the coastal lands, especially in Morocco and Algeria.

3. Dry farming is a technique for conserving moisture in the soil by growing only certain kinds of crops and by growing some crops only every other year.

4. An oasis is a place in the desert that gets enough water for trees and plants to grow. The most important oasis in North Africa is the valley and delta of the Nile River in Egypt.

PAGE 258

1. The Arabs changed North Africa by giving the Arabic language and the Islamic religion to almost everyone in North Africa.

2. *Arabize* means to cause people to adopt Arab ways, including the adoption of the Arabic language, the Islamic religion, and other customs. The Berbers and the Copts are the main groups in North Africa that have not been completely Arabized.

3. The main European colonial effort began in 1830. The Europeans built schools and railroads, made medical care available, caused cities to grow, and improved agriculture. One problem that arose was that the local people rebelled, and the Europeans put down the rebellions with armies. The people of North Africa sometimes had bitter feelings toward the Europeans. Usually, local people could not get the good jobs and good pay in their own country.

PAGE 263

1. The Aswân Dam has created hydroelectric power; it has prevented flooding; and it has helped create irrigated farmlands. Also, the hydroelectric power has made new industries possible and, therefore, more jobs possible. One problem the dam has caused is the shrinking of the Nile Delta and the buildup of salt water in the soil of the delta.

2. Both Tunisia and Egypt have some oil, but not as much as their neighbors, and both have to import food and manufactured goods. Tunisia is not nearly as poor as Egypt; it has about the same amount of resources but a much smaller population than Egypt.

3. After Algeria became independent, French landowners gave up their land. Today more land is used for wheat and other food crops, and less land is used for growing grapes.

4. Morocco has two thirds of the world's supply of phosphates, more agricultural land than other North African countries, and rich fishing grounds in the Atlantic Ocean.

ANSWERS FOR CHAPTER REVIEW

PAGE 264

Vocabulary Quiz

1. h 2. a 3. b 4. c 5. d 6. j 7. e 8. f 9. g 10. i

Review Questions

1. The Sahara is the major desert in North Africa, and the Atlas Mountains form the major mountain range in North Africa.

2. One of the kinds of farming is dry farming. In the dry farming method, farmers try to save moisture in the soil by growing only certain kinds of crops, planting some crops only every other year, and using various other procedures to save moisture. The other kind of farming is called oasis agriculture. In the oasis method, farmers use irrigation for the desert lands and are able to grow many different crops, such as the date palm tree.

3. The Nile Valley is the place where almost all the people live and where most of the farming, which is Egypt's main source of income, takes place.

4. Cities grew up in the inland areas of North Africa because the Arabs were more concerned with land-based travel and trade than with maritime commerce.

5. There has always been friction between Arabs and Berbers in North Africa because the Berbers have resented the Arab conquest of their lands.

ANSWER KEY

6. The Algerians resented French rule and the loss of much of their land to French settlers. The Algerian farmers were not pleased that their land was in foreign hands or that the land was being used to grow grapes. The Algerians revolted and finally won their independence in 1963.

7. Egypt has 46 million people and its only farmland is a narrow strip along the Nile. Also, Egypt's growing cities and industries have taken over land that was once used for farming.

8. The Algerians practice the Islamic religion, which forbids the drinking of alcoholic beverages, so they did not like the idea of the French growing grapes to make wine.

9. The Berbers live in the upland valleys and plateaus of Morocco.

Activities
Answers will vary.

ANSWERS FOR SKILLS DEVELOPMENT

PAGE 265
Skills Practice: Part I
1. a **2.** c **3.** b **4.** c

Skills Practice: Part II
1. Land is often fallow in dry farming because it helps the soil store up moisture.

2. The Algerians had bitter feelings toward the French in Algeria because although the French made up only about ten per cent of the population in colonial Algeria, they held all the political power.

3. The Libyan government has money to invest in economic projects because it has a vast income from oil production.

4. Egypt spends more money on imports than it gets from exports because it exports raw materials and imports more expensive manufactured goods.

CHAPTER 16 The Middle East

ANSWERS FOR CHECKUP QUESTIONS

PAGE 268
1. The region was given the name *Middle East* by the Europeans because it lies east of Europe and is closer than the Far East.

2. A rift valley is a long canyon bounded by two parallel faults.

3. Most of the farming in the Middle East takes place along the valleys of the major streams and rivers.

PAGE 270
1. Mohammed founded the religion of Islam. He began to preach around the year A.D. 610 in the city of Mecca, on the western side of the Arabian Peninsula.

2. Under the rule of the Mongols, the Middle East declined in power. It was set back economically and culturally—no longer a leader in industry, science, art, and architecture.

3. The Europeans influenced the economy of the Middle East by being the first to develop the oil fields there.

PAGE 272
1. Saudi Arabia is a leader in OPEC and has loaned money to its Arab neighbors to help them develop their countries.

2. Saudi Arabia, Kuwait, Qatar, and the United Arab Emirates are all very rich because of oil in their area.

3. Amman is an important city in Jordan; Damascus and Aleppo are important cities in Syria; and Baghdad is an important city in Iraq.

4. Syria and Iraq are both Arabic-speaking, Moslem countries that are strongly anti-Israel and they both get help from the Soviet Union. They are different in that Iraq has oil and most Iraqis are Shiite Moslems, whereas Syria has little oil and most of its people are Sunnis.

1. Mustafa Kemal Atatürk reduced the power of religious leaders and introduced Western ways, such as the use of the Roman alphabet and the concept of equality between men and women.

2. Kurdistan is a region in southeastern Turkey that stretches into adjoining areas of Syria, Iraq and Iran. This is a problem area because the Kurds who live here have not been allowed to have their own country.

3. Iran is a Shiite Moslem country because a sixteenth century ruler did not want his subjects to identify with the Sunni Turks and made them switch from Sunni to Shiite Islam.

4. When Turkish rule of Palestine ended in 1918, the British government promised the Zionists a homeland in Palestine. A number of Jews moved to Palestine and bought land from the Arabs. In the 1930s many Jews fled from Hitler's Germany and went to live in Palestine. After World War II more Jews moved to Palestine. Many Arabs did not want so many Jews coming into Palestine. Britain had difficulty governing both Jews and Arabs peacefully. Palestine was divided, and in 1948 part of Palestine became the independent country of Israel.

5. The Palestinians are the Arabs who lived in Palestine. The PLO is an organization of Arabs whose aim is to retake Palestine from the Jews by force.

6. The religious groups of Lebanon are the Moslems (Sunni, Shiite, and Druse) and the Christians (mainly Catholic). The government of Lebanon was formed in such a way as to keep balance among all the religious groups. Government leaders must be of a certain religion and representation in the Lebanese legislature is based on religion.

ANSWERS FOR CHAPTER REVIEW

Vocabulary Quiz

1. c **2.** d **3.** g **4.** j **5.** f **6.** b **7.** h **8.** a **9.** e **10.** i

Review Questions

1. Bahrain, Iraq, Iran, Israel, Jordan, Kuwait, Lebanon, Oman, Qatar, Saudi Arabia, Syria, Turkey, United Arab Emirates, Yemen, and South Yemen are the countries of the Middle East.

2. The Taurus, Elburz, and Zagros mountains are found in the Middle East. The Tigris and the Euphrates are the most important rivers. The Black, Red, Caspian, and Mediterranean seas touch the coast of the Middle East.

3. Judaism, Christianity, and Islam all had their origins in the Middle East. Islam is the religion practiced by most people in the Middle East.

4. The sudden wealth from oil exploitation has changed life greatly for many of the people living on the Arabian Peninsula.

5. The Bosporus and the Dardanelles are straits that connect the Black Sea and the Aegean Sea. They are important because they provide a water gateway to a large part of Eastern Europe.

ANSWER KEY

Activity

Country	Area	Population	Capital	Exports	Imports
Bahrain	240 sq mi (622 sq km)	400,000	Manama	petroleum products	food products
Iran	636,296 sq mi (1,648,000 sq km)	42,500,000	Tehran	oil	machinery, food
Iraq	167,925 sq mi (434,924 sq km)	14,500,000	Baghdad	oil	chemicals, machinery
Israel	8,019 sq mi (20,770 sq km)	4,100,000	Jerusalem	fruit, chemicals	machinery, iron & steel
Jordan	37,738 sq mi (97,740 sq km)	3,600,000	Amman	farm produce	chemicals, food
Kuwait	7,768 sq mi (20,118 sq km)	1,600,000	Al-Kuwait	oil	food
Lebanon	4,015 sq mi (10,400 sq km)	2,600,000	Beirut	chemicals, fruit	food, oil
Oman	82,030 sq mi (212,457 sq km)	1,000,000	Masqat	oil	food
Qatar	4,247 sq mi (11,000 sq km)	300,000	Doha	oil	meat & other foods
Saudi Arabia	831,313 sq mi (2,153,090 sq km)	10,400,000	Riyadh	oil	food, machinery
Syria	71,498 sq mi (185,180 sq km)	9,700,000	Damascus	oil	food, machinery
Turkey	292,261 sq mi (756,953 sq km)	49,200,000	Ankara	chromite, cotton	machinery, raw material
United Arab Emirates	32,278 sq mi (83,600 sq km)	1,400,000	Abu Dhabi	oil	food
Yemen (Aden)	128,560 sq mi (332,968 sq km)	2,100,000	Aden	refined oil	food
Yemen (San'a)	75,290 sq mi (195,000 sq km)	5,700,000	San'a	coffee	manufactured goods

ANSWERS FOR SKILLS DEVELOPMENT

PAGE 280
Skills Practice
1. **a.** Aden **b.** Arabian

2. **a.** Baghdad **b.** Tigris **c.** Persian

3. **a.** Tehran **b.** Iraq **c.** The Soviet Union

4. **a.** Jordan **b.** Iraq **c.** Kuwait **d.** Qatar **e.** United Arab Emirates **f.** Oman **g.** Yemen (Aden) **h.** Yemen (San'a)

5. **a.** Abu Dhabi **b.** Masqat **c.** Masqat

6. **a.** Syria **b.** Iraq **c.** Iran

7. **a.** Aegean **b.** Greece

8. **a.** Elburz **b.** Iranian **c.** Caspian **d.** Damāvand **e.** 18,834 **f.** 5,571

9. **a.** Persian **b.** Oman

10. **a.** Beirut **b.** Jerusalem **c.** Damascus

11. **a.** Turkey **b.** Syria **c.** Lebanon **d.** Israel

12. **a.** Persian **b.** Manama

13. **a.** Zagros **b.** Iran **c.** Iraq

14. **a.** Al-Kuwait **b.** 29°N,48°E **c.** Tehran

ANSWERS FOR UNIT REVIEW

PAGE 281
Reading the Text
1. The two important features of the Arab way of life that had great impact on North Africa were the Arab language and the religion of Islam.

2. The Bedouins were nomadic Arabs in North Africa. They migrated to find pastureland for their sheep and goats.

3. The fellahin were crop-raising farmers of North Africa. They opposed the Bedouins because the overgrazing of the Bedouin's livestock destroyed farmland.

4. Both the Berbers and the Copts resisted Arab ways.

5. The Arabs established inland cities to serve their land-based caravan trade.

Reading a Map
1. Middle Eastern petroleum deposits are found in the coastal areas surrounding the Persian Gulf.

2. Both countries of Yemen have oasis agriculture.

3. Coal deposits are found in Iran and in Turkey.

4. Phosphates are found near Amman, Jordan, and Damascus, Syria.

5. As the map shows, Iraq has extensive irrigated agriculture.

Reading a Picture
1. The city shown in the picture is Jerusalem.

2. Jerusalem is the capital city of Israel.

3. Jerusalem is a holy place for Jews, Christians, and Moslems.

4. The Damascus Gate is the name of the entrance to the old section of Jerusalem.

5. Walking is the way people get from place to place in the old city. The narrow streets and the wall surrounding the city are barriers to other types of transportation.

Reading a Table
1. The largest country in North Africa and the Middle East is Algeria.

2. Turkey has the largest population of all the countries of North Africa and the Middle East.

3. Bahrain has the highest population density of all the countries of North Africa and the Middle East.

4. The capital cities in North Africa and the Middle East with populations greater than 1 million are Cairo, Egypt; Tehran, Iran; Baghdad, Iraq; and Ankara, Turkey.

5. Masqat, Oman, is the capital city with the lowest population in North Africa and the Middle East.

ANSWER KEY

UNIT 7 AFRICA SOUTH OF THE SAHARA

CHAPTER 17 East and Equatorial Africa

ANSWERS FOR CHECKUP QUESTIONS

PAGE 294

1. The high altitudes of volcanic mountains, such as Mount Kilimanjaro and Mount Kenya, stay cold all year long.

2. The Great Rift Valley.

3. The White Nile begins in the lakes of Uganda and Tanzania; the Blue Nile begins in Ethiopia.

PAGE 295

1. Palm oil and rubber are important export crops that come from plantations.

2. Zaire supplies most of the world's cobalt.

3. Palm oil is used in making soap and margarine.

4. Tourists visiting Tsavo Park would see interesting, sometimes rare, animals in their natural habitat.

PAGE 298

1. The currents of the Indian Ocean allowed traders to sail from Asia and Arabia to East Africa during one part of the year and to sail home from East Africa during the other. (The winds in this area reverse their direction during the year.)

2. Swahili is an East African language that has Arabic, Persian, and Indian words as well as African words.

3. The headquarters of the Organization of African Unity is in Addis Ababa, Ethiopia.

PAGE 301

1. Hydroelectric power can be called white coal.

2. Belgium, France, and Portugal had colonies in this part of Africa (also Germany before 1920).

3. Petroleum is a source of wealth for Angola and Gabon.

ANSWERS FOR CHAPTER REVIEW

PAGE 302

Vocabulary Quiz

1. d 2. g 3. a 4. j 5. h 6. c 7. e 8. i 9. b 10. f

Review Questions

1. The great plateau pulled apart, creating the Great Rift Valley.

2. Mount Kilimanjaro and Mount Kenya are volcanoes.

3. The waterfalls on the Zaire River can provide the white coal of hydroelectric power when capital is there to develop it. But the waterfalls make the river navigable only in places.

4. Most people in Zaire and neighboring countries speak languages belonging to the Bantu family.

5. Belgium colonized Zaire; Portugal colonized Angola; Great Britain colonized Zanzibar.

6. Malaria and sleeping sickness are two serious sicknesses in Tanzania and other parts of tropical Africa.

Activities

Answers will vary.

ANSWERS FOR SKILLS DEVELOPMENT

PAGE 303

Skills Practice

1. The types of vegetation found in Africa are equatorial rain forest (shown as dark green on the map); savanna (shown as light green on the map); desert (shown as yellow on the map); grassland (shown as orange on the map); Mediterranean (shown as medium green on the map).

2. The two areas of Mediterranean climate in Africa are the extreme north and the extreme south of Africa. The same types of crops are grown in both regions.

3. The major rain-forest area is along the Equator.

4. The two largest vegetation areas of Africa are the savanna and desert regions.

5. Savanna borders the rain forest.

6. The Mediterranean vegetation zone lies outside the tropic zones.

7. Yes, the vegetation zones north and south of the Equator are similar.

8. A physical map showing elevation that affects vegetation would be useful in studying vegetation.

CHAPTER 18 Southern Africa

ANSWERS FOR CHECKUP QUESTIONS

PAGE 307
1. The southern part of Southern Africa lies in the middle latitudes.

2. Zimbabwe and Zambia have large amounts of savanna land. So does northern Malawi.

3. South Africa has large amounts of diamonds and gold; Zambia has copper and cobalt; Zimbabwe has coal.

PAGE 308
1. Zimbabwe was a kingdom in precolonial Southern Africa.

2. The Boers were farmers, the white descendants of the Dutch settlers who colonized Southern Africa before British rule.

3. Black nationalism is the idea that black Africans ought to control their own nations.

PAGE 311
1. Resources of the High Veld include water, fertile farmland, diamonds, and gold.

2. Apartheid is forced separation of whites and non-whites, a government policy in South Africa by which different races do not have equal rights and opportunities.

3. Botswana, Lesotho, and Swaziland are South Africa's landlocked neighbors.

4. Namibia is not yet independent.

PAGE 313
1. Zimbabwe's new government needs capital to develop the country's resources. It also needs to resolve conflicts between people of different backgrounds who do not agree about how the country should be run. In addition, participation in world trade is difficult because the country is landlocked and transportation costs are high.

2. The Zambian economy depends on copper.

3. Madagascar is an island nation.

ANSWERS TO CHAPTER REVIEW

PAGE 314
Vocabulary Quiz
1. F 2. T 3. T 4. T 5. F 6. T 7. F 8. T 9. F 10. F

Review Questions
1. One reason Europeans settled here was that the climates of the middle latitudes far to the south were similar to the climates of Europe. European farmers could use the same farming techniques they had used in their homelands. European trading ships that sailed to and from Asia provided a market for the produce of these early European farms in Africa.

2. Three climatic types are semiarid (or steppe), savanna, and Mediterranean.

3. Southern Africa's agricultural products include grapes, wheat, and beef. Mineral resources include copper, cobalt, gold, diamonds, coal, uranium, and chromium.

4. Gold and diamonds were discovered in the High Veld of South Africa.

5. Black homelands are places in South Africa that the South African government has designated as legal residences for many of its black workers. The homelands lack good land, modern transportation and housing, and jobs. Thirteen percent of the land has been set aside for the black majority of the population in South Africa.

6. Most of the countries in Southern Africa were colonies until 1960 or later.

Activities
Answers will vary.

ANSWERS FOR SKILLS DEVELOPMENT

PAGE 315
Skills Practice
Graphs should reflect the same data as shown on the table.

ANSWER KEY

CHAPTER 19 West Africa

ANSWERS FOR CHECKUP QUESTIONS

PAGE 319

1. West African rain forests are on the coastal lowlands. Interior lands are higher and drier.

2. The Sahel is a region that has a semidesert climate and that lies between the Sahara and the moister savanna land.

3. The Niger River has been used for commerce for hundreds of years. It has been a transportation route for the exchange of goods between the northern dry lands and the southern rain forests.

4. West Africa's mineral resources include bauxite, diamonds, gold, iron ore, manganese, phosphate, tin, and uranium.

PAGE 321

1. The Nok people were early residents of Nigeria, people who not only farmed but also manufactured tools and other items from both iron and clay.

2. The English and French colonies often included Africans who spoke different languages. The only common language was the language of the colonizers.

3. Groundnuts are what Americans call peanuts.

PAGE 324

1. Lagos is located on an island in a large lagoon.

2. Most people in the Sahel are farmers who must spend all their time providing food and water for themselves and their families.

3. These four countries are landlocked.

4. Both Ghana and Ivory Coast have aluminum—smelting industries.

ANSWERS FOR CHAPTER REVIEW

PAGE 325
Vocabulary Quiz
1. b 2. c 3. b 4. a 5. c 6. a 7. b 8. c 9. c
10. b

Review Questions

1. The Europeans came to trade with the nations of West Africa.

Eventually the Europeans moved into the interior and established colonies. The colonies ignored the African nations. Sometimes the African population of a colony would consist of nations that had been at war with each other. The nations within a colony often were held together only by the fact that they were a colony. The only language they had in common was the language of the colonizer.

2. The main colonial powers were England and France, although Portugal had the earliest trade interaction with West Africa and retained a colony there.

3. One of Nigeria's important resources is petroleum.

4. Aluminum, cacao, and coffee are exported from Ghana and Ivory Coast.

Activities
Answers will vary.

ANSWERS FOR SKILLS DEVELOPMENT

PAGE 326
Skills Practice

Time line:
100 B.C.—Ethiopia
1847—Liberia
1922—Egypt
1931—South Africa
1951—Libya
1956—Morocco, Sudan, Tunisia
1957—Ghana
1958—Guinea
1960—Benin, Cameroon, Central African Republic, Chad, Congo, Gabon, Ivory Coast, Madagascar, Mali, Mauritania, Niger, Nigeria, Senegal, Somalia, Togo, Upper Volta, Zaire
1961—Sierra Leone
1962—Algeria, Burundi, Rwanda, Uganda
1963—Kenya
1964—Malawi, Tanzania, Zambia
1965—Gambia
1966—Botswana, Lesotho
1968—Equatorial Guinea, Mauritius, Swaziland
1974—Guinea-Bissau

1975—Angola, Cape Verde, Comoros, Mozambique, São Tomé e Principe
1976—Seychelles
1977—Djibouti
1980—Zimbabwe

1. Ethiopia became an independent country before Egypt.

2. 17 African countries became independent in 1960.

3. Liberia became independent before South Africa.

4. Zimbabwe became an independent country most recently.

5. Most African countries became independent in the second half of the twentieth century.

ANSWERS FOR UNIT REVIEW

PAGE 327
Reading the Text
1. T **2.** F **3.** T **4.** T **5.** F

Reading the Map
1. Khartoum, Sudan, is near the junction of the White Nile and the Blue Nile.

2. The height of Mount Kilimanjaro is 19,340 feet (5,895 m).

3. The Zambezi River flows into the Mozambique Channel.

4. Niger, Nigeria, and Chad border Lake Chad.

5. Cape Agulhas is the southernmost point.

Reading a Picture
1. The subject is slash-and-burn farming.

2. Trees and brush—forest growth—is the natural vegetation.

3. Knives, machetes, and hoes are the tools being used.

4. The land is not being cleared permanently.

5. Yes, slash-and-burn farming is subsistence farming.

Reading a Graph
1. A single-export economy is largely dependent on the export of one product.

2. Nigeria is dependent on oil for over 90% of its exports.

3. Sierra Leone's main export is diamonds.

4. Zambia's major export is copper.

5. The single-export economy is too dependent on market fluctuations.

ANSWER KEY

UNIT 8 SOUTH ASIA AND EAST ASIA

CHAPTER 20 China and Its Neighbors

ANSWERS FOR CHECKUP QUESTIONS

PAGE 338

1. The western interior is China's most isolated region.

2. The Yangtze River and the Hwang Ho are two major rivers.

3. The Great Silk Road was a trade route through western China to Europe.

PAGE 340

1. Coal deposits in China are among the largest in the world. Coal is China's greatest source of energy.

2. A flood plain is the flat land near a river that is flooded when the river overflows its banks. Usually a flood plain has rich, fertile soil that produces good crops in times when it is not flooded.

3. Loess is soil that has been carried and deposited by wind. It makes rich farmland of very fine, easily eroded soil.

PAGE 343

1. A dynasty is a family of rulers.

2. Taoism and Confucianism developed in China.

3. The Chinese invented the compass, silk cloth, porcelain, paper, and the idea of printing.

4. The Communists took over the Chinese government in 1949.

PAGE 345

1. No, Mongolia is controlled by the Soviet Union.

2. South Korea has about twice as many people as North Korea.

3. *Hong Kong* is the name of the British colony off the coast of China.

4. The government on the island of Taiwan is called the Chinese Nationalist government.

ANSWERS FOR CHAPTER REVIEW

PAGE 346

Vocabulary Quiz

1. j 2. g 3. b 4. e 5. d 6. a 7. i 8. c 9. h 10. f

Review Questions

1. The Yangtze and the Hwang are two major rivers in China.

2. The western interior is mountainous, with arid, high plateaus.

3. China's energy sources include coal, petroleum, and hydroelectric power.

4. Taoism and Confucianism are religions that began in China. Taoism emphasizes respect for nature, and Confucianism emphasizes respect for social order and authority.

5. The People's Republic of China has been the name of China since a Communist government took over in 1949.

6. In 1948 the Korean peninsula was divided into North Korea and South Korea.

7. Mongolia is the least modern and industrialized of China's neighbors. It is sparsely populated and landlocked.

8. South Korea has become much more industrialized since 1949. So, too, has Taiwan.

Activities

1. Answers will vary.

2. **a.** Soybeans—Illinois, Iowa, Missouri, Indiana, Minnesota, Ohio, Arkansas, Mississippi, Louisiana, Tennessee
b. Sugar beets—California, Colorado, Michigan, Minnesota, North Dakota, Washington
c. Rice—Arkansas, California, Texas, Louisiana
d. Cotton—Texas, California, Mississippi, Arizona, Louisiana, Arkansas, Oklahoma, Alabama, Tennessee, Missouri

3. Answers will vary.

ANSWERS FOR SKILLS DEVELOPMENT

PAGE 347

Skills Practice

1. The black arrows show the route Marco Polo followed.

2. Marco Polo began his journey from Venice.

3. Marco Polo began his journey by sea.

4. Marco Polo traveled to Peking.

5. Yes, Marco Polo traveled on the Great Silk Road on his way to China.

6. The Great Silk Road is near 40°N latitude.

7. Marco Polo did not visit Japan, Borneo, or Russia.

8. No, Marco Polo's description of a city 80°E and 20°N would not be very believable because he did not visit this area.

9. Marco Polo's return journey from Peking was the longer journey in distance.

10. Marco Polo's journey to Peking took more time because more of it was over land.

CHAPTER 21 Japan: An Island Nation

ANSWERS FOR CHECKUP QUESTIONS

PAGE 351
1. An archipelago is a group of islands.

2. Japan's island location gives it a mild climate, since the nearness of the water keeps temperatures from becoming too hot in summer and too cool in winter.

3. Mount Fuji is a dormant volcano known for its beauty.

4. In addition to making the climate mild, the sea is important to Japan as a source of fish. The seas around Japan are some of the best fishing grounds in the world.

PAGE 354
1. The Japanese modeled their style of writing on the one used in China.

2. Portuguese sailors were the first Europeans to reach Japan.

3. Japan became isolated from other countries during the Tokugawa shogunate. Foreigners were banished, and Japanese people were forbidden to travel abroad.

4. Compulsory education was an important social reform of the Meiji Restoration.

5. In World War II, Japan fought the United States, Great Britain, France, the Soviet Union, and China.

PAGE 357
1. GNP stands for gross national product, the total value of all the goods and services a country produces in a year.

2. Japan gets most of the raw materials used in its factories by importing them from other countries.

3. A juku is an extra school that Japanese children attend during after-school or weekend hours to help them prepare for examinations.

4. Japan's largest city is Tokyo.

ANSWERS FOR CHAPTER REVIEW

PAGE 358
Vocabulary Quiz
1. c **2.** c **3.** a **4.** c **5.** a **6.** c **7.** a **8.** b **9.** c **10.** b

Review Questions
1. The four largest Japanese islands, in order of size, are Honshū, Hokkaidō, Kyushu, and Shikoku.

2. Japan's maritime location keeps its climate mild. The water keeps the land temperatures from reaching extremes of either cold or hot.

3. (a) China was Japan's early trading partner. From China, Japan received ideas on which Japanese writing, government, and philosophy were based. (b) The Tokugawa shogunate enforced Japan's isolation from the rest of the world. Foreigners were not allowed to visit Japan (with the exception of some interaction on one small island), and Japanese people were not allowed to travel. As a result, for several centuries Japan developed without influence from other countries. (c) The Meiji Restoration meant that shoguns were no longer in power, that social reforms could begin, and that interaction with the rest of the world could begin again. One important social reform was compulsory education, an attempt to remove illiteracy.

4. We know that Japan is a wealthy country, because it has a high GNP. The people of Japan enjoy a high standard of living, which includes good health care and good schools.

5. Three of Japan's important industries are shipbuilding, textiles, and automobiles. Other industrial products include cameras, tape recorders, and computers.

ANSWER KEY

Activities
Answers will vary.

ANSWERS FOR SKILLS DEVELOPMENT

PAGE 359
Skills Practice
1. Japan's main type of export to the United States is machinery and equipment.

2. Japan's main type of import is foodstuffs.

3. Yes, Japan does buy machinery and equipment from abroad.

4. Yes, the United States does buy foodstuffs from Japan.

5. Japan bought $1,248,000 worth of soybeans from the United States in 1980.

CHAPTER 22 India and Its Neighbors

ANSWERS FOR CHECKUP QUESTIONS

PAGE 364
1. India is the largest South Asian country. The other countries are Pakistan, Bangladesh, Sri Lanka, Nepal, and Bhutan.

2. South Asia's four greats are great mountains (the Himalayas), great rivers (the Indus, the Ganges, and the Brahmaputra), a great plateau (the Deccan), and a great wind (the monsoon).

3. Bangladesh is largely delta land of the Brahmaputra and Ganges rivers.

4. The Indus River flows primarily through Pakistan but also through small portions of India.

5. The monsoon brings South Asia its yearly supply of moisture. Sometimes the monsoon causes destruction by bringing too much or too little moisture, or by arriving too early or too late for successful planting.

PAGE 368
1. The Aryans were a conquering people whose culture was a forerunner of modern Indian culture. They were farmers who brought Sanskrit to the Indus and Ganges valleys.

2. Most people in India today are Hindus.

3. Most people in Sri Lanka today are Buddhists.

4. The British built roads, railways, and ports and brought the English language to the Indian subcontinent. However, they prevented industrial growth so that most Indians had to remain subsistence farmers.

5. The partition was the division of the former British colony of India into two countries—India and Pakistan—largely along religious lines. The partition caused the movement of many Hindus to India and of many Moslems to East or West Pakistan. Later, East Pakistan, which was far removed from West Pakistan, became the separate country of Bangladesh.

PAGE 371
1. The Green Revolution was a series of agricultural discoveries during the 1960s in which scientists created high-yielding varieties of wheat and rice.

2. Jamshedpur, a major steelmaking center, is near Calcutta.

3. When manufacturing is done in workers' homes, it is called cottage industry.

4. Flooding caused by overflowing rivers and tidal waves during tropical storms is a natural danger in Bangladesh.

ANSWERS FOR CHAPTER REVIEW

PAGE 372
Vocabulary Quiz
1. Hinduism
2. Buddhism
3. populous
4. plateau
5. Revolution
6. jute
7. subcontinent
8. linguist
9. industry
10. refugee

Review Questions

1. The seven nations in South Asia are India, Pakistan, Bangladesh, Sri Lanka, Nepal, Bhutan, and Afghanistan.

2. The Ganges, Brahmaputra, and Indus are important rivers that flow across South Asia from the Himalaya Mountains. They have created broad alluvial plains on which half of the region's people live. These three rivers are also important for irrigation. The Ganges is a holy river.

3. Storms frequently bring dangerous flooding, sometimes by causing tidal waves that sweep coastal villages out to sea. In Bangladesh, which is densely populated and too poor to have many safeguards against storm damage, many people have died because of flooding. The monsoon storms, which are seasonal, provide moisture needed to grow crops. Without the monsoons, people would starve.

4. Three religions important to South Asia are Hinduism, Islam, and Buddhism.

5. Many languages developed because early farming villages were isolated from each other and each village had its own language. Today the presence of so many languages hinders trade and communication between people. People in India who have had advanced education usually speak Hindi, the official language, and English. However, this does not aid their communication with citizens who have had less schooling.

6. The partition was a division of the former British colony into the two separate countries as a result of the independence movement. Pakistan was created for people of the Moslem religion, and India for people of the Hindu religion. As part of the partition, whole villages of people moved from one location to another. Many people were killed. The new Moslem country of Pakistan was in two locations, one to the east of India and one to the west. They were 1500 miles (2410 km) apart. The country called Pakistan today used to be West Pakistan. East Pakistan is now a separate country called Bangladesh.

Activity
Answers will vary.

ANSWERS FOR SKILLS DEVELOPMENT

PAGE 373
Skills Practice
1. a **2.** b **3.** a **4.** b **5.** b **6.** b

CHAPTER 23 Southeast Asia

ANSWERS FOR CHECKUP QUESTIONS

PAGE 377
1. The major landforms are mountainous peninsulas that fan out into large lowlands and large volcanic islands.

2. Seas are deepest on the outer edges of the islands. They are shallow between the mainland and the largest islands of Indonesia.

3. Summer is usually the rainy season on the mainland. The wettest areas are west-facing coasts backed by high mountains.

PAGE 379
1. Mongoloid peoples began moving into Southeast Asia 2,000 years ago.

2. Invaders pushed early settlers of Southeast Asia into remote upland areas.

3. Indian and Chinese cultures have had the greatest influence in Southeast Asia.

4. Thailand, Malaysia, Singapore, Indonesia, and Vietnam all have large Chinese populations.

5. The main colonial powers were Great Britain, the Netherlands, Spain, France, and the United States.

PAGE 386
1. The two kinds are dry rice and wet rice, or paddy rice.

2. Java is the most densely populated island.

3. Malaysia is a federation of monarchies.

4. The Philippines was a colony of Spain.

5. Burma, Thailand, Laos, Kampuchea, Vietnam, and part of Malaysia are on the mainland.

ANSWERS FOR CHAPTER REVIEW

PAGE 387
Vocabulary Quiz
1. a **2.** c **3.** g **4.** h **5.** e

Review Questions
1. The deltas of the great rivers have formed the major lowlands of the mainland.

ANSWER KEY

2. Hinduism was replaced by Buddhism in almost all of Southeast Asia.

3. Great Britain controlled Burma and Malaysia; the Dutch held Indonesia; and the Spanish ruled the Philippines. Later on, the French moved into Indochina and the United States took over the Philippines.

4. The people of the lowlands have a denser population; they are paddy rice farmers; often they are late arrivals and control the country's government.

5. The Chinese often earn their living through trade.

6. Wet rice farming, or paddy farming, is the most important agricultural activity today.

7. Rice, palm oil, rubber, tin, petroleum, and products of light manufacturing such as textiles and clothing are the main exports.

Activities
1. The Salween and Mekong rivers are 750 miles (1,200 km) apart at their mouths. They come within 100 miles (161 km) of each other in Laos.

2. Answers will vary.

3. Answers will vary.

ANSWERS FOR SKILLS DEVELOPMENT
PAGE 388
Skills Practice
1. South Asia has a severe shortage. East Asia has an average supply. The United States and Japan have a large surplus.

2. This pattern can be explained by the density of population and the consequent shortage of land. Land is overused and produces less crops.

3. Singapore's surplus results from the wealth that comes into the area from trade. Singapore is a trading center. The population of Singapore is mostly Chinese in origin. The abundance of food is the result of its location as a center of trade.

4. The fastest growing countries in Southeast Asia are Malaysia, Indonesia, and Korea. These countries, along with Vietnam and Thailand, will have severe food-supply problems in the future if their present growth rate continues.

ANSWERS FOR UNIT REVIEW
PAGE 389
Reading the Text
1. The Chinese empire was formed in 221 B.C.

2. China's population reached 100 million during the Sung dynasty.

3. Taoism emphasizes harmony with nature.

4. Confucianism emphasizes respect for the past.

5. The government of China was influenced by Confucianism.

Reading a Map
1. Ten Japanese cities have populations of 1 million or more.

2. The population density in and around Tokyo is 2,500 or more per square mile.

3. Hokkaidō has a population density of under 100 people per square kilometer.

4. Most of the large Japanese cities are on the east coast.

5. The grid coordinates for Tokyo are B-2.

Reading Pictures
1. R **2.** A **3.** H/C **4.** I **5.** R **6.** H/C **7.** I **8.** H/C **9.** R **10.** I **11.** H/C **12.** A **13.** I **14.** A **15.** I

Reading a Table
1. T **2.** F **3.** T **4.** T **5.** F

UNIT 9 OCEANIA AND AUSTRALIA

CHAPTER 24 The Pacific Islands

ANSWERS FOR CHECKUP QUESTIONS

PAGE 399

1. Continental islands are islands that geographers believe were once joined to one of the continents.

2. Volcanic islands are formed by lava that has been pushed above the surface of the water by volcanoes on the ocean floor. Coral islands are formed from the hard outer skeletons of billions of tiny sea animals called coral polyps.

3. A reef is a rocklike ridge or mound formed by coral polyps. An atoll is a coral island consisting of a reef that encloses a lagoon.

4. The main seasons in the tropical Pacific Islands are wet and dry, rather than winter and summer.

PAGE 405

1. The Pacific Islanders grew food and kept animals, used tools of stone and shell, wove mats from palm leaves, built large double canoes, and traveled long distances by sea.

2. When we say that European explorers discovered the Pacific Islands, we mean that they were the first people from Europe to visit and learn about them.

3. Some places in the Pacific were named for places in Europe (New Britain), European explorers (Cook Island), European rulers (Marianas, Carolines), European organizations (Society Islands), or the day that Europeans first visited them (Easter and Christmas islands).

4. Some Europeans went to the Pacific Islands looking for gold. Some Europeans and Americans went to the Pacific Islands to trade manufactured goods—such as guns, cloth, cooking pots, glass beads, steel knives, axes, and other hardware—for pearls, coral, and sandalwood. Others stopped for fresh supplies and refreshment. Missionaries came to teach the islanders about the Christian religion. After the 1850s, Europeans and Americans came seeking land on which to grow sugarcane and coconuts. Some people came seeking out-of-the-way places.

5. The following countries acquired territory in the Pacific: Great Britain, France, Germany, and the United States. After World War I, Australia, New Zealand, and Japan took over the islands that had belonged to Germany.

PAGE 409

1. Before the coming of the Europeans, the Pacific Islanders gathered and grew their food and other materials for their own use.

2. European traders and planters introduced a commercial economy, in which goods are gathered and produced for sale.

3. Some of the exports from the Pacific Islands include coconuts and coconut products, copra, bananas, pineapples, citrus fruit, sugar, coffee, tea, cocoa, vanilla, timber, finished lumber, canned fish, and phosphate.

4. The location of the Pacific Islands has these advantages: Tourists like the location; planes can use the location for refueling; the United States has chosen one of the islands for a huge military base that helps the economy of the island. The location has had these disadvantages: The isolation of the islands caused a lag in development of tools and weapons; the isolation attracted countries to choose the islands as test sites for atomic weapons.

ANSWERS FOR CHAPTER REVIEW

PAGE 410
Vocabulary Quiz
1. T **2.** T **3.** F **4.** F **5.** T **6.** F **7.** T **8.** F **9.** F **10.** T

Review Questions

1. Some of the islands in the Pacific were formed by the tops of mountains that rise from the ocean floor above the surface of the water. Some islands, it is thought, were once joined to one of the continents. These islands are called continental islands. Other islands were formed when submerged volcanoes piled lava above the surface of the water. These are called volcanic islands. Other islands were formed when billions of coral polyps massed together to form mounds, called reefs, which were pushed above the surface of the water. These islands are called coral islands. Some atoll islands were formed by the process of a reef being made around the edge of an island that later became sub-

ANSWER KEY

merged, leaving only the ring-shaped reef enclosing a lagoon.

2. There are only slight seasonal temperature changes in the Pacific Islands, whereas in places outside the tropics there is a much greater difference between summer and winter temperatures.

3. The ancestors of some Pacific Island people received this name because they were good sailors who sailed east, rather than west as the European Vikings did. The early islanders used crude tools to build their canoes, and they made cords from the fibers of plants. They shaped timbers and made canoes that they sailed great distances without the use of a compass, reaching widely separated islands.

4. No, the Europeans did not discover the Pacific Islands. However, Europeans were the first to map the Pacific Ocean.

5. Europeans and Americans went seeking some of the valuable products of the islands. They stopped for fresh supplies while whaling in the Pacific. Whalers often used these stops as opportunities to carry on trade with the islanders. The Europeans and Americans also went to the islands to teach Christianity to the island people. The presence of the Europeans and Americans resulted in a number of the islands being named after places in Europe, manufactured goods being brought to the islands, the people learning to read, and Christianity becoming the major religion in the islands.

6. In a subsistence economy, goods are produced and gathered only for the needs of local people. In a commercial economy, goods are produced and gathered to sell for a profit. The islanders had a subsistence economy before the arrival of outsiders, but today they have a commercial economy.

7. The location of the Pacific Islands has made the islands an attraction for tourists, a supply stop for airplanes, and a test site for explosives.

Activities
Answers will vary.

ANSWERS FOR SKILLS DEVELOPMENT

PAGE 411
Skills Practice I
1. c **2.** a **3.** b **4.** a **5.** a **6.** c **7.** c **8.** b **9.** a **10.** c

Skills Practice II
1. T **2.** T **3.** T **4.** F **5.** F **6.** F **7.** F

CHAPTER 25 Australia, New Zealand, and Antarctica

ANSWERS FOR CHECKUP QUESTIONS

PAGE 416
1. The deserts are largely in the western half of Australia. The southeast receives rainfall throughout the year. Areas along the southwest and north coasts receive plenty of rain during part of the year, but they have seasonal droughts.

2. The Great Dividing Range is a highland belt that parallels the east coast and separates the coastlands from the rest of the continent.

3. The Great Barrier Reef is a large coral structure made up of thousands of individual reefs and islets along the northeast coast of Australia.

4. Australia's wildlife includes platypuses; echidnas; kangaroos; wallabies; koalas; gliders, or flying phalangers, also called flying opossums; emus; mallee fowls; kookaburras; Tasmanian tigers, or wolves; and Tasmanian devils.

PAGE 419
1. The Aborigines hunted and gathered their food, using tools of stone, bone, and wood. They clothed themselves with animal skins. They were always on the move in their neverending search for food, so they erected no permanent buildings.

2. The early explorers included Abel Tasman, who discovered the island named after him; William Dampier, who landed on the northwest coast; James Cook, who discovered the east coast near the vicinity of present-day Sydney.

3. Some of Australia's first settlers were convicts sent to work the land rather than being kept in prison in England. Free settlers also came in order to get land.

4. The Commonwealth of Australia is a federal government made up of six states and one territory. Australia is a member of the Commonwealth of Nations, and the Queen of the United Kingdom is also Queen of Australia.

PAGE 422
1. Australians use the grasslands for raising sheep and cattle.

2. Australia is able to grow a variety of crops because it has a variety of climates.

3. Australia mines gold, iron, bauxite, lead, zinc, nickel, coal, manganese, silver, tin, and uranium.

4. Australia's four largest cities—Sydney, Melbourne, Brisbane, and Adelaide—are located on the southeast coast. Canberra is the capital.

PAGE 427

1. New Zealand is a mountainous island country; Australia is mostly flat. Australia has large deserts; New Zealand has none. Australia lies partly in the tropics; all of New Zealand lies south of the tropics.

2. South Island is very mountainous, with a range of rugged mountains called the Southern Alps that extends the length of the island from north to south. North Island is hilly and mountainous but not so rugged. The center of North Island is a plateau on which an ancient water-filled crater forms a lake.

3. The Maoris were the first inhabitants of New Zealand. Their ancestors had migrated from other Pacific Islands by canoes. Today the Maoris make up part of New Zealand's population.

4. European settlers cleared the forests for cropland and pastures on which they raised sheep and cattle. The settlers created a commercial economy, exporting wool, meat, dairy products, and other foods. They created industries, particularly those that processed food, and they built modern cities. These changes were the basis of New Zealand's economic activity, which has continued to grow.

5. The three largest cities of New Zealand are Auckland, Wellington, and Christchurch. Wellington is the capital.

PAGE 430

1. Although Antarctica is an ice-covered continent, it is quite dry. The yearly snowfall in the center of the continent equals only about 3 inches (7.6 cm) of rainfall.

2. Life in Antarctica consists of some lichen and mosses in which some insects and mites live. The only animals are those that live in the sea, such as whales, dolphins, and seals. Many seabirds spend the summer there, and the emperor penguin remains throughout the year.

3. Antarctica is now used primarily as a base for observing weather, the earth, and wildlife.

ANSWERS FOR CHAPTER REVIEW

PAGE 431

Vocabulary Quiz

1. d **2.** c **3.** b **4.** j **5.** a **6.** h **7.** e **8.** f **9.** g **10.** i

Review Questions

1. About one third of Australia receives less than 10 inches (25 cm) of rainfall a year. Another third gets less than 20 inches (51 cm) of rainfall a year. About one tenth of the continent is well-watered. The remaining areas usually receive plenty of rain, but they do have seasonal droughts. Snow falls regularly only in the higher mountains. The temperatures vary from hot to mild.

2. The Aborigines learned to live on the land without growing crops. They hunted and gathered their food and other materials that they used. The Europeans cleared forests and bushlands and planted crops such as wheat, barley, and oats. They pastured sheep and cattle on the grassy plains.

3. Both Australia and New Zealand belong to the Commonwealth of Nations. The Queen of the United Kingdom is also Queen of New Zealand and Australia.

4. The Aborigines hunted, fished, gathered food, and found other materials they needed, but they did not plant crops or keep livestock. The Maoris also fished and hunted, but unlike the Aborigines, the Maoris grew root crops such as yams, taro, and sweet potatoes. Also, the Aborigines built no permanent homes, whereas the Maoris did.

5. Captain Cook's report on Australia encouraged the British to send new settlers to Australia. Cook's report on New Zealand first encouraged traders. It was after Britain annexed New Zealand that settlers came in larger numbers.

6. Australia's main exports include animals, wool, mutton, and beef. New Zealand's important exports are wool, mutton, beef, dairy products, apples, and kiwi fruit.

7. From above, Antarctica would appear as a sheet of ice.

8. The Antarctic Treaty is an international agreement regarding investigations by various countries in Antarctica. The treaty allows for freedom of scientific investigation throughout Antarctica without regard to national claims. The treaty also prohibits use of the continent for military purposes.

ANSWER KEY

Activities
Answers will vary.

ANSWERS FOR SKILLS DEVELOPMENT

PAGE 432
Skills Practice I
1. Victoria   2. Northern Territory   3. Northern Territory   4. Western Australia   5. Tasmania   6. South Australia   7. New South Wales   8. Queensland

Skills Practice II
1. Australia lies between the Indian and the South Pacific oceans.

2. The Great Barrier Reef is on the east coast of Australia.

3. The two rivers in Australia are the Darling and the Murray rivers. The two deserts in Australia are the Great Victorian and the Great Sandy deserts.

4. Western Australia, Queensland and the Northern Territory are partly within the tropics.

5. Canberra is the national capital of Australia.

Skills Practice III
1. b   2. c   3. a   4. a   5. a. Sunday   b. Monday   c. Monday   d. Monday   e. Monday   f. Sunday   g. Sunday   h. Monday

Skills Practice IV
1. Washington, D.C.   2. Melbourne, Australia   3. Panama, Panama   4. Rangoon, Burma   5. Brisbane, Australia

ANSWERS FOR UNIT REVIEW

PAGE 433
Reading the Text
1. Different countries claimed parts of Antarctica, often the same parts.

2. The present best use of Antarctica is for scientific observation.

3. The agreement was signed in 1959. To date, 16 countries have signed.

4. The countries also agreed not to use Antarctica for military purposes.

5. Weather, earth, and wildlife in a natural state can be studied in Antarctica.

Reading a Map
1. Three cities, all in Australia, have populations of 1 million or more.

2. The International Date Line follows 180°W.

3. It is Monday, March 12, in Wellington.

4. No, there are United States territories on both sides of the date line.

5. The Great Barrier Reef is in the Coral Sea.

Reading a Picture
1. A boat is sinking.

2. The man in front is a harpooner. It is his job to kill the whale.

3. The man facing the rowers is steering the boat.

4. The whale is at least three to four times larger than the rowboats.

5. The ships are sailing vessels, dependent on wind power.

Reading a Graph
1. The temperature in Apia ranges from 74°F to 86°F.

2. The temperature in Melbourne is highest during January and February.

3. The winter months in Melbourne are June, July, and August.

4. Apia has an average annual temperature of 27°C.

5. Sweaters and light overcoats are part of the wardrobe of people in Melbourne.

UNIT 10 TAKING A WORLD VIEW

CHAPTER 26 People and Resources

ANSWERS FOR CHECKUP QUESTIONS

PAGE 442

1. Income from the export of phosphate made Nauru a rich country.

2. After 1600 the world's population began to grow at an increasingly rapid rate.

3. A country's population growth rate is figured by comparing the average number of deaths and births for every 1,000 persons in the country. To obtain the rate in a decimal fraction form, the number of deaths per thousand is subtracted from the number of births per thousand.

4. Population increased rapidly because people learned to check the spread of diseases, through such measures as the purification of water, the pasteurization of milk, vaccination, and the control of disease-spreading insects. Population also increased rapidly because of an increase in food supply, which was the result of new croplands and improved agricultural methods, including use of fertilizers, insecticides, better seeds, and more irrigation.

5. Cities grew because population grew so rapidly that there was no longer room for all the people to work on the land and because the use of machines and chemicals reduced the need for farmers.

The shapes in which cities grew depended partly on how people could travel to work. When people depended on trolleys and trains, cities grew along the tracks. The coming of the automobile made it possible for cities to spread over much greater areas.

PAGE 448

1. The value of a resource depends upon whether people know how to make use of it. The iron ore of Australia, for example, was of no use to the Aborigines because they did not know how to smelt metals.

2. Soil may be preserved through fertilization, con-

trol of floods, and retaining grass cover in places subject to heavy erosion.

3. Water becomes polluted when cities and industries discharge untreated waste into streams and lakes. Smoke from chimneys and smokestacks and gases from automobiles pollute the air.

PAGE 451

1. A population projection is a forecast of future developments on a population growth graph.

2. Nuclear power, wind power, solar power, and power produced from waste are some sources of energy that may take the place of coal and oil.

3. Much of the work once done in factories by human workers can be done by robots, so there may be fewer factory jobs in the future.

ANSWERS FOR CHAPTER REVIEW

PAGE 452

Vocabulary Quiz

1. b 2. d & g 3. h 4. c 5. f

Review Questions

1. In Nauru the value of phosphate depended upon the use people were able to make of it. The same is true of the rest of the world; the value of a natural resource depends upon the use people can make of it. In addition, Nauru, like the rest of the world, has had large increases in population.

2. The growth rate of 1980 in France was 4.7 per 1,000 persons.

3. The rapid growth in the world's population that occurred after 1600 happened for a combination of reasons. Ways were discovered to make water and milk safe to drink, checking the spread of diseases such as typhoid. Vaccination against diseases such as smallpox and the control of disease-spreading insects also aided population growth. New croplands provided more food and, in recent years, the use of fertilizers, insecticides, better seeds, and more irrigation has also increased world food production, thus helping to increase world population.

4. Today over one third of the world's people live in cities. In Europe, the Americas, and Australia, the majority of the people live in cities. In Africa and Asia, however, city-dwellers are a minority of the population.

5. Natural resources are materials useful to people and supplied by nature. Some main natural resources are soil, water, air, minerals, forests, coal, oil, and the energy of the sun.

6. Soil is used carelessly when crops are allowed to continually use up nutrients without efforts being made to replenish the soil. Water is misused when industries empty wastes into streams or rivers from which cities draw water. Air is misused when it is polluted by gases from automobiles, trucks and factories.

7. It is unlikely that the world's population will keep on growing at the same rate as it has in the past. As has been the case in past years, people in the future will probably continue to discover new resources and new ways to use old resources. Many new kinds of jobs will be available in the future. It is forecasted that in the future many more people will work in the service industries.

Activities
Answers will vary.

ANSWERS FOR SKILLS DEVELOPMENT

PAGE 453
Skills Practice
1. Answers will vary.

2. **II.** The Use of Resources
  A. What makes a resource useful?
    1. A natural resource gets its value from the usefulness it provides for people.
    2. All areas of the earth's natural environment include resources that are vital to human survival.
  B. Some resources can be used up.
    1. The island of Nauru is facing a crisis because its main natural resource is almost used up.
    2. The government of Nauru hopes to overcome this crisis by using the income from foreign investments.
    3. Nauru's crisis is one example of a problem common to all the world's peoples.
    4. Oil is a natural resource that became useful to people with the discovery of kerosene in the nineteenth century.
    5. In the late 1800's Pennsylvania was the leading producer of oil.

    6. As more uses for oil were discovered, more sources for the mineral were found in the earth.
    7. Oil is becoming more difficult to get from the earth as the more accessible sources are used up.
    8. The future of the earth's oil supply is in question and demands study.
  C. Soil—valuable dirt
    1. Resources in the soil are used up by the process of growing crops.
    2. There are ways that soils can be preserved or restored.
    3. Erosion is responsible for much soil loss.
    4. Good soil is scarce and of great value.
    5. Many Americans have taken their country's soils for granted and have done things to decrease their value.
  D. Pollution and two essential resources
    1. Of all the natural resources, only two, water and air, are essential for life.
    2. People have damaged their supply of water and air through pollution.
    3. Air pollution has become a serious problem.
      a. The growth of cities has caused the serious spread of air pollution.
      b. Governments have tried, with limited success, to control air pollution.
    4. Air pollution causes acid rain, which increases water pollution.
3. **III.** Looking to the Future
  A. The problem of forecasts and projections
    1. Present information about world population growth, such as the graph on page 33, can be helpful in understanding the future.
    2. Assumptions about the future are essential even though they cannot be proven.
  B. A crowded world
    1. While the world's population probably will not continue to grow at the same rate as it has in the past, the world will continue to have more people than ever before.
    2. Future population growth, centered in urban areas, will continue to create problems related to natural resources.
  C. Search for new ways to use resources
    1. New solutions are continually being sought to the world's limited-resource problem.

2. The nuclear-energy solution to the world's rising costs of coal and oil has created new problems.
3. New solutions are being found for the problems created by nuclear energy.
4. Increased efforts to find new ways to use resources are essential to future growth.
D. What kinds of jobs will there be?
   1. New jobs are continually being created by the discoveries of new ways to use resources.
   2. Recent history indicates the kinds of jobs people will have in the future.
      a. The number of farmers will probably decrease.
      b. Many assembly-line workers will be replaced by robots.
      c. New jobs will develop in designing and operating automated factories.
      d. Computers are both replacing certain workers and creating new jobs.
      e. Many new jobs will be created in service industries.
   3. Forecasts and projections about the future are always subject to change.

CHAPTER 27 An Interdependent World

ANSWERS FOR CHECKUP QUESTIONS

PAGE 459

1. Some products the United States imports are cocoa, tea, bananas, canned meat, sardines, fresh vegetables, apples, grapes, kumquats, kiwis, ugli fruit, nuts, toys, shirts, sweaters, shoes, automobiles, stereos, television sets, flowers, tools, knives, and cooking pots. Some United States exports are airplanes, tractors and other farm machinery, office machines, computers, oil-drilling and pipeline equipment, corn, wheat, soybeans, meat, and poultry.

2. By specializing in making a particular product, a nation may produce goods of higher quality.

3. A country may be able to produce goods more cheaply either because workers are paid less or because the country has newer and more efficient factories and plants.

4. Tariffs on imported goods make them as expensive as the goods produced within a country, and therefore the home industries are not threatened by the cheaper prices of imported goods.

5. Multinational corporations own plants or businesses in more than two countries.

PAGE 466

1. Nations have generally accepted the rule that the high seas cannot belong to a country and that ships from all nations may sail upon them. Each country is responsible for preserving law and order on ships that fly its flag. Nations follow common rules concerning safety at sea and the fixing of responsibility for accidents.

Airspace over a nation is considered as part of its territory, but nations do follow common rules on international flights.

Outer space is considered to be like the high seas, open to all nations for exploration and other peaceful purposes. Nations have agreed not to explode nuclear devices in outer space or to use it for military purposes.

2. In the General Assembly, each member of the United Nations has a seat and a vote. In the Security Council, five nations (France, Great Britain, China, the Soviet Union, and the United States) have permanent seats and ten other members are elected to the Security Council by the General Assembly. Any permanent member of the Security Council may veto an action of the Council.

3. Regional organizations are made up of countries from a particular geographic area, such as the Americas, Western Europe, or Southeast Asia. Regional organizations have such purposes as keeping peace, providing for peaceful settlement of disputes, and making trade agreements.

4. NATO, or the North Atlantic Treaty Organization, is an alliance made up of the United States, Canada, and a group of Western European nations. The Warsaw Pact is an alliance of Communist countries in Eastern Europe.

ANSWERS FOR CHAPTER REVIEW

PAGE 467
Vocabulary Quiz
1. F 2. T 3. T 4. F 5. T 6. T 7. T 8. F
9. F 10. F

ANSWER KEY

Review Questions

1. Independent countries depend on trade with other nations for goods they need or want and in some cases do not produce.

2. The quality and the price may be better on the imported goods.

3. Nations sometimes restrict trade to protect home industries. Quotas and protective tariffs may be used to restrict trade. Quotas limit the amount of goods that may be imported, and protective tariffs raise import prices.

4. Many corporations own plants or businesses in more than two countries.

5. It is necessary that nations have some common rules or understandings in order to trade with each other. Ships from all nations may sail upon the high seas; each country is responsible for keeping law and order on ships flying its flag. Airspace over a country is considered part of that country, and airplanes from one country must have permission to fly into another country's airspace. Outer space is open to all nations for exploration and other peaceful purposes, not for military purposes. Nations have agreed not to explode nuclear devices in outer space.

6. The Universal Postal Union was formed to make the sending of mail easier, through nations working together. The union sets postal standards, such as rates and sizes of letters.

7. The Security Council has 15 members, including 5 permanent members. Each permanent member has veto power. The Security Council cannot act on anything that has been vetoed by any permanent member.

8. Special agencies give nations a means for working together for a better world—providing for refugees, raising funds to help children in the less-developed countries, improving the health of people, and helping nations manage their credit and money systems.

9. The Olympic Games are called an international activity because athletes from many nations take part, because since 1894 the games have been held in 15 different countries on four continents, and because an international committee controls the games.

Activities

Answers will vary.

ANSWERS FOR SKILLS DEVELOPMENT

PAGE 468

Skills Practice I

1. 6,097 **2.** 3,622 **3.** 6,735 **4.** 7,434 **5.** 6,296

Skills Practice II

1. T **2.** T **3.** F **4.** T **5.** F

ANSWERS FOR UNIT REVIEW

PAGE 469

Reading the Text

1. Answers will vary.

2. About 1,000 people lived on Nauru in 1789. They lived by fishing and simple farming.

3. Fertilizer is made from phosphate.

4. About 8,000 people live on Nauru today. They work for the mining company or for the government.

5. Answers will vary.

Reading a Map

1. T **2.** F **3.** F **4.** T **5.** F

Reading Pictures

1. Pictures on pp. 446, 447, and 448 show poor use of resources.

2. Pictures on pp. 458 and 459 show business among many nations.

3. Pictures on pp. 455 and 466 show examples of international cooperation.

4. Pictures on pp. 449 and 450 show energy sources.

5. Either one of the pictures on page 451 shows how technology can affect the future.

Reading a Table

1. Thirteen of the world's 25 largest cities are in Asia.

2. Four cities are in Europe.

3. New York City; it ranks eighth on the list.

4. Six cities are in the Western Hemisphere.

5. Shanghai, the world's largest city, has a population of 11,859,748.

T-80